# Foundation Design
# and Construction

# Foundation Design and Construction

M. J. Tomlinson
C Eng., F.I.C.E., F.I.Struct.E.

*Third Edition*

*A Halsted Press Book*

*John Wiley & Sons*
*New York — Toronto*

*First published in Great Britain in 1963*
*by Sir Isaac Pitman & Sons Limited*
*Second edition 1969*
*Third edition 1975*


Published in the U.S.A. and Canada
by Halsted Press
a division of John Wiley & Sons, Inc
New York

Library of Congress Cataloging in Publication Data
Tomlinson, Michael John.
Foundation design and construction.
"A Halsted Press book."
Includes bibliographies and index.
1. Foundations. I. Title
TA775.T6    1975    624'.15    74–31121
ISBN 0–470–87764–2


Text set in 10/11 pt. Monotype Times New Roman, printed by
photolithography and bound in Great Britain at The Pitman Press, Bath

# Preface to the Third Edition

At the time of preparing this edition, the changeover in the building and civil engineering industry from the Imperial to the metric system was not fully completed. Although many engineers had been familiar with metric force units, few had experience of the S.I. system (Systéme International d'Unités), in particular in the application of the system to expression of force and stress.

In this edition, S.I. units have been adopted in all cases when converting force, pressure and stress from the Imperial units of the Second Edition, but in a few of the more important tables and diagrams, metric force units have also been shown for the benefit of readers in those countries which have not adopted the S.I. system.

The rather slow progress in the adoption of S.I. units by industry has meant that as yet no common usage of terms to express certain compound units has emerged. Differences in the terms used to express density, and confusion between weight, mass and force have unfortunately appeared in various publications. The author hopes that he has foretold correctly the terms which will eventually be adopted.

Those who have experienced the difficulties of converting "rounded-off" Imperial dimensions to similarly treated metric figures will appreciate the Author's problems in preparing this edition. It is inevitable that some inconsistencies have appeared in the text. The metric force unit "tonne" has been used instead of the kilonewton when describing the capacity of plant such as piling hammers and cranes to conform to present practice.

The former Institution of Civil Engineers' Code of Practice for Foundations has been revised and published by the British Standards Institution as B.S. Code of Practice CP 2004, and the text of this edition is in line with the new code. Parts of the book dealing with piling and deep excavations have been revised.

The dimensions and properties of steel bearing piles and sheet piles of British and U.S. manufacture as tabulated in Chapters 8, 9 and

v

10 are the metric equivalents of the standard Imperial sections. At the time of preparing this edition, British steel manufacturers had not commenced to roll sections to international metric standard sizes.

The author is grateful for the help of his colleague, Mr P. F. Winfield, F.I.Struct.E., for revising the sections of Chapter 4 dealing with the structural design of foundations and for converting the worked examples in Chapters 4, 9 and 10 to S.I. units.

Grateful acknowledgment is made to the following who have given permission to reproduce illustrations, photographs, and other information—

John Wiley & Sons Inc.—Figs. 1.14, 1.25, 2.13, 2.31, 6.7, 9.23 and 9.27.

N. V. Goudsche Machinefabriek—Figs. 1.15 and 1.16.

Controller of H.M. Stationery Office—Figs. 2.11, 2.23, 3.1, 3.6, 3.7, 3.24, and 9.29.

Deutsche Gesellschaft für Erd- und Grundbau—Fig. 2.25 and Table 2.2.

South African Institution of Civil Engineers—Fig. 3.3.

*Architectural Forum*—Fig. 3.8.

Royal Institution of Chartered Surveyors—Fig. 3.19.

*Architects Journal*—Figs. 3.27 and 3.28.

The Society of Environmental Engineering—Fig. 3.29.

European Organization for Nuclear Research—Figs. 3.30 to 3.33.

*Engineering News Record*—Figs. 5.13, 6.30, 9.2 and 11.31.

Butterworth & Co. (Publishers) Ltd.—Figs. 5.8 and 10.27.

Institution of Structural Engineers—Figs. 3.24, 12.18 and 12.19.

American Society of Civil Engineers—Figs. 2.26, 5.6, 5.14, 6.29, 7.5 and 7.16.

The Tudor Engineering Company—Fig. 6.16.

L'Institut Technique du Bâtiment et des Travaux Publiques—Fig. 7.17.

B.S.P. International Foundations Ltd.—Figs. 8.5, 8.24, 8.26 and 8.37, Table 8.7 and Plate VIII.

Redhurst Engineering Co. Ltd.—Fig. 8.1.

C.E.T. (Plant) Ltd.—Figs. 8.2, 8.4 and 8.7.

*Dock and Harbour Authority*—Figs. 8.20 and 8.39.

Frankipile Ltd.—Figs. 8.25 and 12.14.

Alphapile Ltd.—Fig. 8.27.

Western Foundation Corporation—Figs. 8.28, 8.29 and 8.40.

Raymond International Inc.—Fig. 8.30.

West's Piling and Construction Co. Ltd.—Fig. 8.31.

Pressure Piling Co. (Parent) Ltd.—Fig. 8.36.

British Steel Corporation—Table 8.5, Table 8.6 and Table 10.1 (*a*) and (*c*).

Edmund Nuttall, Sons & Co. (London) Ltd.—Fig. 9.21.

Norwegian Geotechnical Institute—Figs. 2.32 and 9.24.

Columbia University Press—Fig. 10.7.

Société Technique pour l'Utilisation de la Precontrainte and Société Auxiliaire d'Études et d'Entreprises—Fig. 10.29.

Cementation Co. Ltd.—Figs. 11.34 and 11.35.

Pynford Ltd.—Fig. 12.12.

Brendan Butler (London) Ltd.—Plate IX.

Peter Lind & Co. Ltd.—Plate X.

A. Waddington & Son Ltd.—Plate XI.

Boston Society of Civil Engineers—Table 2.3.

University of Illinois—Table 2.4.

United States Steel International (New York) Inc.—Table 10.1 (*e*).

Thyssen Stahlunion—Export—Table 10.1 (*b*).

Columeta, Luxembourg—Table 10.1 (*d*).

Krupp Stahlexport—Table 10.1 (*f*) Pilcon Engineering Ltd—Plate II.

British Standards Institution—Table 1.1 and extract from C.P.3: Chapter V: Loading. Complete copies of these Codes may be purchased from the British Standards Institution, 2 Park Street, London, W.1.

Institution of Civil Engineers—Illustrations appearing in their Journals and Proceedings, and in *Géotechnique* as listed in the bibliographies at the end of each chapter.

ISLEWORTH
1974

M. J. T.

# Preface to the First Edition

THE author's aim has been to provide a manual of foundation design and construction methods for the practising engineer. The book is not intended to be a textbook on soil mechanics, but it does include examples of the applications of this science to foundation engineering. The principles of the science are stated only briefly; the reader should refer to the relevant textbooks for explanations of its theory. It is hoped that the limitations and pitfalls of soil mechanics have been clearly set out—undue reliance on soil mechanics can be dangerous if foundation designs are based on inadequate data or on the use of wrong investigational techniques.

Professor Peck has listed three attributes necessary to the practice of subsurface engineering; these are a knowledge of precedents, familiarity with soil mechanics, and a working knowledge of geology. He believes the first of these to be by far the most important. Regarding soil mechanics, he states—

"The everyday procedures now used to calculate bearing capacity, settlement, or factor of safety of a slope, are nothing more than the use of the framework of soil mechanics to organize experience. If the techniques of soil testing and the theories had not led to results in accord with experience and field observations, they would not have been adopted for practical, widespread use. Indeed, the procedures are valid and justified only to the extent that they have been verified by experience. In this sense, the ordinary procedures of soil mechanics are merely devices for interpolating among the specific experiences of many engineers in order to solve our own problems, or which we recognize to fall within the limits of previous experience."

The author has included information on ordinary foundations, including the economic design of house foundations, as a help to architects and builders in the use of the present-day techniques of

ix

investigation and construction. The application of soil mechanics science to the carrying capacity of pile foundations of all types is a comparatively new development, but is coming to be recognized as having advantages over older methods using dynamic formulae, and this subject is fully treated. It is hoped that the information given on large-diameter bored-pile foundations will be helpful in aiding the design of foundations of tall multi-storey buildings. Experience in recent years has shown the economies which these high-capacity piles can give over the more conventional types where heavy foundation loads are to be carried.

The background information on soil mechanics has been mainly drawn from Terzaghi and Peck's *Soil Mechanics in Engineering Practice* (John Wiley). For examples of constructional problems the author has drawn freely on his experiences with George Wimpey & Co. Ltd., and he is indebted to Dr. L. J. Murdock, D.Sc., M.I.C.E., manager of their Central Laboratory, for permission to publish this information, together with illustrations and photographs. General information on current design practice in Great Britain has been obtained from the Institution of Civil Engineers Code of Practice No. 4 (1954), "Foundations," with the kind permission of the Institution.

The author gratefully acknowledges the help and criticism of his colleagues in the preparation of the book, and in particular of A. D. Rae, B.Sc., for checking the manuscript and proofs. Thanks are especially due to Professor H. O. Ireland, of the University of Illinois, for critical reading of the manuscript and advice on its application to American engineering practice. The illustrations are the work of Mrs. W. Alder and Mrs. P. Payne.

AMERSHAM                                              M. J. T.
1963

$\bar{K}_s$ coefficient for skin friction on piles

$K_V$ modulus of compressibility

$L$ length of foundation

$L_w$ liquid limit

$L_p$ plastic limit

$l$ span of foundation beam

$l_a$ lever arm of resistance moment

$M$ bending moment

$M_r$ moment of resistance

$m$ Poisson's ratio (and modular ratio)

$m_v$ coefficient of volume compressibility

$N$ number of blows in standard penetration test

$N_c$, $N_q$ and $N_\gamma$ bearing capacity factors

$P_a$ total pressure on back of retaining wall

$p$ total overburden pressure

$p_o$ effective overburden pressure

$p_{cb}$ permissible compressive stress in concrete in bending

$p_{st}$ permissible tensile stress in reinforcement

$Q$ discharge from a pumped well

$Q_d$ ultimate carrying capacity of a deep foundation

$Q_{pr}$ ultimate carrying capacity of base of deep foundation

$Q_p$ ultimate carrying capacity of a single pile

$Q_u$ ultimate carrying capacity of a pile group

$q$ unit total foundation pressure

$q_a$ unit allowable bearing pressure

$q_b$ unit end resistance

$q_e$ unit effective pressure

$q_f$ unit ultimate bearing capacity

$q_n$ unit net foundation pressure

$q_s$ unit maximum safe bearing capacity

$s$ shear strength

$s_p$ safe punching shear strength

$T$ time factor

$t_v$ yield point of reinforcement

$u$   cube crushing strength of concrete

$W$   total vertical load on a foundation

$Z_p$   modulus of section of sheet piling

$z$   vertical distance below a foundation

$\alpha$   adhesion factor

$\delta$   settlement or angle of wall friction

$\phi$   angle of shearing resistance

$\gamma$   density

$\gamma_w$   density of water

$\gamma_{sat}$   saturated density of soil

$\gamma_{sub}$   submerged density of soil

$\lambda$   shape factor

$\mu$   coefficient used for calculating $\rho_c$

$\rho_c$   consolidation settlement

$\rho_f$   final settlement

$\rho_i$   immediate settlement

$\rho_{oed}$   settlement calculated from oedometer tests

$\sigma_z$   vertical stress at any point $z$ below foundation level

$\tau$   shear stress

**Errata**

page 34, line 12, for 'cost' read 'costs'.

page 35, line 34, for 'to surcharge' read 'to the surcharge'.

page 105, Table 2, for 'Reductions in total distributions' read 'Reduction in total distributed'.

page 207, line 41, for 'Naldon' read 'Maldon'.

page 293, line 3 should be deleted.

page 385, line 6, for '457/mm' read '457 mm'.

page 385, line 7, for 'silty overlain' read 'silty sand overlain'.

page 392, line 20, for 'adhesion (Fig. 7.10)' read 'adhesion factors (Fig. 7.10)'.

page 498, line 31, for 'who where responsible' read 'who were responsible'.

page 622. Table 10.1 (cont.) heading, for 'Steel Sheeting Piling' read 'Steel Sheet Piling'.

page 672, line 17, for equation read $= h_{max} = \sqrt[3]{(0\cdot2712 \times 2962)}$.

# Contents

xi

## Contents

*The Plates* (I–XVI) *are positioned at the end of the book.*

# List of Symbols

$A$    base area of foundation

$B$    width of foundation

$b$    width of foundation

$C$    constant of compressibility (for Dutch Cone test)

$C_{kd}$    cone resistance (for Dutch Cone test)

$c$    unit cohesion

$\bar{c}$    average unit cohesion

$C_c$    coefficient of compressibility

$C_v$    coefficient of consolidation

$D$    depth of foundation below ground level

$d$    effective depth

$E$    Young's modulus

$E_f$    efficiency ratio of pile group

$e$    voids ratio (or eccentricity)

$F_1$ and $F_2$    factors for calculating immediate settlement

$f_s$    unit skin friction

$H$    thickness of soil layer

$H_c$    critical height of slope

$I$    moment of inertia

$I_p$    influence factor for calculating immediate settlement

$K$    coefficient of permeability

$K_a$    coefficient of active earth pressure

$K_p$    coefficient of passive earth pressure

# 1

# Site Investigations and Soil Mechanics

A SITE investigation in one form or another is always required for any engineering or building structure. The investigation may range in scope from a simple examination of the surface soils with or without a few shallow trial pits, to a detailed study of the soil and ground water conditions to a considerable depth below the surface by means of boreholes and in-situ and laboratory tests on the materials encountered. The extent of the work depends on the importance and foundation arrangement of the structure, the complexity of the soil conditions, and the information which may be available on the behaviour of existing foundations on similar soils. Thus it is not the normal practice to sink boreholes and carry out soil tests for single or two-storey dwelling houses or similar structures since there is usually adequate knowledge of the required foundation depths and bearing pressures in any particular locality. Sufficient information to check the presumed soil conditions can usually be obtained by examining open sewer trenches or shallow excavations for roadworks, or from a few shallow trial pits or hand auger borings. Only if troublesome foundation conditions such as layers of peat or loose fill material were encountered would it be necessary to sink deep boreholes, possibly supplemented by soil tests. More extensive investigations for light structures are needed when building in ground conditions where there is no information on foundation behaviour; for example in undeveloped territories overseas where there may be climatic or other factors which have an important effect on foundation design.

A detailed site investigation involving deep boreholes and laboratory testing of soils is always a necessity for heavy structures such as bridges, multi-storey buildings, or industrial plants. Even if rock is known to be present at a shallow depth it is advisable to excavate down to expose the rock in a few places to ensure that there are no zones of deep weathering or heavily shattered or faulted rock. Thorough investigations are equally necessary for engineering structures founded in deep excavations. As well as providing information for foundation design, they provide essential information on the soil and ground water conditions to contractors tendering for the work. Thus, money is saved by obtaining realistic and competitive tenders based on adequate foreknowledge of the ground conditions. A reputable contractor will not gamble on excavation work if its cost amounts to a substantial proportion of the whole project; he will add a correspondingly large sum to his tender to cover him for the unknown conditions. Hence the saying "You pay for the borings whether you have them or not."

It follows that contractors tendering for excavation work must be supplied with all the details of the site investigation. It is not unknown for the engineer to withhold certain details such as groundwater level observations under the mistaken idea that this might save money in claims by the contractor if water levels are subsequently found to be different from those encountered in the borings. This is a fallacy; the contractor will either allow in his tender for the unknown risks involved or he will take a gamble. If his gamble fails and the water conditions turn out to be worse than he assumed then he will surely make a claim.

An engineer undertaking a site investigation may engage local labour for trial pit excavation or hand auger boring, or he may employ a contractor for boring and soil sampling. If laboratory testing is required the boring contractor can send the samples to an independent testing laboratory. The engineer then undertakes the soil mechanics analysis for foundation design or he may ask the testing laboratory to do this analysis. Alternatively, a specialist contractor offering comprehensive facilities for boring, sampling, field and laboratory testing and soil mechanics analysis may undertake the whole investigation. This is much to be preferred to the system whereby one organization does the borings, another the testing and yet another the analysis. Only a single organization can provide the essential continuity and close relationship between field, laboratory and office work. It also has the advantage of permitting the boring and testing programme to be readily modified in the light of information made available as the work proceeds. Additional samples can be obtained, as necessary, from soil layers shown by laboratory testing to be particularly significant. In-situ testing can be substituted for laboratory testing if desired.

Whether or not the specialist contractor who undertakes borings and soil tests should also carry out the engineering analysis and foundation design is a rather delicate question to which there can be no general answer. Certainly the specialist contractor is in the most favourable position to do the engineering analysis, since he has first-hand knowledge of the soil conditions and knows when to put full reliance on test data, and when unreliable data should be disregarded. However, there are many engineering organizations such as firms of consulting engineers, local authorities, Government departments and others who employ staff having the necessary specialist knowledge of soil mechanics to undertake analysis of field and laboratory test data. Provided that close liaison is maintained with the single or separate organizations undertaking the boring and testing, this should be a satisfactory procedure. The structural design of the foundations is another matter and it is not the usual practice for a site investigation contractor to undertake this side of the work as it is closely related to the design of the superstructure and the two must be considered together.

The various procedures for undertaking site investigations as outlined above vary from one country to another. In Britain much of the investigation work is performed by organizations offering comprehensive facilities for boring, testing, and engineering analysis, including geological and geophysical work. In North and South America and in European countries it is generally the practice for borings to be done by specialist contractors with the testing and engineering analysis undertaken by universities, technical colleges, or independent testing laboratories, although the larger Government authorities such as the U.S. Bureau of Reclamation and some specialist soil investigation contractors in U.S.A. have their own comprehensive services. In Holland, Denmark, Norway, and Sweden a great deal of the work both for Government and private projects is undertaken by single Government bodies which have full facilities for boring, testing, and analysis.

Whatever procedure the engineer adopts for carrying out his investigation work it is essential that the individuals or organization undertaking the work should be conscientious and completely reliable. Site investigation procedure has advanced considerably since the time when in 1880, the official report on the Tay Bridge disaster commented, "It is said that engineers are always liable to be deceived by borers, and that, therefore, Sir Thomas Bouch could not be held to blame on that account. This does not satisfy me. I should have thought that, if engineers are liable to be deceived by borers, it is all the more important that before designing a bridge they should satisfy themselves beyond a doubt, of the accuracy of the borings."[1.1] Nevertheless the engineer has an important responsibility to his employers in selecting a competent organization and in satisfying himself by checks in the field and on laboratory or office work that the work has been undertaken with accuracy and thoroughness.

### Information Required from a Site Investigation

Assuming a fairly detailed study is required, the following information should be obtained in the course of a site investigation for foundation engineering purposes—

(*a*) The general topography of the site as it affects foundation design and construction, e.g. surface configuration, adjacent property, the presence of watercourses, ponds, hedges, trees, rock outcrops, etc., and the available access for construction vehicles and plant.

(*b*) The location of buried services such as electric power and telephone cables, water mains, and sewers.

(*c*) The general geology of the area with particular reference to the main geological formations underlying the site and the possibility of subsidence from mineral extraction or other causes.

(*d*) The previous history and use of the site including information on any defects or failures of existing or former buildings attributable to foundation conditions.

(*e*) Any special features such as the possibility of earthquakes or climatic factors such as flooding, seasonal swelling and shrinkage, permafrost, or soil erosion.

(*f*) The availability and quality of local constructional materials such as concrete aggregates, building and road stone, and water for constructional purposes.

(*g*) For maritime or river structures information on normal spring and neap tide ranges, extreme high and low tidal ranges and river levels, seasonal river levels and discharges, velocity of tidal and river currents, and other hydrographic and meteorological data.

(*h*) A detailed record of the soil and rock strata and ground water conditions within the zones affected by foundation bearing pressures and construction operations, or of any deeper strata affecting the site conditions in any way.

(*j*) Results of laboratory tests on soil and rock samples appropriate to the particular foundation design or constructional problems.

(*k*) Results of chemical analyses on soil or ground water to determine possible deleterious effects on foundation structures.

A more detailed list of other information required in connexion with general engineering design and construction is given in the *British Standard Code of Practice for Site Investigations* (CP 2001)[1,2].

Items (*a*) to (*g*) above can be obtained from a general reconnaissance of the site and from a study of geological memoirs and maps and other published records. A close inspection given by walking over the site area will often show significant indications of subsurface features. For example, concealed swallow holes (sink holes) in chalk or limestone formations are often revealed by random depressions and marked irregularity in the ground surface; soil creep is indicated by wrinkling of the surface on a hillside slope, or leaning trees; abandoned mine workings are shown by old shafts or heaps of mineral waste; glacial deposits may be indicated by mounds or hummocks (drumlins) in a generally flat topography; and river or lake deposits by flat low-lying areas in valleys. The surface indications of ground water are the presence of springs or wells, and marshy ground with reeds (indicating the presence of a high water table with poor drainage and the possibility of peat). Professional geological advice should be sought in the case of large projects covering extensive areas.

On very extensive sites, aerial photography is a valuable aid in site investigations. Skilled interpretations of aerial photographs can reveal much of the geology and topography of a site. Geological mapping from aerial photographs as practised by specialist firms is a well-established science.

Old maps as well as up-to-date publications should be studied, since these may show the previous use of the site and are particularly valuable when investigating backfilled areas. Museums or libraries in the locality often provide much information in the form of maps, memoirs, and pictures or photographs of a site in past times. Local authorities should be consulted for details of buried services, and in Britain the National Coal Board for information on coal-mine workings. Some parts of Britain were worked for coal long before records of workings were kept, but it is sometimes possible to obtain information on these from museums and libraries. If particular information on the history of a site has an important bearing on foundation design, for example the location of buried pits or quarries, every endeavour should be made to cross-check sources of information especially if they are based on memory or hearsay. People's memories are notoriously unreliable on these matters.

Items (*h*), (*j*), and (*k*) of the list are obtained from boreholes or other methods of sub-surface exploration, together with field and laboratory testing of soils or rocks. It is important to describe the type and consistency of soils in the standard manner laid down in CP 2001. The standard descriptions are based on internationally recognized soil classifications and are shown in Table 1.1. Descriptions are given in the following sequence—

1. Consistency—for cohesive soils, e.g. soft, stiff, etc.
   Density—for non-cohesive soils, e.g. loose, dense, etc.
2. Structure (i.e. fissured, laminated, etc.).
3. Colour.
4. Particle size classification with the predominating type last.

As examples—

Stiff fissured brown clay;
Firm laminated grey clayey silt;
Loose yellow fine sand.

In some cases it may be relevant to state the odour of the soil, such as that caused by organic matter or chemical wastes, to draw attention to possible effects on foundation concrete or steel.

The divisions between the various ranges of particle size as shown in Table 1.1, i.e. gravels, sands, silts, and clays and their sub-divisions, are quite arbitrary but they generally accord with the behaviour of the soils in the engineering sense. For example, clays show quite different behaviour from sands when subjected to foundation pressures, and their drainage characteristics when pumping from foundation excavations are also very different. It is not usual to describe soils by other forms of classification, e.g. the Unified System of the U.S. Corps of Engineers and the Bureau of Reclamation, when considering them as foundation soils; such classifications are generally restricted to road and airfield work.

Rock types are given a simple geological classification descriptive of their engineering characteristics. There may be some confusion in describing the hardness of rocks when considering them in relation to soil consistency. Thus a weak sandstone will have a much higher bearing capacity than a soft clay. To avoid confusion the terms "friable" or "weakly-cemented" should be used to describe weak rocks wherever these terms are applicable. The current revisions of CP 2001 adopt a new system of nomenclature for rock strengths and substitute the terms "weak" and "strong" rocks to replace the previous "soft and hard". This system should help to avoid confusion with descriptions of soil consistency. Examples of engineering descriptions of rock types are—

Friable coarse-grained red sandstone;
Weakly-cemented porous shelly limestone;
Strong fissured purple siltstone;
Loose disintegrated grey shale;
Weak red and white decomposed granite.

## SITE INVESTIGATIONS OF FOUNDATION FAILURES

From time to time it is necessary to make investigations of failures or defects in existing structures. The approach is somewhat different from that of normal site investigation work, and usually takes the form of trial pits dug at various points to expose the soil at foundation level and the foundations themselves, together with deep trial pits or borings to investigate the full depth of the soil affected by bearing pressures. A careful note is taken of all visible cracking and movements in the superstructure since the pattern of cracking is indicative of the mode of foundation movement, e.g. by sagging or hogging. It is often necessary to make long-continued observations of changes in level and of movement of cracks by means of tell-tales. Glass or paper tell-tales stuck on the cracks by cement pats are of little use and are easily lost or damaged. The tell-tales should consist of brass or bronze plugs cemented into holes drilled in the wall on each side of the crack and so arranged that both vertical and horizontal movements can be measured by micrometer gauges. Similarly, points for taking levels should be well-secured against removal or displacement. They should consist preferably of steel bolts or pins set in the foundations and surrounded by a vertical pipe with a cover at ground level. The levels should be referred to a well-established datum point at some distance from the affected structure; ground movements which may have caused foundation failure should not cause similar movement of the levelling datum.

A careful study should be made of adjacent structures to ascertain whether failure is of general occurrence, as in mining subsidence, or whether it is due to localized conditions. The past history of the site should be investigated with particular reference to the former existence of trees, hedgerows, farm buildings, or waste dumps. The proximity of any growing trees should be noted, and information should be sought on the seasonal occurrence of cracking, for example if cracks tend to open or close in winter or summer, or are worse in dry years or wet years. Any industrial plant in which forging hammers or presses cause ground vibrations should be noted, and inquiries should be made about any construction operations such as

| | | Size and nature of particles | |
|---|---|---|---|
| | | Principal soil types | |
| | 1 | 2 | |
| | Types | Field identification | |
| **Coarse grained, non-cohesive** | Boulders<br>Cobbles | Larger than 200 mm in diameter.<br>Mostly between 200 mm and 75 mm. | |
| | Gravels | Mostly between 75 mm and 2·36 mm BS sieve.* | |
| | Uniform<br><br>———<br><br>Graded | Sands | Composed of particles mostly between 2·36 mm and 75 $\mu$m BS sieves, and visible to the naked eye.<br>Very little or no cohesion when dry.<br><br>Sands may be classified as uniform or well graded according to the distribution of particle size.<br>Uniform sands may be divided into coarse sands between 2·36 mm and 600 $\mu$m sieves, medium sands between 600 $\mu$m and 212 $\mu$m sieves and fine sands between 212 $\mu$m and 75 $\mu$m sieves. |
| **Fine grained, cohesive** | Low plasticity | Silts | Particles mostly passing 75 $\mu$m sieve<br>Particles mostly invisible or barely visible to the naked eye. Some plasticity and exhibits marked dilatancy. Dries moderately quickly and can be dusted off the fingers. Dry lumps possess cohesion but can be powdered easily in the fingers. |
| | Medium plasticity<br><br>———<br><br>High plasticity | Clays | Dry lumps can be broken but not powdered.<br>They also disintegrate under water.<br><br>Smooth touch and plastic, no dilatancy. Sticks to the fingers and dries slowly.<br>Shrinks appreciably on drying, usually showing cracks.<br>Lean and fat clays show those properties to a moderate and high degree respectively. |
| **Organic** | Peats | Fibrous organic material, usually brown or black in colour. | |

*Note.* The principal soil types in the above table usually occur in nature as siliceous sands and silts and as alumino-siliceous clays, but varieties very different chemically and mineralogically also occur. These may give rise to peculiar mechanical and chemical characteristics which, from the engineering standpoint, may be of sufficient importance to require special consideration. The following are examples—

Lateritic weathering may give rise to deposits with unusually low silica contents, which are either gravels or clays; but intermediate grades are rare.

| Composite types 3 | Strength and structural characteristics | | | |
| | Strength 4 | | Structure 5 | |
| | Term | Field test | Term | Field identification |
| ·ulder avels ·ggin ·ndy avels | Loose | Can be excavated with spade. 50 mm wooden peg can be easily driven. | Homogeneous | Deposit consisting essentially of one type. |
| ·ty sands ·icaceous ·nds ·teritic ·nds ·ayey ·nds | Compact | Requires pick for excavation. 50 mm wooden peg hard to drive more than 50 to 100 mm. | Stratified | Alternating layers of varying types. |
| | Slightly cemented | Visual examination. Pick removes soils in lumps which can be abraded with thumb. | | |
| ·ams ·ayey silts | Soft | Easily moulded in the fingers. | Homogeneous | Deposit consisting essentially of one type. |
| ·ganic silts ·icaceous ·s | Firm | Can be moulded by strong pressure in the fingers. | Stratified | Alternating layers of varying types. |
| ·ulder ·ys ·ndy clays | Very soft | Exudes between fingers when squeezed in fist. | Fissured | Breaks into polyhedral fragments along fissure planes. |
| | Soft | Easily moulded in fingers. | Intact | No fissures. |
| ·ty clays ·arls | Firm | Can be moulded by strong pressure in the fingers. | Homogeneous | Deposits consisting essentially of one type. |
| ·ganic ·ys | | | Stratified | Alternating layers of varying types. If layers are thin the soil may be described as laminated. |
| | Stiff | Cannot be moulded in fingers. | | |
| ·teritic ·ys | Hard | Brittle or very tough. | Weathered | Usually exhibits crumb or columnar structure. |
| ·ndy, silty or ·yey peats | Firm | Fibres compressed together. | | |
| | Spongy | Very compressible and open structure. | | |

Volcanic ash may give rise to deposits of very variable composition which may come under any of the principal soil types.

Deposits of sand grade may be composed of calcareous material (e.g. shell sand, coral sand) or may contain considerable proportions of mica (where grain shape is important) or glauconite (where softness of individual grains is important).

Deposits of silt and clay grade may contain a large proportion of organic matter (organic silts, clays, or muds) and clays may be calcareous (marls).

\* *See* Appendix I for relationship between British and American sieve sizes and the corresponding sieve openings.

The table in CP 2001 is in imperial units.

deep trenches, tunnels, blasting, or piling which may have been carried out in the locality.

## BOREHOLE LAYOUT

Whenever possible boreholes should be sunk as close as possible to the proposed foundations.  This is important where the bearing stratum is irregular in depth.  For the same reason the boreholes

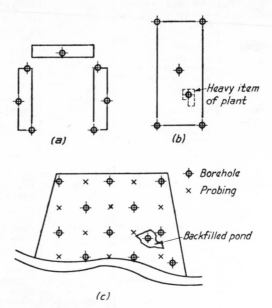

FIG. 1.1. TYPICAL BOREHOLE LAYOUTS
(a) Multi-storey flats.
(b) Factory building.
(c) Large development area where building layout is not decided.

should be accurately located in position and level in relation to the proposed structures.  Where the layout of the structures has not been decided at the time of making the investigation a suitable pattern of boreholes is an evenly spaced grid of holes.  For extensive areas it is possible to adopt a widely spaced grid of boreholes with some form of in-situ probes, such as dynamic or static cone penetration tests or wash probings, at a closer spacing within the borehole grid.  Suitable borehole layouts for various sites are shown in Figs. 1.1 (a), (b), and (c).

The required number of boreholes which need to be sunk on any particular location is a difficult problem which is closely bound up with the relative costs of the investigation and the project for which it is undertaken. Obviously the more boreholes that are sunk the more is known of the soil conditions and greater economy can be achieved in foundation design, and the risks of meeting unforeseen and difficult soil conditions which would greatly increase the costs of the foundation work become progressively less. However, an economic limit is reached when the cost of borings outweighs any savings in foundation costs and merely adds to the overall cost of

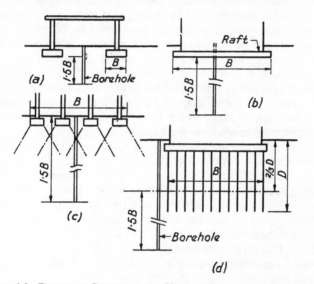

FIG. 1.2. DEPTHS OF BOREHOLES FOR VARIOUS FOUNDATION CONDITIONS

the project. For all but the smallest structures, at least two and preferably three boreholes should be sunk, so that the true dip of the strata can be established. Even so, false assumptions may still be made about stratification.

The depth to which boreholes should be sunk is governed by the depth of soil affected by foundation bearing pressures. The vertical stress on the soil at a depth of one and a half times the width of the loaded area is still one-fifth of the applied vertical stress at foundation level, and the shear stress at this depth is still appreciable. Thus, borings in soil should always be taken to a depth of at least one and a half times the width of the loaded area. In the case of narrow and widely spaced strip or pad foundations the borings are comparatively shallow (Fig. 1.2 (*a*)) but for large raft foundations the borings will have to be deep (Fig. 1.2 (*b*)). Where strip or pad footings are closely spaced so that there is overlapping of the zones of pressure the whole loaded area becomes in effect a raft foundation with correspondingly deep borings (Fig. 1.2 (c)). In the case of piled foundations the ground should be explored below pile-point level to cover the zones of soil affected by loading transmitted through the piles. It is usual to assume that a large piled area in uniform soil behaves as a raft foundation with the equivalent raft at a depth of two-thirds of the length of the piles (Fig. 1.2 (d)).

Where foundations are taken down to rock, either in the form of strip or pad foundations or by piling, it is necessary to prove that rock is in fact present at the assumed depths. Where the rock is shallow this can be done by direct examination of exposures in trial pits or trenches, but when borings have to be sunk to locate and prove bedrock it is important to ensure that boulders or layers of cemented soils are not mistaken for bedrock. This necessitates percussion boring or rotary diamond core drilling to a depth of at least 3 m in bedrock in areas where boulders are known to occur. On sites where it is known from geological evidence that boulders are not present a somewhat shallower penetration into rock can be accepted. In some areas boulders larger than 3 m have been found, and it is advisable to core the rock to a depth of 6 m for important structures. Mistakes in the location of bedrock in boreholes have in many cases led to costly changes in the design of structures and even to failures; a notable example was the failure of the Tay Bridge, which was directly attributable to the mistaking of a compact layer of gravel for bedrock. This error necessitated a change in the design of the bridge supports from massive brick piers to slender cast-iron columns which failed during a winter gale in 1879.[1.1]

Direct exposure of rock in trial pits or trenches is preferable to boring, wherever economically possible, since widely spaced core drillings do not always give a true indication of shattering, faulting, or other structural weakness in the rock.

When boreholes are sunk in water-bearing ground which will be subsequently excavated, it is important to ensure that they are backfilled with concrete or well-rammed puddled clay. If this is not done the boreholes may be a source of considerable inflow of water into the excavations. In a report on an investigation for a deep basement structure in the Glasgow area the author gave a warning about the possibility of upheaval of clay at the bottom of the excavation, due to artesian pressure in the underlying water-bearing rock. After completing the basement the contractor was asked whether he had had any trouble with this artesian water. The answer was that "the only trouble we had with water was up through your borehole." In another case, large bored piles with enlarged bases were designed to be founded within an impervious clay layer which was underlain by sand containing water under artesian pressure. The risks of somewhat greater settlement due to founding in the compressible clay were accepted to avoid the difficulty of constructing the piles in the underlying, less compressible sand. However, considerable difficulty was experienced in excavating the base of one of the piles because of water flowing up from the sand strata through an unsealed exploratory borehole.

## METHODS OF SUB-SURFACE EXPLORATION

### Exploration in Soils

Methods of determining the stratification and engineering characteristics of sub-surface soils are as follows—

Trial Pits
Hand Auger Borings (post-hole auger)
Mechanical Auger Borings
Shell and Auger Borings
Percussion Borings
Wash Borings
Wash Probings
Dynamic Cone Penetration Tests
Static Cone Penetration Tests
Vane Shear Tests
Plate Bearing Tests

*Trial pit* sinking is the cheapest method of exploration to shallow depths. Pits can be excavated by hand using any local labour, but small tractor-mounted mechanical excavators are, if locally available, economical to use and rapid in operation. If it is necessary for men to work at the bottom of pits, say for soil sampling, then support of the sides of pits deeper than 1·2 m will be necessary if there is the slightest risk of collapse. Safety in excavations and methods of timbering are discussed in Chapter 9. In water-bearing soils, particularly in sands, there is likely to be difficulty in excavating below the water table and trial pits may be more costly than borings in such conditions. Methods of timbering trial pits are described on page 577.

Trial pits enable a clear picture to be obtained of the stratification of the soils and the presence of any lenses or pockets of weaker material. They enable hand-cut samples of soil, giving the minimum of disturbance, to be taken. They are particularly valuable in investigating the nature of fill material when voids, loosely deposited layers, or deleterious material can readily be recognized. In fact trial pits or trenches are the only really reliable means of obtaining adequate information on filled ground or very variable natural deposits.

*Hand or mechanical auger borings* are also a cheap means of sub-surface exploration in favourable types of soil, for the soils must have sufficient cohesion to stand unsupported in an unlined borehole and there must be no large cobbles, boulders, or other obstructions which would prevent rotation of the auger. If carefully done, augering gives the least disturbance of any boring method. Hand augers (also known as post-hole augers) are usually of 150 mm or 200 mm diameter for site investigation work and are provided with extension rods. Holes can be sunk to depths of 5 to 7 m in soft to firm clays or sands possessing some cohesion. Holes sunk by the mechanical auger of the type illustrated in Plate IX are limited in depth by the "kelly-bar" to 12 m. Some types have means of extending the drill rods to sink holes to much greater depths (*see* p. 527). Worm flight augers in which the soil cuttings are brought to the surface by a continuously revolving helical screw can be used for site investigation work if they are provided with a hollow central tube down which the sampling apparatus or in-situ testing gear can be lowered.

*Shell and auger borings* can be carried out in all types of soil since the boreholes can be lined where required with steel casing tubes, and a wide variety of tools are used for different soil and rock types. A shell and auger rig employing a friction winch to raise and lower the boring tools is shown in Plate I.

Boring in cohesive soils is effected by augers, "clay-circle" (an open-ended steel tube with cutting edge) or "shell" (an open-ended steel tube with a flap-valve and cutting edge at its lower end). Sands and gravels are removed from the boreholes by the shell. When boring through rock or boulders, chisels of various types are used to break up the rock and the fragments are cleaned out by the shell. In hard rock the progress is slow and it is preferable to employ rotary core drilling as described later in this chapter. The use of water poured in the hole is often unavoidable in shell and auger boring, particularly when boring in gravels. However, it should always be used sparingly and the occasions when water is added should be noted on the site borehole records.

Machines used for *percussion boring* loosen the soil by repeated blows of a heavy chisel or spud, and the resulting slurry is removed by shell or by washing. The stroke of each blow is controlled mechanically by means of a walking beam. This method of drilling for site investigation purposes is deprecated by some engineers on the grounds of possible deep disturbance of the soil and the lack of sensitivity or "feel" in its operation. However, a skilled operator can regulate the force of the blow to a degree at least equal to that obtainable by the friction winch used in shell and auger boring. Therefore, if due attention is paid to adequate soil sampling there is no reason why borings made by the percussion drill should not yield reliable information.

In *wash boring* (Fig. 1.3) the soil is loosened and removed from the borehole by a stream of water or drilling mud issuing from the lower end of the wash pipe which is worked up and down or rotated by

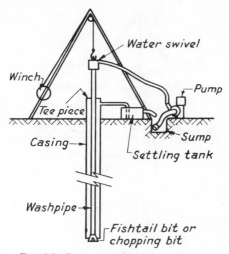

FIG. 1.3. EQUIPMENT FOR WASH BORINGS

hand in the borehole. The water or mud flow carries the soil up the annular space between the wash pipe and the casing, and it overflows at ground level where the soil in suspension is allowed to settle in a pond or tank and the fluid is re-circulated or discharged to waste as required. Samples of the settled-out soil can be retained for identification purposes but this procedure is often unreliable as the cuttings are mixed as they flow up the borehole and in the settling tank, and the structure of the soil is destroyed. However, accurate identification can be obtained if frequent "dry" sampling is resorted to, using undisturbed sample tubes (*see* p. 21) or the split-spoon sampler (*see* p. 27). Wash boring has the advantage that the structure or density of the soil below the bottom of the borehole is not disturbed by blows of the boring tools, but the method cannot be used in large gravels or soil containing boulders. It is best suited to uniform sands or clays. A variety of tools are used for fitting to the end of the wash pipe for different soil types. The use of mud instead of water allows the hole to remain uncased in cohesionless soils.

*Wash probing* (Fig. 1.4) is a simple method of determining the depth to an interface between soft or loose soils and a stiff or compact layer. The wash pipes delivering water at high pressure are worked up and down in an uncased hole. Thus there is no positive identification of the soil since there is often no return of the wash-water. "Dry" sampling through the wash pipes cannot easily be achieved and in many cases is impossible. However, if ample water is available

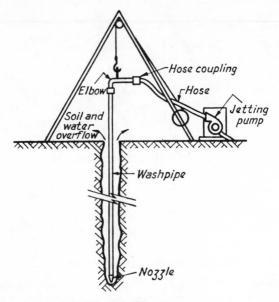

FIG. 1.4. WASH PROBING

and if the soil does not contain large cobbles or boulders, the method is rapid and cheap in establishing the level of a well-defined stratum which can be located by the "feel" of the wash pipes as they are worked up and down. Wash probings must be correlated with boreholes sunk by more positive methods and they should only be regarded as "filling-in" data between widely spaced boreholes. They are a convenient method of rapid sub-bottom exploration for river or marine works; to investigate, for example, the depth of sand or mud over bedrock on a piling or dredging project.

*Dynamic or static cone penetration equipment* is used to determine the characteristics and stratification of soil deposits by measuring either the number of blows required to drive the cone a fixed distance (dynamic cone tests) or the force required to push the cone into the soil at progressively increasing depths (static cone tests). A record of penetration resistance with depth is obtained from which it is possible, by correlation with boreholes, to deduce the stratification of the soils. However, such methods are of more value in determining the bearing characteristics of the soils by direct in-situ measurement and as such they are described later in this chapter.

## Soil Sampling

There are two main types of soil samples which can be recovered from boreholes or trial pits.

*Disturbed samples*, as their name implies, are samples taken from the boring tools: examples are auger parings, the contents of the split-spoon sampler in the standard penetration test (*see* p. 27), sludges from the shell or wash-water return, or hand samples dug from trial pits. The structure of the natural soil may be disturbed to a considerable degree by the action of the boring tools or excavation equipment. The samples are placed in airtight jars or bags and labelled to identify the locality, borehole number, depth of sample, and date of sampling.

*Undisturbed samples* represent as closely as is practicable the true in-situ structure and water content of the soil. The usual method of obtaining undisturbed samples is to drive a thin-walled tube for its full extent into the soil and then to withdraw the tube and its contents. It is important not to overdrive the sampler as this compresses the contents. It should be recognized that no sample taken by driving a tube into the soil can be truly undisturbed. In fact in soft and sensitive soils the true in-situ shear strength as determined by vane tests has been shown to be three or four times the shear strength determined by unconfined compression tests on "undisturbed" tube samples taken from borings. The care in sampling procedure and the elaborateness of the equipment depends on the class of work which is being undertaken, the importance of accurate results on the design of the works, and the funds allowed for the investigation.

The Swedish Geotechnical Institute[1,3] recognizes three main classes of sampling, namely—

*"Research" class.* Highest possible quality of sampling with little regard to costs (i.e. sampling on research projects, or for very important or expensive foundation structures).

*"Routine" class.* A fairly good quality of sample but with some attention paid to keeping both the equipment fairly simple and the time of operation reasonably short in order to avoid excessive costs (i.e. sampling by specialist soil mechanics organizations for fairly important foundation investigations).

*"Simple" class.* The samples must not be seriously disturbed but the chief consideration is given to avoiding delay in boring and the use of simple apparatus to keep costs as low as possible (i.e. sampling by non-specialist organizations without skilled supervision).

The "research" and "routine" classes of sampling require a good design of sampler such as a piston or thin-walled sampler which is jacked or pulled down into the soil and not driven down by blows of a hammer. The "simple" class of sampling employs open-drive tube samplers which are hammered into the soil by blows of a sliding hammer or careful hand-cut samples taken from trial pits. There is a great difference in cost between the three classes but the engineer should recognize the value of good quality sampling if this can result in economies in design; for example good quality sampling means higher indicated shear strengths, with higher bearing pressures and consequently reduced foundation costs. In certain projects good sampling may mean the difference between a certain construction operation being judged possible or impossible, for example the placing of an embankment on very soft soil for a bridge approach. If the shear strength as indicated by poor sampling procedure is low then the engineer may decide it is impossible to use an embanked approach and will have to employ an expensive piled viaduct. On the other hand in "insensitive" clays such as stiff boulder clays the sampling procedure has not much effect on shear strength and the simple class of sampling may give quite adequate information. Also, elaborate samplers such as the fixed piston types may be incapable of operation in clays containing appreciable amounts of gravel.

The engineer should study the foundation problem and decide what degree of elaborateness in sampling is economically justifiable, and he should keep in mind that in-situ tests such as the vane or cone tests may give more reliable information than laboratory tests on undisturbed samples. If in-situ tests are adopted, elaborateness in undisturbed sampling is unnecessary and the "simple" class is sufficient to give a check on identification of soil types. A good practice, recommended by Rowe[1.4] is to adopt continuous sampling in the first boreholes drilled on a site. An open-drive sampler with an internal split sleeve is used to enable the samples to be split longitudinally for examination of the soil fabric. The critical soil layers can be identified and the appropriate class of sampling or *in-situ* testing adopted.

The *piston samplers* as used in the "research" or "routine" classes are of two types, the *floating piston* or the *fixed piston*. In the case of the floating piston sampler (Fig. 1.5), the tube is lowered down the borehole with the piston closing it at cutting edge level. When the tube is driven down, the piston is prevented from moving downwards with the tube by a rod or wire line passing up the borehole to ground level. However, the piston remains in close contact with the top of the sample so aiding retention of the soil in the tube during withdrawal. In the case of the fixed piston samplers (Fig. 1.6 (*a*)) the piston can be held at any desired level by a rigid rod extending to ground level. Thus the sampler, with its end closed by the piston, can be pushed down below the soil at the bottom of the borehole which is disturbed by the boring operations, and on reaching the depth where the ground is considered to be undisturbed the piston can be held in position and the tube pushed down. In fact in soft soils it is possible to push the sampler down through the soil to any desired depth, so allowing a number of samples to be taken without any boring being sunk (Fig. 1.6 (*b*)). Thus the fixed piston sampler has several operational advantages over the free piston type although its construction is rather more elaborate and considerable care is needed to keep the moving parts clean and free of corrosion. Piston samplers should never be driven down by hammer but should be pushed down by hydraulic jack or by a system of ropes and pulleys.

They can be used to recover samples of fine or silty sands having some cohesion, particularly when using some types of equipment which are provided with a ring of spring leaves which are forced into the bottom of the sample to support it.

Standard *open-drive samplers* which come into the "simple" class and are widely used for most investigations in Great Britain are generally made in

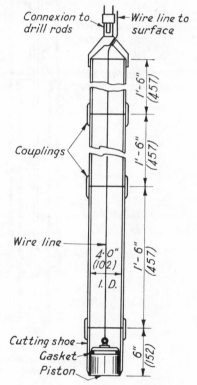

FIG. 1.5. FLOATING PISTON SAMPLER

4 in. and 1½ in. diameters. The widely-used British 4 in. by 18 in. long sampler is shown in Fig. 1.7. The lower end of the tube has a detachable cutting shoe and the upper end an extension piece

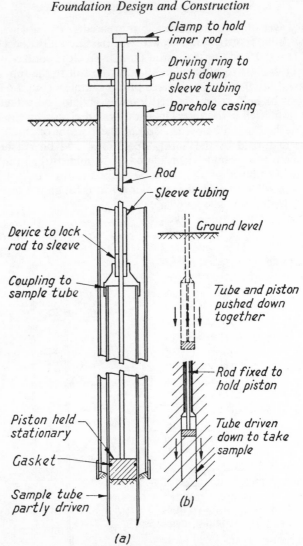

FIG. 1.6. FIXED PISTON SAMPLER
(*a*) Diagrammatic arrangement of sampler.
(*b*) Taking samples without boring.

(overdrive space) and an adaptor to connect the tube to a sliding hammer. The adaptor is fitted with a ball valve which permits air or water to be expelled from the tube as the soil rises within it, but which prevents re-entry of air or water as the tube is withdrawn from the borehole. Although the normal procedure is to drive the tube with blows of a sliding hammer actuated by the drilling rods, a better sample can be obtained if the tube is pushed down into the soil. The quicker the action of thrusting the tube the better the sample, so if a hydraulic jack is used, the ram should have a long stroke with a speed of advance of 0·2 to 0·3 m per s. The type of sampler shown in Fig. 1.7 is very suitable for British soil conditions where appreciable quantities of gravel may be found within clays,

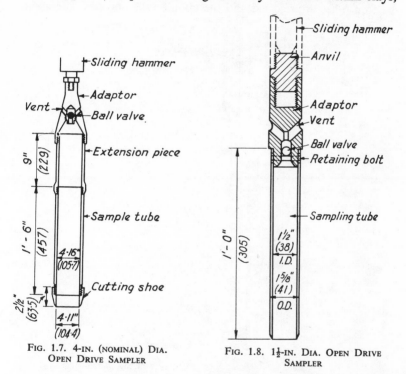

FIG. 1.7. 4-IN. (NOMINAL) DIA. OPEN DRIVE SAMPLER

FIG. 1.8. 1½-IN. DIA. OPEN DRIVE SAMPLER

and the soils are generally firm to stiff. The use of the detachable cutting shoe in particular allows very many re-uses of the tubes, which are simple and robust in construction.

The action of boring in soft and sensitive silts and clays is to disturb the soil for several borehole diameters below the bottom of the hole. Thus the upper part of an open drive sample in such soils will be wholly disturbed. Also, when the sample tube is rotated to shear off the soil at the cutting edge level before withdrawal of the tube, the rotation will cause disturbance of the lower part of the sample. Thus the whole length of a 460 mm long sample may well be fully or partially disturbed. Even straight withdrawal without rotation will cause "waisting" or "necking" of the bottom of the sample and consequent disturbance. The method of overcoming this difficulty is to use either a fixed piston sampler pushed below the zone of disturbance at the bottom of the borehole before fixing the piston and allowing the tube to be projected forward, or to couple three standard 460 mm long tubes together in the manner described by Serota and Jennings.[1.5] The contents of the top and bottom tubes are rejected and the middle tube and its contents are

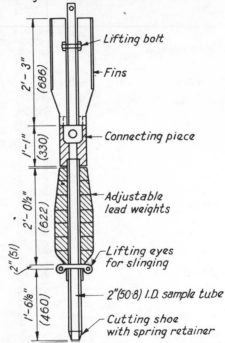

FIG. 1.9. HEAVY (300 kg) DROP SAMPLER FOR SEA-BED SAMPLING

retained. The soil in the top and bottom tubes should be augered out before uncoupling. Another advantage of using three tubes is that soft soils can be retained during withdrawal from the bore-hole, whereas with a single 460 mm tube it is quite likely that the soil will drop out.

Another type of standard open drive sampler is the $1\frac{1}{2}$ in. *diameter thin-walled tube* with an integral cutting edge (Fig. 1.8). It has a ball-valve adaptor similar to that used with the 4 in. diameter sampler. The $1\frac{1}{2}$ in. diameter tube is frequently used in conjunction with hand auger borings or small-diameter wash borings. It has the advantage that it can be driven and extracted with light hand tackle whereas the 4 in. tubes often require hydraulic jacks to extract them from stiff clays. It is standard practice in U.S.A. to use thin-walled open drive samplers with an integral cutting edge. These are generally 2 in. in diameter (Shelby tube samplers). The American practice has been widely copied in other parts of the world, but small-diameter samplers are of little use in soils containing gravel, and hence are not widely used in British practice.

Relatively undisturbed samples of soft sediments can be taken to depths of up to 3 m below the bed of the sea or rivers in a continuous length by means of *gravity* or *drop samplers*. The type developed by the British Institute of Oceanography is shown in Fig. 1.9. It is provided with lead weights to give a total mass of about 270 to 300 kg. This type of sampler has a very limited application to foundation engineering. It can be used for preliminary investigations for docks and harbours and for offshore oil well drilling structures.

Rotary methods using core barrels (including the Denison sampler) are used to obtain undistrubed samples of hard clays. Samplers of these types are described on pages 40 to 42.

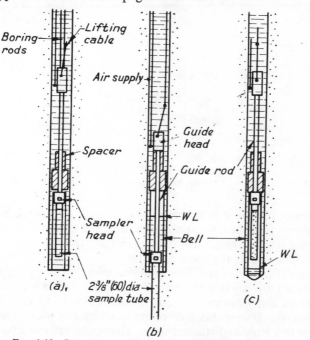

FIG. 1.10. SAMPLING IN SANDS WITH THE BISHOP SAMPLER

(*a*) Lowering sampler.
(*b*) Sampler driven, expelling air from bell.
(*c*) Withdrawing sampler into bell.

It has been noted that piston samplers can be used to retain fine sands or silty sands having some cohesion, especially if the piston samplers are provided with spring leaves just above the cutting edge which can be forced into the bottom of the sample to retain it in the tube. However, a more positive type of sampler which can be used in cohesionless soils below the water table is the *Bishop compressed air sampler*[1.6] shown in Fig. 1.10. This equipment has an inner $2\frac{3}{8}$ in. diameter tube to retain the sampler and an outer tube or "bell."

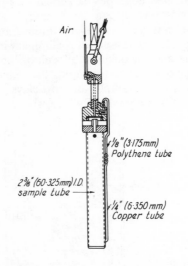

FIG. 1.11. MODIFICATION TO BISHOP SAMPLER BY SEROTA AND JENNINGS[1.5]

The inner tube is driven down into the soil, and compressed air introduced into the bell expels the water. The tube is then carefully retracted into the bell, when the pressure of the air on the underside of the tube retains the soil within it.

A modification of the Bishop device in which compressed air is introduced directly into the base of the inner tube has been described by Serota and Jennings[1.5] and is shown in Fig. 1.11. It is doubtful whether the Bishop sampler or its modification ever produced a sample in a truly undisturbed state. The action of boring (either the dropping of the shell or the suction in withdrawing the shell) inevitably causes disturbance of the soil at the bottom of the borehole (the disturbance is less with wash boring), and thrusting in the tube must cause further disturbance. In the case of a dense sand or a gravelly sand there will be an appreciable increase in density when driving in the tube and it is quite impossible to use the Bishop sampler in a very gravelly sand. In view of these drawbacks and the time taken to operate the compressed air sampler, it is generally preferable to rely on some form of in-situ test such as static or dynamic cone tests to obtain the relative in-situ density of sands and gravels. Only in the case of hand-cut samples in trial pits can truly undisturbed samples of sands and gravels be taken.

For a full description of soil sampling equipment and a discussion of the basic principles of soil sampling the reader is referred to the comprehensive treatise by Hvorslev.[1.7]

Equally important as care with sampling techniques to obtain minimum disturbance is attention to sealing, labelling, and transporting the tubes from the site to the laboratory. The ends of the samples should be trimmed and sealed with a micro-crystalline wax, or in the case of small-diameter tubes, by rubber stoppers. Any remaining space in the tubes should be packed with sand, shavings, or rags, and the tube labelled giving the location of the site, borehole number, depth of sample, and date. An identifying label should also be placed inside the tube in case the outside label becomes detached or illegible. The bottom of the sample should be clearly indicated so that the testing laboratory will know from which end the tube should be opened for extracting the test specimens.

Samples of soft sensitive soils should be carefully handled during transportation. They should be packed in boxes and wedged to stop the tubes rolling about. It is advisable to provide a van or car to take the sample boxes to the laboratory rather than to risk disturbance by vibration or rough handling in rail transport.

IN-SITU TESTING OF SOILS

Tests to determine the shear strength or density of soils in situ are a valuable means of investigation since these characteristics can be obtained directly without the disturbing effects of boring or sampling. They are particularly advantageous in soft sensitive clays and silts or loose sands. However, it is very important to remember that they give only one characteristic, the shear strength in the case of vane tests or the penetration resistance in the case of dynamic or static cone tests. Thus they must not be used as a substitute for borings but only as a supplementary method of investigation. One cannot identify from them the types of soil they encounter and the tests give no information on ground water conditions.

*The Vane Shear Test Apparatus* was developed to measure the shear strength of very soft and sensitive clays but in Scandinavian countries the vane test is also regarded as a reliable means of determining the shear strength of stiff fissured clays. A comprehensive review of the test techniques and their interpretation has been made

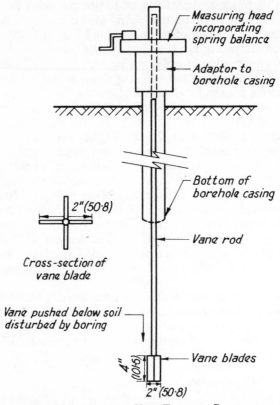

FIG. 1.12. MAKING A VANE TEST IN A BOREHOLE

by Flaate.[1.8] Basically the method consists in pushing a four-bladed vane into the soil and rotating it at a constant rate of 0·1 degree per second. The torque required to rotate the cylinder of soil held within the blades is measured by means of a spring balance on top of the vane rods, which gives a direct reading of the shear strength (Fig. 1.12). Preferably the vane should be pushed down from ground level to the full depth to be investigated, with measurements of shear strength at close intervals, say every 0·3 m. The cohesion on the rod above the vane is allowed for by measuring the torque on a "dummy" rod (i.e. without vanes) pushed down to the same level. Alternatively the vane rod can be enclosed in a casing tube. If the test is done in a borehole it should be made at least 0·6 m, and preferably more in sensitive soils, below the bottom of the hole to get below the zone affected by disturbance during boring. Making tests at close spacing in a borehole delays progress noticeably, and as

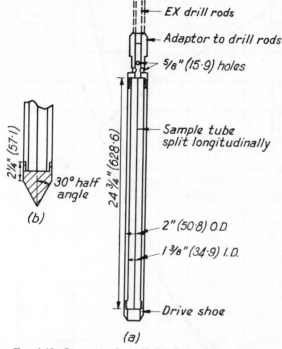

FIG. 1.13. STANDARD 2-IN. (O.D.) SPLIT SPOON SAMPLER
(a) Standard sampler.
(b) Modification by Palmer and Stuart[1.9] for use in gravels.

already mentioned, vane tests are best made independently of boring. The remoulded shear strength of the soil can also be measured by observing the minimum torque required for continued rapid rotation of the vane.

*The Standard Penetration Test* is made in boreholes by means of the standard 2 in. outside diameter split-spoon sampler (sometimes known as the Raymond sampler). It is a very useful means of determining the approximate in-situ density of cohesionless soils and, when modified by a cone end, the relative hardness of rocks. The sampler (Fig. 1.13(a)) is driven to penetration of 450 mm by repeated blows of a 63·5 kg monkey falling through 760 mm. The monkey is operated at ground level on to the top of the normal drilling rods which extend down the borehole to the sampler. Only

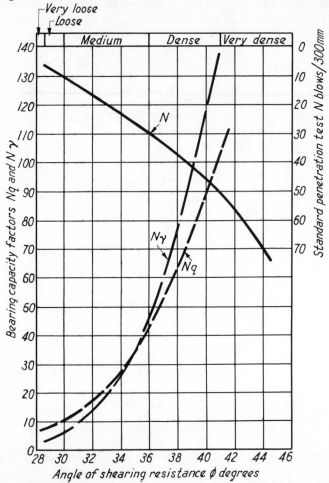

FIG. 1.14. RELATIONSHIP BETWEEN $\phi$, BEARING-CAPACITY FACTORS, AND $N$-VALUES FROM THE STANDARD PENETRATION TEST (PECK, HANSON, AND THORNBURN[1.11]).

the number of blows for the last 300 mm of driving is recorded as the standard penetration number ($N$-value). It is good practice to count the number of blows for every 75 mm of penetration in the full 450 mm of driving. By this means the depth of any disturbed soil in the bottom of the borehole can be assessed and the level at which any obstructions to driving, such as cobbles, large gravel, or cemented layers, are met can be noted. After withdrawal from the borehole the tube is taken apart for examination of the contents, and although the sample is in a disturbed state it is often sufficiently intact to be able to see laminations or similar features.

A modification of the apparatus as devised by Palmer and Stuart[1.9] enables it to be used in gravelly soil and rocks. In this modification the open-ended sampler is replaced by a cone end (Fig. 1.13 (*b*)). Investigations have shown a general similarity in $N$-values for the two types in soils of the same density.

Although the applications of the test are wholly empirical, very extensive experience of their use in U.S.A. and Great Britain has enabled a considerable knowledge of the behaviour of foundations in sands and gravels to be accumulated. Relationships have been established between $N$-values and such characteristics as density, angle of shearing resistance, settlement, and pile driving resistance.

Terzaghi and Peck[1.10] give the following relationship between $N$-values and the relative density of a sand—

| $N$-value | Relative density |
| --- | --- |
| Below 4 | Very loose |
| 4 to 10 | Loose |
| 10 to 30 | Medium |
| 30 to 50 | Dense |
| Over 50 | Very dense |

Peck, Hanson, and Thornburn[1.11] have established a relationship between $N$-values, bearing capacity factors and the angle of shearing resistance of a cohesionless soil as shown in Fig. 1.14. The use of the standard penetration test for calculating allowable bearing pressures of spread foundations is shown on pp. 98–100 and for piled foundations on pp. 374–82. There is a very approximate correlation between the shear strength* of clays and $N$-values quoted by Terzaghi and Peck[1.10] as tabled on p. 30. However, the adoption of the standard penetration test for determining the shear strength of clay soils is not recommended in preference to the direct methods of vane shear tests or making laboratory tests on undisturbed samples.

Consideration is sometimes given to refining the test procedure such as allowing for the length or flexibility of rods. However, such

---

* Shear strength $= \frac{1}{2} \times$ unconfined compressive strength, where angle of shearing resistance $\phi$ is zero.

refinements detract from its general utility and tend to obscure the fact that the test and its correlation with bearing capacity and settlement are wholly empirical and based on observation and experience rather than on scientific theory. In any case the in-situ density of most cohesionless soils is so variable that refinements in test procedure are unjustified. Serious doubts may bear on the validity of standard penetration tests if suitable precautions are not used in

| | | Approximate unconfined compressive strength | |
|---|---|---|---|
| *N*-value | Consistency | U.S. ton/ft² | Approx. equivalent in kN/m² |
| Below 2 | Very soft | Below 0·25 | Below 25 |
| 2 to 4 | Soft | 0·25 to 0·50 | 25 to 50 |
| 4 to 8 | Medium | 0·50 to 1·00 | 50 to 100 |
| 8 to 15 | Stiff | 1·00 to 2·00 | 100 to 200 |
| 15 to 30 | Very stiff | 2·00 to 4·00 | 200 to 400 |
| Over 30 | Hard | Over 4·00 | Over 400 |

boring methods. The test was developed in U.S.A. for use with wash boring, giving minimum disturbance in a sandy soil. If, however, the test is used in conjunction with boring by shelling, it is quite possible that the soil will be disturbed to some depth. Disturbance is mainly caused by suction when withdrawing the shell.[1.12] Before making the test in boreholes advanced by shelling, the soil at the bottom of the borehole should be gently removed to a depth of about 0·5 m, by a shell of much smaller diameter than the borehole. If water is present care should be taken to avoid disturbance by surging. The casing must not be driven below the level of the tests. If heavy driving is needed to advance the casing, the results of in-situ tests in boreholes will be useless.

Experience has shown that various adjustments are necessary to the standard penetration test values before using them to calculate allowable bearing pressures and settlements. These adjustments take account of looseness and fineness of the soil, the effects of overburden pressure, and the position of the water table. The procedure for making such adjustments is described on pages 98 to 100.

*The Continuous Dynamic Cone Penetration Test* employs a cone which is driven down into the soil by blows of a drop hammer. The number of blows per 0·3 m of penetration is recorded. The apparatus is in effect a miniature pile driver and as such is used by piling contractors as a means of predicting empirically the driving resistance and hence the carrying capacity of piles; used in this way it is sometimes known as a "pre-piling test." The author's firm uses a 63·5 mm diameter cone with a 60° apex angle driven through 50·8 mm diameter rods by a 160 kg hammer with a 600 mm drop. It has been found that the number of blows per 0·3 m of penetration with this equipment is roughly the same as that given by the standard penetration test in the same soil.[1.12] The method has no direct application to shallow foundation design, and there is as yet no recognized correlation between dynamic cone resistance and such characteristics as in-situ density, bearing capacity, and settlement as is the case with the standard penetration test. However, the dynamic cone test is a useful one and with increasing experience it may be possible to use empirical formulae relating driving resistance to these characteristics.

*The Static Cone Penetration Test* is widely used. The apparatus developed by the Dutch Government Soil Mechanics Laboratory at Delft and extensively used in Holland is recognized as a standard test procedure (the Dutch cone test) in many parts of the world. The Dutch cone has an apex angle of 60° and an overall diameter of 35·7 mm giving an end area of 1000 mm² (Fig. 1.15). The cone is attached to rods which are protected by a sleeve. The thrust on the rods and on the sleeve can be measured separately. The machine illustrated in Fig. 1.16 is manufactured by N. V. Goudsche Machinefabriek of Gouda, Holland. The cone is thrust down by hydraulic cylinder for a penetration of 75 mm into the soil, the load on the cone being recorded, up to a maximum thrust of 100 kN. Also available is a lorry-mounted machine with a thrust capacity of 200 kN. It utilizes a cone which measures the thrust by means of electrical resistance strain gauges which produce a continuous graph showing the end bearing and frictional resistance of the soil. The results are correlated directly with bearing capacity and settlement of shallow foundations and piles. For applying to shallow foundations and piles see pp. 100–1 and 382–4.

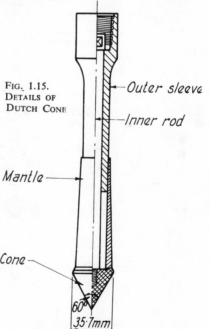

Fig. 1.15. Details of Dutch Cone

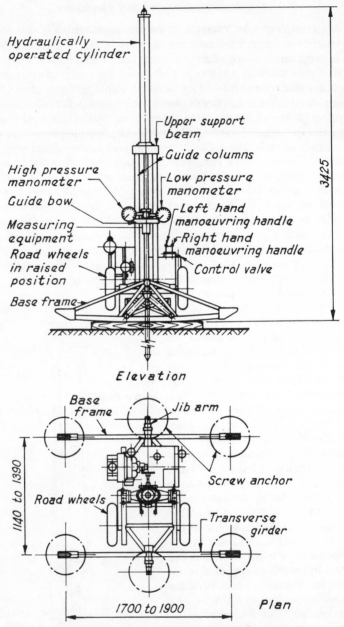

FIG. 1.16. DUTCH DEEP SOUNDING APPARATUS FOR MAXIMUM FORCE OF 100 KN

Long experience of its use and familiarity with their soil stratification have enabled the Dutch largely to dispense with conventional borings in their own country, and they rely almost entirely on cone tests for foundation design.

The static cone test is also a valuable method of recording variations in the in-situ density of loose sandy soils or laminated sands and clays in conditions where the in-situ density is disturbed by boring operations, thus making the standard penetration test unreliable in evaluation. It is unsuitable for gravelly soils, and when used in dense sands the anchorage of the equipment can be cumbersome and expensive.

The relationship between static cone tests and the standard penetration test has been reviewed by Rodin *et al.*,[1.13] who showed that there is no unique relationship between them. In the case of fine sands the static cone resistance (expressed in kilogrammes per square centimetre) has been shown to be three or four times the standard penetration test value. Tests in gravelly soils have given cone resistances on average 6 times the standard penetration test value. Therefore, the relationship between the two types of test must be established for any given site, if it is to be used to aid the interpretation of the field test data.

*Plate Bearing Tests* were once very widely used for foundation investigations but since the advent of soil mechanics science and the development of other forms of soil exploration they have tended to fall into disfavour. The main reasons for this are their high cost compared with boring and laboratory testing of soils, and the limited depth to which they can explore the ground. The procedure in making plate bearing tests is to excavate a pit to the predetermined foundation level or other suitable depth below ground level, and then to apply a static load to a plate set at the bottom of the pit. The load is applied in successive increments until failure of the ground in shear is attained or, more usually, until the bearing pressure on the plate reaches some multiple, say two or three, of the bearing pressure proposed for the full-scale foundations. The magnitude and rate of settlement under each increment of load is measured. After the maximum load is reached the pressure on the plate is reduced in successive decrements and the recovery of the plate is recorded at each stage of unloading. The load test should be taken to failure whenever this is economically possible.

Although the above procedure might, at first sight, appear to answer all the requirements of foundation design, the method is subject to serious limitations and in certain cases the information given by the tests can be wildly misleading. In the first place it is essential to have the bearing plate as near as is practicable equal in size to the width of the proposed foundations. A 300 mm plate is the minimum size which should be used. This is to ensure that the zone of soil below the bearing plate which is stressed by the superimposed loading will, as far as possible, correspond in depth and lateral extent to the zone of soil stressed by the full-scale foundation. This may be possible in the case of narrow strip foundations or small pad foundations but it is clearly impossible to use test plates equal in size to large foundation areas. The misleading information given by small plates in relation to large foundation areas is illustrated in Fig. 1.17. A 600 or 1000 mm plate is generally the economic limit, since a 1000 mm plate loaded say to 800 kN/m$^2$ will require some 63 tonnes of kentledge which is expensive to hire including the cost of

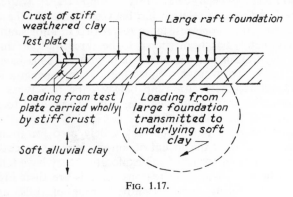

FIG. 1.17.

transport and handling. The cost of a single plate bearing test with a 300 to 600 mm plate with 50 tonnes of kentledge is about three times the cost of a 12 m deep borehole (in soft ground) complete with in-situ and laboratory testing. A single plate bearing test on a site is, in any case, far from sufficient since the ground is generally variable in its characteristics both in depth and laterally. At least three tests, and preferably more, are required to obtain representative results.

Economies in plate bearing tests on rock can be made by jacking against cable or rod anchorages grouted into drill holes in the rock, instead of using kentledge. Single anchors have been used successfully. The anchor cable, which is not bonded to the rock over its upper part, is passed through a hole drilled in the centre of the test plate. A test of this type can be made at the bottom of a borehole.

The level of the water table has an important effect on the bearing capacity and settlement of sands. Thus a plate bearing test made some distance above the water table will indicate much more favourable results than will be given by the large full-scale foundation which transmits stresses to the ground below the water table. The plate bearing test gives no information whereby the magnitude and rate of long-term consolidation settlement in clays may be calculated.

In spite of these drawbacks, the plate bearing test cannot be ruled out as a means of site investigation, since in certain circumstances it can give information which cannot be readily obtained by other means. For example, it may be necessary to found on fill material consisting of slag, broken bricks, and similar materials which cannot be sampled in boreholes and are not amenable to static or dynamic penetration tests. Also, the bearing capacity and consolidation characteristics of certain types of rocks such as broken shales or variably weathered materials cannot be assessed from laboratory tests due to difficulties in sampling. In these ground conditions it is necessary to sink a number of trial pits down to or below foundation level. The pits are carefully examined and three or four are selected in which the ground appears to be appreciably looser than the average, and plate bearing tests are made in these selected pits. Alternatively it may be desirable to select the pits in loosest and densest ground so that a range of settlement data can be obtained to assess likely differential settlement. The largest practicable size of plate should be used and it is advisable to dig or probe below plate level on completion of the test to find out if there are any voids or hard masses of material present which might affect the results. If the ground conditions are reasonably uniform with depth it is possible to use three different sizes of plate on the same test area and extrapolate to the full-scale foundation width provided that the extrapolation is not too great.

The procedure for making plate bearing tests is fully described in *CP 2001*. A typical arrangement for a test is shown in Fig. 1.18. Points to note in this arrangement are—

(*a*) The test should be made with the plate bearing on the general level at the base of the pit, i.e. without surcharge on the plate. Surcharge has a most important effect on the test results, but it is difficult to relate the conditions in plate bearing tests to surcharge conditions in the actual foundation. Therefore it is preferable to make the tests without surcharge, when they will be comparable to other tests made under the same conditions. To avoid the conditions shown in Fig. 1.17, the pit should be taken below any stiff crust and the test made in the underlying soft soil, the pit being at least six times as wide as the test plate.

(*b*) The load should be applied to the plate by jacking against kentledge in increments of one-fifth of the proposed design pressure. The method of applying direct loading to a plate is unreliable since it is difficult to prevent uneven distribution, and it can be dangerous if there is sudden tilting. If anchors are used instead of kentledge they should not be nearer the centre of the test plate than eight times its diameter.

(*c*) A proving ring or pressure capsule should be used to measure the load applied by the jack. Ordinary pressure gauges supplied with hydraulic jacks are unreliable in accuracy especially near the maximum rated loading of the jack.

(*d*) The settlement of the plate should be measured on at least two

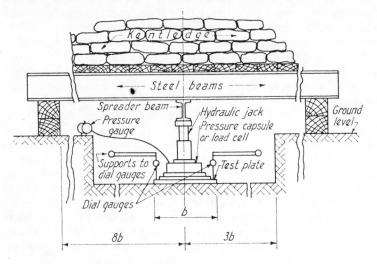

FIG. 1.18. ARRANGEMENT OF PLATE BEARING TEST RIG

points diametrically opposite. The movement should be measured by dial or vernier gauges to an accuracy of at least 0·05 mm.

(*e*) The settlement measuring gauges must be supported independently of the kentledge. It is usual to provide some form of bridge to carry the gauges with the supports to the bridge far enough away from the plate or kentledge supports to avoid ground movements from loading or unloading.

(*f*) The rate of settlement caused by each increment of loading should have decreased to not more than 0·25 mm per h, before applying the next increment.

(*g*) It is desirable to measure the elastic as well as the plastic settlement by unloading the plate after applying each successive increment, or after several selected increments in the loading cycle.

Typical load settlement and time settlement graphs for a plate bearing test are shown in Figs. 1.19 (*a*) and (*b*).

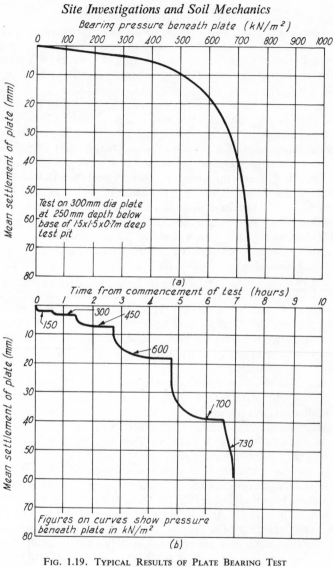

FIG. 1.19. TYPICAL RESULTS OF PLATE BEARING TEST
(*a*) Load–Settlement curve.
(*b*) Time–Settlement curve.

## Exploration in Rocks

Investigations into rock formations for foundation engineering purposes are concerned first with the bearing capacity of the rocks for spread foundations or piles and secondly with the conditions which are likely to be met if excavations have to be taken into the rock strata for deep foundations. The engineer must therefore have information on the depth of any weathering of the rock, the presence of any shattered zones or faults susceptible to movement, the possibility of the occurrence of deep drift-filled clefts, buried glacial valleys, swallow holes or concealed cavities, and the quantity of water likely to be pumped from excavations. Much of this information can be obtained in a general way by advice from a geologist from his knowledge of local conditions and the study of published maps and memoirs. Indeed the advice of a geologist in connexion with the siting of any important project on rock formations is very necessary. An essential part of exploration of rock masses to aid the interpretation of borehole data and field and laboratory tests, is a detailed study of the spacing, thickness, and orientation of joints in the rock mass, together with a study of the composition and consistency of any weathered rock or other material infilling the joints. If detailed observations of joint characteristics are made at locations of plate bearing tests, then the test results will be applicable to other parts of the site where similar jointing conditions exist in the rock formation. A method of surveying and classifying joint systems has been proposed by Duncan and Sheerman-Chase.[1.14] A reference letter is assigned to each joint system, and the spacing, thickness, and nature of the joint surfaces are denoted by suffixes to the reference letters in the tabulated survey sheets.

Weathering or other disturbances of the surface of a rock stratum are likely to necessitate varying foundation levels on a site, and it is often difficult if not impossible to assess from the results of boreholes a definite foundation level for a structure. For example, some types of rock such as marl or limestone soften as a result of seepage of water down fissures forming zones of weakened rock of soft clayey consistency surrounding hard unweathered material. If a few boreholes only are put down in these conditions they may encounter only unweathered rock giving a false picture of the true site conditions. Conversely, boreholes striking only softened weathered rock might suggest the presence of a deep stratum of soft clay overlying hard rock, whereas such soft material might only exist in comparatively narrow fissures. Glacial action can have caused deep and irregular disturbance of the surface of bedrock, for example the breaking-up and bodily movement of shales, or the tilting of large blocks of massively bedded rock.

The surface of friable, and therefore erodible, rocks may be intersected by narrow drift-filled valleys or clefts which again may be undiscovered by borings or trial pits, although a geologist would anticipate their occurrence. These conditions may require major re-design or re-location of foundations when the actual bedrock surface is revealed at the construction stage of the project.

There are two methods in general use for sub-surface exploration in rocks. These are—

(*a*) Test Pits
(*b*) Rotary Core Drilling

TEST PITS

Test pits are the most satisfactory means of assessing foundation conditions in rock, since the exposed bedrock surface can be closely inspected. The dip of the strata can be measured and it is often possible to assess the extent of weathering in layers or fissures. The hardness of the rock and its ease of excavation can be determined by trial with a pick or compressed-air tools. If necessary, blocks or cylinders of the rock can be cut for laboratory tests. However, test pits are only economical when bedrock lies fairly close (say within 3 m) of the ground surface. They should be used instead of boreholes when rock level is shallower than 2 m below ground level, but for depths between 2 and 3 m a few pits can be dug to supplement the evidence given by boreholes. Where rock is deeper than 3 m pits will be too costly, unless it is particularly necessary to assess the character of the rock for important structures or to investigate unusual conditions found in boreholes.

ROTARY CORE DRILLING

Rotary core drilling is regarded as the most satisfactory method of assessing the character of rock formations which lie at depth below the ground surface. Specimens of rock in the form of cylindrical cores are recovered from the drill holes by means of a core barrel. The core barrel is provided at its lower end with a detachable shoe or core bit which carries industrial diamond chips in a matrix of metal. Rotation of the barrel by means of the drill rods causes the core bit to cut an annulus in the rock, the cuttings being washed to the surface by a stream of water pumped down the hollow drill rods. The wash-water also cools the drilling bit.

In soft rocks or hard clays and silts, tungsten carbide inserts can be used instead of diamonds. Another method of achieving the cutting or grinding action is to use chilled steel shot instead of diamonds. The shot is fed down the drill rods and it finds its way to the bottom of the annulus where it is carried round with the shoe of the core barrel, becoming partly embedded in the soft metal of the shoe. A careful regulation of the wash-water is required in order to prevent the shot from being washed away. Shot drilling (also known as calyx drilling) is usually restricted to large diameter boreholes (300 mm or more).

*Core barrels* are made in various types and sizes depending on the depth of hole, type of rock, and size of specimen required. The barrels are also made in various lengths, 1·5 and 3·0 m being common lengths for site investigation work. The simplest form is the *single-tube barrel* in which the wash-water flows down the space between the core and the inner face of the barrel. This results in erosion of a friable core by wash water because of contact between the core and the rotating barrel. Consequently single-tube barrels are only used in hard rocks. It is the usual practice to employ *double-tube barrels* (Fig. 1.20) for all small diameter foundation investigation borings, since this overcomes the risk of erosion of the core and assists in improving the percentage core-recovery. An inner tube is attached to the core barrel head by a swivel connexion which allows the inner tube to remain stationary while the outer barrel and drilling bit rotate. There are variations in the detail design of double-tube barrels depending on the extent to which the inner tube projects into the core bit, so giving protection to the core.

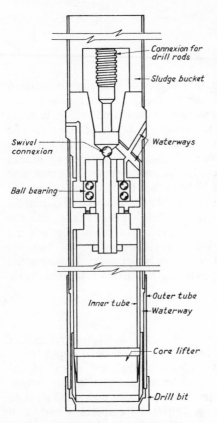

FIG. 1.20.  DOUBLE-TUBE CORE-BARREL

The most efficient design for good core recovery in friable rocks is the *M*-series bottom discharge bits in which the drilling fluid does not come into contact with the core except at its lowest extremity. A spring-steel core catcher is provided in some types of barrel to retain the core, and a reaming shell is provided above the core bit to aid alignment of the barrel in the hole and to prevent wear on the outer face of the barrel. The *Denison sampler* (Fig. 1.21) is a type of double-tube core barrel which can be used for obtaining undisturbed samples of stiff and hard clays, weakly cemented or cohesive sands, and stiff silts by rotary drilling methods. However, this type of sampler cannot recover undisturbed samples of cohesionless sands from below the water table, nor can it be used to sample gravels. The Denison sampler consists of a $5\frac{19}{32}$ in. I.D. sheet metal liner inside a 6 in. I.D. inner tube and then an outer barrel. Both the inner tube and outer barrel are provided with cutting shoes, that on the outer barrel having projecting teeth. The function of the liner is to facilitate handling of the sample after extraction from the borehole. Other features are a spring-steel core

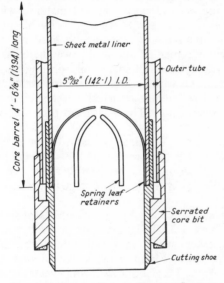

FIG. 1.21. LOWER END OF DENISON SAMPLER

catcher above the bit, and on top of the inner tube a non-return valve which allows expulsion of air and water from above the sample but reduces hydrostatic pressure on top of the sample. The projection of the stationary inner tube below the rotating outer barrel can be varied to suit the type of soil. The Denison sampler produces a $5\frac{1}{8}$ in. diameter by 20 in. long sample. Much care and experimentation is needed in adjusting the speed of rotation, pressure on drilling bit, and velocity of wash-water when drilling in soils and very friable rocks.

The *triple-tube core barrel* can recover good samples of hard clays and friable rocks, and in some conditions it may show a performance superior to the Denison sampler.

The main factor which decides the size of core barrel is the type of rock. Thus, small-diameter cores ($\frac{7}{8}$ in. or $1\frac{1}{8}$ in.) can be satisfactorily recovered in hard intact rocks, whereas in friable rocks or hard much-fissured formations it is necessary to use a larger diameter core, say $2\frac{1}{8}$ in. or even $4\frac{7}{16}$ in. diameter. It is false economy to use a small-diameter core barrel for the sake of cheaper drilling rates if this results in a poor core recovery, or even no recovery at all in weak or shattered rocks. It is most important to recover the *weakest* materials when assessments of safe bearing pressures are being made on rock cores. This requires, as nearly as possible, 100 per cent core recovery. Failure to obtain specimens of the weak rocks in formations consisting of alternating beds of hard and soft material will prevent any reasonable assessment of the bearing capacity of such formations. A case occurred on a building site where a hard red sandstone was overlain by weakly cemented and friable weathered sandstone. For the sake of economy small-diameter core drilling had been used in the site investigation, with the result that the weathered sandstone did not yield a core but was returned to the surface as a sand suspension in the wash-water. The weathered rock was thus identified as a sand and a correspondingly low bearing pressure was adopted for the foundation design. When, at the contruction stage, the foundations were excavated, compressed-air tools were required to break up the friable rock. A much higher bearing pressure could have been used, at least 1000 kN/m², but at that stage it was too late to change the design.

Standard sizes of core barrels as specified in British Standard 4019 are shown in Table 1.2. These sizes are generally used throughout the world and, except where shown, they conform to the American Diamond Core Drill Manufacturers Association (D.C.D.M.A.) standard sizes. Table 1.2 also shows casing sizes which accommodate the core barrels of each designation.

The smallest sizes (XRT and EWX) are only suitable for "proving" hard intact rocks to a limited penetration. Reasonably good recovery of hard intact rocks can be obtained from deep holes with AWX barrels, but if the rock is much fissured or friable it will be necessary to use larger diameters. Good recovery of fairly friable rocks or fissured hard rocks can be obtained with NWX and H core barrels, but for very friable rocks or heavily fissured hard rocks it is advisable to go up to K size.

Since diamond drilling is a fairly expensive procedure it is important to give care and attention to preserving the cores recovered from the drill holes. The value of the investigation is lost if the cores are mislaid or become mixed up in the boxes. The moisture content of weak rocks such as marl or chalk should be maintained at its true in-situ value if laboratory tests are required to be made. This can be done by coating selected cores with wax or wrapping them in plastic sheeting or a rubber envelope.

The type of the *drilling machine* is governed by the depth of drill hole and the size of core required. Rock proving to a limited depth

**Table 1.2**

**BRITISH STANDARD CORE BARREL SIZES**

| Core barrel designation | Approx. dia. of core (mm) | Approx. dia. of drill hole (mm) | Casing outside dia. (mm) | Casing coupling inside dia. (mm) |
|---|---|---|---|---|
| XRT* | 17 | 30 | 36·5 | 30·23 |
| EWX or EWM | 21 | 38 | 46·02 | 38·10 |
| AWX or AWM | 30 | 49 | 57·15 | 48·41 |
| BWX or BWM | 41 | 60 | 73·02 | 60·32 |
| NWX or NWM | 54 | 76 | 88·90 | 76·20 |
| HWX or HWF* | 76 | 100 | 114·30 | 100·00 |
| PF* | 92 | 121 | 139·70 | 123·82 |
| SF* | 113 | 146 | 168·28 | 149·23 |
| UF* | 140 | 172 | 193·68 | 176·20 |
| ZF* | 165 | 200 | 219·08 | 201·60 |

\* Not D.C.D.M.A. standard sizes.

for foundation purposes is generally undertaken by a rotary core drill attachment to a standard shell and auger rig, to enable the rock to be cored after drilling to rockhead by normal soil boring methods. The "Pendant" diamond drill attachment to the Pilcon "Wayfarer" soil exploration rig is shown in Plate II. It is a gravity feed drill powered by a hydraulic motor. For deep boreholes the hydraulic feed drill such as the Boyles BBS-2 is suitable. The BBS-2 (Plate III) can sink an EWX hole to a depth of 750 m or an H hole to a depth of 300 m. Its net mass is 1300 kg. The advantage of the hydraulic feed is that the rate of penetration and thrust on the bit can be controlled by the driller to suit varying rock conditions, whereas there is not the same control with a gravity feed drill.

### Borehole Records

The first stage in the preparation of borehole records is the site log or "journal" which gives a record of the soil or rock strata as determined by visual examination in the field. All relevant data on

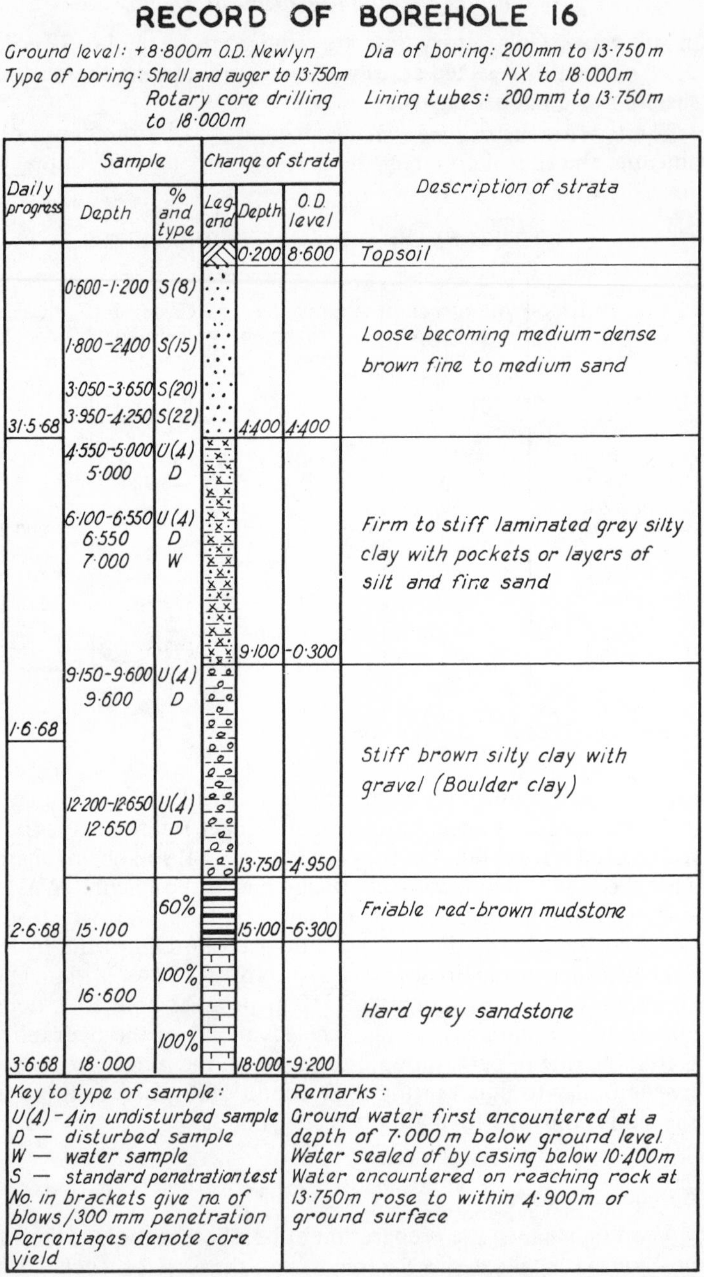

# RECORD OF BOREHOLE 16

Ground level: +8·800m O.D. Newlyn  
Type of boring: Shell and auger to 13·750m  
Rotary core drilling to 18·000m  

Dia of boring: 200mm to 13·750m  
NX to 18·000m  
Lining tubes: 200mm to 13·750m  

| Daily progress | Sample | | Change of strata | | | Description of strata |
|---|---|---|---|---|---|---|
| | Depth | % and type | Legend | Depth | O.D. level | |
| | | | | 0·200 | 8·600 | Topsoil |
| | 0·600-1·200 | S(8) | | | | |
| | 1·800-2·400 | S(15) | | | | Loose becoming medium-dense brown fine to medium sand |
| | 3·050-3·650 | S(20) | | | | |
| 31·5·68 | 3·950-4·250 | S(22) | | 4·400 | 4·400 | |
| | 4·550-5·000 5·000 | U(4) D | | | | |
| | 6·100-6·550 6·550 7·000 | U(4) D W | | | | Firm to stiff laminated grey silty clay with pockets or layers of silt and fine sand |
| | 9·150-9·600 9·600 | U(4) D | | 9·100 | -0·300 | |
| 1·6·68 | | | | | | Stiff brown silty clay with gravel (Boulder clay) |
| | 12·200-12·650 12·650 | U(4) D | | 13·750 | -4·950 | |
| 2·6·68 | 15·100 | 60% | | 15·100 | -6·300 | Friable red-brown mudstone |
| | 16·600 | 100% | | | | Hard grey sandstone |
| 3·6·68 | 18·000 | 100% | | 18·000 | -9·200 | |

| Key to type of sample: | Remarks: |
|---|---|
| U(4) - 4in undisturbed sample<br>D — disturbed sample<br>W — water sample<br>S — standard penetration test<br>No. in brackets give no. of blows/300 mm penetration<br>Percentages denote core yield | Ground water first encountered at a depth of 7·000 m below ground level.<br>Water sealed of by casing below 10·400m<br>Water encountered on reaching rock at 13·750m rose to within 4·900m of ground surface |

FIG. 1.22. TYPICAL BOREHOLE RECORD

ground water levels, reduced levels of strata changes, depths of samples and records of any in-situ tests are shown on these site records which provide preliminary information for the designer and enable the laboratory testing programme to be drawn up. The second stage is the final record which is included in the engineering report on the site investigation. In this record the descriptions of the soils and rocks are amended where necessary in the light of information given by laboratory testing and examination of the samples and detailed assessment by a geologist. In both stages of borehole record presentation it is important to adopt a consistent method of describing soil and rock types. The standard method given in *CP2001* should always be followed. A typical final borehole record is shown in Fig. 1.22.

### Field Permeability Tests

Field tests to determine in-situ the permeability of soils and rocks are used in connexion with ground water lowering schemes when it is necessary to estimate the number and diameter of pumping wells and the size of the pumps, for a given size of excavation (*see* Chapter 11). These tests are also used in investigations for dams and impounding reservoirs when information is required on the rate of seepage beneath the dam or into the surrounding ground. Field permeability tests are time-consuming and quite expensive to carry out; consequently they are usually restricted to investigations for major excavation works where the cost of ground water lowering represents an appreciable proportion of the cost of foundation construction.

The procedure widely followed for the tests is described in the *U.S. Bureau of Reclamation Earth Manual*,[1.15] which describes two main types of test for use in conjunction with boreholes. These are—

1. Open-end tests—gravity or pressure tests made through the bottom of the borehole casing or through the uncased lower section of the borehole.

2. Packer tests—pumping-in tests made in an uncased length of borehole either between a single packer and the bottom of the hole, or between double packers at any selected level.

Open-end tests are made at the required intervals between the stages of deepening the borehole. Water is allowed to flow at a constant rate into the test section, either into the open borehole (gravity test) or through a seal at the top of the borehole casing (pressure test). The single packer test is made in an uncased test length at intervals between stages of deepening the borehole, or it can be made over varying test lengths after completion of boring. The double packer test is made in selected lengths of uncased hole after completion of boring. Details of the test procedure and methods of calculating the in-situ permeability are given in the *Earth Manual*.

The above test methods are useful for obtaining permeability data within specific soil layers on a site. If an excavation requires ground-water lowering on an appreciable scale, it is essential to make trials by pumping from a full-scale well with subsidiary observation wells, as described on page 680.

### Investigations for Foundations of Works over Water

The equipment and techniques for sinking boreholes through water are essentially the same as for land borings. For boring close to land or existing structures or in shallow water, it is economical to use staging to carry the rig. This need only be of light construction such as tubular steel scaffolding (Plate IV) since the drilling equipment is of no great weight. Where the borehole is within about 50 m of the land the platform can be connected to the shore by a catwalk. For greater distances it may be more economical to erect the platform as an island either lowering it as a unit from a crane barge or in the form of a raft which can be sunk by admitting water into buoyancy chambers. For boring in water deeper than about 10 m or at some distance from the shore it is convenient to mount the drilling rig on a platform cantilevered over the side of a barge or pontoon. Dumb craft of this type are suitable for working in sheltered waters or where a harbour is reasonably close to hand to which the craft can be towed at times of storms. However, when boring in open unsheltered waters away from harbours it is advisable to use a powered craft which, at the onset of a gale, can cast off its moorings and ride out the storm at anchor or seek shelter at the nearest available place.

Drilling from a floating craft requires some slight modifications in technique and there are complications in making some of the in-situ tests such as vane tests and static cone tests. For a fuller account of the various methods and techniques in marine site investigations the reader is referred to a paper by the author.[1.16]

### Geophysical Methods of Site Investigation

It is possible to determine stratification of soils and rocks by geo-physical methods which measure changes in certain physical charac-teristics of these materials, for example the magnetism, density, electrical resistivity, elasticity, or a combination of these properties. However, such methods are of limited value in foundation engineer-ing since they only record changes in stratification where the layers have appreciably different geophysical properties, and the only useful information they give is the level of the interfaces between the various strata. Vital information on ground-water conditions is usually lacking. Geophysical methods in their present state of development do not give direct quantitative data on shear strength, compressibility, or particle-size distribution. At best geophysical surveying is a means of filling in data on strata changes between widely spaced boreholes. On large sites geophysical methods can show economies due to the rapidity with which extensive areas can be covered. Before embarking on such surveys, the engineer should consider whether other methods such as wash boring or probing, or static and dynamic cone penetration tests would not be preferable, since these methods are also rapid and have the advantage of giving quantitative data on the in-situ density or the shear strength of soils. Generally, geophysical methods are best suited to deep investigations in rock strata, for example for dams or tunnels where the stratification of rocks at depth is required, and for investigations in soils containing many cobbles or boulders where probings or cone tests are impracticable.

Terzaghi[1.17] gave a warning about the pitfalls inherent in geophysical methods stating "So far as geophysical methods of subsoil exploration are concerned, there can be no doubt about their desirability and merits, because they are extremely cheap: they are even cheaper than geologists. They have only one disadvantage, and that is we never know in advance whether they are going to work or not! During my professional career I have been intimately connected with seven geophysical surveys. In every case the physicist in charge of the exploration anticipated and promised satisfactory results. Yet only the first one was a success; the six others were rather dismal failures."

However, geophysicists are persevering with the development of light and portable apparatus for use on civil engineering sites and it is possible that these methods, when used with discretion and properly correlated with borehole data and skilled geological interpretation, will find increasing use for foundation engineering purposes. The methods in general use are—

(*a*) Electrical Resistivity
(*b*) Seismic Refraction
(*c*) Seismic Reflexion.
(*d*) Magnetic.

*The Electrical Resistivity Method* makes use of the differences in electrical resistance or conductivity between one soil or rock type and another. An electric current is passed through the ground between a pair of electrodes (current electrodes) and the drop in potential is measured by an inner pair of electrodes known as the potential electrodes. The four electrodes are equally spaced in a straight line

(Fig. 1.23) so that by varying the spacing the depth of current penetration can be varied. In the expanding-electrode technique, the distances between the pairs of current and potential electrodes are progressively increased and the drop in potential at each spacing is measured. The results are analysed by graphical or mathematical methods from which the levels of the various strata can be deduced. The equipment is light and portable and the team need only consist of one operator and an assistant. The author's firm have used the equipment to trace the level of the interface between gravels and clay,

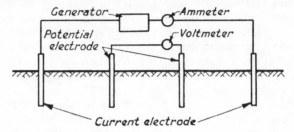

FIG. 1.23. ARRANGEMENT OF ELECTRODES FOR ELECTRICAL RESISTIVITY SURVEY

and between unconsolidated deposits and bedrock. They have also used it to determine the outline of old coalmine workings where the air-filled voids show as a zone of very high resistivity. Care is needed in interpretation of the resistivity data since the water table will appear as a change in stratification, and confusion may result if there are perched water tables; also, certain materials such as peat or iron pyrites have very low resistivities and if such deposits are irregular in extent and thickness the resistivity data may be impossible to interpret. The electrical resistivity method gives useful data on the conductivity of soils in connexion with schemes for protecting buried steel structures against corrosion.

*Seismic Methods* are based on the fact that soils and rocks have differing characteristics in the speed of propagation of vibrations through them. Thus, when an explosive charge is fired at ground level or in a borehole, the waves travel in all directions from the "shot point" and are refracted and reflected by the various strata. They travel at a higher velocity through rocks and highly consolidated soils than through the looser overburden deposits. Therefore by measuring, with a seismometer, the time of arrival of the waves at a point on the surface, the nature and depth of the underlying strata can be deduced.

*The Seismic Refraction Method* is more suited to shallow exploration for civil engineering purposes than the reflexion technique which in conventional seismic surveying is limited to depths greater than

120 or 150 m. The principle of the refraction method is illustrated for a simple two-layer structure in Fig. 1.24. Seismometers are spaced out at increasing distances from the shot point. The time of arrival of the wave front at each seismometer is plotted graphically against the distance of the seismometer from the shot point, from which the velocity of sound in each layer can be measured and the depth to each layer calculated. A seismic refraction team consists of an observer, a shooter, a surveyor, and four labourers. The equipment is complex and expensive, with the result that seismic refraction

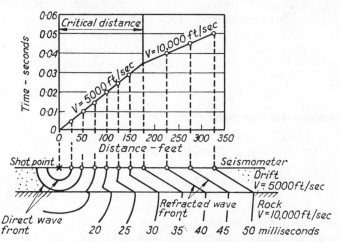

FIG. 1.24. DIAGRAM SHOWING ADVANCE OF WAVE-FRONT THROUGH A TWO-LAYER STRUCTURE AND THE RESULTANT TIME–DISTANCE GRAPH (ROBERTSHAW AND BROWN[1.18]).

surveying is fairly costly, and is suitable only for large sites and complex conditions and where economies are given by the rapidity of the method.

A very light and portable apparatus is available for shallow refraction surveying. The vibrations are produced very simply by hitting the ground with a 6 kg hammer. Surveys for foundation engineering purposes can be carried out by a two-man team at a much lower cost than conventional seismic shooting, but there are serious difficulties in using the equipment in areas of high background "noise" such as traffic vibrations.

The continuous stratification recorder or "sparker" is a seismic method, which is restricted to investigations carried out over water.[1.19] The principle of the method is to produce an intermittent 10,000 volt electric spark at the end of a cable towed by a launch. The spark causes breakdown of the water into its constituent gases, and the resultant collapse of the gas bubbles produces energy waves which are reflected back from the sea bed and the various soil or rock layers below. The reflected waves are picked up by a hydrophone towed on a parallel cable to the spark unit, and analysed in the form of a continuous chart showing the levels of the sea bed and the various reflecting strata. The equipment is light and compact and it requires only a two-man team. Long distances can be covered in a working day. The method is applicable to foundation works of large span bridges, subaqueous tunnels, docks or harbour schemes.

*Magnetic methods* are based on measuring the variation in intensity of the earth's magnetic field. They have been used, but not always with success, for tracing the location of concealed underground cavities such as swallow holes or disused mine shafts. The proton magnetometer is a convenient instrument for this purpose.[1.20]

## LABORATORY TESTS ON SOILS AND ROCKS

### Laboratory Tests on Soils

The physical characteristics of soils can be measured by means of laboratory tests on samples extracted from boreholes or trial pits. The results of shear strength tests can be used to calculate the ultimate bearing capacity of soils or the stability of slopes in foundation excavations and embankments. Laboratory tests also provide data from which soils can be classified and predictions made of their behaviour under foundation loading. From the laboratory test information, methods of treating soils can be devised to overcome difficulties in excavations, especially in dealing with ground-water problems. It is important to keep in mind that natural soil deposits are variable in composition and state of consolidation; therefore it is necessary to use considerable judgment based on common sense and practical experience in assessing test results and knowing where reliance can be placed on the data and when they should be discarded. It is dangerous to put blind faith in laboratory tests, especially when they are few in number. The test data should be studied in conjunction with the borehole records and other site observations, and any estimations of bearing pressures or other engineering design data obtained from them should be checked as far as possible with known conditions and past experience.

Laboratory tests should be as simple as possible. Tests using elaborate equipment are time-consuming and therefore costly, and are liable to serious error unless carefully and conscientiously carried out by highly experienced technicians. Such methods may be quite unjustified if the samples are few in number, or if the cost is high in relation to the cost of the project. Elaborate and costly tests are justified only if the increased accuracy of the data will give worthwhile savings in design or will eliminate the risk of a costly failure.

An important point in favour of carrying out a reasonable amount of laboratory testing is that an increasing amount of valuable data is built up over the years relating test results to foundation behaviour, for example stability and settlement, enabling engineers to use laboratory tests with greater confidence. At the very least the test results give a check on field descriptions of boreholes based on visual examination and handling of soil samples, and are a useful corrective to "wishful thinking" by engineers in their first impression of the strength of a soil as it appears in the borehole or trial pit.

The soil mechanics tests made in accordance with B.S. 1377 which concern the foundation engineer are—

    (*a*) Visual examination
    (*b*) Natural moisture content
    (*c*) Liquid and plastic limits
    (*d*) Particle-size distribution
    (*e*) Unconfined compression
    (*f*) Triaxial compression
    (*g*) Vane
    (*h*) Consolidation
    (*i*) Permeability
    (*j*) Chemical analyses.

*Visual Tests* carried out in the laboratory are for noting the colour, texture, and consistency of the disturbed and undisturbed samples received from the site. This should be undertaken as a routine check on the field engineer or boring foreman's descriptions.

It is the practice of some testing laboratories to make *natural moisture content* tests on all undisturbed samples received at the laboratory. By comparing the results and relating them to the liquid and plastic limits of the corresponding soil types it is possible to arrange the programme for shear strength tests and to ensure that tests on the softer soils (as suggested by the higher moisture content) are not omitted. This procedure assumes that there will be some selection from a large number of samples received at the laboratory. If, however, it is decided that shear strength tests will be made on all the undisturbed samples received, then there is no need to make separate moisture content determinations since they are made as a matter of course as part of the shear strength test procedure. Generally there is no point in making natural moisture content tests on disturbed samples since the results may be unrepresentative of the in-situ condition of the soils as a result of the boring procedure. If for any reason data on moisture content additional to that given from tests on undisturbed samples is required, the samples for this purpose should be specially selected; for example disturbed samples taken from the cutting shoe of tube samplers or from the split-spoon sampler in the standard penetration test.

*Liquid and Plastic Limit Tests* are made on cohesive soils for classification purposes and for predicting their engineering properties. The Casagrande Plasticity Chart (Fig. 1.25) can be used to predict the

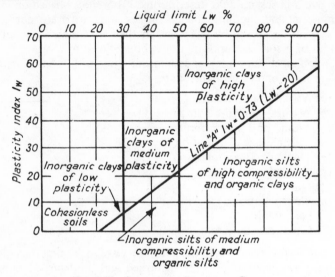

FIG. 1.25. CASAGRANDE PLASTICITY CHART

compressibility of clays and silts. To use this chart it is necessary to know whether the soil is of organic or inorganic origin. Organic soils are usually dark in colour with a characteristic smell of decaying vegetation. When in doubt the liquid limit should be determined on a specimen which has been dried in an oven. If the drying reduces the liquid limit of the fresh specimen by 30 per cent or more the soil is organic. The usual procedure is to make liquid and plastic limit tests on a few selected samples of each main soil type found in the boreholes. By comparing the results and plotting the data on the plasticity chart the various soil types can be classified in a rough order of compressibility and samples selected accordingly for consolidation tests if these are required.

*The Particle-size Distribution Test* is a form of classification test in which sieve analysis or a combination of sieve analysis and sedimentation or hydrometer analysis is used to obtain grading curves which can be plotted on the chart shown in Fig. 1.26. The grading curves are of no direct value in assessing allowable bearing pressure, and generally this type of test need not be made in connexion with any foundation investigation in clays or in the case of sands and gravels where the excavation is above the water table. The particle-size distribution test is, however, of particular value in the investigation of problems of excavation in permeable soils below the water table, when the results can be used to ascertain which of several geotechnical processes are feasible for ground water lowering or grouting treatment, as described on page 681.

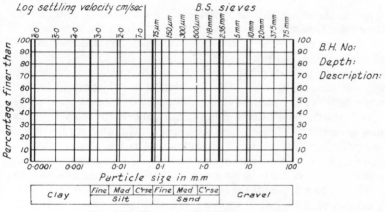

FIG. 1.26. PARTICLE-SIZE DISTRIBUTION CHART

The *shear strength* of soil can be used directly to calculate its ultimate bearing capacity, as described in Chapters 2, 4, and 7, and to calculate earth-pressure on sheeted excavations as described in Chapter 9.

*The unconfined compression test* is the simplest form of shear strength test and in Great Britain is usually performed directly on $1\frac{1}{2}$ in. samples ejected from tube samples of the same diameter, or on $1\frac{1}{2}$ in. test specimens cut from tube samples of larger diameter. In soils containing gravel making it impossible to cut $1\frac{1}{2}$ in. specimens, the unconfined compression test can be made directly on 4 in. specimens ejected from sample tubes of the same diameter.

This type of test cannot be made on cohesionless soils or on clays and silts which are too soft to stand in the machine without collapsing before the load is applied. In the case of fissured or brittle soils the results are lower than the true in-situ strength of these soils.

*The Triaxial Compression Test* is a more elaborate form of shear strength test which can be applied to a wider range of soil types than the unconfined compression test, and the conditions of tests and observations made can be varied to suit a wide range of engineering problems. It is used to determine the cohesion ($c$) and the angle of shearing resistance ($\phi$) of a soil as defined by the Coulomb–Mohr equation—

$$s = c + p \tan \phi \quad . \qquad . \qquad . \qquad . \quad (1.1)$$

The three main types of triaxial test are—

(a) Undrained
(b) Consolidated-undrained
(c) Drained.

In the *undrained test* the specimen is not allowed to drain during the application of the all-round pressure or during the application of the deviator stress, and therefore the pore pressure is not allowed to dissipate at any stage of the test. In the case of a saturated cohesive soil, this test procedure reproduces the conditions which occur when the soil beneath the full-scale foundation is subjected to load or when earth is removed from an open or sheeted excavation. In these conditions the pore pressures in the soil beneath the loaded foundation or in the soil behind the face of an excavation have no time to dissipate during the time of application of stress. The analyses to determine the ultimate bearing capacity of the foundation soil or the initial stability of excavations are carried out in terms of *total stresses*.

The test procedure for the *consolidated-undrained test* is to allow the specimen to drain while applying the all-round pressure; thus the specimen is allowed to consolidate fully during this stage of the test. Drainage is not allowed during the application of the deviator stress.

In the case of the *drained test*, drainage of pore-water from the specimen is allowed both during the stage of consolidation under all-round pressure and during the application of the deviator stress. The time allowed for consolidation under all-round pressure and for application of the deviator stress must be slow enough to ensure that no build-up of pore pressure occurs at any stage of the test. The procedure for consolidated-undrained and drained tests corresponds to the conditions of long-term application of load, for example the loading of the soil beneath an earth dam when the construction takes place relatively slowly (over several seasons). The long-term stability of excavated slopes is also investigated by means of consolidated-undrained or drained tests. These long-term stability problems are analysed in terms of the *effective stress* (the difference between the total stress and the pore pressure). Analyses of this type are not usually made in normal foundation investigations; their application is limited to particular conditions such as foundations of earth dams, and the stability of earth embankments for cofferdams. The foundations of oil storage tanks on soft clays have been analysed by these methods where their stability is critical and it is possible to allow pore pressures to dissipate while loading the tanks in stages over a long period of time. A discussion of this type of analysis is beyond the scope of this work and the reader is referred to a book by Bishop and Henkel[1.21] for a detailed and authoritative account of the triaxial test and an extensive bibliography of the application of the various types of test to the solution of engineering problems.

The undrained, consolidated-undrained, and drained tests are sometimes referred to as "quick," "consolidated-quick," and "slow" tests respectively. This nomenclature is rather misleading since the rate of loading depends on the type of soil and size of specimen (i.e. on the time taken for excess pore pressures to dissipate) rather than on the type of test itself.

Triaxial tests are limited to clays, silts, peats, and soft rocks. It is generally pointless to test sands and gravels since a test cannot in any case be made directly on an undisturbed sample. Even if it is possible to obtain satisfactory undisturbed samples of sands and gravels from boreholes or trial pits, it is impossible to extract specimens for the triaxial tests from the sample tubes without disturbing the soil. The best that can be done is to determine the density of the soil in the tube by weighing the contents and measuring the volume. The test specimen can then be made-up to the same density. It is usually preferable to derive the angle of shearing resistance empirically by means of in-situ tests such as the standard penetration test (p. 27) or the Dutch cone test (p. 31).

*The Vane Shear Test* is more applicable to field conditions than to the laboratory. However, the laboratory vane test has a useful application where satisfactory undisturbed samples of very soft clays and silts have been obtained by the procedures described on pages 21 to 22, and where it is impossible to prepare specimens, because of their softness, from the tubes for shear strength tests using the unconfined or triaxial apparatus.

*Consolidation Test* results are used to calculate the magnitude and rate of consolidation of the soil beneath foundations. The test is more accurately described as a one-dimensional consolidation test, because the sample is enclosed in a metal ring and the load is applied in one direction only. The apparatus used is known as the oedometer, or sometimes as the consolidometer. From the results the coefficient of consolidation ($C_v$) is obtained which enables the *rate* of settlement of the full-scale structure to be calculated. The load-settlement data obtained from the full cycle of loading and unloading are used to draw a pressure-voids ratio curve from which the coefficient of volume compressibility ($m_v$) is derived. This is used to calculate the *magnitude* of consolidation settlement under any

Table 1.3

COMPRESSIBILITY OF VARIOUS TYPES OF CLAYS

| Type | Qualitative description | Coefficient of volume compressibility ($m_v$) m²/MN |
|---|---|---|
| Heavily over-consolidated boulder clays (e.g. many Scottish boulder clays) and stiff weathered rocks (e.g. weathered siltstone), hard London Clay, Gault Clay and Oxford Clay (at depth) | Very low compressibility | Below 0·05 |
| Boulder clays (e.g. Tees-side, Cheshire) and very stiff "blue" London Clay, Oxford Clay, Keuper Marl | Low compressibility | 0·05 to 0·10 |
| Upper "blue" London Clay, weathered "brown" London Clay, fluvio-glacial clays, Lake clays, weathered Oxford Clay, weathered Boulder Clay, weathered Keuper Marl, normally consolidated clays (at depth) | Medium compressibility | 0·10 to 0·30 |
| Normally-consolidated alluvial clays (e.g. estuarine clays of Thames, Firth of Forth, Bristol Channel, Shatt-al-Arab, Niger Delta, Chicago Clay), Norwegian "Quick" Clay | High compressibility | 0·30 to 1·50 |
| Very organic alluvial clays and peats | Very high compressibility | Above 1·50 |

given loading. Typical values of the coefficient $m_v$ are shown in Table 1.3.

Consolidation tests are restricted to clays and silts since the theories on which settlement calculations are based are limited to fine-grained soils of these types. It is not usual to make consolidation tests on heavily preconsolidated clays such as glacial boulder clays since settlement of normally loaded structures on soils of this type is generally negligible. Only in the case of very large and heavy structures on boulder clays need the settlements be investigated on the basis of laboratory tests. The use of consolidation test data to calculate the magnitude and rate of settlement of foundations is described on pages 122 to 138. The settlement of structures founded on sands is usually estimated from field test data as described on pages 118 to 122.

*Permeability Tests* can be made in the laboratory on undisturbed samples of clays and silts, or on sands or gravels which are compacted in cylindrical moulds to the same density as that in which they exist in their natural state (as determined from in-situ tests). The two types of permeability test in general use are the *constant head test* and the *falling head test*. Laboratory tests are liable to errors due to piping of water between the soil and the wall of the tube, and due to bubbles of air entrained in the sample. Also, there is a difference between the horizontal and vertical permeability of natural soil deposits due to the effects of stratification with alternating beds of finer or coarser grained soils. Thus the results of laboratory tests on a few samples from a vertical borehole are of rather doubtful value in assessing the representative permeability of the soil for calculating the quantity of water to be pumped from a foundation excavation. It is preferable to determine the permeability of the soil on a given site by means of field pumping tests as noted on page 45 and on page 680.

*Chemical Analyses* of soils and ground water are required to assess the possibility of deterioration of buried steel and concrete foundation structures. In the case of steel structures such as permanent sheet piling or steel bearing piles it is usually sufficient to determine the pH value and chloride content of the soil and ground water. For concrete structures the sulphate content and pH value are normally required. Although the pH value, which is a measure of the degree of acidity or alkalinity of the soil or ground water, cannot be used directly to determine the nature or amount of acid or alkaline material present, it is a useful index in considering if further information is required to decide on the precautions to be taken in protecting buried concrete structures. For example, a low pH value indicates acid conditions, which might result from naturally occurring matter in the soil or which might be due to industrial wastes dumped on the site. In the latter case, detailed chemical analyses would be needed to determine the nature of the substances present, and to assess their potential aggressiveness towards concrete. A full discussion on the subject of chemical attack on foundation structures, including the procedure for sampling is given in Chapter 13.

## Laboratory Tests on Rocks

Attempts have been made to calculate the bearing capacity of rock from the results of unconfined or triaxial compression tests on cores from drill holes. This procedure is applicable only to intact (i.e. unfissured) rock masses or to rock formations in which the fissures and bedding planes are very widely spaced in relation to the zones of rock affected by the foundation stresses. In the case of fissured rocks, the safe bearing capacity (i.e. the ultimate bearing capacity divided by a nominal safety factor) calculated from the results of laboratory compression tests bears no relation to the allowable bearing pressure as determined by considerations of limiting the settlement of the foundation due to compression of the rock mass. This compression is a combination of the closure of open fissures and bedding planes and the compression of the intact rock and any soft material in or adjacent to fissures. No laboratory consolidation test procedure has been devised which accurately simulates the effects of fissuring and weathered zones within rock formations.

Only in the case of weak rocks, such as chalk, marl or clay shales, can the results of laboratory compression and consolidation tests be used to determine allowable bearing pressures from considerations of shear failure and settlement. The compression tests should not be made on unconfined specimens, since these are likely to exhibit brittle failure, with consequent underestimate of the bearing capacity value. Triaxial compression tests should be made using high lateral pressures comparable with the vertical deviator stresses, so enabling Mohr's circles of stress to be drawn from which the cohesion and angle of shearing resistance can be derived. The results of such tests are also applicable to cases where very high bearing pressures are applied to strong intact rocks, e.g. from steel bearing piles.

Where laboratory tests on rock cores are required the procedure should be as follows—

(*a*) Examine all rock cores.

(*b*) Select cores representative of the weakest and strongest rocks for test.

(*c*) Examine the drilling records to ensure that there is no weaker rock from which there has been no core recovery (if the drilling technique has not been satisfactory the weakest rocks may have crumbled away). If this is the case selected holes should be redrilled with a more careful technique or a larger core barrel to ensure recovery of the weakest rocks. If this cannot be done the idea of laboratory testing should be abandoned.

(*d*) Make triaxial compression tests on the rock cores. Unconfined compression tests may be suitable for the preliminary classification of cores from intact rock masses.

(*e*) On the basis of the test results classify the rock in terms of weak, medium, or strong consistency.

## THE FOUNDATION ENGINEERING REPORT

The engineering report on a foundation investigation is a consideration of all available data from boreholes, trial pits, site observations, historical records, and laboratory tests. Most reports follow a fairly stereotyped pattern under the following headings—

### 1. INTRODUCTION

This should tell the reader for whom the investigation was undertaken, the reason for the investigation, how (briefly) the work was carried out, and the time of year the job was done. It should state the terms of reference, for example whether the investigation was merely to obtain a limited amount of factual data for assessment by the design engineer, or whether a full investigation was required with borings, laboratory tests, and an analysis of the results to consider possible methods of foundation design and construction and to calculate the allowable bearing pressures. If the scope of the investigation has been limited, on the grounds of cost or for other reasons, to such an extent that the engineer regards it as inadequate, he should state the reasons for this limitation in the introduction or at another appropriate point in the report. If, because of such limitations, the soil conditions are subsequently found to be different from those inferred, and the cost of the work is thereby increased, the engineer cannot be held to blame. However, he will be regarded as negligent if he bases his conclusions on inadequate data without qualifying his report.

### 2. GENERAL DESCRIPTION OF THE SITE

This part of the report should describe the general configuration and surface features of the site, noting the presence of any trees, hedges, old buildings, cellars, quarries, mine shafts, marshy ground, ponds, watercourses, filled areas, roads, and tracks. Any useful information derived from historical records on previous usage of the site should be described, and other observations should cover such factors as flooding, sea or wind erosion, subsidence, earthquakes, or slope instability; any nearby buildings showing signs of settlement cracking should be noted.

### 3. GENERAL GEOLOGY OF THE AREA

Notes should be given on the geology of the site, comparing published information on maps, memoirs, etc., with conditions found in the boreholes. Attention should be drawn to any known faults, quarries, springs, shallow holes, mines or shafts, or other features which will have a bearing on the foundation works.

### 4. DESCRIPTION OF SOIL CONDITIONS FOUND IN BOREHOLES (AND TRIAL PITS)

This is a general description of the soil conditions with reference to the configuration of the ground and variations in level of the various strata and the ground water table. A detailed description is not required. The written matter should not be a mere catalogue of the borehole records, for the reader of the report can get a much clearer picture of these by studying the records himself. If a number of boreholes have been sunk on a site it is a good plan to draw one or more sections through the site to show the variations and level of particular strata which may be of significance in the engineering problem (Fig. 1.27). A single drawing is better than pages of written matter.

### 5. LABORATORY TEST RESULTS

A long description of the test results should not be given. The descriptive matter should be limited to a brief mention of the various types of tests which were made and attention drawn to any results which are unusual or of particular significance. For details of the results the reader should be referred to a table of results with charts and diagrams of such tests as particle size analysis, triaxial compression (Mohr's circles of stress), and consolidation tests (pressure–voids ratio curves).

The test procedure should be described only in the case of non-standard tests specially devised for the investigation.

### 6. DISCUSSION OF RESULTS OF INVESTIGATION IN RELATION TO FOUNDATION DESIGN AND CONSTRUCTION

This is the heart of the report and the writer should endeavour to discuss the problem clearly and concisely without "ifs" and "buts." For readability this section of the report should be broken down into a number of sub-headings. First, under "general," a description is given of the main structures and the related loadings which are to be considered together with a general assessment of the ground conditions and the types of foundation which could be adopted, e.g. strip foundations, rafts, or piles. The remainder of the sub-headings can refer either to particular structures (e.g. in the case of an electricity generating station, the boiler house, turbine house, coal or ash handling plants, switchgear, and circulating water culverts, all of which have different foundation characteristics requiring separate consideration) or they can refer to possible types of foundation design for any individual structure or structures.

The writer should come straight to the point. In the case of strip foundations he should state what the required foundation depth is,

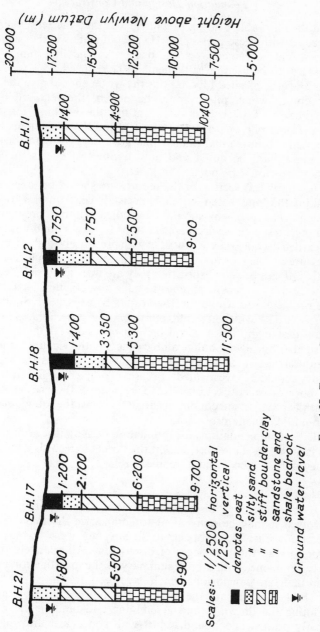

FIG. 1.27. TYPICAL SECTION THROUGH BOREHOLES

then the allowable bearing pressures, and then the settlements to be expected with these pressures. He should state whether any advantage would be gained by going deeper, so enabling higher bearing pressures to be used or settlements to be reduced.

In the case of piled foundations the writer should give the bearing stratum to which piles should be driven, the required or likely penetration of piles into this stratum, the working loads to be adopted per pile or per group of piles, and the settlements likely to occur in the individual pile or pile groups. Possible difficulties in driving should be noted and any detrimental effects on adjacent structures should be pointed out.

In writing this section of the report care should be taken to avoid wishful thinking based on preconceived ideas on the foundation design. The problem should be studied without prejudice. For example, test results which appear to be too low should not be lightly discarded because they do not fit in with preconceived ideas on bearing pressures. The reasons why the results are low should be studied. Only if it can be established that they are due say to sample disturbance or are too few in number to have any practical significance to the problem as a whole can low results be neglected. Similarly any borehole data which are unfavourable to the general ideas on foundation design must not be pushed on one side. If the results of a particular boring are unlike all the others in the vicinity, so upsetting a tidy arrangement of the foundations, the reasons for the discrepancy should be investigated. In cases of doubt a confirmatory boring or borings or check tests should be made. If it is demonstrated that the peculiar soil conditions do in fact exist the foundation design should take them into account.

The recommendations for foundation design must be based on the facts stated in the report, i.e. on the borehole records and test data. They must *not* be based on conjecture.

## 7. CONCLUSION

If the preceding "discussion" section of the report is lengthy or involved it may be convenient to summarize the main findings in itemized form. This is of help to the busy engineer who may not have time to read through pages of discussion. Alternatively the report may commence with a brief summary of the investigation procedure and the main conclusions which have been drawn from it.

The last stages are the final typing and checking of the report, printing the drawings and assembling and binding the whole. A neatly printed and bound report with good clear drawings free of typing and draughtsman's errors reflects the care with which the whole investigation has been done. Slipshod writing and careless typing and drawing may lead the client to think that the whole investigation has been carried out in a similar manner.

## FOUNDATION PROPERTIES OF SOIL AND ROCK TYPES

In the following pages, some notes are given on the engineering properties of various soils and rocks, with special reference to their bearing capacity and behaviour during construction and under foundation loading. Reference to *CP 2001* should be made for geological descriptions of these materials. The physical characteristics of the main groups and sub-groups of soils are given in Table 1.1. (See also reference 1.22.)

### Non-cohesive Soils

*Gravels* in the form of alluvial deposits are usually mixed with sands to a greater or lesser degree. Examples of the range of particle-size distribution are the beach gravels of the south coast of England which contain little or no sand. The sandy gravels which are widespread in the Thames Valley may contain 60 per cent or more of sand.

Gravels and sandy gravels in a medium-dense or denser state have a high bearing capacity and low compressibility. Compact gravelly soils give rise to difficulty in driving piles through them. If deep penetration is required into gravel strata it is usually necessary to adopt steel piles which have a higher penetrating ability than concrete or timber members.

Sandy gravels in a damp state but above the water table have some cohesion and can therefore be excavated to stand at very steep slopes provided that they are protected from erosion by flowing water (Plate XIV). Loose gravels without sand binder are unstable in the slopes of excavations and require to be cut back to their angle of repose of about 30° to 35°.

Heavy pumping is required if deep excavations in open gravels are made below the water table, but the water table in sandy gravel can be lowered by well points or deep wells with only moderate pumping. As an alternative to providing large capacity pumping plant the permeability of slightly sandy or clean gravels can be substantially reduced by injecting cement, clay slurries, or chemicals (*see* p. 699).

Erosion or solution of fine material from the interstices of gravel deposits can result in a very permeable and unstable formation. Open gravels caused by solution are sometimes found in the alluvial deposits derived from limestone formations.

*Sandy soils* have bearing capacity and compressibility characteristics similar to gravels, although very loosely deposited sands (e.g. dune sands) have a high compressibility requiring correspondingly low bearing pressures in order to avoid excessive settlement of foundations.

Dense sands and cemented sands have a high resistance to the driving of piles and steel piles are required if deep penetrations are necessary.

Sands in their naturally deposited state above the water table are usually damp or cemented to a varying degree and thus will stand at a steep slope in excavations. However, support by timbering or sheet piling is necessary in deep and narrow excavations where a sudden collapse—caused by drying out of the sand or vibrations— might endanger workmen.

Excavation in sands below the water table will result in slumping of the sides or "boiling" of the bottom (Plate XV), unless a properly designed ground water lowering system is used. This instability, which is also known as "quick" or "running sand" condition, is due to the erosive action of water flowing towards the excavation. By providing a ground water lowering system to draw water away from the excavation towards filter wells or wellpoints a condition of high stability can be achieved (p. 685). In particular circumstances it may be necessary to stabilize the sands by the injection of chemicals (p. 705), or excavation under compressed air in caissons may be required.

Loosely deposited sands are sensitive to the effects of vibrations which induce a closer state of packing of the particles. Therefore special consideration should be given to the design of machinery foundations on loose to medium-dense sands, and it is necessary to take precautions against the settlement of existing structures due to vibrations arising from such construction operations as blasting or pile driving (p. 167).

In some arid parts of the world the structure of loose deposits of sand is liable to collapse upon wetting, with consequent serious settlement of structures founded on these deposits. Wetting may be due to fracture of drains or leaking water pipes. Collapsing sands are found in some parts of South Africa, Rhodesia, and Angola (p. 166). Sand deposits can be formed as a result of weathering and breakdown of calcareous formations. Examples of these are limestone sands which are found on the coasts and islands of the Mediterranean Sea; shelly sands and coral sands which are found on the coasts and islands of the Persian Gulf and the Pacific Ocean, and on the southeastern seaboard of U.S.A.; and gypsum sands which are found in Iraq and Persian Gulf territories. These deposits which are formed from weathering are nearly always in a loose state except at the surface where they may be weakly cemented by silt or salt spray. Low foundation bearing pressures are required unless the loose deposits can be compacted by vibration or other methods.

Distinct from these products of weathering are the cemented calcareous sands or sandstones which are formed by saline and lime-rich waters being drawn up by temperature effects and evaporation in the surface layers to form a hard crust. These soils are known in various parts of the world as "caliche," "tufa," or "Steppen Kalk"; local names include "gatch" (Iran and Kuwait), "croute calcaire" (French North Africa), "havara" (Cyprus), and "kurkar" (Israel and Jordan). The deposits occur widely in Australia where they are known as "limestone rubble." A feature of their formation is the irregularity in thickness and distribution of the hardened crust. It may exist in several distinct layers of varying thickness separated by loose sands or soft clay, or in irregular masses of varying degrees of cementation. Thus it is difficult to design foundations to take full advantage of the high bearing capacity of the cemented material. Disturbance of the cemented sands by excavating machinery, construction traffic, or flowing water results in rapid breakdown to a material having the texture of a sandy silt which is highly unstable when wet. Cemented sands are highly abrasive to excavation machinery.

### Cohesive Soils

The foundation characteristics of cohesive soils vary widely with their geological formation, moisture content, and mineral composition. It is impossible in this chapter to cover all the types and combinations which exist in nature, and the following notes are restricted to the characteristics of some of the well-known types.

*Boulder Clays* are generally stiff to hard. Because of their heavy preconsolidation in glacial times only small consolidation settlements will occur under heavy foundation bearing pressures. Some boulder clays are highly variable containing lenses (often water-bearing) of gravels, sands and silts. In such conditions, foundation design must take account of the variable bearing capacity and compressibility at any particular locality. When carrying out deep excavations in variable glacial deposits, precautions should be taken against inrushes from water-bearing pockets. Excavations in stiff to hard boulder clays will stand vertically without support for long periods (Plate XIII). The presence of random boulders or pockets of large gravel and cobbles can cause difficulties in driving sheet piles or bearing piles into boulder clays. Another type of glacial deposit is *varved clay* which comprises layers of silty clay separated by thinner layers of sand or silt. These intervening layers are often water-bearing, which causes difficulties in "bleeding" of sand or silt into excavations. Varved clays are usually softer in consistency and more compressible than boulder clays. Driving piles into varved clays may weaken the strength of the clay layer to that of a soft slurry. Also, where varved clays are bordering a lake or river, fluctuations in the water level may be communicated to the sand layers with a detrimental effect on their bearing capacity. For these reasons varved clays are generally held to be troublesome soils in foundation engineering.

*Clay-with-Flints* exists widely in Southern England as a mantle over the chalk formations; it is partly a residual soil composed of the insoluble parts of chalk left after solution of the calcareous material and partly of the clays, sands and pebbles of Tertiary age that once existed with chalk. Below the zone of surface weathering the clay-with-flints is stiff to very stiff in consistency and has a low compressibility. In some deposits there may be difficulties in excavation due to the occurrence of masses of large flints in close contact and bound with hard dry clay. The clay fraction of clay-with-flints is a lean type of clay and consequently does not show marked volume changes with varying moisture content.

*Stiff Fissured Clays* such as London Clay, Barton Clay (in Hampshire), the Lias Clays of the Midlands, and the Weald and Gault Clays of South-eastern England have a relatively high bearing capacity below their softened weathered surface. Also, since they are preconsolidated clays, they have a moderate to low compressibility. They are "fat" clays and heavy structures founded on them show slow settlement over a very long period of years. Stiff fissured clays show marked volume changes with varying moisture content. Thus foundations need to be taken down to a depth where there will be little or no appreciable movement resulting from swell and shrinkage of the clay in alternating wet and dry seasons (*see* p. 156). For the same reason it is necessary to avoid accumulation of water at the bottom of excavations in order to avoid swelling and softening of the soil. Fissuring in these soils can cause a wide variation in shear strength determined by laboratory tests on samples taken by drive tubes, due to random distribution of fissures and their partial opening during sampling. Thus it is difficult to assess the results when assessing bearing capacity (p. 207). Because of these difficulties, shear strengths are often determined by in-situ tests such as the Dutch Cone or a small-diameter plate loading test made in a borehole.[1.23]

The fissured structure of these clays causes difficulties, mainly unpredictable, in the stability of slopes of excavations (p. 562), the stability of the walls of unlined holes sunk by mechanical boring methods for deep piers or piles (p. 529), and in the design of timbering or sheetpiling to excavations (p. 593). Clays having similar characteristics to the British stiff fissured clays include the Fort Union "shale" of Montana and the Bearpaw "shale" of Saskatchewan. Stiff fissured clay also occurs in Northern France, Denmark, and Trinidad.

*Tropical Red Clays* are principally residual soils resulting from physical and chemical weathering of igneous rocks. They are widespread in India, Africa, South America, Hawaii, West Indies, and Far Eastern countries. They are usually "lean" clays with a relatively high bearing capacity and low compressibility. However, in certain tropical conditions, leaching of the clays can occur at shallow depths, leaving a porous material with a fairly high compressibility. Vargas[1.24] has described the settlement of heavy structures on porous red clay at São Paulo, Brazil. Tropical red clays do not show any marked volume changes with varying moisture content and can be excavated to vertical or steeply battered slopes with little risk of collapse.

*Laterite* is a term given to a ferruginous soil of clayey texture, which has a concretionary appearance. It is essentially a product of tropical weathering and occurs widely in Central and South America, West and Central Africa, India, Malaya, the East Indies, and Northern Australia.[1.25] Laterites are characteristically reddish-brown or yellow in colour. They exist in the form of a stiff to hard crust 6 m or more thick overlying rather softer clayey materials followed by the parent rock. Laterites have a high bearing capacity and low compressibility. They do not present any difficult foundation engineering problems.

*Tropical Black Clays* are also developed on igneous rocks, examples being the "black cotton soils" of the Sudan and Kenya, the "vlei" soils of Southern Rhodesia, and the "adobe" of Southwestern U.S.A.[1.26] Black clays are also found in India, Nigeria, and Australia. They are generally found in poorly-drained topography. Unlike the tropical red clays, black clays are very troublesome in foundation engineering in that they show marked volume changes with changes in moisture content, and because of their poor drainage characteristics they become impassable to construction traffic in the wet season. Because these clays exist in countries where there are marked wet and dry seasons, the soil movements brought about by alternate wetting and drying are severe and extend to considerable depths. In many cases it has been found necessary to construct even light buildings on piled foundations to get below the zones of soil movement.

*Saline Calcareous Clays* are widely distributed in the Near and Middle East. They are found in the Mesopotamian Plain of Iraq, the coastal plains of the Levant and South-west Iran, the coast of North Africa, the islands of the Mediterranean, the limestone plateaux of Jordan, and in Utah and Nevada, U.S.A.[1.27] These soils were formed by the deposition of clay minerals in saline or lime-rich waters. The deposits are augmented by wind-blown sand and dust. The profile of calcareous silty clays is similar throughout the arid and semi-arid countries of the Near and Middle East. It comprises a surface crust about 2 m thick of hard to stiff desiccated clay overlying soft moist clay. The surface crust is not softened to any appreciable depth by the winter rains.

The stiff crust has adequate bearing capacity to support light structures, but heavy structures requiring wide foundations which transmit pressures to the underlying soft and compressible layers may suffer serious settlement unless supported by piles driven to less compressible strata. Calcareous clays show marked volume changes with varying moisture content, and where there are marked seasonal changes, as in the wet winter and dry summer of the countries bordering the Mediterranean, the soil movements extend to a depth of 5 m or more below ground level, and special precautions in foundation design are required. In regions where there are no marked differences in seasonal rainfall, as in Southern Iraq, soil movement is not a serious problem. In some regions the stiff crust is a weakly cemented agglomeration of sand or gravel-size particles of clayey material probably resulting from deposition by winds. These soils may suffer collapse on inundation combined with foundation loading.

Excavation in the stiff crust of calcareous clays is not a difficult problem, although there is likely to be some seepage of water from fissures. Excavation in the deeper soft deposits is likely to be troublesome due to slumping of the sides and heaving of the bottom.

*Alluvial (including Marine) Clays* are geologically recent materials formed by the deposition of silty and clayey material in river valleys, estuaries and on the bed of the sea. They are "normally consolidated," i.e. they have consolidated under their own weight and have not been subjected in their geological history to a preconsolidation load as in the case of boulder clays and stiff-fissured clays. Since they are normally consolidated they show a progressive increase in shear strength with increasing depth ranging from very soft near the ground surface to firm or stiff at depth. Atmospheric drying and the effects of vegetation produce a stiff surface crust on alluvial clays. The thickness of this crust is generally 1 to 1·2 m in Great Britain, but it is likely to be much greater and liable to vary erratically in thickness in arid climates. Some regions show several layers of desiccation separated by soft, normally consolidated clayey layers. Moderately high bearing pressures, with little or no accompanying settlement, can be adopted for narrow foundations in the surface crust which do not transmit stresses to the underlying soft and highly compressible deposits. In the case of wide or deep foundations it is necessary to adopt very low bearing pressures, or to use a special type known as the buoyancy raft (p. 268), or to support the structure on piles driven through the soft and firm alluvial clays to a satisfactory bearing stratum.

Alluvial clays, especially marine clays, are "sensitive" to disturbance, i.e. if they are disturbed in sampling or in construction operations they show a marked loss in shear strength. The sensitivity* can range from 2 or 3 in the case of estuarine clays of the Thames and the Firth of Forth to as much as 150 in the post-glacial clays of Eastern Canada. The marine clays of Norway and Sweden are also highly sensitive due to leaching of salts from the pore-water of the soil by the percolation of fresh water, leaving an open lattice structure which is readily broken down on disturbance.

Excavations below the dried-out surface crust require support by timbering or sheetpiling; open excavations require to be cut back to shallow slopes to avoid massive rotational slips. Excavations in soft clays exceeding a certain depth–width ratio are subject to failure by heaving of the bottom or appreciable inward yielding of the side supports (p. 597).

As in the case of stiff fissured clays, precautions must be taken against the effects on foundations of seasonal swelling and shrinkage and the drying action of the roots of vegetation (p. 159).

Alluvial clays are frequently varved or laminated clays interbedded with layers of peat, sand and silt as in the Fens of East Anglia, and in major river deltas.

*Silts* occur as glacial or alluvial deposits, or as windblown deposits. Examples of the latter are the "brickearth" of Southeastern England, and "loess" which is found in widespread tracts in Mid-western and North-western U.S.A., China, India, Russia, and Israel. Glacial and alluvial silts are generally water-bearing and soft in consistency. They are among the most troublesome soils in excavation work, since they are readily susceptible to slumping and "boiling." Being retentive of water they cannot readily be dewatered by conventional ground water lowering systems. Silts are liable to frost heave.

Brickearths are generally firm to stiff and do not normally present

* Sensitivity $= \dfrac{\text{Undisturbed shear strength}}{\text{Remoulded shear strength}}$.

any difficult problems in foundation work. Similarly, loess soils are slightly cemented and have a high bearing capacity. However, they are liable to collapse of their structure on wetting which may occur as a result of flooding or even broken water mains. Loess soils can stand with vertical faces to a great height provided they are protected from erosion by flowing water.

*Peat* consists of dead and fossilized organic matter. It is found in many parts of the world. Extensive deposits occur in Northern Europe, North America and U.S.S.R., where it is overlain by living vegetable matter in "muskeg" terrain. Peat is a permeable fibrous material and is highly compressible. The usual procedure is to take foundations of structures below peat to less compressible strata unless heavy settlements can be tolerated. Lewis[1.28] has described the settlement of a road embankment in Suffolk, where in a little over four years 1·5 m of peat and organic clay were compressed by nearly 0·3 m under the load of a 1·5 m thick embankment. Another undesirable characteristic of peat is its "wasting." The ground surface of the peat in the Fen districts of East Anglia is slowly sinking through the years due to consolidation of the ground under its own weight (accelerated by drainage), to the fibrous peat blowing away in the wind, and to accidental or deliberate burning of the peat. Thus if foundations are taken below peat layers by means of piles or piers the surrounding ground surface sinks relative to the structure with the result that over a long period of years the foundations become exposed. Many instances of this can be seen in the Fens. Peats may contain organic acids which are aggressive to concrete (p. 762).

### Rocks

*Volcanic Rocks* such as granite, basalt, gabbro, gneiss, schist, and porphyry, normally have excellent bearing capacity unless they are heavily faulted or shattered.

In tropical countries, volcanic rocks are often deeply weathered by physical and chemical action. In Hong Kong the granite is weathered to depths up to 60 m. Beneath a surface layer of "red earth," the decomposed granite consists of coarse quartz grains in a porous matrix of decomposed felspar and biotite. In foundations, it behaves as a free-draining coarse sand of low compressibility. Lumb[1.39] states that decomposed granite has an angle of shearing resistance of 35° when fully drained and that unsaturated soils do not show "collapse" phenomena (p. 64) when they become fully saturated. Boulders of undecomposed granite, 3 m or more in size, are found in the deeper layers of partly weathered granite. Decomposed granite is stable in excavations and will stand at a near vertical face over a long period of time.

*Quartzite* has excellent load bearing characteristics. A presumed bearing value of 4000 kN/m² can be taken for "hard sandstones" in which quartzites can be classed. Quartzites are highly abrasive causing heavy wear in drilling equipment and the teeth of excavator buckets or grabs. Quartzite boulders are frequently found in glacial drift in Wales and Scotland.

*Sandstones* in the unweathered state have good load bearing capacity; presumed bearing values of 4000 kN/m² for strong sandstones and 2000 kN/m² for weak sandstones are permissible. However, they can cause considerable difficulty in foundation work due to deep and irregular weathering. The extent and type of weathering depends on the cementing medium. Clayey cement leads to a rock with low strength which is liable to soften on exposure to water or frost, and such sandstones may show frost weathering to a great depth as a result of ice action in glacial times. If the cement is calcareous it may have been dissolved out of the rock to an irregular extent, forming random pockets of loose sand within the sound rock. Great care is needed when undertaking exploratory drilling in sandstones. Percussion drilling is generally unsatisfactory since the thickness and extent of weathered layers or pockets is obscured as the rock is broken up by the percussion tools. Rotary core drilling is the preferred method, but cases have occurred where fairly hard rock has been identified as a loose sand because of careless drilling techniques or the adoption of too small a core size (p. 42). Ample core sizes should be specified, for example N or H for fairly strong sandstones and up to K size for weak weathered rocks. Where exploration in sandstones of the Coal Measures in Great Britain is being undertaken by trial pits without boreholes, it should not be assumed that a bed of hard sandstone found at the bottom of the pit represents sound bedrock capable of carrying high bearing pressures. It is quite possible that the sandstone is underlain at no great depth by weaker mudstones or shale.

*Mudstones or Siltstones* have similar foundation characteristics to sandstones but are not often found in a weathered state. Being structureless deposits mudstones are often difficult to break up by explosives in bulk excavations, since they do not shatter like the harder bedded or fissured rocks.

*Shales* are often found in a weathered state having the consistency of a soft to firm clay, or glacial action may have caused frost-shattering producing deep deposits of loose broken particles. When intact and unweathered, shales have a high bearing capacity, 2000 kN/m² or more for hard shales and mudstones. Some shales are liable to soften in contact with water. The shaly slates (known locally as "shillet") of south-west England are characterized by their steep and contorted dip which can vary in angle and direction over short distances. The shaly slates sometimes contain thin layers weathered to a soft clay consistency, which may be the cause of creep and slips of hillsides and instability in slopes of excavations.

Shale mixed with coal particles is found in large dumps in coal-mining districts of Britain. Usually the shale is found in these dumps in a burnt state due to spontaneous combustion. The reddish burnt shale is useful for filling. However, if the material contains unburnt or partially burnt shale it is liable to swell in contact with water, leading to heavy pressures on retaining walls. Burnt or unburnt shale often contains sulphates in appreciable quantity. Cases have occurred of sulphate attack on foundation walls and floors due to the use of shale filling below ground floors.

*Marl.* The Keuper Marls outcrop widely in the Triassic deposits of the Midlands and West of England. It is difficult to assess their bearing capacity due to variable depth of weathering and interbedding with sandstones. They are often highly fissured and due to the percolation of water, softening takes place about the fissures. Solution of calcareous nodules can also result in frequent small cavities. Near the surface the whole mass of the material may be softened, but with increasing depth the softening is restricted to a narrow zone about the fissures. At greater depths the fissures become tightly closed and free of water, when the rock is in a strong unweathered state. Plate loading tests have shown the unweathered Marl to have an ultimate bearing capacity of 4000 to 5000 kN/m². Chandler and Davis[1.30] have established values of the deformation modulus of Keuper Marl appropriate to spread foundations where the anticipated settlements are in the range of 0·01 to 0·05 per cent of the foundation width. The values are—

|  | MN/m² |
|---|---|
| Zone I (unweathered) | 26–250 |
| Zone II (slightly weathered) | 9–70 |
| Zone III (moderately weathered) | 2–48 |
| Zone IV (heavily weathered) | 2–13 |

Rotary core drilling with large size cores (preferably κ) should be used in Keuper Marl, possibly in conjunction with Denison or open drive samplers in the softer weathered layers.

Heavy ground water flow may be encountered in foundation excavations in fissured water-bearing Keuper Marls. The ground water is also liable to be sulphate-bearing.

*Chalk* varies widely in character from a soft crumbly deposit to a hard, massively bedded rock. In Southern England there are three types: the Upper Chalk which is generally white, crumbly, and much-fissured, and contains many flints; the Middle Chalk is white but more massive in appearance with fewer flints; the Lower Chalk is grey, very massive, and fairly hard with relatively few fissures and bedding planes; it contains very few flints.

The softening is caused by frost action or the downward percolation of water and it can extend to a depth of 20 m or more. Chalk is also subject to softening as a result of mechanical disturbance; for example the action of boring tools such as chisels or shells can change a hard chalk into a material resembling a soft putty due to breakdown of the cellular structure of the rock and the release of water held in the cells. Similarly, driving of sample tubes or piles into chalk can result in the formation of a creamy slurry between the face of the tube or pile and the chalk. Weathered chalk can vary from a soft putty-like material at the surface to a mass of hard lumps in a matrix of putty chalk in its less weathered state. In the transition between weathered and unweathered chalk the soft material is limited to fissures or bedding planes. Pile driving into the partly weathered material tends to squeeze the softened chalk into the fissure system with a consequent low driving resistance.

As a result of these characteristics chalk is a very difficult material to evaluate from the point of view of bearing capacity and settlement and the author is reluctant to use piled foundations in chalk or weathered limestone unless strictly necessary. Because of the effect of boring and sampling operations on the material it is possible to get a misleading impression of its true in-situ strength. Certainly its strength should not be judged from the appearance of the lumpy debris brought up in boring tools. "Undisturbed" samples not less than 4 in. diameter give a better representation of the strength, but ordinary open-drive samplers cannot penetrate the harder unweathered chalk and it is necessary to resort to rotary core drilling to obtain satisfactory samples. Here again a careful technique with large diameter coring is necessary to avoid crumbling and erosion of the cores.

Plate bearing tests are the most useful means of obtaining quantitative data on bearing capacity and settlement. Again the mineralogical structure of chalk gives rise to difficulty in interpretation of load test data. A typical loading test result is shown in Fig. 1.28. The initial straight-line portion of the load-settlement curve represents normal elastic settlement, the steepening portion indicates breakdown of the cellular structure and expulsion of water with consequent softening and plastic yielding of the chalk. With further loading the broken-down chalk cells consolidate with a greatly increased bearing resistance and the final stage is normal failure, as a granular material, of the consolidated mass. The settlements at the various stages of loading are comparatively high—far higher than would be given by any rock and more typical of a soil such as a compact silt. For this reason, the author suggests that weathered chalk should be treated as a soil and its bearing capacity and consolidation should be computed on the basis of data provided by laboratory tests on "undisturbed" samples or by in-situ tests such as the standard penetration test.

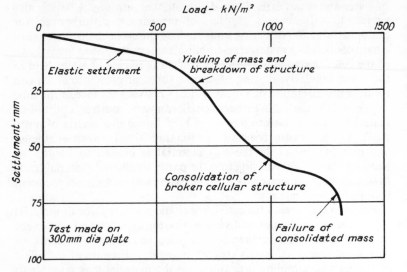

FIG. 1.28. RESULTS OF PLATE LOADING TESTS ON CHALK

This approach was recommended by Wakeling in the 1965 *Symposium on Chalk in Earthworks and Foundations.*[1.31] This symposium and a later review by Hobbs,[1.32] contain much information on the engineering behaviour of chalk.

The surface of chalk concealed by overburden may be highly irregular. A typical section as exposed in a quarry is shown in Plate V. Therefore on the evidence of borehole data alone considerable caution is required in determining the required depth of foundations where these are to be taken down to chalk bedrock below superficial soil deposits. "Swallow holes" or "sink holes" filled with sands, clays, and flints are frequently found in chalk districts. These are described in greater detail under "limestones."

Heavy ground water flow may be encountered in broken fissured chalk, but only small seepages of water need be expected from the massive Lower Chalk. Such seepages occur from bedding planes and fissures which are fairly infrequent in this formation.

Chalk is liable to heaving by frost action so foundations on chalk in Great Britain should be placed at least 0·3 m below ground level to avoid excessive movement at times of severe frosts. Chalk can be cut to a near-vertical face in excavations but it is liable to breakdown by weathering due to frost. For long-term stability a face of 45° to 50° slope is required.

*Limestones* do not have many of the difficult characteristics of chalk (which of course is a form of limestone). They are generally harder and less prone to deep weathering. A bearing pressure of 4000 kN/m² can be used for massively bedded limestones. However, the engineer should always be on the look-out for very deep swallow holes or deep fissures filled with softened material in limestone formations. These are widespread in Derbyshire, Somerset, and Glamorgan. They may be concealed by superficial deposits but they are often indicated by depressions and irregularities in the ground surface. On one site investigated in Derbyshire a mass of swallow holes were found in a small area. The intact limestone occurred as irregularly shaped "islands" or "promontories" wholly or partially surrounded by sands and clays infilling the swallow holes. Borings over 15 m deep did not reach the bottom of the infilling material.

In some areas the overlying rocks may have collapsed into swallow holes in the limestone, the collapsed material forming a mass of loose fragments. Piling is useless in such circumstances, and the usual expedient is to bridge over the swallow holes or to cover them by a dome-shaped slab bearing on its rim around the edge of the subsidence crater. If the swallow holes are very wide it is necessary to re-site the structure since they are always liable to renewed subsidence at quite unpredictable intervals of time.

Ground water flow may be very heavy in excavations taken into water-bearing limestone especially if the rock is cavernous or heavily fissured. It is often necessary to resort to grouting with cement, cement/sand mixture, sawdust, or bitumen in order to reduce the quantity of water to be pumped.

Some limestone formations such as the Forest Marble or Lower (Blue) Lias are thinly bedded and interbedded with clays. Special consideration should be given to foundations on such formations, especially at the investigation stages where the problems are similar to those described for Keuper Marl on page 72.

## REFERENCES

1.1 ROTHERY, H. C., *Report to the President of the Board of Trade on the Tay Bridge Disaster, London*, 30th *June*, 1880.

1.2 British Standard Code of Practice *CP 2001 Site Investigations* (London, British Standards Institution).

1.3 KALLSTENIUS, T., Mechanical disturbance in clay samples taken with piston samplers, *Royal Swedish Geotechnical Institute, Proc. No. 16* (Stockholm, 1958).

1.4   Rowe, P. W., The relevance of soil fabric to site investigation practice, *Geotechnique*, **22**, No. 2, pp. 193–300 (June 1972).

1.5   Serota, S. and Jennings, R. A., Undisturbed sampling techniques for sands and very soft clays, *Proc. 4th Int. Conf. Soil Mech.* (London, 1957), **1**, pp. 245–248.

1.6   Bishop, A. W., A new sampling tool for use on cohesionless soils below ground water level, *Geotechnique*, **2**, pp. 125–131 (Dec., 1948).

1.7   Hvorslev, M. J., *Sub-surface exploration and sampling of soils for civil engineering purposes* (U.S. Waterways Exp. Station, 1949).

1.8   Flaate, K., Factors influencing the results of vane tests, *Canadian Geotech. J.*, **3**, No. 1, pp. 18–31 (Feb., 1966).

1.9   Palmer, D. J. and Stuart, J. G., Some observations on the standard penetration test and a correlation of the test with a new penetrometer, *Proc. 4th Int. Conf. Soil Mech.* (London, 1957), **1**, pp. 231–236.

1.10   Terzaghi, K. and Peck, R. B., *Soil Mechanics in Engineering Practice*,\* pp. 341–347 (New York, John Wiley, 2 ed. 1967).

1.11   Peck, R. B., Hanson, W. E. and Thornburn, T. H., *Foundation Engineering*, p. 310 (New York, John Wiley, 2 ed. 1974).

1.12   Rodin, S., Experiences with penetrometers with particular reference to the standard penetration test, *Proc. 5th Int. Conf. Soil Mech.* (Paris, 1961), **1**, pp. 517–521.

1.13   Rodin, S., Corbett, B. O., Sherwood, D. E. and Thorburn, S., Penetration testing in the United Kingdom, *Proc. European Symp. on Penetration Testing*, State-of-the-Art Report, Stockholm 1974.

1.14   Duncan, N. and Sheerman-Chase, A., Rock mechanics in civil engineering works, *Civ. Eng. and Public Works Rev.*, pp. 1,751–1,756 (Dec., 1965) and pp. 57–59 (Jan., 1966).

1.15   U.S. Bureau of Reclamation, *Earth Manual*, p. 541 (Washington, U.S. Govt. Printing Office, 1963).

1.16   Tomlinson, M. J., Site exploration for maritime and river works. *Proc. Inst. C.E.*, **3**, No. 2, Pt. 2, pp. 225–272 (June, 1954).

1.17   Terzaghi, K., Discussion on Session 3, Techniques of field measurement and sampling, *Proc. 4th Int. Conf. Soil Mech.* (London, 1957), **3**, p. 135.

1.18   Robertshaw, J. and Brown, P. D., Geophysical methods of exploration and their application to civil engineering problems, *Proc. Inst. C.E.*, **4**, No. 5, Pt. 1, pp. 644–690 (Sept., 1955).

1.19   Beckmann, W. C., Roberts, A. C., and Luskin, B., Sub-bottom depth recorder, *Geophysics*, **24**, No. 4, pp. 749–769 (Oct., 1959).

1.20   Raybould, D. R. and Price, D. G., The use of the proton magnetometer in engineering geological investigations, *Proc. 1st Cong. Int. Soc. Rock Mech.*, **1**, pp. 11–14 (Lisbon, 1966).

1.21   Bishop, A. W. and Henkel, D. J., *The Measurement of Soil Properties in the Triaxial Test* (London, Arnold, 1957).

---

\* Future references to this book will state the title only.

1.22 TERZAGHI, K., Influence of geological factors on the engineering properties of sediments, *Harvard Soil Mech. Series No. 50* (Harvard Univ., Cambridge, Mass., 1955).

1.23 WARD, W. H., MARSLAND, A. and SAMUELS, S. G., Properties of the London Clay at the Ashford Common shaft, *Geotechnique*, **15**, No. 4, pp. 321–344 (Dec., 1965).

1.24 VARGAS, M., Foundations of structures in over-consolidated clay layers in São Paulo, *Geotechnique*, **5**, No. 3, pp. 253–266 (Sept., 1955).

1.25 NIXON, I. K. and SKIPP, B. O., Airfield construction on overseas soils: Laterite, *Proc. Inst. C.E.*, **8**, pp. 253–275 (Nov., 1957).

1.26 CLARE, K. E., Airfield construction on overseas soils: tropical black clays, *Proc. Inst. C.E.*, **8**, pp. 223–231 (Nov., 1957).

1.27 TOMLINSON, M. J., Airfield construction on overseas soils: saline calcareous soils, *Proc. Inst. C.E.*, **8**, pp. 232–252 (Nov., 1957).

1.28 LEWIS, W. A., The settlement of the approach embankments to a new road bridge at Lackford, West Suffolk, *Geotechnique*, **6**, No. 3 (Sept., 1956).

1.29 LUMB, P., The residual soils of Hong Kong, *Géotechnique*, **15**, No. 2, pp. 180–194 (June, 1965).

1.30 CHANDLER, R. J. and DAVIS, A. G., Further work on the engineering properties of Keuper Marl, *Constr. Ind. Res. and Inf. Assoc.*, Res. Report No. 47, London, 1973.

1.31 *Symposium on Chalk in Earthworks and Foundations*, Inst. Civ. Eng., (London, 1966).

1.32 HOBBS, N. B., General report and state-of-the-art review, *Proc. Conf. on Settlement of Structures*, Cambridge, Pentech Press, 1974.

# 2

# The General Principles of
# Foundation Design

THE foundation of a structure is defined as that part of the structure in direct contact with the ground and which transmits the load of the structure to the ground.

*Pad Foundations* are usually provided to support structural columus. They may consist of a simple circular, square, or rectangular slab of uniform thickness, or they may be stepped or haunched to distribute the load from a heavy column. Pad foundations to heavily loaded structural steel columns are sometimes provided with a steel grillage.

Various forms of pad foundations are shown in Fig. 2.1 (*a*) to (*d*).

*Strip Foundations* are normally provided for load-bearing walls (Fig. 2.2 (*a*)), and for rows of columns which are spaced so closely that pad foundations would nearly touch each other (Fig. 2.2 (*b*)). In the latter case it is more economical to excavate and concrete a strip foundation than to work in a large number of individual pits. In fact, it is often thought to be more economical to provide a strip foundation whenever the distance between the adjacent square pads is less than the dimensions of the pads.*

*Wide Strip Foundations* are necessary where the bearing capacity of the soil is low enough to necessitate a strip so wide that transverse

---

* The strip foundation may consist of individual pads with a joint between each pad (*see* p. 231).

bending occurs in the projecting portions of the foundation beam
(Fig. 2.3) and reinforcement is required to prevent cracking.

*Raft Foundations* are required on soils of low bearing capacity, or

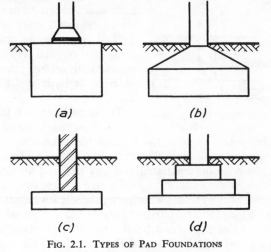

FIG. 2.1. TYPES OF PAD FOUNDATIONS
(*a*) Mass concrete for steel column.
(*b*) Reinforced concrete with sloping upper face.
(*c*) Plain reinforced concrete.
(*d*) Stepped reinforced concrete.

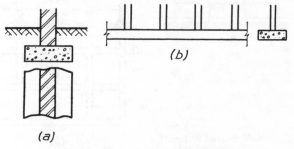

FIG. 2.2. TYPES OF STRIP FOUNDATIONS
(*a*) Strip foundation to load-bearing wall.
(*b*) Strip foundation to row of close-spaced columns.

where structural columns or other loaded areas are so close in both
directions that individual pad foundations would nearly touch each
other. Raft foundations are useful in reducing differential settlement
on variable soils or where there is a wide variation in loading between
adjacent columns or other applied loads. Forms of raft foundations
are shown in Fig. 2.4 (*a*) to (*c*).

*Bearing Piles* are required where the soil at normal foundation level cannot support ordinary pad, strip, or raft foundations (Fig. 2.5 (*a*)) or where structures are sited on deep filling which is compressible and settling under its own weight (Fig. 2.5 (*b*)). Piled foundations are

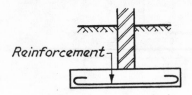

a convenient method of supporting structures built over water (Fig. 2.5 (*c*)) or where uplift loads must be resisted (Fig. 2.5 (*d*)). Inclined or raking piles are provided to resist lateral forces (Fig. 2.5(*e*)).

FIG. 2.3. WIDE STRIP FOUNDATION

The usual approach to a normal foundation engineering problem is first to prepare a plan of the base of the structure showing the various column, wall, and distributed loadings. Dead and live loadings should be differentiated and any bending moments at the base of columns or walls should be noted. Secondly, the bearing characteristics of the ground as given by the site investigation should be studied. From this, tentative allowable bearing pressures can be allocated for the various strata below ground level. The third step is to determine the required foundation depth. This may be the

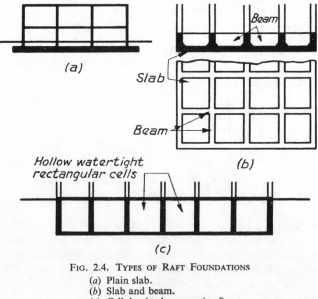

FIG. 2.4. TYPES OF RAFT FOUNDATIONS
(*a*) Plain slab.
(*b*) Slab and beam.
(*c*) Cellular (or buoyancy) raft.

minimum depth to get below surface layers of soil affected by seasonal temperature or moisture changes or by erosion. Structural requirements may involve founding at greater depths than the minimum required solely from soil considerations. For example, the building may have a basement, or there may be heating ducts or culverts below ground level. Having decided upon a minimum depth from either soil mechanics or structural requirements, the dimensions of the foundations are arrived at from a knowledge of the loading

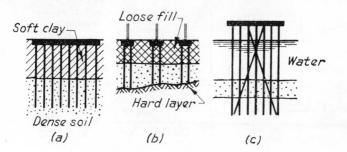

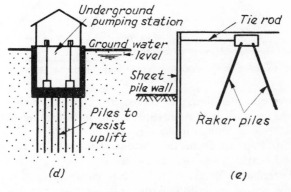

FIG. 2.5. TYPES OF PILED FOUNDATIONS

and the allowable bearing pressures. This usually decides the type of foundation, i.e. pad, strip, or raft foundations. If soil of a higher bearing capacity exists at no great depth below the required minimum depth, consideration could be given to taking foundations to the deeper stratum, with consequent savings in the quantity of excavation and concrete. However, if the deeper stratum lies below the ground water table, the cost of pumping or sheet piling might well outweigh these savings.

With the foundation depth and bearing pressures tentatively

decided upon, the fourth step is to calculate or estimate the total and differential settlements of the structure. If these are excessive, the bearing pressures will have to be reduced or the foundations taken to a deeper and less compressible stratum. If the bearing capacity of the shallow soil layers is inadequate, or if the estimated settlements of shallow foundations are excessive, the structure will have to be founded on piles or other special measures taken.

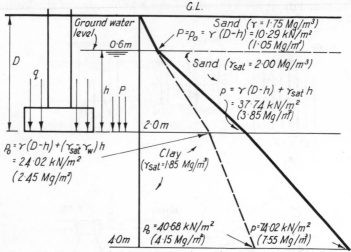

FIG. 2.6. EXAMPLE OF CALCULATING TOTAL AND EFFECTIVE OVERBURDEN PRESSURE

The above considerations are discussed in greater detail in the following pages and in the subsequent chapters dealing with the various methods of foundation design and construction. It will be useful at this stage to define the various terms relating to bearing capacity and bearing pressure. These are—

*Total overburden pressure*, $p$, is the intensity of total pressure, due to the weights of both soil and soil water, on any horizontal plane at and below foundation level before construction operations are commenced (Fig. 2.6).

*Effective overburden pressure*, $p_o$, is the intensity of inter-granular pressure on any horizontal plane at and below foundation level before construction operations are commenced. This pressure is the total overburden pressure ($p$) less the pore-water pressure, which, in the general case, is equal to the head of water above the horizontal plane. For example, for a foundation level at a depth $h$ below the water table—

$$p_o = p - \gamma_w h \qquad . \qquad . \qquad . \qquad . \qquad (2.1)$$

*Total foundation pressure* (or gross loading intensity), $q$, is the intensity of total pressure on the ground beneath the foundation after the structure has been erected and fully loaded. It is inclusive of the gross load of the foundation substructure, the loading from the superstructure, and the gross loading from any backfilled soil and soil water supported by the substructure.

*Net foundation pressure* (or net loading intensity), $q_n$, is the net increase in pressure on the ground beneath the foundation due to the dead load and live load applied by the structure.

$$q_n = q - p \text{ (at foundation depth } D) \qquad . \qquad . \quad (2.2)$$

The term $q_n$ is used for calculating the distribution of stress at any depth below foundation level.

*Ultimate bearing capacity*, $q_f$, is the value of the loading intensity at which the ground fails in shear.

*Net ultimate bearing capacity*, $q_{nf}$, for a particular foundation is that value of the net loading intensity at which the ground fails in shear,

i.e.
$$q_{nf} = q_f - p \quad . \qquad . \qquad . \qquad . \quad (2.3)$$

*Presumed bearing value*, is the net loading intensity considered appropriate to the particular type of ground for preliminary design purposes. The particular value is based either on local experience or by calculation from strength tests or field loading tests using a factor of safety against shear failure.

*Allowable bearing pressure*, $q_a$, is the maximum allowable net loading intensity of the ground in any given case, taking into consideration the bearing capacity, the estimated amount and rate of settlement that will occur, and the ability of the structure to accommodate the settlement. It is therefore a function both of the site and of the structural conditions.

It will be seen from the above definitions that there is an important difference between the terms "bearing capacity" and "bearing pressure." It is important that this distinction is clearly understood and that the terms are correctly used. The *bearing capacity* of a foundation soil is that pressure that the soil is *capable* of carrying, i.e. in the case of ultimate bearing capacity the pressure at which shear failure occurs, and this value, divided by a suitable safety factor, gives the *presumed bearing value*. The *bearing pressure* of a foundation is the loading intensity *imposed* by the foundation on the soil.

The use of the above terms can be illustrated by the following statement: "Calculations based on the shear strength of the soil showed that the *ultimate bearing capacity* for 1·2 m wide strip foundations at a depth of 1·5 m was 600 kN/m². Adopting a safety factor of 3 on this value, the *presumed bearing value* of the soil beneath the strip foundation is 200 kN/m². However, in view of the sensitivity of the structure to the effects of small differential settlements, it was decided to limit the total and differential settlements by adopting an *allowable bearing pressure* of 150 kN/m²."

### ESTIMATION OF ALLOWABLE BEARING PRESSURES

As defined above the allowable bearing pressure imposed by a foundation is a function of the characteristics of the ground, the depth and dimensions of the foundation, and the degree of settlement which can be tolerated by the structure or its installations.

There are two approaches to the estimation of allowable bearing pressures. First, from a knowledge of the shear strength characteristics of the soil, determined in the manner described in Chapter 1, the *ultimate bearing capacity* ($q_f$) of the soil can be calculated for a foundation of given depth and dimensions. An arbitrary safety factor can then be applied to the calculated ultimate bearing capacity to give the presumed bearing value. If it can be shown from experience or by calculation that the settlements given by a foundation pressure equal to the presumed bearing value are not excessive for the type and function of the structure, then the *allowable bearing pressure* ($q_a$) can be taken as equal to the presumed bearing value. If the settlement is excessive then a lower value will have to be taken for the allowable bearing pressure.

The second approach is to determine the allowable bearing pressure from experience and a knowledge of the characteristics of the ground, or by empirical methods based on the results of certain types of in-situ test made on the soil.

The procedure for calculating ultimate bearing capacity from the shear strength characteristics of the soil can be applied to foundations on gravels, sands, silts, clays, and intermediate types. It is widely used for silts and clays since with 30 years of experience in the application of soil mechanics there is ample evidence to substantiate the soundness of this approach. The procedure is less widely used for foundations on sands and gravels and hardly at all for foundations on rocks. In the case of sands and gravels the main drawback to the adoption of the purely theoretical soil mechanics approach is the difficulty of obtaining satisfactory undisturbed samples for laboratory shear strength tests, and the lack of any in-situ test which will give values of shear strength directly.

Fortunately we do not often need to calculate the ultimate bearing capacity of sands and gravels. Only in the case of narrow and shallow foundations on waterlogged sands is there likely to be a risk of general failure in shear under the bearing pressures normally used for foundation work. In all cases of foundations on dry sands, and most cases of wide or deep foundations on waterlogged sands, the *allowable bearing pressures* are governed by considerations of tolerable settlement. In other words, the allowable bearing pressure required to limit settlements to a tolerable value is very much lower than that obtained by dividing the ultimate bearing capacity by an arbitrary safety factor, say of 3. It is therefore preferable, in the case of foundations on sands and gravels, to adopt an empirical design method relating allowable bearing pressures to permissible settlements for foundations of given dimensions. Empirical methods based on experience are the only ones in general use for foundations on rocks. Although it is possible, by the methods described in Chapter 1, to obtain cores of rock from boreholes and to subject them to laboratory shear strength and consolidation tests which simulate conditions of consolidation under foundation loading and overburden pressure, there is as yet no wide experience of the correlation of these tests with foundation behaviour. The effects of fissuring and bedding planes are to a large extent incalculable.

### Calculations for Ultimate Bearing Capacity by Theoretical Soil Mechanics Methods

#### 1. GENERAL CASE

When a load is applied to a foundation, settlement will occur in the form shown in the load-settlement graph (Fig. 2.7). Up to a certain stage, the settlement of the foundation will be comparatively small and mainly elastic (i.e. on removal of the load the foundation will rise nearly to its original level). With increased loading the settlement will increase at a disproportionate rate until ultimately the settlement will increase rapidly without further increase of loading. The ultimate bearing capacity $(q_f)$ of the soil will have been reached, and the foundation will sink

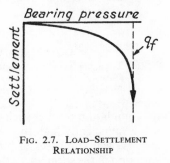

FIG. 2.7. LOAD–SETTLEMENT RELATIONSHIP

and tilt accompanied by heaving of the surrounding soil (Fig. 2.8).

Sinking and tilting of the foundation will continue until the structure overturns, or until a state of equilibrium is reached when

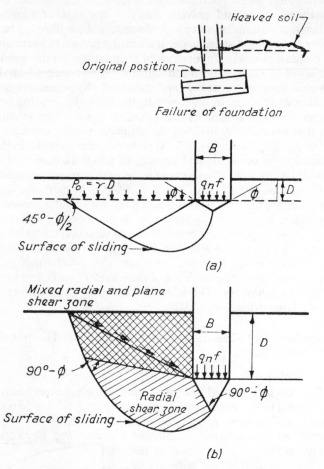

FIG. 2.8. ANALYSIS OF FOUNDATION FAILURE

(a) Terzaghi's approximate analysis of failure of shallow foundation with rough base and surcharge.

(b) Meyerhof's analysis of failure of shallow foundation with surcharge.

the foundation reaches such a depth that the bearing capacity of the soil is sufficiently high to prevent further movement. Tilting nearly always occurs in cases of foundation failure because the inevitable variation in the shear strength and compressibility of the soil from one point to another causes greater yielding on one side or another of the foundation. This throws the centre of gravity of the load towards the side where yielding has occurred, thus increasing the intensity of pressure on this side followed by further tilting.

Various equations have been established for calculating the ultimate bearing capacity of shallow foundations. The most comprehensive one, which takes into account the shape and depth of the foundation, and the inclination of the loading, the base of the foundation and the ground surfce has been derived by Brinch Hansen,[2.1] whose equation is

$$q_f = \tfrac{1}{2}\gamma B N_\gamma s_\gamma d_\gamma i_\gamma b_\gamma g_\gamma + p_o N_q s_q d_q i_q b_q g_q + c N_c s_c d_c i_c b_c g_c \qquad (2.4)$$

where, $\gamma$ = density of soil below foundation level

$B$ = width of foundation

$c$ = undrained cohesion of soil

$p_o$ = effective pressure of overburden soil at foundation level

$N_\gamma$, $N_q$ and $N_c$ are bearing capacity factors

$s_\gamma$, $s_q$ and $s_c$ are shape factors

$d_\gamma$, $d_q$ and $d_c$ are depth factors

$i_\gamma$, $i_q$ and $i_c$ are load inclination factors

$b_\gamma$, $b_q$ and $b_c$ are base inclination factors

$g_\gamma$, $g_q$ and $g_c$ are groundsurface inclination factors.

Values of the above factors can be obtained from Brinch Hansen's paper, but for most normal foundation work where the depth of the foundation is not greater than its width, Terzaghi's equations[2.2] for general shear failure of shallow foundations can be used as follows—

(i) Strip foundation:
Ultimate bearing capacity

$$= q_f = cN_c + p_o(N_q - 1) + \gamma\frac{B}{2}N_\gamma + p \qquad . \qquad . \quad (2.5)$$

or   Net ultimate bearing capacity

$$= q_{nf} = cN_c + p_o(N_q - 1) + \gamma\frac{B}{2}N_\gamma \qquad . \qquad . \quad (2.5a)$$

(ii) Square or circular foundation:
Ultimate bearing capacity

$$= q_f = 1\cdot3cN_c + p_o(N_q - 1) + 0\cdot4\gamma BN_\gamma + p \qquad . \quad (2.6)$$

or   Net ultimate bearing capacity

$$= q_{nf} = 1\cdot3cN_c + p_o(N_q - 1) + 0\cdot4\gamma BN_\gamma \qquad (2.6a)$$

The terms in equations 2.5 to 2.6a are as defined for the Brinch Hansen general equation above.

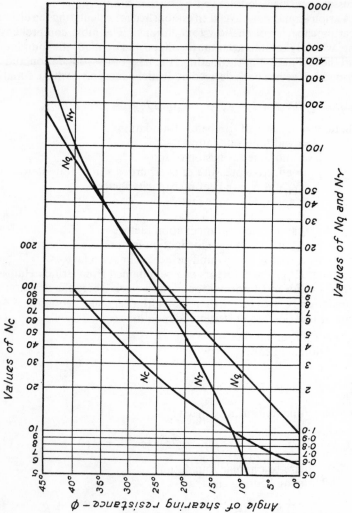

FIG. 2.9. TERZAGHI'S BEARING CAPACITY FACTORS FOR SHALLOW FOUNDATIONS ($D$ not greater than $B$).

$N_c$, $N_q$, and $N_\gamma$ are constants which depend on the angle of shearing resistance of the soil (values given by Terzaghi and Peck are shown in Fig. 2.9). If the water table rises above foundation level the submerged density is taken for the soil below the water table to determine the value of $p_o$ and $\gamma$.

In the case of deep foundations (including basements, shafts, and piles), Terzaghi introduced additional factors to take account of the friction along the sides of the foundation and the shearing stress along the outer boundary of the soil adjacent to the foundation. Thus in Fig. 2.10 his general formula for a circular *deep* foundation of radius $r$ is—

$$Q_d = Q_{pr} + 2\pi r f_s D. \qquad . \qquad . \qquad . \quad (2.7)$$

where $Q_{pr}$ = base resistance calculated from equation 2.6

$f_s$ = skin friction between foundation and soil

$D$ = depth of foundation.

The values of $f_s$ depend on the material of the foundation and the characteristics of the soil. Information on values used in practice are given on pages 313, 375, and 381.

Meyerhof[2.3] has shown that Terzaghi's general equations are conservative, since in the case of shallow foundations he ignores the shearing resistance of the soil along the failure path above the level of the base of the foundation. In the case of deep foundations Terzaghi's method suffers from the disadvantage that when the failure surface does not reach ground level the height over which the shearing resistance of the soil is mobilized becomes very uncertain. Meyerhof[2.3] analysed the conditions of failure along a path shown in Fig. 2.8 (*b*). His general equation is—

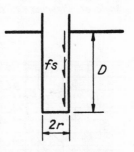

FIG. 2.10. DEEP FOUNDATION ($D/B > 5$)

Net ultimate bearing capacity

$$= q_{nf} = cN_c + p_o(N_q - 1) + \gamma\frac{B}{2}N_\gamma \quad . \qquad . \quad (2.8)$$

This is exactly the same form as Terzaghi's equations 2.5 and 2.6 but, $N_c$, $N_q$, and $N_\gamma$ instead of depending solely on the angle of shearing resistance ($\phi$), in Meyerhof's analysis, also depend on the depth and shape of the foundation and the roughness of its base. Meyerhof's general equation for deep foundations is also similar to

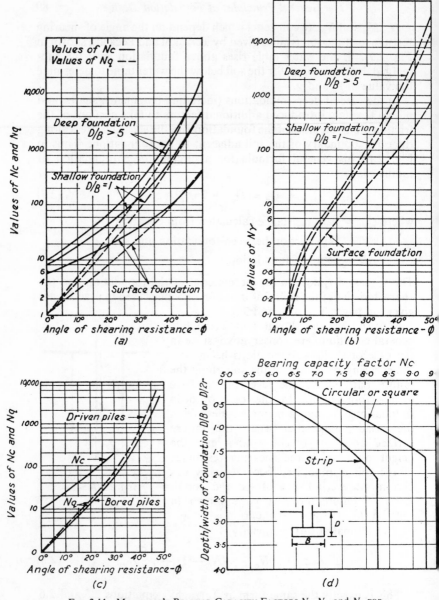

FIG. 2.11. MEYERHOF'S BEARING CAPACITY FACTORS $N_c$, $N_q$, and $N_\gamma$ FOR STRIP AND CIRCULAR FOUNDATIONS

(a) Values of $N_c$ and $N_q$ for strip foundations (rough base and level ground surface).
(b) Values of $N_\gamma$ for strip foundation (rough base and level ground surface).
(c) Values of $N_c$ and $N_q$ for deep circular foundations.
(d) Bearing-capacity factor $N_c$ for strip and circular foundations in clays.

Terzaghi's equation 2.7 but the base resistance is calculated from Meyerhof's values of $N_c$, $N_q$, and $N_\gamma$. These are shown in simplified form in Fig. 2.11.

It will be noted that the factors given in Fig. 2.11 (*a*) and (*b*) are

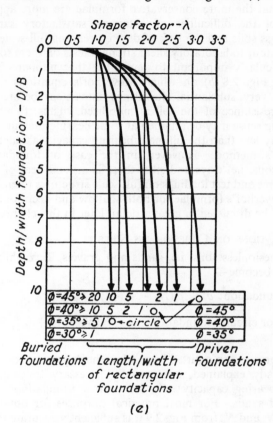

FIG. 2.11 (*continued*)
(*e*) Values of shape factor $\lambda$ for foundations in sand.

for strip foundations only. In the case of rectangular or circular foundations, Meyerhof recommends that the appropriate values of $N_c$, $N_q$, and $N_\gamma$ should be multiplied by an empirical shape factor $\lambda$. Values of $\lambda$ for various values of the depth/width ratio and $\phi$ are shown in Fig. 2.11 (*e*). There is a difference between the values for buried and driven foundations. Meyerhof has calculated values of $N_c$ and $N_q$ for deep circular foundations as shown in Fig. 2.11 (*c*).

Present-day practice in applying soil mechanics methods for

calculating ultimate bearing capacity is to adopt the more conservative equations of Terzaghi, 2.5, 2.6, and 2.7, for foundations on gravels, sands, and c-$\phi$ soils, i.e. gravels and sands having some silt and clay binder giving them cohesive properties. The author believes that the more conservative formulae are more appropriate because of the difficulties of obtaining satisfactory samples of cohesionless soils and the lack of data correlating full-scale foundation behaviour to laboratory shear strength tests on these soils. Also it is particularly important to remember that ultimate failure as shown in Fig. 2.8 (*b*) on which Meyerhof's equations are based implies a very substantial downward movement before the full shearing resistance of the soil is mobilized. Thus, failure in the engineering sense may be attained at some bearing pressure which is appreciably less than the ultimate bearing capacity as calculated by Meyerhof's method. However, in the case of foundations on cohesive soils, i.e. clays and silts, there is a good deal of evidence from failures and test loadings on full-scale structures to enable us to accept Meyerhof's formulae for both shallow and deep foundations. These will be discussed in greater detail later in this chapter.

## 2. FOUNDATIONS ON COHESIONLESS SOILS

For cohesionless soils, i.e. sands and gravels, Terzaghi's general equations become—

Strip foundation: $q_f = p_o(N_q - 1) + \gamma\dfrac{B}{2}N_\gamma + p$ . . (2.9)

Square or circular foundation: $q_f = p_o(N_q - 1) + 0 \cdot 4\gamma B N_\gamma + p$
$$(2.10)$$

The $cN_c$ term is also omitted from Meyerhof's general equation 2.8.

As already explained, it is usually necessary to calculate the ultimate bearing capacity only for narrow foundations on loose submerged sands. For most practical purposes for obtaining the values of $N_q$ and $N_\gamma$ from Fig. 2.9 it is sufficiently accurate to assume a value for the angle of shearing resistance ($\phi$) on the basis of the relative density of the sand as given by empirical in-situ penetration tests. Suitable tests are the standard penetration test (p. 27) or the static or dynamic cone penetration tests (p. 30). Terzaghi and Peck[2.4] give the following values of $\phi$ for *dry* sands, gravels and silts—

| | Round grains uniform | Angular grains well graded | Silty sands | Sandy gravels | Inorganic silts |
|---|---|---|---|---|---|
| Loose . | 27·5° | 33° | 27–33° | 35° | 27–30° |
| Dense . | 34° | 45° | 30–34° | 50° | 30–35° |

Loose sands correspond in the standard penetration test to $N$-values of 0 to 10 blows per 0·3 m. Dense sands correspond to $N$-values of 30 or more. Values of $\phi$ for medium-dense sands ($N = 10$ to 30) can be interpolated between the values in the above table. Terzaghi and Peck state that the $\phi$ values for *saturated* sands are likely to be one or two degrees below the values given in the table, except in the case of very silty sands where $\phi$ may be considerably lower for rapid loading conditions,* when $\phi$ must be determined from shear strength tests in the laboratory or from field loading tests.

The ultimate bearing capacity of deep foundations on cohesionless soils may be calculated from equation 2.7.

### 3. FOUNDATIONS IN COHESIVE SOILS

Most clay soils are saturated and behave as if they are purely cohesive (angle of shearing resistance equal to zero), provided that no water is expelled from the soil as the load is applied. This is true for most normal cases of structural loading, where the load comes on to the foundations relatively quickly. Only in the case of very slow rates of loading, or with very silty soils, can the effect of decrease in water content, and hence increase in shear strength, be taken into account. Gain in shear strength with very slow rates of loading is allowed for when estimating the safe bearing pressures for high earth dams which are likely to take several years to construct. The decrease in water content of the soil is, of course, accompanied by settlement. In the case of an earth dam, such settlement would not be detrimental to the stability of the embankment. However, this procedure cannot be applied to structures which are sensitive to appreciable settlement. It can be used for flexible structures such as steel storage tanks constructed on silty soils. The tanks can be filled in small increments over long periods. The resulting settlement might dish or warp the steel plate floors without causing fracture and loss of the contents.

On the assumption that the angle of shearing resistance of the soil is equal to zero, the formulae for the bearing capacities of strip and pad foundations are as follows—

$$\text{Ultimate bearing capacity} \quad = q_f = cN_c + p \quad . \quad (2.11)$$
$$\text{Net ultimate bearing capacity} = q_{nf} = cN_c . \quad . \quad (2.12)$$

where $\quad c$ = undrained cohesion

$\quad N_c$ = bearing capacity factor

$\quad p$ = total overburden pressure at foundation level.

* *See also* p. 99.

The cohesion (*c*) is determined from the results of laboratory tests on soil samples from below foundation level within the zone which is stressed significantly by the foundation loading. Owing to the appreciable variations in cohesion which usually occur in natural soil deposits, the selection of a representative value of *c* for substitution in the above equations is a matter requiring some experience

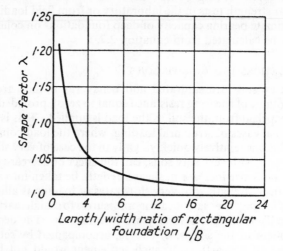

FIG. 2.12. SHAPE FACTOR FOR RECTANGULAR FOUNDATIONS
(MEYERHOF AND SKEMPTON)

and judgment. This is discussed further in the case of spread foundations on page 207, and in the case of piles on page 391.

The value of the bearing capacity factor, $N_c$, depends on the ratio of the depth to width of the foundation. Meyerhof's values of $N_c$ for strip and circular foundations for various values of $D/B$ are shown in Fig. 2.11 (*c*). Values of $N_c$ for a square foundation may be taken as the same as those for a circular foundation. In the case of rectangular areas, values intermediate between those for a strip and for a circle are taken. They are obtained by multiplying the factor ($N_c$) for a strip foundation by a shape factor $\lambda$. Values of $\lambda$ for any ratio of $L/B$ are shown in Fig. 2.12.

The ultimate bearing capacity of deep foundations on cohesive soils may be calculated from equation 2.7. Equation 2.11 is used for calculating $Q_{pr}$; the values of $f_s$ are obtained from page 313 for pier and caisson foundations, and page 387 for piled foundations.

**Estimation of Allowable Bearing Pressures by Empirical Methods**

There are two approaches to the estimation of allowable bearing pressures by empirical methods. The first is to obtain the presumed bearing values from local or national building regulations or from published tables of the type shown in Table 2.1. The second approach is to use an empirical design method based on some form of test performed in situ on the soil or rock.

The presumed bearing values stated in building regulations are usually based on long experience of the behaviour of foundations on soils or rocks in the localities covered by the regulations. They are usually conservative, but not always so. Where, for example, low bearing values are given for rocks, these may well be due to local knowledge of such factors as deep weathering or intensive fissuring of the formation. The engineer is often tempted to adopt a higher bearing value after inspecting what appears to be sound hard rock in trial pits. However, when the foundation trenches are subsequently excavated, the surface of the sound rock may be found to be highly irregular, thus necessitating deep excavation in pockets in a narrow trench to reach sound rock. This delays the construction programme and there may also be protracted delays while discussions are held to define what is the acceptable bearing stratum compatible with the adopted bearing value. It is not unusual to find that the engineer who made the initial site investigation and recommendations has an opinion on an acceptable bearing stratum which is different from that of the engineer supervising the construction on site.

It is nearly always cheaper to construct wide foundations to a uniform and predetermined depth than to excavate narrow trenches or pits to a depth which cannot be forecast at the time of estimating the cost of the work. The values in Parts B and C of Table 2.1 are based on the compressibility of soils as determined by field and laboratory tests. The adoption of these values may result in immediate and long-term settlements totalling up to 50 mm in the case of an isolated foundation. With this order of settlement, the differential movement between adjacent foundations should not exceed the permissible limit for structural damage (*see* p. 108). If this order of settlement is excessive, a detailed settlement analysis should be made following the procedure described on pages 114 to 138.

The values shown in Table 2.1 are based on the assumptions—

(*a*) that the site and adjoining sites are reasonably level;

(*b*) that the ground and strata are reasonably level;

(*c*) that there is no layer of higher compressibility below the foundation stratum;

(*d*) that the site is protected from deterioration.

## Table 2.1

### PRESUMED BEARING VALUES FOR HORIZONTAL FOUNDATIONS UNDER VERTICAL STATIC LOADING SETTLEMENT OF INDIVIDUAL FOUNDATION NOT TO EXCEED 50 mm

**A. Foundations not exceeding 3 m wide on Surface of Rock.**

| Type of rock | Presumed bearing value $kN/m^2$ or $kgf/cm^2 \times 100$ |
|---|---|
| Massive hard igneous and metamorphic rocks, massive hard limestones, hard strongly cemented sandstones | Exceeds safe working stress on concrete or masonry sub-structure |
| Schists or slates free from crumbly or weathered material | 4000 |
| Interbedded hard mudstones, hard shales and sandstones of Coal Measures (free from coal or fireclay), friable weakly cemented sandstones (free from uncemented sand layers) | 3000 |
| Hard unweathered Keuper Marl, hard unweathered Chalk (free from wide fissures) | 2000 |
| Clayey shales and soft mudstones | 1000 |

**B. Foundations in Non-cohesive Soils at a Minimum Depth of 0·75 m below ground Level.**

| Description of soil | $N$-value in standard penetration test | Presumed bearing value ($kN/m^2$ or $kgf/cm^2 \times 100$) for foundation of width | | | Remarks |
|---|---|---|---|---|---|
| | | 1 m | 2 m | 4 m | |
| Very dense sands and gravels | >50 | 600 | 500 | 400 | (1) Corrections to $N$-values to be applied to observed $N$-value before using this table (see p. 99). (2) The water table is assumed not to be close to base of foundation. If the water table is at the base of the foundation or within a depth equal to the width of the foundation then these presumed bearing values should be halved. |
| Dense sands and gravels | 30 to 50 | 350 to 600 | 300 to 500 | 250 to 400 | |
| Medium-dense sands and gravels | 10 to 30 | 150 to 350 | 100 to 300 | 100 to 250 | |
| Loose sands and gravels | 5 to 10 | 50 to 150 | 50 to 100 | 50 to 100 | |

C. Foundations in Cohesive Soils at a Minimum Depth of 1 m below Ground Level.

| Description | Cohesive strength (kN/m² or kgf/cm² × 100) | Presumed bearing value (kN/m² or kgf/cm² × 100) for foundation of width | | |
|---|---|---|---|---|
| | | 1 m | 2 m | 4 m |
| Hard boulder clays, hard fissured clays (e.g. deeper London and Gault clays) hard weathered shales and weathered mud-stones | >300 | 800 | 600 | 400 |
| Very stiff boulder clay, very stiff "blue" London Clay, very stiff weathered Keuper Marl | 150 to 300 | 400 to 800 | 300 to 500 | 150 to 250 |
| Stiff fissured clays (e.g. stiff "blue" and brown London clay), stiff weathered boulder clay, stiff weathered Keuper Marl | 75 to 150 | 200 to 400 | 150 to 250 | 75 to 125 |
| Firm normally consolidated clays (at depth), fluvioglacial and lake clays, upper weathered"brown" London clay | 40 to 75 | 100 to 200 | 75 to 100 | 50 to 75 |
| Soft normally consolidated alluvial clays (e.g. marine, river and estuarine clays) | 20 to 40 | 50 to 100 | 25 to 50 | Negligible |

## DETERMINATION OF THE ALLOWABLE BEARING PRESSURES IN COHESIONLESS SOILS FROM IN-SITU TESTS

Only in the case of narrow foundations on waterlogged sands and gravels is the allowable bearing pressure determined from the ultimate bearing capacity at failure. In other cases the allowable bearing pressure is governed by the permissible settlement of the structure due to consolidation of the soils under the applied loading. The effects of settlement on the structure will be discussed later in this chapter. The four types of in-situ tests which may be used for estimating bearing pressures are—

(*a*) Standard Penetration Test
(*b*) Dynamic Cone Penetration Test

(c) Static Cone Penetration Test

(d) Plate Loading Test.

If the standard penetration test has been carried out in the borings the values of $N$ can be related to allowable bearing pressures for various footings widths as shown in Fig. 2.13. This relationship is

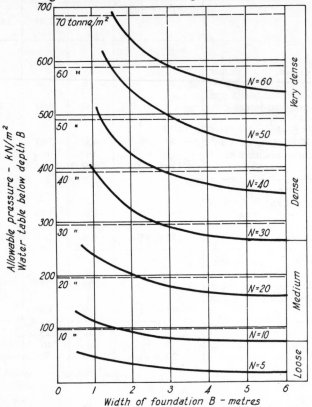

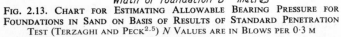

FIG. 2.13. CHART FOR ESTIMATING ALLOWABLE BEARING PRESSURE FOR FOUNDATIONS IN SAND ON BASIS OF RESULTS OF STANDARD PENETRATION TEST (TERZAGHI AND PECK[2.5]) $N$ VALUES ARE IN BLOWS PER 0·3 M

empirical and has been established by Terzaghi and Peck[2.5] from field observations. In preparing the curves shown in Fig. 2.13 Terzaghi and Peck defined the allowable bearing pressure as that causing 25 mm of settlement under the given foundation width. It should also be noted that the allowable bearing pressures are based on the assumption that the water table is at a depth of at least $B$ below foundation level. If the water table is at or close to foundation level and the depth of the foundation is small in relation to its width, the settlements will be doubled, or if the same criterion of a settlement not exceeding 25 mm is to be followed, then the allowable bearing pressures should be halved. Because of the rigidity of raft or deep pier foundations, the total and differential settlements will be less than those of individual spread or strip foundations; therefore twice the allowable bearing pressures given in Fig. 2.13 can be used for large rafts or deep piers on dry sands, and the actual values in Fig. 2.13 for submerged sands.

Terzaghi and Peck state that precautions should be taken to avoid the lateral yield of sand from beneath the edges of rafts at depths of less than 2·5 to 3 m below ground level.

Corrections should be made to the standard penetration test values as measured in the boreholes before using these values in Fig. 2.13. Suitable corrections should be made for the effect of overburden pressure. Several investigators, notably Gibbs and Holtz,[2.6] have found that the standard penetration test seriously underestimates the relative densities of cohesionless soils at shallow depths. To allow for this a correction factor should be applied to the measured values. The correction factors shown in Fig. 2.14 are based on the work of Gibbs and Holtz. As an example of their application, take the case of a 2·5 m wide foundation bearing on dry sand at a depth of 1·2 m below ground level. The average $N$-value measured in boreholes over a depth of 2·5 m (i.e. the foundation width) below foundation level was 17. The average overburden pressure over this depth is 32·7 kN/m$^2$. Fig. 2.14 gives a correction factor of 2·7. Therefore the $N$-value to be used in Fig. 2.13 is 2·7 × 17 = 46. Some engineers do not accept that it is necessary to halve the bearing pressures if the water table is close to foundation level. They consider that the test results themselves automatically allow for reduction in bearing pressure. Certainly some $N$-values when plotted with depth do show a reduction of about 15 per cent when they pass from a dry or damp sand to a saturated sand. However, there is no conclusive evidence to suggest that it is safe to reject the established procedure of halving the bearing pressure for foundations at or below the water table.

A further correction should be applied in the case of very fine or silty sands when the low permeability of these soils may affect the penetration resistance of the split-spoon sampler, giving lower values than would be obtained with a more permeable soil of the same density. This is particularly liable to occur when the voids ratio is above a critical value which is stated by Terzaghi to occur when the $N$-value of very fine or silty sands is about 15. For voids ratio below the critical value, i.e. for values of $N$ higher than 15, the reverse is the case. Terzaghi and Peck state a rule that when the number of blows ($N$) for a fine or silty sand is greater than 15 it should be assumed that the density of the soil is equal to that of a sand having an $N$-value of $15 + \frac{1}{2}(N - 15)$.

Rodin et al.[1.13] state that if the above corrections for overburden pressure and for very fine or silty sands are applied, and if the appropriate precautions are taken to obtain reliable data in the field (*see* p. 30), the standard penetration test method gives realistic values of allowable bearing pressure which are in accordance with values indicated by plate loading tests and those known by experience to be safe.

*Standard Penetration Tests*, as described on p. 27, are generally made at 0·75 m intervals in the boreholes. An approximate depth and width ($B$) of the foundation is assumed, and the average value of $N$ is taken over a depth below foundation level equal to $B$. If several boreholes show different average values of $N$, the lowest average should be taken to assess the value of $\phi$ or to determine allowable bearing pressures from aspects of settlement. Terzaghi and Peck do not themselves regard the test and its calibration with compressibility as anything but rough-and-ready.

*The Continuous Dynamic Cone Penetration Test* (p. 30) procedure is similar to that used for the standard penetration test. Fig. 2.13 can be used directly if the dynamic test gives the same $N$-values as the standard penetration test. If they give different $N$-values the two tests will have to be calibrated and a conversion table drawn up to convert the dynamic cone values to standard penetration test $N$-values. Corrections to the dynamic cone values to allow for overburden pressure or for fine or silty sands should be made in the same way as for the standard penetration tests.

*The Static Cone Penetration Test* (p. 31) in which the cone is thrust into the soil without the necessity of boring provides a much more accurate and detailed record of the variation in the soil. De Beer[2.7] has published relationships between the cone resistance ($C_{kd}$) and the angle of shearing resistance and apparent angle of shearing resistance, respectively, of cohesionless soils. However, since a rough and ready check on ultimate bearing capacity is, in most cases, all that is required, and even that calculation is only needed for narrow foundations on submerged sands, it would seem unnecessary to use De Beer's relationship. It may happen, however, that only static cone tests have been made. In such cases Meyerhof[2.8] has suggested simplified formulae for determining allowable bearing pressures to ensure that a settlement of 25 mm is not exceeded. His formulae are based on Terzaghi and Peck's curves and are applicable to pad or strip foundations of fairly small dimensions on *dry* sands as follows.

For square or strip foundations equal to or less than 1·2 m wide—
Allowable bearing pressure $= q_a = 3\cdot6\ C_{kd}\ \text{kN/m}^2$

$$\left(\text{or approximately } \frac{C_{kd}}{30}\ \text{kg/cm}^2\right) \qquad . \qquad . \ (2.13)$$

where $C_{kd}=$ cone resistance in kg/cm$^2$
For square or strip foundations greater than 1·2 m wide—

Allowable bearing pressure $= q_a = 2\cdot1\ C_{kd} \left(1 + \dfrac{1}{B}\right)^2\ \text{kN/m}^2$

$$\text{or approximately } \frac{C_{kd}}{50} \left(1 + \frac{1}{B}\right)^2\ \text{kg/cm}^2 \qquad . \ (2.14)$$

An approximate formula to cover all foundations irrespective of width is: allowable bearing pressure $= q_a = 2.7\ C_{kd}\ \text{kN/m}^2$

$$\left(\text{or approximately } \frac{C_{kd}}{40}\ \text{kg/cm}^2\right) \qquad . \qquad . \ (2.15)$$

It should be noted that these formulae are based on the approximate rule that the $N$-value is one quarter of the static cone resistance (in kg/cm$^2$). As stated on page 33, however, this relationship may vary with the type of soil.

Values of $q_a$ calculated from formulae 2.13, 2.14, and 2.15 above should be *halved* if the sand within the stressed zone is submerged. Meyerhof suggests that the allowable bearing pressures given by his formulae may be *doubled* for raft or pier foundations, in a similar way to Terzaghi and Peck for allowable bearing pressures calculated from the standard penetration test $N$-values (*see* p. 98).

The procedure recommended by the author when static cone test results are available is to use Meyerhof's formulae 2.13, 2.14, and 2.15 to get an approximate guide to the allowable bearing pressure and hence the likely dimensions of the foundations for given loading conditions, and then to use the cone resistance values in De Beer and Martens' or Schmertmann's method (pp. 122 to 124) to calculate the *settlements* for the assumed allowable bearing pressure. If the calculated settlements are excessive then the allowable bearing pressures should be reduced, although it should be remembered that De Beer and Martens recognize that their method gives somewhat conservative values.

*Plate Loading Tests* can be used to determine the ultimate bearing capacity of cohesionless soils for plates of various dimensions. The ultimate bearing capacity obtained in this way can be used directly, if the plate size is roughly similar to the width of the proposed foundation. It is only necessary to divide the ultimate bearing capacity by an arbitrary safety factor to obtain the allowable bearing pressure; or, if settlement is the criterion, to adopt an allowable bearing pressure for which the permissible settlement will not be exceeded, using the load-settlement relationship obtained from the loading test. Methods of extrapolating from small plate loading tests to wide foundations are discussed later (see p. 118). In these cases, the permissible settlement will govern allowable bearing pressures.

Plate loading tests are best suited to investigating fill materials or soils containing large gravel or boulders in which in-situ penetration tests cannot be made.

The foregoing description of methods of calculating allowable bearing pressures in sandy soils are not applicable to vibratory loading. As explained on page 167 heavy consolidation settlement and loss of bearing capacity may occur if the frequency of the vibrating machinery is in a state of resonance with the foundations and underlying soil. Low values of bearing pressure should be used, and the foundations should be designed to absorb the vibrations (see pp. 193–196).

### Allowable Bearing Pressures for $c$-$\phi$ Soils

Soils intermediate between cohesive and cohesionless are known as $c$-$\phi$ soils. They include sandy clays and sandy silts, gravelly clays, sandy and gravelly silts, and silty sands. It is possible to obtain satisfactory undisturbed samples of these materials. Consequently their cohesion and angle of shearing resistance can be obtained by triaxial compression tests. These values can be substituted in Terzaghi's general equations (2.5, 2.6, and 2.7) to obtain the ultimate bearing capacity. The latter can be divided by an arbitrary safety factor to determine the maximum safe bearing capacity of the soil, which may be adopted as the allowable bearing pressure provided that consolidation settlements will not be excessive.

### Bearing Pressures for Large Raft Foundations in Clays

Allowable bearing pressures for large raft foundations on uniform soils are likely to be assessed from considerations of the permissible total and differential settlements rather than calculated by dividing the calculated ultimate bearing capacity by a nominal safety factor. However, there may be a considerable variation in shear strength and compressibility of natural soil deposits beneath a large raft foundation, particularly in alluvial deposits where a stiff crust of variable thickness may be overlying soft compressible layers of varying extent both horizontally and vertically. In such conditions there is the possibility of failure of a foundation due to overstressing and squeezing out of a wedge-shaped layer of soft soil from one side of the loaded area (p. 211).

Where the shear strength and compressibility of the soil varies over the foundation area, the shear strength/depth relationship and

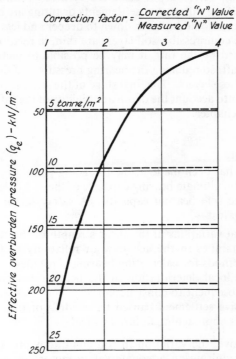

$$\text{Correction factor} = \frac{\text{Corrected "N" Value}}{\text{Measured "N" Value}}$$

FIG. 2.14. CORRECTION FACTORS FOR STANDARD PENETRATION TEST (AFTER GIBBS AND HOLTZ[2·6])

the coefficient of volume compressibility ($m_v$)/depth relationship should be plotted at each borehole position and the information displayed on a soil profile along one or more cross-sections. Inspection of the plotted data will indicate whether or not the potential zones of overstressed soils are sufficiently large in extent to involve a risk of failure by tilting. If this is the case then the foundation should be taken below such zones to deeper and stiffer soils. If, however, the weaker soils are fairly uniformly distributed over the area, or if they are confined to a relatively small zone beneath the centre of the area, then the allowable bearing pressure can be calculated from considerations of settlement. A preliminary value for the allowable bearing pressure should be adopted based on the ultimate bearing capacity of the weaker soil layers divided by a nominal safety factor, say 3. The immediate and consolidation settlements should be calculated corresponding to the maximum, minimum and average compressibility of the soil layers as shown by the various plottings of $m_v$ versus depth using the methods described on pages 114 to 138. If the differential settlements or tilting are excessive then the foundation should be taken down to deeper and less compressible soil, or if the compressible soil layers are thin, in relation to the zone of soil stressed by the raft, it may be possible to increase the plan area of the raft, so reducing the bearing pressure and hence the compression of these layers. The final stage of the settlement calculations should take into account the depth and rigidity of the raft as described later in this chapter.

### Safety Factors

Reference has been made in the foregoing pages to the procedure of dividing the ultimate bearing capacity of the soil by a safety factor to obtain the safe bearing capacity. A safety factor is used as a safeguard against—

(a) Natural variations in the shear strength of the soil.

(b) Uncertainties in the accuracy or reliability of theoretical or empirical methods for calculating bearing capacities.

(c) Minor local deterioration in the bearing capacity of the soil during or subsequent to construction.

(d) Excessive settlement caused by yielding of the soil when the foundation is approaching failure in shear.

Of the above, the variation in soil conditions provides the main reason for requiring an adequate safety factor. A high degree of judgment is required of the foundation engineer in selecting design values of shear strength of the soil on sites where there is a wide scatter of tests results. General rules for guidance cannot be laid down, but the reader is referred to examples of foundation design given in later chapters of this book. A safety factor of 2·5 to 3 is generally used to cover the variations or uncertainties listed above. A value of 2 would only be adopted on sites where very uniform soil conditions were found. Low safety factors of 1·5 to 2 are also used in the design of temporary works such as cribs supporting construction plant, or for calculations of the allowable bearing pressure for earthworks where the effects of settlement are not detrimental to temporary works or adjoining property.

It should be noted that safety factors used in calculations to determine safe bearing pressures are not normally intended to cover accidental increases in structural loading. These contingencies should be considered when calculating the superimposed loading on the foundations. On calculating stability against shear failure it is usual to allow for the maximum intensity of loading from all causes including wind loading except that when the bearing pressure due to wind is less than 25 per cent of that due to dead and live loads it is neglected.

If the bearing pressure due to wind is more than 25 per cent the foundations can be proportioned so that the bearing pressures from the combined dead, live, and wind loading do not exceed the allowable bearing pressure by more than 25 per cent. It is also permissible to allow for the percentage reduction of live loading in multi-storey buildings. The *British Standard Code of Practice* (CP 3), Chapter V, Part I, clause 5, states—

"5.1  Except as provided for in 5.2 and 5.3, the reductions in assumed total imposed floor loads given in Table 2 may be taken in designing

TABLE 2

REDUCTION IN TOTAL DISTRIBUTED IMPOSED FLOOR LOADS

| No. of floors, including the roof, carried by member under consideration | Reductions in total distributions imposed load on all floors carried by the member under consideration |
|:---:|:---:|
| | per cent |
| 1 | 0 |
| 2 | 10 |
| 3 | 20 |
| 4 | 30 |
| 5 to 10 | 40 |
| over 10 | 50 |

columns, piers, walls, their supports and foundations. For the purposes of 5.1 to 5.3, a roof may be regarded as a floor. For factories and workshops designed for 5 kN/m² (510 kgf/m²; 104 lbf/ft²) or more, the reductions shown in Table 2 may be taken provided that the loading assumed is not less than it would have been if all floors had been designed for 5 kN/m² (510 kgf/m²; 104 lbf/ft²) with no reductions."

"5.2  Where a single span of a beam or girder supports not less than 46 m² (495 ft²) of floor at one general level, the imposed load may in the design of the beam or girder be reduced by 5 per cent for each 46 m² (495 ft²) supported, subject to a maximum reduction of

25 per cent. This reduction, or that given in Table 2, whichever is greater, may be taken into account in the design of columns or other types of member supporting such a beam.

"5.3 No reduction shall be made for any plant or machinery which is specifically allowed for or for buildings for storage purposes, warehouse, garages and those office areas which are used for storage and filing purposes."

## SETTLEMENT OF FOUNDATIONS

### Total and Differential Settlements

Settlement due to consolidation of the foundation soil is usually the most important consideration in assessing *allowable* bearing pressures. Even though sinking of foundations as a result of shear failure of the soil has been safeguarded against by an arbitrary safety factor on the calculated ultimate bearing capacity, it is still necessary to investigate the likelihood of consolidation settlements before the allowable bearing pressures can be fixed. In the following pages consideration will be given to the causes of consolidation settlement, the effects on the structure of total and differential settlements, methods of estimating settlement, and the design of foundations to eliminate settlement or to minimize its effects.

The settlement of a structural foundation consists of two parts. The *"immediate"* settlement $(\rho_i)$ takes place during application of the loading as a result of elastic deformation of the soil without change in water content. *"Consolidation"* settlement $(\rho_c)$ takes place as a result of volume reduction of the soil caused by extrusion of some of the porewater from the soil. The *"final"* settlement $(\rho_f)$ is the sum of $\rho_i$ and $\rho_c$. If deep excavation is required to reach foundation level, swelling of the soil will take place as a result of removal of the pressure of the overburden. The magnitude of the swelling depends on the depth of overburden removed and the time the foundations remain unloaded. A diagram illustrating the various stages of swelling and settlement is shown in Fig. 2.15.

In the case of foundations on medium-dense to dense sands and gravels, the "immediate" and "consolidation" settlements are of a relatively small order and take place almost simultaneously, and a high proportion of the total settlement is almost completed by the time the full loading comes on the foundations. Similarly, a high proportion of the settlement of foundations on loose sands takes place as the load is applied; whereas settlements on compressible clays are partly immediate and partly long-term movements. The latter is likely to account for the greater proportion of the movement and may take place over a very long period of years.

Settlement of foundations is not necessarily confined to very large and heavy structures. In soft and compressible silts and clays, appreciable settlement can occur under light loadings. Settlement and cracking occurred in two-storey houses founded on a soft silty clay in Scotland. The houses were of precast concrete block construction and the foundation loading was probably not more than about 3·2 kN/m run of wall. In less than three years from the time of completion, differential settlement and cracking of the blocks of

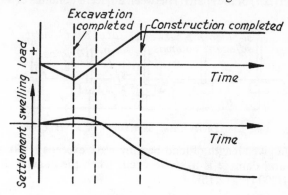

FIG. 2.15. LOAD–SETTLEMENT-TIME RELATIONSHIP FOR A STRUCTURE

houses were so severe that a number of the houses had to be evacuated. One block showed a relative movement of 100 mm along the wall.

The differential, or relative, settlement between one part of a structure and another is of greater significance to the stability of the superstructure than the magnitude of the total settlement. The latter is only significant in relation to neighbouring works. For example, a flood wall to a river might be constructed to a crest level at a prescribed height above maximum flood level. Excessive settlement of the wall over a long period of years might result in overtopping of the wall at flood periods.

If the whole of the foundation area of a structure settles to the same extent, there is no detrimental effect on the superstructure. If, however, there is relative movement between various parts of the foundation, stresses are set up in the structure. Serious cracking, and even collapse of the structure, may occur if the differential movements are excessive.

Skempton and Macdonald[2.9] in a comprehensive study of the settlement of structures have divided damage resulting from settlement into three categories, namely—

1. Structural damage which involves only the frame, i.e. stanchions and beams.

2. "Architectural" damage involving only the panel walls, floors, or finishes.

3. Combined structural and architectural damage.

A study of recorded settlements of structures which have suffered damage to a greater or lesser degree led these authors to the conclusion that structural damage is likely to take place when the angular distortion $(\Delta/l)$ of the span $(l)$ between adjacent columns of a structure

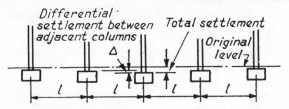

FIG. 2.16. DIFFERENTIAL SETTLEMENT OF A STRUCTURE

or along a given length of load-bearing walls exceeds 1/150, and that architectural damage is likely to occur when the angular distortion exceeds 1/300 (Fig. 2.16).

DIFFERENTIAL SETTLEMENT OF STRUCTURES

The studies of Skempton and Macdonald were elaborated by Bjerrum[2.10] who produced the data shown in Table 2.2, which relates angular distortions to danger limits for various types of structure. The limit of 1/300 for architectural damage corresponds to a relative settlement of 20 mm between adjacent columns at 6 m centres.

Table 2.2

DANGER LIMITS FOR DISTORTION OF STRUCTURES

| Angular distortion | Behaviour of structure |
|---|---|
| 1/750 | Limit where difficulties with machinery sensitive to settlements are to be feared |
| 1/600 | Limit of danger for frames with diagonals |
| 1/500 | Safe limit for buildings where cracking is not permissible |
| 1/300 | Limit where first cracking in panel walls is to be expected |
| 1/300 | Limit where difficulties with overhead cranes are to be expected |
| 1/250 | Limit where tilting of high, rigid buildings might become visible |
| 1/150 | Considerable cracking in panel walls and brick walls |
| 1/150 | Safe limit for flexible brick walls $(h/L < \frac{1}{4})$ |
| 1/150 | Limit where general structural damage of buildings is to be feared |

It is unrealistic to specify that not the slightest cracking shall occur in a structure due to differential settlement. In most buildings where plaster finishes are used, cracking can be seen in internal walls and ceilings resulting from thermal and moisture movements in the structures. The most advanced constructional techniques cannot yet prevent this form of cracking, and therefore a certain amount of cracking due to settlement should be tolerated. However, it is necessary to limit differential settlement to a very small amount in monumental-type buildings with expensive external or internal finishes where cracking would be unsightly.

In some types of building angular distortions exceeding the limits for architectural damage can be tolerated, for example in steel-framed garage or warehouse buildings with corrugated metal cladding, or in timber structures. However, it is inadvisable to allow angular distortions to exceed the limit of 1/150 for structural damage unless special measures can be taken to prevent excessive stresses in the structure, for example by articulation of joints or by levelling devices. Such measures are only justifiable in cases where the cause of settlement is outside the control of the engineer, for example mining or regional subsidence.

In an authoritative review of allowable total and differential settlements and their effects on structures, Burland and Wroth[2.11] noted that while the allowable limit for angular distortion of 1/500 as proposed by Skempton and Macdonald and by Bjerrum is satisfactory for framed buildings both of traditional and modern construction, it is unsafe for buildings with loadbearing walls having a panel length to height ratio of less than 4. The 1955 Building Code of the USSR quoted by Polshin and Tokar[2.12] limited the angular distortion of buildings with loadbearing brick walls (panel length to height ratio less than 3) to not more than 1/3300 and 1/2500 for such buildings on sand and soft clay respectively. Even these criteria can be unsafe where load bearing walls are subjected to hogging movements for which Burland and Wroth have established limits of 1/5000 to 1/2500 for panel length to height ratios ranging from 2 to 7.

Differential settlement between parts of a structure may occur as a result of—

1. VARIATIONS IN SOIL STRATA. One part of a structure may be founded on a compressible soil and the other part on an incompressible material. Such variations are not uncommon, particularly in glacial deposits, where lenses of clay may be found in predominantly sandy material or vice versa. In areas of irregular bedrock surface, parts of a structure may be founded on shallow rock and others on soil or compressible weathered rock. Wind-laid or water-laid

deposits of sands and gravels can vary widely in density in a vertical and horizontal direction.

2. VARIATIONS IN FOUNDATION LOADING. For example, in a building consisting of a high central tower with low projecting wings, differential settlement between the tower and wings would be expected unless special methods of foundation design were introduced to prevent it. Similarly a factory building might have a light super-structure surrounding a very heavy item of machinery.

3. LARGE LOADED AREAS ON FLEXIBLE FOUNDATIONS. The settlement of large flexible raft foundations, or large loaded areas comprising the independent foundations of a number of columns,

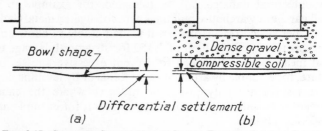

FIG. 2.17. SHAPE OF SETTLEMENT OF LARGE FLEXIBLE LOADED AREAS
(*a*) Raft on uniform compressible soil.
(*b*) Raft on dense incompressible stratum overlying compressible soil.

when constructed directly on a compressible soil, takes a characteristic bowl-shape with the maximum settlement at the centre of the area and the minimum at the corners. The maximum differential settlement is usually about one-half of the total settlement. However, in the case of a structure consisting of a large number of close-spaced equally-loaded columns, even though the maximum differential settlement between the centre and corners may be large, the relative settlement between columns may be only a fraction of the maximum. An example of the form of settlement of a large loaded area is shown in Fig. 2.17 (*a*). Where the large loaded area is founded on a relatively incompressible stratum (e.g. dense gravel) overlying compressible soil (Fig. 2.17 (*b*)), settlement of the structure will occur due to consolidation of the latter layer, but it will not take the form of the bowl-shaped depression. The effect of the dense layer, if thick enough, is to form a rigid raft which will largely eliminate differential settlement.

4. DIFFERENCES IN TIME OF CONSTRUCTION OF ADJACENT PARTS OF A STRUCTURE. This problem occurs when extensions to a structure are built many years after completion of the original structure. Long-term consolidation settlements of the latter may be virtually complete, but the new structure (if of the same foundation loading as

the original) will eventually settle an equal amount. Special provisions in the form of vertical joints are needed to prevent distortion and cracking between the old and new structures.

5. VARIATION IN SITE CONDITIONS. One part of a building area may have been occupied by a heavy structure which had been demolished; or on a sloping site it may be necessary to remove a considerable thickness of overburden to form a level site. These variations result in different stress conditions both before and after loading with consequent differential settlement or swelling.

## METHODS OF PREVENTING EXCESSIVE DIFFERENTIAL SETTLEMENT

Buildings with massive load-bearing walls or heavy structural frames are often sufficiently rigid in themselves to prevent appreciable

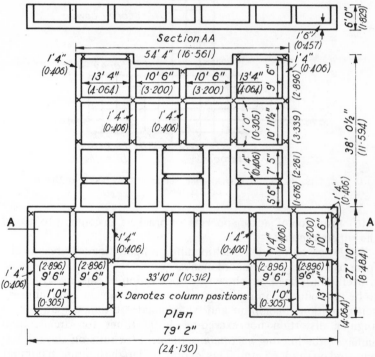

FIG. 2.18. STIFF SLAB AND BEAM RAFT FOUNDATION TO MINIMIZE DIFFERENTIAL SETTLEMENT

differential settlement from occurring. The massively-built Palace of Fine Arts in Mexico City was built in 1904 on a substantial raft foundation. Although it had settled about 2·7 m the differential settlements were only about 150 mm.

If the structures themselves have insufficient rigidity to prevent excessive differential movement with ordinary spread foundations, one or a combination of the following methods may be adopted in order to reduce the total and differential settlements to a tolerable figure—

(*a*) Provision of a rigid raft foundation either with a thick slab or with deep beams in two or three directions.

(*b*) Provision of deep basements to reduce the net bearing pressure on the soil.

(*c*) Transference of foundation loading to deeper and less compressible soil by means of basements, piers, or piles.

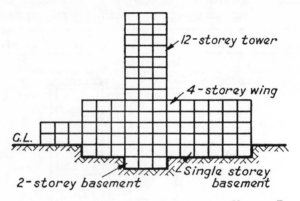

FIG. 2.19. REDUCING DIFFERENTIAL SETTLEMENT BY VARYING DEPTH OF BASEMENTS

(*d*) Provision of jacking pockets, or brackets, in columns to relevel the superstructure.

(*e*) Provision of additional loading on lightly loaded areas in the form of kentledge or embankments.

Method (*a*) has been shown by observation of existing structures to be very effective in reducing differential settlement. For uniform soil conditions Skempton and Macdonald[2.9] estimate that, for an angular distortion not exceeding 1/300 (limit for architectural damage), the limiting *maximum* settlement for rafts on clays is 100 mm, and on sands 65 mm. This is compared to the limiting maximum settlement for individual foundations of 75 mm and 50 mm for clays and sands respectively. A 1·829 m deep reinforced concrete slab and beam raft foundation (Fig. 2.18) was used for eleven-storey flats on fairly compressible London Clay in north-west London. For a fully flexible raft, the maximum and differential settlements were estimated to be 100 mm and 75 mm respectively after a long period of years.

Two years after construction the maximum settlement was 50 mm with an average of 40 mm compared to the estimated 33 mm at the same period of time. However, the differential settlement of the rigid raft was only 10 mm compared to the estimated 25 mm for the flexible raft.

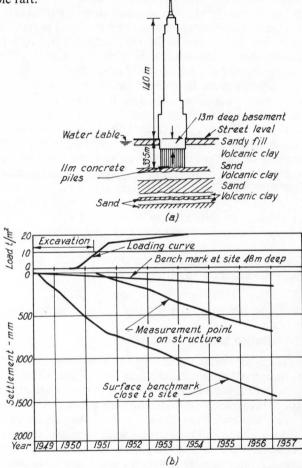

(a)

(b)

Fig. 2.20. Foundation Arrangement and Settlement Observations at Latino Americana Tower, Mexico City (Zeevaert[2.13])

As well as reducing maximum settlements due to relief of over-burden pressure in excavating for deep basements, method (b) is useful in preventing excessive differential settlement between parts of a structure having different foundation loads. Thus the deepest basements can be provided under the heaviest parts of the structure with shallower or no basements in the areas of lighter loading (Fig. 2.19).

An outstanding example of a combination of methods (b) and (c) is given by the foundations of the forty-storey Latino-Americana Building in Mexico City (Fig. 2.20 (a)).[2.13] A 13 m deep basement was constructed to reduce the net bearing pressure on the piled raft. The piles were driven to a depth of 34 m below street level to reach a 5 m thick stratum of sand followed by firm to stiff clays and sands. The settlement observations for this building (Fig. 2.20 (b)) illustrate the high compressibility of the deep volcanic clay layers in Mexico City. These deposits are settling under their own weight as shown by the surface settlement relative to the deep bench mark.

An important point to note in connexion with the excavations of deep basements in clay soils is that swelling will occur to a greater or lesser degree on release of overburden pressure. This causes additional settlement as the swelled ground reconsolidates during the application of the structural load. Measor and Williams[2.14] reported measurements of swelling at the base of 12 m deep excavations for the basements of the Shell Centre. The London Clay at the base of the excavation showed an elastic heave of about 12 mm. Assuming a Poisson's ratio of 0·5, this corresponds to an $E$-value of about 130 $MN/m^2$.

The effects of such swelling are eliminated by the adoption of piled basements as discussed on pages 293 to 297.

## ESTIMATION OF THE SETTLEMENT OF FOUNDATIONS

### Pressure Distribution beneath Foundations

The first consideration in calculating the magnitude of settlements is the distribution of pressure beneath the loaded area. This depends on the rigidity of the foundation structure and the nature of the soil. The variation of *contact pressure* beneath a smooth rigid foundation on a clay (or a soil containing thick layers of soft clay) is shown in Fig. 2.21 (a). A similar foundation on sand or gravel shows a very different contact pressure distribution as in Fig. 2.21 (b), and the distribution for intermediate soil types takes the form shown in Fig. 2.21 (c). When the bearing pressures are increased to the point of shear failure in the soil, the contact pressure is changed tending to an increase in pressure over the centre of the loaded area in each of the above cases.

A fully flexible foundation, such as the steel plate floor of an oil storage tank, assumes the characteristic bowl shape as it deforms with the consolidation of the underlying soil. The contact pressure distribution for a fully flexible foundation on a clay soil takes the form shown in Fig. 2.21 (*d*).

In the calculation of consolidation settlement we are concerned with the pressure distribution for a contact pressure which has a reasonable safety factor against shear failure of the soil. Also, it is

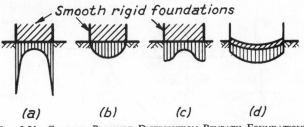

Smooth rigid foundations

*(a)*          *(b)*          *(c)*          *(d)*

FIG. 2.21. CONTACT PRESSURE DISTRIBUTION BENEATH FOUNDATIONS
    (*a*) Clay.
    (*b*) Sand and gravel.
    (*c*) Intermediate soil type.
    (*d*) Fully flexible foundation on clay.

impracticable to obtain complete rigidity in a normal foundation structure. Consequently the contact pressure distribution is intermediate between that of rigid and flexible foundations, and for all practicable purposes it is regarded as satisfactory to assume a *uniform pressure distribution* beneath the loaded area.

The next step is to consider the vertical stress distribution *in depth* beneath the loaded area. In the case of a concentrated load on the surface of the ground, the vertical stress ($\sigma_z$) at any point $N$ beneath the load is given by Boussinesq's equation—

$$\sigma_z = \frac{3Q}{2\pi z^2}\left[\frac{1}{1 + \left(\dfrac{r}{z}\right)^2}\right]^{\frac{5}{2}} \qquad . \qquad . \qquad . \quad (2.16)$$

where $Q$ = concentrated vertical load

    $z$ = vertical distance between $N$ and the underside of the foundation structure

    $r$ = horizontal distance from $N$ to the line of action of the load.

Boussinesq's equation is based on the assumption that the loaded material is elastic, homogeneous, and isotropic. None of these is strictly true for natural soils, but the assumptions are justifiable for practical design. The stress distribution given by the equation is bell-shaped as shown in Fig. 2.22. Influence factors for calculating

$\sigma_z$ for various ratios of the diameter of a circular foundation and $z$ have been calculated by Jurgenson[2.15] and are reproduced in Table 2.3.

In the case of *rigid foundations*, only the mean stress need be determined for settlement calculations. The coefficients for rectangular areas ranging from square to strip foundations for various depths below foundation level are shown in Fig. 2.23.

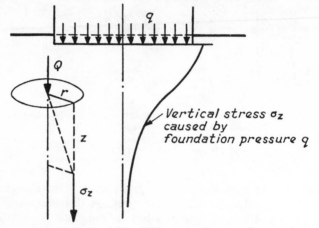

FIG. 2.22. VERTICAL STRESS DISTRIBUTION BENEATH LOADED AREA
CALCULATED BY BOUSSINESQ'S EQUATION

Table 2.3

INFLUENCE FACTORS FOR VERTICAL PRESSURE ($\sigma_z$)
UNDER CENTRE OF UNIFORMLY LOADED FLEXIBLE
CIRCULAR AREA OF DIAMETER $D$

| $\dfrac{D}{z}$ | Influence factor | $\dfrac{D}{z}$ | Influence factor | $\dfrac{D}{z}$ | Influence factor |
|---|---|---|---|---|---|
| 0·00 | 0·0000 | 2·00 | 0·6465 | 4·00 | 0·9106 |
| 0·20 | 0·0148 | 2·20 | 0·6956 | 6·00 | 0·9684 |
| 0·40 | 0·0571 | 2·40 | 0·7376 | 8·00 | 0·9857 |
| 0·60 | 0·1213 | 2·60 | 0·7733 | 10·00 | 0·9925 |
| 0·80 | 0·1966 | 2·80 | 0·8036 | 12·00 | 0·9956 |
| 1·00 | 0·2845 | 3·00 | 0·8293 | 14·00 | 0·9972 |
| 1·20 | 0·3695 | 3·20 | 0·8511 | 16·00 | 0·9981 |
| 1·40 | 0·4502 | 3·40 | 0·8697 | 20·00 | 0·9990 |
| 1·60 | 0·5239 | 3·60 | 0·8855 | 40·00 | 0·9999 |
| 1·80 | 0·5893 | 3·80 | 0·8990 | 200·00 | 1·0000 |

$\sigma_z$ = Influence factor $\times$ contact pressure ($q$)

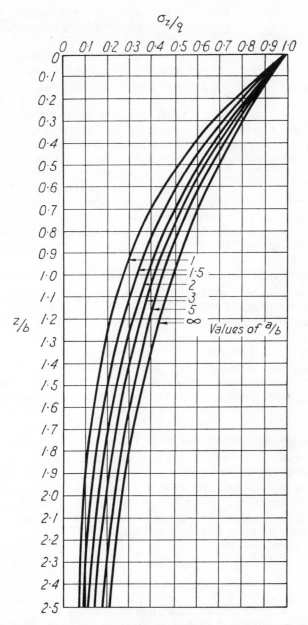

FIG. 2.23. CALCULATION OF MEAN VERTICAL STRESS ($\sigma_z$) AT DEPTH $z$ BENEATH RECTANGULAR AREA $a \times b$ ON SURFACE, LOADED AT UNIFORM PRESSURE $q$

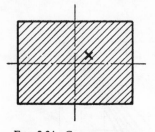

FIG. 2.24. CALCULATION OF SETTLEMENT AT CENTRE OF LARGE FLEXIBLE RECTANGULAR FOUNDATION

In the case of *rectangular flexible foundations* (thin plates, flexible rafts, or close-spaced pad or strip foundations), the stress is determined by Newmark's method.[2.17] The factors for determining the vertical stress at a corner of a rectangle have been tabulated by Newmark, Table 2.4. To obtain the vertical stress at the centre of the loaded area, the area is divided into four equal rectangles (Fig. 2.24). By the principle of superposition, the vertical stress at the point X is equal to four times the stress at any one corner (see example 2.6). The procedure for obtaining the pressure distribution by Newmark's method beneath irregular loaded areas has been described by Terzaghi and Peck[2.18].

### Estimation of Settlements of Foundations on Cohesionless Soils

As already noted, settlements of cohesionless soils such as sands, gravels, and granular fill materials, take place almost immediately as the foundation loading is imposed on them. Because of the difficulty of sampling these soils, there is no practicable laboratory test procedure for determining their consolidation characteristics. Consequently settlements of cohesionless soils are estimated by semi-empirical methods either by extrapolation from plate loading tests or from the results of static cone penetration tests.

#### ESTIMATION OF SETTLEMENTS FROM PLATE LOADING TESTS

The relationship between the settlement $S_o$ of a loaded test plate of diameter $D_0$ under a given load per unit area and the settlement $S$ of a foundation of diameter $D$ at the same load per unit area was originally stated in 1948 by Terzaghi and Peck. Their relationship was expressed approximately in an equation which is shown below in the form given by Bjerrum and Eggestad.[2.19]

$$\frac{S}{S_0} = \frac{4}{\left(1 + \dfrac{D}{D_0}\right)^2} \qquad . \qquad . \qquad . (2.17)$$

where $S$ = settlement of foundation of diameter $D$
$S_0$ = settlement of standard loading plate with diameter $D_0$ for same unit load as under foundation.

## Table 2.4

### INFLUENCE VALUES (I$\sigma$) FOR VERTICAL NORMAL STRESS $\sigma_z$ AT POINT $N$ BENEATH CORNER OF A UNIFORMLY LOADED RECTANGULAR AREA

| $\dfrac{B}{z}$ | $\dfrac{L}{z}$ | | | | | | | | | | | | | |
|---|---|---|---|---|---|---|---|---|---|---|---|---|---|---|
| | 0·1 | 0·2 | 0·3 | 0·4 | 0·5 | 0·6 | 0·7 | 0·8 | 0·9 | 1·0 | 1·2 | 1·4 | 1·6 | 1·8 |
| 0·1 | 0·00470 | 0·00917 | 0·01323 | 0·01678 | 0·01978 | 0·02223 | 0·02420 | 0·02576 | 0·02698 | 0·02794 | 0·02926 | 0·03007 | 0·03058 | 0·03090 |
| 0·2 | 0·00917 | 0·01790 | 0·02585 | 0·03280 | 0·03866 | 0·04348 | 0·04735 | 0·05042 | 0·05283 | 0·05471 | 0·05733 | 0·05894 | 0·05994 | 0·06058 |
| 0·3 | 0·01323 | 0·02585 | 0·03735 | 0·04742 | 0·05593 | 0·06294 | 0·06858 | 0·07308 | 0·07661 | 0·07938 | 0·08323 | 0·08561 | 0·08709 | 0·08804 |
| 0·4 | 0·01678 | 0·03280 | 0·04742 | 0·06024 | 0·07111 | 0·08009 | 0·08734 | 0·09314 | 0·09770 | 0·10129 | 0·10631 | 0·10941 | 0·11135 | 0·11260 |
| 0·5 | 0·01978 | 0·03866 | 0·05593 | 0·07111 | 0·08403 | 0·09473 | 0·10340 | 0·11035 | 0·11584 | 0·12018 | 0·12626 | 0·13003 | 0·13241 | 0·13395 |
| 0·6 | 0·02223 | 0·04348 | 0·06294 | 0·08009 | 0·09473 | 0·10688 | 0·11679 | 0·12474 | 0·13105 | 0·13605 | 0·14309 | 0·14749 | 0·15028 | 0·15207 |
| 0·7 | 0·02420 | 0·04735 | 0·06858 | 0·08734 | 0·10340 | 0·11679 | 0·12772 | 0·13653 | 0·14356 | 0·14914 | 0·15703 | 0·16199 | 0·16515 | 0·16720 |
| 0·8 | 0·02576 | 0·05042 | 0·07308 | 0·09314 | 0·11035 | 0·12474 | 0·13653 | 0·14607 | 0·15371 | 0·15978 | 0·16843 | 0·17389 | 0·17739 | 0·17967 |
| 0·9 | 0·02698 | 0·05283 | 0·07661 | 0·09770 | 0·11584 | 0·13105 | 0·14356 | 0·15371 | 0·16185 | 0·16835 | 0·17766 | 0·18357 | 0·18737 | 0·18986 |
| 1·0 | 0·02794 | 0·05471 | 0·07938 | 0·10129 | 0·12018 | 0·13605 | 0·14914 | 0·15978 | 0·16835 | 0·17522 | 0·18508 | 0·19139 | 0·19546 | 0·19814 |
| 1·2 | 0·02926 | 0·05733 | 0·08323 | 0·10631 | 0·12626 | 0·14309 | 0·15703 | 0·16843 | 0·17766 | 0·18508 | 0·19584 | 0·20278 | 0·20731 | 0·21032 |
| 1·4 | 0·03007 | 0·05894 | 0·08561 | 0·10941 | 0·13003 | 0·14749 | 0·16199 | 0·17389 | 0·18357 | 0·19139 | 0·20278 | 0·21020 | 0·21510 | 0·21836 |
| 1·6 | 0·03058 | 0·05994 | 0·08709 | 0·11135 | 0·13241 | 0·15028 | 0·16515 | 0·17739 | 0·18737 | 0·19546 | 0·20731 | 0·21510 | 0·22025 | 0·22372 |
| 1·8 | 0·03090 | 0·06058 | 0·08804 | 0·11260 | 0·13395 | 0·15207 | 0·16720 | 0·17967 | 0·18986 | 0·19814 | 0·21032 | 0·21836 | 0·22372 | 0·22736 |
| 2·0 | 0·03111 | 0·06100 | 0·08867 | 0·11342 | 0·13496 | 0·15326 | 0·16856 | 0·18119 | 0·19152 | 0·19994 | 0·21235 | 0·22058 | 0·22610 | 0·22986 |
| 2·5 | 0·03138 | 0·06155 | 0·08948 | 0·11450 | 0·13628 | 0·15483 | 0·17036 | 0·18321 | 0·19375 | 0·20236 | 0·21512 | 0·22364 | 0·22940 | 0·23334 |
| 3·0 | 0·03150 | 0·06178 | 0·08982 | 0·11495 | 0·13684 | 0·15550 | 0·17113 | 0·18407 | 0·19470 | 0·20341 | 0·21633 | 0·22499 | 0·23088 | 0·23495 |
| 4·0 | 0·03158 | 0·06194 | 0·09007 | 0·11527 | 0·13724 | 0·15598 | 0·17168 | 0·18469 | 0·19540 | 0·20417 | 0·21722 | 0·22600 | 0·23200 | 0·23688 |
| 5·0 | 0·03160 | 0·06199 | 0·09014 | 0·11537 | 0·13737 | 0·15612 | 0·17185 | 0·18488 | 0·19561 | 0·20440 | 0·21749 | 0·22632 | 0·23236 | 0·23735 |
| 6·0 | 0·03161 | 0·06201 | 0·09017 | 0·11541 | 0·13741 | 0·15617 | 0·17191 | 0·18496 | 0·19569 | 0·20449 | 0·21760 | 0·22644 | 0·23249 | 0·23671 |
| 8·0 | 0·03162 | 0·06202 | 0·09018 | 0·11543 | 0·13744 | 0·15621 | 0·17195 | 0·18500 | 0·19574 | 0·20455 | 0·21767 | 0·22652 | 0·23258 | 0·23681 |
| 10·0 | 0·03162 | 0·06202 | 0·09019 | 0·11544 | 0·13745 | 0·15622 | 0·17196 | 0·18502 | 0·19576 | 0·20457 | 0·21769 | 0·22654 | 0·23261 | 0·23684 |
| $\infty$ | 0·03162 | 0·06202 | 0·09019 | 0·11544 | 0·13745 | 0·15623 | 0·17197 | 0·18502 | 0·19577 | 0·20458 | 0·21770 | 0·22656 | 0·23263 | 0·23686 |

Table 2.4 (contd.)

$\sigma_z = q \times I\sigma$

$q$ per unit area

| $\dfrac{B}{z}$ | $\dfrac{L}{z}$ | | | | | | | | |
|---|---|---|---|---|---|---|---|---|---|
| | 2·0 | 2·5 | 3·0 | 4·0 | 5·0 | 6·0 | 8·0 | 10·0 | $\infty$ |
| 0·1 | 0·03111 | 0·03138 | 0·03150 | 0·03158 | 0·03160 | 0·03161 | 0·03162 | 0·03162 | 0·03162 |
| 0·2 | 0·06100 | 0·06155 | 0·06178 | 0·06194 | 0·06199 | 0·06201 | 0·06202 | 0·06202 | 0·06202 |
| 0·3 | 0·08867 | 0·08948 | 0·08982 | 0·09007 | 0·09014 | 0·09017 | 0·09018 | 0·09019 | 0·09019 |
| 0·4 | 0·11342 | 0·11450 | 0·11495 | 0·11527 | 0·11537 | 0·11541 | 0·11543 | 0·11544 | 0·11544 |
| 0·5 | 0·13496 | 0·13628 | 0·13684 | 0·13724 | 0·13737 | 0·13741 | 0·13744 | 0·13745 | 0·13745 |
| 0·6 | 0·15326 | 0·15483 | 0·15550 | 0·15598 | 0·15612 | 0·15617 | 0·15621 | 0·15622 | 0·15623 |
| 0·7 | 0·16856 | 0·17036 | 0·17113 | 0·17168 | 0·17185 | 0·17191 | 0·17195 | 0·17196 | 0·17197 |
| 0·8 | 0·18119 | 0·18321 | 0·18407 | 0·18469 | 0·18488 | 0·18496 | 0·18500 | 0·18502 | 0·18502 |
| 0·9 | 0·19152 | 0·19375 | 0·19470 | 0·19540 | 0·19561 | 0·19569 | 0·19574 | 0·19576 | 0·19576 |
| 1·0 | 0·19994 | 0·20236 | 0·20341 | 0·20417 | 0·20440 | 0·20449 | 0·20455 | 0·20457 | 0·20458 |
| 1·2 | 0·21235 | 0·21512 | 0·21633 | 0·21722 | 0·21749 | 0·21760 | 0·21767 | 0·21769 | 0·21770 |
| 1·4 | 0·22058 | 0·22364 | 0·22499 | 0·22600 | 0·22632 | 0·22644 | 0·22652 | 0·22654 | 0·22656 |
| 1·6 | 0·22610 | 0·22940 | 0·23088 | 0·23200 | 0·23236 | 0·23249 | 0·23258 | 0·23261 | 0·23263 |
| 1·8 | 0·22986 | 0·23334 | 0·23495 | 0·23698 | 0·23935 | 0·23671 | 0·23681 | 0·23684 | 0·23686 |
| 2·0 | 0·23247 | 0·23614 | 0·23782 | 0·23912 | 0·23954 | 0·23970 | 0·23981 | 0·23985 | 0·23987 |
| 2·5 | 0·23614 | 0·24010 | 0·24196 | 0·24344 | 0·24392 | 0·24412 | 0·24425 | 0·24429 | 0·24432 |
| 3·0 | 0·23782 | 0·24196 | 0·24394 | 0·24554 | 0·24608 | 0·24630 | 0·24646 | 0·24650 | 0·24654 |
| 4·0 | 0·23912 | 0·24344 | 0·24554 | 0·24729 | 0·24791 | 0·24817 | 0·24836 | 0·24842 | 0·24846 |
| 5·0 | 0·23954 | 0·24392 | 0·24608 | 0·24791 | 0·24857 | 0·24885 | 0·24907 | 0·24914 | 0·24919 |
| 6·0 | 0·23970 | 0·24412 | 0·24630 | 0·24817 | 0·24885 | 0·24916 | 0·24939 | 0·24946 | 0·24952 |
| 8·0 | 0·23981 | 0·24425 | 0·24646 | 0·24836 | 0·24907 | 0·24939 | 0·24964 | 0·24973 | 0·24980 |
| 10·0 | 0·23985 | 0·24429 | 0·24650 | 0·24842 | 0·24914 | 0·24946 | 0·24973 | 0·24981 | 0·24989 |
| $\infty$ | 0·23987 | 0·24432 | 0·24654 | 0·24846 | 0·24919 | 0·24952 | 0·24980 | 0·24989 | 0·25000 |

The graphical relationship of Terzaghi and Peck between $S/S_0$ and $D/D_0$ derived from equation 2.17 is shown in the full line in Fig. 2.25. Bjerrum and Eggestad showed somewhat higher settlement ratios. They obtained average and upper and lower limit curves shown by dashed lines in Fig. 2.25. The upper curve is valid for a very loose,

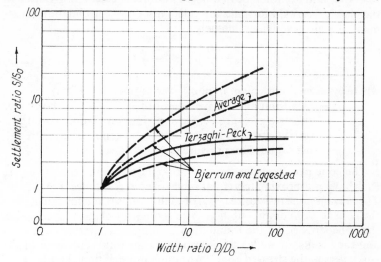

FIG. 2.25. APPROXIMATE RELATION BETWEEN SETTLEMENT RATIO $S/S_0$ AND DIMENSIONS OF LOADED AREA (BJERRUM AND EGGESTAD[2.19])

slightly organic sand. The use of Fig. 2.25 for estimating settlements is based on the assumption that the density of the soil within the zone affected by the foundation loading is similar to that beneath the test plate. This may be approximately true if the plate diameter is roughly the same size as the foundation, but in the case of large foundations, which stress the soil to a considerable depth, it is likely that there will be a considerable difference in the densities. A more exact estimate can be obtained by carrying out plate loading tests throughout the depth which is stressed by the large foundation and taking an average value of the settlement $S_0$ for substitution in equation 2.17.

## ESTIMATION OF SETTLEMENTS FROM STATIC CONE PENETRATION TESTS

De Beer and Martens[2.20] use Buismann's empirical formula as follows—

$$\text{Constant of compressibility} = C = \frac{3}{2}\frac{C_{kd}}{p_o} \qquad . \ (2.18)$$

where $C_{kd}$ = static cone resistance

$p_o$ = effective overburden pressure at point of measurement.*

Values of $C_{kd}$ are read in kg/cm². The readings should be converted to kN/m² and $p_o$ should be in units of kN/m² for calculating $C$ used in the classic Terzaghi formula for calculating the consolidation settlement of a given soil layer, namely—

$$\rho_f = \frac{H}{C} \log_e \frac{p_o + \sigma_z}{p_o} \qquad . \qquad . \qquad . \quad (2.19)$$

where $\rho_f$ = final settlement in m of layer of thickness $H$ (m)

$p_o$ = mean initial effective overburden pressure of layer, i.e. effective pressure before applying foundation loading

$\sigma_z$ = vertical stress in kN/m² induced at centre of layer by the net foundation pressure ($q_n$).

The cone penetrometer curve is broken down into separate layers each having approximately equal values of cone resistance (Fig. 2.26b). The *average* cone resistance ($C_{kd}$) of each layer is taken for calculating the constant of compressibility. The settlement of each layer within the zone stressed by the foundation loading is separately calculated and the results are added together to give the total settlement of the soil layers in the stressed zone. Although not mentioned by De Beer and Martens, it appears logical to reduce the settlements calculated from equation 2.19 by a depth factor and a rigidity factor, if these are applicable to the problem under consideration. These factors are normally applied to the calculated settlement of foundations on clays and the methods of obtaining the factors are described later in this chapter (pp. 129 and 133).

The method of calculating the vertical stress at any depth below foundation level was given earlier in this chapter (p. 115). Where the cone resistance is uniform for a considerable depth within the stressed zone, it may be necessary to subdivide the layer because the values of $\sigma_z$ fall off rapidly with increasing depth below foundation level.

If several cone tests made over an individual foundation area show varying results it is advisable to calculate the maximum, minimum, and average settlements from the highest, lowest, and average values respectively of cone resistance. This will give a guide to the likely tilting or differential settlement of the foundation.

Schmertman's method[2.21] can also be used for calculating settlements from the results of static cone penetration tests using the equation—

---

* *See* p. 82 for definition of effective overburden pressure.

$$\rho = C_1 C_2 \Delta_p \sum_0^{2B} \frac{I_z}{E_d} \Delta_z \qquad . \qquad . \quad (2.20)$$

where  $C_1$ = depth correction factor (see below)
$C_2$ = creep factor (see below)
$\Delta_p$ = net increase of load on soil at foundation level due to applied loading
$B$ = width of loaded area
$I_z$ = vertical strain influence factor (Fig. 2.26(a))
$E_d$ = deformation modulus
$\Delta_z$ = thickness of soil layer
The depth correction factor is given by—

$$C_1 = 1 - 0.5 \left( \frac{p_o}{\Delta_p} \right) \qquad . \qquad . \quad (2.21)$$

where $p_o$ = effective overburden pressure at foundation level.

Schmertmann states that although settlements on cohesion-less soils are regarded as immediate, observations frequently show long-term creep, calculated by the factor—

$$C_2 = 1 + 0.2 \log_{10} \left( \frac{\text{time}_{\text{years}}}{0.1} \right) \qquad . \qquad . \quad (2.21\text{a})$$

The vertical strain influence factor is obtained from a simplified curve (2B $-$ 0·6 curve) related to the dimensionless depth factor $z \Big/ \dfrac{B}{2}$ as shown in Fig. 2.26(a). The deformation modulus is obtained by multiplying the static cone resistance $C_{kd}$ by an empirical factor $N$ for which Schmertmann suggests the following values—

Silts, sandy silts, and slightly cohesive silty sands—$N = 2$
Clean fine to medium sands, slightly silty sands —$N = 3.5$
Coarse sands and sands with a little gravel      —$N = 5$
Sandy gravel and gravels                         —$N = 6$

The cone resistance diagram is divided into layers of approximately equal or representative values of $C_{kd}$ as shown in Fig. 2.26(b) and the 2B $-$ 0·6 curve is placed alongside this diagram beneath the foundation which is drawn to the same scale (Fig. 2.26(c)). The settlements in each layer resulting from the loading $\Delta_p$ are then calculated using the values of $\bar{E}_d$ and $I_z$ appropriate to each layer. The sum of the settlements in each layer is then corrected for the depth factor and creep factor using equations 2.21 and 2.21a.

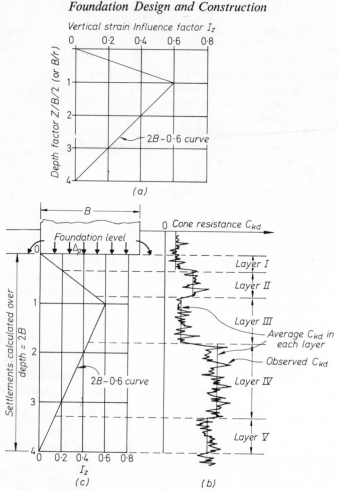

FIG. 2.26. SCHMERTMANN'S METHOD FOR CALCULATING SETTLEMENTS
FROM STATIC CONE PENETRATION TESTS

## Estimation of Settlements on Clay Soils

The procedure described in the following pages is based on Skempton and Bjerrum's modification[2.22] of Terzaghi's theory of consolidation.[2.23] The latter assumes that consolidation is a process of one-dimensional strain. Comparison of observed and calculated settlements indicates that the method underestimates the rate of settlement. Other theories have been published which claim to represent more accurately the consolidation process but in most cases these are difficult to apply in practice. In any event the magnitude of settlement of engineering structures on most firm to stiff soils is relatively small. For this reason, refinement of calculations is hardly justifiable, especially as natural variations in soil compressibility can produce settlement variations of greater significance than differences in values calculated by the various methods. Only in cases of soft compressible soils carrying large heavy structures is it justifiable to adopt the more elaborate calculation methods based on three-dimensional strain. The steps in carrying out the settlement analysis are as follows—

1. CHOICE OF THE SOIL PROFILE. A soil profile should be drawn for the site, on which is marked the average depths of the various soil strata and the average values of the compression index (or the coefficient of volume compressibility) and coefficient of consolidation for each stratum or each division of a stratum. In the case of thick clay strata, it must not be assumed that the compressibility is constant throughout the depth of the strata. Clays usually show progressively decreasing compressibility and increase in elastic modulus with increasing depth. It frequently happens that the borehole records and soil test results show wide variations in the depths of the strata and compressibility values. In these circumstances the choice of a representative soil profile involves exercise of careful judgment. For large and important structures it is worthwhile to make settlement analyses for the highest compressibility and maximum depth of compressible strata and the lowest compressibility with the minimum depth of strata, and then to compare the two analyses to obtain an idea of the differential settlement if these two extremes of conditions occur over the area of the structure.

2. ASSESSMENT OF THE LOADING CAUSING SETTLEMENT. When considering long-term consolidation settlement it is essential that the foundation loading used in the analysis should be realistic and representative of the *sustained* loading over the time period under consideration. This is a different approach to that used when calculating safe bearing pressures. In the latter case the most severe loading conditions are allowed for, with full provision for maximum live loading. The live loading used in a settlement analysis is an *average value* representing the continuous live load over the time period being considered.

Wind loading is only considered in settlement analyses for high structures where it represents a considerable proportion of the total loads, and then only the wind loads representing the average of continuous winds over the full period are allowed for.

The calculation of consolidation settlement is based on the increases in effective vertical stresses induced by the loads from the structure. At foundation level, the effective vertical pressure before construction is $p_0$; after completion of the structure, the effective vertical stress becomes—

$$q - \gamma_w h$$

Thus the increase in effective vertical stress at foundation level is—

$$q - \gamma_w h - p_0 = q - \gamma_w h - (p - \gamma_w h)$$
$$= q - p$$
$$= q_n \text{ from eqn. 2.2}$$

3. CALCULATION OF PRESSURE AND STRESS DISTRIBUTION. The distribution of *effective* vertical pressure of the overburden ($p_o$) and the vertical stress ($\sigma_z$) resulting from the net foundation pressure ($q_n$) is shown in Fig. 2.27. Values of $\sigma_z$ at various depths below foundation level are obtained by the methods described earlier in this chapter (p. 115).

In the case of deep compressible soils the lowest level considered in the settlement analyses is the point where the vertical stress ($\sigma_z$) is relatively small, say of the order of 10 to 20 kN/m².

4. CALCULATION OF CONSOLIDATION SETTLEMENT ($\rho_c$). If the variation in compressibility of a soil is known from the result of a number of oedometer tests (*see* p. 55) the consolidation settlement

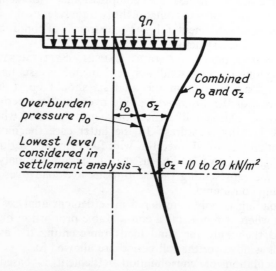

FIG. 2.27. VERTICAL PRESSURE AND STRESS DISTRIBUTION FOR DEEP CLAY LAYER

($\rho_c$) is calculated preferably from the values of the coefficient of volume compressibility ($m_v$) as determined from the oedometer tests.

Skempton and Bjerrum [2.22] have shown that the actual consolidation settlement ($\rho_c$) may be less than the calculated values based on oedometer tests. They give the formula—

$$\rho_c = \mu \rho_{oed} \qquad . \qquad . \qquad . \qquad . \qquad (2.22)$$

where $\mu$ = a coefficient which depends on the type of clay

and $\rho_{oed}$ = settlement as calculated from oedometer tests.

Skempton and Bjerrum have related $\mu$ to the pore pressure coefficient of the soils as determined from undrained triaxial compression tests, and also to the dimensions of the loaded area. However, for most practical purposes it is sufficient to take the following values for $\mu$—

| *Type of clay* | *$\mu$ value* |
|---|---|
| Very sensitive clays (soft alluvial, estuarine, and marine clays) | 1·0 to 1·2 |
| Normally-consolidated Clays | 0·7 to 1·0 |
| Over-consolidated clays (London Clay, Weald, Kimmeridge, Oxford, and Lias Clays) | 0·5 to 0·7 |
| Heavily over-consolidated clays (boulder clay, Keuper Marl) | 0·2 to 0·5 |

The $\mu$ value for London Clay is generally taken as 0·5.

The oedometer settlement ($\rho_{oed}$) in metres of a soil layer is calculated from the formula—

$$\rho_{oed} = m_v \times \sigma_z \times H \qquad . \qquad . \qquad . \qquad (2.23)$$

where $m_v$ = average coefficient of volume compressibility obtained for the effective pressure increment in the particular layer under consideration

$\sigma_z$ = average effective vertical stress imposed on the particular layer resulting from the net foundation pressure $q_n$

$H$ = thickness of the particular layer under consideration.

The values of $\rho_{oed}$ and hence $\rho_c$ obtained for each layer are added together to obtain the total consolidation settlement beneath the loaded area.

If only one or two oedometer test results are available for a given loaded area it is more convenient to calculate $\rho_{oed}$ directly from the *pressure–voids ratio* curves obtained in the tests. The procedure is then as follows—

For normally consolidated clays such as estuarine or marine clays, the virgin compression curve should be used for the settlement calculations. For preconsolidated or over-consolidated clays such as boulder clays and the London, Woolwich and Reading, Gault, Weald, Kimmeridge, Oxford and Lias Clays, the actual pressure–voids ratio curves should be used. Typical curves for normally consolidated clays and for over-consolidated clays are shown in Fig. 2.28.

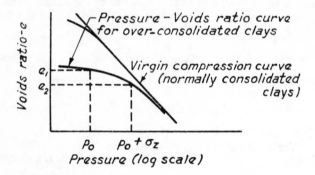

FIG. 2.28. USE OF PRESSURE–VOIDS RATIO CURVES IN SETTLEMENT ANALYSIS

For ordinary clays of low or medium compressibility, a rough guide to the compression index $(C_c)$, i.e. the slope of the virgin compression curve when plotted to a semi-logarithmic scale, is given by the equation—

$$C_c = 0\cdot009 \, (L_w - 10\%) \qquad . \qquad . \qquad . \quad (2\cdot24)$$

where $L_w$ = liquid limit of the clay.

Referring to Fig. 2.29, the change in voids ratio due to an increase in vertical stress resulting from the foundation loading is considered at the centre of the clay layer having a thickness $H$. Thus for the initial (unloaded) condition, the initial voids ratio $(e_1)$ is read off the $p–e$ curve (Fig. 2.28) corresponding to the initial overburden pressure $(p_o)$ at the centre of the layer. After foundation loading is applied, the initial vertical pressure $(p_o)$ is increased by the vertical stress $(\sigma_z)$

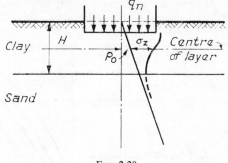

FIG. 2.29

induced at the centre of the layer by the net foundation pressure ($q_n$). Thus the final voids ratio ($e_2$) is read off the *p–e* curve corresponding to a pressure of $p_o + \sigma_z$. The decrease in thickness of the layer, i.e. the oedometer settlement $\rho_{oed}$, after full consolidation is then given by the equation—

$$\rho_{oed} = \frac{H}{1 + e_1}(e_1 - e_2) \qquad . \qquad . \qquad . \quad (2.25)$$

or if the compression index has been used as the basis for the settlement computations, the final settlement is calculated from the equation—

$$\rho_{oed} = \frac{H}{1 + e_1} C_c \log_{10} \frac{p_o + \sigma_z}{p_o} \qquad . \qquad . \quad (2.26)$$

As before,       $\rho_c = \mu \rho_{oed}$

If the clay layer shows appreciable change in compressibility with depth, the settlement within each layer should be separately calculated. Then the total net final settlement is given by the sum of the settlements of each individual layer. For deep clay layers it is usually necessary to consider separate layers to allow for variations in compressibility with depth, and also to provide for the effect of variation in voids ratio with the rapidly decreasing vertical stress with increasing depth. The net final settlement is calculated for each layer and the sum of the values so obtained gives the total net final settlement for the whole depth of the clay stratum affected by the foundation loading.

A correction is applied to the calculated $\rho_c$ in the form of a "depth

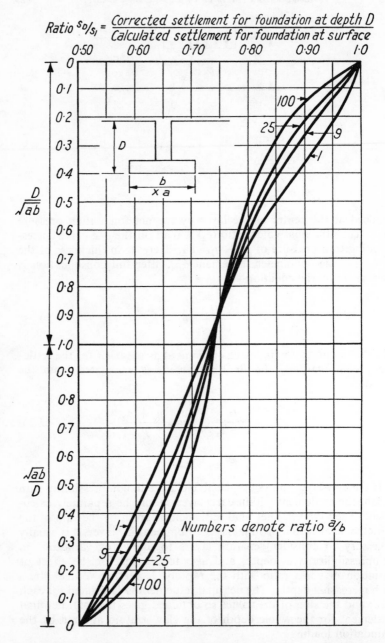

FIG. 2.30. Fox's Correction Curves for Elastic Settlement of Flexible Rectangular Foundations at Depth

factor." This depends on the depth-to-area ratio and the length-to-breadth ratio of the foundation. Values of the depth factor—

$$\text{Depth factor} = \frac{\text{corrected settlement for a foundation at depth } D}{\text{calculated settlement for a surface foundation}}$$

are obtained from Fox's[2.16] correction curves which are as shown in Fig. 2.30. Theoretically, Fox's curves apply only to elastic or "immediate" settlements, but it is logical to correct consolidation settlements to allow for the depth of the foundation and Fox's curves provide a convenient method of doing this.

5. CALCULATION OF NET IMMEDIATE SETTLEMENT ($\rho_i$). The net immediate settlement ($\rho_i$), i.e. the elastic settlement beneath the centre of a flexible loaded area, is calculated from the equation—

$$\rho_i = q_n \times 2B \times \frac{(1 - m^2)}{E} \times I_p \qquad . \qquad . \ (2.27)$$

where $B$ = width of foundation (see note on Fig. 2.31)

$E$ = modulus of elasticity of clay

$m$ = Poisson's ratio of clay (generally taken as 0·5)

$q_n$ = *net* foundation pressure

$I_p$ = influence factor.

Because of sample disturbance, values of $E$ obtained from laboratory compression tests are unreliable and it is preferable to obtain $E$ values from plate loading tests made in the field or from established empirical ratios of the $E$ value to the undrained cohesion of the clay. Butler[2.26] gives an $E/c$ ratio of 400 for London Clay while Bjerrum[2.27] quotes ratios in the range of 500 to 1500 for normally consolidated clays. The lowest range is for clays of high plasticity and the highest for clays of low plasticity. Bjerrum's ratios were based on measurements of undrained cohesion by the vane test.

$I_p$ is a function of the length-to-breadth ratio of the foundation, and the thickness ($H$) of the compressible layer. Terzaghi[2.24] has given a method of calculating $I_p$ from curves derived by Steinbrenner.[2.25]

For Poisson's ratio of 0·5,  $I_p = F_1$

For Poisson's ratio of zero, $I_p = F_1 + F_2$

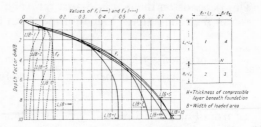

FIG. 2.31. CALCULATION OF IMMEDIATE SETTLEMENTS DUE TO A FLEXIBLE LOADED
AREA ON THE SURFACE OF AN ELASTIC LAYER
Note: When using this diagram to calculate $\rho_i$ at *centre* of rectangular area, take $B$ as
half foundation width to obtain $H/B$ and $L/B$.

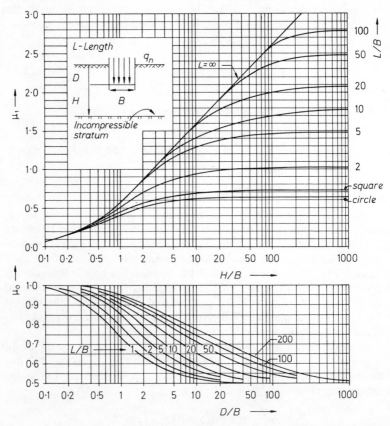

FIG. 2.32. FACTORS FOR CALCULATING THE AVERAGE IMMEDIATE
SETTLEMENT OF A LOADED AREA
(after Janbu, Bjerrum and Kjaernsli[2.28])

Values of $F_1$ and $F_2$ for various ratios of $H/B$ and $L/B$ are given in Fig. 2.31. Elastic settlements should not be calculated for thicknesses ($H$) greater than $4B$. If it is desired to calculate $\rho_i$ at the corner of the loaded area, the following formula should be used—

$$\rho_i \text{ at corner} = q_n \times B \times \frac{(1 - m^2)}{E} \times I_p \qquad . \ (2.28)$$

The immediate settlement at any point $N$ (Fig. 2.31) is given by—

$$\rho_i \text{ at point } N = \frac{q_n}{E} (1 - m^2)(I_{p_1}B_1 + I_{p_2}B_2 + I_{p_3}B_3 + I_{p_4}B_4) \ . \ (2.29)$$

Generally, it will be found more convenient to use the method of Janbu, Bjerrum, and Kjaernsli[2.28] to obtain the *average* immediate settlement of a foundation where

$$\text{Average settlement} = \rho_i = \frac{\mu_1\mu_0 q_n B}{E} \qquad . \qquad . \ (2.30)$$

In the above equation Poisson's ratio is assumed to be 0·5. The factors $\mu_1$ and $\mu_0$ are related to the depth $D$ of the foundation, the thickness $H$ of the compressible layer and the length/width $L/B$ ratio of the foundation. Values of these factors are shown in Fig. 2.32.

It is the usual practice to calculate $\rho_i$ for the various representative soil layers beneath the foundation and to add them together to obtain the total immediate settlement. In the case of a rigid foundation, for example a heavy beam and slab raft or a massive pier, the immediate settlement at the centre is reduced by a rigidity factor. The commonly accepted factor is 0·8; thus—

$$\frac{\text{Immediate settlement of rigid foundation}}{\text{Immediate settlement at centre of flexible foundation}} = 0\cdot8 \text{ approx.}$$

A correction is also applied to the immediate settlements to allow for the depth of foundation by means of the "depth factor" (*see* p. 129 and Fig. 2.30).

6. ESTIMATION OF FINAL SETTLEMENT ($\rho_f$). The final settlement is the sum of the corrected values of the immediate settlement and the consolidation settlement, i.e.

$$\rho_f = \rho_i + \rho_c \qquad . \qquad . \qquad . \qquad . \ (2.30)$$

7. ESTIMATION OF THE RATE OF CONSOLIDATION SETTLEMENT. It is usually necessary to know the rate at which the foundations will

settle during the long process of consolidation. This is normally calculated as the time period required for 50 per cent and 90 per cent of the final settlement.

The time required is given by the equation—

$$t = \frac{Td^2}{C_v} \qquad \qquad . \qquad (2.31)$$

or expressed in m/year units—

$$t \text{ (years)} = \frac{Td^2 \times 10^{-7} \quad \text{(m)}}{3{\cdot}154 \times C_v \quad \text{(m}^2\text{/s)}} \qquad . \qquad (2.31a)$$

where $T$ = time factor

> $d = H$ (thickness of compressible stratum measured from foundation level to point where $\sigma_z$ is small, say 10 to 20 kN/m$^2$) for drainage in one direction

or   $d = \dfrac{H}{2}$ for drainage at top and bottom of clay stratum

and   $C_v$ = average coefficient of consolidation over the range of pressure involved (obtained from the oedometer test).

The values of the time factor ($T$) for various degrees of consolidation ($U$) are given in Fig. 2.33.

The total settlement at any time $t$ is given by—

$$\rho_t = \rho_i + U\rho_c \qquad . \qquad . \qquad (2.32)$$

The type of curve to be used depends on the pressure distribution. The standard cases of pressure distribution are shown in Fig. 2.34. When there is two-way drainage, i.e. when there is a permeable layer above and below the compressible stratum, there is only one type of curve for all types of pressure distribution.

When considering drainage of the clay layer it is always assumed that the concrete of the foundation acts as a permeable layer. In fact concrete is much more pervious than most clays. Where the foundation is constructed from impermeable material, e.g. asphalt tanking around a concrete sub-structure or a buried steel tank, the rate of settlement should, strictly, be based on three-dimensional theory of consolidation. However, this procedure is rarely needed in practice

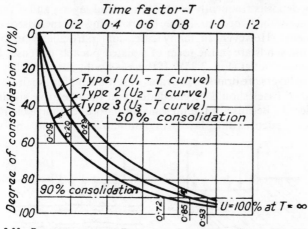

FIG. 2.33. RELATION BETWEEN DEGREE OF CONSOLIDATION AND TIME FACTOR

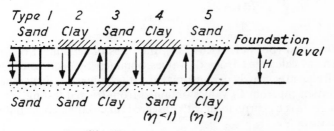

FIG. 2.34. TYPES OF PRESSURE DISTRIBUTION

Arrow indicates direction of drainage

$$\eta = \frac{\text{Pressure at permeable surface}}{\text{Pressure at impermeable surface}}$$

For Case 4— $\qquad U_4 = U_1 - \left(\frac{1-\eta}{1+\eta}\right)(U_1 - U_2$

i.e. intermediate between $U_1$ and $U_3$.

For Case 5— $\qquad U_5 = U_1 + \left(\frac{\eta-1}{\eta+1}\right)(U_1 - U_2)$

i.e. intermediate between $U_1$ and $U_2$.

since asphalt tanking is nearly always laid on a mass concrete blinding layer, and similarly steel tanks are usually placed on a bed of sand or crushed stone. Therefore in nearly all cases the standard one-dimensional theory of consolidation can be followed.

Clay deposits frequently contain thin sand layers, and if these are continuous they form drainage layers giving an increased rate of settlement. However, in many cases and particularly in boulder clays, the sands are in the form of isolated pockets or lenses having no drainage outlet (Fig. 2.35). If there is doubt as to whether or not the sand layers are drained, the rates of settlement for the drained and undrained cases should be calculated and their relative significance considered. Because of the presence of natural drainage channels in clay soils, such as thin layers or laminations of sand and silt, or

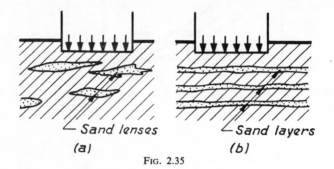

Sand lenses
(a)

Sand layers
(b)

Fig. 2.35

fissures and root holes (Rowe[1.4]), the rates of settlement of foundations as calculated from $C_v$ values obtained by oedometer testing are frequently grossly over-estimated. It is better to estimate the rate of settlement from $C_v$ values obtained from triaxial testing.[1.21] The best guide is by correlation with observed time-settlement of full-scale structures.

## 8. ESTIMATION OF SETTLEMENTS OVER THE CONSTRUCTION PERIOD.

Typical curves for the loading and settlement of a structure over the period of construction and after completion are shown in Fig. 2.36. The curve of the net settlement, assuming the final foundation loading to be instantaneously applied, is first plotted as shown by the lower curve in Fig. 2.36. The first point $C$ on the corrected curve (allowing for progressive increase of load over the construction period) is obtained by dropping a perpendicular from a point $A$ on the time abscissa, where $OA$ is the time for completion of construction (time $t_1$). A perpendicular is dropped from a point equal to half $t_1$, to intersect the instantaneous loading curve at $B$. Then $BC$ is drawn parallel to the time scale to intersect the perpendicular from $A$ at $C$. Intermediate points for any other time $t$ are similarly obtained. A perpendicular is dropped from $\frac{1}{2}t$ to intersect the instantaneous loading curve at $D$. A line drawn parallel to the time scale is extended to the perpendicular $AC$ to intersect at the point $E$. Then the

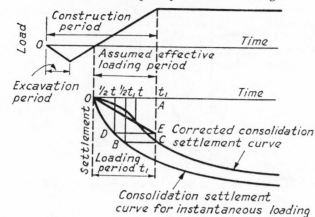

FIG. 2.36. CONSOLIDATION SETTLEMENT CURVE DURING THE CONSTRUCTION
PERIOD

intersection of $OE$ with the perpendicular from the point $t$ gives the intermediate point on the corrected curve for the time $t$. Beyond $C$ the settlement curve is assumed to be the instantaneous curve offset to the right by half the loading period, i.e. offset by the distance $BC$.

The corrected *total* settlement curve can be obtained by adding the immediate settlement (as calculated from equations 2.27 to 2.29) to the corrected consolidation settlement as shown in Fig. 2.36. Assuming that the applied loading increases linearly during the construction period, the immediate settlement also increases roughly linearly.

## SWELLING OF EXCAVATIONS

Removal of the overburden when excavating to foundation level causes swelling of the soil below the excavation. After applying the loading the soil is re-compressed and after the loading has increased beyond the original overburden pressure further consolidation takes place. This swelling and re-compression is usually insignificant in the case of shallow foundations and it can be neglected. It must, however, be taken into consideration for deep foundations and it is discussed further in Chapter 5.

## SETTLEMENT DATA IN AN ENGINEERING REPORT

The accuracy obtainable in settlement computations does not justify quoting exact calculated figures. It is usual to give settlement to the nearest 15 mm where the settlement is 25 mm or less, or to use some such expression as "less than 25 mm" or "about 25 mm."

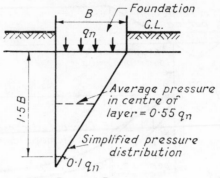

FIG. 2.37. APPROXIMATE PRESSURE DISTRIBUTION BENEATH A FOUNDATION

For settlements greater than 25 mm the quoted figures should be to the nearest mm stating "25 to 50 mm" or "about 100 mm." Settlements greater than 150 mm should be quoted to the nearest 50 to 100 mm.

### AN APPROXIMATE METHOD OF ESTIMATING CONSOLIDATION SETTLEMENTS OF FOUNDATIONS ON CLAYS

In many cases it is unjustifiable to adopt the rather lengthy method given in the preceding pages for calculating immediate and consolidation settlements, particularly when foundations of fairly small dimensions are to be constructed on uniform stiff and relatively incompressible clays. The approximate method given below is based on consolidation theory but the procedure for calculating the pressure distribution is simplified.

The vertical stress distribution shown in Fig. 2.22 (p. 116) can be represented approximately by a triangular distribution (Fig. 2.37). Thus from equation 2.23—

$$\text{Oedometer settlement} = \rho_{oed} = m_v \times \sigma_z \times H$$
$$= m_v \times 0 \cdot 55 q_n \times 1 \cdot 5B \quad (2.33)$$

where $q_n$ = net foundation pressure
$B$ = width of foundation.

If consolidation test results are available, the average value of $m_v$ should be taken over the depth $1 \cdot 5B$. If there are no test results the $m_v$ values given in Table 1.3 (p. 56) should be used.

It should be noted that the above method gives only the oedometer settlement and it ignores immediate settlement. Also, because it is approximate, it is unrealistic to apply any "geological" or rigidity factors. If the value of $\rho_{oed}$, as calculated from equation 2.33, gives some concern about the possibility of excessive total and differential settlements, then the full procedure described on pages 121 to 132 should be followed.

## EXAMPLES ON CHAPTER 2

EXAMPLE 2.1

A water tank 5 m wide by 20 m long is to be constructed at a depth of 0·8 m below ground level. The depth of water in the tank is 7·5 m. Borings showed a loose, becoming medium-dense, sand with the water table 2 m below ground level. Standard penetration tests made in the boreholes gave the values shown in the table below. It is desired to keep settlements down to a small value. Determine the required width of the concrete foundation slab.

From Appendix A, the density of the sand may be taken as 1·70 Mg/m³.

Net bearing pressure at base of tank $= q_n = q - p$

$$= (7·50 - 0·80 \times 1·70)$$
$$\times 9·807$$

$$= 60·2 \text{ kN/m}^2$$

Applying the correction factors to the standard penetration test values (*see* Fig. 2.14) we get—

| Depth below ground level m | Uncorrected N-value | Corrected N-value |
|---|---|---|
| 1·50 | 5 | 15 |
| 2·50 | 7 | 20 |
| 3·50 | 10 | 26 |
| 4·50 | 12 | 29 |
| 5·50 | 12 | 28 |
| 6·50 | 13 | 30 |

Taking the average corrected penetration resistance ($N$) of 25, reference to Fig. 2.13 shows that the allowable bearing pressure for a foundation 5 m wide is 105 kN/m². (The value corresponding to $N = 25$ is halved because of the proximity of the water table to the foundation.) Therefore it will be convenient to adopt a slab width equal to the width of the tank.

EXAMPLE 2.2

Strip foundations supporting a wall are to be constructed on a medium dense silty fine sand. The loading on the foundations is 100 kN per metre run. The water table is 3 m below ground level and records show that it does not rise above this height. Triaxial compression tests on undisturbed samples showed that the cohesion of the sand was 12 kN/m² and its angle of shearing resistance 25°. The natural densities of the dry and saturated soils were 1·75 and 1·90 Mg/m³ respectively. Determine the required foundation depth and width.

FOUNDATION DEPTH. Appreciable movements due to seasonal rainfall or temperature conditions do not occur in a sandy soil. Therefore a foundation depth of 0·7 m should be satisfactory from the point of view of surface erosion by winds, and the need to have the foundation level below any excavations for drains or other services entering the building.

BEARING PRESSURE. For an angle of shearing resistance of 25° the value of $N_c$, $N_q$, and $N_\gamma$ from Fig. 2.9 are 24, 13, and 9 respectively. Take $B = 1·0$ m. For $D = 0·7$ m we have from equation 2.5a—

Net ultimate bearing capacity

$$= q_{nf} = 12 \times 24 + \{1·75 \times 0·7 \times (13 - 1) + \tfrac{1}{2} \times 1·75 \times 1·0 \times 9\}$$
$$\times 9·807 = 509 \text{ kN/m}^2$$

For a safety factor of 3, allowable bearing pressure

$$= q_a = \frac{509}{3}$$
$$= 170 \text{ kN/m}^2$$

For 100 kN per metre run of loading, required foundation width

$$= \frac{100}{170} = 0·59 \text{ m}$$

Therefore our first approximation of $B = 1·0$ m was over-conservative. Take B = 0·6 m, and substitute again in equation 2.5a—

$$q_{nf} = 12 \times 24 + \{1·75 \times 0·7 \times (13 - 1) + \tfrac{1}{2} \times 1·75$$
$$\times 0·6 \times 9\} \times 9·807 = 478 \text{ kN/m}^2$$

For a safety factor of 3, $q_a = \dfrac{478}{3} = 159 \text{ kN/m}^2$

Required foundation width $= \dfrac{100}{159} = 0·63$ m, say 0·60 m nominal.

The combined weight of wall, wall footing, and strip foundation minus the weight of soil displaced by the foundation must not exceed 159 kN/m$^2$ or approximately 100 kN per metre of footing.

The dry density of 1·75 Mg/m$^3$ was taken in the above calculations since the water table was too low to influence the bearing capacity.

If the water table rises to within 0·3 m of ground level,

$$\text{Then } p = \gamma_{dry}(D - h) + \gamma_{sat}h = \{1\cdot75\,(0\cdot7 - 0\cdot4) + 1\cdot90 \times 0\cdot4\}$$
$$\times\ 9\cdot807$$
$$= 12\cdot5 \text{ kN/m}^2$$

and from equation 2.1, $p_o = p - \gamma_w h = 12\cdot5 - 1\cdot0 \times 0\cdot4 \times 9\cdot807$
$$= 8\cdot6 \text{ kN/m}^2$$

Substituting in equation 2.5a—
  Net ultimate bearing capacity

$$= q_{nf} = 12 \times 24 + 8\cdot6\,(13 - 1) + \tfrac{1}{2}\,(1\cdot90 - 1.00) \times 0\cdot60$$
$$\times\ 9 \times 9\cdot807$$
$$= 415 \text{ kN/m}^2$$

Therefore the safety factor for 159 kN/m$^2$ bearing pressure has been reduced to $\dfrac{415}{159} = 2\cdot6$.

### EXAMPLE 2.3

A public building consists of a high central tower with three-storey wings projecting on each side. The central tower structure is carried by four widely spaced columns each carrying a combined dead load and representative sustained live load of 2500 kN inclusive of the substructure. Trial borings showed that below a shallow surface layer of topsoil was stiff fissured London Clay followed by dense sand. Tests made on undisturbed samples from several boreholes gave a shear strength–depth relationship shown in Fig. 2.38. For an $E/c$ ratio of 400 the $E$ value at foundation level is, conservatively, 30 MN/m$^2$. Determine the required foundation depths and allowable bearing pressures for the tower and the three-storey wings.

Because of the difference in loading conditions between the tower and the wings, we shall have to investigate the possibility of differential settlement between these parts of the building.

Dealing first with the central tower, inspection of Fig. 2.38 shows that it will be desirable to take the column foundations to a depth of about 2 m to take advantage of the stiffer soil. Founding at a higher level would require excessively large foundations, thus complicating

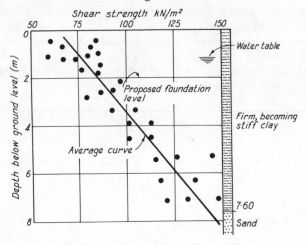

FIG. 2.38. SHEAR STRENGTH–DEPTH CURVE

the foundations of the wings at their junction with the tower. At a depth of 2 m the fissured shear strength is about 85 kN/m².

The approximate bearing capacity factor $N_c$ for shallow square or circular foundations is 7·5. Therefore from equation 2.11,

Ultimate bearing capacity, $q_f = 85 \times 7.5 + 37 = 675$ kN/m²

As the fissured shear strength is considerably below the average shear strength a safety factor of 2·5 should be adequate to keep the settlements within tolerable limits, and therefore the presumed bearing value will be about 270 kN/m².

$$Required\ size\ of\ column\ foundation = \frac{2500}{270} = 9.3\ \text{m}^2$$

say 3 m square

It is now necessary to check the bearing capacity factor by referring to Fig. 2.11.

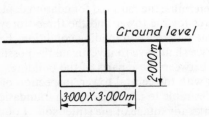

FIG. 2.39. FOUNDATION ARRANGEMENT FOR TOWER

For $\qquad \dfrac{D}{B} = \dfrac{2}{3} = 0.66 \qquad N_c = 7.6$

Therefore it is unnecessary to change our presumed bearing value of 270 kN/m². The foundation arrangement is shown in Fig. 2.39. We must now calculate the total settlement under this pressure.

CALCULATION OF NET IMMEDIATE SETTLEMENT AT CENTRE OF LOADED AREA.

Net foundation pressure $q_n = 270 - 1.90 \times 2 \times 9.807$
$$= 233 \text{ kN/m}^2$$
Influence factor, for $m = 0.5$, is $I_p = F_1$. From Fig. 2.31,

$$F_1 = 0.46 \text{ for } \frac{2L}{B} = 2, \text{ and } \frac{2H}{B} = \frac{2 \times 5.6}{3} = 3.7$$

From equation 2.27, $\rho_i = \dfrac{233 \times 6 \times 0.75 \times 0.46 \times 1000}{30 \times 1000}$ mm

$$= 16 \text{ mm}$$

Checking immediate settlement from equation 2.30, for $\dfrac{L}{B} = 1$,

$\dfrac{H}{B} = \dfrac{5.6}{3} = 1.9$, and $\dfrac{D}{B} = \dfrac{2}{3} = 0.66, \mu_1 = 0.57$ and $\mu_0 = 0.80$ (Fig. 2.23)

Therefore $\rho_i = \dfrac{0.57 \times 0.80 \times 233 \times 3 \times 1000}{30 \times 1000} = 11 \text{ mm}$

The higher value of 16 mm will be taken.

From Fig. 2.30, depth factor for $D\sqrt{ab} = 0.66$ is $0.80$.
Therefore corrected settlement $= 0.80 \times 16 = 12.8$ mm, say 15 mm. Since the immediate settlement is small it will not be worthwhile to reduce it by a rigidity factor (p. 133).

CALCULATION OF CONSOLIDATION SETTLEMENT $\rho_c$. The soil above the water table will be nearly saturated and allowing for hydrostatic uplift in the clay below the water table, we have—

Original overburden pressure before applying foundation loading,

$$p_o = [1.90 \times 1.2 + (1.90 - 1.00) \, 0.8] \times 9.807$$
$$= 29 \text{ kN/m}^2$$

As already calculated, net foundation pressure, $q_n = 233$ kN/m². We must now calculate the distribution of effective overburden

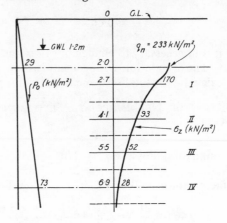

FIG. 2.40. VERTICAL PRESSURE DISTRIBUTION

pressure $p_o$ and the induced vertical stress $\sigma_z$ throughout the full depth of the clay stratum as shown in Fig. 2.40. The vertical stress distribution is obtained from the factors shown in Fig. 2.23. Since we have only one consolidation test result we must base our calculations for $\rho_c$ on the $p$–$e$ curve shown in Fig. 2.41. Because the clay stratum is relatively thick, we must divide it into 1·4 m thick horizontal layers, and calculate separately the settlement for each layer. The calculation is shown in tabular form on page 145.

To obtain the net consolidation settlement $\rho_c$ we must reduce the oedometer settlement $\rho_{oed}$ by a factor which we can take as 0·5 for London Clay.

Therefore, $\qquad \rho_c = 0\cdot5 \times 43 = 22$ mm

$\rho_c$ can be reduced by a depth factor (*see* p. 129). From Fig. 2.30, depth factor for $D/\sqrt{ab} = 0\cdot66$ is 0·80. Therefore corrected settlement is $22 \times 0\cdot80 = 18$ mm.

CALCULATION OF RATE OF CONSOLIDATION SETTLEMENT. From laboratory tests, coefficient of consolidation $c_v = 0\cdot0139 \times 10^{-6} \mathrm{m^2/s}$. The sand underlying the clay acts as a drainage layer, and also the concrete of the foundation can be taken as being more pervious than the clay; thus the drainage is in two directions. Since the sand is much more pervious than the concrete, the majority of the water expelled during the process of consolidation will travel downwards to the sand layer. However, for the purposes of calculating the rate of settlement it will be sufficiently accurate to assume equal drainage in each direction.

Calculation of Consolidation Settlement for Each Layer

| Layer no. | Depth of layer (m) | Depth to centre of layer (m) | Thickness of layer $H$ (m) | Original effective overburden pressure $p_o$ at centre of layer ($kN/m^2$) | Vertical stress $\sigma_z$ due to net pressure $q_n$ ($kN/m^2$) | Resultant effective pressure at centre of layer $p_o + \sigma_z$ ($kN/m^2$) | Voids ratio at $p_o$ $e_1$ | Voids ratio at $p_o + \sigma_z$ $e_2$ | $\dfrac{e_1 - e_2}{1 + e_1}$ | Settlement of layer (mm) $= \dfrac{e_1 - e_2}{1 + e_1} \times H \times 1000$ |
|---|---|---|---|---|---|---|---|---|---|---|
| 1 | 2·0–3·4 | 2·7 | 1·4 | 36 | 170 | 206 | 0·858 | 0·827 | 0·0167 | 23 |
| 2 | 3·4–4·8 | 4·1 | 1·4 | 48 | 93 | 141 | 0·856 | 0·839 | 0·0092 | 13 |
| 3 | 4·8–6·2 | 5·5 | 1·4 | 60 | 52 | 112 | 0·855 | 0·848 | 0·0038 | 5 |
| 4 | 6·2–7·6 | 6·9 | 1·4 | 73 | 28 | 101 | 0·854 | 0·851 | 0·0016 | 2 |

Total oedometer settlement of clay layer $\rho_{oed} =$  43 mm

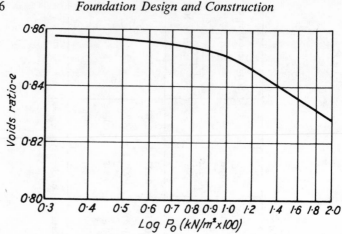

FIG. 2.41. PRESSURE–VOIDS RATIO CURVE

For two-way drainage, the time factors $T_{50}$ and $T_{90}$ for 50 and 90 per cent consolidation from the Type 1 $U_1$–$T$ curve in Fig. 2.33 are—

$$T_{50} = 0.20$$

$$T_{90} = 0.85$$

$$d = \frac{H}{2} = 2.8 \text{ m}$$

Therefore, by equation 2.31a, time required for 50 per cent consolidation,

$$t_{50} = \frac{T_{50}d^2 \times 10^{-7}}{3.154 \times c_v}$$

$$= \frac{0.20 \times 2.8^2 \times 10^{-7}}{3.154 \times 0.0139 \times 10^{-6}} = \underline{\underline{3.5 \text{ years (approx.)}}}$$

Similarly, $\quad t_{90} = \dfrac{0.85 \times 2.8^2 \times 10^{-7}}{3.154 \times 0.0139 \times 10^{-6}} = 15 \text{ years (approx.)}$

Net total settlement after 4 years
$\quad = \rho_i + 50\% \, \rho_c$
$\quad = 15 + 0.5 \times 18,$
$\quad$ say 25 mm

Net total settlement after 20 years
$\quad = 15 + \dfrac{90}{100} \times 18,$
$\quad$ say 30 mm

With the relatively small order of settlement there is no particular need to calculate the rate of settlement over the construction period or to draw a time–settlement curve.

If the sand stratum were not present, drainage would be one-way only (i.e. vertically upwards). We would then use the Type 3 $U_3$–$T$ curve in Fig. 2.33. From this curve—

$$T_{50} = 0\cdot09$$

$$T_{90} = 0\cdot72$$

and $$d = H = 5\cdot6 \text{ m}$$

Therefore, time required for 50 per cent consolidation—

$$t_{50} = \frac{0\cdot09 \times 5\cdot6^2 \times 10^{-7}}{3\cdot154 \times 0\cdot0139 \times 10^{-6}}$$

$$= \underline{\underline{6\cdot5 \text{ years (approx.)}}}$$

Similarly $$t_{90} = \frac{0\cdot72 \times 5\cdot6^2 \times 10^{-7}}{3\cdot154 \times 0\cdot0139 \times 10^{-6}}$$

$$= \underline{\underline{50 \text{ years (approx.)}}}$$

STRIP FOUNDATION TO THREE-STOREY WINGS. Since the structure is founded on a stiff fissured clay it will be subject to seasonal swell and shrinkage. Since this is a public building, presumably with high standards of finish and workmanship, any cracking due to seasonal movements would be unsightly. If we take the foundations to 1·2 m depth this will get below the zone of any soil movement. However, this is the water table level and we do not want the clay in the foundation trench bottom to become puddled and soft during excavation. Therefore it is best to select a foundation level a few inches above the water table, i.e. at 1·15 m. From Fig. 2.38 the fissured shear strength at this level is 75 kN/m².

For a shallow strip foundation, the net ultimate bearing capacity $q_{nf}$ is of the order of 6 × shear strength. Therefore,

$$q_{nf} = 6 \times 75 = 450 \text{ kN/m}^2$$

For a net loading of 120 kN/m run of wall and a safety factor of 2·5, the approximate foundation width $B$ will be given by—

$$B = \frac{120 \times 2\cdot5}{450} = 0\cdot66 \text{ m}$$

Using this first approximation of the width, the bearing capacity factor $N_c$ is read from Fig. 2.11 for the depth width ratio $\dfrac{D}{B}$ of

$$\frac{1 \cdot 15}{0 \cdot 66} = 1 \cdot 75$$

Fig. 2.11 gives $N_c = 7 \cdot 9$, and using this value,

$$q_{nf} = 7 \cdot 9 \times 75 = 592 \text{ kN/m}^2$$

Therefore, with a safety factor of $2 \cdot 5$,

$$\text{Required foundation width} = \frac{120 \times 2 \cdot 5}{592} = 0 \cdot 51 \text{ m}$$

In practice we shall require a wider foundation, since the base of the wall will be in 328 mm of brickwork, and we must have our concrete foundation 150 mm wider than the wall on each side to give room for the bricklayers to work in the trench. Therefore,

$$\text{Actual design foundation width} = 328 + 2 \times 150$$
$$= 628 \text{ mm}$$

$$\text{Actual bearing pressure} = \frac{120}{0 \cdot 63} = 190 \text{ kN/m}^2$$

For $\qquad \dfrac{D}{B} = \dfrac{1 \cdot 15}{0 \cdot 63} = 1 \cdot 8$, $N_c$ from Fig. 2.11 is $8 \cdot 0$

Therefore, $\quad q_{nf} = 8 \cdot 0 \times 75 = 600 \text{ kN/m}^2$

$$\text{Actual safety factor} = \frac{600}{190} = 3 \cdot 15$$

With this safety factor the settlements are likely to be small, but it will be advisable to get a rough idea of the settlement in order to estimate the differential movement between the tower and the wings. Using the approximate method given on page 137, we get from equation 2.33—

$$\rho_{oed} = 0 \cdot 0001 \times 0 \cdot 55 \times 190 \times 1 \cdot 5 \times 628$$

(obtaining value of $m_v$ from Fig. 2.41)

$$= 10 \text{ mm}$$

The general order of *total* settlement of the wings will therefore be roughly between 10 and 15 mm.

Thus the differential settlement between tower and wings will be negligible.

### EXAMPLE 2.4

Columns supporting a steel-framed workshop building with steel sheet cladding carry a load of 320 kN. Borings show estuarine clay extending to a depth of 20 m or more. Determinations of shear strength by tests on undisturbed samples gave an average shear strength of 40 kN/m² below a 1·2 m thick crust of desiccated stiff clay. Calculate the allowable bearing pressure and required size and depth of the column foundations.

The surface crust of stiff clay is typical of estuarine conditions but we cannot utilize it to support the column foundations because the minimum width of the bases will cause shear stresses to be set up in the underlying firm clay. The shear strength and compressibility of the latter will govern the allowable bearing pressure.

FOUNDATION DEPTH. A foundation depth of 1·1 m is desirable to get below the zone affected by seasonal moisture changes and below the level of ducts and other services below the workshop floor.

BEARING PRESSURES. As a first approximation the bearing capacity factor $N_c$ for a pad foundation will be about 7·5.

$$\text{Net ultimate bearing capacity } q_{nf} = 7\cdot5 \times 40 = 300 \text{ kN/m}^2$$

For a safety factor of 3, the required width $B$ of a square foundation is given by—

$$B = \sqrt{\left(\frac{320 \times 3}{300}\right)} = 1\cdot79 \text{ m}$$

Checking the bearing capacity factor from Fig. 2.11 we have

$$\frac{D}{B} = \frac{1\cdot10}{1\cdot79} = 0\cdot6$$

This gives $N_c = 7\cdot5$ which is the value assumed in our first approximation.

Practical dimensions of the column base are 1·80 × 1·80 m.

$$\text{Actual bearing pressure} = \frac{320}{1\cdot8^2} = 99 \text{ kN/m}^2$$

$$\text{Safety factor} = \frac{300}{99} = 3$$

In view of the fairly large size of the base it will be advisable to consider possible settlements. For a firm estuarine clay the value of $m_v$ from Table 1.3 will be about 0·0003 to 0·001. From equation 2.33

$$\rho_{oed} = 0·0003 \times 0·55 \times 99 \times 1·5 \times 1·8 \times 1000 = 44 \text{ mm}$$

Therefore the settlement is likely to be more than 40 mm but less than 120 mm. Since the building is in steel-frame construction and with steel sheet cladding, it is not sensitive to differential settlement of the order of 50 to 75 mm. Therefore the dimensions of 7·80 m square should be satisfactory.

EXAMPLE 2·5

Calculate the immediate and long-term settlement of a bridge pier with a base 8·50 m long by 7·50 m wide, founded at a depth of 3·0 m. The base of the pier imposes net foundation pressures of 220 kN/m² for dead loading and 360 kN/m² for combined dead and live loading. Borings showed dense sand and gravel with cobbles and boulders to a depth of 9 m below ground level, followed by very stiff over-consolidated clay to more than 25 m below ground level. Because of the presence of large gravel cobbles and boulders it was impossible to make any static or dynamic penetration tests. However, plate bearing tests were made in pits at two locations ($A$ and $B$) at depths of 3 m and 4·5 m below ground level. A number of oedometer tests were made on samples of the stiff clay. Triaxial tests on undisturbed samples of the clay gave a minimum shear strength of 120 kN/m², and a modulus of elasticity ($E$) of 40 MN/m².

CALCULATING IMMEDIATE SETTLEMENTS IN SAND AND GRAVEL STRATUM. The settlements of the 300 mm test plate corresponding to 220 kN/m² and 360 kN/m² loading were obtained from the load settlement curves as shown in the table on p. 151.

From the average values of $S_0$ in the table we can determine the settlement of the 7·50 m wide pier base from Fig. 2.25.

Settlement of 7·50 m wide foundation $= 4 \times S_0$.

(i.e. from $D/D_0 = 25$ and corresponding value of $S/S_0 = 4$ taken between average curve and lowest curve for densest soils.)

These settlements will take place as the dead load on the pier base is built up during the construction of the bridge and as the live loading is increased to its maximum value.

| Test | Depth below ground level (m) | Settlement ($S_0$) of 300 mm square plate (mm) | |
| :---: | :---: | :---: | :---: |
| | | 220 kN/m² pressure | 360 kN/m² pressure |
| A | 3 | 1 | 4 |
| | 4·5 | 2 | 7 |
| B | 3 | 2 | 5 |
| | 4·5 | 1 | 4 |
| Average $S_0$ = | | <u>1·5 mm</u> | <u>5·0 mm</u> |

Settlement for 220 kN/m² loading = 4 × 1·50 = <u>6 mm</u>

Settlement for 360 kN/m² loading = 4 × 5·0 = <u>20 mm</u>

BEARING CAPACITY OF STIFF CLAY

The vertical stress distribution curves (Fig. 2.42) from the curves for rigid foundations (Fig. 2.23) show that the vertical stress on the surface of the clay is 137 kN/m² for combined dead and live loading. The bearing capacity factor from Fig. 2.11 for a foundation 12 m wide at a depth of 9 m (on the surface of the clay) is 7·7. Thus the ultimate bearing capacity of the clay is 7·7 × 120 = 924 kN/m² which gives an ample safety factor against shear failure in the clay. However, it will be necessary to calculate the immediate and long-term consolidation settlements of the clay stratum to ensure that the total settlements of the bridge pier are not excessive.

CALCULATING SETTLEMENTS IN CLAY STRATUM. From the vertical stress distribution curves (Fig. 2.42) the stresses transmitted to the surface of the clay stratum are 83 and 137 kN/m² for the 220 and 360 kN/m² loadings respectively. These are transmitted over an area of approximately 12 by 15 m. The vertical stress below 18 m is only 10 per cent of the applied stress. Therefore we need not consider settlements below a depth of 18 m.

From equation 2.27, in centre of loaded area—

$$\text{Net immediate settlement} = \rho_i = \frac{q_n \times 2B \times (1 - m^2)I_p}{E} \text{ mm}$$

Taking $m = 0.5$, Fig. 2.32 gives $I_p = 0.20$ for $\dfrac{2H}{B} = \dfrac{18}{12} = 1.5$ and $\dfrac{2L}{B} = \dfrac{30}{12} = 2.5$. The immediate settlements must be reduced by a depth factor which, from Fig. 2.30 for $D/\sqrt{ab} = 0.68$, is $0.8$.

Thus, for 220 kN/m² loading,

$$\rho_i = 0.8 \times \frac{83 \times 24 \times 0.75 \times 0.20 \times 1000}{40 \times 1000} = 6\ \text{mm}$$

and for 360 kN/m² loading,

$$\rho_i = 0.8 \times \frac{137 \times 24 \times 0.75 \times 0.20 \times 1000}{40 \times 1000} = 10\ \text{mm}$$

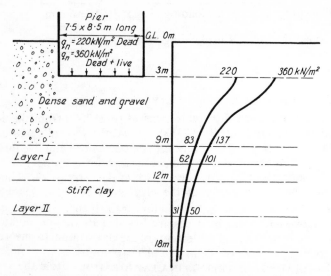

FIG. 2.42. VERTICAL STRESS DISTRIBUTION FROM PIER LOADING
(STRESS IN TON/FT²)

CALCULATION OF NET CONSOLIDATION SETTLEMENTS. Since a number of consolidation tests were made we can use the coefficient of volume compressibility ($m_v$) for calculating the oedometer settlement ($\rho_{oed}$). The 9 m thick clay layer which is appreciably affected by the foundation pressures is divided into a 3 m thick layer from 9 to 12 m below ground level and a 6 m thick layer from 12 to 18 m below ground level. The $m_v$ values corresponding to the respective increments of pressure in each layer are shown in the table below. The oedometer settlement is calculated from

$$\rho_{oed} = m_v \sigma_z H \qquad \text{(eqn. 2.23)}$$

and the net consolidation settlement from

$$\rho_c = \mu \rho_{oed} \qquad \text{(eqn. 2.22)}$$

Since this is an overconsolidated clay, we can take $\mu = 0.5$ and the depth factor as before $= 0.8$. The calculations for $\rho_{oed}$ are:

| Net foundation pressure $q_n$ (kN/m²) | Depth of layer below ground level (m) | Thickness of layer (m) | $m_v$ (m²/kN) | Average vertical stress on layer $\sigma_z$ (kN/m²) | Oedometer settlement $\rho_{oed}$ (mm) |
|---|---|---|---|---|---|
| 220 | 9–12 | 3 | 0·00011 | 62 | 20 |
|     | 12–18 | 6 | 0·00003 | 31 | 6 |
| 360 | 9–12 | 3 | 0·00020 | 101 | 61 |
|     | 12–18 | 6 | 0·00004 | 50 | 12 |

From the above table—

Total consolidation settlement for 220 kN/m² load

$$= 0.8 \times 0.5 \times (20 + 6) = 10 \text{ mm}$$

Total consolidation settlement for 360 kN/m² load

$$= 0.8 \times 0.5 \times (61 + 12) = 29 \text{ mm}$$

SUMMARIZING TOTAL SETTLEMENTS. The total final settlement of the bridge pier is given by—

$\rho_f =$ Immediate settlement in sand and gravel

+ Immediate settlement in clay

+ Consolidation settlement in clay

For *dead loading* of 220 kN/m²—

$$\rho_f = 6 + 6 + 10 = 22, \underline{\underline{\text{say 25 mm}}}$$

For *combined dead and live loading* of 360 kN/m²—

$$\rho_f = 20 + 10 + 29 = 59, \underline{\underline{\text{say 60 mm}}}$$

A settlement of 15 mm will take place as the pier is constructed and this will increase to about 30 mm if and when the bridge sustains its maximum live load. The remaining settlement due to long-term consolidation of the clay under the dead load and sustained live load may take one hundred years or more to attain its final value of 30 mm.

EXAMPLE 2.6

If the foundation in the previous example is a flexible raft calculate the pressure distribution beneath the centre of the raft on the surface of the stiff clay stratum for the net foundation pressures of 220 kN/m² and 360 kN/m².

Referring to Fig. 2.24 the raft can be divided into four equal rectangles each 4·25 × 3·75 m. Using Newmark's coefficients (Table 2.4), for—

$$\frac{B}{z} = \frac{3\cdot75}{6} = 0\cdot62, \quad \text{and} \quad \frac{L}{z} = \frac{4\cdot25}{6} = 0\cdot71, \quad \text{coefficient} = 0\cdot12$$

Therefore, for 220 kN/m² loading, vertical stress at corner $= \sigma_z = 0\cdot12 \times 220$.

Vertical stress at centre $= 4 \times 0\cdot12 \times 220 = \underline{\underline{105 \text{ kN/m}^2}}$.

For 360 kN/m² loading, vertical stress at centre $= 4 \times 0\cdot12 \times 360 = \underline{\underline{173 \text{ kN/m}^2}}$.

This may be compared with the values of 83 and 137 kN/m² respectively calculated for the rigid foundation in Example 2.5.

REFERENCES

2.1  HANSEN, J. BRINCH, A revised and extended formula for bearing capacity, *Danish Geotechnical Institute*, Bulletin No. 28, October, 1968.

2.2  TERZAGHI, K., *Theoretical Soil Mechanics* (New York, J. Wiley, 1943).

2.3  MEYERHOF, G. G., The ultimate bearing capacity of foundations, *Geotechnique*, **2**, No. 4, pp. 301–332 (1951).

2.4  *Soil Mechanics in Engineering Practice*, p. 107.

2.5  *Soil Mechanics in Engineering Practice*, p. 491.

2.6  GIBBS, H. J. and HOLTZ, W. G., Research on determining the density of sands by spoon penetration testing, *Proc. 4th Int. Conf. Soil Mech.*, **1**, pp. 35–39 (London, 1957).

2.7  DE BEER, E., Données concernant la résistance au cisaillement déduites des essais de pénétration en profondeur, *Géotechnique*, **1**, No. 1, p. 22.

2.8  MEYERHOF, G. G., Penetration tests and bearing capacity of cohesionless soils, Paper No. 866, *J. Soil Mech. and Found. Div. Amer. Soc. Civ. Eng.* (1956).

2.9  SKEMPTON, A. W. and MACDONALD, D. H., The allowable settlement of buildings, *Proc. Inst. C.E.*, **5**, No. 3, Pt. 3, pp. 727–784 (Dec., 1956).

2.10 BJERRUM, L., Discussion on compressibility of soils, *Proc. Europ. Conf. Soil Mech. and Found. Eng.*, *Wiesbaden*, 1963, **2**, pp. 16–17.

2.11 MEYERHOF, G. G., The settlement analysis of building frames, *Struct. Eng.*, **25**, p. 309 (1947).

2.12 THOMAS, F. G., The strength of brickwork, *Struct Eng.*, **31**, No. 2, pp. 35–46 (Feb., 1953).

2.13 ZEEVART, L., Foundation design and behaviour of Tower Latino Americana Building in Mexico City, *Geotechnique*, **7**, No. 3, pp. 115–133 (Sept, 1957).

2.14 MEASOR, E. O. and WILLIAMS, G. M. J., Features in the design and Construction of the Shell Centre, London, *Proc. Inst. C.E.*, **21**, pp. 475–502 (Mar. 1962).

2.15 JURGENSON, L., The application of theories of elasticity and plasticity to foundation problems, *J. Boston Soc. C.E.*, **21**, pp. 206–211 (1934).

2.16 FOX, E. N., The mean elastic settlement of a uniformly loaded area at a depth below the ground surface, *Proc. 2nd Int. Conf. Soil Mech.* **1**, pp. 129–132 (Rotterdam, 1948).

2.17 NEWMARK, N. M., Simplified computations of vertical pressure in elastic foundations, *Univ. Ill. Eng. Expt. Station, Bul. No. 429* (1935).

2.18 *Soil Mechanics in Engineering Practice*, pp. 271–276.

2.19 BJERRUM, L. and EGGESTAD, A., Interpretation of loading tests on sand, *Proc. Eur. Conf. Soil Mech. and Found. Eng.*, *Wiesbaden*, 1963.

2.20 DE BEER, E. and MARTENS, A., Method of computation of an upper limit for the influence of the heterogeneity of sand layers in the settlement of bridges, *Proc. 4th Int. Conf. Soil Mech.* (London), **1**, pp. 275–282.

2.21 SCHMERTMANN, J. H., Static cone to compute static settlement over sand, *J. Soil Mech. and Found. Div. Amer. Soc. Civ. Eng.*, **96**, SM3, pp. 1011–1043 (May, 1970).

2.22 SKEMPTON, A. W. and BJERRUM, L., A contribution to the settlement analysis of foundations on clay, *Géotechnique*, **7**, No. 4, pp. 168–178 (Dec., 1957).

2.23 *Soil Mechanics in Engineering Practice*, pp. 56–78 and 233–244.

2.24 TERZAGHI, K., *Theoretical Soil Mechanics*, p. 425 (New York, J. Wiley, 1943).

2.25 STEINBRENNER, W., Tafeln zur Setzungsberechnung, *Die Strasse*, **1**, 121–24 (1934).

2.26 BUTLER, F. G., Heavily overconsolidated clays, General report, Session 3, *Proc. Conf. on Settlement of Structures*, Cambridge, Pentech Press, 1974.

2.27 BJERRUM, L., Problems of soil mechanics and construction on soft clays and structurally unstable soils, General report, *Proc. 8th Int. Conf. Soil Mech.*, **3**, pp. 111–159 (Moscow, 1973).

2.28 JANBU, N., BJERRUM, L. and KJAERNSLI, B., Veiledning Ved Iøsning avfundamenteringsoppgarer, *Publ. No. 16 Norwegian Geotech. Inst.*, Oslo, 1956.

# 3

# Foundation Design in Relation to Ground Movements

In the previous chapter we have considered foundation design in relation to bearing capacity and consolidation of the soil. However, ground movements which are independent of stresses imposed by the foundation loading can occur. Examples of these are movements due to swell and shrinkage of the soil under varying moisture and temperature conditions, frost heave, hillside creep, mining and regional subsidence and settlements due to shock and vibration.

It is necessary to take precautions against the effects of these movements on the structure, either by deepening the foundations to place them on ground which is not susceptible to movement, or if this is not economically possible, to adopt special forms of construction which will allow appreciable movement without damaging the structure.

The various types of ground movement are described in this chapter and the foundation designs appropriate to these movements are discussed.

## SOIL MOVEMENTS

### Wetting and Drying of Clay Soils

Some types of clay soil show marked swelling with increase of moisture content, followed by shrinkage after drying out. In Great

156

Britain, the clays showing this characteristic are mainly the stiff fissured heavy clays such as the London, Gault, Weald, Kimmeridge, Oxford and Lias Clays, and the clays of the Woolwich and Reading Beds. The leaner glacial clays and marshy clays do not show marked swell and shrinkage, except for the chalky boulder clay of East Anglia which is derived from the stiff fissured clays mentioned above. The effect of this seasonal volume change is to cause a rise and fall in the ground surface accompanied by tension cracks in the soil in drying periods and closing of the cracks in the wet season. The results of measurements made by the Building Research Station at Garston, Hertfordshire,[3.1] on plates buried at various depths below the ground surface are shown in Fig. 3.1.

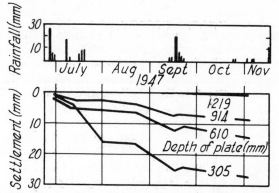

FIG. 3.1. MOVEMENT OF BURIED PLATES AT VARIOUS DEPTHS BELOW GROUND LEVEL IN LONDON CLAY AT GARSTON, HERTS (COOLING AND WARD[3.1])

The movement at a depth of 1·2 m below ground level was less than 6 mm in a year which was drier than normal for British conditions. It was concluded by the Building Research Station[3.2] that foundations placed at a depth of 1·1 to 1·2 m below ground level in shrinkable clay soils should be little affected by swell and shrinkage movement. The general practice is to place foundations of structures which are not particularly sensitive to movements, e.g. ordinary dwelling houses, at a depth of 0·9 m below ground level. It is desirable to go deeper in the case of foundations of structures sensitive to small movements, say for buildings with expensive wall finishes.

Precautions are also necessary in the construction of ground floors on shrinkable clays. Although it is a reasonable precaution to take strip or pad foundations to a depth of 0·9 to 1·2 m below ground level, it will be uneconomical to excavate to this depth for the full ground floor area of a building. The most effective and economical procedure is to allow freedom of movement between the foundation walls and ground floor slab. Following the very dry summer of 1959, the ground floor slabs of houses in Hertfordshire were lifted some 5 to 20 mm above the foundation brickwork due to swelling of the clay in the autumn rains. The concrete floors were cast against the brickwork without any separating membrane, with the result that the brickwork was lifted, forming wide horizontal cracks around the foundation walls. It is also desirable to provide some form of drainage of hardcore or gravel filling below solid ground floors on clay soils, since accumulations of water at the construction stage (before the building is roofed-in) will cause long-term swelling of the clay, resulting in upheaval of the floors and walls carried by them.

## CLIMATIC FACTORS

There are, however, two further factors which greatly increase the problem of swell and shrinkage and which may necessitate special methods of foundation design. The first factor is the effect of a wide difference in seasonal rainfall and soil temperature conditions. These conditions are met in the Sudan, the Levant coast of the Mediterranean, South Africa, and in the south-western parts of the United States of America.

Seasonal differences in the moisture content of the clay soil at Lydda airport in Israel are shown in Fig. 3.2 and measured ground movements at various depths at Leuhof, South Africa,[3.3] are shown in Fig. 3.3.

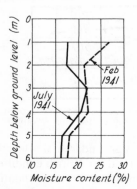

FIG. 3.2. SEASONAL DIFFERENCES IN MOISTURE CONTENT IN CLAY SOIL, ISRAEL

In Israel and Jordan, the winter rainfall from October to April amounts to about 600 mm, while the months of May to September are practically rainless. The measurements shown in Fig. 3.2 were made by the Palestine Public Works Department after well-built dwelling houses on the airport had cracked severely soon after construction. It will be noted that appreciable moisture content changes occur to a depth of 3 m below ground level. Although the soil type is a silty clay, it is not a particularly heavy clay, having a liquid limit of about 50 per cent. It should be noted that the severe movement is due almost wholly to the climatic conditions rather than to the type of clay.

EFFECTS OF VEGETATION

The second factor which aggravates the swell and shrinkage problem is the effect of the roots of vegetation. The roots of trees and shrubs can extract considerable quantities of water from the soil. Cooling and Ward[3.1] have noted that root systems of isolated trees spread to a radius greater than the height of the tree, and in southern England they have caused significant drying of fat clay soils to a depth of about 3 m. Differential movements of 100 mm have been recorded in houses 25 m from a row of black poplars.

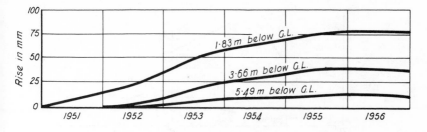

FIG. 3.3. MOVEMENTS OF MEASURING POINTS AT VARIOUS DEPTHS BELOW GROUND LEVEL AT LEUHOF, SOUTH AFRICA (COLLINS[3.3])

The problems caused by root systems are two-fold. First there is the problem of foundations on sites which have recently been cleared of trees and hedges, and secondly there is the problem of cracking in existing structures caused by subsequent planting of trees and shrubs close to them.

The pronounced shrinkage which accompanies removal of water from clay soils can take place both vertically and horizontally. Thus, precautions must be taken not only against settlement but also against forces tending to tear the foundations apart.

An example of movements following clearance of vegetation was the cracking of a block of flats in south-west London in 1952. The site of the buildings had been crossed by a well-grown hedgerow which was grubbed up about one month before the foundation excavation was commenced. The brick footings of the cracked block were constructed in June and July during a fairly long dry spell. August was a rainy month, and by September the dried-out clay soil in the vicinity of the root system had absorbed moisture to such an extent that the corner of the building nearest to the hedge line had risen by 25 mm, causing severe cracking of the foundations and walls before construction had been taken above first floor level. Levels taken along the ground floor are shown in Fig. 3.4.

As already mentioned, foundations constructed at depths of 0·9 to 1·2 m are satisfactory for sites in shrinkable clays in Great Britain where the soil is not affected by trees or shrubs. Where trees and hedgerows are cleared from a site swelling of the desiccated clay can continue for a very long period of years until the moisture content reaches equilibrium with the surrounding ground. Samuels and Cheney[3.3a] observed swelling of London Clay continuing over a period of 20 years after cutting down mature trees. The soil beneath

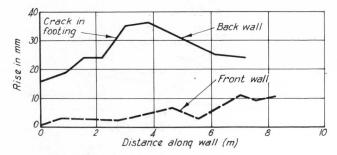

FIG. 3.4. RISE IN 1·22 m DEEP STRIP FOUNDATION DUE TO SWELLING OF CLAY FOLLOWING REMOVAL OF HEDGEROW CLOSE TO WALL OF BUILDING IN SURREY, 1952

areas previously occupied by old buildings and paved areas must also be allowed to come to an equilibrium moisture content with the adjoining uncovered ground.

### PILED FOUNDATIONS

Delays of 20 years or more after cutting down trees on a clay site are not usually admissible and the only satisfactory procedure is to adopt piled foundations as described on p. 527. It must be remembered that swelling takes place beneath the ground floor of a building as well as beneath the foundations and to avoid damage by uplift to the interior of the building it is essential to provide a suspended floor carried by the piles. A clear space should be left beneath the floor and alongside ground beams. In South Africa and Israel bored piles are extensively used even for light single-storey structures. The design of foundations of this type must take into consideration appreciable uplift forces which result from the adhesion of the clay to the pile shaft when the soil is swelling in the rainy season. Reinforcement must be provided to prevent transverse cracking and lifting of the pile shaft as discussed in Chapter 8. To economize in the shaft length required to resist bearing and uplift forces it is usual to provide an under-reamed bulb end on the bottom of the pile (Fig. 3.5).

Piled foundations have been found to be more economical than rafts for the foundations of houses in swelling clays in Western Canada.[3.3b] In these desiccated clays the swelling can occur at a rate of 25 mm a year for several years. It is usually the result of watering gardens. Where there have been plumbing leaks swelling has been at a rate of 75 mm a year. Space is provided beneath suspended floors and beams to allow for the rise in level of the ground surface.

Investigations made at Leuhof in South Africa[3.3] showed that movements in a clay soil were significant to a depth of 5·5 m below ground level, causing failure in tension of 228 mm diameter bored and cast-in-place concrete piles reinforced with four $\frac{1}{2}$ in. vertical bars. The area of vertical steel was 1·24 per cent of the cross-section. Failure occurred at a depth of 5·5 m indicating an uplift of 138 kN on the pile shaft.

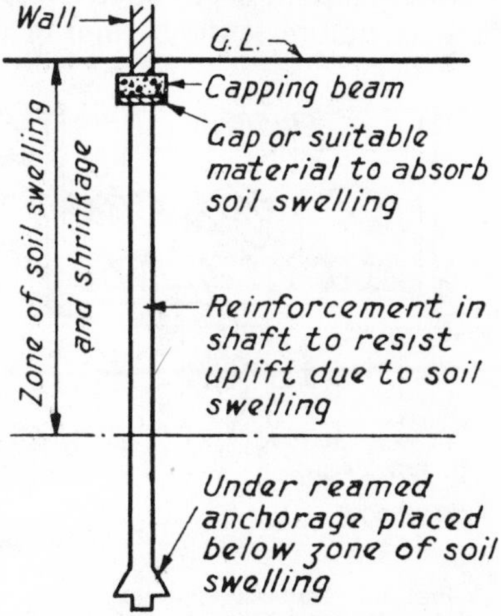

Fig. 3.5. Under-reamed Bored Pile used for Foundations of Light Structures in Soils Subject to Swelling and Shrinkage to Considerable Depth below Ground Level

Provision must also be made for relative movement between the walls of the structure (supported on piles) and the ground floor where it is constructed directly on the soil. It may be advantageous to provide a suspended ground floor carried on the piles.

### Shrinkage of Clays due to High Temperatures

Severe shrinkage of clay soils can be caused by the drying-out of the soil beneath the foundations of boilers, kilns, and furnaces. Cooling and Ward[3.1] reported that the heat from a 61 m by 30·5 m brick kiln had penetrated through 2·7 m of brick rubble filling and then for the full 19·5 m thickness of the underlying Oxford Clay. The kiln was demolished and a cold process building was erected in its place. Seven years later one corner of the new building had settled 330 mm, and elsewhere the building had risen 178 mm. In the same

paper, Cooling and Ward quote the case of a battery of three Lancashire boilers 2·75 m diameter by 3 m long, where settlements up to
150 mm at the centre and 75 mm at the sides had occurred after two
winter seasons of firing. The temperature and moisture conditions in
the London Clay beneath the boilers are shown in Fig. 3.6.

Where furnaces, boiler houses, and the like are constructed on
clay soils it is necessary to provide an insulating air-gap between the
source of heat and the foundation concrete, or alternatively to
provide sufficient depth of concrete or other material to ensure that
the temperature at the bottom of the foundation is low enough to

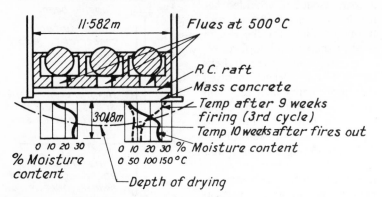

FIG. 3.6. TEMPERATURE AND MOISTURE CONDITIONS BENEATH LANCASHIRE
BOILERS FOUNDED ON LONDON CLAY (COOLING AND WARD[3.1])

prevent appreciable drying of the soil. The procedure for calculating
the required thickness of insulation has been described by Ward and
Sewell.[3.4]

**Ground Movements due to Low Temperatures**

In some soils and rocks appreciable ground movement can be
caused by frost. In Great Britain, chalk and chalky soils and silty
soils are liable to frost heave, but the effects are not noticeable in
heavy clays or sandy soils. Severe frost in the winter of 1954–55
caused a heave in chalk filling beneath the floors of partly-constructed
houses near London; the concrete ground floors were lifted clear of
the brick footing walls by about 25 mm and frost expansion of the
chalk fill caused displacement of the brickwork. In Norway, frost
heave effects are experienced to depths of 1·2 to 2 m below ground
level, resulting in heaving of 100 mm to 300 mm of the ground surface.
Frost effects can be severe below cold-storage buildings. Cooling and
Ward[3.1] have described the heaving of the floor and columns of a

cold-storage building over a period of four to five years. The temperature and ground movement are shown in Fig. 3.7.

A foundation depth of 0·5 m is generally regarded as satisfactory as a safeguard against frost heave in the climate of Great Britain. Greater depths will of course be required in regions where frosts are more severe and prolonged. To avoid harmful effects in cold storage buildings, the floors should be constructed above ground level. If this is not practicable for structural or other reasons, a heating element may be provided below foundation level to prevent freezing of the

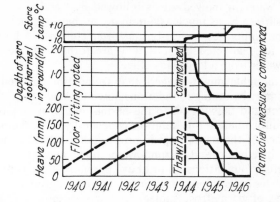

FIG. 3.7. FOUNDATION MOVEMENTS AND TEMPERATURE CONDITIONS BENEATH COLD STORAGE BUILDING (COOLING AND WARD[3.1])

soil. The procedure for calculating the required thickness of insulation beneath floors of cold storage buildings in direct contact with the soil has been described by Ward and Sewell.[3.4] Skaven-Haug[3.5] has described the use of blocks of compressed peat around the retaining walls of basements and tunnels to act as a frost-retarding layer and as a filter to prevent fine silty soils entering materials which are not susceptible to frost movements.

EFFECTS OF PERMAFROST

Frost heave effects are very severe in Arctic and Antarctic regions where ground conditions known as "permafrost" are widespread. Permafrost means permanently frozen ground, which can vary in thickness from a few metres to thousands of metres. About 50% of the land mass of the U.S.S.R. is a permafrost region, generally lying north of the fiftieth parallel of latitude. Permafrost areas are also widespread in Northern Canada, Alaska, and Greenland. The most difficult foundation problems occur where permafrost is overlain by soils subject to seasonal freezing and thawing. The thickness and lateral extent of this overburden do not depend solely on seasonal temperatures. Factors such as the type of soil or rock, the cover of vegetation, exposure to the sun, surface configuration, and ground water movements, all have important effects on the zone subject to freezing and thawing. Permafrost can also occur in distinct layers, lenses, sheets or dikes separated by thawed material. These thawed zones separating permafrost are known as "taliks." It is evident that severe movement will occur in the ground surface of these regions where the soils and rocks are susceptible to frost heave. In fact movement of water in thawed zones followed by freezing can raise the ground surface by as much as 6 m in dome-shaped structures. These "suffusion complexes" or ice-blisters often consist of a hollow dome of clear ice blanketed by soil; they are formed by the escape of thawed water from a large lens of ice.

First thoughts might suggest that foundation problems can be solved simply by taking foundations down through the zones subject to freezing and thawing on to the permafrost by means of piers or piles. Unfortunately this solution is generally unworkable because the surface of the permafrost is rarely stable. It varies with cyclic changes in climate and ground water flow, and the very fact of constructing foundations on or above permafrost can cause appreciable changes in its extent with consequent severe ground movements. The zone of permafrost subject to these variations is known as "active permafrost."

Where structures cannot be sited on rock types which are not susceptible to frost movement, the main principle to be followed in foundation design is to cause the absolute minimum of change in the ground conditions beneath the structure. At the U.S. Air Force base at Thule within the Arctic Circle the active permafrost is 1 m thick overlying non-thawing permafrost 300 m deep.[3.6] The methods used for foundation construction at this base varied with the type of structure. Light buildings were constructed on short piers bearing on a 0·9 m layer of non-frost-susceptible gravel placed on the active permafrost. The air gap beneath the building prevented thawing of the ground due to heating of the building (Fig. 3.8 (a)). Heavy structures were constructed directly on the gravel blanket but air ducts and pipes were provided beneath the floor to allow the circulation of air at freezing temperatures. The inlets to the air ducts were set at a high level to avoid blockage by snow (Fig. 3.8 (b)). Underground buildings (including missile launching bases) had refrigeration coils embedded in the base slabs (Fig. 3.8 (c)).

Rathjens[3.7] recommends that piles should not be driven into permafrost nor should explosives be used in excavation work. This is because of the risk of fracture of the permafrost, allowing thawing waters to seep down into the cracks with consequent deep-seated ground movements. Bored piles can, however, be used provided that in-situ concrete is not placed in direct contact with the frozen ground.

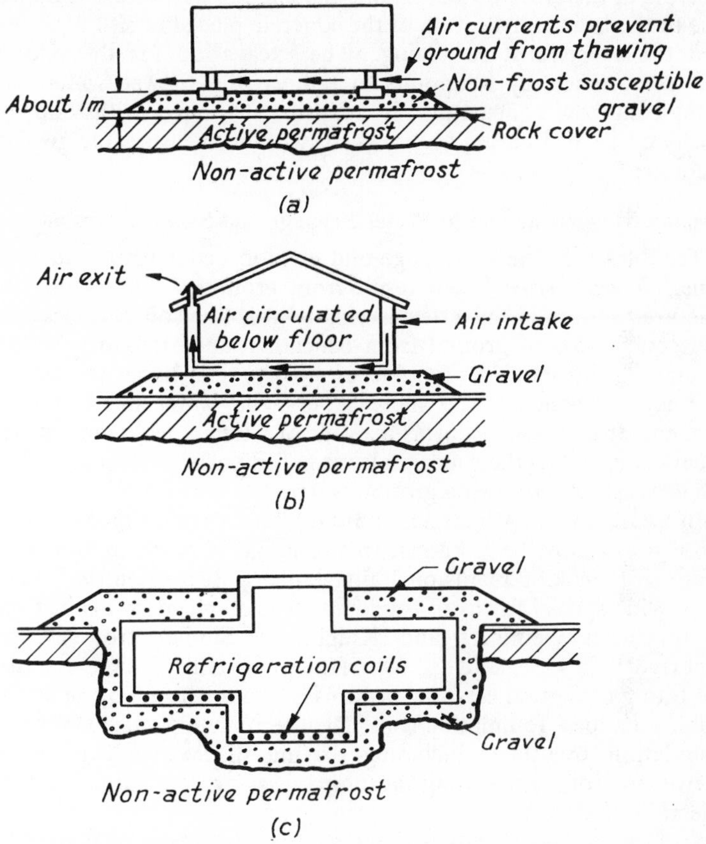

(a)

(b)

(c)

FIG. 3.8. FOUNDATIONS TO BUILDINGS OF U.S. AIR BASE ON ARCTIC PERMAFROST

(a) Light buildings on piers.
(b) Heavy buildings founded directly on gravel blanket.
(c) Underground buildings.

*(Courtesy Architectural Forum)*

Thus the foundations of a 200-tonne steel tower on permafrost in Northern Alaska were supported on steel tube piles set in holes drilled 9 m into the permafrost (Roberts and Cooke[3.8]). The holes were drilled by rotary flush methods through frozen silt, sand, and clay separated by lenses of ice. Nine 200 mm diameter by 9 m long steel tubes were provided for each of the four legs of the tower structure. The required length was based on an estimated adhesion of 517 kN/m² between the frozen ground and the smooth wall of the tubes, with a safety factor of 10. Precautions were taken against heaving of the ground surrounding the pile cap as a result of thawing due to the heat of hydration of the concrete placed in situ in the cap, and the subsequent refreezing. The excavation for the pile cap was surrounded by wellpoints to remove the thawed water. The completed tower structure is reported to have withstood two yearly cycles of freezing and thawing without measureable displacement.

### Ground Movements due to Water Seepage and Surface Erosion

Troubles with water seepage and erosion occur mainly in sandy soils. *Internal erosion* can result from ground water seeping into fractured sewers or culverts carrying with it fine soil particles. The consequent loss of ground from beneath foundations may lead to collapse of structures. Trouble of this kind is liable to occur in mining subsidence areas where sewers and water mains may be broken. It can also occur as a result of careless technique in deep excavations below the water table when soil particles are carried into the excavation by flowing ground water.

In South Africa, Rhodesia, and the Luanda region of Angola dry loose sands have been known to subside as a result of seepage of water from leaking mains or drainage pipes. It is often the practice to provide special forms of foundations as a safeguard against such contingencies (Jennings and Knight[3.9]). Similar troubles have occurred with loess soils (p. 69). Holtz and Hilf[3.10] have described the tilting of a grain elevator in Kansas due to the action of surface water on a loess foundation soil. They recommend various forms of foundation treatment including driving displacement piles into prewetted soil, prewetting accompanied by surcharge and the injection of silt slurry.

Surface erosion may take place as a result of loss of material in strong winds or erosion by flowing water. Fine sands, silts, and dry peat are liable to erosion by the wind. The possibility of undermining of foundations can readily be provided for by a minimum foundation depth of about 0·3 m, and by encouraging the growth of vegetation or by blanketing the erodible soil by gravel, crushed rock, or clay. Surface erosion by flowing water may be severe if structures are sited in the bottom of valleys, especially in regions of tropical rainstorms. Normal foundation depths (say 0·9 to 1·2 m) are inadequate for cases of erosion by floodwaters, but this possibility can be provided for by attention to the siting of structures, adequate drainage and paving or other forms of surface protection, of paths taken by periodical discharges of flood water. Severe erosion can take place around the foundations of bridges or other structures in waterways subjected to heavy flood discharges. The required depths of such foundations can be obtained by hydraulic calculations and local observations.

From time to time cases are reported of subsidence due to solution of minerals from the ground as a result of water seepage. Subsidence and the formation of swallow holes are not uncommon in Britain in the Carboniferous Limestone and Chalk districts (*see* p. 74). Beles and Stanculescu[3,11] described an unusual case of subsidence of a group of buildings constructed on a salt massif in Rumania. Seepage of fresh water beneath the massif had caused solution of the salt, resulting in 750 mm of settlement which was continuing at the rate of 25 mm per month. The rate of settlement was reduced to 1·5 mm per month by the construction of an impermeable barrier around three sides of the affected building. The barrier was formed from a double row of boreholes at 1 m centres, with a dry mixture of clay and sulphite lye rammed down the boreholes into the water-bearing zone. Troubles with solution cavities can best be avoided by careful geological investigations before any construction is commenced.

### Ground Movements due to Vibrations

The processes of using vibrators for consolidating concrete or vibratory rollers and plates for compacting sandy or gravelly soils are well-known. If a poker vibrator is pushed into a mass of loosely placed concrete, the surface of the concrete will subside as its density is increased by the vibrations transmitted to it. It has been found that high frequency in vibrating plant is more effective than low frequency for consolidating concrete or soils.

The same effects of consolidation and subsidence can occur if foundations on sands or sandy gravels (or if the soils themselves) are subjected to vibrations from an external source. Thus, vibrations can be caused by out-of-balance machinery, reciprocating engines, drop hammers, pile driving, rock blasting, or earthquakes. Damage to existing structures resulting from pile-driving vibrations is not uncommon, and it is usual to take precautions against these effects when considering schemes for piled foundations in sands adjacent to existing structures.

Experiments in the field and laboratory and records of damage have shown that the most serious settlements due to vibrations are caused by high-frequency vibrations in the range of 500 to 2,500 impulses per minute. This is also within the range of steam turbines and turbogenerators. Terzaghi and Peck[3.12] record a case of turbo-generator foundations on a fairly dense sand and gravel in Germany. The frequency of the machinery was 1,500 r.p.m. and settlements exceeded 0·3 m within a year of putting the plant to work. Terzaghi and Peck also mention long-continued traffic vibrations and earth-quakes as causes of foundation settlement. If the foundations of structures carrying vibrating machinery cannot be taken down to a stratum not sensitive to vibration (clays for example do not usually settle under vibrating loads), then special methods of mounting the machinery to damp down the vibrations must be adopted. Consolidation of sands beneath foundations by vibration processes are described in Chapter 11. Methods of designing machinery foundations to absorb or damp down vibrations are described later in this chapter.

### Ground Movements due to Hillside Creep

Certain natural hillside slopes are liable to long-term movement which usually takes the form of a mass of soil on a relatively shallow surface of sliding or slipping downhill. Typical of such movements are hillsides in London Clay with slopes of 10° or steeper. Their effects can be seen in parallel ridges in the ground surface and in leaning trees.

Normally, the weight of structures erected on these slopes is insignificant in relation to the mass of the slipping ground. Consequently foundation loading has little or no influence on the factor of safety against slipping. However, other construction operations may have a serious effect on the slope stability, for example regrading operations involving terracing the slopes may change the state of stress both in cut and fill areas, or the natural drainage of subsoil water may be intercepted by retaining walls.

Instability of slopes may occur on rocky hillsides where the strata dip with the ground surface, especially where bedding planes in shales or clayey marls are lubricated by water. Again the risk of instability is increased by regrading operations or alteration of natural drainage conditions rather than by the foundation loading.

There is little that can be done to restore the stability of hillside slopes in clays since the masses of earth involved are so large, and regrading operations on the scale required are usually impossible. The best advice is to avoid building in such areas, or if this cannot be done, to design the foundations so that the whole structure will move as one unit with provision for correcting the level as required. Suitable methods of construction are discussed in the next section of this chapter.

Local instability in rocky slopes can be corrected by grouting or by rock bolting as described on page 565.

## GROUND MOVEMENT DUE TO MINING SUBSIDENCE

### Forms of Subsidence

The magnitude and lateral extent of subsidence due to mineral extraction depends on the method used for winning the minerals from the ground whether by mining, pumping, or dredging. The main problems in Great Britain arise from coal mine workings, and these will be discussed in some detail in the following pages. An early method of mining coal was by sinking "bell-pits," practised in medieval times. A vertical shaft was sunk to the level of the coal seam, and mining then proceeded in all directions radially from the shaft. The bottom of the shaft was "belled-out" as necessary to support the roof (Fig. 3.9) and mining continued until the roof was in imminent danger of collapse or the accumulation of ground water became too much for the primitive baling or pumping equipment. The shafts were filled with spoil from other workings or were used as rubbish tips. Most of the traces of these workings were lost over the centuries but they still remain,

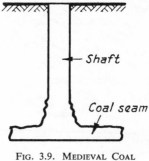

FIG. 3.9. MEDIEVAL COAL WORKINGS

notably in the Northumberland Coalfield, as a source of trouble in foundation design. Their presence can sometimes be detected by depressions in the ground. The author has successfully used electrical resistivity and proton magnetometer equipment to trace the whereabouts of concealed bell-pits and disused mine shafts. Having established the location of workings of this type, structures can be re-sited as necessary to avoid them, or they can be suitably bridged with beams or domed structures or backfilled using injection techniques.

Similar workings were excavated in many coalfields throughout the country in the 1926 coal strike. These workings in the form of shafts, drifts, or deep trenches were excavated at or near the outcrops of coal seams. No records of their location were kept, but local inquiry will sometimes establish their presence.

### PILLAR AND STALL WORKINGS

As mining techniques improved, in particular with the development of steam pumping plant in the eighteenth and nineteenth centuries, workings were extended to greater distances from the shafts. Support to the roof was given by methods known variously as "pillar and stall," "room and pillar," or "bord and pillar." Galleries were driven out from the shaft with cross-galleries leaving rectangular pillars of unworked coal to support the roof (Fig. 3.10). Only 30 to 50 per cent of the coal was extracted in this way in the first advance of the workings from the shaft. On the return workings towards the shaft the pillars were removed either in entirety, to allow full collapse of the roof, or partially, to give continued support. Large pillars were left beneath churches and similar public buildings and sometimes beneath the colliery headworks.

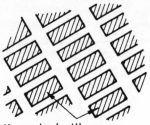

Unworked pillars

FIG. 3.10. PLAN OF PILLAR AND STALL WORKINGS

In many coalfields in Britain the presence of these old pillar and stall workings with partially worked pillars remain as a constantly recurring problem in foundation design where new structures are to be built over them. If the depth of cover of soil and rock overburden is large, the additional load of the building structure is relatively insignificant and the risk of subsidence due to the new loading is negligible (Fig. 3.11 (a)). If, however, the overburden is thin, and especially if it consists of weak crumbly material, there is a risk that the additional load imposed by the new structure will cause a breakdown in an arched and partially collapsed roof, leading to local subsidence (Fig. 3.11 (b)). There is an increased risk of subsidence,

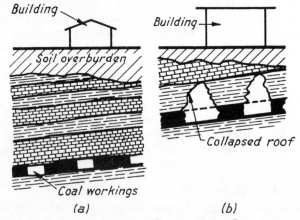

FIG. 3.11. STABLE AND UNSTABLE CONDITIONS FOR CONSTRUCTION ON PILLAR AND STALL WORKINGS
(a) Stable conditions.
(b) Potentially unstable conditions.

or renewal of past subsidence, of pillar and stall workings if under-lying seams are being worked by longwall methods.

There is also a risk of subsidence if flooded workings are pumped dry, when the effective weight of the overburden will be increased as a result of removing the supporting water pressure. This will increase the load on the pillars, possibly to the point of their collapse.

## LONGWALL WORKINGS

The present-day method of coalmining is by "longwall" working whereby the coal face is continuously advanced over a long front. The roof close to the face is supported by props, and the "goaf" or cavity left by the coal extraction is partially filled by waste material ("stowage"). As the props are removed or allowed to crush down, the roof subsides, resulting in slow settlement of the ground surface. The surface subsidence takes the form of an advancing wave moving at the same rate as the advancing coal face (Fig. 3.12). The amount of subsidence at ground level is usually less than the depth of the underground gallery due to bulking of the collapsing strata. Solid packing of the gallery with crushed mine dirt may reduce the sub-sidence to only one-half of that given by the unfilled gallery. The trough or basin of subsidence occurs all round the area of coal extraction, and the affected area at ground level is larger than the area of extraction. The angle between the vertical and a line drawn from the coal face to intersect the ground surface at the edge of the subsidence wave is known as the *limit angle* (Fig. 3.12); it is common-ly 35°. Movement of the ground surface is not only vertical; horizontal strains are caused as the subsidence wave advances. Thus the building at *A* in Fig. 3.13 first experiences a tilting towards the trough accompanied by tensile strains in the ground surface which tend to pull the building apart. As the wave continues to advance, the ground becomes concave. When the concave part of the subsi-dence wave reaches the building, the direction of tilting will have been reversed and the ground surface will be in a compression zone tending to crush the building. As the wave advances further the building will finally right itself and the horizontal strains will eventually die away. Vertical and horizontal movements resulting from longwall mining are severe. The amount of tilting depends on the surface slope but it may vary from 1 in 50 or steeper over shallow workings to practically nothing over deep workings. Horizontal strains may be as much as 0·8 per cent for shallow workings, but are more commonly 0·2 per cent or less.

The protection in one form or another of structures cannot be neglected. It must be appreciated that the movements are rarely uniform. It is possible to predict with reasonable accuracy the

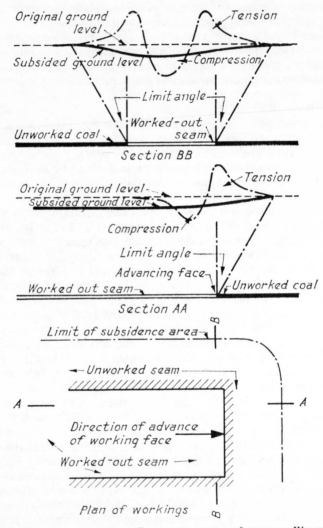

Original ground level

Tension

Subsided ground level

Compression

Limit angle

Worked-out seam

Unworked coal

Section BB

Original ground level

Tension

Subsided ground level

Compression

Limit angle

Advancing face

Worked out seam

Unworked coal

Section AA

Limit of subsidence area

B

Unworked seam

A

A

Direction of advance
of working face

Worked-out seam

Plan of workings

B

FIG. 3.12. FORM OF GROUND SUBSIDENCE GIVEN BY LONGWALL WORKING

Building foundation
in compression
zone

Building foundation
in tension zone

FIG. 3.13

172

amount of settlement and the extent of the subsidence zone if the coal is horizontal or nearly so, and if the overburden conditions are reasonably uniform. If, however, the coal seam is dipping steeply, no reasonable predictions can be made. Variations in the overburden, especially in the depth of soil cover, can cause differential vertical and horizontal movements across individual structures. Faulting can cause severe movement of the ground surface. The problem is further complicated if seams are worked at deeper levels, at different times, and in different directions of advance.

OTHER FORMS OF SUBSIDENCE

Other forms of underground mineral extraction by mining or pumping methods give rise to similar subsidence problems. In Cheshire, brine is extracted by pumping from salt-bearing rocks. In earlier years indiscriminate pumping caused heavy long-term subsidence over a wide area due to removal of buoyant support of the overburden strata, and the formation of large cavities due to the solution of the salt in the rock. Similar subsidence is caused by the removal, by pumping, of mineral oil and natural gas.

The extent and depth of subsidence can be greatly reduced by carefully planned extraction accompanied by "recharge" or recuperation pumping whereby water or gas is pumped in simultaneously with the extraction of the minerals. In some brine-pumping areas of the North of England the quantity pumped from a borehole is limited and the boreholes are spaced at such intervals that individual cavities are separated by pillars of salt of sufficient thickness to give support to the overburden.

### Protection against Subsidence due to Longwall Mining

Schemes for protection against subsidence should be drawn up in consultation with the local mine authorities. A great deal can be done to reduce the slope of the subsidence trough, and hence to reduce the tensile and compressive ground strain, by planning the extraction of the mineral in successive strips of predetermined width. The slopes can also be reduced considerably by concurrent mining of two or more seams beneath a site, advancing the working face in different directions. The opinion of a consulting mining engineer or geologist with knowledge of the area is advisable. The measures to be taken depend to a great extent on the type and function of the structure. Complete protection can be given by leaving a pillar of unworked coal beneath the structure (Fig. 3.14). This involves payments to the mine owners for the value of the unworked coal. Even for an isolated structure this is liable to cost many tens of thousands of pounds, and the subsidence effects around the fringe of the pillar are increased in severity. Therefore, protection by unworked pillars is only considered in the case of structures such as dams where structural damage might have catastrophic effects. Measures for protection of structures and full bibliographies on the subject are given in the Institution of Civil Engineers *Report on Mining Subsidence*,[3.13] and in the *Subsidence Engineers' Handbook*, published by the National Coal Board.

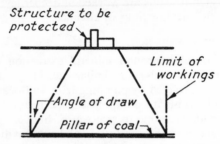

FIG. 3.14. PROTECTION OF STRUCTURE BY PILLAR OF UNWORKED COAL

The general principles recommended in the report are—

(*a*) Rigid frame or similar statically indeterminate structures should be avoided. Simply supported spans and flexible super-structures should be used whenever possible.

(*b*) The shallow raft foundation is the best method of protection against tension or compression strains in the ground surface.

(*c*) Large structures should be divided into independent units not exceeding 18 m by 18 m in plan. Gaps between the units should be at least 50 mm (or more for tall structures where tilting could cause closure of the gap).

(*d*) Bearing pressures beneath the foundations of heavy structures should be as *high* as possible.

Although the orientation of a structure in relation to the direction of advance of the subsidence wave has, theoretically, an effect on the distortion of the structure (Fig. 3.15), the National Coal Board handbook states that there is little point in trying to orient the structure in any particular direction relative to the mine workings unless the mining is to be undertaken in the near future to a definite plan. The handbook states that there is not enough difference between the maximum slope in a transverse profile and that in a longitudinal profile materially to affect the design of a structure. The design should allow for the maximum normal movements which are predicted for the seams to be worked.

Structures should not be sited within 15 m of known geological faults, since subsidence is likely to be severe near fault planes.

PROTECTION BY RAFT FOUNDATIONS

*Raft foundations* should be as shallow as possible, preferably above the ground, so that compressive strains can take place beneath them instead of transmitting direct compressive forces to their edges, and they should be constructed on a membrane so that they will slide as ground movements occur beneath them. It is then only necessary to provide enough reinforcement in the rafts to resist tensile and compressive stresses set up by friction in the membrane. In the case

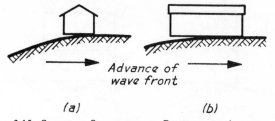

FIG. 3.15. SITING OF STRUCTURES IN RELATION TO ADVANCE OF SUBSIDENCE WAVE

(*a*) Building parallel to wave-front.
(*b*) Building at right angles to wave-front.

of light structures such as dwelling houses, it is not usually practicable to make the raft any smaller than the plan area of the building. However, in the case of heavy structures it is desirable to adopt the highest possible bearing pressures so that the plan dimensions of the raft are the smallest possible (Fig. 3.16). By this means the total horizontal tensile and compressive forces acting on the underside of the raft are kept to a minimum, and the lengths of raft acting as a cantilever (Fig. 3.16 (*a*)) at the "hogging" stage, or as a beam (Fig. 3.16 (*b*)) at the "sagging" stage, are also a minimum. Mauntner[3.14] has analysed the conditions of support shown in Figs. 3.16 as follows—

Maximum pressure on foundation

$$q_{max} = \frac{4qb}{3(b-2l)} \text{ for cantilevering} \qquad . \qquad (3.1)$$

and

$$q_{max} = \frac{qb}{b-l} \text{ for free support} \qquad . \qquad (3.2)$$

where $b$ is the length of the structure in the vertical plane under consideration, $q$ is the uniformly assumed design pressure in undisturbed ground and $l$ is the unsupported length for cantilevering or free support. The value of $q_{max}$ depends on the length $l$ which in turn depends on the ratio $\frac{q_{max}}{q}$. As soon as the value of $q_{max}$ approaches the ultimate bearing capacity of the ground, yielding of the ground will occur, causing the structure to tilt in the case of the cantilever (Fig. 3.16 (*a*)) and to settle more or less uniformly in the free support case (Fig. 3.16 (*b*)). In both cases the effect is to increase the area of support given to the underside of the foundation, hence reducing the

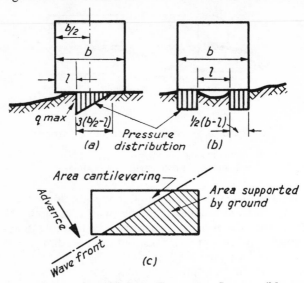

FIG. 3.16. CALCULATION OF MAXIMUM FOUNDATION PRESSURE (MAUNTNER[3.14])
(*a*) Raft acting as cantilever.
(*b*) Raft acting as beam.
(*c*) Wave-front oblique to structure.

length of the cantilever, or the span of the beam, and reducing the stresses in the foundation structure or superstructure. It is clear from equations 3.1 and 3.2 that the smaller the ratio of the ultimate bearing capacity to the design bearing pressure, the less will be the length of cantilever or the unsupported span length of the beam. In other words the design bearing pressure should be kept as close as possible to the ultimate bearing capacity $q_{max}$. The value of $q_{max}$ can be determined from soil mechanics tests or by plate bearing tests on the ground; hence the value of $l$ can be estimated approximately. It can be assessed only roughly because the assumed straight line pressure distribution shown in Fig. 3.16 (*a*) or the uniform distribution at each end of the free support case in Fig. 3.16 (*b*) is not necessarily true. It should also be noted that the alignment of the front of the subsidence wave in relation to the foundation plan is not known in advance. It is therefore necessary to analyse various positions of the subsidence wave and calculate the worst condition of support for the structure (Fig. 3.16 (*c*)). Because the design bearing pressure is made close to the ultimate, the consolidation settlement may be severe if the ground is compressible (e.g. a clay or loose sand). However, the magnitude of the consolidation settlements will be small in relation to the mining subsidence movements.

A typical design of a light raft for a dwelling house as recommended by the British Government authorities[3.15] is shown on Fig. 3.17. The design features are—

(*a*) A 150 mm layer of compacted sand or other suitable granular material is placed on the ground surface.

(*b*) A layer of waterproofed paper* is placed over the granular sub-base layer to act as a surface of sliding.

(*c*) Reinforcement is provided to resist the frictional forces acting on the underside of the slab as it slides over the sub-base.

(*d*) The frictional forces may be in a transverse or longitudinal direction and may be taken as the product of half the weight of the structure and the coefficient of friction between the slab and the granular material.

(*e*) The coefficient of friction may be taken as $\frac{2}{3}$.

(*f*) The permissible tensile stress in the steel may be taken as 200 N/mm² and the permissible compressive stress on the concrete as 14 N/mm².

(*g*) Snow loads and wind loads on the building may be neglected and the floor superload may be taken as 480 N/m².

(*h*) The reinforcement is placed in the centre of the slab to allow both for hogging and sagging of the ground surface, but the thickness of the raft and the percentage of reinforcement is such that the raft will deform under vertical movements rather than remain in one rigid plane.

(*i*) The design makes allowance for resistance to movement given by the superstructure, i.e. the windows and doors are arranged so as not to weaken the walls, internal load-bearing walls are tied with external walls, floors and roofs are secured to all walls, plasterboard (or fibreboard) is used for ceilings instead of plaster, and lime mortar is used for brickwork instead of cement mortar to allow movement to take place along joints instead of in wide infrequent cracks.

The Government publication[3.15] states that these rafts cost thirteen to twenty pounds more than normal strip foundations (based

---

* Polythene sheeting can also be used.

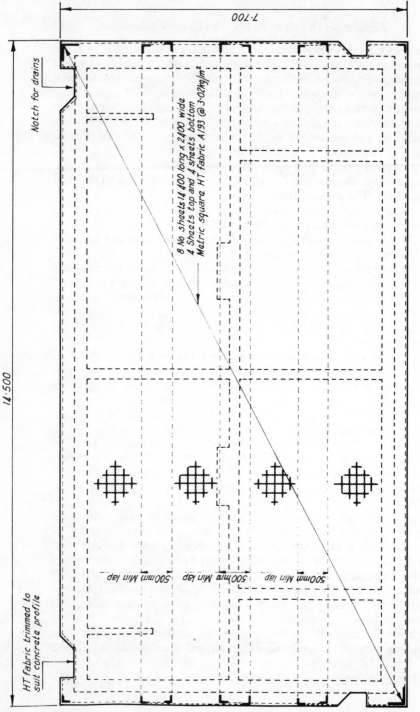

FIG. 3.17. MINISTRY OF WORKS DESIGN FOR 150 mm SLAB RAFT FOUNDATION FOR LIGHT BUILDINGS SUBJECTED TO MINING SUBSIDENCE

on 1949 prices). Thin slab rafts of this type are only satisfactory for light structures such as dwelling houses. Heavier slab and beam or cellular rafts are required for multi-storey structures or heavy plant installations. It is important that these stiffened rafts should be constructed on a membrane laid over a granular base, and that the underside of the raft should be a flat slab, i.e. the beams should be designed as upstanding beams. The stiffened rafts should be designed for the conditions of support shown in Fig. 3.16.

Because of the large movements which take place with longwall mining, appreciable deflexion of rafts cannot be avoided, and the appropriate precautions are necessary in the design of the super-structure such as flexibility in the design or provision for jacking the superstructure of a suitably strengthened raft.

PROTECTION BY ARTICULATION

Articulation has been extensively used for the construction of schools in Great Britain. In the well-known "Nottinghamshire construction," described by Lacey and Swain,[3.16] the superstructure consists of a pin-jointed steel frame designed to "lozenge" in any direction. The cladding of hung tiles, precast concrete slabs, timber panels, or vitreous enamelled sheets is designed to move relative to the frame, as is the internal wall construction of heavy gypsum slabs. Cracking of the lightly reinforced floor slab is expected and the floor finishes designed accordingly.

Buildings of special importance have been erected on sets of roller bearings allowing movement in two directions at right angles.[3.17] The Institution of Civil Engineers *Report on Mining Subsidence* suggests a form of construction for buildings which cannot be split up into units or constructed on a rigid base. This method provides for a stiff column acting as a self-supporting bastion to which all other members are attached by flexible hinges. A variation of this method provides a stiff corner to the structure at a high level arranged so that no bending moments are transferred to the ground.

Instead of articulating the superstructure it is possible to provide articulated foundations with a rigid superstructure. This is the "three-point support" method as used in Germany, Holland, and Poland and described by Mauntner.[3.14] The foundations consist of three piers or pads. The superstructure is constructed on columns resting on spherical bearings on the pads (Fig. 3.18). As the foundations tilt with the passing of the subsidence wave they always remain in the same plane. Therefore, although the superstructure must tilt, there is no differential movement causing racking or twisting. Another important principle of the three-point method is to use the highest possible bearing pressures in order to keep the foundation blocks as small as possible. By this means tilting of the blocks relative to each other is minimized, and the horizontal tensile and compressive forces acting on the underside of the blocks are also kept to a minimum.

### OTHER METHODS

Patented jacking systems incorporating several hydraulic jacks under walls or columns of structures have been devised. In the Pynford "Pedatifid" System[3.18] the jacks are connected to a central

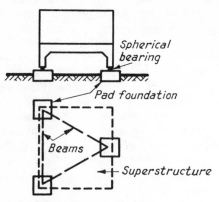

FIG. 3.18. THREE-POINT SUPPORT METHOD

control system which automatically adjusts them individually as settlement takes place. In such systems it is important that they should be designed to withstand horizontal movements as well as subsidence.

Wardell[3.19] has described the use of trenches around structures to relieve horizontal compression. He states that although more cases of damage are caused by tension, the really serious cases are often irreparable damage to traditional structures caused by the compression strain which could be twice the tensile strain. Wardell also described a two-layer slab for small structures in which the bottom slab is separated along the diagonal into four independent units. The upper slab is in one unit separated from the bottom slab by a layer of sand covered with building paper (Fig. 3.19).

Piled foundations should not be used under any circumstances in areas of longwall mining subsidence, since horizontal forces will either shear through the piles or else cause failure in tension of the tie beams or raft connecting the heads of the piles. Structures sited on soft ground or fill, where piling would be used in normal conditions, should be constructed on rafts designed to accommodate differential movement resulting from both consolidation of the fill and mining subsidence. The latter movements are likely to be the greater.

### Protection against the Effects of Pillar and Stall Mining

The problems of protection against subsidence arising from the collapse of pillar and stall workings are very different from those involved in longwall mining. In the latter case the engineer is dealing with certain subsidence caused by mining in current progress or proposed for the future, and the amount and extent of the movements

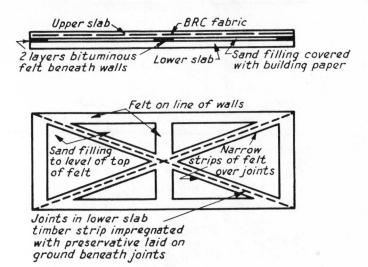

FIG. 3.19. TWO-LAYER SLAB RAFT FOR SEMI-DETACHED HOUSES (WARDELL[3.19])

are to a large extent predictable. In the case of pillar and stall workings the engineer is concerned with past workings, possibly made a hundred years or more ago. All subsidence may be complete or subsidence may never have taken place, but the workings are in a state of incipient instability such that the additional load of the building on the ground surface or changes in underground water levels might cause the collapse of a pillar or a cave-in of an arched roof weakened by erosion or oxidation. In some cases partial subsidence may have occurred due to pushing of a pillar into the soft pavement, and the additional load of a structure may increase this form of subsidence.

The first step in considering schemes of protection is to make a detailed exploration of the workings in consultation with a geologist. All available records in the hands of the mining authorities, local museums or libraries, and the Institute of Geological Sciences, should be consulted first.  Vertical boreholes using rotary core drills should be sunk to establish the depth and dip of the worked seam and the nature of the overburden.  If intact coal and not cavities are found, it should not be assumed that the seam has not been worked.  The depth of the seam being known, the engineer should decide whether subsidence is likely to be a serious risk.  If the overburden is

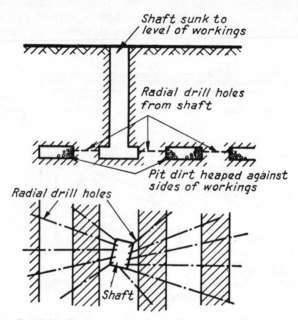

FIG. 3.20. EXPLORATION OF PILLAR AND STALL WORKINGS

deep so that the load imposed by the new structure is small in comparison, he may decide that the risk is negligible, especially if there are massive sandstone layers forming a sound roof over the cavities. If, however, the overburden is thin and consists mainly of soil or weak shales, or if there is surface evidence of past subsidence in the form of random depressions, then the engineer may decide that some form of protection is necessary.  Detailed mapping of the galleries is best made by driving a heading from the outcrop if this is close at hand, or by sinking a shaft to the level of the coal seam to obtain access to the workings.  There may be existing mine shafts in the vicinity which can be used.  If the roof of the workings is unstable, the exploration should be limited to jackhammer holes drilled radially in all directions from the shaft to establish the width of the galleries and pillars (Fig. 3.20).  In any case, due safety precautions should be taken against roof falls and gas accumulations. The work should preferably be undertaken under the supervision of an experienced mine surveyor. Jackhammer holes drilled vertically from the surface have been used to map galleries, but very close spacing is required to obtain adequate information. The method is only suitable for sites where the galleries have not collapsed and are free of heaped pit dirt (Fig. 3.20). In such cases the location of the workings is revealed by the sudden drop of the drill rods. If, however, the roof of the workings has collapsed, forming numerous small cavities above the worked seam, then the vertical jackhammer holes will not give any useful information on the extent of the galleries.

If the exploration shows that a large proportion of the foundation area has been mined, and the thickness or stability of the roof gives cause for concern, the engineer may decide that precautions against subsidence due to crushing of a pillar or roof collapse should be taken. Three methods have been used—

(*a*) The provision of a heavy raft foundation designed to bridge over a local collapsed area.

(*b*) Piles or piers taken down through the overburden and coal workings to the underlying "solid" strata.

(*c*) Filling the workings with cement grout or other imported filling.

## RAFT FOUNDATIONS

These can consist either of massive reinforced concrete slabs or stiff slab and beam cellular rafts. The latter type is suitable for the provision of jacking pockets in the upstand beams to permit the columns or walls to be re-levelled if subsidence distorts the raft. A 600 mm thick slab raft was used beneath 8-storey buildings at Gateshead where workings in the 0·9 to 1·2 m thick seam were only 2·3 m beneath the foundations. It was decided that such rafts could bridge the cavities and any future local subsidence zones, since the 2·75 to 3 m wide galleries were supported by wider intact pillars and the roof to the workings consisted of massive sandstone.

## PIER FOUNDATIONS

These are used for sites where the overburden is too weak to support surface foundations. The piers must be taken through the overburden to a bearing stratum beneath the old workings, because founding at a higher level would involve a risk of concentrating load on potentially unstable strata above the workings. Precautions must be taken against drag-down on the piers from vertical movement of the overburden or horizontal shear forces on the piers caused by lateral ground movement. Such movements may take place at any time in the future as a result of crushing of pillars or roof collapse.

A space must be provided between the piers and the overburden, and the space must be filled with a plastic material to prevent it from being filled with accumulated debris which might transmit heavy forces on to the piers. Bitumen is the best type of filling material. Dutch mining engineers use pre-formed slabs of bitumen up to 330 mm thick between the inner reinforced concrete and the outer brick-work linings of colliery shafts to give them protection against mining subsidence, as described by Weehuizen.[3.20]

PILED FOUNDATIONS

If piled foundations are necessary because of weak overburden conditions, they should be installed in holes drilled through the overburden to a suitable bearing stratum beneath the workings. For reasons given in the previous paragraph, they must not be terminated above the roof of the old workings. Piles should consist of precast concrete units or steel tubes filled with concrete. Concrete cast-in-place in an unlined borehole must not be used in any circumstances, because of the possible drag-down and shear forces mentioned above. The space between the concrete units or steel tubes and the over-burden should be filled with a viscous bitumen mix or other plastic material. Because of the complications in providing safeguards against drag-down forces on piles, large diameter cylinder foundations or massive piers are preferable to conventional slender piles.

Piled foundations were used for the Metropolitan-Vickers Electrical Company's factory at Sheffield. Four seams had been worked below the site. The shallowest of them outcropped beneath one end of the factory. It had been extensively worked by pillar and stall methods, and a number of shallow drifts had been made at the outcrop during the 1926 Coal Strike. Further complications were caused by the presence of deep filling over the eastern part of the site either side of the Car Brook (Fig. 3.21). A large area of this fill was burning and it blanketed the outcrop workings. Exploration showed extensive collapsed areas near the outcrop, but as the seam dipped towards the west it was roofed by sandstone and the galleries appeared to be intact. Because of the great extent of the workings it was decided that filling would be unduly slow and expensive. The method adopted was to take the foundations of the building in the collapsed areas down to a stratum of siltstone beneath the coal seam. At and near the outcrop precast concrete piles were driven without difficulty through the overburden of boulder clay and broken mudstone. Further to the west where the roof was mainly intact the piles were lowered down holes pre-bored through the clay, mudstone and silt-stone. Where the depth of overburden exceeded 12 m it was considered unnecessary to take any precautions because of the presence of the sandstone roof.

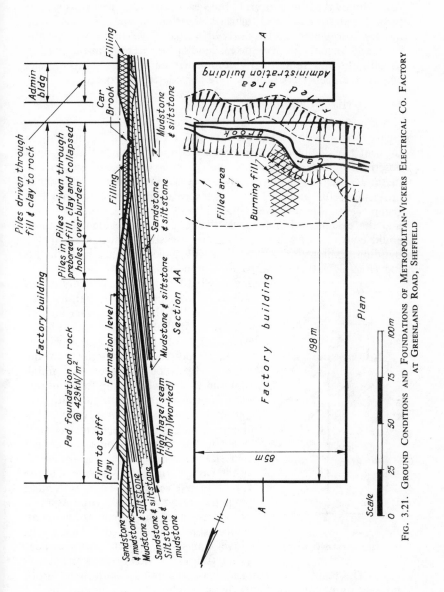

FIG. 3.21. GROUND CONDITIONS AND FOUNDATIONS OF METROPOLITAN-VICKERS ELECTRICAL CO. FACTORY
AT GREENLAND ROAD, SHEFFIELD

Accordingly the foundations to the west of the piled area consisted of piers bearing on the rock beneath the shallow clay deposits. The factory floor which carried fairly light loading was not piled, but the weak and burning fill over the east end of the factory was removed in its entirety and replaced by compacted hard filling. Precautions against the deeper coal seams were considered unnecessary.

FILLING THE WORKINGS

Method (c), involving filling the workings, was used to protect an eight-storey building forming part of the College of Technology in the centre of Sheffield. The procedure adopted in filling the workings described by Scott[3.21] provides an interesting example of a variety of methods used to achieve a low-cost solution to the subsidence problem. Pillar and stall workings were a minimum of 10 m below ground level, and because of the width of the galleries (up to 4·5 m) and the evidence of collapse of the roof it was decided that there could be a risk of subsidence resulting in structural damage to the building. Exploration showed four wide galleries beneath the building (Fig. 3.22 (a)). Comparison with old maps of the workings indicated that there were continuous pillars of coal beneath the parallel galleries and that the workings terminated close to the building site. These conditions were favourable for filling the workings by the introduction of material from the surface. In order to prevent the filling material escaping down-dip to the north-east, dams were formed in galleries 1, 3, and 4 by dropping pea gravel down 250 mm boreholes. The gravel formed conical piles in the galleries, and the rounded material aided dispersion over the width of the cavity. Increased dispersion at the top of the pile was achieved by water and air jetting and the use of a rotating plate at the bottom of the boreholes having an action similar to a road gritter. The gravel dams were injected with cement grout using calcium chloride as an accelerator. The main filling material was an aerated sand/cement grout injected by pneumatic placer down boreholes at the up-dip ends of the galleries (Fig. 3.22 (b)). The 3·5:1 sand/cement mix was aerated by premixed foam to give 1440 kg/m³ density. This gave adequate strength with the advantage of greatly increased yield per unit weight

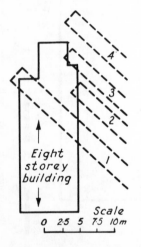

FIG. 3.22 (a). LOCATION OF OLD MINE-WORKINGS

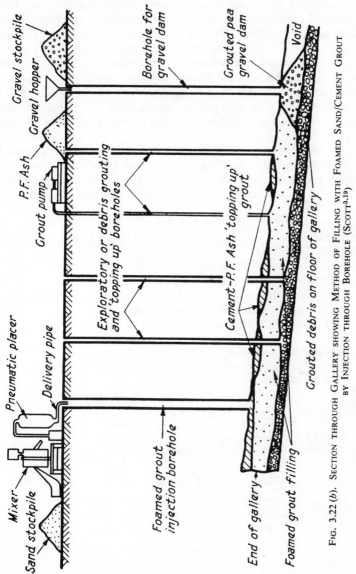

Fig. 3.22 (b). Section through Gallery showing Method of Filling with Foamed Sand/Cement Grout by Injection through Borehole (Scott[3.19])

Labels within figure:

Sand stockpile

Mixer

Pneumatic placer

Delivery pipe

Foamed grout injection borehole

Gravel stockpile

Gravel hopper

P.F. Ash

Grout pump

Borehole for gravel dam

Grouted pea gravel dam

Void

Exploratory or debris grouting and 'topping up' boreholes

Cement–P.F. Ash 'topping up' grout

Grouted debris on floor of gallery

End of gallery

Foamed grout filling

of cement compared with non-aerated mixes. Filling of the galleries was indicated by a rise in grout level in the injection borehole. Additional jackhammer holes were drilled at intermediate points to "top-up" the filling in roof cavities which had not been reached by the main injections. The topping-up grout was a 2:1 PF-ash/cement mix injected by cementation pump. Exploration in gallery 2 showed extensive accumulations of debris which prevented effective formation of the pea gravel dam. Filling in this gallery was effected by washing-in 35 tonne of sand followed by aerated sand/cement grout and finally neat cement grout.

It should be noted that it may not be necessary to fill completely all cavities beneath a building area. It may be sufficient to form a number of "grout piers" over the area. The foundation would then be in the form of a stiff raft designed to span across the piers.

### FOUNDATIONS ON FILLED GROUND

Settlement of foundations constructed on fill material can be caused in three ways—

(*a*) Consolidation of compressible fill under foundation loading.

(*b*) Consolidation of the fill under its own weight.

(*c*) Consolidation of the natural ground beneath the fill under the combined weight of the fill and the structure.

These movements are illustrated in Fig. 3.23.

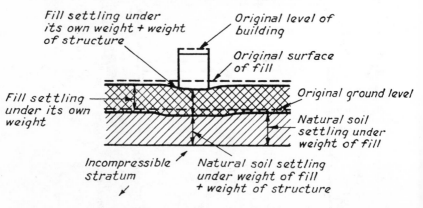

Fig. 3.23. Settlements of Filled Ground

If the structure is light the movement due to (*a*) above will be small even in a poorly compacted fill (it is presumed that founding on very soft clayey fill would not be considered). The movement due to (*b*) depends on the depth and compaction of the fill layer and the

conditions under which it was placed. Meyerhof[3.22] has published
the curves shown in Fig. 3.24 which illustrate the beneficial effect of
compacting the fill in layers at the time of placing. Well-compacted
sand, gravel, shale, chalk and rock fills show settlements of only
one-half per cent of their height, whereas poorly compacted chalk

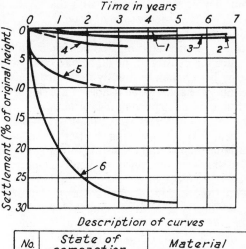

| No. | State of compaction | Material |
|---|---|---|
| 1 | Well compacted | Well-graded sand |
| 2 | Medium | Rock fill |
| 3 | Lightly compacted | Clay and chalk |
| 4 | Uncompacted | Sand |
| 5 | Uncompacted | Clay |
| 6 | Well compacted | Mixed refuse |

FIG. 3.24. OBSERVATIONS OF THE SETTLEMENT OF VARIOUS TYPES OF FILL
DUE TO CONSOLIDATION UNDER OWN WEIGHT (MEYERHOF[3.22])

fills may settle up to 1 per cent. Well-compacted clay fills show settlements up to one-half per cent of their height compared with 1 to 2 per
cent for lightly compacted clay placed in deep layers. Sand fills
placed by pumping show very small settlements above ground water
level due to the consolidating effect of the downward percolating
water. On the other hand pumped clay fills show very severe settlement (*see* curve 5 in Fig. 3.24). With controlled tipping in layers the
settlement of domestic refuse can be restricted to about 10 per cent of
the height, and settlement of a 3 m deep fill can be expected to be
complete in about five to ten years.

Uncompacted backfilling to opencast coal workings settle by about
0·5 to 1·5 per cent of the backfilled depth for fills 10 to 40 m deep.

The settlement takes about 10 years for near completion.[3.23]

Movement due to consolidation of the underlying natural soil again depends on the composition of the soil and the thickness of the compressible layers. Where the natural soils are highly compressible, e.g. soft clay or peat, the settlement due to consolidation of the natural ground may be high compared with that of the fill material. If the natural soil is a fairly dense sand or gravel, or a stiff to hard clay, its consolidation under the weight of filling will be of a very small order.

Buildings can be constructed on well-compacted fill with normal foundations, since the density of the fill should be in no way inferior to, or it may be better than, naturally deposited soils. Where the density of the fill is variable it is advisable to provide some reinforcement to strip foundations to prevent the formation of stepped cracks. When building over poorly compacted fill, it is advisable to use raft foundations. Three-storey dwelling houses were constructed at Bilston, on variable fill material consisting of mineral waste. The age and depth of the fill were unknown but it was suspected to be more than 12 m deep. One block of three-storey dwellings settled 100 mm with a differential movement of 75 mm over a $1\frac{1}{4}$-year period. The ribbed raft foundation (Fig. 4.36) prevented any cracking of the superstructure. On another site in Bilston two-storey houses were constructed on ash and clinker fill which had been placed two years previously without any special compaction. One block of houses were founded on fill varying in thickness from 2·5 m to less than 0·25 m. There was a maximum settlement of 20 mm in a $1\frac{1}{2}$-year period. Again the raft foundation with edge beams prevented any cracking.

Preloading is a useful expedient to allow building on normal foundations in areas of deep uncompacted fills. A factory was constructed on a back-filled clay pit at Birtley, Co. Durham.[3.24] The 15 m deep colliery waste fill had been end-tipped through water some 35 years before, and it was still in a loose state (average $N$ value 10 blows/300 mm). The overall loading on the factory floor of 86 kN/m$^2$ would have caused excessive settlement of foundations on untreated fill. Accordingly it was decided to adopt preloading by a mound of colliery waste some 3·5 to 5·5 m high moved progressively across the site by scrapers and bulldozers at a rate controlled by observations on settlement plates. In areas of deep fill the surcharge mound remained in place for periods between 50 and 108 days when the average settlement of the fill surface was about 0·5 m (3·3 per cent of the fill thickness) under a surcharge of 1000 kN/m$^2$.

Heavy structures, including factory buildings containing plant or machinery which is sensitive to settlement, are best supported on piles taken through the fill to a relatively incompressible stratum.

This procedure may not be necessary where the fill is known to be well-compacted and is bearing on natural ground having a compressibility less than or not appreciably greater than that of the filling. It is common practice to construct oil storage tanks on hydraulically placed sand fill or compacted earth fill.

Where piled foundations are used in filled areas, the consolidation of the filling under its own weight or under superficial loads may cause a load to be transferred to the pile shafts due to the adhesion or skin friction of the fill material in contact with them. This phenomenon is discussed in Chapter 7.

## MACHINERY FOUNDATIONS

Machinery foundations should be designed to spread the load of installed machinery on to the ground so that excessive settlement or tilting of the foundation block relative to the floor or other fixed installations will not occur; they should have sufficient rigidity to prevent fracture or excessive bending under stresses set up by heavy concentrated loads, or by unbalanced rotating or reciprocating machinery; they should absorb or damp down vibrations in order to prevent damage or nuisance to adjacent installations or property; and they should withstand chemical attack or other aggressive action resulting from manufacturing processes.

If the shear strength and the compressibility of the soil are known, the proportioning of the base of a foundation block is generally a simple matter where non-vibrating loads are carried. The allowable bearing pressures to prevent excessive settlement can be calculated by one of the procedures described in Chapter 2. Tilting can be avoided by placing the centre of gravity of the machinery at or reasonably close to that of the foundation block.

### Machinery Vibrations

The problems of foundation design for machinery having unbalanced moving parts are much more difficult. Unbalanced moving parts, such as large flywheels, crankshafts, or the pistons of reciprocating engines, set up vibrations in the foundation blocks which if not absorbed by anti-vibration mountings are transmitted to the ground. Strong ground vibrations may cause loss of bearing capacity and settlement of the soil beneath the foundations; they may also cause damage to adjacent buildings or machines. The problems of vibrations in structures, soils, and rocks are highly complex, but an understanding of the general principles will help the engineer in designing foundations for the simpler machinery installations. In the case of foundations for the heavier types of vibrating machines such as large forging presses or hammers it will be advisable to obtain expert advice if these machines are sited in localities where vibrations may cause nuisance or damage.

### VIBRATION THEORY

A body subjected to a single impulse or a series of impulses is set in vibratory motion. The number of movements in any one direction per unit of time is known as the *frequency* of the vibrations, and it is usually expressed in cycles per second, or hertz (Hz). The maximum distance through which the body moves from its equilibrium position is known as the *amplitude* of the vibrations. If the frequency of vibrations can be varied it will be found that at one particular frequency the amplitude is a maximum. This frequency is known as the *natural frequency* of the system comprising the vibrating mass and any soil beneath the mass that vibrates with it. The natural frequency of a system is defined as the frequency of vibrations that are set up when a body with well-defined boundaries is subjected to a single impulse. When the same body is subjected to periodic impulses (e.g. vibrating machinery) the amplitude of vibration will increase as the frequency of the impulse approaches the natural frequency of the system. At a frequency close to the natural frequency the amplitude is a maximum and the system is in a state of *resonance*.

The impulses in the ground set up by vibrating machinery spread outwards from the foundation block in a series of waves (Fig. 3.25).

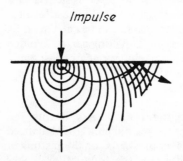

*Impulse*

FIG. 3.25. SPREAD OF WAVE-FRONT FROM IMPULSE AT GROUND SURFACE (CROCKETT AND HAMMOND[3.25])

The shape of the wave-front varies from hemispherical immediately beneath the foundation to roughly ellipsoidal gradually developing to a spherical form and finally to egg-shapes. As the waves pass through the ground they become *attenuated*, i.e. they decrease in amplitude. The waves pass through different materials at different speeds. When they pass from one stratum to another, or from the foundation block to the ground, they are refracted, i.e. the direction of the wave-front is changed. Also, they are partly *reflected* at the boundaries between different materials. Thus waves are reflected by the base and sides of the foundation block, and at the changes of strata beneath the foundation. They are also reflected back into the ground as they strike the ground surface. As would be expected the greater part of the wave energy is reflected when the wave meets a hard stratum such as rock or an adjacent foundation block. Because of this refraction and reflection of the waves within the foundation block and in the various underlying strata, it is evident that at any given point in the ground surrounding the block there will be the "direct arrival" of the energy wave from the impulse of the machine, followed at different time intervals by the arrivals of the refracted and reflected waves. Crockett and Hammond[3.25] state that a single blow from a pile driver may produce a dozen or more vibrations at a point 30 m away. It is also evident that at certain points there will be resonance when the frequency of the various arrivals will approximate to the natural frequency of the ground at that point. The effect of this resonance may be to produce vibrations of such amplitude that structural damage or nuisance will be caused. The resonance effects may also cause settlement of foundations on loosely deposited materials.

It is usually impossible to predict whether or not machinery vibrations will cause resonance and ill-effects in adjacent areas. The reasons are the complexity of the various reflections and refractions in the foundation block and the surrounding ground, and the difficulty in determining the natural frequency of the adjacent structures or installations. The aim, therefore, of the engineer should be to absorb vibrations within the foundation block, or, if this cannot be wholly achieved, to transmit them to deeper strata whereby they will be much attenuated before they reach the surface. Advice on the foundations of reciprocating machinery is given in Part I of the B.S. Code of Practice for Foundations of Machinery, *CP 2011.*

## Absorbing Vibrations

Amongst the methods of absorbing vibrations one of the simplest is to provide sufficient mass in the foundation block, so that the waves are attenuated and absorbed by reflections within the block itself. A long-established rule in machinery foundations is to make the weight of the block equal to or greater than the weight of the machine. This procedure is generally satisfactory for normal machinery where there are no large out-of-balance forces. However, in the case of heavy forging hammers and presses, or large reciprocating engines, it is quite likely that the vibrations cannot be absorbed fully by the foundation block. Also, in some circumstances a large and heavy foundation block may be impracticable; for example where the machinery is carried on a suspended floor or structural framework, or where space is limited by service ducts or other foundations. In these circumstances, absorption of vibrations can be achieved by special mountings.

The aim of anti-vibration mountings for machinery or foundation blocks is to reduce the amplitude of the vibrations transmitted to the supporting foundation block or to the ground. Thus the mounting should have a much lower frequency than that of the induced vibrations of the machine. When the frequency of the mounting is very

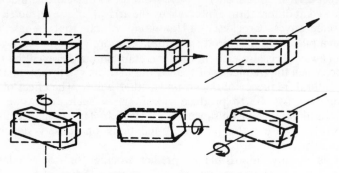

FIG. 3.26. SIX DEGREES OF FREEDOM OF MOVEMENT
(CROCKETT AND HAMMOND[3.25])

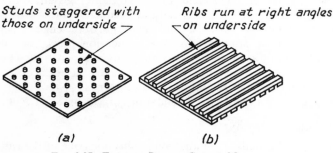

Studs staggered with those on underside ⌐

Ribs run at right angles ⌐on underside

(a)                    (b)

FIG. 3.27. TYPES OF RUBBER CARPET MOUNTINGS
(a) Stud type.
(b) Ribbed type.

low it is said to be a "soft mounting." The mountings must also allow freedom for the six degrees of movement illustrated by Crockett and Hammond[3.25] in Fig. 3.26. These movements comprise translations in three dimensions and rotations in planes at right angles to these dimensions. Types of anti-vibration mountings in general use include—

CORK SLABS AND RUBBER PADS. These are suitable for vibrating machines which do not produce severe shock or high amplitude vibrations and where the intensity of loading on the cork slab or rubber carpet is not so high that the materials will become "hard" under compression. Cork and rubber are reasonably durable materials and can be expected to have a life of at least twenty-five years.

RUBBER CARPET MOUNTINGS. These are designed for heavier machines such as compressors, power-hammers, presses, and generators. A type consisting of studs on either side of a rubber sheet (Fig. 3.27 (*a*)) can be loaded to 36 kN/m² and a heavier type with close-spaced ribs running at right angles on either side of a rubber sheet can be loaded to 430 kN/m² (Fig. 3.27 (*b*)).

BONDED RUBBER MOUNTINGS. These are used for direct connexion of machines to concrete or steel bases. They consist of various steel sections, e.g. plates, angles, pedestals and plugs, which are bonded to

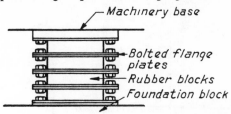

FIG. 3.28. RUBBER-STEEL SANDWICH SPRING MOUNTING

rubber blocks. They can be used for the lightest to the heaviest machines. The sandwich type consisting of layers of rubber separated by steel is illustrated in Fig. 3.28. This mounting is designed to carry 300 kN at a frequency of 2·8 Hz. Rubber-steel sandwich mountings were used to insulate a complete 5-storey building from the vibrations caused by railway trains running beneath the building. The mountings were installed beneath columns as shown in Fig. 3.29. Column loads were up to 2·7 MN. It was stated that the cost of the anti-vibration installation was £3,000 or 5 per cent of the total building cost.[3.26]

LEAF SPRINGS. These were used in the past for forging hammers, but they have been superseded by the simpler rubber mountings.

The blow of heavy hammers is likely to cause considerable oscillation of the anvil block or base when it is supported by anti-vibration mountings. In such cases it may be necessary to provide dampers in horizontal and/or vertical positions between the anvil and base or between the base and the surrounding pit to damp down the oscillations and so bring the anvil to rest before the next blow of the hammer. Such dampers are usually a hydraulic dashpot arrangement whereby movement of the piston forces oil in a cylinder through a small hole. The energy is absorbed in compression and heat in the oil. It is also the practice to provide an air gap between the foundation block of heavy hammers and the surrounding ground by placing the block inside a lined pit. The object of this is to prevent direct transmission of shock waves to adjacent machines or enclosing buildings through the shallow soil layers. Instead the energy waves are transmitted to deeper strata and become considerably attenuated before they reach the surface; hence they are less likely to cause damage or nuisance.

It is desirable to avoid projections from machinery foundation blocks such as thin cantilever brackets in concrete or steel, since these

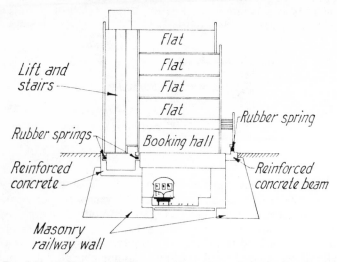

FIG. 3.29.  A FIVE-STOREY BUILDING MOUNTED ON RUBBER-STEEL SPRINGS

may resonate with the machine vibrations. Similarly any light removable steel floor-plates or decking surrounding the foundation block should be bedded on felt or rubber if there is a risk of these light units vibrating in resonance with the machinery. Problems of resonance and interference with close-spaced machinery installations can often be overcome by providing a combined foundation for a number of machines.

### EFFECTS OF SOIL CONDITIONS

In the foregoing notes, little has been said about the effects of different soil or rock types beneath the foundation blocks of heavy vibrating machinery. The most difficult problems are: avoiding excessive amplitude of vibrations within the machinery bedplate and the foundation block causing fatigue and failure of these units; and the transmission of high energy vibrations to the surrounding ground causing damage to adjacent machinery and building structures and annoyance to people nearby. Both these problems are to a great extent independent of the conditions below the foundations. However, certain soil types are more liable than others to consolidate under vibrations, and if the settlement is uneven, tilting of the foundation block will occur. As noted on page 168, even dense sands are liable to consolidate under vibratory loading. Thus, machinery foundations on sands are likely to tilt if out-of-balance moving parts result in eccentricity of loading on the soil; for example if the anvil of a forging hammer is eccentric to the centre of gravity of the concrete base, or if a long foundation block has a large out-of-balance flywheel or crank shaft at one end. Bearing stresses from static and dynamic loading should be kept to low values on loose water-bearing sands. An investigation by Eastwood[3.27] showed that "for a footing on dry sand subjected to severe vibration, a normal failure can occur at about 50 per cent of the static failure load after rather more than $10 \times 10^6$ cycles. For mean loads greater than 50 per cent of the static ultimate load, failure took place after appropriately less cycles of loading."

Eastwood also showed that a loading slightly less than 50 per cent of the static ultimate on dry sand gave heavy settlement at $12 \times 10^6$ cycles, and that inundation of the sand gave marked reductions in bearing capacity compared with that of dry sands.

**Design of Special Machinery Foundations**

Some machinery installations are highly sensitive to slight settlements. An example of the design of foundations for a gear cutting installation is given on pages 429 to 432. The foundations of the proton synchrotron at the CERN Nuclear Research Establishment at Meyrin, near Geneva, described by Adams[3.28] are an outstanding example of the achievement of a high degree of accuracy both in construction and in measures taken to avoid any appreciable differential settlement. The design of the proton synchroton required that units forming a large circular magnet should be set up on a prescribed figure (very nearly a circle) with a mean radius of 100 m in a perfect plane with a tolerance of only 0·1 mm. The foundations had to be designed so that the units could be set up within this tolerance and subsequent distortions had to be less than 1 mm to prevent the machine from being put out of operation. The general arrangement of the structure is shown in Fig. 3.30.

GROUND EXPLORATION

Extensive ground investigations showed 4·5 to 7·5 m of glacial moraine overlying "molasse" rock. The latter consists of interbedded hard and soft marls and sandstones of variable thickness. Compression tests in the laboratory gave the following information on elastic and plastic deformation—

| Load | | Total compressive strain (per cent) | Strain after removal of load (per cent) |
|---|---|---|---|
| Soft marl | 8 kg/cm² | 1·4 | — |
| | 16 kg/cm² | 2·4 | 0·9 |
| | Repeated cycles 8 kg/cm² to zero | 1·9 | 1·2 |
| Hard marl | 8 kg/cm² | 0·6 | — |
| | 16 kg/cm² | 0·9 | 0·3 |
| | Repeated cycles 8 kg/cm² to zero | 0·7 | 0·3 |
| Sandstone | 16 kg/cm² | 0·6 | zero |
| | Repeated cycles 8 kg/cm² to zero | 0·4 | zero |

To investigate the relative horizontal and vertical movements of the moraine and underlying molasse rock, six survey monuments were set up over the site at a depth of 1 m below ground level.

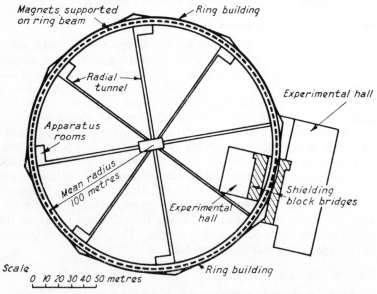

Fig. 3.30. General Arrangement Plan of Proton Synchrotron at Meyrin, Geneva (Adams[3.28])

Measurements of their relative positions to an accuracy of 0·1 mm showed that the horizontal movements in the first year of measurement in the moraine equivalent to a 100 m radius ring were 10 mm. Movements in subsequent years were much smaller and it was thought that the initial movements were due to various excavations over the site. The vertical movements in the moraine were relatively small. The horizontal and vertical movements of the molasse rock were negligible. A study of seismic movements in the area showed that the site was subject to occasional earth tremors of one-half second period giving accelerations of 0·01 to 0·1 *g*. Surface waves with periods of ten to sixty seconds were also liable to occur.

### Design of Foundations

Although the functioning of the machine would not be affected either by tilting in any plane or by lengthening of one diameter and shortening on a diameter at right angles by up to 38 mm, localized distortion of the ring by settlement or horizontal movement of only 1 mm would be detrimental to its performance. It was realized, therefore, that it would be necessary to found the supports to the magnets on the hard marl or sandstone of the molasse to keep relative plastic deformation within these limits.

The magnets were to be enclosed in a ring building covered with several metres of earth to prevent the escape of harmful radiations. One section of the ring was occupied by two experimental halls. Within these buildings shielding had to be provided in the form of movable concrete blocks with a total mass of some 10 000 tonne. It was decided to found the ring building on the moraine, but the experimental halls were founded on the molasse rock by means of large cellular box structures (Fig. 3.31). These were necessary to

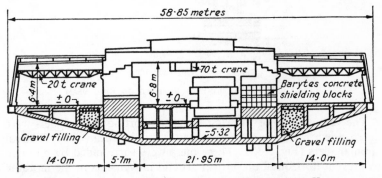

Fig. 3.31. Cellular Box Foundation to Experimental Halls

keep the bearing pressures on the rock to a low value to avoid plastic deformation, and to obtain a high degree of stiffness to avoid distortion when the shielding blocks were moved from point to point to suit the various experiments.

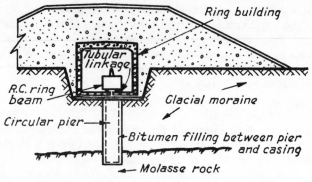

FIG. 3.32. CROSS-SECTION THROUGH RING BUILDING

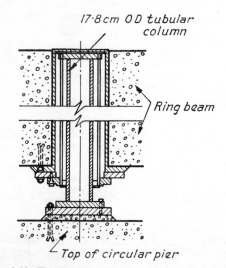

FIG. 3.33. TUBULAR LINKAGE SUPPORTS TO RING BEAM

The foundations of the ring beam supporting the magnets were taken down to the hard marl or sandstone by means of individual circular piers (Fig. 3.32). These piers were surrounded by bitumen to prevent horizontal or vertical ground movements in the moraine being transmitted to them. Each pier was surmounted by a pair of steel columns and the 2 m square ring beam was suspended by tubular steel linkages from the tops of these columns (Fig. 3.33). This suspension arrangement allowed freedom of movement for the ring beam so avoiding high stresses and local distortions in the beam resulting from tilting of the piers consequent on temperature or shrinkage movements of the beam. The alternative of taking the entire ring beam down to the rock was rejected on account of the high cost of construction and the likelihood of uncontrollable temperature variations in the ring. The ring beam was cast in sections to avoid a large total shrinkage; the ring building operates under controlled temperature conditions to avoid excessive expansion or contraction of the ring while the machine is operating. Because the ring beam is on elastic supports it is liable to oscillate under the action of earth tremors or machinery vibrations. Calculations for varying conditions of support showed that the period of oscillation of the undamped ring varied from 3·3 to 43 Hz. It was therefore necessary to provide for damping of oscillations by means of I-beams cast into the ring beam and projecting into boxes filled with bitumen in the floor of the ring building.

SETTING-OUT

Setting-out the magnets on the ring required a very high degree of accuracy. The setting-out was facilitated by constructing eight radial tunnels to the ring building to allow simple triangulation of the survey points on an octagonal figure. These tunnels also served the purpose of service and ventilation tunnels which allowed flow of temperature-controlled air to eight points around the ring beam. Calculations showed that the radius of the beam would increase by 0·5 mm for every 1° C increase in its temperature, but that it would take two days for the ring to heat up by 0·5° C. It was considered that the survey for setting-out purposes could be completed in less than a day, and therefore to allow setting-out to within 0·1 mm it was necessary to control the temperature of the beam to within $\pm 1°$ C. Close control was facilitated by water tubes cast into the ring beam concrete.

A number of the problems of distortion, settlement, and oscillation of the ring beam were investigated in a full-scale trial section of 17 m of the ring building containing a 15 m section of the ring beam on a pair of pier supports. Measurements of all possible modes of movement were made, and in addition the earth pressure on the ring building was measured. Great care was taken in stockpiling and disposal of excavated soil to avoid excessive loading of any part of the site of the building.

REFERENCES

3.1  COOLING, L. F. and WARD, W. H., Some examples of foundation movements due to causes other than structural loads, *Proc. 2nd Int. Conf. Soil Mech.* 2 (Rotterdam, 1948).

3.2  House foundations on shrinkable clays, *B.R.S. Digest No. 3* (London, H.M.S.O., 1950).

3.3  COLLINS, L. E., Some observations on the movement of buildings on expansive soils in Vereeniging and Odendaalrus, *Proc. S.Afr. Inst. C.E.*, pp. 273–285 (Sept. 1957).

3.3a  SAMUELS, S. G. and CHENEY, J. E., Long-term heave of a building on clay due to tree removal, *Proc. Conf. on Settlement of Structures*, Cambridge, Pentech Press, 1974.

3.3b  HAMILTON, J. J., Swelling and shrinking subsoils, *Canadian Bldg. Dig.*, CBD 84, Nat. Res. Council, Ottawa (Dec., 1965).

3.4  WARD, W. H. and SEWELL, H. C., Protection of the ground from thermal effects of industrial plant, *Geotechnique*, **2**, No. 1, pp. 64–81 (June, 1950).

3.5  SKAVEN-HAUG, S. V., Protection against frost heave in the Norwegian Railways, *Geotechnique*, **9**, No. 3, pp. 87–135 (Sept., 1959).

3.6  *Architectural Forum*, Building below zero, pp. 117–121 (U.S.A., Feb., 1958).

3.7  RATHJENS, G. W., Arctic engineering requires knowledge of permafrost behaviour, *Civ. Eng.*, pp. 645–647 (U.S.A., Nov., 1951).

3.8  ROBERTS, P. W. and COOKE, F. A. F., Arctic tower foundations frozen into permafrost, *Eng. News Record*, pp. 38–39 (9th Feb., 1950).

3.9  JENNINGS, J. E. and KNIGHT, K., The additional settlement of foundations due to collapse of structure of sandy soils on wetting, *Proc. 4th Int. Conf. Soil Mech.*, **1**, pp. 316–319 (Zürich, 1953).

3.10  HOLTZ, W. G. and HILF, J. W., Settlement of soil foundations due to saturation, *Proc. 5th Int. Conf. Soil Mech.*, pp. 673–679 (Paris, 1961).

3.11  BELES, A. A. and STANCULESCU, I. T., Moderating the rate of settlement of a building founded on a salt massif, *Geotechnique*, **8**, No. 2, pp. 92–99 (June, 1958).

3.12  *Soil Mechanics in Engineering Practice*, p. 586.

3.13  INST. C. E., *Report on Mining Subsidence* (London, 1959).

3.14  MAUNTNER, K. W., Structures in areas subjected to mining subsidence, *Proc. 2nd Int. Conf. Soil Mech.* **1**, pp. 167–177 (Rotterdam, 1948).

3.15  NAT. BLDG. STUDIES, Mining subsidence effects on small houses, *Special Report No. 12* (London, H.M.S.O., 1951).

3.16  LACEY, W. D. and SWAIN, H. T., Design for mining subsidence, *Architects Journal*, **126**, No. 3287 (10th Oct., 1957); *also* The development of the Nottinghamshire system of construction, *Architects Journal*, **126**, No. 3288 (24th October, 1957).

3.17  VENTER, J., PIRNAY, L., and LESSAGE, G., The protection of buildings against earth movements, *Ann. Min. Belg.*, NCB Translation A. 978/DJB (unpublished), **53**, p. 511 (1954).

3.18 PRYKE, J. S. S., Eliminating the effects of subsidence, *Colliery Eng.*, pp. 501–508 (Dec., 1954).
3.19 WARDELL, K., The protection of structures against subsidence, *Journal R.I.C.S.*, **90**, Pt. 10, pp. 573–579 (April, 1958).
3.20 WEEHUIZEN, J. M., New shafts of the Dutch State mines, *Proc. Symposium on Shaft Sinking and Tunnelling*, Inst. Mining Eng., pp. 28–60 (London, 1959).
3.21 SCOTT, A. C., Sheffield College of Technology: locating and filling old mine working, *Civ. Eng. and Public Works Rev.* (Sept., 1957).
3.22 MEYERHOF, G. G., Building on fill with special reference to the settlement of a large factory, *Struct. Eng.*, **29**, No. 2, pp. 46–57 (Feb., 1951), and discussion, **29**, No. 11, pp. 297–305 (Nov., 1951).
3.23 KILKENNY, W. M., A study of the settlement of restored opencast coal sites and their suitability for building development, *Dept. of Civ. Eng. Bulletin No. 38, Univ. of Newcastle-upon-Tyne* (May, 1968).
3.24 TOMLINSON, M. J. and WILSON, D. M., Preloading of foundations by surcharge on filled ground, *Geotechnique*, **23**, 1, pp. 117–120 (March, 1973).
3.25 CROCKETT, J. H. A. and HAMMOND, R. E. R., Reduction of ground vibrations into structures, *Inst. C.E. Struct. Paper, No. 18* (1947).
3.26 WALLER, R. A., A block of flats isolated from vibration, *Proc. Symposium, Society Environmental Eng.* (April, 1966).
3.27 EASTWOOD, W., Vibrations in foundations, *Struct. Eng.*, **26**, No. 3, pp. 82–98 (March, 1953).
3.28 ADAMS, J. B., The design of foundations for the magnet of the CERN Alternating Gradient Proton Synchrotron, *European Organization for Nuclear Research Publicn. No. CERN. 56–21* (Geneva, 1956).

# 4

# Spread Foundations

THE term "spread foundation" has been used to distinguish between foundations of the strip, pad, and raft type, and deep foundations such as basements, caissons, or piles. Terzaghi and Peck[4.1] define a shallow footing as one which has a width equal to or greater than its depth. This is a reasonable definition for normal pad or strip foundations but it is unsatisfactory for narrow or very wide foundations. In order to avoid possible misunderstandings when writing engineering reports, it is advisable to avoid using the term "shallow foundation" unless the limiting depths are clearly defined in terms of the depth to width ratio. Definitions and general descriptions of strip, pad, and raft foundations are given at the beginning of Chapter 2.

## DETERMINATION OF ALLOWABLE BEARING PRESSURES

### Foundations on Cohesionless Soils

The allowable bearing pressures of spread foundations on cohesionless soils, i.e. gravels, sands and other granular materials, are governed by considerations of the tolerable settlement of the structures. Thus, it is the normal practice to use empirical methods as described in Chapter 2 (pp. 95–101) based on the results of in-situ tests or plate loading tests. The former are generally preferred since they are cheaper and rapid in execution. Plate loading tests are usually restricted to "difficult" soils, i.e. variable fill materials or stony

ground where the obstructions prohibit any form of in-situ penetration tests. Only in the case of narrow foundations on waterlogged
sands need we concern ourselves with making calculations for
ultimate bearing capacity by equations 2.9 or 2.10 (p. 92).

## DEPTH OF FOUNDATIONS

If borehole or in-situ test records show a marked increase in
density of sands with increasing depth below ground level, it may be
tempting to take the foundations deeper than normal in order to take
advantage of the much higher allowable bearing pressures. This
procedure is unlikely to be economical if it involves excavating below
the water-table. Even excavating as little as 0·5 m below the water-
table in a fine sand will give considerable trouble with slumping of
the sides and instability of the base of the excavation. In fact
uncontrolled inflow of water is likely to loosen the ground and hence
decrease the allowable bearing pressures. Stability of excavations
below the water-table in sands can only be achieved by wellpointing
or similar methods (pp. 681 to 699). The cost of these measures is
likely to be higher than founding on looser sands at the higher level
above the water-table even though the lower bearing pressures require
wider foundations.

There is not the same risk of instability when pumping from
gravelly soils, but since these are usually very permeable the pumping
rate will be heavy and the cost of excavation correspondingly
high.

If satisfactory bearing conditions cannot be obtained above the
water table, it is often more economical to pile the foundations than
to excavate for spread foundations below ground water level.

## SETTLEMENTS

An example of the settlement of spread foundations on loose sand
is given by three-storey flats which were built on site at Kirkcaldy in
Fifeshire. The site was near the seashore and the sand was probably
a wind-blown dune deposit. In view of its looseness, as shown by
the standard penetration test which gave $N$-values (uncorrected for
overburden pressure) varying between 1 and 8, a raft foundation was
adopted. This gave an overall bearing pressure on the 61 by 8·2 m
raft of 35 kN/m². The settlements were measured on this block.
They increased immediately the foundation loading increased and the
average, maximum, and maximum differential values were 13, 19,
and 6 mm respectively. On an adjacent block a bearing pressure of
45 kN/m² was given by strip foundations 1·4 m wide in external
walls and 1·8 m wide in the central longitudinal wall. The measured

average, maximum, and maximum differential settlements were 25, 44, and 6 mm respectively. Although these measurements showed that tilting had occurred, the movements were not detrimental to the structure since a rigid form of load-bearing wall construction was used. Such differential settlements would, however, have produced unsightly cracking in any form of "hard-faced" wall panels. On the strength of these results some confidence can be placed in the use of the standard penetration test in dry sands, and they indicate the need for caution in assessing allowable bearing pressures for structures sensitive to settlement which are founded on loose or even medium-dense sands.

## FOUNDATIONS ON LOOSE SATURATED SANDS AND VERY FINE OR SILTY SANDS

If a sand is very loose (value of $N$ of 5 or less) and also in a saturated state, then any form of shock loading may cause spontaneous liquefaction followed by subsidence of the foundation. A rapid change in water-level, such as a sudden rise caused by severe flooding, can give the same effect. Therefore very loose sands in a saturated state should be artificially compacted by vibrators or "vibroflotation" (p. 717). If the size of the foundations and other conditions make such methods impracticable or uneconomical then the load should be carried to underlying denser strata by means of piers or piles.

### Foundations on Cohesive Soils

The ultimate bearing capacity of strip or pad foundations on cohesive soils can be calculated from equations 2.11 and 2.12. In the case of foundations of fairly light structures on firm to stiff clays it is unnecessary to make any calculations to determine consolidation settlement, especially if they are founded on boulder clays. A factor of safety of 2·5 to 3 will ensure that settlements are kept within tolerable limits. It is desirable to make computations of consolidation settlements by the methods described on pages 124 to 138 in all cases of heavy structures, and in cases where there is no previous experience to guide the engineer.

## ESTIMATION OF SHEAR STRENGTHS

One of the chief difficulties in calculating the ultimate bearing capacity of spread foundations at a shallow depth is making a reasonable assessment of the shear strength of the soil. The soil to a depth of 1·2 to 1·5 m in Great Britain, or deeper in tropical or subtropical conditions, is affected to a variable extent by seasonal wetting and drying and the effects of vegetation. Below this surface crust, normally consolidated clays, e.g. estuarine clays, usually show a fairly uniform variation in shear strength with depth. The scatter in laboratory test values is relatively small and is mainly due to disturbance caused by sampling. There is usually a smaller scatter when shear strengths are determined by field vane tests (p. 25).

In British climatic conditions, foundations will normally be placed beneath or at the lower levels of the surface crust which is subject to seasonal wetting and drying (*see* p. 156). Consequently, the minimum values of shear strength which are normally found immediately beneath the surface crust should be taken for the calculation of the ultimate bearing capacity. It is usually found that there is a progressive increase in shear strength with increasing depth below the surface crust, and the engineer may decide to take advantage of this by placing the foundation at a depth below that at which the minimum shear strength occurs. It is not always necessary to take the very lowest values of shear strength, since, as mentioned above, they may be random soil samples which have been affected by excessive sample disturbance.

The alternative to placing the foundations below the zone of seasonal moisture changes (and therefore on soil which has a minimum shear strength) is to place them at a fairly high level within the surface crust. This will enable relatively higher bearing pressures to be used, and because the foundations will have correspondingly smaller dimensions there will not be significant stressing of the softer soil below the surface crust. This procedure entails the risk of detrimental foundation movements, but this can be assessed in the light of available rainfall data, evidence of similar trouble in the locality, susceptibility of the soil to swelling and shrinkage, and the sensitivity of the superstructure to differential movement.

The problem of variation in shear strength is a difficult one in the case of foundations on fissured over-consolidated clays (p. 66) where, in addition to variations within the surface crust, a wide scatter in shear strength test results occurs throughout the full depth of the stratum owing to the effects of random fissuring on sampling and subsequent laboratory testing (*see* Bishop[4.2] and Rowe[1.4]). It has been found that shear strengths derived from plate loading tests or tests on full-scale foundations reflect the fissured strength of the clay, i.e. failure takes place partly through the fissure planes. The scatter of triaxial compression test results on samples from boreholes and trial pits is typically shown in Fig. 4.1 for a site at Naldon in Essex. The shear strengths derived from plate loading tests in a pit on the same site are also shown. These shear strengths correspond to the lowest limits of the triaxial compression test results. Similar results have been found elsewhere in London Clay.

Therefore in the case of foundations on stiff fissured clays, values of shear strength corresponding to the lower limits should be used in conjunction with the appropriate bearing capacity factors for substitution in equations 2.11 and 2.12.

Boulder clays also show wide variations in shear strength due to random inclusions of sands and gravels within the test specimens.

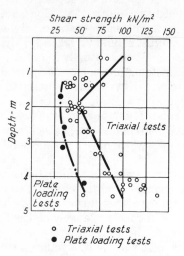

○ *Triaxial tests*
● *Plate loading tests*

FIG. 4.1. VARIATION OF SHEAR STRENGTH WITH DEPTH IN LONDON CLAY AT MALDON (AFTER BISHOP)[4.2]

However, the in-situ strength as determined by full-scale foundation behaviour is usually higher than that indicated by triaxial tests in the laboratory. Therefore, if the *average* shear strength from triaxial tests is taken, the calculated bearing capacity will be on the safe side. Nevertheless, it is advisable to make a careful study of the in-situ characteristics of the boulder clay in case low shear strengths may be the result of lenses of weak clay of appreciable extent which might cause local failure of foundations sited immediately above them.

FOUNDATIONS ON STIFF SOIL OVERLYING A SOFT CLAY STRATUM

In the case of a foundation constructed within a stratum of stiff soil overlying a stratum of soft clay, if the foundation is close enough to the soft layer, it may break through to the latter and result in failure. This danger can arise in normally consolidated clays such as estuarine clays. Normally consolidated clays usually have a crust of stiff dry soil at the surface. Although the stiff crust may have a reasonably high shear strength enabling relatively high bearing pressures to be used, the foundation may be placed sufficiently close to the underlying soft clay for the bearing pressure transmitted through the crust to exceed the ultimate bearing capacity of the soft material.

With normal foundations, it is sufficiently accurate to estimate the bearing pressure on the underlying layers by assuming the load to be spread at an angle of 30° to the vertical as shown in Fig. 4.2. The pressure on the surface of the soft stratum is then given by—

Square (or circular) foundations: $q_1 = q_n \left( \dfrac{B}{B + 1 \cdot 15d} \right)^2$ . (4.1)

Strip foundation: $q_1 = q_n \left( \dfrac{B}{B + 1 \cdot 15d} \right)$ . (4.2)

The values of $q_1$, as calculated from the above equations, should not exceed the safe bearing capacity of the soft stratum. If the foundations are widely spaced (for example if the distance between them exceeds four times the width), it is possible to reduce, to some extent, the bearing pressure on the underlying stratum by increasing the size of the foundation. However, if the footings are closely spaced, the pressures transmitted to the underlying stratum will overlap, as shown in Fig. 4.3. Where they overlap,

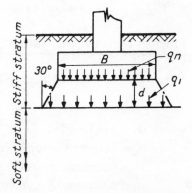

FIG. 4.2. STRIP OR PAD FOUNDATION FOUNDED IN STIFF STRATUM OVERLYING SOFT STRATUM

the bearing pressure on the buried stratum is double that for an isolated foundation. If it is greater than the safe bearing capacity of the soft clay, it may be possible to reduce the applied pressure still further by combining the footings to form a raft foundation or, in the case of a row of footings, to form a strip foundation, but if the bearing pressures are still excessive, consideration will have to be given to piling through the soft layer to a deeper bearing stratum. It should be noted that the stiff stratum in itself acts as a raft beneath the foundations. This natural raft, if thick enough, prevents the soft soil from heaving up beyond the loaded area. Therefore, if the thickness of the stiff stratum between the underside of a pad foundation and the top of the soft clay exceeds half the width of the foundation, the resistance of the stiff layer in

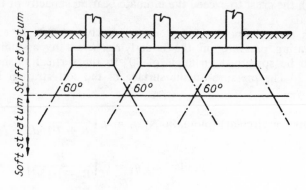

FIG. 4.3. CLOSE-SPACED FOUNDATIONS

forming a natural raft should be allowed for by the following procedure—

Pressure on surface of buried soft stratum $= q$

$$= \frac{W - p_s}{A} . \qquad . \qquad (4.3)$$

where $W =$ total load at base of foundation

$p_s =$ perimeter shearing resistance

$\quad =$ peripheral area of stiff clay $\times$ shear strength of stiff clay

$A =$ base area of foundation.

The value of $q$ should not exceed the safe bearing capacity of the soft clay. Also, as in all cases of foundations on clay soils, the settlement of the foundation due to consolidation within both the stiff and the soft strata should be considered. The peripheral area of stiff clay is obtained by multiplying the peripheral length of the foundation by the depth of stiff clay *below* foundation level. It is inadvisable to allow for any transfer of load from the foundation sides to the stiff clay because shrinkage of the soil or of the foundation concrete, or a combination of both, will open up a gap between the soil and the concrete. If the zone of soil affected by seasonal moisture content changes extends below foundation level, cracking of the soil in the dry season will destroy the perimeter shearing resistance. Therefore, the latter should be calculated only over the thickness of the clay layer *below* the zone of seasonal moisture changes.

## FOUNDATIONS CONSTRUCTED ON A THIN CLAY STRATUM

When foundations are constructed on a thin surface stratum of clay overlying a relatively rigid stratum, there may be a tendency for the thin layer to be squeezed from beneath the foundation, particularly if the soft layer is of varying thickness. Fig. 4.4 shows a foundation of width $B$ on a thin clay layer overlying a stratum of different characteristics and appreciably higher bearing capacity,

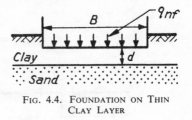

Fig. 4.4. Foundation on Thin Clay Layer

for example a sand layer. The net ultimate bearing capacity of the thin clay layer is given by the formulae—
For a strip foundation of width $B$:

$$q_{nf} = \left(\frac{B}{2d} + \pi + 1\right)c \quad \text{for } \frac{B}{d} \geqslant 2 \quad . \quad . \quad (4.4)$$

For a circular foundation of diameter $B$:

$$q_{nf} = \left(\frac{B}{3d} + \pi + 1\right)c \quad \text{for } \frac{B}{d} \geqslant 6 \quad . \quad . \quad (4.5)$$

For smaller values of $B/d$ than those given above, $q_{nf}$ can be obtained from equations 2.11 and 2.12, i.e. the formulae for a thick clay layer.

It should also be noted that, with a thin clay layer, plastic deformation resulting from overstressing begins at a lower foundation pressure than with a thick clay layer. For both strip and circular foundations, the maximum shear stress induced in the clay stratum is approximately $\frac{1}{2}q_n$.

### Spread Foundations Carrying Eccentric Loading

Examples of foundations subject to eccentric loading are column foundations to tall buildings where wind pressures cause appreciable bending moments at the base of the columns, foundations of stanchions carrying brackets supporting travelling crane girders, and the foundations of retaining walls.

The pressure distribution below eccentrically loaded foundations is assumed to be linear as shown in Fig. 4.5 (*a*), and the maximum pressure must not exceed the maximum pressure permissible for a centrally loaded foundation. For the pad foundation shown in Fig. 4.5 (*a*), where the resultant falls within the middle third of the base,

$$\text{Maximum pressure} = q_{max} = \frac{W}{BL} + \frac{My}{I} \quad . \quad . \quad . \quad (4.6)$$

which for a centrally loaded symmetrical pad becomes—

$$q_{max} = \frac{W}{BL} + \frac{6M}{B^2L} \qquad . \qquad . \qquad . \quad (4.6a)$$

Similarly,

$$\text{Minimum pressure} = q_{min} = \frac{W}{BL} - \frac{6M}{B^2L} \qquad . \qquad . \quad (4.6b)$$

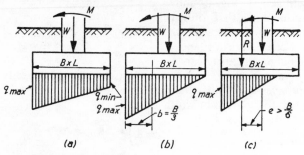

FIG. 4.5. ECCENTRICALLY LOADED PAD FOUNDATION

When the resultant of $W$ and $M$ falls outside the middle-third of the base, equation 4.6b indicates that tension will occur beneath the base. However, no tension can in fact develop and the pressure distribution is as shown in Fig. 4.5 (*c*)—

$$q_{max} = \frac{4W}{3L(B - 2e)} \qquad . \qquad . \qquad . \quad (4.6c)$$

where $W$ = total axial load

$M$ = bending moment

$y$ = distance from centroid of pad to edge

$I$ = moment of inertia of plan of pad

$e$ = distance from centroid of pad to resultant loading

If the criterion for the allowable bearing pressure is the ultimate bearing capacity against shear failure, the value of the latter should be calculated from equations 2.5, 2.6, 2.9, 2.10, 2.11, or 2.12 for the width $B$, the depth $D$ and values of $c$ or $\phi$ obtained from field or laboratory tests. The maximum edge pressure should then have a safety factor of at least 3 on the ultimate bearing capacity except where the eccentric loading is due to wind pressure when the procedure given on page 105 should be followed. If allowable settlement is the criterion for determining bearing pressures then the bearing pressures determined from the curves in Fig. 2.13 should be the maximum edge pressure and not the average pressure. In the case of triangular loading (Fig. 4.5 (*b*)), Peck, Hanson, and Thornburn[4.3] recommend that the allowable bearing pressures should be based on the maximum bearing pressure ($q_{max}$) but the effective foundation width for use in Fig. 2.13 can be taken as one-third of the overall foundation width ($B/3$). Settlement is an important consideration for eccentrically loaded foundations on sands, since if it is excessive the tilting of the foundation will cause an increase in eccentricity with higher edge pressure, followed by further yielding and possible

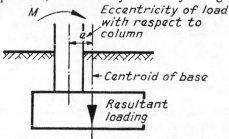

FIG. 4.6. PLACING COLUMN ECCENTRIC TO BASE TO OBTAIN UNIFORM BEARING PRESSURE

failure. If the foundation is restrained against tilting it may be permissible for the maximum edge pressure to exceed that permissible for a centrally loaded foundation.

In cases where eccentric loading on a column is produced by sustained bending moments, for example dead-load bending moments, it may be advantageous to place the column off-centre of the base so that the resultant of the axial load and the bending moments passes through the centroid of the base (Fig. 4.6). Thus there is no eccentricity of loading on the foundation and the pressures are uniformly distributed.

## STRUCTURAL DESIGN AND CONSTRUCTION

In this part of the chapter some of the practical aspects of structural design and methods of construction of shallow foundations are discussed. The structural design methods follow those of CP114 to conform to the foundation design philosophy of the CP2004 code (1972 ed). As yet no procedure has been formulated for bringing soil mechanics design methods into line with the limit state approach of the structural code CP110.

### Strip Foundations for Load-bearing Walls

UNREINFORCED CONCRETE STRIP FOUNDATIONS

The unreinforced concrete strip foundation using a mix of one part of cement to 9 parts of aggregate* is very widely used to support load-bearing walls of dwelling houses, boundary walls, and the wall panels of the ground floor of framed structures. The loading per metre run of wall on this type of foundation is usually quite low, and in the case of strip foundations supporting brick walls, the width of the foundation is governed by the minimum width in which a bricklayer can lay the footing courses, rather than by the bearing capacity of the soil. Thus, in Fig. 4.7, the 281 mm cavity brick wall requires a projection or "oversail" in the concrete base of about 150 mm on each side of the wall, which gives an overall width of 580 mm. The load per metre run of wall of a two-storey dwelling house is about 30 kN, which gives a bearing pressure of little more than 50 kN/m² for the 580 mm wide foundation. For this value, the factor of safety on the ultimate bearing capacity of a stiff clay or a dense sand may be 10 or more. Thus the maximum safe bearing capacity of soils of good supporting value is not utilized, and in these soils it may be advantageous to adopt a narrow strip foundation as illustrated in Fig. 4.8.

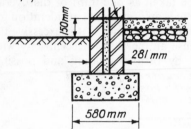

FIG. 4.7. STRIP FOUNDATION TO 11 IN. CAVITY BRICK WALL

NARROW STRIP FOUNDATIONS

The essential feature of the narrow strip foundation is that the trench is too narrow to be dug by labourers working in the trench. It depends for its success on the ability of a mechanical excavator, such as a light tractor-mounted back-acter with a specially narrow bucket, or a bucket-ladder type of trencher to dig the trench, which must be self-supporting until it can be backfilled with concrete. Either hand or mechanical excavation will be ineffective if the ground contains many large stones or thick roots. Also narrow strip foundations cannot economically be used in very soft clays or water-bearing sands which require support by close-timbering.

However, given suitable and reasonably level ground conditions, the narrow strip foundation can result in worthwhile economies in labour and materials. Take for example the foundations of a house with load-bearing walls at 30 kN per metre run of wall on a stiff fissured

---

* A mix as lean as 1 to 9 would not be used if sulphates or other aggressive substances were present in the soil in sufficient quantity to be deleterious to concrete (*see* Chapter 13).

clay. A suitable foundation depth to guard against seasonal swell and shrinkage would be 1 m, and the ultimate bearing capacity of the soil for a strip foundation 0·6 m wide at this depth is 7·8 times

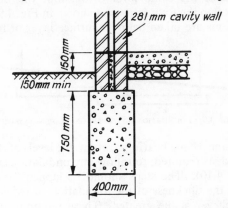

FIG. 4.8. NARROW STRIP FOUNDATION TO 11 IN. CAVITY BRICK WALL

the shear strength (*see* Fig. 2.11 (*c*)). Assuming a shear strength of say 50 kN/m², the ultimate bearing capacity is 390 kN/m². Therefore the conventional strip foundation with a 281 mm brick footing wall, which requires a minimum width for construction purposes of 580 mm, has a bearing pressure of 52 kN/m², which gives a safety factor of 7·5 on the ultimate value.

For a narrow strip foundation of the type shown in Fig. 4.8, a higher proportion of the bearing capacity can be utilized. A practical width of 0·4 m would be required for the 281 mm cavity wall carried by the strip foundation. The quantities for the two types of foundation per metre run of wall can be compared as follows—

|  | Conventional strip | Narrow strip |
|---|---|---|
| Overall width | 0·58 m | 0·4 m |
| Overall depth | 1 m | 1 m |
| Total excavation | 0·58 m³ | 0·40 m³ |
| Concrete | 0·58 × 0·30 = 0·17 m³ | 0·40 × 0·75 = 0·30 m³ |
| Brickwork | 0·7 m² | 0·25 m² |
| Formwork to top edges of strip | nil | May be required on irregular ground |
| Return and ram excavated soil | 2 × 0·7 × 0·15 = 0.21 m³ | 2 × 0·25 × 0·06 = 0·03 m³ |
| Disposal of surplus soil | 0·37 m³ | 0·37 m³ |

## STEPPED FOUNDATIONS

When building on sloping ground, strip foundations need not necessarily be at the same level throughout the building. It is permissible to step the foundations as shown in Fig. 4.9. Similarly if strip foundations are taken below a surface layer of filling or weak

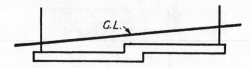

FIG. 4.9. FOUNDATIONS STEPPED ON SLOPING GROUND

soil on to the underlying bearing stratum, the levels of the foundation can be stepped, as required, to follow any undulations in the bearing stratum (Fig. 4.10). The steps should be lapped for a distance at least equal to the thickness of the foundation or twice the height of the step whichever is the greater. These requirements are shown

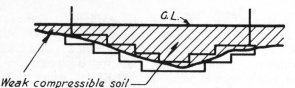

FIG. 4.10. FOUNDATIONS STEPPED TO FOLLOW UNDULATIONS IN BEARING STRATUM

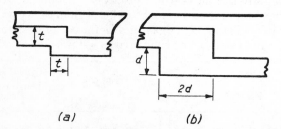

*(a)*       *(b)*

FIG. 4.11. REQUIREMENTS FOR OVERLAPPING STEPPED FOUNDATION

in Fig. 4.11 (*a*) and (*b*). The steps should not be of greater height than the thickness of the foundations unless special precautions are taken. For example, it might be necessary to step foundations to get below an old cellar. It would be clearly unwise to step the foundations as shown in Fig. 4.12 (*a*). The shallow foundations in Fig. 4.12 (*a*) are on natural soil which may be loose and of fairly high compressibility at a shallow depth, whereas the foundations below the cellar are on dense or stiffer soil which has consolidated under the weight of the building carried on the cellar. The foundations could be stepped as shown in Fig. 4.12 (*b*), or, to save excavation

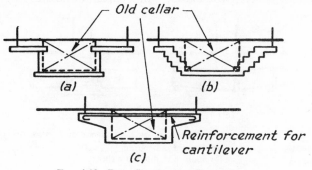

FIG. 4.12. DEEP STEPPING OF FOUNDATION

and materials, they could be constructed as shown in Fig. 4.12 (*c*), but in this case the special precautions would take the form of reinforcement to allow the shallow portions to cantilever from the deep central portion.

### REQUIREMENTS FOR THICKNESS

The thickness of concrete in a lightly-loaded conventional strip foundation is, more often than not, governed by the local authorities' bye-law requirements. The British 1972 *Building Regulations* require the thickness to be at least equal to the projection from the face of the wall or footing with a minimum thickness of 150 mm. This minimum is necessary for rigidity, to enable the foundations to bridge over loose pockets in the soil, and to resist longitudinal forces set up by thermal expansion and contraction, and moisture movements of the footing walls. On clay soils swelling pressures can be of a fairly high order.

When strip foundations carry heavy loading, the criterion for the width of the foundations is then likely to be the allowable bearing pressure, and the thickness of the strip is governed by its strength to resist failure of the projecting portions in bending or shear. The mode of failure in bending is illustrated in Fig. 4.13 (*a*), and in punching shear in Fig. 4.13 (*b*). In an unreinforced strip foundation failure in bending will be the governing factor. This can be prevented by an adequate thickness of concrete, with or without a stepped or sloping transition from the wall to the bottom width. A conservative design rule is to proportion the thickness of the strip so that no tension is developed on the underside of the strip. This is achieved by the rule of thumb procedure of making the thickness equal to twice the projection. However, The *B.S. Code of Practice 101*:1963[4.4] allows a distribution of loading at an angle of 45° from the base of the wall for concrete foundations, or a spread of load through brick

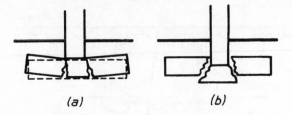

FIG. 4.13. STRUCTURAL FAILURE OF UNREINFORCED FOUNDATIONS
(*a*) Failure in bending.
(*b*) Failure in punching shear.

footings of a quarter of a brick per course (51 to 75 mm). This procedure is illustrated for plain strip, stepped, and sloping foundations in Fig. 4.14 (*a*) to (*d*).

The 45° load distribution implies a small order of tension on the underside of the foundation, but its magnitude cannot be determined since it depends on the bending of the strip and the eccentricity of loading. These cannot be calculated with any pretence of accuracy; for this reason, the nominal 45° distribution is preferred to design

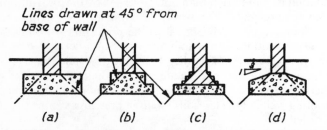

FIG. 4.14. PROPORTIONING THICKNESS OF UNREINFORCED STRIP FOUNDATIONS
BASED ON 45° LOAD DISTRIBUTION
(*a*) Plain strip.
(*b*) Stepped concrete.
(*c*) Stepped brick footings.
(*d*) Concrete with sloping upper face.

procedures which are based on permitting a certain tensile stress to develop.

In wide and deep foundations consideration must be given to economies in concrete quantities that can be achieved by stepping or sloping the footings. It will be seen from Fig. 4.14 (*a*) that there is a considerable area of concrete which is not contributing to the distribution of the load from the wall. The wastage is less if the concrete is stepped as shown in Fig. 4.14 (*b*). However, the construction of such a stepped form would mean concreting in two lifts with formwork to the upper step. The cost of these operations is likely to be more than a simple addition to the thickness of the foundation. In the case of brick or stone-masonried load-bearing walls, the stepping can conveniently be carried out in the wall materials (Fig. 4.14 (*c*)). Sloping the upper face of the projections (Fig. 4.14 (*d*)) will give savings in concrete and will enable the concrete to be placed in one lift, but if the slope is steeper than about 1 vertical to 3 horizontal it will require formwork. Such formwork is costly to construct in a trench and requires weighting down. However, the savings given by haunching at flat slopes as in Fig. 4.14 (*d*) are problematic except for very long continuous foundations, and in most cases the plain strip (Fig. 4.14 (*a*)) is the most economical.

In wide or heavily loaded strip foundations it is always worthwhile to keep in mind the economies that unreinforced may have over reinforced concrete foundations. This is especially the case if foundations have to be taken to a greater than nominal depth, to get below a layer of filling or weak soil for example. In such circumstances it may well be more economical to backfill the trench with a sufficient depth of lean concrete to conform to the requirement of the 45° load distribution rather than incur the expense of providing and bending reinforcement and assembling it in a deep timbered trench, with the extra care that is necessary in placing the concrete in such conditions. Savings in cement are also given, because in non-aggressive soils 1:9 concrete can be used in unreinforced foundations, whereas concrete made in accordance with *CP 114*[4,5] and other structural codes usually requires to be richer.

## Reinforced Concrete Strip Foundations

Reinforced concrete strip foundations are likely to show an advantage in cost over unreinforced concrete where weak soil and heavy wall loading require a wide strip at a comparatively shallow depth. Reinforcement in the form of *longitudinal* bars is also desirable in strip foundations on highly variable soils when the foundation is enabled to bridge over local weak or hard spots in the soil at foundation level; or when there is an abrupt change in loading.

The transverse reinforcement in a wide strip foundation is designed on the assumption that the projection behaves as a cantilever with its critical section on the face of the wall (line *XX* in Fig. 4.15), and with a loading on the underside of the cantilever equal to the actual net bearing pressure under the worst conditions of loading (i.e. maximum eccentricity if the loading is not wholly axial). The main reinforcement takes the form of bars at the bottom of the slab. The slab must also be designed to withstand punching shear, calculated on the faces of the wall, and also shear and bond stresses. The resistance to

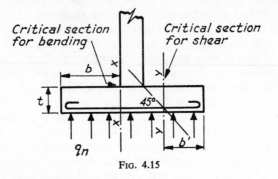

FIG. 4.15

punching shear stress gives an approximate guide to the required thickness of the strip, namely—

$$\text{Required thickness (Fig. 4.15)} = t = \frac{q_n \times b}{1000 \times s_p} \text{ mm} \quad . \text{ (4.7)}$$

where $q_n$ = net pressure on underside of strip (kN/m²)
  $b$ = width of projecting part of strip (mm)
  $s_p$ = safe punching shear stress (N/mm²).

The *CP 114*[4.5] does not recognize punching shear and gives no values of safe stress. However, this criterion gives a useful guide to the thickness requirements and a value of $s_p$ of 1·4 N/mm² may be taken as suitable for the classes of concrete given in Tables 4 and 5 of *CP 114*. Having obtained a preliminary figure for the overall thickness it is then necessary to check the required effective depth to resist bending and shear. If the economical depth to resist bending and shear stresses is less than the depth for punching shear, then the latter should be disregarded. In calculating bending stresses, the projecting portion $b$ in Fig. 4.15 is taken as a cantilever, i.e. bending moment at face of wall where $b$ is in m—

$$M_b = \frac{q_n \times b^2}{2} \text{ kNm per m length of wall} \quad . \text{ (4.8)}$$

It is further necessary to check the shear stress at the critical section $YY$ in Fig. 4.15 given by the intersection of a line drawn at

* See *Amendment* No. 1, dated 19th February, 1965.

45° from the base of the wall with the centre of the layer of bottom reinforcement.

$$\text{Shear stress} = \frac{q_n \times b'}{l_a} \text{ N/mm}^2 . \qquad . \qquad . \quad (4.9)$$

where $l_a$ = lever arm at section $YY$ and $b'$ are in mm.

If the shear stress is greater than the values given in Tables 6 and 10 of *CP 114* it should be reduced by increasing the effective depth of the strip. Shear reinforcement in the form of stirrups or inclined bars should be avoided if at all possible.

As noted for unreinforced concrete foundations, economy in concrete quantities can be made by sloping or stepping the upper face of the projections. The former shape is usually preferred but if the foundation is short, the cost of formwork to the slope or constructing it without formwork in a dry concrete, will exceed the cost of the extra concrete in a rectangular section. However, for long lengths of strip foundation, where travelling formwork or other methods of repetitive construction can be used, the savings in the quantity of concrete given by a sloping face may well show savings in the overall costs.

CONSTRUCTIONAL DETAILS

It is good practice to lay a blinding coat of 50 to 75 mm of lean-mix concrete over the bottom of the foundation trench in order to provide a clean dry surface on which to assemble the reinforcement and pack up the bars to the correct cover. The blinding concrete should be placed as quickly as possible after trimming the excavation to the specified levels: it will then serve to protect the foundation soil from deterioration by rain, sun, or frost. If the excavated material is a reasonably clean sand or sand/gravel mixture, it can be mixed with cement for the blinding layer. There is no need to use imported graded aggregates if the excavated soil will itself make a low-grade concrete.

To protect the reinforcing steel against corrosion, a minimum cover of 50 mm is desirable between the surface of the blinding concrete and the bottom layer of reinforcement. If concrete is placed against rough timber or untimbered soil the nominal cover should be increased to 75 mm. If blinding concrete is not provided the cover should be 75 to 100 mm depending on the type of soil. The latter requirement refers to the ease with which the soil can be trimmed to a true surface which will not deteriorate under the weather or the feet of workmen. Thus a loose sand is easily disturbed and displaced, and 75 mm of cover could not easily be maintained, whereas a compact sand/gravel mixture or a hard clay (if prevented from softening) would give a stable surface enabling the 75 mm cover to be maintained. Further information on methods of excavating and protecting foundation trenches is given in Chapter 9. It should be noted that *CP 114* (clause 307) requires a cover of only 40 mm between reinforcing bars and the soil. The author recommends that his larger figures should be adopted, although a cover of as much as 100 mm should rarely be required.

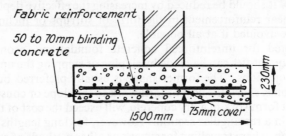

FIG. 4.16. REINFORCED CONCRETE STRIP FOUNDATION FOR 440 mm BRICK WALL

A typical arrangement of a reinforced concrete strip foundation for a brick footing wall is shown in Fig. 4.16. The fabric reinforcement is wholly in the bottom of the slab and the "mat" of reinforcement

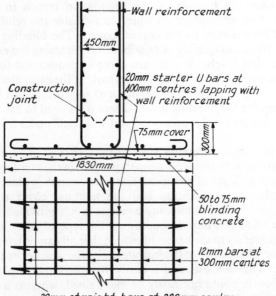

FIG. 4.17. STRIP FOUNDATION TO REINFORCED CONCRETE LOAD-BEARING WALL

may be assembled on the surface, concrete spacer blocks wired on, and the whole assembly lowered on to the blinding concrete.

Fig. 4.17 shows the reinforcement for a wide strip foundation supporting a load-bearing wall also in reinforced concrete.

### Unreinforced Concrete Pad Foundations

The methods of design of unreinforced and reinforced concrete pad foundations are similar in principle to those described in the preceding pages for strip foundations. Thus the minimum size of the pad is given by the practical requirement of being able to excavate by hand to the required depth and level off the bottom and to lay bricks or fix steelwork for the columns. The minimum size for a 215 mm square brick pier is a base 510 mm square. The design corresponding in constructional technique to the narrow strip foundation is the circular pad in which a mechanical earth auger is used to drill a hole to the required depth which is backfilled with concrete. A brick pier may be built off the levelled surface, or a pocket may be cast into the pad to receive a steel or precast concrete column. The savings in mechanically augered excavations are more in terms of labour and time than in quantities of excavation or concrete. They are most favourable in the case of deep pier foundations.

As in the case of strip foundations, the thickness of unreinforced concrete pad foundations is given by the necessity of preventing development of tension on the underside of the base or reducing it to a small value. The former criterion is given by the rule of thumb procedure of making the thickness twice the projection, while the latter can be determined by the normal British practice of a 45° distribution of loading (as Fig. 4.14).

The considerations for determining the choice of stepped or sloping foundations or a plain rectangular section are the same as those described for strip foundations.

### Reinforced Pad Foundations

The procedure for the design of reinforced concrete pad foundations is as follows—

(*a*) Determine the base area of the foundation by dividing the total load of the column and base by the allowable bearing pressure on the soil.

(*b*) Determine the overall depth of the foundation required by punching shear, based on the column load only.

(*c*) Select the type of foundation to be used, i.e. simple slab base, or sloping upper surface. Assume dimensions of slope.

(*d*) Check dimensions by computing beam shear stress at critical sections, on the basis that diagonal shear reinforcement should not be provided.

(*e*) Compute bending moments and design the reinforcement.

(*f*) Check bond stresses in steel.

### CALCULATION OF REQUIRED THICKNESS OF PAD TO RESIST PUNCHING SHEAR

An approximate guide to the required overall thickness of the pad at the column is given from considerations of punching shear. As

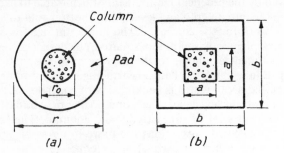

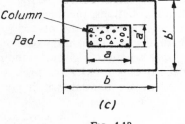

FIG. 4.18

already mentioned on page 220, this criterion is not recognized by *CP 114*. For circular pads and columns (Fig. 4.18 (*a*)),

$$\text{Required thickness, } t = \frac{W\left(1 - \dfrac{r_o^{\,2}}{r^2}\right)}{2\pi r_o s_p} \text{ mm.} \qquad . \qquad . \qquad . \ (4.10)$$

For square pads and columns (Fig. 4.18 (*b*)),

$$t = \frac{W\left(1 - \dfrac{a^2}{b^2}\right)}{4 \times a \times s_p} \text{ mm.} \qquad . \qquad . \qquad . \ (4.11)$$

For rectangular pads and columns (Fig. 4.18 (*c*)),

$$t = \frac{W\left(1 - \dfrac{aa'}{bb'}\right)}{2(a + a')s_p} \text{ mm.} \qquad . \qquad . \text{ (4.11a)}$$

where $r_o$, $r$, $a$, $a'$, $b$, and $b'$ are the dimensions *in mm* of the columns and pads as shown in Fig. 4.18 (*a*) to (*c*), $W$ is the column load in Newtons, and $s_p$ the safe punching shear stress in $N/mm^2$. A value of $s_p$ of $1 \cdot 4$ $N/mm^2$ can be taken for the classes of concrete given in Tables 4 and 5 of *CP 114*. Having obtained an approximate value of thickness, it must be checked by calculating the shear stress at critical sections as required by clause 340*c* of *CP 411* and if necessary the thickness required by punching shear can be disregarded as noted on page 220.

CALCULATION OF SHEAR STRESS AT CRITICAL SECTIONS

In the case of pads of uniform thickness, the critical section is at the intersection of lines drawn at 45° from the base of the column

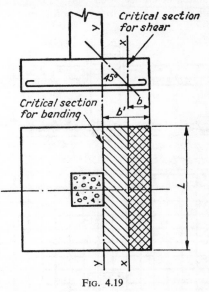

FIG. 4.19

with the bottom layer of reinforcement of the pad, i.e. section $XX$ in Fig. 4.19.

$$\text{Shear stress} = \frac{q_n \times b \times L}{L \times l_a} \qquad . \qquad . \qquad . \text{ (4.12)}$$

where $q_n$ = net bearing pressure on area outside section under consideration

$\quad b$ = width of section under consideration

$\quad l_a$ = lever arm of section

$\quad L$ = length of pad.

In the case of stepped footings, other critical sections may exist at the face of each step, and the shear stress should be checked at the reduced thickness at each step. Where pads have a sloping upper face it may be necessary to check the shear stress at two or three points. If the shear stress is greater than the permissible values given in Tables 6 and 10 of *CP 114*, then it will be necessary to increase the thickness of the base. Shear reinforcement in the form of stirrups or inclined bars should be avoided if at all possible.

### CALCULATION OF BENDING MOMENTS IN CENTRALLY-LOADED PAD FOUNDATIONS

The *CP 114* states in clause 340*a* that "The bending moments at any section of a base for a reinforced concrete column or wall should

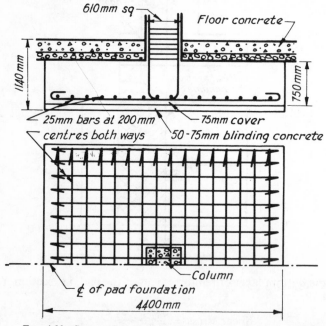

FIG. 4.20. SQUARE PAD FOUNDATION (*see* example 4.5, p. 254)

be taken to be the moment of the forces over the entire area on one side of the section. The critical section for bending in the base should be taken at the face of the column or wall."

Thus in Fig. 4.19—

Bending moment at critical section $YY$

$$= q_n \times b' \times \frac{b'}{2} \text{ per unit width of pad . } . \quad (4.13)$$

Square or rectangular base slabs are preferred to circular slabs since the latter require reinforcing bars of varying lengths, and formwork, if required for circular steps or sloping faces, is expensive. Typical reinforcement details for a pad foundation are shown in Fig. 4.20. For rectangular bases, *CP 114* requires the reinforcement parallel to the short side to be more closely spaced near the column (clause 340*b*).

### PAD FOUNDATIONS FOR L-SHAPED COLUMNS

Columns at the corners of reinforced concrete framed structures are often L-shaped for architectural reasons. The foundation slab must be made concentric with the centroid of the column, as in the column base shown in Fig. 4.21. The foundation slab is designed in a similar manner to square or rectangular bases. The punching shear is small because of the large perimeter of the column in relation to the load carried.

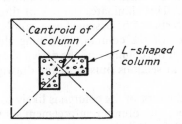

FIG. 4.21. PAD FOUNDATION TO L-SHAPED COLUMN

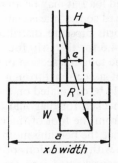

FIG. 4.22. ECCENTRICALLY LOADED PAD FOUNDATION

### ECCENTRICALLY LOADED PAD FOUNDATIONS

Where the lateral loads or bending moments on a column come from any direction, for example from wind loads, a square foundation slab is desirable; unless, for reasons of limitation of space, a rectangular foundation must be provided. However, where the bending moments always act in the same direction, as in columns supporting rigid framed structures, the foundation slab can be lengthened in the direction of the eccentricity. Thus in Fig. 4.22, if the resultant $R$ of the vertical load $W$ and the horizontal load $H$ cuts the base at a distance $e$ from its centroid, then when $e$ is smaller than $\frac{a}{6}$.

Maximum bearing pressure at toe of slab

$$= \frac{W}{ab}\left(1 + \frac{6e}{a}\right) \qquad . \qquad . \qquad . \qquad . \quad (4.14)$$

Minimum bearing pressure at heel of slab

$$= \frac{W}{ab}\left(1 - \frac{6e}{a}\right) \qquad . \qquad . \qquad . \quad (4.14a)$$

When $e$ is greater than $\frac{a}{6}$

Maximum bearing pressure at toe of slab

$$= \frac{4W}{3b(a - 2e)} \qquad . \qquad . \qquad . \qquad . \quad (4.15)$$

The dimensions of the base slab, $a$ and $b$, are proportioned in such a way that the maximum bearing pressure at the toe does not exceed the allowable bearing pressure (*see* p. 211). If a column carries a permanent bending moment, for example a bracket carrying a sustained load, it may be an advantage to place the column off centre on the pad so that the eccentricity of the resultant loading is zero, giving uniform pressure distribution on the base in a similar manner to Fig. 4.6 for the strip foundation. This eliminates the risk of tilting.

The long toe section of the slab should be designed as a cantilever about a section through the face of the column. Punching shear should be calculated on the faces of the column and the design should be checked for diagonal tension at sections outside a line drawn at 45° from the foot of the column.

Since the bending moment at the foot of the column is likely to be large with foundations of this type, the column reinforcement should be properly tied into the base slab. Reinforcement details for an eccentrically loaded pad foundation are shown in Fig. 4.23.

In the case of large eccentricity from any direction on square or rectangular pad foundations, consideration can be given to the passive resistance of the soil in contact with the foundation block to resist overturning. For this to be taken into account it is necessary that the foundation block should be cast against the undisturbed soil, and that the soil itself should not yield appreciably under the lateral load, or that the backfilling can be rammed between the face of the block and the excavation to a density equal to or greater than that of the surrounding soil. Thus, a dense sand or sand and gravel would have a high resistance to overturning of a foundation block. No resistance to overturning could be given by a clay soil if the block were sited within the zone of seasonal moisture movements, when

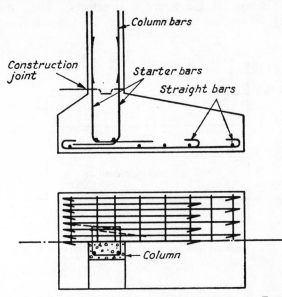

Fig. 4.23. Reinforcement Details for Pad Foundation with Eccentrically Placed Column

shrinkage might open a gap between the soil and the block. For a discussion of the design methods involved the reader is referred to the paper by Hamilton.[4.6]

### Foundations Close to Existing Structures

Where space for the base slab of foundations is restricted, for example where a strip foundation is to be built close to an existing wall (Fig. 4.24), there may not be room for a projection on both sides

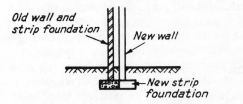

Fig. 4.24. Strip Foundation close to Existing Structure

of the column or wall. If the projection is on one side only, eccentric loading is inevitable. This may not matter in the case of light loadings or if the foundation material is unyielding, but eccentric loading on compressible soils may lead to tilting of the foundation with consequent transmittal of dangerous horizontal forces on the walls or columns of the abutting structures. Some degree of eccentricity of loading on the soil may be permitted in framed

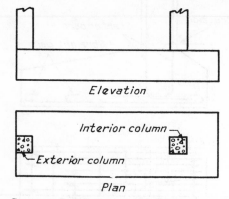

FIG. 4.25. COMBINED PAD FOUNDATION FOR EXTERIOR AND INTERIOR
COLUMNS

structures which are properly tied together, or in deep foundations where the tilting can be resisted by the passive resistance of the soil against the vertical surfaces of the foundation wall.

A method used to counteract tilting in column foundations of framed structures is to combine the exterior foundation with the adjoining interior foundation as shown in Fig. 4.25. Because of the eccentricity of loading on the base of such a combined foundation, there will be unequal distribution of pressure on the soil and consequently a tendency to relative settlement between the columns. This must be resisted by the structural rigidity of the base slab. Top and bottom reinforcement is required and since shear forces are likely to be large, link steel will probably be necessary.

If there are wide differences in the loading of adjacent columns in a combined foundation, the desirability of having uniform bearing pressures would theoretically require a trapezoidal base slab (Fig. 4.26 (*a*)). In practice the trapezoidal base slab should be avoided if possible, since it requires cutting and bending bars of differing lengths. In many cases it is possible to provide the additional bearing area for the more heavily loaded column by extending the

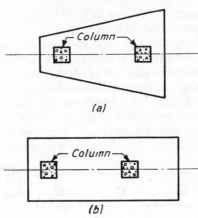

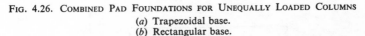

FIG. 4.26. COMBINED PAD FOUNDATIONS FOR UNEQUALLY LOADED COLUMNS
(*a*) Trapezoidal base.
(*b*) Rectangular base.

cantilevered portion of the base slab whilst keeping the sides parallel
(Fig. 4.26 (*b*)).

### Continuous Pad and Beam Foundations

It may often be more economical to construct the foundations of
a row of columns as a row of pad foundations with only a joint
between each pad, rather than to provide individual excavations at a
close spacing. Foundations of this type with individual but touching
pads are more economical in reinforcing steel than continuous beam
foundations, since the latter require a good deal of reinforcement to
provide for the stresses due to differential settlement between
adjacent columns. However, continuous beam foundations may be
required to bridge over weak pockets in the soil or to prevent
excessive differential settlement between adjacent columns. The
advantages of the continuous pad or beam foundation are: ease of
excavation by backacter or other machines; any formwork required
can be fabricated and assembled in longer lengths; and there is
improved continuity and ease of access for concreting the foundations. These foundations have the added advantage of providing
strip foundations for panel walls of the ground floor of multi-storey
framed buildings.

STRUCTURAL DESIGN OF CONTINUOUS BEAM FOUNDATIONS

Continuous beam foundations may take the form of simple
rectangular slab beams (Fig. 4.27 (*a*)) or, for wider foundations with

heavy loads, inverted T-beams (Fig. 4.27 (*b*)). Structural design problems are complicated by factors such as varying column loads, varying live loads on columns, and variations in the compressibility of the soil. In most cases it is impossible to design the beams on a satisfactory theoretical basis. In practice, soil conditions are rarely sufficiently uniform to assume uniform settlement of the foundations even though the column loads are equal. Inevitably there will be a tendency to greater settlement under an individual column, which will then transfer a greater proportion of the load to the soil beneath adjacent columns until the whole foundation eventually reaches

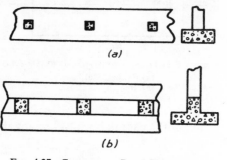

FIG. 4.27. CONTINUOUS BEAM FOUNDATIONS
(*a*) Rectangular slab.
(*b*) Inverted T-beam.

equilibrium. The amount of load transfer and of yielding of individual parts of the foundation beam is determined by the flexural rigidity of the beam and the compressibility of the soil considered as one unit.

For reasonably uniform soil conditions and where maximum settlement will, in any case, be of a small order, a reasonably safe design method is to allow the maximum combined dead and live load on all columns, to assume uniform pressure distribution on the soil, and to design the foundation as an inverted beam on unyielding columns. However, if the compressibility of the soil is variable, and if the live load distribution on the columns can vary, this procedure could lead to an unsafe design. The structural engineer must then obtain from the soil mechanics engineer estimates of maximum and differential settlements for the most severe conditions of load distribution in relation to soil characteristics. The soil mechanics engineer must necessarily base his estimates on complete flexibility in the foundation, and the structural engineer then designs the foundation beam on the assumption of a beam on yielding supports.

A description of methods of calculating bending moments for these conditions is beyond the scope of this book, and the reader is referred to textbooks on reinforced concrete design for guidance on this aspect of the design. However, it may be helpful to give a few illustrations of the forms which foundation settlements and deflexion of continuous beams can take for various conditions of column loading and soil compressibility (Fig. 4.28 (*a*) to (*h*)). It will be seen from Fig. 4.28*d* (i), *f*(i), and *h*(i) that certain arrangements of column load distribution in relation to variable soil conditions can lead to heavy bending moments or excessive deflexions in the foundation beam. Conversely, other distributions of column load can give lower bending moments or less deflexion than uniform load distribution (compare Fig. 4.28*d* (ii), *f*(ii), and *h*(ii) with the corresponding effects of equal load distribution in (*c*), (*e*), and (*g*).

The degree of rigidity which must be given to the foundation beam is governed by the limiting differential movements which can be tolerated by the superstructure and by considerations of economies in the size and amount of reinforcement in the beams. Too great a rigidity should be avoided since it will result in high bending moments and shearing forces, and the possibility of a wide crack forming if moments and shears are underestimated (this is always a possibility since close estimate of settlements cannot be relied on from the soil mechanics engineer and it may be uneconomical to design on the worst conceivable conditions). The general aim should be a reasonable flexibility within the limits tolerated by the superstructure, and in cases of high bending moments the junctions of beams, slabs, and columns should be provided with generous splays and haunches to avoid concentrations of stress at sharp angles. When considering the effects of settlements of columns on the superstructure the structural designer should keep in mind the data on limiting distortions given on page 108.

### Foundations to Structural Steel Columns

The traditional design of bases of structural steel columns consisted of a rectangular steel base plate, rigidly connected to the stanchion by gussets and angles, while holding-down bolts secured the plate to the concrete foundations. The size of the base plate was, more often than not, dictated by the size of the column and the space taken up by the gussets and angles, rather than by the allowable bearing pressure on the concrete beneath the base plate. However, the general adoption of welding in steel structures has led to a reduction in the size of base plates (since clearances need not be allowed for bolt holes), and the use of hinged ends to columns in such structures as portal framed buildings and guyed masts permits base plates of minimum area, which are then governed in size by the allowable bearing pressure which can be imposed on the

Equal column loading

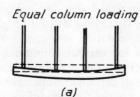

(a)

Unequal column loading
Heavy columns

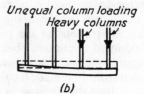

(b)

Uniform soil compressibility

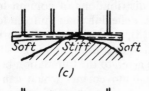

Soft    Stiff    Soft

(c)

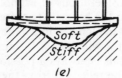

Soft    Stiff    Soft

d(i)

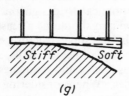

Soft
Stiff

(e)

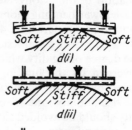

Soft    Stiff    Soft

d(ii)

Soft
Stiff

f(i)

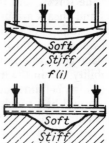

Stiff    Soft

(g)

Soft
Stiff

f(ii)

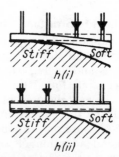

Stiff    Soft

h(i)

Stiff    Soft

h(ii)

Variable soil compressibility

FIG. 4.28. SETTLEMENT OF CONTINUOUS BEAM FOUNDATIONS FOR VARIOUS SOIL AND LOADING CONDITIONS

concrete. Also there is an increasing tendency to embed the feet of steel or precast concrete columns in pockets formed in the concrete foundations.

Designers often assume that the ultimate bearing capacity of the surface of the concrete foundation is equal to its unconfined compressive cube strength. This is clearly a very conservative procedure since the confining effect of the surrounding concrete is neglected. Investigations by Meyerhof at the Building Research Station[4.7] into different sizes and thickness of blocks showed that the ultimate bearing capacity of the concrete was several times the cube strength. Indeed for wide foundations reinforced against splitting, the ultimate bearing capacity was seven times the cube strength.

The results of these researches have not yet been expressed in practical rules for design. It is the usual practice to check the permissible stress on the surface of the foundation by referring to British Standard Code of Practice CP111.[4.8] This states that the maximum stresses resulting from concentrated loading, e.g. a column base on a concrete pad, should not exceed the permissible uniform distributed stress on a plain concrete wall by more than 50 per cent. The permissible distributed stress is defined as 25 per cent of the works cube crushing strength or not more than $10.5$ N/mm² whichever is less. Therefore—

$$p_{cc} = \not> 1.5 \times \frac{u}{4} \not> 10.5 \text{ N/mm}^2 \qquad . \qquad . \quad (4.16)$$

where $p_{cc}$ = maximum bearing pressure on concrete pad at plane of contact

$u$ = cube crushing strength of concrete.

### EMBEDMENT OF COLUMNS IN CONCRETE PAD FOUNDATIONS

Design methods to determine the required depth of embedment of a column to provide fixity in its concrete foundation block are given in the paper by Hamilton.[4.6] Referring to Fig. 4.29, the criteria determining the depth of embedment are the permissible compressive and tensile stresses in the concrete.

If the maximum compressive stress ($p_{cc}$) in the concrete is not to exceed one-quarter of the minimum works cube strength ($u$)

$$h \text{ must not be less than } \sqrt{\frac{Q_2 M}{bu}} \qquad . \qquad . \quad (4.17)$$

and if the permissible tensile stress of $0.03u$ is not to be exceeded, then

$$h \text{ must not be less than } \sqrt{\frac{Q_1 M}{(B - b)u}} \qquad . \qquad . \quad (4.18)$$

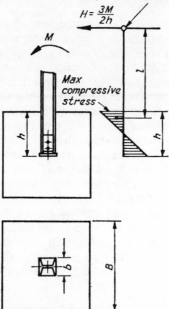

FIG. 4.29. EMBEDMENT OF STEEL STANCHIONS IN CONCRETE PAD FOUNDATION

In general cases the constants $Q_1$ and $Q_2$ can be taken as 210 and 17 respectively, but if the horizontal force $H$ is large and $\dfrac{l}{h}$ is small then $Q_1$ and $Q_2$ should be taken from the following table—

Table 4.1

| $\dfrac{l}{h}$ | $Q_1$ | $Q_2$ Forces on 2 faces Width $=\dfrac{3}{2}\times b$ | Forces on one face |
|---|---|---|---|
| $\infty$ | 200 | 16 | 24 |
| 12 | 208 | 16·7 | 25 |
| 8 | 212 | 17·0 | 25·5 |
| 6 | 217 | 17·3 | 26 |
| 4 | 225 | 17·9 | 27 |
| 3 | 233 | 18·6 | 28 |

It will be noted that two values are given for the constant $Q_2$. The constants for forces on two faces would be used for columns of *H*- or channel-shape where two flanges act in compression against the concrete. For square or box section columns the values of $Q_2$ shown for forces on one face would be used.

## BASES FOR PRECAST CONCRETE COLUMNS

Precast concrete columns at Acton Lane "B" Power Station, were placed in recesses formed in the concrete foundations.[4.9] The main columns of the turbine house were 762 mm square sections and carried maximum loads of 7·6 MN. The stress at the foot of the columns was reduced to 3·17 N/mm² (the design bearing pressure on the concrete foundations) by bulbing, notching, and splaying at the foot as shown in Fig. 4.30. A steel pin 38 mm in diameter was set into the base of the recess. This engaged in a ferrule cast into the

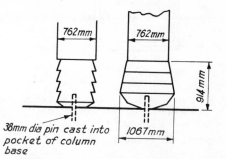

FIG. 4.30. DETAIL OF BASE OF PRECAST CONCRETE COLUMNS FOR FIXED-END CONDITIONS (DERRINGTON AND LANCE[4.9])

underside of the column foot, thus accurately locating the column in position. After setting and plumbing the column, the space in the recess around the column was filled with concrete using a vibrated mix with 9·5 mm maximum sized aggregate. The underside of the column was splayed so that concrete could flow under the column without entrapping air.

The 610 mm by 381 mm columns of the Workshops and Stores Block at the same site were designed with pin-jointed ends. Splayed recesses, 686 mm deep, were cast into the foundation and a centering pin was set into the bottom of the recess (Fig. 4.31). After setting the column, 76 mm of grout were run into the bottom of the recess, followed by sand filling to within 76 mm of the top of the foundation block. The remaining space was filled with concrete. This served to hold the column upright until the ends of the roof beams were

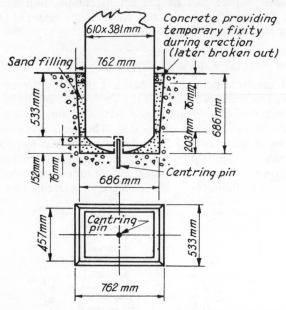

FIG. 4.31. DETAIL OF BASE OF PRECAST CONCRETE COLUMNS FOR HINGED-END CONDITIONS (DERRINGTON AND LANCE[4.9])

cast into the tops of the columns. Then the concrete was broken out.

### HOLDING-DOWN BOLTS

Typical designs for riveted and bolted, and for welded bases of steel I-section columns are shown in Fig. 4.32. A design for an enlarged base for a plated column carrying large bending moments is shown in Fig. 4.33. The holes for the holding-down bolts are formed in the concrete foundation block of sufficient size to accommodate the bolts and the upset ends or bottom washer plates. It is desirable to form the pockets with one pair of faces sloping inwards (Fig. 4.32, Detail *X*). This involves minor intricacy in the formwork, therefore if the holding-down bolts are available at the time of concreting the foundation blocks it is preferable to cast them into the foundations during the main concreting operations. The bottom washers are wholly embedded in the concrete as shown in the detail *Y* and a sleeve is provided around the bolts to give 10 mm or more of clearance around the bolts. The tops of the latter are held in position by a

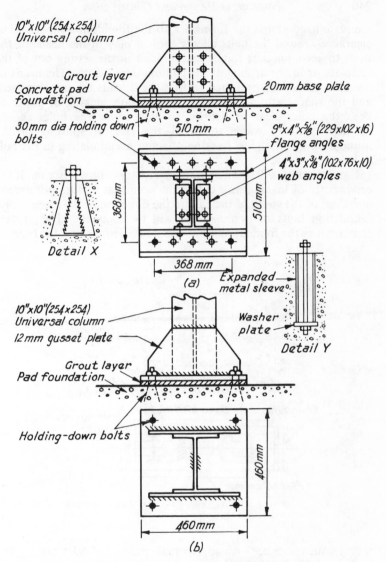

10"x10" (254x254) Universal column

Grout layer
Concrete pad foundation

20mm base plate

30mm dia holding down bolts

510mm

9"x4"x5⁄8" (229x102x16) flange angles

4"x3"x3⁄8" (102x76x10) web angles

368mm

510mm

*Detail X*

368mm

*(a)*

Expanded metal sleeve

10"x10"(254x254) Universal column

12mm gusset plate

Washer plate

*Detail Y*

Grout layer
Pad foundation

Holding-down bolts

460mm

460mm

*(b)*

Fɪɢ. 4.32. Tʏᴘɪᴄᴀʟ Bᴀsᴇs ғᴏʀ Sᴛʀᴜᴄᴛᴜʀᴀʟ Sᴛᴇᴇʟ Cᴏʟᴜᴍɴs

(*Top*) Riveted and bolted column bases.

(*Bottom*) Welded column base.

Detail *X*: pockets for ragged holding-down bolts.

Detail *Y*: holding-down bolt and washer plate cast into base before placing column.

239

template fixed across the formwork to the foundation blocks. The clearance around the bolts allows enough play in the heads of the bolts to accommodate minor inaccuracies in the setting out of the template or in the drilling of the column base plates. The heads of the bolts should be protected so that the threads are not damaged, and the spaces around the bolts packed with sacking or paper to keep the holes clear of debris. In winter-time the holes should be kept clear of water to avoid the risk of splitting of the foundation block due to freezing of water accumulating in the bolt holes.

CALCULATION OF REQUIRED SIZES OF HOLDING-DOWN BOLTS. If the eccentricity of loading in a column is such that it does not exceed one-third of the width of the base in the direction of the eccentricity, foundation bolts of nominal size will be adequate. For greater eccentricities the foundation bolts should be designed on the basis of

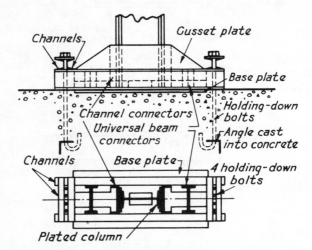

FIG. 4.33. BASE TO PLATED COLUMN CARRYING LARGE BENDING MOMENTS

their tensile resistance. An approximate method of calculation given by Kent and Lovejoy[4.10] is based on conventional theory of reinforced concrete design.

From the pressure diagram in Fig. 4.34—

Depth to neutral axis from compression edge

$$= n = \frac{mp_{cb}d}{mp_{cb} + p_{st}} \qquad . \qquad . \qquad . \quad (4.19)$$

Taking moments about the line of the holding-down bolts—

$$\text{Total compression in concrete} = C = \frac{M_{x-x} + W \times y}{d - \dfrac{n}{3}} \qquad . \ (4.20)$$

$$\text{Total tension in steel} = T = C - W \qquad . \qquad . \qquad . \ (4.21)$$

$$\text{Maximum compressive stress on concrete} = \frac{C}{\frac{1}{2} \times n \times b} \qquad . \ (4.22)$$

$$\text{Therefore, required width } (b) \text{ of base plate} = \frac{2C}{n \times p_{cb}} \qquad . \ (4.23)$$

The safe tensile stress in the bolt can be increased by 25 per cent if the bending moments are due to wind loading. The cross-sectional area

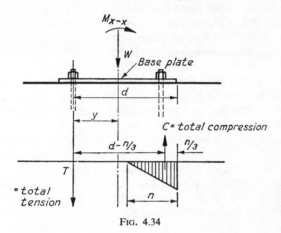

FIG. 4.34

of the bolt should be calculated at the root of the thread which is approximately $0 \cdot 7 \times$ the gross cross-sectional area.

The calculated cross-sectional area of the holding-down bolts and the required width of the base plate should be increased by 40 per cent, to conform to the requirements of B.S. 449. This states that there must be a safety factor of $1 \cdot 4$ on the stability of the structure as a whole against the overturning moment due to imposed loads which are deemed to include wind loading.

In calculating the required sizes of the holding-down bolts the maximum bending moment should be taken in conjunction with the minimum vertical load on the column. If the concrete is stressed to the limit $p_{cb}$, then the safe tensile stress ($p_{st}$) in the holding-down bolt may be exceeded. In practice $p_{cb}$ is calculated for an assumed size of steel base. If the calculations show that $p_{cb}$ is higher than the permissible stress, the size of the steel base must be increased, or a richer mix of concrete must be used.

If the compressive stress on the concrete pad $p_{cb}$ is considerably less than the permissible stress, then a smaller steel base should be used.

### GRILLAGE FOUNDATIONS

Where very heavy loads from structural steel columns have to be carried on a wide base, and where the overall depth of the foundation is restricted (to enable the base slab to be sited above the ground water table, for example) a steel grillage may be required to spread the load. A typical design for a grillage base is shown in Fig. 4.35. The girders of the lowermost tier are designed to act as cantilevers carrying a distributed loading equal to the bearing pressure on the foundation slab. The upper tier distributes the column load on to the lower tier. An intermediate tier may be required. In large grillages the girders in each tier are located by tie bolts passing through holes drilled through their webs with gas barrel spacers threaded over the bolts between the webs. Attention must be given to the stability of the girder webs in bearing under concentrated loading from the column or upper tier of girders. Web stiffeners should be provided as required.

Adequate space must be provided between girder flanges to allow the concrete to flow between and underneath them. The grillage must be set very accurately in location and must be quite level before the concrete is placed, and it must not be allowed to move during concreting, since any errors due to inaccurate setting or displacement will be highly expensive to rectify once the concrete has hardened.

### Raft Foundations

The commonest use of raft foundations is on soils of low bearing capacity, where the foundation pressures must be spread over as wide an area as possible. They are also used for foundations on soils of varying compressibility where the partial rigidity given by stiff slab and beam construction is utilized to bridge over areas of more compressible soil, and thus differential settlement of the foundation slab is minimized. Raft foundations can be used as a matter of constructional convenience in structures supported by a grid of fairly close-spaced columns. In such cases an overall raft will avoid obstruction of the site by a number of individual excavations with their associated heaps of spoil. Some designers work on the rule that

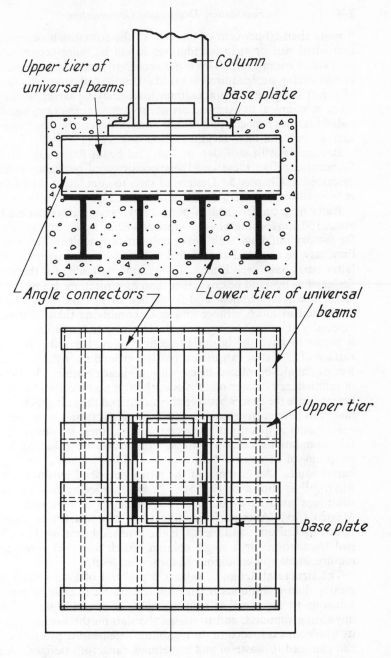

FIG. 4.35. GRILLAGE BASE FOR HEAVILY LOADED STEEL COLUMN

if more than 50 per cent of the area of the structure is occupied by individual pad or strip foundations it will be more economical to provide an overall raft. This is not necessarily true since the quantity of reinforcing steel required to avoid excessive deflexion and cracking of a raft carrying unequal column loads may be large. It may be more economical to excavate the site to a level formation, construct individual close-spaced pad foundations (if necessary they can touch each other), and then backfill around them.

Basements with stiff slab or slab and beam floors are forms of foundation rafts; these and the special case of buoyancy rafts are described in Chapter 5. Designs of rafts to counteract the effects of mining subsidence were described on page 175.

Rafts may be designed as plain slabs varying in thickness from about 150 mm for single or two-storey dwelling houses to 1 m or more for factory buildings with heavy column or machinery loadings, or they may be designed as stiffened slab and beam structures. If the latter types have deep beams, it is usually preferable for them to be designed as upstand beams rather than as projections below the base slab. The reinforcement and formwork of upstand beams can be assembled in much cleaner and drier conditions than in trenches, especially in water-bearing ground. However, for dwelling houses it is better to have the beams projecting below the slab; the upper surface of the latter can then act as the ground floor for the houses. Beams should be placed below all load-bearing walls. In the case of multi-storey flats or office blocks there is no objection to upstand beams, since the spaces between the beams and the suspended ground floor can be used to accommodate heating ducts and other services.

Economy in quantities of concrete and lightness in construction of raft foundations can, in suitable conditions, be achieved by the adoption of structural forms such as folded plates, or inverted barrel vaults. An example of the latter, described by Enriquez and Fierro,[4.11] is shown in Fig. 5.6. In this particular case the barrel vault was used as a buoyancy raft in highly compressible soil in Mexico City. Another interesting form of construction also described by Enriquez and Fierro, is the inverted hypar used as a large pad foundation for a single column. Such forms of construction require stable soil conditions at formation level.

The structural design of rafts is a problem of even greater complexity than continuous beam foundations. It is entirely wrong in principle to assume that a raft acts as an inverted floor slab on unyielding supports, and to design the slab on the assumption that its whole area is loaded to the maximum safe bearing pressure on the soil can lead to wasteful and sometimes dangerous designs. Allowance must be made for deflexions under the most unfavourable combinations of dead and live loading and variations in soil compressibility. Guidance is required from the soil mechanics engineer on the estimated total and differential settlements for dead and live loading considered separately.

Some flexibility is desirable to keep bending moments and shear stresses to a minimum, but the degree of flexibility must be related to

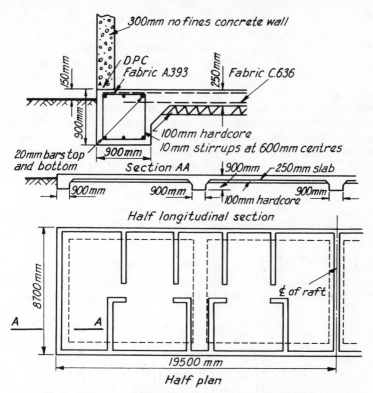

Fig. 4.36. Raft Foundation for Three-storey Houses on Filled Ground

the allowable distortion of the superstructure as discussed on page 108. The inter-related effects of varying load distribution and varying soil conditions on the deflexion of rafts will be somewhat similar to those illustrated in Fig. 4.28 (*a*) to (*h*), but it must be noted that the curvatures will be in both longitudinal and transverse directions. For a uniform load distribution on a fully flexible raft with uniform soil conditions, the resulting settlement will be bowl-shaped as illustrated in Fig. 2.17 (*a*).

For a detailed treatment of the structural design of raft foundations, the reader is referred to Professor A. L. L. Baker's textbook.[4.12] A simple method of design is described by Manning.[4.13]

### RAFT TO WITHSTAND LARGE SETTLEMENTS ON MADE GROUND

A raft of a type similar to Fig. 4.36 was used to support three-storey blocks of flats of load-bearing wall construction on fill at Bilston, Staffordshire. The depth and consistency of the fill were such that piled foundations were out of the question on grounds of cost. However, since the fill varied in composition from a soft clay to a compact mass of hard slag boulders, the raft had to be designed to be stiff enough to resist a tendency towards considerable differential settlement even though the loading at the base of the walls was only about 30 to 45 kN per metre run. Stiffness was achieved by means of beams beneath and longitudinal and cross walls and fabric reinforcement in the top and bottom of the 254 mm thick slab. The beams were placed at the bottom of the slab to enable the latter to form the ground floor of the flats. The total dead load of the superstructure was equivalent to a uniformly distributed load over the raft of 600 kN/m², and the total design dead and live load was 643 kN/m². In one of the blocks the raft withstood a total settlement of 100 mm and a differential settlement of 65 mm without distress to the foundations or superstructure.

### RAFT FOR TWELVE-STOREY GARAGE, JOHANNESBURG

A special design of a raft for a twelve-storey garage at Johannesburg, South Africa, is shown in Fig. 4.37. This design by Professor

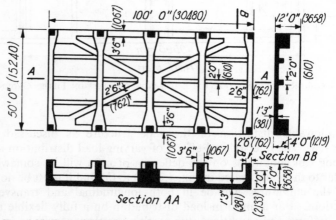

FIG. 4.37. BAKER'S DESIGN OF RAFT FOUNDATION FOR HIGH BUILDING CARRYING HEAVY LIVE LOADING

A. L. L. Baker[4,14] allowed for a wide range of live loading given by different loading arrangements of the parked cars on soil of widely varying compressibility. Diagonal beams were provided to resist possible diagonal bending moments caused by heavy live loading over compressible soil at the corners.

## RAFT FOUNDATIONS FOR OIL STORAGE TANKS

Oil storage tanks for refineries, gathering grounds, fuel depots, etc., are usually provided in large numbers on any given site; it is therefore essential to achieve economy in foundation construction. Oil companies are very reluctant to provide piled foundations for their tanks, even in very poor soil conditions, except in cases where very large differential settlement must be prevented, i.e. for the floating roof kind of storage tank. The normal type of fixed-top cylindrical storage tanks are nevertheless not insensitive to differential settlement since they are usually of welded steel plate construction. Excessive differential settlement around the periphery of welded tanks is liable to cause splitting of the plates in the walls or the bottom.

Any form of rigidity in the foundation raft should be avoided since deflexion and cracking of a concrete slab could cause excessive stresses to develop in the bottom plates. However, some form of base is required for oil tanks, since it is desirable to raise the bottom plates above ground level in order to prevent surface or subsoil water from collecting around the plates and corroding them. It is also desirable to have a clean smooth surface on which to lay the plates and weld their joints. Resilience in the surface is required to prevent local stress concentrations in the plates and to allow the plates to "breathe" or move radially and circumferentially under varying conditions of temperature and stress. Compacted small stone chippings are frequently used, but the most satisfactory surface is a 50 mm thick layer of bitumen/sand mixture as recommended in B.S. 2654: 1956. This is laid on the overall raft or tank base. Various types of materials are used for the base depending on its thickness and the materials available in the locality. Sand is used for thin bases, say a thickness of 250 to 500 mm of compacted sand. For thicker bases, materials such as crushed brick or stone, chalk, or gravel/sand mixtures are frequently used. The essential feature is to avoid any form of rigidity; lean-mix concrete or stabilized soil would be unsuitable. The minimum thickness of the base is dictated by the need to maintain the bottom plates at a level 10 mm or so above the ground surface after consolidation settlement of the soil below the tank bottom is complete. Thus, if it is estimated that the ultimate settlement of a tank and its base will be about 600 mm, then the base would be made 750 mm thick. If hard materials, bricks or crushed stone, are used in the base, it is essential to interpose a layer of sand, quarry dust, or graded stone chippings between the hard materials and the bitumen/sand layer. The function of this intermediate course is to prevent the stones pushing through the bitumen/sand and causing local stress concentrations in the plates during settlement of the tank.

Where tanks are founded on soft silts or clays, it is useful to increase the thickness of the base, and thus to take advantage of the spread of load through the fill to reduce the bearing pressure on the

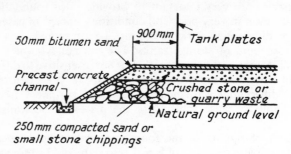

FIG. 4.38. BASE FOR OIL STORAGE TANK

soil. Thus for a tank 25 m in diameter on a 1·5 m thick base, the area in contact with the soil is increased from the net base area of the tank of 491 m² to 616 m²; assuming a forty-five degree spread of load through the fill. A projection of the toe beyond the tank walls greater than is given by the stable slope of the fill plus a top marginal width of 1 to 1·5 m is not justifiable because the load-spreading in a flexible fill material is unlikely to be at an angle flatter than 45°. Also, increases in thickness of the fill beyond a certain amount will merely increase the bearing pressure on the soil without any useful gain in spread of load. The thick base also serves the useful function of reducing concentrations of stress in the soil below the periphery of the tank. Soft alluvial silts and clays often have a crust of stiff dried-out soil at the ground surface (p. 68). This crust should be preserved as far as possible in its full thickness, as it serves to spread the tank loads still further so reducing the shear stresses in the underlying soft layers.

Surcharging the sites of tanks, or slow filling of the tank (a filling period of a year or more can be contemplated) can make it possible to construct heavy oil tanks on very soft silts and clays.

The slope of the filling should be protected from erosion by a layer of bitumen/sand and a drain should be provided at the toe of the slope to collect surface water and any seepages of oil from the tank pipes or valves. A design for a tank base is shown in Fig. 4.38.

The use of a 3 m thick layer of compacted clay filling to support 42·7 m diameter by 14·6 m high oil tanks at the Avon Refinery in San Francisco Bay has been described by Roberts.[4.15] On this site some 1·5 to 3 m of soft organic clay containing peat were overlying stiffer material. The shear strength of the soft clay varied from 9·5 to 14 kN/m² and the bearing pressures imposed by the full tanks would have caused serious overstressing. However, by placing the tanks on a layer of imported clay filling 3 m thick the stresses on the soft material were reduced, and the frictional forces developed at the top and bottom of the soft layer between the surface fill and the lower stratum respectively, prevented the soft clay from flowing away. The method was successful in this particular case because of the relatively thin layer of soft clay. If deep soft deposits had been present the overstressed zones would have been very large and would probably have resulted in tilting and overturning of the tanks. As it was, the tanks had to be filled slowly over a three-month period. On one tank a maximum settlement of 70 mm was recorded over the filling period and 90 mm three months after completing the filling. The maximum differential settlement between points on the periphery was 50 mm. On another site where the soft deposits contained a thick peat layer on one side of the tank, a maximum settlement of 305 mm was recorded five months after commencement of filling. The differential settlement was 254 mm. It was necessary to re-level this tank by jacking the walls from brackets welded to the tank plates followed by the injection of mud beneath the bottom plates.

Another method of containing a relatively thin layer of soft clay is to construct a ring of compacted rock fill around the periphery of the tank. This method was described by Roberts[4.16] in a comprehensive review of foundation methods for oil storage tanks. He states that piled foundations are rarely used since the cost of such a foundation is likely to exceed the cost of the tank itself. If piles must be used, the cost of a pile cap can be saved by surmounting the piles with compacted rock fill. A typical design consists of a 1·4 m thick layer of compacted crushed rock with the heads of the piles projecting 0·46 m into this layer. The crushed rock layer is covered by a 2 m thick layer of compacted granular fill.

## EXAMPLES ON CHAPTER 4

### EXAMPLE 4.1

An isolated column carries a load of 600 kN. It is founded at a depth of 0·9 m in a 2 m thick stiff clay stratum having a shear strength of 130 kN/m² overlying a deep layer of firm clay having a shear strength of 70 kN/m². Determine the required size of the column foundation.

The approximate bearing capacity factor $N_c$ for the square column base is 7·5.

Therefore for a safety factor of 3, presumed bearing value from equation 2.12 $= q_{nf}$

$$= \frac{7 \cdot 5 \times 130}{3}$$

$$= 325 \text{ kN/m}^2$$

Required size of square column base $= \sqrt{\dfrac{600}{325}}$

$$= 1 \cdot 36 \text{ say } \underline{1 \cdot 40 \text{ m}}$$

Checking the assumed value of $N_c$,

$$\frac{D}{B} = \frac{0 \cdot 9}{1 \cdot 4} = 0 \cdot 64, \text{ from Fig. 2.11 } (d)$$

$N_c = 7 \cdot 6$, which is close enough to our chosen value.

Since the thickness of stiff clay beneath the base exceeds half the foundation width, the pressure on the surface of the firm clay stratum is given by equation 4.3.

Bearing pressure on surface of firm clay

$$= \frac{600 - 4 \times 1 \cdot 4 \times 1 \cdot 1 \times 130}{1 \cdot 4 \times 1 \cdot 4}$$

This is a negative value; therefore the foundation width of 1·40 m at a depth of 0·9 m, is satisfactory.

It will be noted that the weight of the column base was not calculated. The weight of the base will be roughly equal to the weight of soil displaced by it. Thus the *net* pressure will be given approximately by the column load of 600 kN divided by the area of the 1·40 m square base as shown above.

EXAMPLE 4.2

In the above example, the columns are spaced at 2·0 m centres in a single row. Determine the required size of the foundation for these conditions.

The pressure distribution in Fig. 4.39 shows that there is overlapping of bearing pressures on the surface of the firm stratum, therefore we cannot use equation 4.3. From equation 4.1 we have for a single column base—

Pressure on surface of buried stratum of firm clay

$$= q'$$

$$= \frac{600}{1\cdot4^2}\left(\frac{1\cdot4}{1\cdot4 + 1\cdot15 \times 1\cdot1}\right)^2$$

$$= 85 \text{ kN/m}^2$$

Where the pressures from adjoining columns overlap, the total pressure on the surface of the firm clay layer

$$= 170 \text{ kN/m}^2$$

For the purpose of calculating the presumed bearing value of the firm

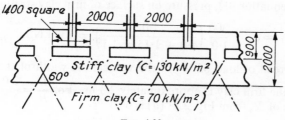

FIG. 4.39

clay, we must assume a strip footing 2·67 m wide on the surface of the clay at a depth of 2·0 m below ground level.

For $\dfrac{D}{B} = \dfrac{2\cdot0}{2\cdot67} = 0\cdot75$, the value of $N_c$ from Fig 2·11 (d) is 6·6.

Therefore, for a safety factor of 3, the presumed bearing value of the firm clay stratum

$$= \frac{6\cdot6 \times 70}{3}$$

$$= 154 \text{ kN/m}^2$$

Thus where the pressures distributed by the pad foundation overlap on the surface of the firm clay layer, the maximum safe bearing capacity is exceeded. The best expedient therefore will be to combine the column bases into a strip foundation.

Load on strip foundation $= \dfrac{600}{2\cdot0} = 300$ kN/metre-run

The bearing capacity factor for the strip foundation at a depth of 0·9 m will be about 6.

Maximum net safe bearing capacity of stiff clay

$$= \frac{6}{3} \times 130 = \underline{\underline{260 \text{ kN/m}^2}}$$

Required width of foundation $= \dfrac{300}{260} = \underline{\underline{1 \cdot 15 \text{ m}}}$

For $\dfrac{D}{B} = \dfrac{0 \cdot 9}{1 \cdot 15} = 0 \cdot 78$, value of $N_c$ from Fig. 2.11 $(d)$ is 6·6.

Using this higher factor, presumed bearing value

$$= \dfrac{6 \cdot 6}{3} \times 130 = 286 \text{ kN/m}^2$$

Required width of foundation $= \dfrac{300}{286} = 1 \cdot 05 \text{m, say } \underline{\underline{1 \cdot 0 \text{ m}}}$

From equation 4.2, pressure on surface of firm clay stratum

$$= q_1 = \dfrac{300}{1 \cdot 0} \left( \dfrac{1 \cdot 0}{1 \cdot 0 + 1 \cdot 15 \times 1 \cdot 1} \right) = 132 \text{ kN/m}^2$$

For a spread of load of 30° to the vertical the width of the loaded area on the firm clay is approximately 2·3 m. For $\dfrac{D}{B} = \dfrac{2 \cdot 0}{2 \cdot 3} = 0 \cdot 87$, the value of $N_c$ from Fig. 2.11 $(d)$ is 6·8.

Net ultimate bearing capacity of firm clay $= 6 \cdot 8 \times 70$
$$= 476 \text{ kN/m}^2$$

$$\text{Factor of safety} = \dfrac{476}{132} = 3 \cdot 6$$

Thus a foundation width of 1·0 m should not give excessive settlement but it will be necessary to reinforce the strip to minimize differential settlement, and if a total settlement of say 75 mm and a differential settlement of 25 mm is likely to be detrimental to the structure, it would be advisable to make a settlement analysis to obtain a closer estimate of the settlement before revising the foundation width.

EXAMPLE 4.3

A total of 64 columns as in Example 4.2 are spaced on a grid at 2 m centres both ways. Investigate the requirements for foundation design.

We know from Example 4.2 that pad footings cannot be used; if we use rows of strip footings running in one direction only the pressure distribution on the surface of the firm clay stratum is similar to that shown in Fig. 4.39. Thus the stiff clay stratum acts as a large raft, and we must consider the stress distribution below this raft in relation to the shear strength of the firm clay.

Approximate average loading on surface of firm clay

$$= \frac{600}{2^2} = 150 \text{ kN/m}^2$$

Considering the stiff clay stratum to act as a surface foundation, from Fig. 2.11($d$).

Ultimate bearing capacity of firm clay

$$= 6 \cdot 25 \times 70 = 437 \cdot 5 \text{ kN/m}^2$$

This gives a safety factor of 2·9 and since the firm clay layer extends to some depth, it is evident that there will be appreciable settlement. It will therefore be advisable to make a settlement analysis, and if the total and differential settlements are excessive, it will be necessary to provide piled foundations to the columns taken down to a stiffer stratum beneath the firm clay.

### EXAMPLE 4.4

An oil storage tank 36 m diameter by 6·5 m high is to be constructed on a 4 m thick layer of soft clay overlying a deep stratum of medium-dense to dense sand. Calculate the safety factor on the ultimate bearing capacity of the soft clay stratum. From the shear strength data a minimum value of 30 kN/m² may be taken for calculating the ultimate bearing capacity of the clay layer. The average shear strength is 45 kN/m².

$$\frac{B}{d} = \frac{36}{4} = 9 \cdot 0$$

Since $\frac{B}{d}$ is greater than 6 we must use equation 4.5 to determine the ultimate bearing capacity of the clay layer. From this equation we have—

Net ultimate bearing capacity, $q_{nf}$

$$= \left( \frac{36}{3 \times 4} + \pi + 1 \right) \times 30$$

$$= 214 \text{ kN/m}^2$$

Net load on foundation will be a maximum when the tank is filled with water for testing.

Pressure due to water $= 6 \cdot 5 \times 1 \times 9 \cdot 807 = 64 \text{ kN/m}^2$
Pressure due to tank structure $\quad = 1 \text{ kN/m}^2$

Total pressure $\quad = 65 \text{ kN/m}^2$

$$\text{Factor of safety} = \frac{214}{65} = 3 \cdot 3$$

Therefore the factor of safety is adequate against ultimate failure of the tank foundation. We must also investigate the possibility of overstressing of the clay.

Maximum shear stress induced in clay stratum

$$= \frac{q_{nf}}{2} = \frac{65}{2} = 32 \cdot 5 \text{ kN/m}^2$$

This is slightly greater than the minimum shear strength of the clay. However, since the average shear strength is appreciably greater at 45 kN/m² the zone of overstressing will be relatively small, and if the tank is filled slowly, allowing induced pore water pressures to dissipate, failure should not occur as a result of the overstressed clay flowing away from beneath the foundation. Nevertheless, appreciable settlement and tilting (100 mm or more) would be expected.

### EXAMPLE 4.5

A structure is supported on widely-spaced reinforced concrete columns 610 mm square, which carry combined dead and live loads of 1800 kN. Borings and static cone penetration tests (Fig. 4.40 (*a*) to

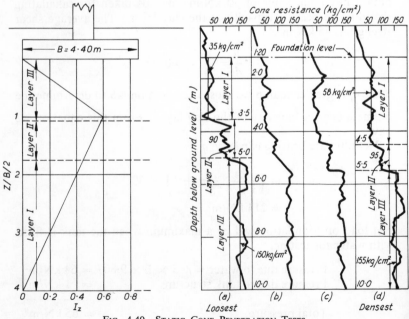

FIG. 4.40. STATIC CONE PENETRATION TESTS

(*d*)) show that the ground is a fairly loose becoming a medium-dense sand. Determine the depth and dimensions of square pad foundations and design the reinforcement.

Because of the variability in density of the sand deposits it will be necessary to design the foundations for the loosest conditions. The calculated allowable bearing pressure can then be used to compare settlements for the loosest and densest conditions, and hence to obtain the maximum differential settlements between any pair of columns. Taking the cone penetration test for the loosest conditions (Fig. 4.40 (*a*)), this can be simplified to give average cone resistances of 35, 90, and 150 kg/cm² in three layers.

A first guide to the allowable bearing pressure is given by Meyerhof's approximate equation (2.15), namely—

Allowable bearing pressure $= 2 \cdot 7 \, C_{kd} \, \text{kN/m}^2$

$$= 2 \cdot 7 \times 35 = 94 \cdot 5 \, \text{kN/m}^2$$

An allowable bearing pressure of $94 \cdot 5 \, \text{kN/m}^2$ requires a foundation approximately 4·40 m square for 1800 kN column load.

A foundation depth of 1·20 m below ground level will be assumed for the purpose of estimating settlements. This is deeper than is required purely from soil considerations. However, a pad of substantial thickness may be required and it is necessary to keep the pad wholly below the ground floor of the structure. Therefore, it will not alter the estimated settlements very much if the final foundation depth is made 0·5 m or so above or below the selected 1·20 m depth.

Calculating settlements in each layer—

*Layer I*

$$p_o = 1 \cdot 9 \times 2 \cdot 35 \times 9 \cdot 807 = 43 \cdot 8 \, \text{kN/m}^2 \text{ at centre of layer}$$

Constant of compressibility, from equation 2.18,

$$= C = \frac{3}{2} \frac{C_{kd}}{p_o} = \frac{3 \times 35 \times 9 \cdot 807 \times 10}{2 \times 43 \cdot 8} = 118$$

Values of $\sigma_z$ are obtained from Fig. 2.23 as follows—

$$\frac{z}{b} = \frac{1 \cdot 15}{4 \cdot 40} = 0 \cdot 26, \text{ giving } \sigma_z = 0 \cdot 71 \times 94 \cdot 5 = 67 \cdot 1 \, \text{kN/m}^2$$

Therefore, settlement in layer I, from equation 2.19,

$$= \frac{2\cdot3 \times 1000}{118} \log_e \frac{43\cdot8 + 67\cdot1}{43\cdot8} = 18 \text{ mm}$$

*Layer II:—*  $\quad p_o = 1\cdot9 \times 4\cdot25 \times 9\cdot807 = 79\cdot2 \text{ kN/m}^2$

$$C = \frac{3}{2} \frac{C_{kd}}{p_o} = \frac{3 \times 90 \times 9\cdot807 \times 10}{2 \times 79\cdot2} = 167$$

From Fig. 2.23,

$$\frac{z}{b} = \frac{3\cdot05}{4\cdot40} = 0\cdot69, \text{ giving } \sigma_z = 0\cdot40 \times 94\cdot5 = 37\cdot8 \text{ kN/m}^2$$

Settlement in layer II

$$= p_f = \frac{1\cdot5 \times 1000}{167} \log_e \frac{79\cdot2 + 37\cdot8}{79\cdot2} = 3\cdot5 \text{ mm}$$

*Layer III*

This is considered to a depth of 10 m below ground level since below this depth the vertical stress resulting from the applied load is less than 10 kN/m² as obtained from Fig. 2.23.

$$p_o = 1\cdot9 \times 7\cdot5 \times 9\cdot807 = 140 \text{ kN/m}^2$$

$$C = \frac{3 \times 150 \times 9\cdot807 \times 10}{2 \times 140} = 158$$

From Fig. 2.23, $\dfrac{z}{b} = \dfrac{6\cdot30}{4\cdot40} = 1\cdot4$, giving $\sigma_z = 16 \text{ kN/m}^2$

Settlement in layer III

$$= p_f = \frac{5\cdot0 \times 1000}{158} \log_o \frac{140 + 16}{140} = 3\cdot5 \text{ mm}$$

Therefore, the sum of the settlements in the three layers is equal to the estimated settlement for loosest conditions

$$= 18 \text{ mm} + 3\cdot5 \text{ mm} + 3\cdot5 \text{ mm} = 25\cdot0 \text{ mm}$$

Considering now the densest conditions as shown in Fig. 4.40 (*d*), we will take the same bearing pressure of 94·5 kN/m², and the same pad foundation 4·40 m square at a depth of 1·20 m below ground level.

In a similar manner to that shown above it can be calculated that the sum of the settlement of the three layers

$$= \text{settlement for the densest conditions}$$
$$= 15 \text{ mm} + 2 \text{ mm} + 3 \text{ mm} = 20 \text{ mm}$$

Maximum differential settlement between columns founded on loosest and densest soils $= 25 - 20 = 5·0$ mm
which is well within safe limits for the R.C. structure.

The settlements for the loosest conditions will be checked by Schmertmann's method, for which the depth correction and creep factors by equations 2.21 and 2.21a are—

$$C_1 = 1 - \frac{0·5(1·9 \times 1·2 \times 9·807)}{94·5} = 0·88$$

and $C_2 = 1 + 0·2 \log_{10} \left( \dfrac{25}{0·1} \right) = 1·48$ for 25 years

Layer *I*, from Fig. 4.40, $I_z$ at centre of layer $= 0·3$, $E_d = 3·0 \times 35 = 122·5 \text{ kg/cm}^2 = 12·0 \text{ MN/m}^2$.

Therefore

$$\rho = 0·88 \times 1·48 \times 94·5 \times \frac{0·3}{12 \times 1000} \times 2·3 \times 1000 = 7·0 \text{ mm}$$

Similarly in Layer II, $I_z = 0·51$, $E_d = 3·5 \times 90 =$
$315 \text{ kg/cm}^2 = 30·89 \text{ MN/m}^2$, $\rho \quad = 3·0$ mm
and in Layer III, $I_z = 0·22$, $E_d = 3·5 \times 150 =$
$525 \text{ kg/cm}^2 = 51·48 \text{ MN/m}^2$, $\rho \quad = 2·6$ mm

$$\text{Total settlement} = 12·6 \text{ mm.}$$

Therefore by Schmertmann's method the settlement for the loosest layers is about 15 mm (the De Beer and Martens' method is known to give conservative values).

STRUCTURAL DESIGN OF PAD FOUNDATIONS. In view of the large dimensions of the pad it will save in quantities of excavation and concrete if they are designed in reinforced concrete.

For 1:2:4 nominal mix concrete as Table 6 of *CP 114* the working stresses and other design data are—

Max. compressive stress in concrete $= p_{cb} = 7 \text{N/mm}^2$

Max. tensile stress in steel $\quad = p_{st} = 140 \text{ N/mm}^2$

Modular ratio $\quad = m \quad = 15$

Max. shear stress $\quad = 0·7 \text{ N/mm}^2$

Max. average bond stress $\quad = 0·83 \text{ N/mm}^2$

Max. local bond stress                    $= 1·25$ N/mm²

Lever arm                     $= l_a = 0·86 \times$ effective depth

Moment of resistance of most

economical section          $= M_r = 1·27bd_i^2$ in N/m units

From equation 4.11, required overall thickness of base slab at face of column for allowable punching shear stress of $1·4$ N/mm².

$$= \frac{1800 \times 1000 \left(1 - \dfrac{610^2}{4400^2}\right)}{4 \times 610 \times 1·4} = \underline{\underline{520 \text{ mm}}}$$

Bending moment per metre width at face

of column (from equation 4.13) $= \dfrac{94·5 \times 10^3 \times 1·895^2 \times 10^3}{2}$ Nm

Required effective depth $= d_i = \sqrt{\left(\dfrac{94·5 \times 10^3 \times 1·895^2 \times 10^3}{2 \times 1·27 \times 10^3}\right)}$

    $= 365$ mm

Overall depth required

$= 365 + (75$ mm cover $+ 25$ mm bar $+ \frac{1}{2}$ of 25 mm bar$) = 478$ mm

In order to keep the base clear of congested reinforcement and to provide a reasonably substantial thickness of base to allow for

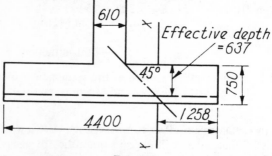

FIG. 4.41

unequal pressure distribution on the variable sand, it will be desirable to use a thicker base than calculated above. An overall thickness of 750 mm is desirable. The effective depth is 637 mm.

Checking shear stress at critical section $XX$ (Fig. 4.41),

Shear stress on $bl_a$ area $= \dfrac{94·5 \times 10^3 \times 1·258 \times 1·000}{10^3 \times 0·86 \times 637} = 0·22$ N/mm²

which is within safe limits.

Required area of main steel per metre width in upper layer

$$= \frac{94 \cdot 5 \times 10^3 \times 1 \cdot 895^2 \times 10^3}{2 \times 140 \times 0 \cdot 86 \times 637} = 2210 \text{ mm}^2$$

This requires 25 mm bars at 200 mm centres (2455 mm² per metre), and the same reinforcement should be placed transversely in the bottom layer. Checking local bond stress at face of column,

$$\text{Bond stress} = \frac{94 \cdot 5 \times 10^3 \times 1 \cdot 895 \times 1 \cdot 000}{0 \cdot 86 \times 637 \times \pi \times 25 \times \dfrac{1000}{200}} = 0 \cdot 83 \text{ N/mm}^2$$

which is well within the permissible value given by *CP 114*.

The complete design of the pad foundation is shown in Fig. 4.20.

## EXAMPLE 4.6

A foundation wall of a rigid-frame building is 400 mm wide. The wall carries a combined dead and live loading of 320 kN/metre run and a reversible bending moment of 200 kN/m/metre run at its base. Borings and standard penetration tests showed that below a 0·2 m layer of topsoil there was medium-dense sand with a corrected $N$-value of 25 blows per 0·3 m for the upper 3 m below ground level followed by rock. The ground water table was 1·1 m below ground level. Design suitable foundations.

The bending moment will produce eccentric loading on the base of the foundation. In order to limit settlements to less than 25 mm, Fig. 2.13 gives an allowable bearing pressure of about 230 kN/m² for a foundation roughly 3m wide on a dry sand. Because of the shallow water table we must halve this bearing pressure, which will require a width of 2·8 m for the vertical loading and an added width to take care of the eccentric loading. Taking a trial width of 3·5 m, from equation 4.6 (*a*)—

$$\text{Maximum edge pressure} = q_{max} = \frac{320}{3 \cdot 5} + \frac{6 \times 200}{3 \cdot 5^2} = 189 \text{ kN/m}^2$$

From page 213 it will be seen that we can take this bearing pressure as acting over an effective foundation width of $\frac{1}{3} \times B = 1 \cdot 17 \text{ m}$. From Fig. 2.13, allowable bearing pressure for a foundation of this width and an $N$-value of 25 is about 300 kN/m². We must halve this value, giving an allowable bearing pressure of 150 kN/m². Thus a 3·5 m wide foundation is too narrow.

$$\text{For a width of 4·5 m, edge pressure} = \frac{320}{4 \cdot 5} + \frac{6 \times 200}{4 \cdot 5^2} = 130 \text{ kN/m}^2.$$

Fig. 2.13 gives an allowable bearing pressure of 280 kN/m² for a 1·5 m effective foundation width. Taking the water table into account, we get an allowable bearing pressure of 140 kN/m². Therefore the 4·5 m wide foundation will be satisfactory.

STRUCTURAL DESIGN OF STRIP FOUNDATION. The pressure diagram on the underside of the slab is shown in Fig. 4.42. It will be convenient to scale from this figure to get the pressure at any point.

Because of the high load intensity at the edge of the strip, it is probable that the required base slab thickness will be governed by the bending moment at the face of the wall (section $XX$). At this section, pressure on base of slab

$$= 77 \text{ kN/m}^2$$

Bending moment at $XX$ from uniformly distributed load of 77 kN/m²

$$= 77 \times 10^3 \times 2\cdot050 \times \frac{2\cdot050}{2} \text{ Nm} = 162\,000 \text{ Nm}$$

Bending moment at $XX$ from triangular loading from zero at $XX$ to 53 kN/m² at edge of slab

$$= \tfrac{1}{2} \times 53 \times 10^3 \times 2\cdot050 \times \tfrac{2}{3} \times 2\cdot050$$
$$= 74500 \text{ Nm}$$

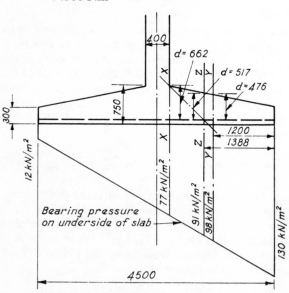

FIG. 4.42

Total bending moment at XX

$$= 162\,000 + 74\,500$$
$$= 236\,500 \text{ Nm}$$

For stress in steel $\quad p_{st} = 140 \text{ N/mm}^2$
For stress in concrete $p_{cb} = 7 \text{ N/mm}^2$
and $m = 15$

Required effective depth $= \sqrt{\dfrac{236\,500 \times 10^3}{1 \cdot 27 \times 10^3}}$

$$= 430 \text{ mm}$$

Allow 75 mm cover and say half of 25 mm bar giving an overall depth of 518 mm. However, for the reasons given in the previous example it will be desirable to give a substantial thickness say 750 mm at *XX*. The effective depth will be 662 mm.

If the upper surface of the strip is sloped down to an edge thickness of 300 mm, pressure at a point 1·20 m from edge of slab (section *YY*) scaled from Fig. 4.42 is 98 kN/m².

Bending moment due to uniformly distributed load of 98 kN/m²

$$= \frac{98 \times 10^3 \times 1 \cdot 200^2}{2} = 70\,500 \text{ Nm}$$

Bending moment due to triangular loading from zero at *YY* to 32 kN/m² at edge

$$= \tfrac{1}{2} \times 32 \times 10^3 \times \tfrac{2}{3} \times 1 \cdot 200^2 = 15\,300 \text{ N/mm}^3$$

Total bending moment at $YY = 70\,500 + 15\,300$
$$= 85\,800 \text{ Nm}$$

Required effective depth $= \sqrt{\dfrac{85\,800 \times 10^3}{1 \cdot 27 \times 10^3}}$

$$= 260 \text{ mm}$$

Checking shear stress—

For edge thickness of 300 mm, actual effective depth at *ZZ*

$$= 605 - (75 + \tfrac{1}{2} \times 25) = 517 \text{ mm}$$

Shear stress on $bl_a$ area at *ZZ*

$$= \frac{\dfrac{91 + 130}{2} \times 10^3 \times 1 \cdot 388}{10^3 \times 0 \cdot 86 \times 517} = 0 \cdot 35 \text{ N/mm}^2$$

which is within safe limits.

Required area of reinforcement at section $XX$

$$= \frac{236\,500 \times 10^3}{140 \times 0.86 \times 662}$$

$$= 2970 \text{ mm}^2/\text{m run}$$

Provide 25 mm bars at 150 mm centres (3272 mm²/m)

Checking average bond stress in steel,
Length from section $XX$ should not be less than

$$\frac{140 \times 25}{4 \times 0.83} = 1050 \text{ mm—this requirement is satisfied}$$

At critical section for maximum local bond stress (section $XX$ in Fig. 4.42),

| | |
|---|---|
| Overall depth | = 750 mm |
| Effective depth | $= 750 - (75 + \frac{1}{2} \times 25)$ |
| | = 662 mm |
| Width of slab beyond $XX$ | = 2050 mm |
| Average bearing pressure | $= \dfrac{77 + 130}{2}$ |
| | = 103 kN/m² |

Local bond stress at $XX$ $= \dfrac{103 \times 10^3 \times 2.050 \times 1.000}{0.86 \times 662 \times \pi \times 25 \times \dfrac{1000}{150}}$

$$= 0.71 \text{ N/mm}^2$$

Therefore permissible local bond stress of 1·25 N/mm² is not exceeded.
The arrangement of the reinforcement is shown in Fig. 4.43.

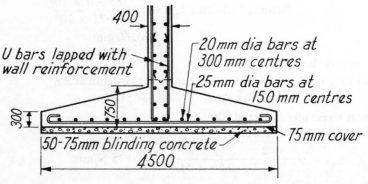

400

U bars lapped with
wall reinforcement

20 mm dia bars at
300 mm centres

25 mm dia bars at
150 mm centres

300

750

50-75mm blinding concrete

75mm cover

4500

FIG. 4.43

EXAMPLE 4.7

The column shown in Fig. 4.44 has a base plate 600 mm wide by 900 mm long. It carries an axial load of 700 kN, a dead and sustained live load bending moment of 240 kNm, and a wind load bending moment of 90 kNm. The sustained bending moments act always in the same direction. The soil consists of stiff boulder clay (shear strength = 105 kN/m²). Design a suitable unreinforced concrete column base to avoid appreciable tilting.

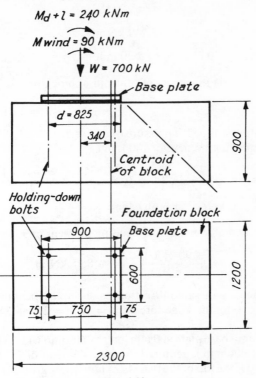

FIG. 4.44

We can avoid appreciable tilting by placing the column off-centre of the base so that the resultant of the axial load and *sustained* bending moment passes through the centroid of the base. Thus only the wind load bending moments cause unequal pressures on the soil, and since these are only intermittent they will not cause any appreciable settlement and tilting.

In Fig. 4.44 the axial load and sustained bending moment can be replaced by a single vertical load of 700 kN acting at a distance of

$\frac{240}{700} = 0.34$ m from the axis of the column. The centroid of the base can then be made to coincide with the line of action of this load. It will be advantageous to make the base longer in the direction of the bending moments to minimize the unequal pressures given by the wind load moments.

The appropriate presumed bearing value of the clay for a pad foundation

$$= \frac{7.5}{3} \times 105$$

$$= 262 \text{ kN/m}^2$$

Assume a base 1·20 m wide by 2·30 m long.

Moment of inertia in respect of centroid of block $= \dfrac{1.2 \times 2.3^3}{12}$

$$= 1.21 \text{ m}^4$$

From equation 4.14, edge pressure due to vertical load of 700 kN and sustained bending moment of 240 kNm

$$= q = \frac{700}{1.2 \times 2.3} \left( 1 + 6 \times \frac{0.34}{2.3} \right) - \frac{240 \times 1.150}{1.21}$$

$$= 250 \text{ kN/m}^2 \text{ at both edges}$$

Edge pressure due to wind load bending moment of 90 kNm

$$= + \frac{90 \times 1.150}{1.21} = + 85.5 \text{ kN/m}^2$$

when moment is in same direction as sustained bending moment. Therefore maximum edge pressure $= q_{max} = 249 + 85.5 = 335.5$ kN/m².

For a column base plate 900 mm long by 600 mm wide, a foundation thickness of 900 mm is required to give a 45° load distribution on to the base, and if the top of the pad is 225 mm below ground level overall foundation depth is 1·125 m.

From Fig. 2.12, for $\quad \dfrac{L}{B} = \dfrac{2.3}{1.2} = 1.92$

and from Fig. 2.11 (d) for $\dfrac{D}{B} = \dfrac{1.125}{1.2} = 0.94$

Bearing capacity factor $= N_c = 1.1 \times 7 = 7.7$

Therefore, ultimate bearing capacity allowing for 25 per cent increase due to wind loading

$$= 7 \cdot 7 \times 105 \times 1 \cdot 25 = 1010 \text{ kN/m}^2$$

The safety factor on the maximum edge pressure $335 \cdot 5$ kN/m²
is $3 \cdot 0$.
Uniform bearing pressure due to axial load and sustained bending
moment $= 250$ kN/m².
Therefore, factor of safety on ultimate bearing capacity

$$= \frac{1010}{250} = 4 \cdot 0$$

With these safety factors, the settlement should be less than 25 mm,
and the tilting due to wind loading should be negligible.
DESIGNING HOLDING-DOWN BOLTS. For most economical design
the dimension $n$ in Fig. 4.34 becomes from equation 4.19—

$$n = \frac{m p_{cb} d}{m p_{cb} + p_{st}}$$

Assuming the bolt diameter will exceed 25 mm the safe tensile stress
($p_{st}$) will be 123 N/mm².
Safe compressive stress on concrete ($p_{cb}$) = 7 N/mm².

Therefore from Fig. 4.44, $n = \dfrac{15 \times 7 \times 825}{15 \times 7 + 123} = 380$ mm

From equation 4.20,

$$\text{Total compression on concrete} = \frac{M_{x-x} + W \times y}{d - \dfrac{n}{3}}$$

$$= \frac{330 + 700 \times 0 \cdot 375}{0 \cdot 825 - \dfrac{0 \cdot 380}{3}}$$

$$= 850 \text{ kN}$$

From equation 4.21,

$$\text{Total tension in steel} = 850 - 700$$
$$= 150 \text{ kN} + 40 \text{ per cent} = 210 \text{ kN}$$

Trying 40 mm holding-down bolts, the total resistance of two bolts at
123 N/mm² safe tensile stress is 216 kN (at root of thread). Since
we can increase the safe tensile stress by 25 per cent in respect of
wind moments, we can increase it by $25 \times \dfrac{90}{240}$ in the present case,
i.e. by $9 \cdot 4$ per cent.

∴ Resistance of two 40 mm bolts $= 216 \times 1\cdot094 = 236$ kN.

From equation 4.22, maximum compressive stress on concrete

$$= \frac{C}{\frac{1}{2} \times n \times b} = \frac{850 \times 10^3}{\frac{1}{2} \times 380 \times 600} = 7\cdot5 \text{ N/mm}^2$$

As before we can increase the safe compressive stress of 7 N/mm² by 9·4 per cent giving a safe stress of 7·7 N/mm², which is not exceeded. However, the base width must be increased by 40 per cent, giving a total width of 840 mm, to provide the safety factor against over-turning required by B.S. 449. Alternatively we could increase the length of the plate thereby reducing the total tension in the holding-down bolts and compression on the concrete.

### EXAMPLE 4.8

In the preceding example, the column which has 460 mm wide flange plates is designed to be embedded in the foundation block. Determine the required depth of embedment.

From equation 4.17, if the maximum compressive stress in the concrete is not to be exceeded, depth of embedment ($h$) must not be less than $\sqrt{\dfrac{Q_2 M}{bu}}$.

$$\text{Taking } Q_2 = 17, h = \sqrt{\left( \frac{17 \times (240 + 90) \times 10^6}{460 \times 21} \right)}$$

$$= 760 \text{ mm}$$

From equation 4.18, if tensile stress of 0·03$u$ in concrete is not to be exceeded, $h$ must not exceed

$$\sqrt{\frac{Q_1 M}{(B - b)u}}$$

$$\text{Taking } Q_1 = 210, h = \sqrt{\left( \frac{210 \times (240 + 90) \times 10^6}{(1200 - 460) \times 21} \right)}$$

$$= 2110 \text{ mm}$$

Therefore, column will have to be embedded for 2·1 m.

### REFERENCES

4.1 *Soil Mechanics in Engineering Practice*, p. 217.
4.2 BISHOP, A. W., The strength of soils as engineering materials, *Géotechnique*, **16**, No. 2, pp. 89–128 (June, 1966).
4.3 PECK, R. B., HANSON, W. E. and THORNBURN, T. H., *Foundation Engineering*, p. 314 (New York, John Wiley, 2nd edn, 1974).

4.4 British Standard Code of Practice *CP 101*:1963, *Foundations and substructures for non-industrial buildings of not more than four storeys* (London, B.S.I).

4.5 British Standard Code of Practice *CP 114*:1969, *The structural use of reinforced concrete in buildings*, Part 2, Metric Units.

4.6 HAMILTON, S. B., The design of independent foundations, *Struct. Engr.*, **23**, No. 9, pp. 403–436 (Sept., 1945).

4.7 MEYERHOF, G. G., The bearing capacity of concrete and rock, *Magazine of Concrete Research* (April, 1953).

4.8 British Standard Code of Practice *CP 111*, Structural recommendations for loadbearing walls, Part 2, 1970′ Metric units.

4.9 DERRINGTON, J. A. and LANCE, A. C. S., The application of precast concrete to the construction of Acton Lane 'B' Power Station, *Proc. Inst. C.E.*, Pt. 3 (Aug., 1953).

4.10 KENT, E. and LOVEJOY, E. G., Examples of structural steel design, *Brit. Constr. Steelwork Assoc. Publicn. No. 13* (1960).

4.11 ENRIQUEZ, R. and FIERRO, A., A new project for Mexico City, *Civ. Eng. (U.S.A.)*, pp. 36–38 (June, 1963).

4.12 BAKER, A. L. L., Raft foundations: the Soil Line Method, *Concrete Publicns.* (1937).

4.13 MANNING, G. P., *Reinforced Concrete Design* (London, Longmans Green & Co.).

4.14 BAKER, A. L. L., High building frames and foundations, *Proc. Inst. C.E.*, **4**, No. 2, Pt. 3, pp. 228–245 (Aug., 1955).

4.15 ROBERTS, D. V., These floating roof tanks were built on "floating foundations," *Petroleum World and Oil*, pp. 10–14 (25th April, 1957).

4.16 ROBERTS, D. V., Foundations for cylindrical storage tanks, *Proc. 5th Int. Conf. Soil Mech.* (Paris, 1961), **1**, pp. 785–788.

# 5

# Buoyancy Rafts and Basements (Box Foundations)

As described in the last chapter, the function of a raft foundation is to spread the load over as wide an area as possible, and to give a measure of rigidity to the sub-structure to enable it to bridge over local areas of weaker or more compressible soil. The degree of rigidity given to the raft also reduces differential settlement. Buoyancy rafts and basements (or box foundations) are designed on the same principles, but they have an additional and important function in that they utilize the principle of buoyancy to reduce the net load on the soil. In this way the total settlement of the foundation is reduced and it follows that the differential settlements will also be reduced. Buoyancy is achieved by providing a hollow sub-structure of such a depth that the weight of the soil removed in excavating for it either balances or is only a little less than the combined weight of the superstructure and sub-structure. In the example shown in Fig. 5.1, excavation to a depth of 4·5 m for the basement relieves the soil at foundation level of a pressure of about 80 kN/m². The sub-structure itself weighs about 25 kN/m²; thus a loading of 50 kN/m² can be placed on the basement before any additional loading causing settlement comes on to the soil at foundation level. A bearing pressure of 50 kN/m² is roughly equivalent to the overall loading of a four-storey block of flats or offices.* Thus, a building of this height can

* A useful approximate rule for calculating the weight of a multi-storey block of

268

be supported on a basement founded in very soft and highly compressible soil, theoretically without any settlement occurring. However, in practice it is rarely possible to balance the loadings so that no additional pressure comes on to the soil. Fluctuations in the water table affect the buoyancy of the foundation; also in most cases the intensity and distribution of live loading cannot be predicted with accuracy. Another factor causing settlement of a buoyant foundation is re-consolidation of soil which has swelled as a result of the removal of overburden pressure in excavating for the sub-structure. Swelling, whether by elastic or long-term movements, must be followed by re-consolidation as loading is replaced on the soil when the super-structure is built up. The order of swelling movements and measures which may be taken to reduce them are discussed later in this chapter.

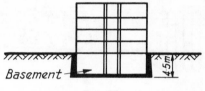

FIG. 5.1

For economy in the depth of foundation construction it is the usual practice to allow some net additional load to come on to the soil after the total of the dead load of the structure and its full live loading has been attained. The allowable intensity of pressure of this additional loading is determined by the maximum total and differential settlements which can be tolerated by the structure.

### Uplift on Buoyant Foundations

It is necessary to prevent the sub-structure from floating and tilting before the superstructure loads are sufficient in magnitude to prevent uplift. Floating only occurs in water-bearing ground or in a very soft silt or clay. During construction it can be prevented by keeping the water table drawn down by continuous pumping or by ballasting the sub-structure by flooding or other means. In some building structures it is possible to overcome the flotation problem by constructing the basement *after* the superstructure has reached a height sufficient to provide the necessary dead weight against uplift.

flats is that a reinforced concrete framed structure with brick and concrete external walls, light-weight concrete partition walls, and plastered finishes weighs 12·5 kN/m² per storey. This figure is inclusive of 100 per cent dead load and 60 per cent maximum design live load.

In some underground structures there may be a net uplift because of light superstructure loading and it is necessary to provide some positive anchorage to prevent flotation. An example of this is the underground pumping station shown in Fig. 5.2. Uplift may be resisted by providing sufficient dead weight in the structure which may result in massive and costly construction, or by means of anchor piles. If anchor piles are embedded wholly in soil, as in Fig. 5.2 (*a*), they must be designed as friction piles. Where the sub-structure is founded on rock as in Fig. 5.2 (*b*), the anchorage can take the form

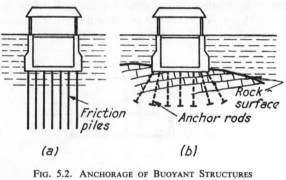

FIG. 5.2. ANCHORAGE OF BUOYANT STRUCTURES
(*a*) Anchorage in soil.
(*b*) Anchorage in rock.

of steel rods grouted into holes drilled into the rock. If rock is present at a moderate distance below the base of the sub-structure, a composite anchorage can be formed by driving open-ended hollow piles to rock and then grouting anchor rods into holes drilled at the bottom of the cleaned-out piles as shown in Fig. 7.27. The anchorage could, alternatively, be made up of groups of high tensile steel wires tensioned by post-stressing. Information on the design of piles or drilled anchorages to resist uplift is given on pages 420 to 425.

## Drag-down Effects on Deep Foundations

When calculating the net bearing pressure at the base of a buoyancy raft or basement the *total* foundation pressure $q$ is reduced by the total overburden pressure $p$. Any skin friction or adhesion between the walls of the sub-structure and the surrounding soil should not be regarded as reducing the net bearing pressure on the soil. In most cases the tendency is for the surrounding soil to produce a limited negative skin friction or drag-down effect on the sub-structure as a result of the construction procedure.

If a basement is constructed in a timbered excavation, as in Fig. 5.3 (*a*), the backfilling which is placed between the walls and the timbered sides consolidates with the passage of time, thus giving a drag-down effect on the walls. In the case of a cellular buoyancy raft (Fig. 5.3 (*b*)) sunk through a soft clay or silt by grabbing or hand excavation from open wells, the downward movement of the structure will cause extensive disturbance of the soil, possibly augmented by

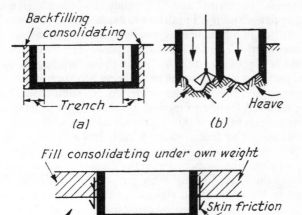

FIG. 5.3. DRAG-DOWN EFFECTS ON BASEMENT STRUCTURES
   (*a*) Basement walls constructed in timbered trenches.
   (*b*) Cellular raft sunk by grabbing.
   (*c*) Basements in filled ground.

slumping of the surrounding soil consequent on upward heave of the soil beneath the cells. The re-consolidation of this disturbed soil will again cause a drag-down effect on the walls. Thus in most cases the tendency will be for the soil in contact with the walls of the sub-structure to add to the load on the base slab rather than to relieve it of load. In practice, the normal design procedure is to ignore any support or drag-down in calculating net bearing pressures at foundation level. However, to minimize drag-down effects, the backfilling around the walls should be carefully placed and well-compacted. Where an appreciable depth of filling is placed over a compressible soil (Fig. 5.3 (*c*)) the drag-down effects may be marked and should be allowed for in the design. The drag-down forces should be calculated as described on pages 313 to 314.

When considering resistance against uplift, the skin friction or adhesion in the surrounding ground can be taken into account. Conservative values should be used (*see* Chapter 7 on Piled Foundations).

## BUOYANCY RAFT FOUNDATIONS

The terms "basement" and "buoyancy raft" have been used in the preceding pages and it is important to explain the differences between them. Although a basement is, in effect, a form of buoyancy raft, it is not necessarily designed for that purpose. The main function of a basement is to provide additional space in the building for the owner, and the fact that it reduces the net bearing pressure by the weight of the displaced soil may be quite incidental. In some cases, basements may be required for their function in reducing net bearing pressures and advantage is taken of this to provide additional floor space in the sub-structure. The true buoyancy raft, however, is a foundation which is designed solely for the purpose of providing support to the structure by the buoyancy given by the displaced soil without regard to utilizing the space for any other purpose. To this end the raft is designed to be as light and rigid as possible. Lightness combined with stiffness is best achieved by cellular or "egg-box" construction. This structural form limits the usefulness of the space within the substructure to accommodate any pipework or service ducts passing through holes in the walls of the cells.

### Buoyancy Rafts at Grangemouth Refinery

Examples of true buoyancy rafts are the cellular structures which support the power station and other plant installations at the Grangemouth Refinery of Scottish Oils Ltd.[5.1] On this site, recent alluvial silts and clays of the estuary of the River Forth extend to depths varying from 25 m to as much as 75 m, and overlie stiff boulder clay. Because of the depth to the boulder clay, cellular rafts were selected as an economical alternative to long piles. Below a 1 to 2 m stiff clay surface crust, the shear strength of the alluvial deposits was only 10 to 15 $kN/m^2$ for a considerable depth.[5.2] Thus the ultimate bearing capacity of the soil for surface rafts was little more than 50 $kN/m^2$, and large loaded areas with overall bearing pressures as low as 25 $kN/m^2$ would have been liable to excessive settlement.

As far as possible, the cellular rafts were designed so that the weight of the displaced soil balanced the combined loading of the rafts and their superstructures. The superstructure loads were carefully positioned to ensure practically uniform bearing pressure over the foundation area. If this had not been done there would have been a risk of tilting. In practice it was found that 3 tonne of displaced earth gave sufficient buoyancy to support 2 tonne of super-structure. The loadings of the buildings and plant required excava-tion to a depth of 6 m, which if undertaken in open cut with sloping sides or sheetpiled supports would probably have led to difficulties with slips or base heaving. Consequently, the rafts were designed to be assembled in shallow excavations, and then sunk to the required depth by grabbing from the open cells. On reaching founding level the cells were plugged with concrete and the superstructure erected on them. By this method, the depth of open excavation was kept to a minimum and, since all the cells were not grabbed out simultaneously, there was always a surcharge of soil within the cells to prevent general heaving of the bottom of the excavation.

POWER STATION FOUNDATIONS

The largest structure on the site was the power station. This was designed to be founded on a group of four cellular rafts. Each raft was sunk independently then rigidly interconnected by in-situ re-inforced concrete panel walls. A total of 240 cells were provided in the 52 m by 52 m combined foundation. The mass of soil displaced at a founding depth of 4·72 m was 23 500 tonne, and the combined mass of the four cellular rafts was only 8 250 tonne. A photograph of the four cellular rafts during sinking operations is shown in Plate VI.

CASTING AND ASSEMBLY OF UNITS. The standard procedure adopted for sinking the rafts was first to excavate to a depth of 2 m through the 0·6 m thick surface layer of burnt colliery shale filling to just below the stiff surface crust of the alluvial clay. The slopes remained stable at batters of about 1 to 1, and a 150 mm thick layer of shale was spread over the working area. Simultaneously with the bulk excavation, the 3 m wide by 150 mm thick precast concrete slabs for the cell walls were being made close by. A thirty-cell raft required sixty slabs, and they were cast horizontally in stacks of six or seven with building paper between each two slabs.

To support the external walls, which were cast in-situ, 1 m wide concrete strips were placed around the external walls. A 1·5 m square pad was also cast at the intersections of the cell walls as shown in Fig. 5.4 (*a*).

When the precast wall slabs were five days old they were lifted from their casting beds by lorry-mounted crane and set vertically on the pads. Four slabs were first set to form a cell in the centre of the raft and were strutted internally and shored externally. The subse-quent slabs were placed symmetrically in turn around the first four,

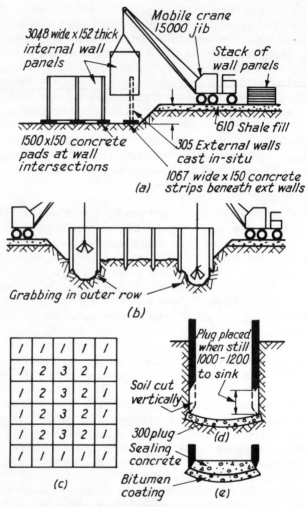

FIG. 5.4. CONSTRUCTION OF BUOYANT RAFT FOUNDATIONS AT GRANGEMOUTH REFINERY

(a) Assembly of precast wall panels.
(b) Sinking unit by grabbing.
(c) Order of excavating cells in a 6 × 5 cell unit.
(d) Plugging cells.
(e) Sealing cells.

the object being to avoid tilting due to non-uniform loading of the soft clay. After assembly of the slabs, the projecting reinforcing bars were tack-welded at the intersections. When all precast slabs had been erected, the concreting of the first 1·22 m lift of the external walls was commenced simultaneously with the electric arc-welding of the bars at the cell intersections. Concreting of the succeeding 1·22 m lifts proceeded, and at the same time the intersections between the precast slabs were concreted. The concrete was placed uniformly around the structure to keep the loading as symmetrical as possible. The rate of concreting of the external walls and the cell intersections was phased so that all parts of the structure were completed at the same time.

SINKING THE RAFTS. Five days after the last lift of concrete was placed, a start was made with sinking the rafts by breaking out the concrete strips beneath the external walls. A short length of strip was left at the junction with the internal walls. The pads beneath the wall intersections were next broken out simultaneously with the remaining portions beneath the external walls. The rafts then commenced to sink through the shale layer, and movement continued until the walls had penetrated far enough to build up skin friction, thus slowing down the sinking. Movement was continued by grabbing from the cells. Two mobile cranes were used, each operated on opposite sides of the raft, excavating with ½ or ⅝ cu. yd. Priestman double-rope clamshell grabs (Fig. 5.4 (*b*)). Grabbing commenced at the corners, continued with the remaining outer cells, and then proceeded towards the centre. The central row of cells was left unexcavated until the rafts had been sunk nearly to founding level. A continuous check was kept on line and level throughout all stages of sinking. The order of grabbing from the cells is shown in Fig. 5.4 (*c*). As soon as the rafts were within 1·2 m of the founding level, two of the outside cells on opposite sides were grabbed out to their full depth and the mass concrete plugs were placed. The vertically cut soil remained stable during the day or two required for the rafts to sink to their final level (Fig. 5.4 (*d*)). On the day after concreting these first two plugs, two more cells were grabbed out and concreted; by this time the raft probably had another 0·6 m to sink. The corner cells were not generally selected among the first four to be plugged. It was usual to select a cell next to a corner one. For a thirty-cell raft (six cells by five cells), it was necessary to grab out and concrete eight cells before the downward movement could be arrested. By the time the eighth cell had been plugged the raft was within 25 to 50 mm of its final level. After the raft had come to rest on the eight plugged cells, the remaining ones were grabbed out and plugged, working towards the centre row. During the plugging of the centre row the outer cells were pumped dry of any water which had seeped through the mass concrete or beneath the cutting edges. They were thoroughly cleaned out and the surface of the mass concrete was given a heavy coat of bitumen. Reinforcing steel was then placed in two directions and wired to splice bars passing through holes in the internal walls of the cells. The reinforced sealing concrete, 0·6 m thick at the centre of each cell and 0·3 m thick at the walls, was then placed (Fig. 5.4 (e)). The top surface of the concrete was given a fall towards a pumping sump at one selected cell. Any leakage through the external walls or plugs gravitated across the floor passing through holes cut through the internal walls to the sump.

Kentledge was not required to aid sinking. Control of level was achieved by grabbing from one side or one corner as required to correct any tendency to tilting. Downward movement could be slowed down or stopped altogether by clearing all men and mechanical plant or transport from the vicinity of the raft for a few hours. The "take-up" or restoration of shear strength of the disturbed clay was sufficient to arrest the movement.

The final stage of the foundation construction was to cast the structural deck, which consisted of a 300 mm reinforced concrete slab cast in situ on permanent formwork provided by 76 mm thick prestressed concrete planks. The upper surface of the latter was corrugated to bond into the in-situ slab since their combined action had been allowed for in the design. Precautions were taken to prevent accumulations of explosive gas in the cells, resulting from leakage from the refinery plant. The structural decks were provided with air-tight manhole covers set on raised plinths.

MEASUREMENTS OF SKIN FRICTION. The author made a study of the skin friction by measuring the depth of soil in the cells at three stages of sinking. The shear stress between the walls and the soil, i.e. the sinking effort, was plotted against the remoulded shear strength of the soil. The results are shown in Fig. 5.5.

The shear stress was obtained by dividing the net weight of the cellular raft (i.e. the total weight minus the buoyancy of the embedded portions of the walls and the resistance given by the bearing area of the walls) by the total vertical area of the walls in contact with the soil. Fig. 5.5 also shows the sinking effort for a trial cylinder sunk on the site, and for Larssen box piles which sank under their own weight to depths of between 3 and 6 m below ground level. It will be seen that in the case of the trial cylinder the shear stress had to be higher than the remoulded shear strength to initiate the downward movement, and, when the cylinder had come to rest at the end of each stage of sinking, the shear stress was slightly lower than the remoulded shear strength. To maintain movement of the cellular rafts, the shear stress had, at all stages, to be greater than the remoulded shear strength.

Settlements were measured on five of the structures founded on the cellular rafts. The results of these measurements were reported

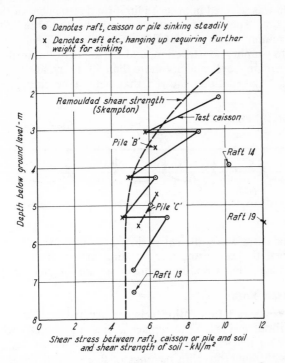

FIG. 5.5. SINKING EFFORT ON CELLULAR RAFT AND OTHER STRUCTURES COMPARED TO SHEAR STRENGTH OF SOIL AT GRANGEMOUTH REFINERY

by Pike and Saurin[5.1] and showed settlements varying from 13 to 6 mm over a period of one and three-quarter years from commencement of the superstructures. Although the buoyancy raft foundations at Grangemouth have performed satisfactorily, deep piled foundations were generally preferred for most of the refinery and petrochemical installations subsequently constructed in the same area. This indicates that under these conditions piled foundations about 30 m deep were cheaper than the buoyancy rafts for industrial structures.

## Buoyancy Rafts in Mexico City

Thin reinforced-concrete barrel shell construction can give substantial savings in the weight of a buoyancy raft structure. Barrel shells were used for the foundations of apartment buildings in Mexico City in soil conditions similar to those described on page 114. Enriquez and Fierro[4.11] claim that this design, which is illustrated in Fig. 5.6, saved 50 per cent of the materials which would have been used in a conventional two-way slab and beam raft. The net pressure on the soil was selected in order to limit total settlement of the buildings to 0·2 m. The shell axes run across the width of the buildings in order to minimize the span of the edge girders. Circular arcs were adopted to simplify construction, and the angle of the surface of the shell at springing level was not more than 40° to avoid the use of top formwork. Calculations showed that with a bearing pressure of

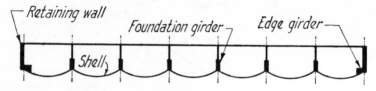

FIG. 5.6. BUOYANCY RAFTS IN BARREL SHELL CONSTRUCTION, MEXICO CITY

100 kN/m² there was sufficient re-distribution of pressures in a 9 m square shell to keep transverse bending moments to a negligible value, provided that a small measure of plastic hinging was allowed.

### Pier 57, New York

A buoyancy raft foundation was constructed at Pier 57 in New York Harbour in 1951–52 to replace a timber piled jetty which was burned down in 1947.[5.3,5.4] The soil strata consisted of 18 m of soft silt with numerous thin partings of fine sand at the shoreward end of the pier, and 60 m of similar material at the pierhead. Bedrock was at 30 m depth at the shore and at 120 m depth at the pierhead. The remaining stumps of the timber piles could not be relied upon to carry the new pier with its cargo sheds, passenger buildings, and cranes. However, it was decided to leave the piles in place since their withdrawal would have weakened the structure of the soft silt which had been partly consolidated by the loading of the former pier. The piles also served to carry the live loading on the new pier. Thus, any tendency to tilting under the variable distribution of live loading was eliminated.

Bedrock was too deep for end-bearing piles to be economical and the silt was too soft to support friction piles. Therefore it was decided that the new pier structure should consist of two 110 m by 25 m wide buoyancy rafts sunk end-to-end along the pier with a third 113 m by 26·5 m raft forming the T-head. It was impossible to design a fully balanced structure because of tidal levels in the harbour. A positive bearing pressure of 10 kN/m² was required at high water to prevent flotation, which resulted in a bearing pressure of 80 kN/m² at low water. Appreciable settlements were likely, due to consolidation of the soft silt under this loading. Consequently, it was decided

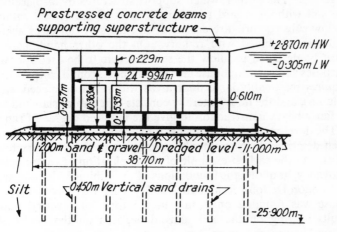

FIG. 5.7. BUOYANCY RAFT AT PIER 57, NEW YORK

to accelerate the settlement by preloading the buoyancy raft. Further acceleration was given by vertical sand drains at 6 m centres beneath the raft (Fig. 5.7). It was calculated that 90 per cent of the consolidation would be achieved in ninety days, after which the superstructure could be erected. The silt was dredged to −11 m M.L.W. and the timber piles cut off at dredged level. A 0·6 m thick blanket of sand was then placed and the 0·46 m diameter vertical sand drains were installed to a depth of −26 m and covered by a 0·6 m thick blanket of gravel. The three pontoons forming the buoyancy rafts were built in a basin on the Hudson River some 60 km away from the pier site. They were floated in and sunk on to the gravel blanket by pumping water into the cells. Pumping-in of water ballast continued until the bearing pressure on the blanket was equal to that of the total weight of the superstructure, including live loading from cargo. Only after the silt had consolidated were anchorages formed by sinking 36 in. diameter pipe casings through the cantilevered projecting portions of the base slabs to a depth of 9 m into the silt. These anchorages gave restraint to uplift and horizontal forces. The final stages were grouting the sand and gravel blanket followed by erection of the superstructure. The water ballast was then pumped out of the cells as the superstructure loading increased.

## BASEMENT OR BOX FOUNDATIONS

The difference between buoyancy rafts and basements is defined on page 272. The former, which support structures by displacement of the soil without regard to the utilization of the spaces within the hollow substructure, are designed with the sole object of achieving lightness combined with rigidity. On the other hand, basements must be designed to allow the sub-structure to be used for various purposes such as warehouse storage or underground car parks. This requires reasonably large floor areas without close-spaced walls or columns, and the floor generally consists of a slab or slab and beams of fairly heavy construction to give the required degree of rigidity.

The development of basements for supporting heavy buildings has been described by Skempton[5.5] who refers to them as box foundations. As the earliest example of the application of the principle of buoyancy, he quotes the foundations of the Albion Mills, constructed in London by John Rennie in 1785.[5.6] This heavy five-storey warehouse was founded on a raft in the form of inverted masonry vaults bearing on the soft alluvial deposits on the banks of the River Thames.

### Basements for Shell Centre, London

The proportioning of the depth of a basement to correspond to variations in superstructure loads was mentioned on page 113. These principles were adopted for the Shell Centre on the South Bank of the River Thames, London.[2.14] This group of high buildings consists of two ten-storey structures separated by a railway viaduct, with a twenty-eight storey tower block in the area upstream of the viaduct. The spaces between the buildings are occupied by underground garages in basements 9 m to 16 m deep. The soil strata consist of made-ground followed by soft clay, sand and gravel, a very thick stratum of London Clay, then the Woolwich and Reading beds, followed by the Thanet Sands and the Upper Chalk (Fig. 5.8). It would have been possible to found the tower block on a relatively shallow raft bearing on the sand and gravel, but the estimated settlement of about 125 mm for a shallow raft was considered to be excessive, in view of the risk of tilting of the tall building. This could have occurred as a result of the loading on one side of the block imposed by the adjacent ten-storey wing and the relief of overburden pressure on the other side given by the construction of

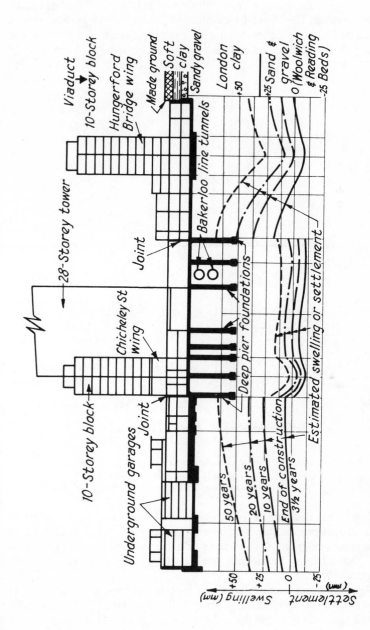

FIG. 5.8. CROSS-SECTION THROUGH SHELL CENTRE, SOUTH BANK, LONDON (MEASOR AND WILLIAMS[2.14])

the underground garage. The estimated maximum differential move-ment between the tower block and the underground garage was as much as 180 mm. Estimates made of swelling of the soil beneath the underground garage showed an upward movement of 75 mm in fifty years. In view of the large differential movements and the risks of

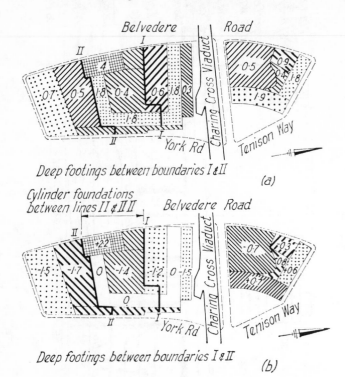

*Deep footings between boundaries I & II*   (a)

*Deep footings between boundaries I & II*   (b)

FIG. 5.9. LOADING CONDITIONS, SHELL CENTRE, SOUTH BANK, LONDON
(a) Approx. average total weight per unit area (kN/m² × 100).
(a) Approx. average total weight per unit area (kN/m² × 100).

tilting it was decided to found the tower block on a deep basement. The reduction in the net bearing pressure greatly reduced the estimated settlement. The values of gross and net bearing pressures for the various basements are shown in Fig. 5.9 (a) and (b) respectively.

Another complicating factor on this site was the presence of four tube railway tunnels running beneath the site (*see* Figs. 5.8 and 5.9). There was only 0·9 m of cover between the basement excavation and the crown of the shallowest tunnel. It was considered that the tunnels, constructed in bolted cast-iron segments, were sufficiently flexible to withstand the estimated rise in the tunnels of 40 mm due to excavation for the basements. Buildings adjacent to the tunnels were constructed on deep piers taken below tunnel level in order to prevent unequal radial pressures which might have distorted the tunnel rings. The deep piers were in the form of cylindrical shafts with belled-out bases. The bases were terminated at a sufficient height above the water-bearing Woolwich and Reading beds to avoid upheaval of the London Clay by sub-artesian water pressure in the water-bearing stratum. Vertical joints were provided between structures founded on deep piers and those on relatively shallow foundations to allow for the expected differential movement.

Extensive measurements were made by the Building Research Station[5.7] of pressures and movements in the tube railway tunnels in the course of construction of the buildings. A rise of nearly 40 mm took place without noticeable distress in the tunnel segments, and no distortion was observed as a result of excavation for the deep belled-out piers. However, driving heavy section steel sheet piling to support the trench excavation for the basement retaining walls caused 5 mm inward deflexion of the sides of a tunnel and a similar elongation of the vertical diameter at the soffit and invert. This movement occurred when the piles were driven parallel to and 3 m away from the tunnel lining. The movement corresponded to an increase in stress on the tunnel lining of about 110 $kN/m^2$.

### Soil Swelling in Deep Excavations

The problem of soil swelling is the chief difficulty to be overcome in the design of deep basements. Although it is possible to balance the superstructure loading by the weight of soil removed in excavating for the basement, so theoretically preventing settlement, in practice the swelling caused by removal of the overburden pressure must be overcome as the loading on the soil increases. Therefore foundation movement does occur, and it may be large enough to cause severe stresses in the superstructure if it is accompanied by correspondingly large differential movement.

In the excavation for three of the piers of Waterloo Bridge[5.8], the London Clay swelled 25 mm after 6 to 7·5 m of overburden had been removed. In the Chelsea Bridge piers, the London Clay swelled 6 to 14 mm during and after removal of the last 1·7 to 2·4 m of overburden. A swelling of 6 mm was measured at the bottom of a 5 m deep excavation in sand and gravel for the basement of the headquarters of the author's firm at Hammersmith. About 1·5 m of sand and gravel remained between the bottom of the excavation and the stiff blue London Clay.

MINIMIZING THE EFFECTS OF SWELLING

Swelling of the bottom of excavations in stiff fissured clays can be greatly reduced by excavating and placing the base slab in small areas at a time. This was done at Waterloo Bridge after excessive swelling had occurred on the first pier to be excavated (Pier 4). The excavation for this pier was taken out in a 35 m by 8·2 m sheet piled cofferdam to a depth of about 8·2 m below river bed. Measurements of swell commenced when the excavation had reached a depth of 1·5 to 3 m above the final level. A rise of 75 mm was measured in the centre of the cofferdam and 25 mm near the sheet piling. The 75 mm thick sealing concrete was cracked and water seeped into the underlying stiff fissured clay. In the other three piers the excavation which was about 6 m deep was taken out in bulk within 1·5 m of the final level. The remaining clay was taken out in narrow strips running the full width of the sheet pile cofferdam. An 0·5 m thick layer of sealing concrete was placed over each strip before the adjoining strip was excavated. The resulting swelling amounted only to about 25 mm in the centre and 8 mm at the sheet piling. The severe swelling at Pier 4 was generally thought to have been due to water seeping into opened-up fissures, but an alternative view was that it had been due to inward yielding of the sheet piles which forced up the clay. In the subsequent piers the 0·5 m of sealing concrete would have effectively prevented this movement. Inward yielding of the sheet piling was thought to be the principal cause of 50 mm of swelling in a 15 m deep foundation trench at the Shell Centre, London. Swelling can however be further minimized by excavating the retaining wall trenches in very short lengths with soil left between them. The soil is removed after the retaining wall in the excavated portions has been completed. This was done for the 15 m deep retaining walls for the basement of the National Provincial Bank building in London.[5.9]

Swelling of the ground over the general area of a basement excavation within the completed retaining wall can be minimized by excavating over limited areas, the base slab being concreted as quickly as possible after completing the excavation in each individual area.

If floors are very thick, as in the case of deep basements in water-bearing ground where deadweight must be provided to resist uplift, it may be necessary to excavate for a concrete floor in alternate strips in order to allow shrinkage of the thick slabs to take place before the intervening portions are concreted. After the soil is taken out in bulk to a level at which there is sufficient overburden pressure remaining to prevent heaving or swelling, the further depth is excavated in sheet piled or timbered trenches and a section of floor slab concreted. The sheet piles are then withdrawn and the intervening excavation is taken out and the floor slab concrete poured in the space between the completed sections. This technique is used for the heavy floors of dry docks constructed in water-bearing soil or in ground liable to swelling.

## CONSTRUCTING BASEMENTS CLOSE TO EXISTING PROPERTY

Excavation for deep basements may cause settlement of the surrounding ground surface. The settlement may be sufficient to cause structural damage to buildings near the excavation, and cracking of drains and other services. This settlement may be caused by—

(*a*) Lateral movement of the face of the excavation due to the cumulative effects of yielding of the sheeting members, walings and struts, or anchors which support the face.

(*b*) Lateral movements due to elastic deflexion of the basement retaining wall after completion of backfilling.

(*c*) Lowering of the water table surrounding the excavation due to pumping during construction.

(*d*) Loss of ground due to slips, heave of the base, erosion etc. as a result of ill-conceived construction methods or carelessness of execution.

### Avoiding Settlement due to Yielding of Excavation Supports

Normal methods of supporting excavations by strutting or tie-back anchors, no matter how carefully done, cannot prevent inward yielding of the face of the excavation. The inward movement may be of the order of 2·5 per cent of the excavation depth in soft clays to 0·05 per cent in dense granular soils or stiff clays accompanied by corresponding settlement of the ground surface (p. 599). One method of safeguarding existing structures is to underpin them, while supporting the excavations. It is generally assumed that settlement of the ground surface will not occur to any appreciable extent beyond a line drawn at a slope of 1(horizontal) to 2(vertical) from the base of excavation. Underpinning of structures is carried out within this line (Fig. 5.10). The possibility of settlements extending to a wider limit beyond the excavation is discussed on page 729. In shallow or only moderately deep excavations it may be justifiable to accept a small amount of settlement and to repair any consequent cracking or other minor damage to existing structures. The degree of risk involved will depend on the value of the property and the effects on any activities such as manufacturing processes within the premises.

The construction of basement retaining walls by placing concrete *in-situ* in a trench excavated with support by a bentonite slurry can be an economical method of combining temporary and permanent support to the sides of the basement excavation, not only close to existing property but also in open ground. An alternative method is to construct the retaining wall in the form of a row of close-spaced bored and cast-in-place piles (the "contiguous" or "secant" pile methods). These cast-in-place concrete wall systems are not economical compared with a conventional reinforced concrete wall constructed inside an excavation supported by strutted steel sheet piling, if the soil conditions permit the extraction of the sheet piling for subsequent re-use. However if extraction of the piles is not feasible, or if noise control regulations prohibit pile driving, then the cast-in-place wall methods can be a favourable method of construction which is relatively free of noise and vibration and can be carried out very close to existing foundations.

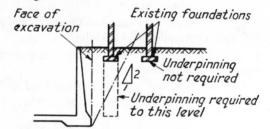

FIG. 5.10. UNDERPINNING ADJACENT TO BASEMENT EXCAVATIONS

The first step in diaphragm wall construction is to form a pair of reinforced concrete guide walls some 150 to 300 mm wide and at least one metre deep. These walls act as guides for the excavating machinery and as a means of maintaining a head of bentonite at least one metre above ground water level in order to prevent collapse of the sides of the excavation. The guide walls also serve to prevent collapse of the trench sides due to the surging of the slurry caused by the excavating tools, and in soft or loose soils they must be taken deep enough or be made sufficiently wide to perform this essential task. The construction of the guide walls can represent a substantial proportion of the total cost of a diaphragm wall and in some site conditions, e.g. in areas of buried foundations and old cellars, they can be prohibitively costly.

Excavation of the trench between the guide walls is undertaken in alternate panels, the length of which depends on the stability of the soil and the dimensions of the basement. A panel length of about 4 to 6 m is quite usual for stable ground. The excavation is performed with the support of the slurry either by grabbing or by reverse-circulation rotary drilling. Grabs operated in conjunction with a power-assisted "kelly" are efficient in a wide range of soil types. Rotary drilling is effective in granular soils. The bentonite slurry is circulated continuously during excavation by pumping from the trench to an elevated settling tank from which it returns to the trench. The slurry can be circulated through a reconditioning plant to remove sand and grit, or its use may be confined to a single panel and then it is pumped into a tank vehicle for disposal off-site. In either case continuous monitoring of the viscosity, density, shear strength, and pH value of the slurry is necessary to ensure that it does not become excessively diluted or contaminated by soil particles.

After completing the excavation of a panel vertical tubes are placed at each end, which form a semi-circular recess at the ends of each concrete panel. The reinforcing cage is then lowered into the slurry and suspended from the tops of the guide walls after which the concrete is placed using a tremie pipe, when the rising concrete displaces the slurry. After a period for hardening of the concrete, the intermediate panels are excavated and then concreted to form the completed wall. The final stages are removal of the inner guide wall followed by bulk excavation within the enclosing wall, trimming off any protuberances caused by "overbreak" during excavation and, finally, casting the facing wall. The model specification prepared by the Federation of Piling Specialists defines the face of the wall as the inside face of the inner guide wall and a tolerance of $\pm 15$ mm in a 3 m length is allowed from this face. Also a deviation from the vertical of 1 in 80 is allowed and protuberances of more than 100 mm from the face must be cut away at the expense of the diaphragm wall contractor. According to the model specification the latter only applies in "homogeneous clays". In highly fissured clays, sands, gravels, and soft or loose soils the removal of the protuberances must be paid for as an extra.

The stages of excavating and concreting for a cast-in-place diaphragm wall are shown in Fig. 5.11, and the methods of bulk excavation and support for a deep basement wall are described in Chapter 9.

Instead of placing concrete *in-situ*, precast concrete panels can be lowered into the slurry-filled trench. Support to the soil behind the panels is provided by a bentonite-cement grout which also forms the seal between the grooved ends of the abutting panels. In the S.I.F.-Bachy system the bentonite slurry is replaced by the grout immediately before placing the panels. In the Soletanche system the excavation is performed with the bentonite-cement as a supporting fluid.

Both the cast-in-place or precast concrete panel systems can achieve watertight basements. The formation of the bentonite gel in the soil behind the wall and between the panels acts as a seal against the entry of water. In rectangular or circular structures the earth pressure induces longitudinal compression in the wall which tends to close-up the vertical joints. Problems with leakage can occur where there are re-entrants in the wall where the vertical joints tend to open.

Where inclined anchors are used to support a diaphragm wall the width of the wall at the toe must be sufficient to prevent failure as a

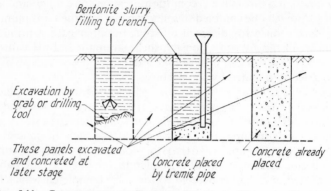

FIG. 5.11. CONSTRUCTION OF BASEMENT RETAINING WALLS BY DIAPHRAGM METHOD

strip foundation under the loading produced by the vertical component of the stress in the anchors. Also the depth of the toe below final excavation level must be such as to provide the required passive resistance in front of the wall to the earth pressure and hydrostatic pressure behind the wall.

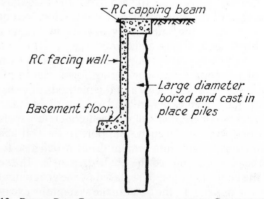

FIG. 5.12. BORED PILE COFFERDAM INCORPORATED IN PERMANENT BASEMENT WALL

In the *contiguous bored pile* system of retaining wall construction, bored piles are installed in a single or double row and positioned so that they are touching or are in very close proximity to each other. Alternate piles are first drilled by power auger (Plate X) or grabbing rig

(Plate XI) and concreted. Then the intermediate piles are installed. The use of casing to guide the drill results in a space some 50 to 75 mm wide between piles. The space may be wider if the drilling deviates from the vertical (up to 1 in 80 tolerance is usual). These gaps between piles can be very troublesome in water-bearing granular soils which bleed through into the excavation. Grouting can be used to seal the gaps but it may not be completely effective.

The problem of watertightness can be overcome by the *secant pile* method of interlocking bored piles. Alternate piles are first drilled and concreted at a closer spacing than the contiguous method. The intermediate piles are then installed by drilling out the soil between each pair followed by chiselling a groove down the sides of their shafts. Concrete is then placed to fill the drilled hole including the grooves so forming a fully interlocking and watertight wall.

The secant pile system is, of course, more costly than the contiguous bored pile wall. However, either of these types may be preferred to the diaphragm wall in conditions unfavourable to the latter, such as in ground intersected by deep sewers or basements which would result in complete loss of slurry from a trench and collapse of the sides. With both types a facing wall is necessary as shown in Fig. 5.12.

Much useful information on the design and construction of diaphragm walls, bored pile walls and anchorages is given in the Proceedings of the Institution of Civil Engineers Conference on this subject.[5.10]

It is possible to avoid underpinning of adjacent structures by adopting specially rigid forms of excavation supports. These consist of heavy steel or concrete sheeting members which are supported at one or more levels by heavily braced struts and walings. Jacking of struts may be used to counteract inward yielding (p. 589). Economy in steelwork in struts and walings is achieved by using the permanent ground floor structure or any intermediate basement floor structures to strut the sheeting. This method was used for constructing a 16 m deep combined basement and underground garage beneath the City National Bank Building in Los Angeles.[5.11] The first operation was to install 300 mm H-beam soldier piles in boreholes drilled at 2·1 m centres along the boundary of the excavation. The space between the soldier piles and the walls of the boreholes was filled with a soil–cement mix. The first 3 m of excavation was then taken out using horizontal timber laggings to support the face between the soldier piles. From this level a well 2·4 m in diameter was drilled at each column position down to the level of the base of the building columns. A total of 20 such wells were drilled and lined with steel casing. A 1·8 m thick plug of concrete forming part of the column base was placed in each well. The steel column base plate was set on the concrete plug, and the

20 m long lower column section was bolted to the base plate. The columns were braced together at ground floor level by the permanent steel ground floor beams and the space between the exterior columns and the soldier piles was spanned by a horizontal truss. The excavation was thus completely strutted across at ground floor level. The soil was then removed to the intermediate basement floor level and the permanent floor beams were erected at this level. The casing to the 2·4 m wells was burned away as necessary. A permanent reinforced concrete slab was cast between the exterior columns and the soldier piles to complete the strutting at this level. The third stage of excavation was down to the general bottom level, but a bank of earth at a 1:1 slope was left to support the lower part of the excavation. An excavation was then made around each plug of concrete to the column bases to enable them to be extended to their final dimensions. The sloping earth bank was finally removed in stages, and the excavated face was supported by concrete placed pneumatically between the

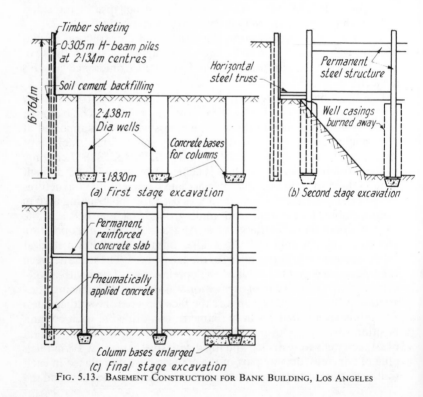

(a) *First stage excavation*

(b) *Second stage excavation*

(c) *Final stage excavation*

Fig. 5.13. Basement Construction for Bank Building, Los Angeles

soldier piles. The final stages of basement construction comprised completion of the basement and garage floor structures. The sequence of construction is shown in Fig. 5.13.

### Avoiding Yielding of Basement Retaining Walls

Backfilling of the excavation behind the basement retaining wall and restoration of the ground-water table to its original level may result

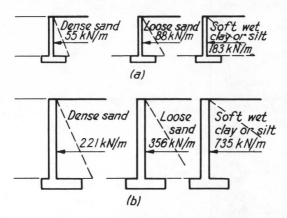

FIG. 5.14. PRESSURE ON RETAINING WALLS DUE TO BACKFILLING
(PECK AND IRELAND[5.12])
(*a*) 4·6 m high retaining walls.
(*b*) 9·1 m high retaining walls.

in lateral pressures of sufficient magnitude to cause inward deflexion of the retaining wall.

The materials used for backfilling behind retaining walls and the compaction given to the backfill material has an important bearing on the magnitude of earth pressure on the wall and its consequent yielding. The material used should not be inferior to that assumed by the designer in his earth pressure calculations. Peck and Ireland[5.12] have described the effect of varying the conditions of materials, placement, compaction and ground water on retaining walls. They give the examples shown in Fig. 5.14 (*a*) and (*b*).

Prestressing of cantilevered retaining walls was undertaken for the 21 m deep basement walls of the Western District Post Office, London.[5.13] The prestressing scheme, shown in Fig. 5.15, was designed in conjunction with jacking the bracing frames supporting the sheet piling driven around the excavation. On completion of the wall the earth pressure was systematically transferred from the bracing frames to the wall.

### Avoiding Settlement due to Ground-Water Lowering

If pumping from within an excavation causes a general lowering of the water table the ground surrounding the excavation may settle

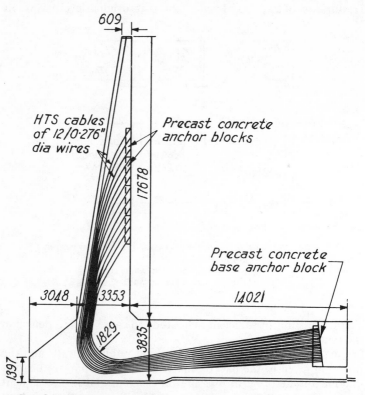

FIG. 5.15. PRESTRESSING OF RETAINING WALL AT WESTERN DISTRICT POST OFFICE, LONDON (BLACKFORD AND CUTHBERT[5.13])

appreciably as a result of the change in hydrostatic conditions (*see* page 709). Settlement can be avoided by constructing the basement within a sheet piled cofferdam or other watertight diaphragm, toed into an impervious stratum (Fig. 5.16).

By this means the head of water outside the excavation is unchanged. Alternatively, a system of "recharging wells" may be used to maintain the water table at its original level (page 711). Construction "in the wet" is another possibility but this is rarely economical. this is rarely economical.

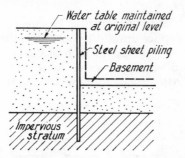

FIG. 5.16. BASEMENT CONSTRUCTION IN SHEET PILED COFFERDAM

### Avoiding Settlement due to Incorrect Construction Methods

It is often desirable for the engineer to indicate a suitable construction method on the contract drawings. The method should, of course, be based on the soil and ground-water conditions as revealed by the site investigations. The scheme need not be detailed. It should show sheeting members, walings, and strutting but the dimensions and spacing of these could be left to the contractor. By showing a construction method the engineer is obliged to take full note of all possible difficulties in construction and he may be able to make some economies in the permanent structure by simplifying the design or by utilizing some of the permanent structure as excavation supports. The engineer's construction scheme also provides a basis for comparing competitive tenders but contractors should be permitted to submit alternative tenders based on their own construction schemes.

### Piled Basements

Basement rafts carrying heavy buildings on weak soil are often founded on piles. The normal function of the piles is to transfer the loading to stronger and less compressible soil at greater depth, or, if economically possible, to transfer the loading to bedrock or other relatively incompressible strata. The piles also have the effect of stiffening the raft and reducing or eliminating re-consolidation of ground heave, thereby reducing differential settlements or tilting.

The question of whether to allow for the full load of the building to be carried by the underside of the base slab of a raft supported by piles is a much debated one which has never been satisfactorily answered. It is probable that in many cases where appreciable settlements of piles have occurred either part or the whole of the building loads has been carried by the raft. There can be no general guidance on the problem and each case must be considered on its merits.

CASE A (Fig. 5.17 (*a*))

In the course of excavation for the basement, considerable heave takes place with further upward movement caused by displacement due to pile driving. After completion of the piling, the swelled soil will be trimmed off to the specified level of the underside of the basement slab. After concreting the basement slab there will be

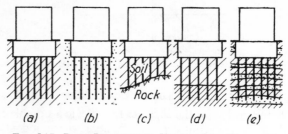

FIG. 5.17. PILED BASEMENTS IN VARIOUS SOIL CONDITIONS
(*a*) Wholly in soft compressible clay.
(*b*) Wholly in loose sand.
(*c*) Bearing on rock.
(*d*) Through soft clay into stiff clay.
(*e*) Alternating layers of soft clay and sand.

some tendency for pressure to increase on the slab due to long-term swelling of the soil, but this will be counteracted to some extent by the soil displaced by the pile driving settling away from the slab as it re-consolidates around the piles. However, as the load on the basement increases with increasing superstructure loading, the piles themselves will settle due to consolidation of the soil in the region of the pile toes. The soil surrounding the upper part of the piles will follow the downward movement of the underlying soil and thus there will be no appreciable tendency for the full structural loading to come on to the basement slab. After completion of the building, long-term settlement due to consolidation of the soil beneath the piles will continue, but at all times the overlying soil will move downwards and will not develop appreciable pressure on the basement slab. Thus, it can be stated that the maximum load which is likely to come on the underside of the slab will be that due to soil swelling in the early days after pile driving together with water pressure if the basement is below ground water level. If, however, the working loads on the piles were to exceed their ultimate carrying capacity they would move downwards relative to the surrounding soil. The slab would then carry the full load of the building, until the consolidation of the soil throws the load back on to the piles with progressive movement continuing until equilibrium is reached.

The net downward movement resulting from the algebraic sum of heave, re-consolidation, and further consolidation will be lower for the piled basement than for an unpiled basement. This is illustrated in Fig. 5.18.

Consider first the unpiled basement. If *AB* represents the designed level of the underside of the basement floor slab, then as excavation

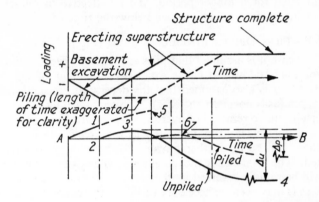

Fig. 5.18. Comparison of Settlement of Piled and Unpiled Basement
Walls

proceeds the soil at level *AB* will rise to point 1 as the ground beneath swells due to reduction in overburden pressure. The excavation will then be trimmed back to the specified level *AB* (point 2) and the slab concreted. Long-term swelling will continue until point 3 is reached when the superstructure loading has increased to an extent corresponding to the original overburden pressure and re-consolidation of the swelled ground will take place. Long-term consolidation settlement will then continue until ultimate settlement is attained (point 4). The total downward movement is then $\Delta u$.

In the case of the piled basement the excavation will remain open and unconcreted for a longer period until all piles have been driven. The displacement caused by pile driving may cause some steepening of the swelling curve. After completion of pile driving (point 5) the soil is trimmed off to the specified level *AB* and the floor slab constructed over the piles. There will be some continuing upward movement at basement level as the soil at the lower end of the pile shafts and beneath the piles continues to swell, but if the piles are long in relation to the width of the building such movement will be very small. When the superstructure loading reaches the original over-burden pressure (point 6) re-consolidation will take place. The net downward movement ($\Delta p$) will be less, since the swelling is less and the consolidation due to net additional superstructure loading will be also less since the piles will have been driven into soil of lower compressibility. If, however, the piles are relatively short there will be no appreciable reduction in net settlement as compared to an unpiled basement. The piles will then be wholly within the zone of swelling which may well be greater because the excavation will remain open for a longer period. To be effective in reducing net settlements, piles should be driven below the zone of swelling.

### Case B—Piles Driven into Loose Sand (Fig. 5.17 (*b*))

In this case it is assumed that piles are required because the loose-ness of the sand would cause excessive settlement of an unpiled basement. It is also assumed that the density of the sand increases with depth (as is normally the case). The only swelling will be elastic movement due to removal of overburden pressure during excavation. This will take place instantaneously as the excavation is deepened, and there will be no further movement after the bottom has been reached. The total elastic movement will, in any case, be quite small and will be rapidly reversed by the consolidation of the sand by pile driving. It may even be necessary to fill up the cone-shaped depressions around the piles with sand before concreting the basement raft. As the superstructure is erected the entire loading of the super-structure and basement will be carried on the piles. This loading is thrown on to the denser sand at depth, and the settlement due to consolidation of the deeper sand strata will take place more or less instantaneously as the loading on the piles increases. The sand sur-rounding the piles will settle as the underlying sand compresses and thus there will be no transfer of load to the underside of the basement slab. It would, of course, be necessary to allow for water pressure.

### Case C—Piles Driven through Compressible Soil to Bedrock (Fig. 5.17 (*c*)).

The soil beneath the basement excavation will swell due to removal of overburden pressure, with further swelling due to displacement by the piles. After completion of pile driving the heaved-up soil will be trimmed down and the basement floor slab concreted. There will be no further swelling because heave due to pile driving will be greater than any residual swelling movement. At some stage during erection of the superstructure, the heaved-up soil will re-consolidate and it may settle away from the underside of the floor slab. There will be no settlement of the piles other than slight elastic shortening of the pile shafts and elastic compression of the rock beneath the pile toes. Thus at no stage will any load come on to the underside of the basement slab other than that from water pressure (if any). If, however, bored piles were to be used there would be no displacement by the piles and it is quite likely that long-term swelling would cause pressure on the basement slab even with some lifting of the piles. This movement would be reversed as soon as the superstructure load exceeded the original overburden pressure.

### Case D—Piles Driven through Soft Clay into Stiff Clay (Fig. 5.17 (*d*))

This case is intermediate between cases A and C. Swelling of the soil will occur because of excavation for the basement and displacement by pile driving. After trimming off the heaved soil and concreting the floor slab there will be no further swelling. Reconsolidation of the displaced soil will proceed as the superstructure load increases. There will be a tendency for the soil to settle away from the underside of the slab since the settlement due to re-consolidation of the soft compressible soil will be greater than the consolidation of the stiff clay soil beneath the piles. Thus at no time will any soil pressure be carried by the underside of the basement floor slab, except when bored piles are used as described in Case C.

Hooper[5.14] measured the inter-action between the basement raft and bored piles supporting the 31-storey Hyde Park Cavalry Barracks, constructed on stiff London Clay. At the end of construction 60 per cent of 121 MN net load was carried by the raft and 40 per cent by the piles. With time there was a slow transfer of load to the piles, the increase being about 6 per cent in three years after construction.

### Case E—Piles Driven into Alternating Layers of Soft Clay and Sand (Fig. 5.17(*e*))

This case gives heave and subsequent consolidation conditions which are intermediate between those of cases A and C.

### The Structural Design of Basement Rafts

Basement walls should generally be designed as self-supporting cantilevered retaining walls even though they may eventually be strutted by the floor construction, and additional stability against overturning given by superstructure loading on top of the walls. It is inconvenient, and often impossible, to provide temporary raking struts to support a basement retaining wall until such time as the strutting given by ground floor or intermediate basement floor is completed. Thus, the walls must be stable against overturning and sliding. However, economies may be achieved by utilizing the strutting of intermediate floors in very deep basements. Earth pressures on basement retaining walls should be calculated by methods in B.S. *Code of Practice* CP2002.

### DESIGN OF HEEL

Since bending moments at the junction of walls and floors of a cantilevered retaining wall are high it is often the practice to provide a substantial heel at this point. Various forms of heel and stepping of retaining walls are shown in Fig. 5.19 (*a*) to (*c*).

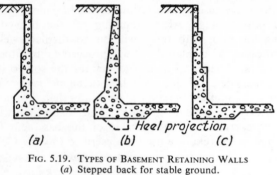

FIG. 5.19. TYPES OF BASEMENT RETAINING WALLS
(*a*) Stepped back for stable ground.
(*b*) Sloping back for stable ground.
(*c*) Stepped face for weak ground.

### DESIGN OF CANTILEVER WALLS

The choice of providing steps on the back or front of a retaining wall to reduce its thickness depends on—
(*a*) the value of the space within the basement;
(*b*) limitations in space available for excavation on the outside of the basement wall;
(*c*) whether or not waterproof asphalt tanking is required;
(*d*) the arrangement of reinforcing steel.
With regard to (*a*) it is obvious that steps on the inner face will reduce the floor area of the basement. If, however, the basement is built close to existing property there may not be space available to excavate on the outside face for steps, and there is then no alternative to putting them on the inside. The problems involved in point (*c*) will be discussed in greater detail on page 307. If the asphalt is applied to the inside of a protecting wall rather than to the outside of the basement wall, it is necessary to have a vertical back to the basement wall as shown in Fig. 5.19 (*c*).

The main reinforcing steel in a cantilevered retaining wall is placed at the back of the wall. Thus, the vertical or uniformly sloping back favours a tidy arrangement of straight bars, whereas a stepped back requires that the bars which extend from top to bottom should be cranked at each step. The alternative of lapping bars at each step is wasteful in steel.

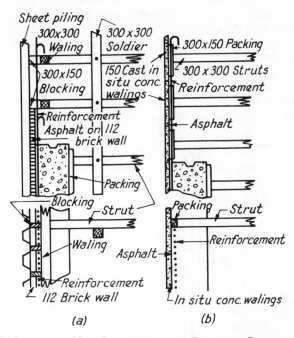

FIG. 5.20. PLACING OF MAIN REINFORCEMENT IN CANTILEVER RETAINING WALLS
(a) Sheet piled trench.
(b) Trench with in-situ concrete facing wall.

There is little to choose between a stepped or sloping face from the aspect of ease of formwork. Against the former it might be said that the location of steps determines the height of lifts of concrete which in turn fixes the spacing of the frames of walings and struts supporting the excavation. The contractor, therefore, has rather more freedom of action with uniform vertical or sloping faces to walls, since he can arrange the lifts of concrete to suit the most desirable spacing of struts and walings determined from considerations of resistance to earth pressure and other forces on the bracing.

Retaining walls should not depend on their connexion to the basement floor slab for stability against overturning or sliding. The width of the base constructed within the trench should be sufficient to keep the bearing pressure at the toe of the base slab within safe limits and to ensure that the resultant of the pressure on the back of the wall and the weight of the wall falls within the middle third of the base. If necessary a projection should be provided beneath the wall to prevent sliding as shown in Fig. 5.19 (*b*).

To save an unnecessarily wide trench excavation, it is the usual practice to locate the main reinforcing bars between the walings and the inner face of the sheeting or facing wall. The walings are blocked out to give the required space to accommodate the bars. The arrangements of reinforcing bars and walings for a sheet piled trench and for a trench with a permanent concrete facing wall are shown in Figs. 5.20 (*a*) and (*b*).

The alternative of keeping the reinforcement wholly inside the walings is uneconomical. Either excessive concrete will be needed

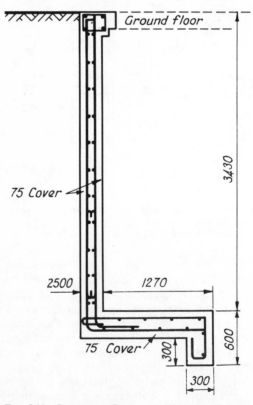

FIG. 5.21. CANTILEVER RETAINING WALL FOR BASEMENT

between the reinforcement and the sheeting or back-formwork will be required together with an additional width of excavation to allow for fixing and striking the formwork. If, however, asphalt tanking is applied directly to the outside of the retaining wall then working space must be provided for the asphalters. In such cases there will be adequate room to bring the reinforcement up inside the walings.

Where reinforcement is placed outside the walings, as shown in Fig. 5.20 (*a*), care must be taken to arrange the spacings of walings and struts to suit the levels of hooks or cranks in the reinforcing steel. The designer should keep this in mind and avoid providing hooks or cranks at a number of differing levels. Typical arrangements of reinforcing steel in a cantilevered retaining wall are shown in Fig. 5.21.

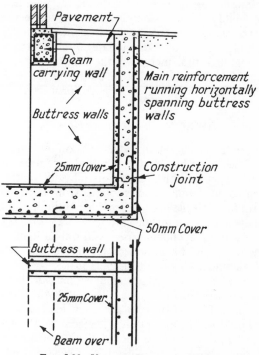

FIG. 5.22. VAULTED RETAINING WALL

## VAULTED RETAINING WALLS

In some circumstances a vaulted type of retaining wall will be advantageous. This type can be used in buildings where the basement is permitted to extend in front of the main walls of the building. In the example shown in Fig. 5.22 the basement extends beneath a footpath, and partial illumination is given by glass and concrete pavement lights. This type of construction is sometimes useful in providing direct access for handling of goods to and from vehicles in the street outside the building. The overall width of the vault at the base is usually governed by the width required by the owner. This should be calculated for conditions without the superstructure loading on the vault and without connexion to the basement floor slab. The quantities of formwork and reinforcement for a vaulted retaining wall are greater than for cantilever walls although the quantity of concrete may be less. Also, the work is probably carried out in a trench with the complications given by the interference of struts and walings. Vaulted walls are therefore, in most cases, more costly than the simple cantilever types and are only advantageous when the planning of the building requires the basement to extend outside the building line. Counterforted or tee-section retaining walls are not often used for basements, since the additional excavation outside the building line to accommodate counterforts and base slabs has to be backfilled, thus increasing the cost of excavation without gaining space in the basement. Also, in built-up areas the counterforts and base slabs might encroach on adjacent property.

## DESIGN OF FLOOR SLABS

Basement floor slabs are designed as rafts on the lines described in Chapter 4. They must be able to withstand pressures on the underside of the slab together with stresses caused by differential settlement, non-uniform column loads, and reactions from the retaining walls. An important factor is the need to provide continuity in the base slab if the basement acts as a buoyancy raft (Fig. 5.23 (*a*)). If the columns are provided with independent bases with only a light slab between them, there would be likelihood of failure of the slabs from the pressure of the underlying soil (Fig. 5.23 (*b*)).

For light or moderate bearing pressures the floor slab may consist of a slab of uniform thickness or a "flat slab" with thickened areas beneath columns (Fig. 5.24). In order to avoid cracking of the floor slab there should not be abrupt changes from thin to thick parts of the slab and the junction of the floor slab with the column bases and wall foundations should be provided with a generous splay as shown in Fig. 5.24. This will avoid concentrations of stress at the junction. For high bearing pressures it is usually necessary to provide a grid of heavily reinforced upstanding beams (Fig. 5.23 (*a*)). The system of independent column bases with a light floor slab (Fig. 5.23 (*b*)) can be used in ground where settlements and ground heave are expected to be negligible, i.e. where the basement is not required for buoyancy

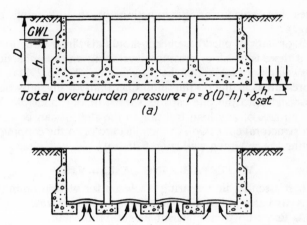

$$\text{Total overburden pressure} = p = \gamma(D-h) + \gamma_{sat}\frac{h}{}$$
(a)

(b)

FIG. 5.23. DESIGN OF BASEMENT FLOOR SLABS WHERE BASEMENTS ACT AS BUOYANCY RAFTS

(a) Slab designed to resist total overburden pressure + net bearing pressure.
(b) Wrong method of design—slabs unable to resist total overburden pressure.

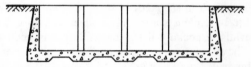

FIG. 5.24. BASEMENT FLOOR DESIGNED FOR LIGHT SUPERSTRUCTURE LOADINGS

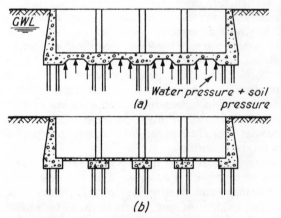

FIG. 5.25. DESIGN OF FLOORS FOR PILED BASEMENTS
(a) Where load is transferred to underside of floor.
(b) Where no load is transferred to underside of floor.

303

purposes but solely for its function in the planning of the building.

The floor slabs of piled basements should also have structural continuity if there is a risk of pressure developing on the underside due to soil swelling or yielding of the piles (*see* pp. 293 to 297) or where water pressure is acting on the slab. Continuity is given by bonding the floor slab into the pile caps as shown in Fig. 5.25 (*a*). Where there is no risk of any load transfer to the slab, it can be designed without structural connexion to the pile caps or to the capping beam supporting the retaining wall (Fig. 5.25 (*b*)).

## WATERPROOFING BASEMENTS

The first essential in preparing a scheme for waterproofing basements is to ensure that the membrane or other water-excluding barrier is taken up to a sufficient height. Information on ground-water levels obtained from boreholes is not always a reliable guide to determining the rest level of the ground water around the walls of the completed basement. For example, the basement may be constructed on a sloping site and so form a barrier to the seepage of ground water across the site. This will result in a rise in ground-water level on the uphill side of the structure. Borings on a clay site may show only random seepages of water at depth. However, after completing the basement, water may collect in the backfilled space around the walls, especially if the backfilling has been placed in a loose state. The space may act as a sump for surface water around the walls, and this water may rise nearly to ground level.

The only satisfactory method of ensuring watertightness in an nderground structure below the water table is to surround it with impervious membrane. This process is called "tanking," and alt is the normal material used for the membrane. Patent 'ives to cement are sold for "waterproofing" concrete. Some of re useless, while others may be satisfactory for a time and then ir effect. However, good quality dense concrete may some- produced for the only reason that the directions given by ufacturers include careful proportioning of the materials g and compaction of the concrete, whereas when normal ent is used for basement concrete such precautions are llowed faithfully.

eers believe that tanking of basements with asphalt is ' expense. It costs some 20 per cent more than an ent and if only part of this money is applied to uality of the concrete and to ensuring close cing and joint preparation then the resulting st as watertight. They claim that just as many cases of leakage occur with tanked basements as with untanked structures. This may well be true. It is certain that leaks in a tanked basement are much more difficult to seal because it is impossible to determine the point of ingress of the water, whereas in an untanked basement the point of leakages can readily be seen and sealed.

Although good quality concrete is to all intents and purposes impervious, the construction joints are always a potential source of leakage. The joint at the base of the walls is a particular case as the reinforcement is nearly always congested at his point. Pre-formed water-stops at joints are often ineffective because of the difficulty in compacting the concrete around them. The Author would adopt tanking to waterproof a basement in preference to an untanked structure. Imperfections in placing concrete and preparation of joints are more likely to occur with the usual standard of unskilled labour employed, than imperfections in asphalt tanking laid by experienced craftsmen who appreciate the need for care in details of workmanship.

### Tanking Materials

Asphalt tanking can be applied either by three coats of hot mastic asphalt trowelled on to the surfaces, or by several layers of bituminous felt. The latter method is generally regarded as inferior to trowel application because of the difficulty in ensuring complete sealing at joints and laps, especially with complicated details of lapping at internal angles. Plastic sheeting made from synthetic resins has been used to some extent, particularly on the Continent of Europe, but it has not supplanted asphalt tanking. A comparatively recent innovation in membrane construction is to use thin panels of bentonite clay contained by a double skin of paper.[5.15] The panels are lapped by about 25 mm and held to the wall surface by stapling or adhesives. This type of membrane maintains its "gel" condition indefinitely and is therefore useful where differential settlements are appreciable in the basement structure.

The materials for asphalt tanking are covered by British Standard 1097, *Mastic asphalt for tanking and damp-proof courses (limestone aggregate)*, and British Standard 1418, *Mastic asphalt for tanking and damp-proof courses (natural rock asphalt aggregate)*.

#### APPLICATION OF TANKING

The mastic asphalt is heated on site by melting broken-up blocks in cauldrons or mixers or, for small jobs, it can be brought to the site in a heated condition in mechanically agitated mixers. The temperature of the molten asphalt should at no time exceed 215°C. The following points on workmanship are made in British Standard

CP 102 :1963, *Protection of buildings against water from the ground*—

1. The foundations must be kept dry, with continuous pumping, as necessary until all asphalt is applied and protective coats have set.

2. Horizontal asphalt should be protected by 50 mm of cement-sand mortar laid as soon as each section of the asphalt is completed, to protect the asphalt against damage by traffic, building materials, and reinforcing bars.

3. The asphalt should be continuous and it should therefore be taken below all columns.

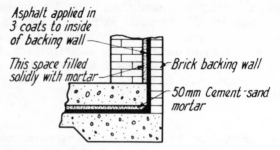

Asphalt applied in 3 coats to inside of backing wall

This space filled solidly with mortar

Brick backing wall

50mm Cement-sand mortar

FIG. 5.26. ASPHALT TANKING TO BRICK BASEMENT WALL WHERE ASPHALT IS APPLIED TO BRICK BACKING WALL (INTERNALLY APPLIED)

4. If the asphalt is applied to a backing wall (internally applied), the space between the inside of the asphalt and the inner (structural) wall should be solidly grouted to prevent movement under external water pressure (Fig. 5.26).

5. Where the asphalt is applied to the external surface of the retaining wall (externally applied), a working space of 0·6 m should be provided, in which to execute the work, and a 100 mm thick protective wall should be built outside the asphalt to protect it from damage by sharp stones, bricks, and similar material in the backfilling.

6. For externally applied asphalt, a horizontal set-off at least 150 mm wide should be provided to make a satisfactory double angle fillet and connexion to be formed with the vertical asphalt.

7. Internal and external angles should be suitably splayed to allow the asphalt to be carried evenly round the angle without variation in thickness.

8. Brickwork should have all horizontal joints raked out and brushed clean to provide a good key for the asphalt; concrete should *not* have a smooth surface.

9. Asphalt tanking should be applied in three coats to a total thickness of not less than 30 mm for horizontal work and not less than 20 mm for vertical work.

10. Internal angles should be provided with asphalt angle fillets applied in two coats and finishing approximately 50 mm wide on the face (Fig. 5.27).

FIG. 5.27. FORMING INTERNAL ANGLE FILLETS

It is not always easy to decide whether asphalt tanking should be applied to the outer face of the structural wall or to the inner face of an external protecting or backing wall. What is certain is that asphalt is useless on the inner face of the structural wall. As pointed out on page 305, concrete can never be made to be completely leak-proof, and water pressure transmitted through the structural wall will readily push off the asphalt, forming large water-filled blisters which eventually break, thus destroying the watertightness of the tanking.

If the asphalt is applied to the outer face of the completed structural wall, it can be easily inspected for imperfections before the protective brick wall is built. Once the wall is in position the tanking cannot be damaged unless major foundation movement causes wide cracks in the structure. This method of applying the tanking is preferred if the basement is built in an excavation with sloping sides where ample room is available for applying the asphalt. However, if the method is used where the retaining wall is constructed in a trench, the excavation requires to be at least 0·6 m wider on the outer face which is wasted excavation and has to be backfilled. Therefore, for economy in trench excavation costs the alternative

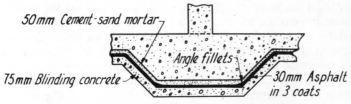

FIG. 5.28. ASPHALT TANKING BENEATH COLUMN BASES

method of applying tanking to the inner face of the protective wall should be adopted. When placing concrete in the structural wall great care is necessary in keeping tamping rods, shovels or poker vibrators away from the asphalt, otherwise there may be unseen damage to the tanking. The ground water lowering pumps should not be shut down until the structural concrete walls have been concreted and have attained their designed strength.

The usual method of treating the waterproofing of column bases is to form pits in the tanking (Fig. 5.28). On the other hand, the asphalt is usually carried over the top of piled bases (Fig. 5.29).

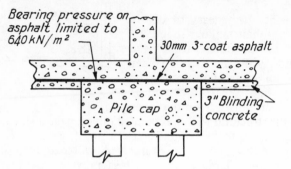

Bearing pressure on asphalt limited to 640 kN/m²

30mm 3-coat asphalt

Pile cap

3" Blinding concrete

FIG. 5.29. ASPHALT TANKING ABOVE PILE CAPS

When mastic asphalt is not fully confined to prevent extrusion, grillages to columns and pile caps should be designed to limit the pressure on the asphalt to 640 kN/m² at normal temperatures.

### Dealing with Leaking Basements

Waterproofing a tanked basement which is leaking can be a lengthy, difficult, and often fruitless task. If leaks occur through imperfections in the tanking, the water creeps between the tanking and the outer face of the structural wall or floor and emerges on the inner face. The point of emergence can be a considerable distance away from the point of leakage in the tanking, making the source of leakage impossible to trace. An inner skin of asphalt or cement mortar to seal off the inflow is, in most cases, ineffective in a deep basement since the water pressure merely forces it off the wall, but such measures can be effective for low heads of water. Pressure grouting can be resorted to and is sometimes effective or partially effective if undertaken by experienced operators. The grouting should be done from the outside with the aim of forming an impervious skin of grout outside the tanking and forcing the latter into closer contact with the structural wall. If grouting is carried out on the inside of the tanking the pressure used to inject the cement may cause the asphalt to burst outwards, thus worsening the situation. If grouting fails the only remedy (other than reconstructing the basement) is to try and tap the source of water by chases and conduits and lead it to a pumping sump or, if surface water drains exist at a suitable level outside the basement, a drainage layer can be provided at the back of the wall connected to the piped drainage system. Even if this drainage layer cannot extend to the full depth of the wall it is often of value in reducing the head causing seepage into the basement. From this brief account of the difficulties in stopping leaks it is obvious that every care must be taken with the tanking during construction of the basement. Careful inspection of every stage of the work will be amply repaid.

## REFERENCES

5.1 PIKE, C. W. and SAURIN, B. F., Buoyant foundations in soft clay for oil refinery structures at Grangemouth, *Proc. Inst. C.E.*, **1**, No. 3, Pt. 3, pp. 301–334 (Dec, 1952).

5.2 SKEMPTON, A. W., Vane tests in the alluvial plain of the River Forth, near Grangemouth, *Geotechnique*, 1:111 (1948).

5.3 Buoyant box foundations to carry New York Pier, *Eng. News Rec.*, p. 46 (11th Jan., 1952).

5.4 BUCKLEY, J. M., and VERPILLOT, E. N., New York's Pier 57 founded on two 27,000-ton reinforced concrete boxes, *Civ. Eng.* (U.S.A.), **22**, No. 3, pp. 36–42 (March, 1952).

5.5 SKEMPTON, A. W., Foundations for high buildings, *Proc. Inst. C.E.*, **4**, No. 2, Pt. 3. pp, 246–269 (Aug., 1955).

5.6 FAREY, J., *A Treatise on the Steam Engine*, p. 55 (London, Longmans, 1827).

5.7 WARD, W. H., Discussion on ref. 2.14, *Proc. Inst. C.E.*, **24**, pp. 411–413 (Mar., 1963).

5.8 COOLING, L. F., Settlement Analysis of Waterloo Bridge, *Proc. 2nd Int. Conf. Soil Mech.*, II, pp. 130–134 (Rotterdam, 1948).

5.9 HARDING, H. J. B., Discussion on paper "Methods of construction of deep land foundations," by F. N. G. Taylor, *Inst. C.E. Works Constr. Div. Paper No. 1* (1945).

5.10 VARIOUS AUTHORS and DISCUSSION, *Proc. Conf. on Diaphragm Walls and Anchorages*, Inst. Civ. Eng., London (1974).

5.11 Upside-down basement cuts cost of 26-storey Los Angeles Building, *Eng. News. Rec.*, **175**, pp. 72–74 16 (14th Oct., 1965).

5.12 PECK, R. B. and IRELAND, H. O., Backfill guide, *A.S.C.E. Struct. Div. Paper No. 1321* (Feb., 1957).

5.13 BLACKFORD, S. and CUTHBERT, E. W., Underground Station for Western District Post Office, London, *Proc. Inst. C.E.*, **15**, pp. 81–94 (Feb., 1960).

5.14 HOOPER, J. A., Observations on the behaviour of a piled raft foundation on London Clay, *Proc. Inst. C.E.*, **55**, 2, pp. 855–877 (Dec., 1973).

5.15 LAZARR, T. R., Waterproofing below the ground line, *Civ. Eng.* (U.S.A.), p. 73 (June, 1965).

# 6

# Pier and Caisson Foundations

THE function of pier and caisson foundations is to enable structural loads ιο be taken down through deep layers of weak soil on to a firmer stratum which will give adequate support in end bearing and resistance to lateral loads. Pier and caisson foundations are also used in river and maritime construction to enable foundations to be taken below zones of soil affected by scour. They fulfil a similar function to piled foundations, the main difference being in the method of construction. In the strictest sense of the word, a pier is a heavy structural member acting as a massive strut, for example piers supporting a bridge over a waterway, or the supports to the heavy gate structures of a barrage or spillway. However, the term "pier foundation" is widely used to describe a pad foundation and the buried column above it which are constructed in-situ in a deep excavation. This definition distinguishes the pier foundation from a caisson or monolith in which the foundation structure is built *above* ground level and sunk to the required founding level as a single unit.

The following definitions are given—

*Caisson:* a structure which is sunk through ground or water for the purpose of excavating and placing the foundation at the prescribed depth and which subsequently becomes an integral part of the permanent work.

*Caisson, box:* a caisson which is closed at the bottom but open to the atmosphere at the top (Fig. 6.1).

*Caisson, open:* a caisson open both at the top and the bottom (Fig. 6.2).

*Caisson, pneumatic:* a caisson with a working chamber in which the air is maintained above atmospheric pressure to prevent the entry of water into the excavation (Fig. 6.3).

*Monolith:* an open caisson of heavy mass concrete or masonry construction, containing one or more wells for excavation (Fig. 6.4).

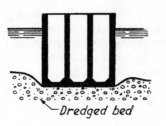

FIG. 6.1. BOX CAISSON

FIG. 6.2. OPEN CAISSON

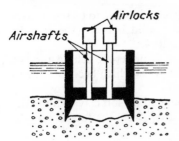

FIG. 6.3. PNEUMATIC CAISSON

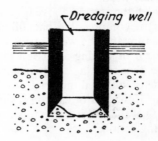

FIG. 6.4. MONOLITH

Calculations to determine allowable bearing pressures and resistance to lateral and uplift loads are common both to pier and caisson foundations; consequently they will be discussed together, after which the aspects of design and construction are discussed separately with examples of piers and caissons in their various categories.

## BEARING PRESSURES FOR PIER FOUNDATIONS AND CAISSONS

The ultimate bearing capacity of the soil beneath pier foundations and caissons can be calculated from a knowledge of the shear strength and density of the soil as described on pages 87 to 94. The design and construction of deep foundations without any form of sub-surface investigation must not be contemplated, and a detailed investigation with comprehensive in-situ and laboratory tests on the soil is amply repaid, since the foundation can be designed and its construction planned in the light of full knowledge of the soil and ground water conditions.

### Skin Friction

In addition to the support given by the soil beneath the base of a deep foundation, in certain circumstances it gains additional support by skin friction with the ground surrounding the outer face of the substructure. The total carrying capacity is then given by the sum of the base resistance and the skin friction as given by equation 2.7 (p. 89). However, there are many circumstances in which skin friction or adhesion should be ignored in contributing to the carrying capacity. These include—

(*a*) if the depth of caisson or pier below founding level is less than its least width;

(*b*) if the ground above founding level is liable to be scoured away;

(*c*) if compressible backfilling is placed between the foundation structure and the walls of the excavation;

(*d*) if in sinking a caisson the soil is undercut behind the cutting edge, thus forming a gap around the walls which becomes filled with loose or softened material;

(*e*) if the pier or caisson is surrounded by soft clay or fill material;

(*f*) if the soil is liable to shrink away from the foundation due to drying action.

Pier foundations and caissons are provided to get below soft or erodible soil, consequently skin friction plays little part in contributing to their carrying capacity in the majority of cases. In the cases where skin friction can be allowed, for example where timbered shafts are backfilled with concrete to form pier foundations to buildings, or where caissons are sunk in ground conditions where erosion or "negative skin friction" (pp. 270 to 271) cannot occur, there is little point in making elaborate calculations of skin friction based on the undisturbed shear strength of the soil. This is because the soil always suffers some disturbance either by loosening or swelling in an open excavation, or by grabbing and drag-down during caisson sinking. Therefore, for all practical purposes it is satisfactory to adopt "rule of thumb" values of skin friction. These can be checked during the sinking of caissons by actual measurements of sinking effort at various stages in the downward movement. Terzaghi and Peck[6.1] give the following values—

**Table 6.1**

**OBSERVED VALUES OF SKIN FRICTION FOR CAISSONS**

| Type of soil | Skin friction $(kN/m^2)$ |
|---|---|
| Silt and soft clay | 7–30 |
| Very stiff clay | 50–200 |
| Loose sand | 12–36 |
| Dense sand | 33–67 |
| Dense gravel | 50–100 |

The higher ranges of the above values should be used with considerable caution. For example, the value of 200 $kN/m^2$ given for a stiff clay is more or less equivalent to its undisturbed shear strength. While a skin friction of this order could occur if the clay were allowed to remain in tight contact with the caisson walls, in actual practice it would only be possible to sink a caisson for a very limited depth in such conditions. To enable sinking to continue, the cutting edges would have to be undercut thus forming a slurry-filled gap which would never regain the shear strength of the undisturbed clay. Dense sands may be considerably loosened by grabbing and drag-down during caisson sinking. Therefore when assigning a value of skin friction to give support to a deep foundation, due account should be taken of the method of construction, and in cases of doubt it is better to err on the side of safety. However, when considering *sinking effort*, i.e. the requirements of dead weight plus any kentledge required to maintain downward movement of a caisson, the skin friction should not be under-estimated.

### NEGATIVE SKIN FRICTION

In some conditions negative skin friction can occur on caissons as described for basements or buoyancy rafts on pages 270 to 271.

The values given in Table 6.1 can be used to calculate negative skin friction. Closer estimates are unrealistic in view of the many uncertain factors. In many circumstances it can be ignored; for example, the downward passage of a caisson through a sensitive clay would cause disturbance followed by re-consolidation. This would theoretically cause negative skin friction, but in practice because of its short duration this effect is ignored or is covered by the safety factor normally allowed on the ultimate bearing capacity. Similarly, it is not taken into consideration when caissons are sunk through sand which is loosened by grabbing and surges into the dredging wells. Re-consolidation of a sand is rapid and thus the negative skin friction is again a relatively short-term effect.

### Pier Foundations and Caissons on Rock

The presumed bearing values given in Table 2.1 (Chapter 2) may be used for pier foundations and caissons taken down to rock. When sinking open caissons by dredging under water it is difficult to assess the nature of soft or weathered rocks at founding level. It is impossible to get the water clear enough for a diver to see the rock and his assessments have to be made by touch. Even though the action of the grabs or the diver's probings may indicate a hard material, there is no certainty that the hard layer is of adequate thickness to distribute the loading to bring it within the allowable bearing capacity of possible underlying soft bands. If the caissons can be pumped dry, or if compressed air is used for sinking, then a close inspection can be made of the material at cutting edge level and trial pits or probings can be made to investigate the quality of the rock with depth. The alternative is to adopt allowable bearing pressures on the assumption that the caisson is founded on the softer weathered layers. However, this might result in uneconomically large foundations.

### Resistance of Pier Foundations and Caissons to Lateral Loads

Pier foundations and caissons are often required to carry horizontal or inclined loads in addition to the vertical loading. Examples of this are piers to river bridges which have to carry lateral loading from wind forces on the superstructure, from the traction of vehicles using the bridge, from currents in the river, and in some cases heavy pressure from floating debris or ice. Caissons in jetty structures may have to be designed to carry very heavy lateral loads from the impact of berthing ships.

The horizontal forces on the foundation structure shown in Fig. 6.5 create an overturning moment about the base of the caisson. This is resisted by the restoring moment given by the dead weight of the pier, caisson, and superstructure. Due allowance must be made for buoyancy of the submerged portion of the pier. Theoretically tension will occur on the underside of the base if the resultant thrust acts outside the middle third of the base and it is common practice to proportion the base width so that the line of action of the resultant falls within the middle third. However, tension cannot in fact develop, and the pier will be safe against overturning provided that the maximum bearing pressure at the edge of the base does not exceed the bearing capacity of the foundation soil. Methods of calculating maximum and minimum bearing pressures beneath

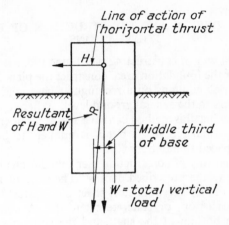

Fig. 6.5. Condition for no Overturning of Pier subjected to Horizontal Loading

foundations carrying lateral or eccentric loads are described on pages 227 to 229. Resistance to sliding under horizontal forces is given by friction on the base of the caisson and the passive resistance of the soil above the cutting edge. The passive resistance is governed by the depth of embedment (allowing for reduction of depth by scour) and the shear strength of the soil. As an alternative to widening the base or increasing the depth of the foundation, the resistance to lateral loads can be increased by driving vertical and raking piles at the bottom of the foundation (Fig. 6.6). Raking piles are often provided below the piers of river bridges where the depth of scour cannot be assessed with any certainty.

Although piers and caissons are, in many cases, sufficiently

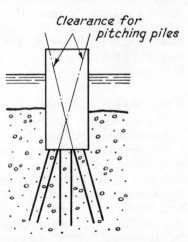

Fig. 6.6. Resistance to Lateral Forces in Caisson Pier by Raking Piles

heavy in themselves to resist uplift forces, in certain circumstances additional anchorage may be necessary using the methods described on page 270.

## THE DESIGN AND CONSTRUCTION OF PIER FOUNDATIONS

The simplest way of constructing pier foundations is to remove all weak soil over the foundation area, construct the piers in the form of concrete or brick columns on a rectangular base, and then backfill around the piers to the general ground level. Where the foundations are at close spacing, this method can save a large number of individual excavations in timbered shafts but it is unlikely to be economical with widely spaced foundations.

A more usual way of constructing pier foundations is to excavate vertical shafts to the prescribed depths. The sides of the shafts are supported by timber sheeting, steel sheet piling, steel tube rings, or bolted steel, cast-iron, or concrete segments. A concrete base is formed at the bottom of the shaft and the column section of the foundation is constructed within the shaft. The space around the column is backfilled as the sheeting is withdrawn. Where the pier bases are small, formwork and reinforcement can be saved by filling the whole of the shaft with mass concrete. In the case of deep piers a considerable volume of excavation for the shaft can be saved if the bottom of the excavation can be belled-out by hand excavation or machine to form the base. This can only be done in ground which will stand unsupported for a sufficient length of time to enable the excavation to be cleaned out and concrete placed. Due regard must be paid to the safety of the workmen if the belling-out is done by hand excavation.

### Hand Excavation Methods

At one time, pier foundations were nearly always constructed by hand excavation methods. However, several types of large-diameter boring machines have been designed in recent years. These machines have sufficient versatility to deal with almost any type of soil or rock with the result that hand methods of excavation have been, to a great extent, superseded. Hand methods have the disadvantages of being slow, ground support is often costly, and there is always a risk of loss of life due to sudden inrushes of water or leakages of gas into the excavations. The latter may come from fractured gas mains, from decomposing organic matter, or from concentrations of natural gas. Adequate safety equipment, including hoisting gear, breathing apparatus and resuscitation equipment must always be kept close at hand on any deep shaft excavation scheme where hazards from water or gas may be present.

There is no established dividing line between a large diameter bored pile and a pier foundation constructed in a mechanically excavated shaft. However, since the latter procedure is very similar in technique to the construction of bored and cast-in-situ piles, it will be described in Chapter 8. Hand excavation methods only will be described in this chapter. These methods still have their uses for small jobs where it may be uneconomical to bring a large machine on to the site, or for work in countries where there are no suitable machines available and where wage rates for labour are comparatively low.

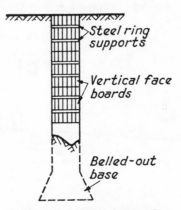

FIG. 6.7. CONSTRUCTING DEEP PIER FOUNDATIONS BY THE "CHICAGO" METHOD

Of the various methods of supporting the sides of shaft excavations, timber sheeting is the simplest and cheapest, provided that the ground will stand unsupported for a metre or so of depth while the timbering is set in position and strutted. The method of timbering commonly used in Great Britain for shaft sinking is the "middle board" method (Fig. 9.9, p. 577). In the U.S.A. the "Chicago" method of timbering is used for deep shafts. This method was introduced by Wm. Sooy-Smith for the Chicago Stock Exchange in 1894. A circular hole is taken out for the depth to which the soil will stand unsupported, i.e. about 0·5 m for soft clays to 2 m for stiff clays. Vertical boards are set in position around the excavated face and held tightly against the soil by two or more steel rings. The shaft is then deepened for 1 to 2 m and another setting of boards and rings is placed. This process is continued until founding level is reached when the base of the shaft is belled-out if the soil is sufficiently stable (Fig. 6.7). Using the "middle board" or "Chicago" methods, shafts can be sunk to a considerable depth but reasonably good ground is necessary. In restricted site conditions and with experienced crews these methods of shaft sinking can be cheaper than the mechanical methods described on pages 527 to 530. Details of methods of timbering and sheet piling and limitations in depth of the various methods are given in Chapters 9 and 10.

## Segmental-lined Shafts

In all the methods of shaft sinking described above, there is a risk of settlement of the ground surface around the excavation caused by yielding or "draw." This is due to inward deflexion of the sheeting or of the unsupported face before the sheeting is placed. Settlement of the ground surface may endanger adjacent structures or underground services such as water mains and sewers. The movement can be greatly reduced, if not totally eliminated, by lining the shaft with cast-iron or concrete segments. By this method only a small area of ground is exposed at any time and, because of the arching of the

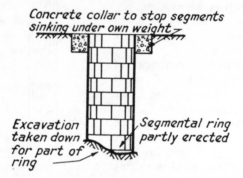

FIG. 6.8. CONSTRUCTING SHAFT FOR PIER WITH SEGMENTAL LINING BY UNDERPINNING

soil, the circular form of the segmental-lined shaft itself is resistant to inward yielding. Pressure grouting with cement behind the segments is undertaken to fill in gaps and to re-consolidate any loosened ground. There are very few examples of segmental-lined shafts being used for building foundations. Their use is mainly restricted to deep foundations in special circumstances where it is essential to avoid loss of ground.

In normal ground, segmental-lined shafts are sunk by the underpinning method, i.e. the first two or three rings of segments are assembled and bolted up in an open excavation. The excavation is backfilled and the segments anchored against sinking by grouting or by a suitable collar. Excavation then continues at the bottom of the shaft but only sufficient ground is taken out for assembly of the complete ring before lifting and bolting to the one above. The whole ring is treated in a similar manner and the dumpling at the centre is removed (Fig. 6.8). After pressure grouting behind the segments, excavation is commenced for the next ring and so on until foundation level is reached. It is essential to grout behind the rings at frequent intervals during shaft sinking. If grouting is unduly delayed the downdrag forces on the back of the segments will cause excessive tension to develop around the ring leading to fracture of the bolts or circumferential cracking of the segments.

If it is desired to bell-out the base of a segment-lined shaft, special trapezoidal segments can be used. Fig. 6.9 shows the belled-out shafts for the foundations of the Asia Insurance Building at Singapore.[6.2]

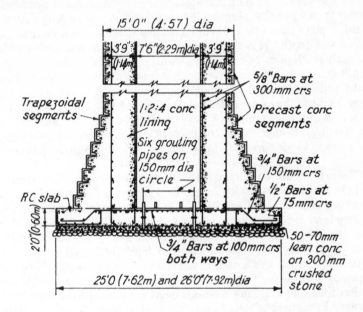

Fig. 6.9. Belling-out Base of Segmental-lined Piers, New Asia Insurance Building, Singapore (Nowson[6.2])

## DESIGN AND CONSTRUCTION OF CAISSON FOUNDATIONS

The essential feature of caissons is that they are constructed above ground or water level and then sunk as a single unit to the required depth, and also that this unit forms part of the permanent works. Because extensive temporary works, such as sheet piled cofferdams, are not required, they are specially suited to work in deep and fast-flowing waterways. In fact the first recorded instance of caisson construction is on work of this kind for the foundations of the Tuileries Bridge constructed in 1685. The river bed was first prepared by dredging, then the caisson, which was merely a barge filled with stones, was sunk at the site of the pier. The masonry forming the piers was then lowered through the water on to these primitive box caissons. Timber box caissons were used in 1738 by Labelye for the foundations of Westminster Bridge. Open well-type caissons were used by the inhabitants of India, Burma, and Egypt for many centuries for the foundations of river bridges. The masonry of the wells was built on timber curbs, and the caissons sunk by hand excavation from within the wells. "Skin divers" doing the excavation could not work deeper than 6 m, which limited the usefulness of caisson foundations of this type to sites where a firm inerodible stratum could be reached within this depth. However, British engineers who were responsible for such prodigious constructional works in India in the late nineteenth and early twentieth centuries, adapted the methods by using grabs and sand pumps for underwater excavation in the wells. By these methods they were able to sink caissons to depths of more than 30 m. A notable example of this construction was the caissons for the Hardinge Bridge[6.3] over the Lower Ganges, where the river piers were sunk to depths varying between 32 and 36 m below river level.

Compressed air was first used in bridge caissons by John Wright in 1851 for the piers of Rochester Bridge, and a few years later by Isambard Brunel at Saltash Bridge. Its first use for the foundations of very large bridges was by James B. Eads for the St. Louis Bridge over the River Mississippi commenced in 1869.[6.4] The two river piers were sunk under compressed air to depths of 26 and 28 m below water level, which was a notable achievement since the physiological effects of working under high air pressures were more or less unknown at that time. The sinking methods devised by Eads have only been changed in matters of detail up to the present day. A new development in caisson construction known as the "flotation caisson" principle was introduced in 1936 by Daniel E. Moran for the San Francisco–Oakland Bay bridge.

Usually the limiting depth of cofferdams is about 25 m. Caissons are therefore essential for constructing foundations through water or through unstable shifting ground to depths greater than this. They are also essential for sites where deep river-bed scour would necessitate very long piles to support falsework for cofferdams, and for waterways where floating ice, logs, or debris might result in destruction of a cofferdam and its associated falsework. It is generally possible to plan the sinking of caissons during the low water season of rivers to enable them to reach a safe depth before the onset of the flood season. Floating plant used in caisson sinking can be towed away to a safe place before the flood season, and if necessary a partly sunk caisson can be submerged beneath the flood waters without harm.

As a result of development of construction methods which avoid appreciable yielding of the ground in deep excavations, caissons are now rarely used for foundations on land.

## Types of Caissons

### BOX CAISSONS

As already mentioned, box caissons are structures with a closed bottom designed to be sunk on to prepared foundations below water level. Box caissons are unsuitable for sites where erosion can undermine the foundations, but they are eminently suitable for founding

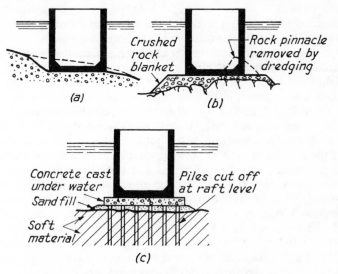

FIG. 6.10. METHODS OF FOUNDING BOX CAISSON
(*a*) On dredged gravel or rock formation.
(*b*) On crushed-rock blanket over rock surface.
(*c*) On piled raft.

on a compact inerodible gravel or rock which can be trimmed by dredging (Fig. 6.10 (*a*)). They can be founded on an irregular rock surface if all mud or loose material is dredged away and replaced by a blanket of sound crushed rock (Fig. 6.10 (*b*)). Where the depth of soft material is too deep for dredging they can be founded on a piled raft (Fig. 6.10 (*c*)). An account of the construction of a box caisson is given on page 358.

## OPEN CAISSONS (AND MONOLITHS)

Open caissons (including monoliths) are suitable for foundations in rivers and waterways where the predominating soil consists of soft clays, silts, sands, or gravels, since these materials can be readily excavated by grabbing from the open wells, and they do not offer high resistance in skin friction to the sinking of the caissons. Open caissons are essential where the depth of sinking requires air pressures exceeding about 3·5 bar (350 kN/m$^2$), since for physiological reasons men cannot work under compressed air at greater pressures than this. Open caissons are unsuitable for sinking through ground containing large boulders, tree trunks, and other obstructions. They can only be founded with difficulty on an irregular bedrock surface, and when sunk on to steeply sloping bedrock, they are liable to move bodily out of the vertical.

On reaching founding level, open caissons are sealed by depositing a layer of concrete under water in the bottom of the wells. The wells are then pumped dry and further concrete is placed, after which the caissons can be filled with clean sand or concrete, or where their dead weight must be kept low, by clean fresh water. Because the sealing is done under water, open caissons have the disadvantage that the soil or rock at foundation level cannot usually be inspected before placing the sealing concrete. Only in rare cases is it possible to pump the wells dry for inspection of the bottom. Another disadvantage is that the process of grabbing under water in loose and soft materials causes surging and inflow of material beneath the cutting edge with consequent major subsidence of the ground around the caisson. In sinking the 69 by 39 m open well caissons for the Verrazano Narrows Bridge, New York City,[6.5] the measured volume of soil removed by grabbing was 120 per cent of the theoretical volume when sinking one of the caissons from 39 to 52 m below river bed level. This large inflow occurred in spite of there being a positive head of water in the dredging wells above mean tide level in the river. Therefore open caissons are unsuitable on sites where damage might be caused by subsidence beneath adjacent structures.

Caissons should, wherever possible, be constructed as isolated units, separated by some distance from adjacent caissons or other deep structures. The effect of sinking and grabbing inevitably causes displacement of the surrounding soil, with the result that it is difficult, if not impossible, to maintain the verticality and plan location of caissons sunk close together.

Monoliths are essentially open caissons of reinforced or mass concrete construction with heavy walls. They are unsuitable, due to their weight, for sinking in deep soft deposits. Their main use is for quay walls where their massive construction and heavy weight is favourable for resisting overturning from the retained backfilling and for withstanding impact forces from berthing ships.

### Design Features of Open Caissons and Monoliths

The principal design features of open caissons and monoliths are shown in Fig. 6.11. The *cutting edge* forms the lowermost extremity

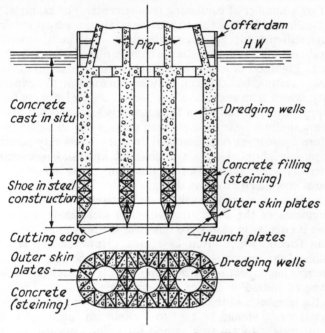

FIG. 6.11. DESIGN FEATURES OF OPEN WELL CAISSON

of the shoe (or curb). The latter usually has vertical steel *outer skin plates,* and sloping inner steel *haunch plates* (or cant plates). The skin plates are braced internally with steel trusses in vertical and horizontal planes. The trusses prevent distortion of the shoe during fabrication, towing to site, and the early stages of sinking. As soon as possible after the initial sinking the space between the skin plates is filled with concrete (*steining*). When the structure has attained sufficient rigidity by reason of the concrete filling, the skin plating can be terminated and the steining carried up in reinforced concrete placed between formwork. At or below low water level in a bridge pier the caisson proper is completed and the pier carried up in concrete, masonry, or brickwork. If the water level rises above the top of the caisson at its finally sunk level, a *cofferdam* is constructed above the caisson in which to build the piers. The space within the walls may form a single *dredging well* or it may be divided by cross walls into a number of wells. Monoliths usually have only one or two small dredging wells.

In the following comments on the design of open caissons it must be realized that in most practical cases there is no ideal solution to the problem, and the final design is usually a compromise brought about by a number of conflicting requirements. For example, thick heavy walls may be desirable to provide maximum weight for sinking through stiff ground; but thick walls mean small dredging wells and the grabs cannot reach beneath the haunch plates to remove the stiff ground. Lightness of weight is desirable in the first stages of floating out the caissons, but this can only be obtained at the expense of rigidity, which is so essential at the second stage of sinking through the upper layers of soil when the caisson is semi-buoyant and may not have uniform bearing, and when stresses due to sagging of the structure consequent on differential dredging levels may be critical. Maximum height of skin plates is desirable when sinking caissons in a waterway where there is a high tidal range, but the extra height of plates may mean excessive draught for towing to site.

The *shape* of a caisson will, in most cases, be dictated by the requirements of the superstructure. The ideal shape for ease in sinking is circular in plan since this gives the minimum surface area in skin friction for a given base area. However, the structural function of the caisson is, in most cases, the deciding factor.

The *size and layout of the dredging wells* is dependent mainly on the type of soil. For sinking through dense sands or firm to stiff clays the number and thickness of cross walls, and the thickness of the outer walls, should be kept to a minimum consistent with the need for weight to aid sinking and for rigidity against distortion. Grabs can excavate close to the cutting edge in caissons with fairly thin walls. This is important in firm or stiff clays since these soils do not slump towards the centre of a dredging well; whereas in sands and soft silts, grabbing below cutting edge level will cause the ground readily to slump away from the haunch plates towards the deepest part of the excavation, especially if assisted by water jetting. However, as already noted, thin walls mean reduced sinking effort and it is inconvenient to have to take kentledge on and off the top of the steining for each lift of concrete that is placed.

Control of verticality in large caissons is facilitated by the provision of a number of wells. To give control in two directions at right angles to one another they should be disposed on both sides of the centre lines (Fig. 6.12 (*a*) and (*b*)) but for a narrow caisson there may only be room for one row since sufficient width must be provided for a grab to work. Heavy monoliths sunk through soft material on to but not into a firm or hard stratum need only have small wells (Fig. 6.13).

Crosswalls need not extend to cutting edge level (Fig. 6.14). They may be stopped at a height of say 8 m above the cutting edge in a

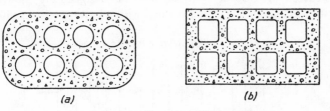

(a)                                      (b)

FIG. 6.12. LAYOUT OF DREDGING WELLS IN CAISSON
(a) Circular wells.
(b) Square wells.

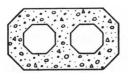

FIG. 6.13. DREDGING
WELLS FOR MONOLITH

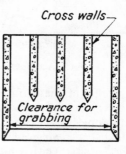

FIG. 6.14

deep caisson, thus reducing the end bearing resistance of the walls and enabling the grab to be slewed beneath the cross walls to excavate over the whole base area. Such a design has the serious limitation of requiring a deep draught at the initial sinking stage. Experiences in sinking open caissons for the piers of the Lower Zambesi Bridge[6.6] showed that straight walls were preferable to circular walls when sinking through stiff clay, since with circular walls there was a tendency for the clay to arch and wedge itself around the cutting edge rather than to be forced towards the centre of the well.

If occasional obstructions to sinking are expected and are such that they cannot be broken up underwater, it will be advisable to make provision for air decks in all the cells (Fig. 6.15). By such means it is possible to put individual cells under compressed air to allow obstructions to be cleared from beneath the cutting edge by men working "in the dry." The use of air decks or air domes also facilitates control of draught and verticality during sinking. This is the "flotation caisson" method used by Dan Moran for the San Francisco–Oakland Bay bridge. Fig. 6.16 shows a section through the 40·7 by 18·1 m caisson used for Pier 4 of the Tagus River bridge constructed in 1960–66.[6.7] The caisson, designed by the Tudor Engineering Company, was provided with a cutting edge "tailored"

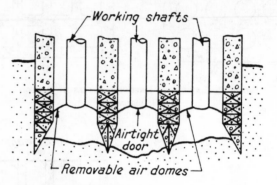

FIG. 6.15. AIR DOMES INSTALLED IN OPEN WELL CAISSON

to the profile of the surface of the rock at founding level. This resulted in a deep draught when in the floating position. However, the use of air domes on the twenty-one dredging wells enabled the caisson to be floated with air pressure in the wells from the launching ways to the bridge site. The irregular weight distribution and submergence also gave problems in sinking but, by varying the air pressure in the different wells, it was possible to control listing and to maintain verticality in the crucial later stages of sinking.

### General Arrangement of Pneumatic Caissons

Pneumatic caissons are used in preference to open well caissons in situations where dredging from open wells would cause loss of ground around the caisson, resulting in settlement of adjacent structures. They are also used in sinking through variable ground or through ground containing obstructions where an open caisson would tend to tilt or refuse further sinking. Pneumatic caissons have the advantage that excavation can be carried out by hand in the "dry" working chamber, and obstructions such as tree trunks or boulders can be broken out from beneath the cutting edge. Also the soil at foundation level can be inspected and if necessary bearing tests made directly upon it. The foundation concrete is placed under ideal conditions in the dry, whereas with open well caissons the final excavation and sealing concrete is almost always carried out under water.

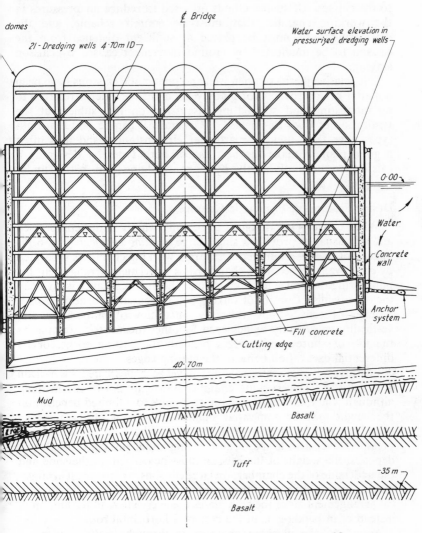

FIG.. 6.16. FLOTATION CAISSON FOR TAGUS RIVER BRIDGE[6.7]

Pneumatic caissons have the disadvantage, compared with open well caissons, of requiring more plant and labour for their sinking, and the rate of sinking is usually slower. There is also the important limitation that men cannot work in air pressures much higher than 3·5 bar, which limits the depth of sinking to 36 m below the water table, unless some form of ground water lowering is used externally to the caisson. If such methods are used to reduce air pressures in the working chamber they must be entirely reliable, and the dewatering wells must be placed at sufficient distance from the caisson to be unaffected by ground movement caused by caisson sinking.

The relative merits of open well and pneumatic caissons have been a matter of controversy for many years and the reader is referred to an interesting and stimulating discussion on this subject at the Institution of Civil Engineers.[6.8] Generally it can be said that both types have their uses for particular circumstances and it is often a good plan to make the best use of both types by designing a caisson to be sunk partly by open dredging and partly under compressed air.

### Design Features of Pneumatic Caissons

When caissons are designed to be sunk wholly under compressed air, it is usual to provide a single large *working chamber* (Fig. 6.17) instead of having a number of separate working chambers separated by cross walls. The single chamber is a convenient arrangement for minimizing resistance to sinking, since the only resistance is given by the outer walls. Control of sinking by differential excavation from a number of cells is not necessary since control of position and verticality can readily be achieved by other means, for example by the use of shores and wedges beneath the cutting edges, or by differential excavation beneath the cutting edges.

Features of pneumatic caissons have been described by Wilson and Sully.[6.9] The working chamber is usually 2·3 to 2·4 m high, although where the caisson chamber is sunk to a limited penetration the height may be somewhat smaller. The roof of the working chamber must be strongly built as it may have to resist high air pressures over a wide span; also during initial sinking through soft deposits, the weight of the caisson must be carried on the shoe and the underside of the chamber. In large caissons, a convenient arrangement is to arch the roof of the working chamber. This is an economical arrangement since the skin plates are everywhere in tension only, instead of in bending as in the case of a horizontal roof.

Access to the working chamber is through *shafts*. Since all excavated material must be lifted through the shafts or through "*snorer*" *pipes*, the shafts must have adequate capacity in size and numbers to pass the required quantity of spoil in buckets through the *air-locks* to meet the programmed rate of sinking. The air-shaft is usually oval or figure-of-eight in plan, and is divided into two compartments by a vertical ladder. One compartment is used for hoisting and lowering spoil buckets and the other is for the workmen. The shaft is built up in 1·5 or 3 m lengths to permit its heightening

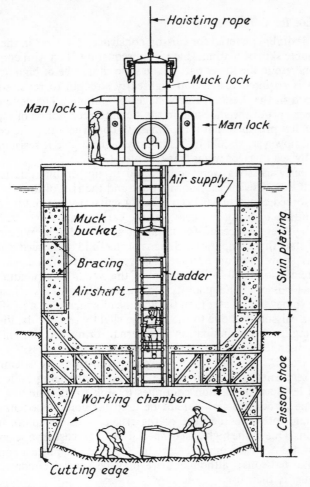

FIG. 6.17. GENERAL ARRANGEMENT OF PNEUMATIC CAISSON (WILSON AND SULLY[6.9])

as the caisson sinks down. The air-locks are mounted on top of the shafts, and it is essential for the safety of the workmen to ensure that the locks are always above the highest tidal or river flood levels with sufficient safety margin to allow for unexpected rapidity in sinking of the caisson. Alternatively, the air-locks can be protected against flooding by building up the skin plating or providing a cofferdam around the top of the caisson to the required height. Details of air-shafts and air-locks are given later in this chapter.

## Materials for Caissons

The desirable material for caisson construction is steel in the form of a double skin of plating which is subsequently filled with concrete. The concrete in the lower part of the shoe should be of high quality, since it is required to develop high early strength to resist stresses developed in the "tender" early stages of sinking. The concrete in the upper part of the shoe and in the steining need not be of especial high quality provided that it is of massive construction. The cement content, however, should be sufficiently high to give it resistance to attack by sea or river water (*see* Chapter 13).

The early caissons were constructed in timber but this is now rarely, if ever, used because of its bulk and the risk of fire.

Reinforced concrete has been used for caisson shoes but it has the disadvantage of being too heavy at the early stages of construction where lightness is needed for flotation and handling. Wilson and Sully[6.9] state that comparative designs of steel and reinforced concrete caissons show that on average the weight of reinforcement in a concrete caisson is 60 to 70 per cent of the weight of structural steel in a steel caisson. The quantity of concrete filling in a steel caisson may be somewhat greater than the volume of concrete in a reinforced concrete caisson, but due to the use of a slightly leaner mix, the ease in placing, and the elimination of external formwork, the unit cost of the concrete filling in a steel caisson is appreciably less.

Cast iron is only used for open-well caissons sunk by assembly of bolted segments on a cutting shoe, the segments being built up at ground level as the caisson continues to sink to its founding level. This type of construction cannot be used for compressed-air work under high pressures because of the risk of tension failure in the cast iron. Due to the high cost of special castings, cast-iron segmental caissons are not used in preference to steel plate or precast concrete segmental caissons; although there may be special circumstances which justify their use.

## Skin Friction in Caissons

The problems of skin friction in the design and construction of piers and caissons have been discussed in a general way earlier in this chapter (pp. 312 to 314). It was noted that while a conservative approach should be used when assessing the contribution of skin friction to the carrying capacity of a caisson, when considering the dead weight to be provided to *sink* the caisson, the skin friction *should not be underestimated*. When sinking caissons through soft sensitive clays and silts, the skin friction will generally be found to be less than the *remoulded* shear strength, possibly two-thirds of this value when the caissons are sunk rapidly and not allowed to come to rest. However, it is usual to adopt skin friction values based on actual observations of caissons sunk in soil conditions similar to the problem being studied. Table 6.1 (p. 313) gives Terzaghi's typical values for use in calculating carrying capacity. Some observed values in sinking caissons are given in Table 6.2.

Wiley[6.14] also gives values for open-well and pneumatic caissons for thirty-four bridges. His values and those in Table 6.2 show that the skin friction is very erratic and generally ranges from 9·6 to 29 kN/m² with very few higher values. There appears to be little difference in the skin friction given by the various soil types, and it is likely that the wide variations are due to the presence of boulders, the effects of air escaping from beneath the cutting edge, the "take-up" effects if sinking is allowed to stop for more than a few hours, and the shape of the caisson. There is no increase in skin friction with increasing depth of penetration in any given caisson, but Handman[6.15] states that the deeper the *designed founding level* of a caisson the higher the average sinking effort required to bring it to its final level. This observation is confirmed by Wiley[6.14] who states: "The skin friction on the lower section of the caisson increases directly as the depth sunk but unless the material is very unstable or practically in the liquid state the friction at any given depth on successive sections of a caisson is not as great as that exerted on the cutting edge and lower section of the caisson while at that point: or in other words the passage of the lower part of the caisson smooths, lubricates, or in some other manner tends to decrease materially the friction on the following sections. A wall thickness of 1·52 to 1·83 m gives weight enough to overcome any friction that may develop ordinarily unless the material penetrated be exceptionally difficult."

Some caisson designs incorporate water and air jets near cutting edge level to reduce skin friction. The arrangement of the water and air jets for the Hawkesbury River bridge[6.16] is shown in Fig. 6.18. The main disadvantage of external jet pipes is that they readily become clogged, especially when they are used for sinking through tight ground, and this is their main use. In an effort to overcome clogging troubles, inclined pipes were provided for the pneumatic caissons on the Kafr-el-Zayat bridge. They were provided with an internal blow-out valve to clear sand which had fallen into the inclined pipes.

**Table 6.2**

**OBSERVED VALUES OF SKIN FRICTION IN CAISSONS**

| Site | Type of caisson | Approximate size (m) | Soil conditions | Observed skin friction (kN/m$^2$) | Reference |
|---|---|---|---|---|---|
| Lower Zambesi Bridge | Open well and pneumatic (steel plates) | 11 × 6 | Mainly sand | 22·75 | Howorth[6.6] |
| Howrah Bridge | Open well and pneumatic (steel plates) | 55 × 25 | Soft clays and sands | 28·75 | Howorth and Shirley Smith[6.10] |
| Uskmouth Power Station | Pneumatic (steel plates) | 50 × 33·5 | 12·2 m soft clay 6·1 m sand | 55·0 | Wilson and Sully[6.11] |
| Grangemouth | Open well (concrete walls) | 13 × 13 | Very soft clay | 4·75 | Murdock, discussion on paper by Pike and Saurin[5.1] |
| | (concrete walls) | 19·5 × 10 | Very soft clay | 5·75 to 10·0 | |
| Kafr-el-Zayat | Pneumatic (steel plates) | 15·5 × 5·5 | Sand and silt | 18·7 × 26·3 | Hyatt and Morley[6.12] |
| Grand Tower (Mississippi River) | Open well (concrete walls) | 19 × 8·5 | Medium fine sand and silt | Above W.L. 51·0 Below W.L. 29·7 | Newall[6.13] |
| Verrazano Narrows | Open well (steel plates) | 69·5 × 39 | Medium dense to dense sand and fine gravel | 84·75 to 95·4 | Yang[6.5] |
| Gowtami | Open well (concrete walls) | 9 × 6 | 9·1 m sand and 13·7 m stiff clay 7·6 m sand | 12·6 | Ramayya[6.25] |

* At lowest stage of sinking to 40 m.

Generally, engineers view built-in jetting arrangements with suspicion, doubting their effectiveness, and many hold the view that independently operated external jet pipes worked down the outside of the caisson wall is the only sure method. Present-day practice is to inject thixotropic clay slurries (e.g. bentonite) above cutting edge or shoe level, thus providing a membrane of slurry around the walls. Successive injections are made as the caisson is sunk to its final level.

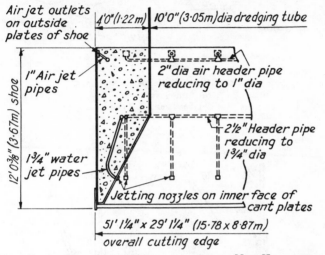

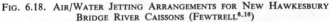

FIG. 6.18. AIR/WATER JETTING ARRANGEMENTS FOR NEW HAWKESBURY BRIDGE RIVER CAISSONS (FEWTRELL[6.16])

This reduces the skin friction very considerably and enables the dead weight of the caisson to be reduced, with the likely elimination of the need for kentledge to assist sinking.* Pipes in caisson walls used for slurry injection or for air/water jetting should be interconnected by a header at shoe level because individual vertical pipes may become damaged or blocked as the walls are built up.

### Design Details of Caissons

SHOE

The depth of the shoe (or curb) is governed by the thickness of the main walls and the angle given to the inner haunch (or cant) plates. This angle should be determined by the type of ground through which the caisson is sunk (Fig. 6.19). Generally the angle should be decided to suit the dominant factor in sinking, whether soft ground at the

* A notable example of this is given on p. 362.

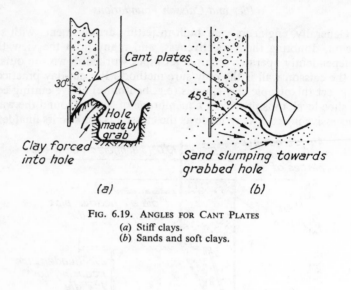

FIG. 6.19. ANGLES FOR CANT PLATES
(a) Stiff clays.
(b) Sands and soft clays.

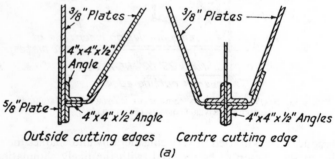

(a)

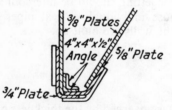
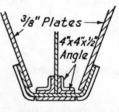

(b)

FIG. 6.20. CUTTING EDGES FOR LOWER ZAMBESI BRIDGE CAISSONS
(HANDMAN[6,15])
(a) Cutting edges for sand.
(b) Cutting edges for rock.

early stages or stiff or bouldery ground at later stages. The usual thickness of skin plating is 19 mm and bracing is provided both in horizontal and vertical planes. Welded joints in the skin plating are now universally employed.

The design of the cutting edge and its attachment to the shoe is an important feature. High concentrations of stress on the cutting edge are experienced when sinking through boulders, and buckling at this point would hinder sinking and might even result in the caisson splitting. Cutting edges are usually made up from 13 mm thick steel angles backed by 19 mm steel plates. The vertical plate projecting below the angle is advantageous in preventing escape of air in pneumatic caissons. Vertical stiffeners are provided on the upstanding part of the plate above the horizontal leg of the angle. Two types of cutting shoe were used on the Lower Zambesi bridge. For founding on sand a vertical plate was used as shown in Fig. 6.20 (*a*), but for founding on rock the lowermost parts were stiffened plates in angles for the outer walls and a plated channel with the web horizontal for the central walls (Fig. 6.20 (*b*)). It was found that the last mentioned two designs gave difficulties in tucking poling boards behind the cutting edge while excavating beneath the cutting edge under compressed air to remove boulders. Caisson shoes are sometimes flared as shown in Fig. 6.21, either with the object of reducing skin friction or preventing adjacent caissons rubbing together and jamming when they are constructed close together. However, experience has shown that the flaring does little or nothing to reduce skin friction and there is increased difficulty in maintaining verticality while sinking.

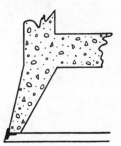

Fig. 6.21. Flaring of Caisson Shoe

## WALLS

The walls of caissons should be set back for a distance of 25 or 50 mm from the shoe. The thickness of the wall is dictated by the need for great rigidity to resist severe stresses which may occur during sinking, and the need to provide sufficient weight for overcoming skin friction. Lightness of the wall construction for the stages of floating-out and lowering is achieved by hollow steel plate construction, using 6 to 7 mm thick skin plates stiffened by vertical and horizontal trusses, as provided in the caisson shoes. The plating should be arranged in strakes about 1·2 m high with welded joints. This is a convenient height of lift for sinking and concreting in a 24-hour cycle.

Vertical reinforcement must extend from the shoe up through the full height of the walls to prevent the tendency for the shoe to part company from the walls and continue its downward progress while the walls are held up by skin friction at higher levels. Shear reinforcement must also be provided to withstand the racking stresses which occur during sinking.

Great care must be taken in constructing the walls and shoe of a caisson to ensure truly plane surfaces in contact with the soil. Bulging of the steel plates due to external ground or water pressure or internal pressure from air or concrete filling will greatly increase the resistance to sinking.

### Design Details for Compressed-air Sinking

AIR DOMES

As previously mentioned, air domes can be provided for the individual wells of open caissons to give buoyancy and control in

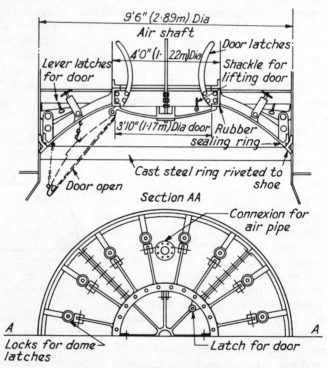

FIG. 6.22. AIR DOMES FOR LOWER ZAMBESI BRIDGE CAISSONS (HANDMAN[6.15])

sinking and to enable obstructions to be cleared from beneath the cutting edge by men working under compressed air.

Air domes for the Lower Zambesi bridge are shown in Fig. 6.22, and for the New Howrah bridge, Calcutta[6.17] in Fig. 6.23. The domes

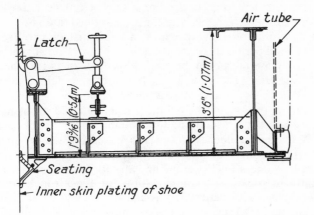

FIG. 6.23. TEMPORARY AIRTIGHT DIAPHRAGMS FOR CAISSONS OF NEW HOWRAH BRIDGE (WARD AND BATESON[6.17])

or diaphragms for both these bridges were designed by H. J. Fereday who originally designed them for the Kalabagh Bridge over the River Indus.

AIR-LOCKS

The number of air-locks required in a caisson depends on the number of men employed in any one working chamber in the caisson. The size of the air-locks and air-shafts is governed largely by the quantity of material to be excavated, i.e. by the size of the "muck bucket." Reid and Sully,[6.18] and later Wilson and Sully,[6.9] have given much valuable factual data on this. Their main points are—

1. For excavating in hard material, one man can be effectively employed in $3.25$ m² of working area of a caisson, but in loose material such as sand or gravel one man may be allowed $6.5$ to $7.4$ m².

2. Generally the number of men in a caisson per shaft will range from five to ten except in the smallest caissons. The optimum number is ten men per shaft.

3. Sufficient air-locks should be provided to allow the whole shift to pass out of the caisson in reasonable time. This depends on the working pressure. For moderate pressures an air-lock should be provided for every 93 to 111 m² of base area. For high pressures two

locks would be considered for 93 to 111 m² of base area because of the longer time spent in locking each shift in and out of the caisson.

4. The size of the lock is governed by the rate of excavation and the number of men to be accommodated. Thus the main chamber (or muck-lock) has to accommodate a skip of sufficient size to pass through the excavated material at the programmed rate. For example with a base area of 93 m² per lock, a large air-lock can deal with 9·5 m³ of spoil per hour; for continuous shift working at say 2·0 bar, 188 m³ of material would be passed through in twenty hours of effective working. This gives about 113 m³ of material "in the solid" or 1·2 m of sinking per day. With a smaller air-lock under similar conditions the output would be 6·8 m³ per hour or 123 m³ of material in twenty hours, corresponding to a sinking rate of 0·79 m per day.

5. The present tendency is towards increasing size in air-locks. The Dorman Long type (Fig. 6.24) can accommodate four men in the man-lock and a bucket of 0·7 m³ capacity in the main lock. The top platform provides accommodation for the air-lock operator. Passage of men and materials through the lock is controlled by a signalman stationed inside the main compartment of the lock.

The "Gowring" type air-lock (Fig. 6.25), originally designed by Holloway Bros., has double man-locks and a 1·12 m diameter by 1·83 m high main lock. Each man-lock can accommodate six workers, and the main lock a 1 m³ muck skip, the same skip carrying 0·8 m³ of concrete to keep the mass within the capacity of the 2-tonne crane. The lock is of welded construction, and is divided into two parts for ease in transport from site to site.

AIR SUPPLY

In Britain the air supply to caissons and the equipment in man-locks and medical locks, and the operation of locks, is governed by the Ministry of Labour and National Service in the Factories Acts, of 1961. The Work in Compressed Air Special Regulations, 1958, requires that the plant for the production and supply of compressed air to the working chamber shall deliver a supply sufficient to provide at the pressure in the chamber 0·30 m³ of fresh air per minute per person for the time being in the chamber. CP2004 recommends that whenever work involving compressed air at pressures greater than 1 bar (14·7 lb/in²) above atmospheric pressure is undertaken the Medical Research Council's Decompression Sickness Panel should be consulted for advice on decompression rates.

If the air supplied in accordance with the above rule is more than the amount lost under the cutting edge and through the air-locks, the surplus should be exhausted from the caisson through a control valve.

Compressors for air supply are usually stationary types. Ideally, they should be driven by variable speed motors to enable the supply to be progressively increased as the caisson sinks deeper. The type of plant in general use is a twin-cylinder single stage piston compressor of 8·5 m³/min capacity motor-driven through a vee belt. Rotary compressors can be used for supplying low-pressure air. At least 50 per cent spare compressor capacity should be provided for emergency

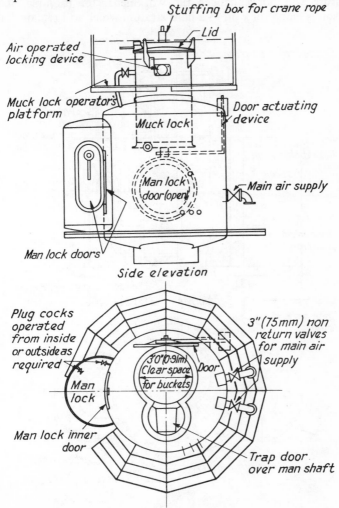

FIG. 6.24. GENERAL ARRANGEMENT OF DORMAN LONG SINGLE MAN-CHAMBER AIR-LOCK (WILSON AND SULLY[6.9])

purposes. Consideration should be given to alternative means of power supply, for example diesel generators for electrically-driven compressors normally supplied from the mains system, or a standby steam plant. The total available air supply may require to be twice the actual requirement if failure is liable to cause danger to life or property. However, a standby supply need not be provided if the loss in air pressure will not endanger the workmen: for example, if the caisson is being sunk on to a hard stratum which will remain stable,

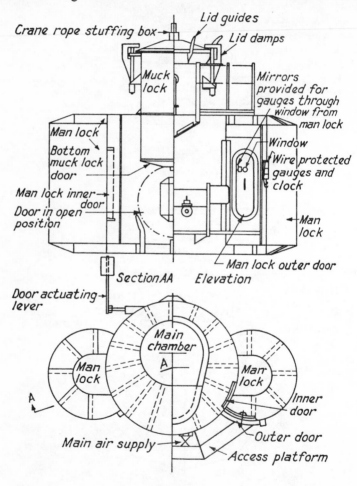

FIG. 6.25. GENERAL ARRANGEMENT OF "GOWRING" TYPE AIR-LOCK WITH DOUBLE MAN-LOCKS (WILSON AND SULLY[6.9])

and if workmen have ample time to escape from the working chamber.

## AIR TREATMENT

Improved working conditions and greater immunity to caisson sickness is given by treatment of the air supply. The air-conditioning plant should aim to remove moisture and oil, and to warm the air for cold weather working, or to cool it for working in hot climates. The need to supply cool dry air is especially important for compressed-air work in hot and humid climates. The air supply to the caissons of the Baghdad Bridges described by Reid and Sully[6.18] had two stages of cooling, and a silica-gel dehumidifier which reduced the wet-bulb temperature to less than 26·6°C at all times, even though the outside dry bulb shade temperature was at 48·8°C. The relative humidity in the working chamber of these caissons rarely exceeded 75 per cent. In cool climates it is advantageous to provide heating in man-locks since the cooling of the air which always takes place during decompression can cause discomfort to the occupants.

## CAISSON CONSTRUCTION AND SINKING METHODS

### Construction Site for Shoe

The normal practice in caisson construction is to build the shoe on land and slide or lower it into the water for floating out to the site, or to construct it in a dry dock which is subsequently flooded to float out the shoe. Land caissons are of course constructed directly in their final position. Caisson shoes constructed on the bank of a river or other waterway are slid down launching ways into the water, or rolled out on a horizontal track and then lowered vertically by a system of jacks and suspended links. Gently sloping banks on a waterway with a high tidal range favour construction on sloping launching ways (Fig. 6.26 (*a*)), whereas steep banks either in tidal or non-tidal conditions usually require construction by rolling out on a horizontal track (Fig. 6.26 (*b*)).

Care must be taken to avoid distortion of the shoe during construction. On poor ground the usual practice is to lay a thick blanket of crushed stone or brick rubble over the building site and to support the launching ways on timber or steel piles.

Economy in temporary works is given by constructing caissons in their final position. This can be done for land caissons, and for river work it is sometimes possible to take advantage of low water stages by constructing caissons on the dry river bed or on sand islands. This is only advisable when the low water periods can be predicted reasonably accurately and there is no risk of sudden "flash" floods.

In some circumstances it may be economical to construct a dock specially for building caisson shoes. Three caissons for the Kafr-el-Zayat railway bridge[6.12] were constructed by Dorman Long and Co. at their final location in a floating dock (Fig. 6.27). The floating dock was assembled from concrete pontoons on which the caisson shoe,

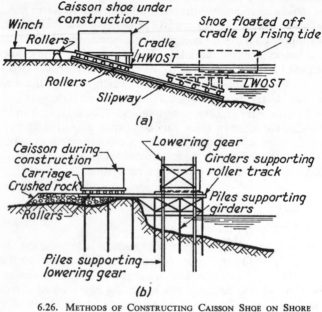

(a)

(b)

6.26. METHODS OF CONSTRUCTING CAISSON SHOE ON SHORE

(a) On gently sloping river bank.
(b) On steeply sloping river bank.

working chamber, and the necessary strakes of skin plating were riveted and welded together. The pontoons were then flooded to sink them below the caisson, which was floated clear, and the pontoons were blown up to the surface again by compressed air.

### Towing to Sinking Site

The operation of towing a caisson from the construction site to its final location must be carefully planned. Soundings must be taken along the route to ensure an adequate depth of water at the particular state of tide or river stage at which the towing is planned to take place. An essential requisite of the launching, towing, and sinking programme is a stability diagram for the caisson. This shows the draught at each stage of construction. The stability diagram used for the Kafr-el-Zayat caissons is shown in Fig. 6.28. In these diagrams the draught is plotted against the weight of the caisson for various conditions of free floating or floating with compressed air in the working chamber. The weight of each strake of skin plating and concrete in the walls to be added to give a desired draught can be read from the diagram. Also the air pressures in the working

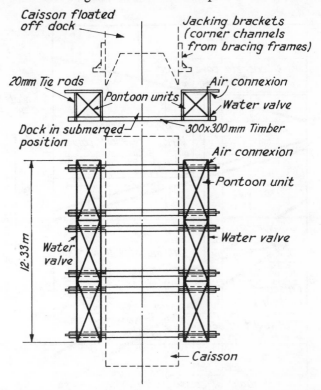

FIG. 6.27. FLOATING DOCK FOR CAISSON CONSTRUCTION AT KAFR-EL-ZAYAT RAILWAY BRIDGE (HYATT AND MORLEY[6.12])

chamber required to give any desired internal water level can be read off the appropriate lines.

### Bed Preparation

The first operation is to take soundings over the sinking location to determine whether any dredging or filling is required to give a level bed for the caisson shoe. A study should be made of the regime of the waterway to determine whether any bed movement is caused by vagaries of current. Such movement can cause difficulty in keeping a caisson plumb when landing it on the bottom, especially at the last stages when increased velocity below the cutting edge may cause non-uniform scour. Difficulties with bed movement can be overcome by sinking flexible mattresses on the sinking site. Willow

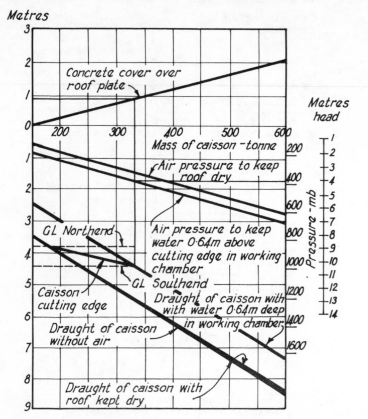

FIG. 6.28. STABILITY DIAGRAM FOR CAISSON No. 8 AT KAFR-EL-ZAYAT RAILWAY BRIDGE (HYATT AND MORLEY[6.12])

mattresses 61 m by 97·5 m weighted down with a 0·6 m layer of crushed stone were used for the bridge over the Mississippi River at Memphis.[6.19]

Nylon mattresses were used for caisson sinking for the Dutch Delta Plan works. The mattresses were assembled in concertina folds and a specially designed equipment mounted on a barge unfolded them on the sea bed.

## Supporting Structures

The various methods used to hold a caisson in position during lowering include—

(*a*) An enclosure formed by piling.

(*b*) Dolphins formed from groups of piles or circular sheet pile cells.

(*c*) Sinking through a sand island.

(*d*) Wire cables to submerged anchors.

The choice of method depends on the size of caisson, the depth of water, and particularly on the stability of the bed of the waterway. River-bed conditions at the site of the Mackinac Bridge, U.S.A.[6.20]

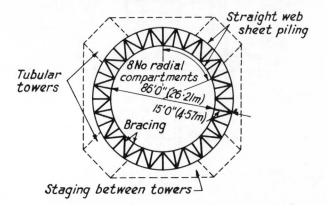

FIG. 6.29. CAISSON FOR NORTH TOWER PIER, MACKINAC BRIDGE (BOYNTON[6.20]

were favourable for the construction of a *piled enclosure* for the circular caissons on two pier sites (Fig. 6.29). The 4·6 m wide space between the two steel shells was divided radially into eight watertight compartments. Four steel tubular towers were spaced at equal distances around the caissons. The towers were prefabricated and taken by barge to the site where they were lowered on to the river bed. Then 12 in. by 74 lb H-beam piles were lowered down each of the 20 in. pipe piles and driven to refusal. The space between the pipes and piles was grouted. Three towers were constructed in this way and connected by horizontal box-type trusses. After floating in the caisson the fourth tower was constructed and the enclosure completed by additional connecting trusses. A clearance of one foot was provided between the caisson and the towers.

The 67 m by 29 m caisson for the west anchorage of the Delaware Memorial Bridge, U.S.A.[6.21] was enclosed by a rectangular pen formed by two 9 m diameter sheet pile cells filled with sand on each long side of the caisson, and two steel pile dolphins formed from three vertical and three battered piles on the short (shoreward) side. Fendering spanned between the cells and dolphins to give a 1·2 m clearance around the caisson. After towing in the caisson another

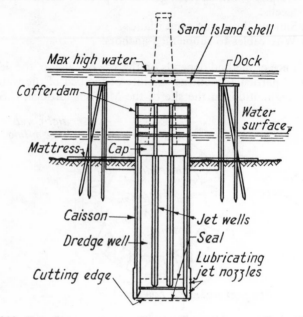

FIG. 6.30. SAND ISLAND USED FOR CAISSON CONSTRUCTION AT BATON ROUGE BRIDGE (BLAINE[6.22])

pair of dolphins was driven to complete the fourth side of the enclosure.

*Sand islands* were used for four of the caisson piers of the Baton Rouge bridge over the Mississippi River.[6.22] The fast flowing river was known to cause deep scour and bed protection was given to the sites of the two deepest piers in the form of 137 m by 76 m woven board mattresses. The islands were 34 m and 37 m respectively in diameter and were formed by steel plate shells filled with sand. The shells were surrounded by a double row of piles (Fig. 6.30). The sand islands narrowed the 730 m waterway to 97 m between the islands, and this caused deep scour which the mattresses did little to prevent. The scour at Pier 3 was 12 m deep, and a similar depth of scour at Pier 4 caused the whole of the sand filling in the island to disappear in two or three minutes.

The external water pressure on the shell then pushed in the ⅜ in. plating which was torn apart. The caisson, which at that time had only penetrated 4·6 m into the river bed, tilted by 2·1 m in line with the bridge and 0·6 m in the other direction, and was only plumbed with great difficulty. These experiences emphasize the hazards resulting

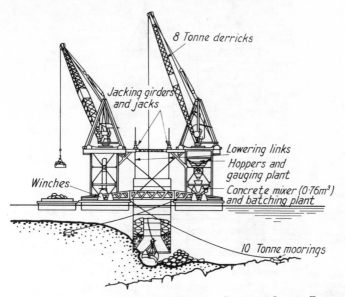

FIG. 6.31. LOWERING CAISSON FROM FLOATING PLANT AT LOWER ZAMBESI BRIDGE (HOWORTH[6.6])

from obstructions to flow caused by substantial temporary works in a river with an erodible bed.

The minimum of temporary construction and the lowest risk of bed erosion is given by the method of securing a floating caisson to *submerged anchors*; the caisson being moored between *floating pontoons*. This method is particularly suited to a multi-span structure when the high capital cost of an elaborate pontoon-mounted sinking plant can be spread over a number of caissons; whereas if fixed stagings are provided for the piers of a multi-span structure, much time will be spent in driving and extracting piles for construction of the stagings at each pier site, with inevitable damage due to repeated re-use. Floating plant is highly mobile, and can be rapidly switched from one pier site to another to suit changing conditions of river level and accessibility at low water stages. It is advantageous in these conditions to design the floating plant to be adaptable to working in the dry.

The arrangement of floating plant designed by Cleveland Bridge and Engineering Ltd. for the Lower Zambesi bridge[6.6] is shown in Fig. 6.31. The two upstream moorings consisted of 10 tonne

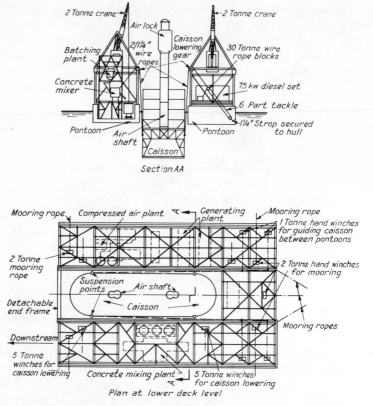

FIG. 6.32. LOWERING CAISSON FROM FLOATING PLANT FOR RIVER TIGRIS
BRIDGES, BAGHDAD (REID AND SULLY[6.18])

concrete or cast-iron sinkers, and the four crossed breast moorings were similar 5-tonne sinkers. The downstream moorings consisted of a single 5-tonne sinker.*

A steel staging to carry the caisson shoe was erected on the twin barges. Two 8-tonne steam derrick cranes were mounted on the staging, together with concreting plant, air compressors, pneumatic

---

* When mooring floating plant in tidal waters it is necessary to provide equal moorings upstream and downstream if the ebb and flood tide velocities are more or less the same.

sinking and riveting tools, hydraulic pumps, lighting sets, and steam boilers providing steam for all purposes. Four such floating sets were provided.

The floating sets used for the King Feisal and King Ghazi bridges over the River Tigris at Baghdad[6,18] were rather more elaborate in design (Fig. 6.32). A 2-tonne electric derrick crane was mounted on the top of the superstructure over each pontoon. One of these derricks handled the excavated material through the two air-locks and the other conveyed concrete from the batching plant to the air-locks. On the upstream side a 5-tonne derrick crane was provided to erect the caisson steelwork, to convey concrete aggregate from barges to the concreting plant, and to handle the caisson air-locks and air-shaft. Also on the upper deck were a large fresh-water tank, a shed to hold 50 tonne of cement, and a medical hut and medical air-lock.

The concreting plant erected on one of the pontoons comprised two $0.38$ m$^3$ mixers at pontoon deck level feeding the skips running on bogie track in the bottom of the pontoon. A storage hopper was erected within the superstructure with a volume batching device. On the opposite pontoon were an electrically-driven $8.5$ m$^3$/min air compressor, a stand-by diesel $8.5$ m$^3$/min compressor, and a portable diesel compressor for pneumatic tools. Electric power was provided by three 75 kW diesel generators, two being run at moderate load and the third a standby.

The pontoons were moored from one upstream and four breast moorings. The upstream mooring consisted of three 3-tonne concrete blocks (with projecting steel channels) placed in series, the 50 mm diameter mooring wire being connected to a six-part 30-tonne tackle leading to a 5-tonne hand winch on the superstructure. The breast moorings were each a 3-tonne concrete block connected directly to 2-tonne hand winches.

## Lowering Caissons

Four main methods are used for maintaining position and verticality of caissons during sinking. They are—

(a) Free sinking using guides between caissons and fixed stagings or floating plant.

(b) Lowering by block and tackle from piled stagings or floating plant.

(c) Lowering by suspension links and jacks from piled stagings or floating plant.

(d) Lowering without guides but controlling verticality by use of air domes.

The block and tackle arrangements used for the River Tigris bridges, Baghdad, are shown in Fig. 6.32. The caissons were suspended at four points by double wire ropes passing over pulleys on top of the superstructure. The ropes were spliced to six-part 30-tonne tackles led to 5-tonne hand winches. Control in a fore-and-aft direction was given by tackles running along the sides of the caisson attached to 1-tonne hand winches on each pontoon. Timber guides between the pontoons and caissons gave lateral positioning. As sinking and concrete filling proceeded, weight was always kept on the lowering tackle in order to maintain full control of verticality until the cutting edge had penetrated a few feet into the river bed.

Suspension links were used by the author's firm for lowering two pneumatic caissons on to the bed of the River Clyde at Plantation Quay, Glasgow. The links were attached to the caisson and the jacks were operated from brackets carried by piled stagings (Plate VII, *upper*).

## Sinking Open Well Caissons

When a caisson reaches the stage where concrete has to be added to maintain downward movement, the rate of sinking should be governed by a fixed cycle of operations. The usual procedure is to maintain a 24-hour cycle comprising excavation from the wells, erecting steel plating or formwork in the walls, and concreting a 1·2 to 1·5 m lift of the walls. Sinking should proceed continuously but the assembly and welding of steelwork should be scheduled for the daylight hours. The level of the concrete should be controlled by reference to stability diagrams.

The top of the skin plating should always be maintained about 1 m above water level to guard against an unexpected rise in level. However, the freeboard should not be so much that the centre of gravity is too high to give proper control of verticality.

Control of verticality can be achieved by one or a combination of the following methods—

    (*a*) Adding concrete on one side or the other.
    (*b*) Differential dredging from beneath the cutting edge.
    (*c*) Pulling by block and tackle to anchorages.
    (*d*) Jetting under the cutting edge on the "hanging" side.
    (*e*) Placing kentledge on one side or the other.

## Excavation Methods

Grabbing is the most commonly used method of excavating from the open wells although ejectors operated by compressed air or water pressure have been used. Arrangements of compressed air ejectors are shown in Figs. 6.33 (*a*) and (*b*). An ejector of the type shown in (*a*) was used by the author's firm for sinking large-diameter cylinders in sands and cemented sands. Compressed air is injected into the riser pipe through holes in a manifold, and the aerated water, being of lighter density than the surrounding water, flows up the riser pipe to the surface. Air or water jets are used to loosen the

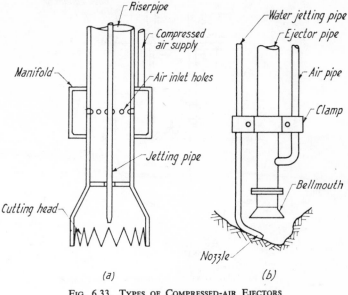

FIG. 6.33. TYPES OF COMPRESSED-AIR EJECTORS
(*a*) Air lift pump.
(*b*) Air/water ejector.

sand at the base of the excavated area. The ejector shown in (*b*) was used for excavating in cylindrical cofferdams at Bonahaven Pier, Islay, as described on page 651.

The Gwynnes's ejector excavator (Fig. 6.34) is operated wholly by water pressure. High pressure water is fed through nozzles in the lower hemispherical head, the water jets churn up the soil, and it is drawn through a contracting orifice to the riser pipe. A second high pressure water jet creates suction around the orifice. Ample supply of water at fairly high pressure is required at the orifice (about 60 l/s at 6·9 bar pressure is satisfactory). An essential factor in the success of ejector excavation is that the material must be cohesionless, i.e. gravels, sands, or sandy silts. If ejectors are lowered into soft clays or clayey silts they merely form a vertical-sided hole and the material does not tend to slump towards the ejector unless assisted by independent water jets.

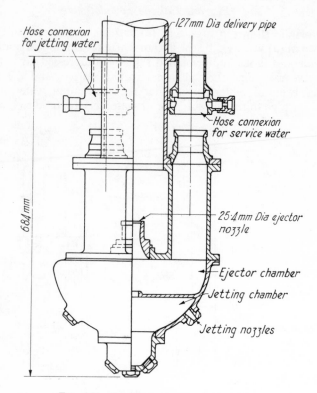

Hose connexion for jetting water

127mm Dia delivery pipe

Hose connexion for service water

684mm

25·4mm Dia ejector nozzle

Ejector chamber

Jetting chamber

Jetting nozzles

FIG. 6.34. GWYNNE'S EJECTOR EXCAVATOR

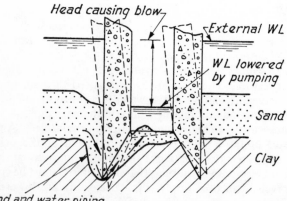

Head causing blow

External WL

WL lowered by pumping

Sand

Clay

Sand and water piping under cutting edge

FIG. 6.35

## Freeing a "Hanging" Caisson

If excavation becomes difficult, a caisson can be partially pumped out. This increases its effective weight so increasing the sinking effort. In Indian practice this is known as "running the wells." The procedure may be dangerous where the cutting edge has only just penetrated a clay stratum overlain by water-bearing sand (Fig. 6.35). The water in the sand may then force its way through a limited

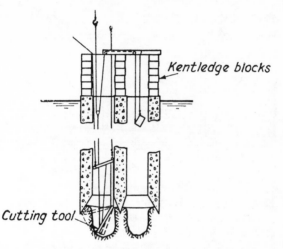

FIG. 6.36. TOOL FOR CUTTING STIFF CLAY AT LOWER ZAMBESI BRIDGE
(HOWORTH[6.6])

thickness of clay causing a localized "blow" followed by tilting of the caisson.

Explosives fired in the wells can be used to cause a temporary breakdown in skin friction but they are rarely effective in breaking down stiff material from beneath the cutting edge. Explosive charges carefully placed by divers can be used to break up boulders or other obstructions to sinking. An ingenious underwater cutting tool was used to clear stiff clay away from the cutting edges of the Lower Zambesi bridge caissons (Fig. 6.36).

Water jetting is not usually effective in freeing hanging caissons, since "sticky" sinking conditions usually occur in stiff clays or boulder clays which are not amenable to removal by jetting.

## Cofferdams

In some caissons, the permanent caisson structure terminates below low water level and the piers are constructed on the decking over the

caisson. In such cases it is necessary to provide a temporary cofferdam on top of the caisson in which the piers can be constructed in
the dry. Cofferdams may be constructed in tongued and grooved

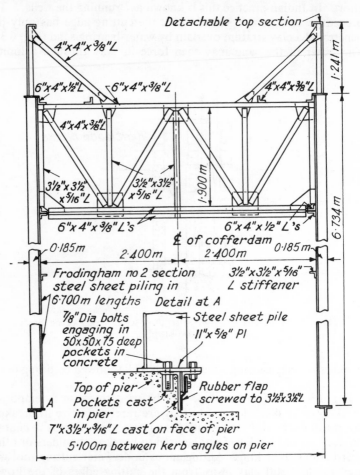

FIG. 6.37. COFFERDAM ERECTED ON CAISSONS FOR RIVER TIGRIS BRIDGES,
BAGHDAD (REID AND SULLY[6.18])

timber, in timber sheeted with bituminous felt, or in cases of repetition
work, by a movable steel trussed section sheeted with steel plating or
interlocking sheet piling. The latter method was used for the River
Tigris bridges (Fig. 6.37). The lower ends of the sheet piles were
made watertight by arranging them to bear against a 178 mm high

raised concrete kerb cast on the top of the caisson. The kerb was faced by a steel angle bent to the shape of the cofferdam. Another angle frame was bolted to the bottom of the sheet piles to fit over the kerb angle and to complete the seal a rubber flap extended loosely below the angle frame on the cofferdam. External water pressure forced this against the kerb angle. When the cofferdam was to be removed it was flooded so releasing the rubber flap seal. As a precaution against a sudden rise in river level a steel plate extension section was kept on hand, and if necessary it could have been bolted quickly in position on top of the sheet piling.

### Sinking Pneumatic Caissons

Control of position and verticality of pneumatic caissons is more readily attainable than with open well caissons. It is possible to maintain control by careful adjustments of the excavation beneath the cutting edge, and if this is insufficient, raking shores can be used in the working chamber, or the caisson can be moved bodily at early stages of sinking by placing sliding wedges or "kickers" beneath the cutting edge.

Excavation in the working chamber is usually undertaken by men hand shovelling into crane skips, compressed-air tools such as clay spades or breakers being used in stiff clays or boulder clays. When excavations are in sands or gravels, hand-held water jets can be used to sluice the material into a sump from where it is raised to the surface by a "snorer." The latter is merely an open-ended pipe with its lower end dipping into water in the sump. By opening a valve on the snorer pipe, the water and soil are forced by the air pressure in the working chamber out of the caisson. The snorer also performs a useful function in clearing water from the floor of the excavation if the soil is too impermeable for the air pressure to drive the water down into it.

The compressed-air supply must be regulated to provide adequate ventilation for the workmen. In permeable ground this is readily attained by allowing it to escape through the soil and beneath the cutting edge. However, when sinking in impermeable clays and silts, ventilation must be maintained by opening a valve to allow air to escape through the caisson roof. Careful regulation of air pressure is necessary when sinking in ground affected by changes in tidal water levels.

Smoking or naked lights should not be permitted in the working chamber because of the risk of encountering explosive gases, e.g. methane (marsh gas), during sinking. A careful watch should be maintained in neighbouring excavations. Accidents have been known to happen by compressed air passing through beds of peat and becoming deprived of oxygen due to oxidation of the peat. The escape of this oxygen-deficient air into the confined spaces of excavations has caused asphyxiation of workmen in them.

In very permeable ground the escape of air may be so great as to overtax the compressor plant. The quantity escaping can be greatly reduced by pre-grouting the ground with cement, clay or chemicals as described on pages 699 to 707.

### Blowing down Caissons

If a pneumatic caisson stops sinking due to build-up of skin friction, it can be induced to move by the process known as "blowing down." This involves reducing the air pressure to increase the effective weight of the caisson, so increasing the sinking effort. The process is ineffective if the ground is so permeable that air escapes from beneath the cutting edge at a faster rate than can be achieved by opening a valve.

The procedure in blowing down a caisson is, first, to remove the men from the working chamber. The control valve is then opened and the caisson should begin to move at a reduction of about one-quarter of the gauge pressure. If it does not do so, the skin friction is too high, and either kentledge must be added or further excavation should be taken out below the cutting edge.

Careful control should be exercised when blowing down in ground containing boulders, or when blowing down a caisson to land it on an uneven rock bed. In some circumstances, it may be necessary to excavate high spots in the rock and fill them with clay and then blow the caisson down into the clay.

An example of difficulties in sinking on to rock is the pneumatic caisson pier for a pipe bridge over the Mississippi River at Grand Tower, Illinois, which has been described by Newell.[6.13]

If at all possible a caisson should not be blown down in soft or loose ground, as this might result in soil surging into the working chamber, so increasing the quantity to be excavated. There is also the risk of loss of ground into the working chamber causing settlement of adjacent structures. It must be remembered that pneumatic caissons are, in many instances, used as a safeguard against such settlement. Blowing down, if properly controlled, is a safe procedure in a stiff clay.

If a caisson is sinking freely without the need for blowing down, measures must be taken to arrest the sinking on reaching founding level. This can be achieved by casting concrete blocks in pits excavated at each corner of the working chamber at such a level that the caisson comes to rest on the blocks at the desired founding level (Plate VII, *lower*).

### Sealing and Filling Caissons

#### Open Well Caissons

Divers are usually employed to seal the bottoms of open well caissons. The caissons at the Delaware Memorial Bridge[6.21] were sealed without the aid of divers. The soil was levelled by a rotary jetting device and high spots removed by an airlift pump. Where caissons are founded on sand it is permissible to level up the sandy bottom at a finished height about 0·5 m above the cutting edge. Where caissons are founded on stiff clay or rock it is likely that the area around the centre of the well will be at a lower level than the cutting edge. Such deeper areas should be backfilled with concrete. The sealing concrete in wells is placed by tremie pipe or bottom-opening skip to the required thickness and roughly levelled by a diver; after which sand or water is pumped in to fill the remaining space in the wells.

#### Pneumatic Caissons

Concrete in pneumatic caissons is placed "in the dry." The procedure as described by Wilson and Sully[6.9] is first to place a 0·6 m thick layer of fairly workable concrete over the floor of the working chamber, ramming it well under the cutting edge. Stiff concrete is

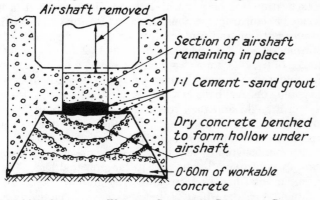

FIG. 6.38. Concreting Working Chamber of Pneumatic Caisson
(Wilson and Sully[6.9])

then carefully packed under the haunch plates and worked back towards the air-shaft, the upper layers being well rammed against the roof of the working chamber. The space beneath the air-shaft is filled with a fairly wet concrete levelled off just below the bottom of the shaft. A 1 to 1 cement-sand grout is then placed in the shaft and allowed to fill up the lower 1·5 m section which is left in permanently.

Air pressure is then raised to 0·3 or 0·6 bar above the normal working pressure to force the grout into the concrete and fill any voids underneath the roof of the chamber. The shaft is recharged with grout as necessary and it is usually found that the total amount of grout required corresponds to a volume equal to a 40 mm thick layer beneath the roof of the working chamber. After the grout has been under air pressure for two days the remaining space to the top of the 1·5 m length of air-shaft is filled with concrete. About three or four days after completion of grouting air pressure can be taken off the caisson and the remaining lengths of air-shaft and air-locks dismantled. The method of concreting is illustrated in Fig. 6.38.

## EXAMPLES OF CAISSON DESIGN AND CONSTRUCTION

### Box Caisson for Hong Kong Power Station

The site of the cooling water pumphouse for the extension of the Hong Kong Electric Power Company's North Point Generating Station, constructed in 1956–57 was below a mound of rubble forming the foundation of a masonry sea wall. The entire wall had to be demolished to make room for the pumphouse. It was impossible to construct the pumphouse in the normal way inside a cofferdam since sheet piles could not penetrate the rubble mound, and the base of the excavation was on permeable sand. The author's firm therefore decided to construct the pumphouse in the form of a box caisson, floated into position and sunk on to a level bed prepared by divers. The bottom section measuring 20·6 m by 12·2 m by 2·6 m deep with a mass of over 400 tonne was constructed on a slipway across the harbour and rolled down launching ways supported on a timber cradle running on steel balls in a rail section track. It was floated off with 1·7 m draught and then towed across the harbour by tug to a wharf close to its final location. Here the walls were heightened to increase the mass to 1400 tonne and the draught to 5·8 m (Fig. 6.39). It was then manoeuvred by tugs into the space opened in the sea wall and sunk by controlled flooding on to the prepared bed. The wall and rubble mound had been excavated by grabbing from 7-tonne cranes mounted on the wharf. Limited explosive charges placed by divers were used to loosen the masonry. The foundation area was levelled by carefully screeding between pairs of steel rails by divers, and finished with a layer of granite chippings. The underside of the caisson was grouted through 2 in. pipes cast into the base slab.

### Monoliths for Quay Wall, No. 1 Berth, Tilbury Dock

Monolith construction was selected for the 256 m long quay wall of the extensions to Tilbury Dock constructed in 1953–56.[6.23] The

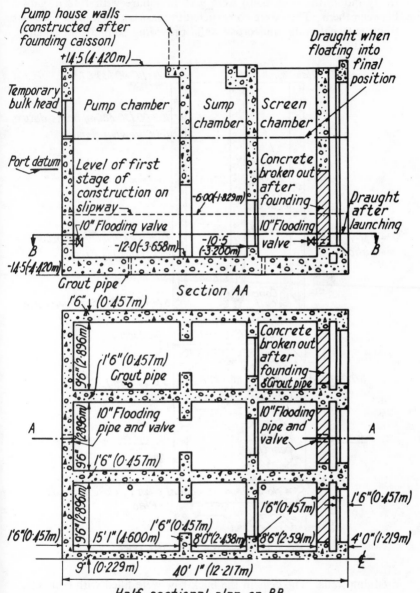

Section AA

Half sectional plan on BB

FIG. 6.39. BOX CAISSON FOR C.W. PUMPHOUSE, NORTH POINT GENERATING
STATION, HONG KONG

359

thirty monoliths (Fig. 6.40) were 9·14 m square with 1·32 m gaps between them. They were constructed in mass concrete with 0·91 m thick external walls and cross walls providing four 3·2 m square

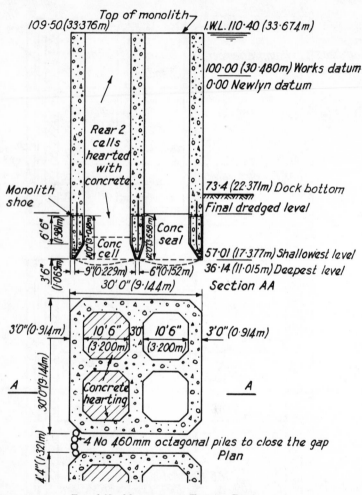

FIG. 6.40. MONOLITH AT TILBURY DOCK

dredging wells. The cells in the back row were filled with concrete, the front row being left empty except for water. The monoliths were designed to be founded on ballast (sand and gravel) overlying chalk, with a minimum penetration of 0·6 m into the ballast. In the event it was found that the gravel thinned out towards the east end and the monoliths had to be taken deeper to found them on chalk. The monoliths were surmounted by a reinforced concrete deck structure cantilevering back from the rear of the monolith wall. The gaps between monoliths were closed by four 457 mm octagonal piles.

The contractors, Holloway Bros. (London) Ltd., decided to sink alternate monoliths to give uniform soil conditions on all four sides of the first ones to be sunk, so aiding control of verticality. The bottom 1·5 m of the reinforced concrete shoe was constructed in a trench on a 6·9 m wide concrete mat laid on a blanket of hardcore. A further 1·83 m of concrete was then added in the walls using formwork specially designed for the work. At this stage the mass of monolith and forms was 320 tonne. After a seven-day curing period the concrete mat and hardcore foundation were broken away from beneath the cutting edge in a symmetrical manner internally and externally, and sinking commenced. Usually the monolith tilted slightly in one direction, then broke through on the opposite side. The sinking was maintained by grabbing from the wells using 0·76 m³ grabs handled by a 7-tonne travelling derrick crane. Kentledge blocks, in the form of 1·22 m by 1·07 m by 0·69 m by 6·3 tonne cast-iron blocks were added by the 7-tonne derricks and sinking continued until the top of the last concrete lift placed was 0·6 m above the sinking trench. The kentledge was then removed, formwork fixed and the next 1·83 m lift of concrete was placed. To safeguard against sinking during the placing of the concrete, it was arranged that the weight of kentledge exceeded the weight of concrete and formwork in the subsequent lift. The forms remained in position for at least seven days, then they were struck and the kentledge replaced to allow sinking to continue. When a depth of 9 m had been reached the full remaining height of the walls was concreted in 1·83 m lifts. This additional weight, together with the added kentledge, gave the necessary sinking effort for the deeper monoliths.

The intermediate monoliths were commenced when the alternate ones had been sunk to 9 m. On reaching founding level the kentledge was left on for twenty-four hours and if movement had stopped it was removed. The monolith was then left for a further twenty-four hours to allow hanging matter on the walls to drop off. A diver then cleaned off any clay or peat from the walls, and the wells were finally cleared by grabbing and pumping.

After adjacent monoliths had been sunk to the final depth, they were sealed by placing concrete from 0·76 m³ bottom-opening skips. After six days the wells were pumped out and cleared and the back wells hearted with concrete.

Grabbing from the wells, loading and unloading kentledge, and sealing and hearting operations were undertaken continuously throughout each working day. A typical sinking diagram for a monolith is shown in Fig. 6.41.

Monoliths of almost identical design were used in 1963–66 for extensions to the berths at Tilbury.[6.24] The contractors, John Howard and Co., used a 7 per cent bentonite slurry to lubricate the space between the monolith walls and the soil. The slurry was injected at three points on each face immediately above the 50 mm setback of the monolith shoe. The lubrication acted so well that it reduced the total time of sinking a monolith by 32 per cent of the average time taken in 1954. Instead of using kentledge of up to 1000 tonne, lifted on and off at each stage of sinking, the lubricated casing required only 100 tonne or so at the early stages to maintain verticality.

### Pneumatic Caissons, Plantation Quay, Glasgow

Two caissons were constructed and sunk by the author's firm in 1949 to form a new quay wall on the River Clyde at Glasgow. They were sited between the existing Plantation and Mavisbank Quays on the south bank of the river. Caissons were required since the presence of three tunnels at a fairly shallow depth below the river bed precluded driving sheet piles for constructing the quay in an open cofferdam.

The two caissons were sunk end to end. The west caisson shoe was 15·2 m long by 7·6 m wide and the east caisson was 18·9 m long by 6·7 m wide. Fig. 6.42 shows a section through the west caisson surmounted by a 10·16 m high temporary steel plate cofferdam within which the lower part of the quay wall was constructed. The caisson shoe, when finally filled with concrete, formed the foundation to the wall. Each caisson was provided with two air-shafts giving access to the 2·3 m high working chamber.

The shoes and working chambers in $\frac{5}{16}$ in. steel plate construction were assembled on a piled trestle at a nearby wharf. They were lowered in 0·23 m stages by four 120-tonne hydraulic jacks operating the suspension links (Plate VII). The west caisson was ballasted with 35 tonne of concrete to give a total mass of 92 tonne when it was lowered on a rising tide. This ballast gave it sufficient buoyancy to float at high tide with the desired freeboard for towing to the sinking site.

After mooring the caisson, the steel plate cofferdam was constructed, the two air-shaft extensions were erected, and concreting of the wall structure was commenced within formwork assembled inside the cofferdam. The final lift of concrete prevented flotation when air at a pressure of 1·03 b was introduced to the working chamber at the first stage of sinking through 0·9 m of mud into stiff

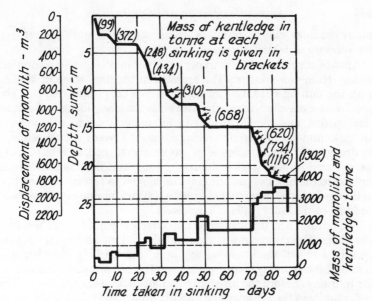

FIG. 6.41. SINKING DIAGRAM FOR MONOLITH FOUNDED ON CHALK AT TILBURY DOCK (PEEL, CARMICHAEL, AND SMEARDON[6.23])

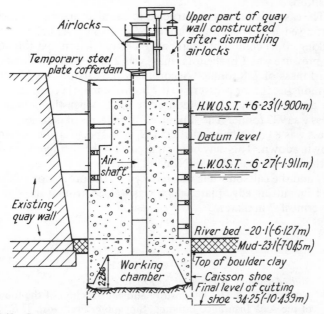

FIG. 6.42. CROSS-SECTION THROUGH PNEUMATIC CAISSON, PLANTATION QUAY, GLASGOW

sandy boulder clay continuing about 40 per cent of gravel and boulders up to 1·2 m³ in volume.

Air was supplied to the working chamber by a single-stage double-acting steam compressor. The pressure at the final stage of sinking with the cutting edge 12·3 m below H.W.O.S.T. was 1·45 b. The spoil was excavated from the working chamber using pneumatic clay spades, and loaded into 0·35 m³ buckets raised through the air-locks and discharged down chutes into the river for later removal by dredger. When founding level was nearly reached, concrete blocks were placed in tiers so that the roof of the working chamber would sink on to the blocks thus bringing the caisson to rest on an even keel at the desired level, after allowing 50 to 100 mm for crushing down and bedding of the blocks (Plate VII, *lower*).

The bottom was then trimmed and concrete placed in the working chamber. The concrete was distributed by skips on bogies running on a 0·61 m rail track. Final sealing of the working chamber was achieved by grouting under pressure. The air pressure was left on for four days before the air-shafts and air-locks were removed. The cofferdam was then dismantled and the upper part of the walls above H.W.O.S.T. were constructed. The caisson was true to level within 3 mm in 15 m, and the cutting edge was within 20 mm of its intended position.

The east caisson was constructed in a similar manner, but when the cutting edge had penetrated about 2·6 m below river bed the available sinking effort could not overcome the skin friction. At this stage the air pressure was 1 b, the total mass was 2 000 tonne with a net downward mass of 758 tonne. Accordingly the caisson was blown down by reducing the air pressure to 0·7 b. Movement recommenced when the air pressure had been reduced to 0·8 b, when the net downward mass was 933 tonne. The sinking effort in terms of perimeter shearing stress was 83·3 kN/m² and 102·5 kN/m² respectively before and after blowing down. This may be compared with the average shear strength of the boulder clay of 139 kN/m². The adhesion between the boulder clay and the caisson walls was reduced by the projection of the 15 in. by 1 in. cutting edge plate which was welded around the skirt of the lowermost skin plates.

REFERENCES

6.1 *Soil Mechanics in Engineering Practice*, p. 563.
6.2 NOWSON, W. J. R., The history and construction of the foundations of the Asia Insurance Building, Singapore, *Proc. Inst. C.E.*, **3**, Pt. 1, No. 4, pp. 407–56 (July, 1954).

6.3 BELL, J. R., The Empress Bridge over the River Sutlej, *Min. Proc. Inst. C.E.*, **65**, pp. 242–257 (1881).

6.4 STEINMANN, D. B. and WATSON, S. R., *Bridges and Their Builders*, pp. 173–206 (New York, G. P. Putnam & Sons, 1941).

6.5 YANG, N. C., Condition of large caissons during construction. *Highway Res. Rec.*, No. 74, pp. 68–82 (Washington D.C., 1965).

6.6 HOWORTH, G. E., The construction of the Lower Zambesi Bridge, *J. Inst. C.E.*, **4**, No. 3 (1936–37: Jan., 1937).

6.7 RIGGS, L. W., Tagus River Bridge—Tower piers, *Civ. Eng.* (U.S.A.), pp. 41–45 (Feb., 1965).

6.8 "Relative methods of sinking bridge foundations" (Discussion), *Inst. C.E. Works Constr. Div.* (1951).

6.9 WILSON, W. S. and SULLY, F. W., Compressed-air caisson foundations, *Inst. C.E. Works Construction Paper No. 13* (1949).

6.10 HOWORTH, G. E. and SHIRLEY SMITH, H., The New Howrah Bridge, Calcutta: Construction, *J. Inst. C.E.*, **28**, No. 7, pp. 211–257 (May, 1947).

6.11 WILSON, W. S. and SULLY, F. W., The construction of the caisson forming the foundations to the circulating water pumphouse for the Uskmouth Generating Station, *Proc. Inst. C.E.*, Pt. 3, pp. 335–356 (Dec., 1952).

6.12 HYATT, K. E. and MORLEY, G. W., The construction of Kafr-el-Zayat Railway Bridge, *Inst. C.E. Works Constr. Paper No. 19* (1952).

6.13 NEWELL, J. N., Pneumatic Caisson Pier, *Civ. Eng.* (U.S.A.), pp. 307–311 (May, 1956).

6.14 WILEY, H. L., Reply to discussion on paper "The sinking of the piers for the Grand Trunk Pacific Bridge at Fort William, Ontario, Canada," *Trans. Am. Soc. C.E.*, pp. 132–133, **LXII** (March, 1909).

6.15 HANDMAN, F. W. A., The Lower Zambesi Bridge, *J. Inst. C.E.*, **4**, No. 3 (1936–37: Jan., 1937).

6.16 FEWTRELL, A. C., The new Hawkesbury River Railway Bridge, New South Wales, Australia, *J. Inst. C.E.*, **32**, No. 8, pp. 419–460 (Oct., 1949).

6.17 WARD, A. H. and BATESON, E., The new Howrah Bridge, Calcutta: design of the structure, foundations, and approaches, *J. Inst. C.E.*, **28**, pp. 167–210 (1946–47: May, 1947).

6.18 REID, A. E. and SULLY, F. W., The construction of the King Feisal Bridge and the King Ghazi Bridge over the River Tigris at Baghdad, *Inst. C.E. Works Constr. Div. Paper. No. 4* (1945–46).

6.19 Piers by sunk open-well dredging for Mississippi River Bridge Memphis, *Eng. News Rec.*, pp. 449–454 (20th March, 1947).

6.20 BOYNTON, R. M., Mackinac Bridge foundations constructed at record speed by unusual methods, *Civ. Eng.* (U.S.A.), pp. 301–306 (May, 1956).

6.21 Crossing the Delaware—from Delaware, *Eng. News Rec.*, pp. 36–38 (13th Jan., 1950).

6.22 BLAINE, E. S., Practical lessons in caisson sinking from the Baton Rouge Bridge, *Eng. News Rec.*, pp. 213–215 (6th Feb., 1947).

6.23 PEEL, C., CARMICHAEL, A. J., and SMEARDON, R. F. J., No. 1 Berth Tilbury Dock, *Proc. Inst. C.E.*, **8**, pp. 331–362 (Dec., 1957).

6.24 O'DONNELL, J. R., Port of London Authority, Tilbury Docks Development, *Dock and Harbour Authority*, **46**, No. 541 (Nov., 1965).

6.25 RAMAYYA, T. A., Well-sinking in Gowtami Bridge Construction, *J. Inst. Eng. (India)*, **45**, No. 7, pp. 665–686 (Mar., 1965).

# 7

# Piled Foundations—I
# The Carrying Capacity of Piles and Pile Groups

PILES are relatively long and slender members used to transmit foundation loads through soil strata of low bearing capacity to deeper soil or rock strata having a high bearing capacity. They are also used in normal ground conditions to resist heavy uplift forces or in poor soil conditions to resist horizontal loads. Piles are a convenient method of foundation construction for works over water, such as jetties or bridge piers. Sheet piles perform an entirely different function; they are used as supporting members to earth or water in cofferdams for foundation excavations or as retaining walls. The design and construction of foundation works in sheet piling will be described in Chapters 9 and 10.

If the bearing stratum for foundation piles is a hard and relatively impenetrable material such as rock or a very dense sand and gravel, the piles derive most of their carrying capacity from the resistance of the stratum at the toe of the piles. In these conditions they are called *end-bearing* or *point-bearing* piles (Fig. 7.1, *left*). On the other hand, if the piles do not reach an impenetrable stratum but are driven for some distance into a penetrable soil, their carrying capacity is derived partly from end-bearing and partly from the skin friction between the embedded surface of the pile and the surrounding soil. Piles which obtain the greater part of their carrying capacity by skin friction or adhesion are called *friction piles* (Fig. 7.1, *right*).

The main types of piling in general use are—

*Driven Piles.* Preformed units, usually in timber, concrete, or steel, driven into the soil by the blows of a hammer.

*Driven and Cast-in-Place Piles.* Formed by driving a tube with a closed end into the soil, and filling the tube with concrete. The tube may or may not be withdrawn.

*Screw Piles.* Steel or concrete piles which are screwed into the soil.

*Jacked Piles.* Steel or concrete units jacked into the soil.

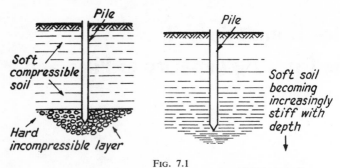

FIG. 7.1

(*Left*) End-bearing pile          (*Right*) Friction pile

*Bored and Cast-in-place Piles.* Piles formed by boring a hole into the soil and filling it with concrete.

*Composite Piles.* Combinations of two or more of the preceding types, or combinations of different materials in the same type of pile.

The first four of the above types are sometimes called *displacement piles* since the soil is displaced as the pile is driven, screwed, or jacked into the ground. In all forms of bored piles and in some forms of composite piles, the soil is first removed by boring a hole into which concrete is placed or various types of precast concrete or other proprietary units are inserted. This basic difference between displacement and non-displacement piles requires a different approach to the problems of calculating carrying capacity, and the two types will therefore be discussed separately.

### The Behaviour of Piles and Pile Groups Under Load

The load-settlement relationship for a single pile in a uniform soil when subjected to vertical loading to the point of failure is shown in

Fig. 7.2 (*a*). At the early stages of loading, the settlement is very small and is due almost wholly to elastic movement in the pile and the surrounding soil. When the load is removed at a point such as *A* in Fig. 7.2 (*a*) the head of the pile will rebound almost to its original level. If strain gauges are embedded along the length of the pile shaft they will show that nearly the whole of the load is carried by skin friction on the upper part of the shaft (Fig. 7.2 (*b*)). As the load is increased, the load-settlement curve steepens, and release of

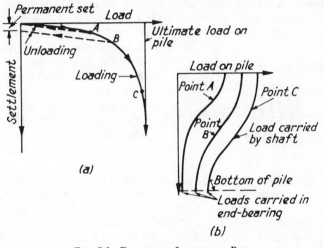

Fig. 7.2. Effects of Loading a Pile

(*a*) Load–Settlement curve.
(*b*) Strain gauge readings on pile shaft.

load from a point *B* will again show some elastic rebound but the head of the pile will not return to its original level, indicating that some "permanent set" has taken place. The strain gauge readings will show that the shaft has taken up an increased amount of skin friction but the load carried by the shaft will not equal the total load on the pile, indicating that some proportion of the load is now being carried in end-bearing. When the load approaches failure point *C*, the settlement increases rapidly with little further increase of load. The strain gauge readings show rather less load carried in skin friction than that just before failure, especially near the toe where the soil tends to flow away from the pile as failure takes place.

The relative proportions of load carried in skin friction and end-bearing depend on the shear strength and elasticity of the soil.

Generally, the vertical movement of the pile which is required to mobilize full end resistance is much greater than that required to mobilize full skin friction. If the total load on the shaft and the load on the base of a pile are measured separately, the load/settlement relationships for each of these components are as shown in Fig. 7.11. It will be seen that the skin friction on the shaft increases to a peak value, then falls with increasing strain. On the other hand the base load increases progressively until complete failure occurs.

Because of elastic movement in the pile shaft the upper part of the pile moves relatively to the soil. Thus in the case of a pile driven on to a hard and almost incompressible rock, the strain gauge readings along the pile shaft will show some load transferred to the soil towards the top of the pile due to mobilization of skin friction as the shaft compresses elastically.

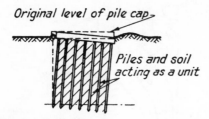

*Original level of pile cap*

*Piles and soil acting as a unit*

FIG. 7.3. FAILURE OF PILES BY GROUP ACTION

When piles are arranged in close-spaced groups (Fig. 7.3) the mechanism of failure is different from that of a single pile. The piles and the soil contained within the group act together as a single unit. A slip plane occurs along the perimeter of the group and "block failure" takes place when the group sinks and tilts as a unit. The failure load of a group is not necessarily that of a single pile multiplied by the number of piles in the group. In sand it may be more than this; in clays it is likely to be less. The "efficiency" of a pile group is taken as the ratio of the average load per pile when failure of the group occurs to the load at failure of a comparable single pile.

It is evident that there must be some particular spacing at which the mode of failure changes from that of a single pile to block failure. The change is not dependent only on the spacing but also on the size and shape of the group and the length of the piles (p. 410).

Group effect is also important from the aspect of consolidation settlement, because in all types of soil the settlement of the pile group is greater than that of the single pile carrying the same working load as each pile in the group. The ratio of the settlement of the group to that of the single pile is proportional to the number of piles in the group, i.e. to the overall width of the group. The group action of piles in relation to carrying capacity and settlement will be discussed in greater detail later in this chapter.

DEFINITIONS OF FAILURE LOAD ON PILES

In the foregoing discussion we have taken the failure load as the load causing ultimate failure of a pile. However, in the engineering sense failure may have occurred long before reaching the ultimate load since the settlement of the structure will have exceeded tolerable limits.

Terzaghi's suggestion that, for practical purposes, the ultimate load can be defined as that which causes a settlement of one-tenth of the pile diameter or width, is widely accepted by engineers. However, if this criterion is applied to piles of large diameter and a nominal safety factor of 2 is used to obtain the working load, then the settlement at the working load may be excessive.

In almost all cases where piles are acting as structural foundations, the allowable load is governed solely from considerations of tolerable settlement at the working load. An ideal method of calculating allowable loads on piles would be one which would enable the engineer to predict the load/settlement relationship up to the point of failure, for any given type and size of pile in any soil or rock conditions. So far this desirable method has only been established for piles in London Clay as a result of very extensive research. In most cases, the procedure is to calculate the ultimate bearing capacity of the isolated pile and to divide this value by a safety factor which experience has shown will limit the settlement at the working load to a value which is tolerable to the structural designer.

In all cases where piles are supported wholly by soil and are arranged in groups, the steps in calculating allowable pile loads are as follows—

1. Determine the base level of the piles which is required to avoid excessive settlement of the pile group. This level is obtained by the methods described on pages 408 and 411. The practicability of attaining this level with the available methods of installing the piles must be kept in mind.
2. Calculate the required *diameter* of the piles such that settlement of the individual pile at the predetermined working load will not result in excessive settlement of the *pile group*.
3. Examine the economics of varying the numbers and diameters of the piles in the group to support the total load on the group.

The general aim should be to keep the numbers of piles in each group as small as possible, i.e. to adopt the highest possible working load on the individual pile. This will reduce the size and cost of pile caps, and will keep the settlement of the group to a minimum. However, if the safety factor on the individual pile is too low excessive settlement, leading to intolerable differential settlements between adjacent piles or pile groups, may result.

In the case of isolated piles, or piles arranged in very small groups, the diameter and length of the piles will be governed solely from consideration of the settlement of the isolated pile at the working load.

## CALCULATION OF ALLOWABLE PILE LOADS BY SOIL MECHANICS METHODS

Techniques of installation have a very important effect on the carrying capacity of piles. Factors such as whether a pile is driven or cast in situ in a bored hole, whether it is straight-sided or tapered, whether it is of steel, concrete or timber, all have an effect on the interrelationship between the pile and the soil. The advantage of the soil mechanics method of calculating carrying capacity is that it enables allowable loads to be assessed from considerations of the characteristics of the soil and the type of pile. These predictions do not have to wait until the actual piling or test piling work is put in hand, although confirmation of the design assumption must be made at some stage by test loading of piles. Soil mechanics methods are, however, in an early stage of development and much research still needs to be done. It often appears to the author that engineers expect too much from formulae in calculating carrying capacity of piles and are disappointed when soil mechanics methods indicate failure loads which are in error by plus or minus 50 per cent of the failure load given by test loading. It should be remembered that when a pile is subjected to test loading a full-scale foundation is being tested. Because of normal variations in ground conditions and the influence of installation techniques on ultimate resistance it is not surprising that there should be quite wide variations in failure loads on any one site. Engineers would not be surprised if such wide variations were experienced if full-scale pad or strip foundations were loaded to failure.

The alternative is to calculate allowable loads by dynamic formulae. These will give even wider variations than soil mechanics methods and, in any case, these dynamic formulae are largely discredited by experienced foundation engineers. The author's views on them are stated on page 432.

## CALCULATING ULTIMATE LOADS ON ISOLATED DRIVEN PILES IN COHESIONLESS SOILS

When a pile is driven by hammering, jacking or screwing into a cohesionless soil it displaces the soil. A loose soil is compacted to a higher density by the pile and very little, if any, heave of the ground surface takes place. In very loose soils a depression will form in the ground surface around the pile due to the compaction of the soil by the pile driving. In dense cohesionless soils very little further compaction is possible, with the result that the pile will displace the soil and heaving of the ground surface will result. Such displacement involves shearing of the mass of soil around the pile shaft. Resistance to this is very high in a dense cohesionless soil, so that very heavy driving is required to achieve penetration of piles in dense sands or gravels. Heavy driving may lower the shearing resistance of the soil beneath the pile toe owing to degradation of angular soil particles. Thus no advantage is gained by over-driving piles in dense cohesionless soils. In any case this is undesirable because of the possible damage to the pile itself.

The compaction of loose or medium dense cohesionless soils by pile driving gives this type of pile a notable advantage over bored pile types. Boring operations for the latter are likely to loosen cohesionless soils and thus lower their end bearing resistance.

The shaft frictional resistance of piles in cohesionless soils is small compared with the end resistance. This is thought to be due to the formation of a ring or "shell" of compacted soil around the pile shaft, with an inner ring of soil particles in a relatively loose or "live" state. The skin friction is governed by this inner shell. In the case of straight-sided piles the soil particles may stay in a loose condition on cessation of driving. In tapered piles the ring is re-compacted with each blow of the pile hammer.

Because of difficulties in obtaining undisturbed samples of cohesionless soils from boreholes, it is the usual practice to estimate loads on piles in these soils from the results of in-situ tests. Four methods will be described; two of these are based on the standard penetration test and two others on the static cone penetration test. In all four methods the failure load is calculated and this must be divided by a safety factor to obtain the working load. The safety factor is not constant. It depends on the permissible settlement at the working load, which is in turn dependent on the pile diameter and the compressibility of the soil. Experience shows that a safety factor of $2\frac{1}{2}$ will ensure that an isolated pile with a shaft diameter of not more than 600 mm driven into a cohesionless soil will not settle by more than 15 mm. There is no reliable published information relating safety factors to settlement of large-diameter piles bearing on cohesionless soils.

Except where previous experience provides a reliable guide, the allowable loads calculated by the four methods described below should be confirmed by load tests on selected piles. The methods do not depend on the procedure for installing the pile. They are applicable to piles driven by single or double-acting hammers, by diesel hammers or by vibrating equipment. Although the method of driving may have some significant effect on failure loads, calculation methods are not yet sufficiently refined to take such effects into account.

## Methods Based on Standard Penetration Test

The basis of the "static" or soil mechanics method of calculating the ultimate carrying capacity of a pile is that the *ultimate carrying capacity is equal to the sum of the ultimate resistance of the base of the pile and the ultimate skin friction over the embedded shaft length of the pile.* This is expressed by the equation—

$$Q_u = Q_b + Q_s \qquad . \qquad . \qquad . \quad (7.1)$$

where $Q_b$ = base resistance

$Q_s$ = shaft resistance

Knowing the angle of shearing resistance of the soil at base level, $Q_b$ can be calculated from Terzaghi's general equation 2.10 (p. 92). Because the diameter of the pile is small in relation to its depth the term $0.4\gamma BN_\gamma$ can be neglected. Therefore—

Net unit base resistance $= q_{nf} = q_f - p = p_d(N_q - 1)$

$\therefore$ Total base resistance $= Q_b = A_b p_d(N_q - 1)$ . (7.2)

where $p_d$ = effective overburden pressure at pile base level.

The total ultimate skin friction on the pile shaft is given by the general expression—

Unit skin friction $= f = K_s p_d \tan \delta$ . . (7.3)

where $K_s$ = an earth pressure coefficient.

$\delta$ = angle of wall friction.

Broms[7.1] has related the values of $K_s$ and $\delta$ to the effective angle of shearing resistance of cohesionless soils for various pile materials and relative densities as shown in Table 7.1.

### Table 7.1
### VALUES OF $K_s$ AND $\delta$

| Pile material | $\delta$ | Value of $K_s$ for | |
|---|---|---|---|
| | | Low relative density | High relative density |
| Steel | $20°$ | 0·5 | 1·0 |
| Concrete | $\frac{3}{4}\phi$ | 1·0 | 2·0 |
| Wood | $\frac{2}{3}\phi$ | 1·5 | 4·0 |

Broms used the effective angle $\phi'$ instead of the undrained angle $\phi$ as shown in Table 7.1, but for practical purposes the $\phi$ value can be used as obtained from standard penetration tests (Fig. 1.14). Where static cone penetration tests (p. 31) have been made, the $C_{kd}$ values can be used in conjunction with Table 7.1 as follows—

| Values of $C_{kd}$ | $\phi$ | $K_s$ corresponding to |
|---|---|---|
| 0–50 kgf/cm² | 28–30° | Low relative density |
| 50–100 kgf/cm² | 30–36° | Medium relative density |
| Greater than 100 kgf/cm² | Above 36° | High relative density |

Equation 7.3 implies that in a uniform cohesionless soil the unit skin friction continues to increase linearly with increasing depth. This is not the case. Vesic[7.2] showed that at some penetration depth between 10 and 20 pile diameters, a peak value of unit skin friction is reached which is not exceeded at greater penetration depths. Thus equation 7.3 gives increasingly unsafe values as the penetration depth exceeds about 20 diameters. Research has not yet established whether the peak value is a constant in all conditions, or is related to factors such as soil grain size or angularity. At the present time a peak value of 110 kN/m² is used for straight-sided piles. In many cases the skin friction on a pile in cohesionless soil is only a small proportion of its total resistance to compression loading and where piles are driven deeper than 20 diameters it may be satisfactory to use the following "rule of thumb" values for the average skin friction over the whole shaft.

| Relative density | Average unit skin friction (kN/m²) for straight-sided piles |
|---|---|
| Less than 0·35 (loose) | 10 |
| 0·35 to 0·65 (medium–dense) | 10–25 |
| 0·65 to 0·85 (dense) | 25–70 |
| More than 85 (very dense) | 70 to not more than 110 |

Where the skin friction is critical, e.g. where uplift loads are resisted, pulling tests should be made to confirm the above values are adequate.

The failure load on the pile, $Q_u$, is equal to the load at failure applied to the pile, $Q'_u$, plus the weight of the pile, $W_p$.

$$Q'_u = Q_u - W_p = Q_b + Q_s$$
$$= A_b p_d (N_q - 1) + Q_s \quad \text{(from equation 7.2)}$$
$$= A_b p_d N_q - A_b p_d + Q_s$$

Since the weight of the concrete in the pile is not much greater than the weight of soil displaced by the pile, then for all practical purposes $W_p$ and $A_b p_d$ are roughly equal for straight-sided or moderately tapered piles. Therefore

$$Q'_u = A_b p_d N_q + Q_s$$

$$= A_b p_d N_q + K_s \bar{p}_d \tan \delta A_s \quad . \quad . \quad (7.4)$$

where $A_s$ = embedded surface area of pile

$\bar{p}_d$ = average effective overburden pressure over embedded depth of pile.

## CALCULATING THE BASE RESISTANCE

Meyerhof's values of $N_q$ for driven piles for use with Equations 7.2 and 7.4 are shown in Fig. 2.11 (c) on page 90. However, comparisons of observed base resistances of piles by Nordlund[7.3] and Vesic[7.4] have shown that $N_q$ values established by Berezantsev et al[7.5] which take into account $D/B$ ratios, most nearly conform to practical criteria of pile failure. Berezantsev's values of $N_q$ as adapted by the author are shown in Fig. 7.4. Values of $\phi$ are obtained from standard penetration tests (corrections as described on page 99 should *not* be applied) using Fig. 1.14 (p. 28) or from the simple values shown on page 92. It may be argued that because driving compacts the soil beneath the pile, the value of $\phi$ should in all cases represent the densest conditions. This is not always the case. For example, when piles are driven into loose sand the resistance is low and little compaction is given to the soil. However, when they are driven into a dense soil the resistance builds up quickly and the soil is compacted to a denser state, but because of possible weakening effects due to soil breakdown mentioned on page 373 it would be unwise to assume $\phi$ values higher than those represented by the in-situ state of the soil before pile driving.

It will be seen from Fig. 7.4 that there is a rapid increase in $N_q$ for high values of $\phi$, giving high values of base resistance. However, research shows that at some depth a maximum value of base resistance is reached which is not exceeded no matter how much deeper the pile is driven. Published pile test results indicate that the maximum value is 11 000 kN/m² (1100 tonne/m²). As a general rule *the allowable working load on an isolated pile driven to virtual refusal (by normal driving equipment) in a dense sand or gravel is given by the allowable load on the pile considered as a structural member rather than by a consideration of failure of the supporting soil*, or, if the permissible working stress on the material of the pile is not exceeded then the pile will not fail.

The base resistance of tapered piles is calculated on the base area at tip level. The base resistance of H-beam piles is calculated on the gross cross-sectional area because a plug of highly compacted soil is carried down by the pile. It is possible to add considerably to the base resistance by enlarging the cross-section at base level. In the

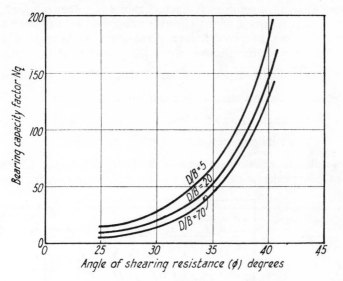

FIG. 7.4. BEREZANTSEV'S BEARING CAPACITY FACTOR, $N_q$

case of precast concrete piles an enlargement is cast on, and plates or "wings" can be added to steel piles (p. 501). However, the permissible working stresses on the least cross-section of pile shaft must not be exceeded and it must also be noted that driving a pile with an enlargement at the tip will reduce the skin friction on the shaft above the enlargement to that corresponding to loose soil conditions.

Equation 7.4 can be used for jacked and screwed piles. Berezantsev's values of $N_q$ can be used provided it is possible to drive the piles to a penetration into the bearing stratum greater than five times the shaft diameter. For lesser penetrations Meyerhof's values of $N_q$ in Fig. 2.11 (*a*) should be used. If soft clay or silt overlies the bearing stratum of sand or gravel then the $D/B$ ratio should be calculated on the penetration into the bearing stratum only.

## CALCULATING THE SKIN FRICTION

The skin friction may be calculated roughly from Equation 7.3 using the values of $\delta$ from Table 7.1. Nordlund[7.3] has developed an empirical method which takes into account the volume of soil displaced by the pile, the material of the pile and the shape of the pile. Nordlund's equation for skin friction is—

$$Q_s = \sum_{d=0}^{d=D} K_\delta p_d \sin \delta \, C_d d . \qquad . \qquad (7.5)$$

where $K_\delta$ = a dimensionless factor expressing the ratio of the resultant of the effective normal and shear stresses on an incipient failure plane passing through a point and the effective overburden pressure at that point,

$d$ = depth of pile over which skin friction is calculated,

$p_d$ = average effective overburden pressure over depth $d$

$\delta$ = angle of wall friction,

$C_d$ = minimum perimeter of pile over depth $d$.

Nordlund's equation is used with confidence by the Raymond Pile Co. for calculating the skin friction on tapered piles but there is

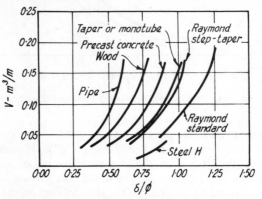

Fig. 7.5. Design Curves for Calculating Skin Friction on Piles in Cohesionless Soils (after Nordlund[7.3])

(a) Relationship between $V$ and $\delta/\phi$ for various types of piles.

little evidence of its reliability when applied to straight-sided piles. The steps in using Nordlund's method are—

(1) Divide the length of the pile shaft into sections corresponding to the different soil characteristics.

(2) For each section calculate the volume displacement $V$ in m³ per m of pile (for tapered piles $V$ is calculated on the minimum cross-section, for H-beam piles on the gross cross-section).

(3) Obtain the value of $\delta/\phi$ from Fig. 7.5 (a), which relates $V$ to

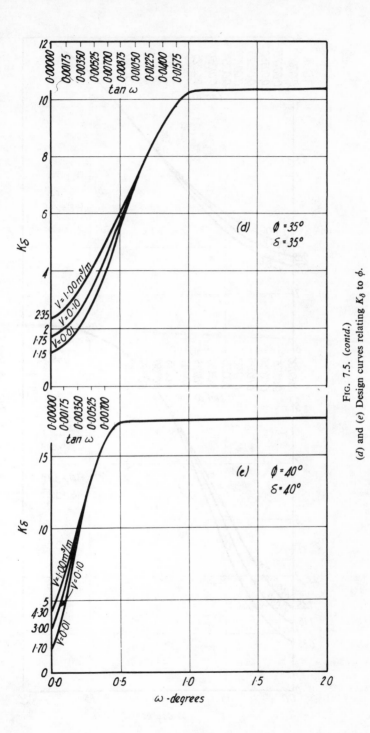

FIG. 7.5. (contd.)

(d) and (e) Design curves relating $K_\delta$ to $\phi$.

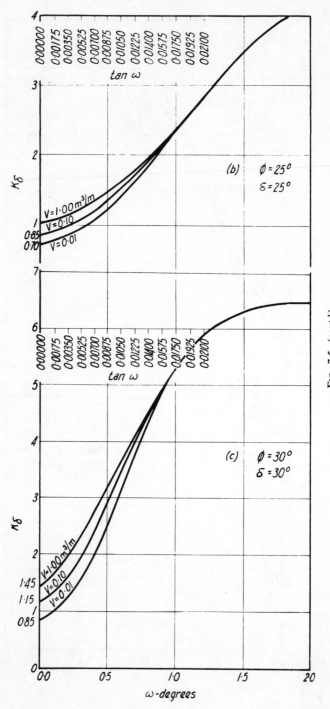

FIG. 7.5. (contd.)

(b) and (c) Design curves relating $K_\delta$ to $\phi$.

$\delta/\phi$ for various shapes of pile and various pile materials. This gives the value of $\delta$, the $\phi$ value being obtained from standard penetration tests or other means.

(4) Obtain $K_\delta$ from Figs. 7.5(*b*) to (*e*) which relate $K_\delta$ to $V$ for various angles of pile taper ($\omega$) and various values of $\phi$.

(5) Using Fig. 7.5 (*f*), correct $K_\delta$ for $\delta/\phi$ obtained from Fig. 7.5 (*a*). (Figs. 7.5 (*b*) to (*e*) assume that $\delta/\phi = 1$).

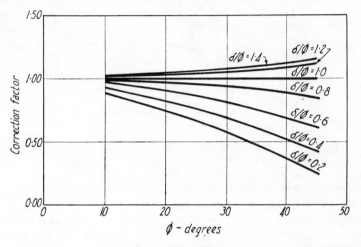

Fig. 7.5. (*contd.*)
(*f*) Correction factor for $K_\delta$ when $\delta$ is not equal to $\phi$.

(6) Multiply the corrected $K_\delta$ by sin $\delta$, and $p_d$ and $C_d$ by the length ($d$) of pile under consideration to obtain the skin friction on this length.

(7) Repeat steps (2) to (6) for the remaining sections of the pile.

(8) Add the components of skin friction to obtain the total skin friction on the pile shaft.

Examples 7.1 and 7.2 (pages 434–6) will make the procedure clear.

Equation also suggests that the deeper the pile is driven the greater will be the rate of increase in skin friction. Research has not yet been undertaken to show whether or not there is a limiting value in skin friction for tapered piles in addition to the attainment of a maximum value of end bearing resistance as mentioned on page 376. Skin friction values much higher than 200 kN/m² (21 tonne/m²) have not been recorded for tapered piles. Therefore higher ultimate values should not be used unless load testing confirms that such values are suitable for the site conditions.

## Methods Based on Static Cone Penetration Test

In extensive areas of Holland and Belgium, all heavy structures are founded on piles driven through peats and soft clays to a suitable bearing on medium dense to dense sands. In these countries an immense amount of experience has been gained in the interpretation of the static (Dutch) cone penetration test (p. 31) in relation to piled foundations in sands. The ultimate end bearing resistance of the

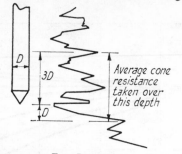

FIG. 7.6. CALCULATION OF END RESISTANCE OF PILE FROM STATIC CONE PENETRATION TEST BY VAN DER VEEN'S METHOD

pile is taken, quite simply, as being equal to the resistance of the cone. To allow for the variation in cone resistance which normally occurs it is usual to use Van der Veen's method[7.6], in which an average is taken of the cone resistance over a depth equal to three times the diameter of the pile above pile point level and one pile diameter below pile point level (Fig. 7.6). Experience has shown that if a safety factor of $2\frac{1}{2}$ is applied to the ultimate end resistance as determined from the cone resistance, the pile is unlikely to settle by more than 15 mm under the working load.

The skin friction on the pile shaft can also be obtained from the cone resistance using the simple empirical relationships established by Meyerhof.[7.7]

For displacement piles,

Ultimate unit skin friction =

$$\frac{\bar{q}_c}{2} \text{ kN/m}^2 = \text{approx.} \frac{\bar{q}_c}{20} \text{ tonne/m}^2 \qquad . \qquad . \quad (7.6)$$

For H-beam piles,

Ultimate unit skin factor =

$$\frac{\bar{q}_c}{4} \text{ kN/m}^2 = \text{approx.} \frac{\bar{q}_c}{40} \text{ tonne/m}^2 \qquad . \qquad . \quad (7.7)$$

where $\bar{q}_c$ = average cone resistance (kg/cm²) over the length of pile shaft under consideration.

Meyerhof states that for straight-sided displacement piles the ultimate unit skin friction has a maximum value of 107 kN/m² and for H-beam piles a maximum of 54 kN/m² (calculated on all surfaces of flanges and web).

The procedure for using the static cone test is then—

(1) Inspect the cone resistance/depth diagram and select a provisional depth for pile tip level which will, as far as possible, utilize the maximum permissible stress on the material of the pile shaft.

(2) Take the average cone resistance over the range of depth shown in Fig. 7.6.

(3) Calculate the end resistance of the pile from the average cone resistance obtained from (2).

(4) Calculate the skin friction from the average cone resistance along the pile shaft using equations 7.6 or 7.7.

(5) Obtain the total ultimate pile resistance from the sum of the end resistance and skin friction and divide by a safety factor of 2½ to obtain the working load.

If the working load obtained in (5) is less than that required for the structural designer's loading conditions then the pile must be taken to a greater depth to increase the skin friction value or to reach a level where the end resistance may be higher. Alternatively an enlargement may be provided at the toe of the pile. However, driving a pile with an enlargement will reduce the skin friction above the enlargement to that corresponding to a loose soil.

Although experience has shown that the above method of equating cone resistance with ultimate end resistance of piles is a reliable one for piles of small or medium diameter (say up to 18 in.), in the case of

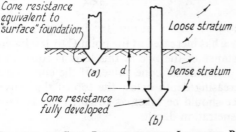

FIG. 7.7. INCREASE OF CONE RESISTANCE WITH INCREASED PENETRATION INTO BEARING STRATUM

a large-diameter pile the tip, in order to achieve its ultimate resistance, must penetrate to a greater depth into the selected bearing stratum than that penetrated by the cone. It can be shown theoretically and confirmed experimentally that if the standard 35·5 mm diameter cone penetrates the bearing stratum to a depth $d$ such that its ultimate end resistance increases from the value corresponding to a surface foundation (Fig. 7.7$a$) to the value at which its ultimate resistance is fully developed (Fig. 7.7$b$), then a pile say of 355 mm diameter (i.e. 10 times the cone diameter) must penetrate the bearing stratum by a distance equal

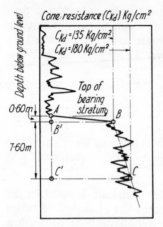

to 10$d$ before its ultimate resistance is fully developed. On the basis of this relationship, De Beer[7.8] has devised a graphical method for determining the required penetration into the bearing stratum. A typical cone resistance/depth diagram is shown in Fig. 7.8. The line AB represents the transition of the cone resistance from the "surface" condition (i.e. the surface of the bearing stratum) to 135 kg/cm² representing the fully developed condition. Below B the cone resistance fluctuates due to variations in density of the soil and the effects of local crushing of the sand grains at high cone pressures. Usually there is an increase in average cone resistance due to increase in overburden pressure. If the vertical depth AB′ from A to B is

FIG. 7.8. METHOD OF OBTAINING PENETRATION OF LARGE DIAMETER PILES INTO BEARING STRATUM TO DEVELOP END BEARING RESISTANCE EQUAL TO STATIC CONE RESISTANCE

equal to 0·6 m then for a pile of 450 mm diameter—

$$AC' = \frac{450}{35 \cdot 5} \times AB' = \frac{450}{35 \cdot 5} \times 0 \cdot 6 = 7 \cdot 6 \text{ m}$$

At a penetration of 7·6 m into the bearing stratum, the average cone resistance has increased at the point C to 180 kg/cm². Therefore the end resistance of the pile at this level is equal to the base area multiplied by this higher cone value. If the cone resistance were to fall with increasing depth below the top of the dense stratum, the end resistance should be taken as equal to the average value at the calculated penetration depth.

## TIME EFFECTS

The carrying capacity of piles in sands and gravels does not normally show any change with time as it does in clays. However, in some circumstances, probably where piles are driven into water-bearing fine or silty sands, the time effect does seem to have some significance.

Terzaghi and Peck[7.9] have noted that occasionally the carrying capacity decreases conspicuously during the first two or three days after driving. They state that it is probable, but not certain, that the high initial bearing capacity is due to a temporary state of stress that develops in the sand surrounding the point of the pile during driving. Feld[7.10] has described the case of 457/mm diameter steel pipe piles driven to depths of 15 to 18 m into varved silty overlain by about 3 m of medium sand. The piles withstood static load tests of 1200 kN and 1600 kN. However, load tests made on the same piles about a month after driving and after further piles had been driven adjacent to them showed excessive settlement under loads of only 800 kN.

Errors made in overestimating the carrying capacity of piles in sands due to time effect can only occur if the capacity is based on calculations by dynamic formulae based on observed driving resistances. They are not likely to occur when the design has been based on static methods taking due account of the effects of pile driving on the characteristics of the soil. However, because of possible time effects, the load tests on piles in sands should not be made until at least four days have elapsed after driving.

### Calculating Ultimate Loads on Driven and Cast-in-place Piles in Cohesionless Soils

Driven and cast-in-place piles (p. 511) are formed by driving a tube into the ground. On reaching founding level the tube is filled with concrete. In some types of pile the tube is withdrawn while concreting the shaft. Also it may be possible to form a bulb at the base of the pile. For pile types where a steel tube or precast concrete cylinder is left in position the shaft friction load can be calculated quite simply by the methods given in the preceding sections of this Chapter. Where the drive tube has a closed end, the end resistance is calculated on the base area at the pile tip. Calculation of the base resistance is more difficult for pile types in which a bulb is formed since only the piling contractor knows the size of bulb which can be formed in any given soil conditions. Thus only the piling contractor is in a position to give reliable estimates of carrying capacity. All that the engineer can do is to obtain a preliminary idea of the range in capacity by assuming that in a dense soil the bulb will be little, if at all, larger than the shaft, and in a loose soil it may be possible to form a bulb of twice the shaft diameter. It should be kept in mind that settlement at the working load may be excessive if the pile is terminated in loose soil conditions.

In calculating the shaft friction on pile types in which the drive tube is withdrawn, it is difficult to assess whether the soil in contact with the shaft will be in a loose or dense state. This depends on the degree of compaction given to the concrete, or on the efficacy of other devices for compacting the soil while withdrawing the tube. It is also possible that the process of withdrawing the tube and compacting the concrete will enlarge the shaft, thus increasing its skin friction value. As these are essentially points of constructional technique, the engineer must be guided by the piling contractor on the proportion of the load which will be carried in skin friction. As a rough check on the contractor's estimates, the engineer can assume that for techniques in which no compaction is given to the concrete the soil will be loosened by the withdrawal of the tube. Where the concrete is compacted the soil can be assumed to be in a medium dense state.

### Calculating Ultimate Loads on Bored and Cast-in-place Piles in Cohesionless Soils

Bored piles are formed in cohesionless soils by drilling with rigs of the type described on pages 527 and 528. Concrete is placed in the drilled hole and the casing is normally withdrawn during or after placing the concrete. In sóme ground conditions the casing is left in position, or precast concrete sections may be inserted in the drilled hole.

In all cases of bored piles formed in cohesionless soils it must be assumed that the soil will be loosened as a result of the boring operations, even though it may initially be in a dense or medium-dense state. Equation 7.5 may be used for calculating the skin friction on the assumption that the $\phi$ value will be representative of loose conditions. Similarly the $\phi$ value used to obtain the bearing capacity factor $N_q$ for calculating the base resistance from the first part of equation 7.4 must correspond to loose conditions.

The assumption of loose conditions for calculating skin friction and end resistance means that the ultimate carrying capacity of a bored pile in a cohesionless soil will be considerably lower than that of a pile driven into the same soil type. This is illustrated by a comparison of bored and driven piles on a factory site in the south of England. On this site 2·4 to 2·7 m of peat and fine sand of negligible bearing value were overlying 2·7 m of dense sand and gravel (standard penetration test $N$ value = 35 to 50 blows/0·3 m), followed by very dense silty fine sand ($N$ value greater than 50 blows/0·3 m). Bored and cast-in-place piles of 482 mm shaft diameter were installed at 4·6 and 9·1 m depth and these failed at loads of 219 and 349 kN respectively. A pile formed from 508 mm diameter hollow precast concrete units was driven to 4·0 m below ground level, where the driving resistance was 4 blows of a 4 tonne hammer for the last 16 mm of penetration. The total settlement under a 747 kN test load was

7·5 mm and the residual settlement after removing the load was only 2·5 mm. At 747 kN the end bearing pressure was estimated to be 3 220 kN/m². Based on an $N$ value of 40 blows/0·3 m, the base resistance was calculated by equation 7.4 to be 4830 kN/m². The total skin friction on the shaft of the 4·6 m bored pile and the driven pile is unlikely to have been more than 50 kN in either case. Thus the loosening effect of boring operations on the base resistance of the bored pile was clearly demonstrated.

Whereas both driven and driven and cast-in-place types can be provided with an enlarged base, it is impossible to enlarge the base of bored piles unless costly ground consolidation techniques (e.g. freezing or chemical injections) are employed.

## Ultimate Loads on Piles Driven into Cohesive Soils

### SKIN FRICTION ON PILE SHAFT

The carrying capacity of piles driven into cohesive materials such as silts and clays is given by the sum of the skin friction* between the pile surface and the soil, and the end resistance. The skin friction is not necessarily equal to the cohesion of the soil, since driving a pile into a cohesive soil can alter the physical characteristics of the soil to a marked extent. The skin friction also depends on the material and shape of the pile.

Piles driven, jacked, or screwed into the ground cause displacement of the soil. As a result, consolidation takes place and pore-water is squeezed out under the lateral pressures set up when the piles are forced into the ground. This pore-water takes some time to dissipate. Consolidation of the soil is relatively slow and a heave of the ground surface is inevitable at the early stages after driving. As consolidation proceeds the excess pore-water pressure is dissipated into the surrounding soil or into the material of the pile and the heaved-up ground surface subsides. Soft clays and soft silts are sensitive to the effects of remoulding by pile driving (*see* p. 69); thus there is an immediate and considerable drop in shear strength of the soil around the pile, depending on the value of the sensitivity. However, the shear strength is generally restored with the passage of time, since loading tests at increasing intervals of time on piles driven into soft sensitive soils show that ultimately the skin friction is approximately equal to the undisturbed shear strength. The effect of time on the increase in skin friction in soft sensitive clays is shown in Fig. 7.9 for steel, concrete, and timber piles driven into such soils at Gothenburg (Sweden)[7.11], San Francisco[7.12] and Drammen (Norway)[7.13]. There

---

* In a purely cohesive soil ($\phi = 0$) there is, in simple terms, no skin friction. However, the term is widely used to denote adhesion or cohesion on the shaft of a pile in a cohesive soil.

is little difference in the rate of increase in carrying capacity for the
three different materials. Fig. 7.9 shows that at least 75 per cent of
the ultimate carrying capacity is achieved within 30 days of driving.
This points to the need for delaying test loading of piles for at least
30 days in cases where a relatively high proportion of their carrying
capacity is gained from skin friction in soft sensitive silts and clays.

When piles are driven into stiff over-consolidated clays such as
boulder clays or London Clay, little or no consolidation takes place
and the soil cracks and is heaved up around the pile. It is known that

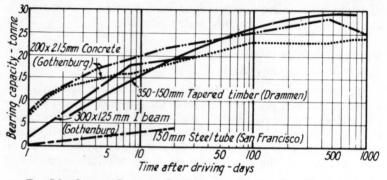

FIG. 7.9. GAIN OF CARRYING CAPACITY WITH TIME OF PILES DRIVEN INTO
SOFT CLAYS

a skin of clay from the softer zones near the ground surface adheres
to the pile shaft following the downward movement and rebound
of the pile with each blow of the hammer.[7.14] It is also known that
an enlarged hole is formed in the upper part of the shaft due to lateral
vibration of the pile under the hammer blows.* Ground-water or
exuded pore water can collect in such an annular hole and lubricate
the shaft. The possibility of "strain-softening" of the clay due to
the large strain to which the soil on the contact face is subjected by
the downward movement of the pile should also be considered.
Tests have shown that the residual shear strength of an over-
consolidated clay after high strain can be as little as 50 per cent of
the peak shear strength at low strain. This is believed to be due to
the effects of re-orientation of the clay particles. Normally-consoli-
dated clays also show these "strain-softening" effects.

Therefore, because of the combined effects in varying degree of
ground heave, the formation of an enlarged hole and strain softening,
it is not surprising that the unit skin friction is often only a fraction

* An enlarged hole can also be caused by deviations in the cross-sectional
dimensions or straightness of a pile.

of the undisturbed shear strength of the clay and that wide variations in the "adhesion factor" (i.e. the ratio of the shear strength of the clay mobilized in skin friction on the pile shaft to the undisturbed shear strength of the clay) can occur on any one site.

The problem of variation of the adhesion factor has been the subject of research by the author[7.15], by Woodward, Lundgren and Boitano[7.16] and by Nordlund.[7.17] From these and other published and unpublished records, the author has collected data which establish a relationship between the adhesion factor and the shear strength of clay for three different conditions as shown in Fig. 7.10. The highest adhesion factors are obtained in Case I in which piles are driven through sands or sandy gravels into a clay. The gap which tends to form between the pile and clay is filled with dragged-down granular material and no skin friction is lost. The greater the penetration into the clay the less becomes the effect of the granular material with consequent reduction in adhesion factor. The reverse is true for Case 2 (soft clay over stiff clay) where the dragged-down soft clay skin has a weakening effect on skin friction. The smaller the penetration depth into the stiff clay the greater is the proportionate reduction in skin friction. For Case 3 (piles driven into a firm to stiff clay without different overlying strata) a gap forms around the upper part of the pile and no skin friction is mobilized. The smaller the penetration and the stiffer the clay the greater is the effect of the gap.

It may be asked why the adhesion factors should be based on the undisturbed shear strength. Although the clay is extensively re-moulded at the time of driving the piles, the author believes that the undisturbed shear strength is the appropriate criterion having regard to the carrying capacity in the long term. In the case of soft sensitive clays, the skin friction increases with time (*see* Fig. 7.9) until it is eventually equal to or greater than the original undisturbed shear strength. In the case of stiff fissured clays there is likely to be a reduction in shear strength due to "strain-softening" but there is no clear evidence of regain in strength with time. Pile tests in London Clay made by Meyerhof and Murdock[7.18] showed that nine months after driving, the ultimate loads on precast concrete piles were only 80 to 90 per cent of the ultimate loads one month after driving. There was a similar decrease in the carrying capacity of piles driven into stiff fissured clays in Denmark[7.19] after 103 days. It is possible that boulder clays which have been subjected to intensive "reworking" may not show appreciable "strain-softening" effects. The remoulded shear strengths of clays of this type are not less than their undisturbed shear strengths. Piles driven into stiff glacial clays in Ontario showed a 50 per cent increase in carrying capacity one year after driving.

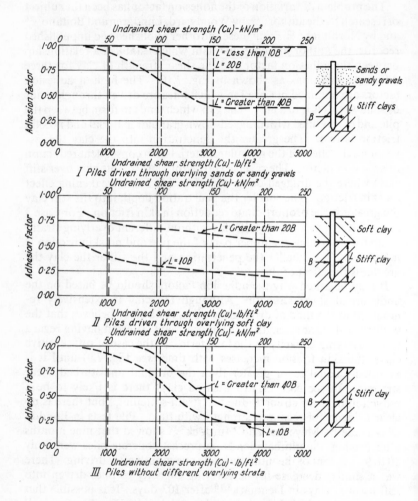

FIG. 7.10. ADHESION FACTORS FOR DRIVEN PILES IN CLAY

Lateral vibration or "whip" set up during pile driving cannot, by itself, account for low adhesion values. Nordlund[7.17] found little difference in adhesion factors between piles installed by driving and those pushed into the ground by static loading in stiff clays in Lake Maracaibo.

The author believes that all the factors such as pore pressure, ground heave (and re-consolidation), lateral vibration, smearing, and "strain-softening" are of significance but each may vary in its effect *even on the same site*. The latter point must be emphasized, because the author has experienced variations in adhesion factor for piles of the same type on the same site of between 0·4 and 1·0 for clays of 72 kN/m² shear strength and between 0·25 and 0·45 for clays of 120 to 144 kN/m² shear strength. Similar variations were experienced by Woodward, Lundgren and Boitano[7.16] and by Nordlund.[7.17]

## Calculating Ultimate Carrying Capacity

The carrying capacity of piles driven into clays and clayey silts is equal to the sum of the end bearing resistance and the skin friction of that part of the shaft in contact with the soil. The end resistance is given by the equation—

$$Q_b = N_c \times c_b \times A_b \qquad . \qquad . \qquad . \qquad (7.8)$$

The bearing capacity factor $N_c$ can be taken as being equal to 9 provided that the pile is driven at least five diameters into the bearing stratum. The shear strength $c_b$ at the base of the pile is taken as the *undisturbed* shear strength provided that time is given for a regain from remoulded to undisturbed shear strength conditions. In the case of stiff fissured clays $c_b$ must be taken as representative of the *fissured* strength, i.e. the lower range of values if there is appreciable scatter in shear strength results. Reduction due to "strain-softening" should not be taken into account, since this effect is restricted to the contact face between the pile and soil.

The skin friction on the pile shaft is given by the equation

$$Q_s = \alpha \times \bar{c}_d \times A_s \qquad . \qquad . \qquad . \qquad (7.9)$$

where $\alpha$ = adhesion factor (*see* Fig. 7.10)

$\bar{c}_d$ = average undisturbed shear strength of the clay adjacent to the shaft,

$A_s$ = surface area of the shaft.

In the case of uniform clays or clays increasing progressively in shear strength with depth the average value of shear strength over the whole shaft length is taken for $\bar{c}_a$. Where the clay exists in layers of appreciably differing consistency, e.g. soft clay over stiff clay, the skin friction is separately calculated for each layer using the adhesion factor appropriate to the shear strength and overburden conditions. For piles in shrinkable clays (*see* Chapter 3) allowance must be made for the clay shrinking away from the pile shaft within the zone subjected to seasonal swelling and shrinkage. In the case of H-beam piles dragdown effects from a soft clay overburden into the stiff clay may cause a greater reduction in skin friction than would be suffered by a solid or hollow-section pile. The presence of a weak skin in the trough of the pile may cause yielding of the soil plug at the toe thus reducing the end bearing resistance. Because of these uncertain effects adequate loading testing is necessary to check the validity of design calculations for H-piles. As a rough guide the skin friction is calculated on a perimeter equal to twice the flange width plus twice the web depth. The end bearing resistance is calculated on the gross cross-sectional area (i.e. flange width × web depth).

The working load for all pile types is equal to the sum of the base resistance and the shaft friction divided by a suitable safety factor taking into account the range of adhesion (Fig. 7.10). A safety factor of $2\frac{1}{2}$ is reasonable on this sum, viz.—

$$\text{Allowable load} = Q_a = \frac{Q_b + Q'_s}{2 \cdot 5} \qquad . \qquad . \quad (7.10)$$

where $Q'_s$ is the skin factor calculated from the adhesion factors shown in Fig. 7.10 using the *average* shear strength. Also $Q_a$ should be not more than—

$$\frac{Q_b}{3} + \frac{Q''_s}{1 \cdot 5} \qquad . \qquad . \qquad . \quad (7.11)$$

where $Q''_s$ is the skin friction calculated from the adhesion factors in Fig. 7.10 using the lowest range of shear strength.

It is permissible to take a safety factor equal to $1 \cdot 5$ for the skin friction because the peak value of skin friction on a pile in clay is obtained at a settlement of only 3 to 8 mm, whereas the base resistance requires a greater settlement for full mobilization.

## DRIVEN AND CAST-IN-PLACE PILES IN COHESIVE SOILS

For piles in which a steel tube or precast concrete shell remains in the ground the skin friction on the shaft is calculated from equation 7.9, using the adhesion factor appropriate to the undisturbed shear strength. For piles in which the drive tube is withdrawn, allowing the concrete to slump against the walls of the hole, the skin friction conditions are intermediate between those for a driven pile and for a bored and cast-in-place pile. Because the driving of the tube compacts the soil, and further compaction is given by tamping the concrete, there is no reason to suppose that the skin friction values will be less than those for precast concrete piles. Therefore equation 7.9 can be used to obtain a rough check on calculations submitted by the contractor for the proprietary piles concerned.

When it is known with certainty that compaction of the concrete during withdrawal of the drive tube can result in appreciable enlargement of the pile shaft in a soft or firm clay, the skin friction can be calculated on the enlarged shaft diameter.

Because of the frequently low skin friction values associated with piles driven into stiff clays, proprietary piles which incorporate an enlargement at the base formed by hammering out the concrete (*see* pp. 511–19) have a notable advantage over straight-sided piles. In all cases the end resistance is calculated from equation 7.8 and the bearing capacity factor $N_c$ may be taken as being equal to 9, provided that the base of the pile is driven at least five diameters into the bearing stratum.

## BORED AND CAST-IN-PLACE PILES IN COHESIVE SOILS

The base resistance and skin friction of bored piles have been extensively studied for London Clay and the adhesion and end bearing capacity factors for this deposit have been reliably established. The researches have shown that a bearing capacity factor $N_c$ of 9 can be used in equation 7.8 provided that $c_b$ is representative of the fissured shear strength (i.e. the lower range of values). The same value of $N_c$ can be taken for all types of clay, provided that the base of the pile penetrates at least 5 diameters into the bearing stratum.

Research on bored piles in London Clay by Skempton[7.20] has shown that an adhesion factor of 0·45 may be taken on the *average* shear strength for use in equation 7.9. It is thought that the reasons for only about half the shear strength being mobilized in skin friction are due to the combined effects of swelling (and hence softening) of the clay in the walls of the borehole, the seepage of water from fissures in the clay and from the unset concrete, and "work softening" from the boring operations. Skempton[7.20] recommended that the maximum adhesion value should be not more than 96 kN/m² and that in the case of short bored piles in London Clay, where the clay may be heavily fissured at a shallow depth, the adhesion factor should be taken as 0·3.

There is little published work on adhesion factors appropriate to other types of clay. The author has experienced adhesion factors as low as 0·1 for bored piles in very stiff to hard Lias Clay. Woodward, Lundgren and Boitano[7.16] have quoted values of 0·49 to 0·52 for clays in California having shear strengths of about 96 kN/m².

When there is no previous experience of adhesion factors in any particular type of clay, the author recommends adopting Skempton's value of 0·45 (but not more than 100 kN/m²) for the skin friction of firm to stiff clays, with adequate load testing to confirm the design value. However, there is no reason to suppose that the full shear strength of very soft to soft clay should not be mobilized in skin friction provided that time is given for the regain of shear strength lost by remoulding during boring operations.

A safety factor of 2½ on the ultimate load as given by the sum of the base resistance and skin friction should ensure that the settlement at the working load will not exceed a tolerable value.

### Large-Diameter Bored Piles in London Clay

A considerable volume of soil is subjected to stress beneath the base of a large-diameter pile, and elastic and consolidation settlements are thus of considerable significance in assessing the allowable load. The design methods must take into account these settlements, and it is not sufficient merely to divide the ultimate load by a nominal safety factor.

The extensive researches carried out on large-diameter piles with and without enlarged bases as described in the 1966 Large Bored Pile Symposium[7.21] have provided a sound basis for the practical design of such piles in London Clay.

The first step is to select a base level for the piles from the aspect of overall settlement of the pile group (p. 411). Having thus established the required length, the engineer can carry the superstructure load on to the piles in a variety of ways. He may carry a column on a single straight-sided pile of large diameter, or he may use a shaft of smaller diameter but with an enlarged base, or he may use a group of piles of smaller dimensions with or without enlarged bases.

The governing consideration in the selection of a shaft and base diameter is, of course, the settlement at the working load and this is determined by a rather complex interaction between the shaft and base. The load/settlement relationship of these two components for a typical pile is shown in Fig. 7.11. It will be seen from this figure that the full shaft resistance is mobilized at a settlement of only 15 mm whereas the full base resistance, and the ultimate resistance of the entire pile, is mobilized at a settlement of 120 mm. Therefore, if the structure can tolerate a settlement of 15 mm at a working load of 2000 kN, the full shaft resistance, but only 57 per cent of the base resistance, will have been mobilized at the working load. The safety factor of the whole pile shown in Fig. 7.11 is 2·1. In most cases, the

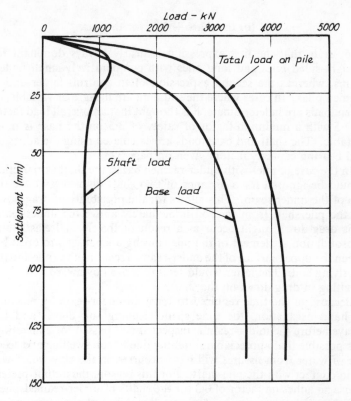

FIG. 7.11. LOAD/SETTLEMENT RELATIONSHIPS FOR LARGE-DIAMETER BORED AND CAST-IN-PLACE PILES

full shaft resistance is mobilized at a settlement less than that acceptable to the structural designer at the working load.

The separate effects of shaft and base resistance have been considered by Burland, Butler and Dunican in their paper to the 1966 Symposium.[7.21] They present a simple stability criterion which they say can be used to obtain the maximum safe load on any bored pile.

In general terms they state that "in addition to an overall load factor, a factor of safety in end-bearing must be satisfied." If an overall load factor of 2 is stipulated, together with a minimum factor of safety in end bearing of 3, then the maximum safe load is the lesser of the two expressions—

$$\frac{Q_{ult}}{2} \text{ for the pile}$$

and

$$Q_{ult} \text{ for the shaft} + \frac{Q_{ult}}{3} \text{ for the base}$$

They state that the first expression is nearly always dominant for straight-sided piles and long piles with comparatively small under-reams, whereas the second expression often controls larger under-reamed piles. In cases where the soil data are meagre or variable, or when loads are indeterminate, it is thought that an overall load factor of 2·5 with a minimum factor of safety of 3·5 on the base is more suitable. The shaft and base loads are calculated using the adhesion and bearing capacity factors given on page 393.

In the case of piles with under-reamed bases, the shaft skin friction should be ignored for a distance of two shaft diameters above the top of the under-ream. This allows for the possibility of drag-down on the pile shaft from the soil immediately above the under-ream. This drag-down might occur as a result of the normal elastic and consolidation settlement of the pile causing a small gap to open between the upper surface of the under-reamed section of the pile and the overlying soil. The latter would tend to move downward with time, resulting in drag-down on the shaft.

Because of the time required to form an under-ream by machine or hand excavation, the time spent cleaning soil debris and the delays before the under-ream is inspected and passed for concreting, it is possible that appreciable softening due to soil swelling and seepage of water from fissures will have occurred in the clay which will be in contact with the pile shaft. For this reason, the author prefers to use an adhesion factor of 0·3 for the shafts of under-reamed piles.

Using the above criterion for overall stability, the relative dimensions of the shaft and base are governed by considerations of elastic settlement at the working load. The load/settlement relationship for the base of the pile can be obtained directly by making plate bearing tests at the bottom of boreholes or trial shafts. By plotting the settlement of the plate divided by plate diameter ($\rho_i/B$) against the plate bearing pressure divided by the ultimate bearing capacity of the soil beneath the plate ($q/q_r$), a curve of the type shown in Fig. 7.12 is obtained. For a base safety factor greater than 3, Burland, Butler and Dunican have shown that a curve of this type can be expressed as—

$$\frac{\rho_i}{B} = K(q/q_r) \quad . \quad . \quad . \quad . \quad (7.12)$$

Thus from a plate bearing test of any appropriate diameter the $K$ value for $q/q_f > \frac{1}{3}$ is obtained, enabling the engineer to calculate $\rho_i$ for any given pile base diameter. Values of $K$ for London Clay have been found to lie principally between 0·01 and 0·02. The higher value can be used for sites in London Clay where no plate bearing tests have been made. This will give a conservative prediction. Equation 7.12 can be used to determine the base settlement for any

type of clay provided sufficient plate bearing tests are made to ensure that the relationship is unique for the particular site.

If the settlement obtained from equation 7.12 is excessive it will be necessary either to reduce the working load on the pile, or to decrease the load on the base by increasing the shaft diameter, or to take the pile down to deeper, less compressible soil. Increasing the size of the base will not reduce the settlement.

It will be found that straight-sided piles show less elastic settlement than under-reamed piles carrying the same working load. However, the final decision as to whether or not straight-sided or under-reamed piles should be adopted and the selection of the relative shaft and base diameter

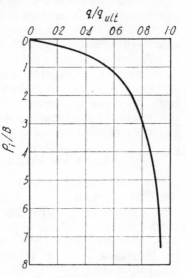

FIG. 7.12. SETTLEMENT RELATIONSHIP FOR PILES IN CLAY

of under-reamed piles is not always made from considerations of settlement alone. Economic factors often have a dominating influence. For example, consideration must be given to the relative volumes of soil and concrete involved, the practicability of forming under-reams in very silty or fissured clays, and the feasibility of forming very large under-reamed bases with the available drilling equipment. These factors will be discussed in Chapter 8 (p. 529).

A method described by Whitaker and Cooke in the 1966 Symposium is considerably more refined. It takes into account the shaft friction mobilized by the elastic compression of the pile shaft and enables predictions of the maximum, minimum and mean settlements, based on a statistical analysis of pile loading tests using several base to shaft diameter ratios, to be made. This method provides a guide to the expected differential settlement between adjacent piles, which is of considerable value to the structural designer especially in the frequently used procedure of providing a single large pile beneath each column of a structure. However, the method of Whitaker and Cooke is only applicable to sites where extensive load test data are available.

### Calculation of the Carrying Capacity of Piles in Soils Intermediate between Sand and Clay

The end resistance can be calculated from Terzaghi's general equation 2.6 (p. 87) using the undisturbed values of $c$ and $\phi$ from tests on soil samples. As previously noted, this formula is likely to give conservative results. There are no available data on the skin friction or adhesion of the pile shaft in $c$-$\phi$ soils. However, it may be taken as the sum of the adhesion and skin friction based on experience and using as a guide the values given in Fig. 7.10, the skin friction being calculated by the methods given on pages 377 to 394. In the case of bored piles, due allowance should be made for likely softening or loosening effect caused by the boring operations.

### SCREWED PILES IN COHESIVE SOILS

The shaft friction on a screwed pile in a cohesive soil can be obtained by treating it as a driven pile and using the adhesion factors shown in Fig. 7.10. The end-bearing resistance is calculated on the diameter of the base plate using the bearing capacity factor $N_c$ of 9, provided that the plate can be screwed at least 5 diameters into the bearing stratum. It is unlikely that plates of large diameter could be screwed for this distance into a stiff or hard clay, and in these cases $N_c$ should be obtained from Fig. 2.11 (*d*). (See also p. 526.)

### THE CARRYING CAPACITY OF PILES FOUNDED ON ROCK

#### Driven Piles

When founding piles on rock it is usual to drive the piles to refusal in order to obtain the maximum carrying capacity from the piles. If the rock is hard at its surface, the piles will refuse further driving at a negligible penetration. In such cases the carrying capacity of the piles is governed by the strength of the pile shaft regarded as a column. When piles are driven on to hard rock through fairly stiff clays or sands, the piles can be regarded as being supported on all sides from buckling as a strut; therefore the carrying capacity is calculated from the safe load on the material of the pile at the point of minimum cross-section. In practice, it is necessary to limit the safe load on piles regarded as short columns because of the possibility of damage to the pile during driving, and the subsequent deterioration of the material by the action of soil or ground water over a long period of years. The limitations in working stresses are usually laid down in Codes of Practice or local by-laws. Values in general use are given in the description of various types of pile in Chapter 8.

Piles driven into certain types of rock such as chalk or marl, or into weathered rocks, may penetrate to a considerable depth before a satisfactory driving resistance is obtained. Chalk is a particularly difficult material in which to estimate pile driving resistance, since the pile breaks down the cell-structure of the chalk, freeing the contained water. This water forms a slurry around the pile, giving a very low frictional resistance while driving. It is probable that the slurried chalk (water and silt-size particles) settles around the pile, giving increasing frictional resistance with time after cessation of driving because piles in chalk are known to carry high working loads if a suitable period of time is allowed after driving before the pile is allowed to carry its full load (*see also* p. 72). Some useful information on the carrying capacity of piles in chalk is given in the 1965 *Symposium on Chalk in Earthworks and Foundations*.[1.31] From this information, the author recommends *allowable* values of 30 kN/m² in skin friction and 2200 kN/m² in end-bearing for piles driven into a chalk of Grade III or better consistency (N value greater than 20 blows/0·3 m).

Marls frequently consist of alternating bands of hard rocky material and stiff clay. Unless rock bands can be proved to be of appreciable thickness over the piled area, it is advisable to base the end resistance of the pile on the shear strength of the clay bands. Strong unweathered marl can carry allowable values of 50 kN/m² in skin friction and 2200 kN/m² in end-bearing for piles.[1.30]

If it is possible to obtain undisturbed samples of marl or chalk either by the open drive sampler or by coring, then the carrying capacity of piles can be obtained by treating them as driven into $c$-$\phi$ soils, using laboratory tests to determine values of $c$ and $\phi$ for substitution in equation 2.6. Weathered rocks such as decomposed granite or limestone can generally be treated as soils from the point of view of estimation of carrying capacity which is based on the results of laboratory tests on undisturbed samples, or in-situ tests in the case of cohesionless materials.

### Bored Piles

The action of boring a hole in rock to form a socket for a pile may weaken the bearing capacity of some types of rock. For example, the action of boring tools in chalk or marl causes considerable breakdown and slurrying of these rock types. Therefore, low values of skin friction should be used for bored piles in contact with slurried chalk or marl. The actual value chosen will depend on the hardness and susceptibility to breakdown of these materials. In soft friable chalk or marl, complete softening may result and the ultimate skin friction may not be more than, say, 12 kN/m². In hard chalk or marl where casing is not required to support the borehole, the walls of the hole (if drilled by percussion rather than rotary methods) will be rough. Thus, the concrete will key into the walls of the hole and the full shear strength of the rock will be developed in skin friction on the rock socket. Some useful information on the carrying capacity of rock sockets is given in the paper by Thorburn in the 1966 *Symposium on Large Bored Piles*.[7.21] Thorburn quotes *allowable* values ranging from 107 kN/m² for fragmented shale to 429 kN/m² for a widely fissured hard sandstone.

Where it is possible to drive sample tubes into chalk or marl, or to obtain cores from holes drilled by rotary methods, the angle of shearing resistance and cohesion of the material can be obtained by triaxial compression tests at high lateral pressure in the laboratory (p. 58). These values may be substituted in equation 2.6 to obtain a first estimate of the end resistance of the pile. This should be confirmed by full-scale loading tests at the construction stage.

In the absence of laboratory test data the allowable bearing pressures given in Table 2.1 (p. 96) can be used for calculating the safe end resistance.

Where the depth of soft weathered rock over hard unweathered rock is small, it will usually be economical to take the pile down to unweathered rock when its ultimate carrying capacity should not be less than the ultimate strength of the pile shaft. Since bored piles are usually wholly buried in the ground, and cannot be formed in highly fluid mud, the working load on the pile shaft can be calculated as for a short concrete column. The choice between either founding a pile at the surface of a weak rock stratum, with a correspondingly low end bearing value, or taking a smaller diameter pile deep into the stratum to utilize its rock socket skin friction is usually governed by the relative costs. Take, for example, a pile required to carry a working load of 1500 kN which is to be drilled through 12 m of soft overburden into shale with an end bearing value of 1600 kN/m² (allowable) and a rock socket value of 160 kN/m² (allowable). For a pile taken only just into the surface of the rock, the diameter must be 1·10 m. This might cost £520 all-in based on £40 per metre in overburden and £70 per metre for drilling 0·6 m into rock. The alternative of a 600 mm pile would provide 448 kN in end bearing, the remaining 1052 kN being taken up in a rock socket 3·5 m deep. This might cost £475 based on £25 per metre in overburden and £55 for drilling into rock. Thus the smaller diameter pile would be cheaper.

If it is decided to utilize the full carrying capacity of the pile shaft by taking the pile down to hard unweathered rock, it will be advisable to sink boreholes with rotary core drilling through the rock to obtain a guide to the likely variation in thickness of the weathered material. Cores should be retained for inspection by the piling contractor. If rock strata consist of *thinly bedded* hard and soft layers (such as may be found in limestone and marls), the end resistance of the pile should be calculated from the resistance of the softer layers, no matter whether the pile finishes on a hard or soft layer.

## PILES IN FILL—NEGATIVE SKIN FRICTION

If driven or bored piles are installed in compressible fill or any soil showing appreciable consolidation under its own weight, a load additional to the working load on the head of the pile is transmitted in skin friction, i.e. "negative skin friction," to the pile surface. Additional consolidation of the fill or soil is given by superimposed loading. Negative skin friction must be allowed for when considering the safety factor on the ultimate carrying capacity of the pile.

The calculation of the total negative skin friction or "drag-down" force on a pile is a matter of great complexity, and the time factor is of importance. The maximum unit negative skin friction on a pile is the maximum skin friction which is mobilized on the contact face, and this peak value can be calculated in exactly the same manner as that used for calculating the support in skin friction given to bearing piles. However, as stated on pages 370 and 394, the maximum skin friction will not be mobilized until the soil has moved relatively to the pile by an appreciable amount, and this may be of the order of one per cent of the shaft diameter. Thus if we take the simple case of a fill settling under its own weight and placed on an incompressible stratum as shown in Fig. 7.13 (*a*), the fill immediately above the incompressible stratum will not move at all and consequently it will not cause any drag-down on the pile. In fact, the elastic compression of the pile due to the superimposed and drag-down loads may cause the pile to move downwards relatively to the fill and so cause the fill to act in *support* of the pile. The maximum settlement of the fill will be at the ground surface, but here the movement may be so large that the skin friction will have passed its peak value and the final drag-down will then be that corresponding to the residual value (p. 370). Nevertheless, at some earlier stage in the settlement of the fill the movement at the ground surface will have been such as to mobilize the peak skin friction whereas the movement at lower levels would not have been such as to mobilize the peak value. If a load is then superimposed on the pile above ground level the pile will compress elastically, the movement being a maximum at the ground surface. This will reduce the relative movement between pile and soil, which may result in mobilization of peak skin friction in support of the pile (Fig. 7.13 (*b*)) or the relative movement may be so low that the peak value is not reached.

Take now the case of a pile bearing on a compressible stratum, say a stiff clay. In this case the whole pile will settle and is likely to

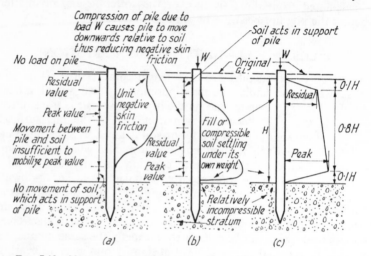

FIG. 7.13. NEGATIVE SKIN FRICTION ON PILES DRIVEN INTO RELATIVELY INCOMPRESSIBLE STRATUM

(*a*) Early stages of settlement of compressible layer.
(*b*) Late stages of settlement of compressible layer.
(*c*) Average curve for design purposes.

mobilize the peak value of skin friction and a proportion of the base resistance in the bearing stratum. The pile will move downwards relatively to the fill immediately above the bearing stratum and thus the fill will act in support of the pile over this length. Figs. 7.14 (*a*) and (*b*) show the distribution of drag-down forces and stresses in the pile shaft for early and late stages in consolidation of the fill.

It will be seen from the foregoing that because of the uncertainties in the magnitude of the drag-down forces mobilized in the time-dependent relative movement between pile and soil, it is impossible to obtain a close estimate of the total drag-down force. All that can be said with certainty is that peak value of skin friction will not at any time act on the whole length of shaft embedded in the fill. Figs. 7.13 (*c*) and 7.14 (*c*) will enable the engineer to make an intelligent guess at a reasonable drag-down load to be allowed for design purposes.

The distribution of negative skin friction forces on a steel box pile of 1640 mm periphery driven through about 45 m of soft clay, on which was later superimposed 10 m of fill, was measured by Johannessen and Bjerrum.[7.22] It was estimated that the total drag-down force at the toe of the pile, which was driven into hard rock, was about 250 tonne and this caused a further penetration of more

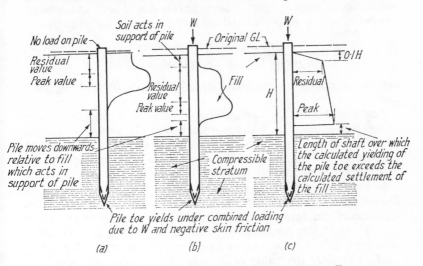

Fig 7.14. Negative Skin Friction on Piles Driven through Fill into Compressible Stratum

(a) Early stages of settlement of fill.
(b) Late stages of settlement of fill.
(c) Average curve for design purposes.

than 50 mm into the rock. It was found impossible to relate the stress distribution along the pile shaft to the shear strength of the clay. However, good agreement was found from the relationship—

$$\text{Negative skin friction} = \sigma'_v K \tan \phi_a' \qquad (7.13)$$

where $\sigma'_v$ = effective vertical stress

The function $K \tan \phi'_a$ was assumed to be constant throughout the length of the pile and its value at the final stage of consolidation was found to be 0·20 for the medium soft marine clay at the test site.

In cases where negative skin friction is so high that it causes difficult problems in pile design, it may be possible to eliminate the drag-down in its entirety or to control it within pre-determined limits. This can be done by sleeving the pile through the compressible stratum, or by surrounding the pile by a plastic membrane which has a comparatively low frictional value. Claessen and Horvat[7.23] describe the coating of precast concrete piles with 10 mm of soft asphalt (penetration 4 to 5 mm at 25°C). This reduced the calculated negative skin friction by more than 50 per cent. If the fill has been in place for a very long period of years or has otherwise been well-consolidated, the negative skin friction can be ignored in estimating the total working load on the pile, but the skin friction of the fill should not be allowed to act in *support* of the pile. For cases intermediate between recently placed and old fill the safety factor given by

$$\frac{\text{Ultimate carrying capacity}}{\text{Working load} + \text{negative skin friction}}$$

may be reduced below the value normally adopted for working loads alone.

Negative skin friction can also occur when fill is placed over peat or soft clay strata. The superimposed loading on such compressible strata causes heavy settlement of the fill with consequent drag-down on piles. The skin friction to be added to the working load includes that from the peat or soft clay as well as the fill.

In some circumstances, negative skin friction can be caused by driving piles into normally consolidated clays which causes extensive remoulding and upheaval of the ground surface but as remarked on page 387 the soil re-consolidates quite quickly and regains its original strength before the pile is normally required to carry its full working load. Certainly the value of driving piles wholly into soft clays without reaching any firm bearing stratum is questionable. In the case of piles driven into stiff over-consolidated clays, although re-moulding takes place there is little or no loss of shear strength. However, the broken up masses of clay re-consolidate very slowly (possibly never within the life of the structure). Thus, the stiff clays will continue to give support to the piles throughout the long period of consolidation. This consolidation will inevitably be accompanied by some settlement.

### THE CARRYING CAPACITY OF PILE GROUPS

As stated at the beginning of this chapter, it is important to consider the effect of driving and loading piles in groups. Only if piles are taken down to a hard incompressible stratum is the settlement of a group of piles equal to that of a single pile under the same working load as each pile in the group (the settlement of piles driven to a hard incompressible stratum is due to elastic shortening of the pile shaft and some elastic yielding of the material under the toe of the pile).

If piles are driven into a compressible bearing stratum, such as a layer of stiff clay, or if the bearing stratum is itself relatively incompressible (a dense sand, for example) but is underlain by a compressible stratum, then the carrying capacity of a group of piles may be very much less than that of the sum of the individual piles. Also, the settlement of the group of piles is likely to be many times greater than that of the individual pile under the same working load. This is illustrated by Fig. 7.15 (*a*) and (*b*). In the case of the single pile

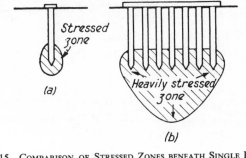

FIG. 7.15. COMPARISON OF STRESSED ZONES BENEATH SINGLE PILE AND BENEATH PILE GROUP

(*a*) Single pile
(*b*) Pile group

(Fig. 7.15 (*a*)) only a small zone of compressible soil around or below the pile is subjected to vertical stress; whereas with the large pile group (Fig. 7.15 (*b*)), a considerable depth of soil around and below the group is stressed and settlement of the whole group may be large.

An example of the effects of heavy settlement due to consolidation of deep layers of soft clay beneath large pile groups is given by the case of the Campus Buildings of the Massachusetts Institute of Technology.[7.24] These buildings were constructed in 1915 and were founded on piles, which in most cases were terminated in a layer of sand and gravel found beneath organic silt and peat at a depth generally of 3 to 6 m below ground level. The sand and gravel layer was very variable in thickness up to a maximum of about 7·6 m (Fig. 7.16). In places the layer was only about 1 m and the piles were driven through it to enter the underlying deep stratum of soft and compressible Boston Blue Clay, which was 21 m or more in thickness and was underlain by glacial till and rock. Thus the large piled areas transmitted their loads through the sand and gravel to the underlying compressible clay and this resulted in heavy settlement and extensive cracking of the buildings. The settlements varied widely over the loaded area. Between 1915 and 1943 the

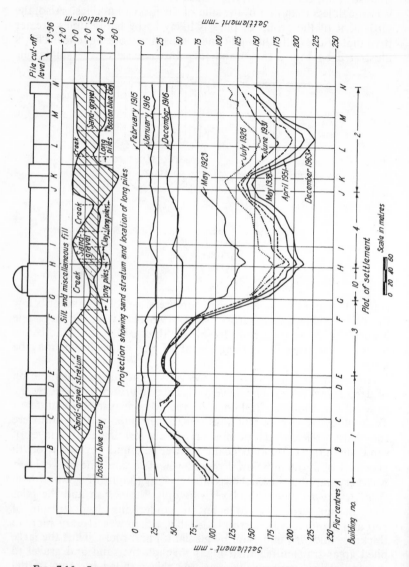

FIG. 7.16. SETTLEMENT OF PILE GROUPS BENEATH CAMPUS BUILDINGS OF THE MASSACHUSETTS INSTITUTE OF TECHNOLOGY (AFTER HORN AND LAMBE[7.24])

settlements increased progressively, the minimum being about 40 mm and the maximum 230 mm (Fig. 7.16). The variations were due mainly to the variation in thickness of the sand and gravel stratum and the lengths of the piles. The heaviest settlements occurred where the piles were driven into the Boston Blue Clay stratum.

It will be appreciated from the foregoing that the problems of the stability of pile groups are, first, the ability of the soil around as well as below the block of soil containing the pile group to support the whole load of the structure and, secondly, the effects of consolidation of the soil for a considerable depth below the pile group. Therefore, the manner in which the individual pile is installed, whether by driving, boring, jacking, or screwing, has little effect on these two problems. This is because the zone of soil affected by the method of installing the pile is very small compared to the very large mass of soil affected by the vertical pressures transmitted to it by the piles in the group.

## Pile Groups in Sands and Gravels

### Driven Piles and Driven and Cast-in-Place Piles

The action of driving piles or pile tubes into sands and gravels is to compact the soil around the pile to a radius of at least three times the pile diameter. Thus, when piles are driven in a group at close spacing the soil around and between them becomes highly compacted. The efficiency ratio* of the group is thus greater than unity. Model tests on groups of piles by Kezdi[7.25] have shown that the maximum efficiency of 2 is given by piles in groups of nine and sixteen at a spacing of two diameters. However, more recent tests by Vesic[7.26] on larger-scale models have shown lower efficiency ratios. He recommends that bearing in mind the effects of soil compressibility, it is advisable not to count, in design, on efficiency ratios higher than unity. Even so, care should be taken when considering efficiency ratios for sites where piles are driven into sands and gravels overlying compressible clays, when stresses transferred to the clays from the pile group might result in over-stressing or excessive consolidation. The carrying capacity of pile groups under these conditions is governed by the shear strength and compressibility of the clays, rather than by the "efficiency" of the group within the sand or gravel stratum. It should also be noted that the ultimate carrying capacity of the group obtained from the efficiency ratio should be used only to obtain a preliminary guide to the working load. Even when driven into sands and gravels the working loads on piles will be

---

* Efficiency ratio = $E_f = \dfrac{\text{Average load per pile in group at failure}}{\text{Failure load of single comparable pile}}$.

governed by considerations of the settlement of the group as described below.

## Spacing of Driven and Driven and Cast-in-Place Piles

The spacing of piles in large groups in sands and gravels requires careful consideration. If the piles are at close centres, the first few piles drive easily, but as the density of the soil increases so driving of additional piles becomes increasingly difficult. A spacing of 2 to 3 diameters is commonly specified. When driving piles in sands or gravels, the best procedure to avoid difficulty with "tightening-up" of the ground is to start driving at the centre of the group and then work outwards in all directions.

## Bored Piles

Tests on groups of full-scale or model bored piles in sands or gravels have not been made in a similar manner to those described above for driven piles. However, it is reasonable to assume that the same compacting effect and high efficiencies at close spacing will *not* apply in the case of bored piles. In fact, there is likely to be a general loosening of the ground around and between the piles if they are installed at close spacing. In the absence of other evidence, the author suggests that bored piles in sands and gravels should not be installed at a spacing closer than 750 mm or twice the least width, whichever is the greater. The efficiency may be taken as unity.

## Settlement of Pile Groups in Sands and Gravels

For most engineering structures the load to be applied to a pile group will be calculated from considerations of consolidation settlement rather than by calculating the ultimate carrying capacity of the group and dividing it by an arbitrary safety factor of 2 or 3. Skempton, Yassin, and Gibson[7.27] have published curves (Fig. 7.17) relating the settlement of pile groups of a given width to that of a single pile. These curves can be taken as applying to driven or bored piles.

Actual observations of the settlement of pile groups in sands include the twenty-storey hotel at São Paulo, Brazil, where Da Costa Nunes and Vargas[7.28] observed that the settlement of a large group was ten times the average of test loadings on three single piles. Other observations by the same authors at the Banes do Estado, also in São Paulo, showed that a group of piles settled fifteen times that of the single pile. In the case of the Deptford Creek Bridge, the east abutment was founded on ninety-three precast concrete piles 6·1 m long driven through 2·1 to 4·0 m of stiff clay into the Thanet Sands.

The maximum loading on any pile was 837 kN. The average settlement of about 20 mm was approximately five and ten times that of two test piles each under the same working load as that of the piles in the

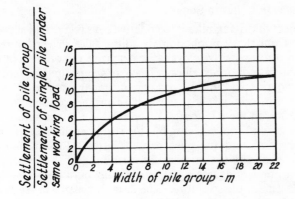

Fig. 7.17. Settlement of Pile Groups in Sands (Skempton, Yassin, and Gibson[7.23])

group. The west abutment was founded on eighty-five similar piles with a maximum working load of 897 kN per pile. Loading and measured settlement curves from a paper by Fuller and Couper[7.29] are shown in Fig. 7.18. The average settlement of 23 mm for the eastern end of this abutment was approximately four to seventeen times that of a single pile under 897 kN test load. The least

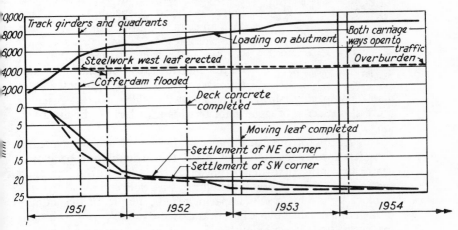

Fig. 7.18. Settlement Records of West Abutment, Deptford Creek Bridge (Fuller and Couper[7.29])

width of the pile groups in both the east and west abutments was about 12 m. For this width, the curves in Fig. 7.17 give the ratio of the settlement of the group to that of the single pile as 10.

## Pile Groups in Cohesive Soils

The effect of driving piles into cohesive soils (clays and silts) is very different from that in cohesionless soils. Piles driven or bored in groups into soft sensitive clays cause extensive remoulding of the soil and, in the case of driven piles, a heave of the ground surface occurs around the group. With the passage of time the soil re-consolidates and regains its original shear strength. Thus, re-consolidation causes a drag-down on the pile shaft. When piles are driven into stiff clays the same ground heave occurs but the soil is pushed up in lumps or cracked masses and the piles may be lifted. Re-consolidation is extremely slow and the original shear strength of the whole mass of ground around and within the pile group may never be restored within the life of the structure. The drag-down effects are small and in the case of bored piles they do not occur.

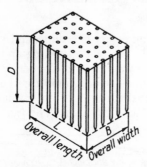

When loading is applied to a group at close spacing the soil contained within the piles moves downwards with the piles and at failure, piles and soil move together to give the typical "block failure." The same mechanism of failure occurs with driven or bored piles. Model tests by Whitaker[7.30] at the Building Research Station showed that block failure occurred at spacings closer than $1\frac{1}{2}$ diameters for groups of 3 by 3 piles and closer than $2\frac{1}{4}$ diameters for 9 by 9 piles. For wider spacings the piles failed individually but the efficiency ratio (see p. 407) was only about 0·7 at $2\frac{1}{2}$

FIG. 7.19. CALCULATION FOR BLOCK FAILURE OF PILE GROUP IN CLAY

diameters spacing, slowly increasing with wider spacing, reaching unity at a spacing of eight diameters for piles forty-eight diameters long.

The spacing of piles in groups is largely governed by structural considerations. Generally, for clays they should not be closer, centre to centre, than the perimeter of the piles, with a minimum spacing of 1100 mm centre to centre. This rule will avoid the risk of block failure but a closer spacing may be adopted if the stability of the group against block failure and excessive settlement is checked by the methods given below.

The stability of a group of driven or bored piles against *block failure* is given by the sum of the perimeter shearing resistance and the end bearing resistance of the block of soil contained by the piles (Fig. 7.19), as expressed in the following equation—

Ultimate carrying capacity of group $= Q_u$

$$= 2D(B + L) \times \bar{c} + 1 \cdot 3cN_c \times B \times L \qquad . \qquad . \quad (7.14)$$

where $D$ = length of piles

$B$ = width of group

$L$ = length of group

$\bar{c}$ = average cohesion of clay around the group

$c$ = cohesion of clay beneath group

$N_c$ = bearing capacity factor (from Fig. 2.11(*d*), p. 90).

The remoulding caused by the pile driving or boring only takes place to a relatively small distance around and beneath the pile group; thus the undisturbed shear strength beneath the group may be taken for the second term in equation 7.14. However, when considering the perimeter shearing resistance, the time effect should be taken into account allowing the fully remoulded shear strength for $\bar{c}$, if the piles are required to carry their full working load a short time after driving, or the original shear strength if full loading can be delayed for six months or more.

For spacings wider than, say, two diameters, the ultimate carrying capacity of the group is given by the equation—

$$Q_u = E_f \times n \times Q_p \qquad . \qquad . \qquad . \quad (7.15)$$

where $E_f$ = efficiency ratio of the group

$n$ = number of piles in the group

$Q_p$ = ultimate carrying capacity of a single pile.

In the absence of evidence from tests on full-scale pile groups, values of $E_f$ may be taken as $0 \cdot 7$ for a spacing of 2 to 3 diameters increasing to unity at a spacing of 8 diameters. This is a reasonable procedure to give an approximate guide to the required number of piles to support a given total load on the group, since the actual working load per pile will most likely be governed by consideration of immediate and consolidation settlements of the group.

IMMEDIATE AND CONSOLIDATION SETTLEMENTS

There are no published data on the relationship between immediate and long-term consolidation settlement of groups of piles and those of individual piles. It is the usual practice to compute the settlement of pile groups on the basis of laboratory consolidation tests on soil samples. The method usually followed is to assume that a group of friction piles behaves as a pier having dimensions in plan equal to the overall dimensions of the group plus the additional width given by the 1 in 4 spread of the load. The base of the "virtual pier" foundation is assumed to be at a depth of two-thirds of the length of the piles, as shown in Fig. 7.20.

Where the piles are wholly end-bearing, the settlements are considered as given by a raft foundation at the level of the base of the piles and equal in area to the plan area of the pile group.

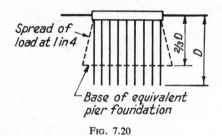

Spread of load at 1 in 4

2/3 D

D

Base of equivalent pier foundation

FIG. 7.20

### EFFECTS OF GROUND HEAVE

The effect of driving piles in groups in clays to cause ground heave has already been noted. In some circumstances this can cause lifting of piles already driven. Cases have occurred where both precast and driven and cast-in-place piles have been lifted 100 mm or more. In the case of driven and cast-in-situ piles, it is virtually impossible to drive them down again to their original position if they are of the type in which the tube is withdrawn. However, piles which incorporate a steel shell which remains in the ground can be re-driven by reinserting the mandrel, before they are finally filled with concrete. Lifting of piles is most likely to occur when the pile shafts are wholly in firm to stiff clays. When the major portion of the shaft is in a very soft clay which is remoulded during driving, the adhesion is insufficient for the heaving ground to lift the piles. Therefore, when considering driving piles in groups in firm to stiff clays, the engineer should use precast concrete, steel, or shell piles which can be re-driven if necessary, or alternatively, he should adopt bored piles, or partly bored and partly driven and cast-in-place piles. The ground displaced by the piles driven in groups can cause high lateral pressures to develop on nearby buried culverts, sewers, or tunnels, with consequent risk of serious damage.

### THE EFFICIENCY OF PILE GROUPS IN SOFT COMPRESSIBLE CLAYS

The possible detrimental effect of driving piles wholly into soft compressible clays has been mentioned briefly on page 404. It will be as well, therefore, to discuss in more detail the advantages and disadvantages of pile groups in this type of ground. It is as well to point out at this stage that *short* piles in such conditions are worse than useless. A comparison of the stress distribution in Fig. 7.21 (*a*) and (*b*) between a shallow raft foundation and a short pile foundation shows that, virtually, the same volume of compressible soil is stressed in each case. In fact, the short pile group may show greater settlement than the shallow raft, due to re-consolidation of the heaved and

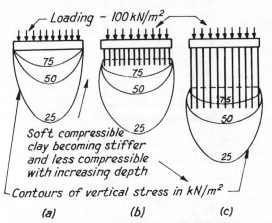

FIG. 7.21. COMPARISON OF VERTICAL STRESS DISTRIBUTION BETWEEN (*a*) SURFACE RAFT, (*b*) RAFT WITH SHORT PILES, (*c*) RAFT WITH LONG PILES

remoulded soil. However, most normally consolidated clays show a progressive increase in shear strength and decrease in compressibility with increasing depth. Therefore, in the case of the long pile group (Fig. 7.21 (*c*)) the stresses are transferred to deeper and less compressible soil and the settlement of the structure is correspondingly less.

Piles driven wholly in soft compressible clays have been used extensively in Shanghai to support tall buildings on the river front where the compressible clays extend to a depth of nearly 300 m In pre-war years the buildings were constructed on tapered wood piles (China fir) at close spacing. It is likely that the buoyancy given by the material of the piles was an important factor in avoiding failure of the pile groups, since the piles were short in relation to the width of the structures and the high compressibility of the clays, as described by Clarke.[7.31]

Long friction piles are used in highly compressible lacustrine volcanic clays in Mexico City, as described by Zeevaert.[7.32] The Azteco building had a total weight of 79 300 kN. A basement was constructed to a depth of 6 m which relieved the soil of 57 691 kN, and the remaining 21 522 kN was carried by eighty-three concrete piles 410 mm in diameter and 18 m long, giving a working load of 259 kN per pile. The observed settlement ten months after com-

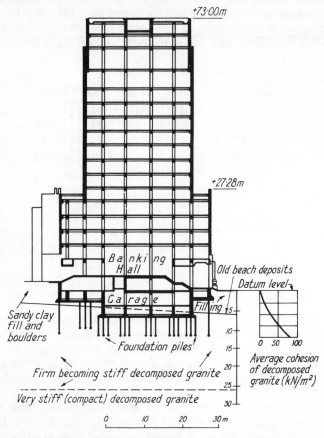

FIG. 7.22. PILED FOUNDATIONS TO BANK OF CHINA, HONG KONG

pletion of the building and two years after commencement of loading was 200 mm compared to a computed 250 mm. The computed settlement at eight years was a little over 300 mm. The observed and estimated settlements are only about one-half of the settlements calculated by Zeevaert for a basement foundation without piles.

An example of a similar reduction in settlement given by a basement foundation in conjunction with piles is the foundation of the Bank of China at Hong Kong.[7.33] Borings showed that below a stratum of fill and boulders was decomposed granite extending to more than 30 m below ground level (Fig. 7.22). The decomposed granite had the characteristics of a sandy clay of medium plasticity. Near the surface of this stratum it was rather soft and compressible but it became increasingly stiff and less compressible with increasing depth. A basement was provided, which reduced the net bearing pressure to about 188 kN/m² over the base of the substructure, but the factor of safety against shear failure of the clay was very low and calculations showed that a settlement of as much as 150 mm might occur. The differential settlements between the seventeen-storey central tower and the five-storey wings would have been excessive, and, in addition, headroom for the access to an underground garage in the basement was strictly limited and the total settlement was excessive from this point of view. Accordingly, piled foundations were recommended, with the object of transferring the foundation loading to less compressible soil at depth. Because of boulders in the decomposed granite, it was impracticable to drive long piles to bedrock, so a total of about 350 driven and cast-in-place piles (Franki piles) was provided. The average depth of the piles was nearly 12 m below the lowest ground surface level on the site, or 5 m below driving level at the bottom of the basement excavation. The record of the settlement observations, together with the estimated time–settlement curve based on laboratory tests on the soil samples, are shown in Fig. 7.23.

The gross final settlement was about twelve times the settlement of the test pile under the same average dead load of 947 kN per pile for a foundation width of 43 m. The net settlement (i.e. the gross settlement less the estimated settlement caused by re-consolidation of the ground after putting back a load equivalent to the weight of the soil removed in the basement excavation) was about six and a half times that of the test pile under the average load of 947 kN. The maximum working load (dead *plus* live *plus* wind) on any pile was 1395 kN. The test pile withstood a total load of 1993 kN with a settlement of only 11 mm.

## GROUPS OF DRIVEN PILES IN SOFT CLAYS AND SILTS OVERLYING STIFF CLAYS

In a close-spaced pile group, the upper part of the mass of soil enclosed by the group is heaved up during pile driving (Fig. 7.24). Therefore, when re-consolidation takes place the weight of the heaved-up soil is transferred to the piles thus increasing the load on them. It is thus evident that the upper soft clays and silts do not contribute to the carrying capacity of the piles. The problem is to assess how much of this load should be taken as increasing the working load on the pile from the point of view of the carrying capacity of the individual pile.

The weight of the mass of soil causing drag-down should be divided up between the piles in the group and added to the working load on

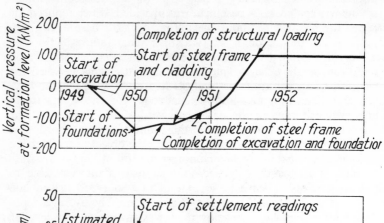

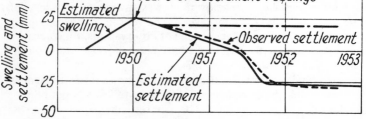

Fig. 7.23. Foundation Loading and Observed and Estimated Settlements, Bank of China, Hong Kong

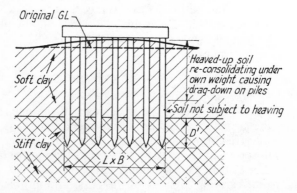

Fig. 7.24. Effects of Ground Heave on Groups of Driven Piles in Clay

each pile. The total load should not exceed the ultimate carrying capacity of the individual pile as determined by calculation or loading test, but the safety factor need not necessarily be high. A safety factor less than 2 would be accepted if the settlement of the individual pile is not excessive under the total load. It should be noted that the drag-down on any individual pile in a group caused by consolidation of the soil around the pile will not be greater than can be carried in skin friction on the pile shaft, i.e. the surface area of the pile embedded in the soft clay multiplied by the adhesion corresponding to the shear strength of the soft clay (*see* Fig. 7.10). Also in considering the drag-down on an individual pile it should be remembered that heave and re-consolidation sufficient to cause negative skin friction is only likely to occur in the upper part of the pile shaft (*see* Fig. 7.14). The safety factor of the whole group of piles under the working load plus the weight of the consolidating mass of soft clay should also be calculated. The carrying capacity of the group is given by—

$$Q_u = 2D'(B + L) \times \bar{c} + cN_c \times B \times L \qquad . \ (7.16)$$

where $D' = $ penetration into stiff clay stratum.

Safety factor $= Q_u \div$ (Total working load on pile group + Load transferred by consolidation of soft clay)

Here again the safety factor need only be low since the drag-down due to the consolidating soil will not increase the consolidation of the soil beneath the whole group because the only additional load at the base of the pile group is the working load imposed on the group from the structure plus the net weight of the piles themselves, i.e. the weight of the overburden soil on the stiff clay beneath the pile group has not been increased by the pile driving.

The procedure should be therefore—

(*a*) For calculating the carrying capacity of individual piles in the group or the whole group, neglect any support given by the soft clay.

(*b*) There should be a safety factor on the expression—

$$\frac{\text{Ultimate carrying capacity of individual pile}}{\substack{\text{Working load on individual pile + Load transferred to} \\ \text{individual pile from consolidating overburden}}}$$

but the safety factor can be lower than that used for

$$\frac{\text{Ultimate carrying capacity of individual pile}}{\text{Working load on an individual pile}}$$

(*c*) There should also be a safety factor on the expression—

$$\frac{\text{Ultimate carrying capacity of pile group}}{\text{Working load on group} + \text{Load transferred to pile group from consolidating overburden}}$$

Again the safety factor can be lower than that used for

$$\frac{\text{Ultimate carrying capacity of pile group}}{\text{Working load on pile group}}$$

### PILE GROUPS EMBEDDED IN A FIRM STRATUM UNDERLAIN BY COMPRESSIBLE CLAY

The case of the M.I.T. Campus Buildings, as described on page 405, is an example of the dangers involved in terminating piles in a relatively thin stiff stratum underlain by compressible clay. If these conditions exist, the stability and consolidation settlements of the whole group should be calculated on the basis that the pile group represents a raft foundation with its base at a level two-thirds of the length of the piles (Fig. 7.20). If the piles are driven through deep soft deposits to a relatively small penetration in a sand or stiff clay stratum, the equivalent raft should be taken as being located at a level of two-thirds of the depth of penetration into the bearing stratum ($\frac{2}{3}D_1$) plus the depth of the soft deposits ($D_2$) as shown in Fig. 7.25.

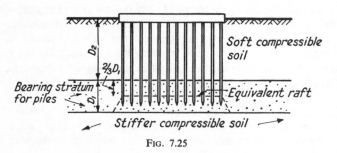

FIG. 7.25

This procedure is applicable both to driven and bored piles.

### Pile Groups in Filled Ground

In the case of pile groups driven or bored in fill which is consolidating under its own weight, or under the weight of surface load, the weight of the whole mass of fill enclosed by the periphery of the group is transferred to the piles, as shown in Fig. 7.26 (*a*). Where the fill is underlain by a compressible stratum as shown in Fig. 7.26 (*b*), the weight of that part of the soft stratum enclosed by the pile group from which the downward movement is sufficient to cause drag-down must be added to the weight of the superimposed fill, since the latter causes the soft clay to consolidate resulting in additional drag-down.

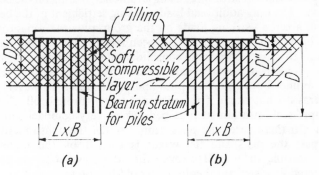

FIG. 7.26. PILE GROUPS IN FILLED GROUND

Thus, in Fig. 7.26 (*a*)—
Total load on pile group at level of bearing stratum,

$$Q_1 = \text{Working load} + L \times B \times \gamma'D' \qquad (7.17)$$

where  $\gamma'$ = density of fill

  $D'$ = depth of fill over which the movement is sufficient to cause drag-down.

In Fig. 7.26 (*b*)—
Total load on pile group at level of bearing stratum,

$$Q_2 = \text{Working load} + L \times B \times \gamma'D' + L \times B \times \gamma''D''$$
$$. \quad . \quad . \ (7.18)$$

where  $\gamma''$ = density of soft stratum

  $D''$ = depth of soft stratum over which movement is sufficient to cause drag-down.

However, total load on pile group will not exceed ultimate skin friction on piles from fill and soft clay, i.e.

$$Q_2 \text{ will not exceed working load} + S_1f' + S_2f'' \quad . \quad (7.19)$$

where $S_1$ = sum of surface area of piles embedded in fill

  $S_2$ = sum of surface area of piles embedded in soft clay

  $f'$ = skin friction between fill and piles

  $f''$ = skin friction between soft clay and piles.

The consolidation settlement of the bearing stratum due to loads imposed by the pile group should be calculated on the basis of the working load on the group plus the maximum load transferred on to the piles from the fill only. Thus, in Fig. 7.26 (*b*) there is no increase in weight of the soft stratum causing additional loading on the bearing stratum. The only additional loads causing settlement of the bearing stratum are the working loads on the group plus the weight of the fill. This assumes that the fill has been recently placed and has not had time to cause appreciable consolidation of the underlying strata.

The problem of negative skin friction from the consolidation of filling applies both to driven piles and bored piles. However, these problems do not occur if the piles are taken through fill on to an incompressible stratum such as bedrock or very compact sand and gravel. In these cases the piles cannot settle, the consolidating fill slips past the piles, and its weight is carried by the underlying incompressible stratum. However, the drag-down effect on the pile considered as a structural column should not be neglected.

### The Design of Axially Loaded Piles Considered as Columns

Piles embedded wholly in the ground need not be considered as long columns for the purposes of structural design. Where, however, they project above the ground as in the case of jetties or piled trestles, the portion above the ground or the sea or river bed must be considered as a column and it is then necessary to consider their effective length and conditions of end fixity. The *Code of Practice for Foundations CP 2004* makes the following recommendations—

(*a*) In good ground the lower point of contraflexure can be taken as about 1 m below the ground surface.

(*b*) When the top stratum is soft clay or silt, this point may be taken at about half the depth of penetration into this stratum, but not necessarily more than 3 m.

(*c*) A stratum of liquid mud should be treated as if it were water.

Reduction factors for working stresses in piles acting as columns for various ratios of effective length to least radius of gyration are shown in Table 7.2.

### Piles Resisting Uplift

In certain circumstances, piles are required to resist uplift forces, such as in foundations to structures subject to considerable overturning moment, for example tall chimneys, transmission towers, or jetty structures. Resistance to uplift is given by the friction between the pile and the surrounding soil; it may be increased in the case of bored piles by "under-reaming" or belling-out the bottom of the piles, or by the bulb end of a driven and cast-in-place pile. A method of calculating the uplift resistance of piles with enlarged bases has been established by Meyerhof and Adams.[7.34] Various published test results have indicated that the skin frictional resistance of piles to uplift loads is appreciably lower than that mobilized in resistance to compression loading. A reduction of 50 per cent has been suggested for granular soils and the same order of reduction for long-term sustained loading for clays. The latter reduction is particularly significant for short piles due to relaxation of stresses induced in the

**Table 7.2**

**REDUCTION FACTORS FOR PILES ACTING AS COLUMNS**

| Ratio of effective length to least radius of gyration | Timber (1) | Rein-forced concrete (2) | Steel to B.S. 15 (3) | Steel to B.S. 548 (3) | Steel to B.S. 968 (3) | Cast iron (4) |
|---|---|---|---|---|---|---|
| 0 | 1·00 | — | 1·00 | 1·00 | 1·00 | 1·13 |
| 10 | 0·98 | — | 0·95 | 0·94 | 0·94 | 0·94 |
| 20 | 0·95 | — | 0·89 | 0·87 | 0·88 | 0·80 |
| 30 | 0·93 | — | 0·84 | 0·81 | 0·82 | 0·64 |
| 40 | 0·89 | — | 0·78 | 0·75 | 0·75 | 0·50 |
| 50 | 0·82 | 1·00 | 0·73 | 0·68 | 0·69 | 0·39 |
| 60 | 0·72 | 0·88 | 0·68 | 0·62 | 0·63 | 0·31 |
| 70 | 0·61 | 0·76 | 0·62 | 0·56 | 0·57 | — |
| 80 | 0·50 | 0·67 | 0·57 | 0·49 | 0·51 | — |
| 90 | 0·41 | 0·59 | 0·51 | 0·43 | 0·44 | — |
| 100 | 0·34 | 0·52 | 0·46 | 0·37 | 0·38 | — |
| 110 | 0·28 | — | 0·41 | 0·32 | 0·33 | — |
| 120 | 0·24 | — | 0·36 | 0·27 | 0·29 | — |
| 130 | 0·21 | — | 0·32 | 0·24 | 0·25 | — |

(1) *CP 112: The structural use of timber in buildings.*
(2) *CP 114: The structural use of normal reinforced concrete in buildings.*
(3) *CP 113: The structural use of steel in buildings.*
(4) Recommendation of the British Cast Iron Research Association.

soil during installation. Therefore the appropriate safety factor should be applied to the skin friction values calculated by the methods described earlier in this chapter, and if the uplift load on piles necessitates mobilization of skin friction approaching the ultimate values, it will be advisable to carry out uplift tests on selected full-scale piles to ensure that there is an adequate safety factor against the pile pulling out of the ground. The uplift resistance in shaft friction given by sands or gravels will be of a low order and should be neglected if piles driven to a small depth of penetration are subjected to vibration. Jetty and wharf structures are subjected to lateral forces from berthing ships and from wave action. If these forces are transferred to supporting piles the resulting lateral movement of the upper part of the embedded length of the piles may destroy most of the skin friction, for example an enlarged hole may be formed if the piles are embedded in stiff clays. This progressive deterioration in uplift resistance due to skin friction will not be reflected by a pull-out test made soon after driving; therefore, a generous safety factor on the ultimate pull-out load should be adopted for piles carrying both lateral and uplift loads.

### Anchoring Piles to Rock

Piles driven to rock, although they have a high bearing resistance, may have a low uplift resistance if they are driven through soft or loose materials to a small penetration into rock. Thus, if a pile is driven only a few feet into hard rock it will so shatter the material around the pile that uplift resistance will be negligible and due almost wholly to friction in debris and the overburden soil. The uplift resistance may be increased by driving a large diameter hole deep into the rock and concreting or grouting the pile into this hole or socket or, in the case of hollow tube or box piles or bored piles, by

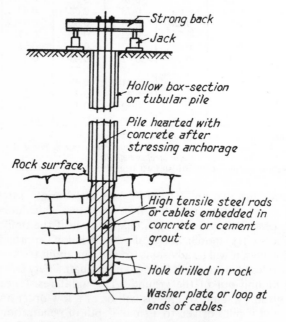

FIG. 7.27. PRESTRESSING ANCHORAGE TO TENSION PILE

drilling a deep hole into the rock at the bottom of the pile, followed by concreting in steel rods or cables made up from high-tensile wires lowered into the drilled hole (Fig. 7.27).

The uplift resistance of this type of anchorage is given by—

(*a*) The tensile strength of the anchor rods or cables;

(*b*) The bond resistance between the rods or cables and the concrete or grout which surrounds them;

(*c*) The bond resistance between the concrete or grout and the surrounding rock;

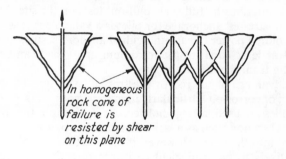

(*a*)                    (*b*)

FIG. 7.28. FAILURE OF ANCHOR PILES DUE TO UPLIFT OF CONE OF ROCK
(*a*) Single pile.
(*b*) Group of piles.

(*d*) The dead weight (or submerged weight if the anchorage is below water level) of a cone of rock which must be lifted by the anchor if failure does not occur by (*a*), (*b*), or (*c*). The typical shape of a cone failure of a single pile anchorage is shown in Fig. 7.28 (*a*).

The uplift resistance given by (*a*), (*b*), or (*c*) can be determined by experiment or by calculations based on the known properties of the steel, concrete, or grout. If the surface of the anchor rod is roughened or if the rod has a hook or washer at its lower end, then anchor to grout failure should not theoretically occur. However, experiments made by the author's firm showed that steel to grout failure took place under these conditions by the grout flowing plastically around the washer or projections on the rod. This type of yielding took place before any grout to rock failure. The bond stress at failure between smooth rods and grout was about 2 N/mm² increasing to about 5·5 N/mm² between roughened rods and grout. These results indicate that an allowable bond stress of at least 0·7 N/mm² can safely be used for deformed anchor bars provided with an end hook or washer. For bars set in concrete the normal design requirements for embedment should be followed. With regard to (*d*) above the estimation of the angle and depth of the cone for the purpose of calculating its weight is largely a matter of judgment based on experience. A 30° half-angle is likely to be on the conservative side but the shape of the cone is dependent on the friability, bedding and joint planes, and angle of dip of the rock. Uplift of a cone of rock is unlikely to occur in a dense homogeneous rock, because of the high resistance in shear given by the surface of the cone. However, this type of failure may take place in a heavily jointed or shattered rock. Where uplift on anchorages is a critical factor in design, it is advisable to check the design assumptions by full-scale pull-out tests on the site. The adoption of pre-stressed anchorage for piles is a valuable means of checking the holding power of each individual anchorage since a prestressing load at least equal to the maximum uplift load can be applied by jacking from the top of the pile.

A disadvantage of the rod or prestressed cable type of anchorage is the risk of corrosion particularly in marine work. If large-diameter hollow piles are used, a large hole can be drilled into the rock and a heavy steel section such as a large-diameter bar or rail section can be concreted into the hole. However, if the aperture in the pile is small there is likely to be insufficient clearance to enable concrete to be used to surround the anchor, which must then be grouted in. Neat cement grout of a consistency which can be pumped through a small diameter pipe is of necessity a weak material in comparison with concrete.

If the anchorage is not prestressed, the anchor rod or cable need only extend for sufficient height up the pile to develop the required strength in bond between the inner surface of the pile and the concrete or grout. However, if prestressing is used the cables must be carried up the pile to enable them to be stressed using the top of the pile as the reaction for the jack. It is then necessary to protect the cable with a plastic sheath or with concrete or cement grout. If space is adequate, concrete placed by tremie pipe is preferable to grouting. Another method is to place a perforated pipe in the pile for its full depth, then to surround this pipe with clean single sized aggregate, say 50 to 25 mm stone. The interstices of the stone are then filled by grouting with cement through a flexible pipe which is lowered down for the full depth of the perforated pipe then slowly withdrawn.

If uplift piles are placed in a group, allowance should be made for the overlapping of the individual uplift cones in heavily jointed or broken rock formations, and the anchorages of the group should be deep enough to ensure that there is sufficient weight in the cone of rock encompassing the whole group (Fig. 7.28 (*b*)).

Uplift on piles used as foundations to light structures on swelling clay soils has been described on page 161.

## Piles Subjected to Horizontal or Inclined Loads

Foundation piles are frequently required to carry inclined loads which are the resultant of the dead load of the structure and horizontal loads from wind, water pressure, or earth pressure on the structure. Where the horizontal component of the load on the piles is small in relation to the vertical load, it can be carried safely by vertical piles. Thus, special provision is not usually made in piled foundations to buildings for the horizontal loading resulting from wind pressure.

However, in the case of piles in wharves and jetties carrying the impact forces of berthing ships, and piled foundations to bridge piers, trestles to overhead travelling cranes, tall chimneys and retaining walls, the horizontal component is relatively large and vertical piles cannot generally be relied on to withstand the horizontal forces. Raking or batter piles have a very much higher resistance to horizontal loading since a large proportion of the horizontal component is carried axially by the pile. Typical arrangements of raker piles are shown in Fig. 7.29 (*a*) to (*d*).

In the case of the retaining wall (*a*), the earth pressure always acts in the same direction and forward raking piles only are required to carry the horizontal loading, while vertical piles are provided to support the dead weight of the wall and vertical forces transmitted to the back of the wall by the retained earth. Horizontal forces in the bridge trestle (*b*) are caused by braking and traction of the moving loads. These forces are reversible in direction and raking piles in two directions are required. If the bridge pier is in a deep fast-flowing river the pressure from the water may require rakers in a direction transverse to the line of the bridge. Horizontal forces in the piled wharf (*c*) are caused by the impact of berthing ships and by wave action and are high in relation to the dead load of the superstructure requiring a large number of raking piles. The tie rod supporting the earth forces on the sheet pile retaining wall in (*d*) is always in tension, but a combination of forward and backward rakers is provided in the anchorage in cases where the load would be too much for a single pile. A large pile cap is provided to counteract the uplift on the backward raker.

Where the lateral loading is intermittent, as in the case of piles to wharves and jetties or in bridge trestles, the full value of skin friction on the shaft should not be allowed when calculating the resistance to axial loading along the pile. Thus, where short piles are driven into stiff clays the deflexion and rebound under intermittent loading will result in an enlarged hole for the pile reducing the friction to a negligible amount, and the resistance to axial loading should be calculated on end-bearing only. Where the piles are in soft clays, silts, or sands and gravels, the soil will partially close around the pile if the frequency of loading is low; thus the remoulded shear strength of clays or silts

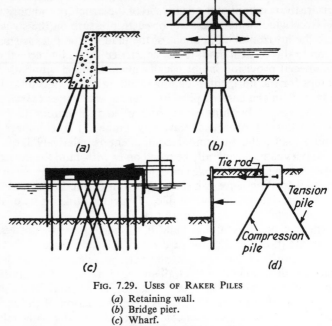

FIG. 7.29. USES OF RAKER PILES
(a) Retaining wall.
(b) Bridge pier.
(c) Wharf.
(d) Sheet pile retaining wall.

may be used for the skin friction, and a low value of skin friction in sands and gravel should be adopted. The required value may be obtained from pulling tests when the skin friction should be calculated from the load required to maintain steady upward movement of the pile. Where short raking piles are carrying vibrating loads in soft silts and clays or cohesionless soils, skin friction will be negligible and the end-bearing resistance only should be used to carry the axial loading. Higher values of skin friction may be allowed in the case of long piles because vibrations or lower frequency movements will be, for the most part, absorbed in the upper embedded parts of the piles.

The resistance of rakers to the axial loads caused by lateral loading is often a critical factor in design since small yielding might result in serious tilting of a structure. Driving piles to batters of 1 in 3 or 1 in 4 is common, but driving to angles flatter than 1 in 2 is a difficult procedure, and is impossible for bored or driven and cast-in-place piles. It is therefore necessary to provide a larger number of rakers driven to a small batter. Wherever possible, raking piles carrying compression loads should be driven to a hard unyielding stratum.

### Calculation of Resistance of Piles to Inclined Loading

The resistance to failure of piles subjected to horizontal loading is given by the passive resistance of a wedge of soil in front of the piles (Fig. 7.30 (*a*)) and in the case of raking piles, additional resistance is given by skin friction and end-bearing (Fig. 7.30 (*b*)). Methods of calculating this resistance or the deflexion of piles under a given inclined load are described by Broms.[7.35] The required factor of safety is governed by the allowable horizontal deflexion of the

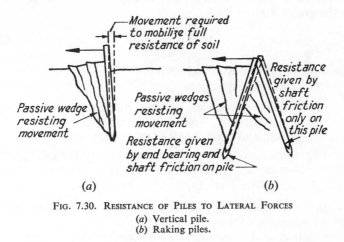

FIG. 7.30. RESISTANCE OF PILES TO LATERAL FORCES
(*a*) Vertical pile.
(*b*) Raking piles.

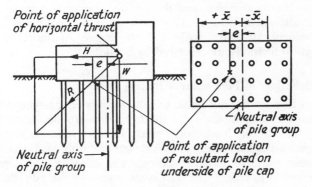

FIG. 7.31

structure. The allowable movement may be quite large in the case of temporary structures or tied retaining walls, but only small movements can be tolerated in such structures as tied abutments to bridges or in tall structures where tilting is undesirable. The deflexion of a pile under an inclined load is dependent on the elasticity and compressibility of the soil and the rigidity of the pile itself. It is always advisable to check the design assumptions by full-scale lateral loading tests on the site. These can be done simply and comparatively cheaply by pulling a pair of piles together or pushing them apart. The deflexions should preferably be measured at two or more points on the pile shaft to obtain the curvature of the pile.

In the group of vertical piles shown in Fig. 7.31, the vertical component ($V$) of the load on any pile from the resultant load ($R$) on the group is given by—

$$V = \frac{W}{n} + \frac{We\bar{x}}{\Sigma\bar{x}^2} \qquad . \qquad . \qquad . \qquad . \quad (7.20)$$

where $W$ = total vertical load on pile group

$n$ = number of piles in group

$e$ = distance between point of intersection of resultant of vertical and horizontal loading with underside of pile cap, and neutral axis of pile group

$\bar{x}$ = distance between pile and neutral axis of pile group; $\bar{x}$ is positive when measured in the same direction as $e$ and negative when in the opposite direction.

The above equation is applicable only when the resultant load ($R$) cuts the underside of the pile cap.

Calculation of the compressive and tensile forces on a group of raking piles or combined vertical and raking piles under inclined loading is very complex, and there is no established procedure with any sound theoretical basis, since a piled foundation is a three-dimensional structure with a high degree of indeterminancy. Analytical methods are described by Bowles.[7.36]

### The Behaviour of Piles under Vibrating Loads

Piles in clays are not liable to settlement when carrying vibrating loads, other than that due to the normal consolidation of the soil under the working load on the piles. However, there is a likelihood of severe settlement when piles carrying vibrating loads are bearing on loose or medium-dense sands. The effect of the machinery vibrations is to reduce the skin friction around the pile thus transferring load to the toe. The vibrating load on the toe causes further compaction of the sand below the toe with consequent settlement. The risks of settlement are much greater in the case of bored and cast-in-place piles than with driven piles, since the former method does not compact the soil. Indeed, the effect of boring the hole for the pile may result in loosening of the sand.

Investigations were made by Dodge and Swiger[7.37] into the effect of vibrations on test piles driven into medium-loose silty sands and silts at the General Electric Company's plant at Schenectady, N.Y. At this site, tilting of precision tools was attributed to vibrations from heavy overhead travelling cranes. Various types of piles driven into the sand were tested by subjecting them to a dead load on to which was imposed vibrations of varying frequency for different periods of time. The piles tested were a composite driven pipe and cast-in-place concrete pile, a composite pipe pile, a composite wood and driven and cast-in-place concrete pile, and a cased concrete pedestal pile. All but the last-mentioned type showed settlement under the static load and further settlement on vibration. Varying the frequency showed that the piles had a resonant frequency between 500 and 600 cycles per minute at which the amplitude was a maximum. For the composite pipe pile and the composite wood and concrete pile, the maximum amplitude at resonant frequency was about 0·09 mm.

The pedestal pile installed by the method described on page 518 was driven through about 6 m of soft sandy clay, 6 m of medium loose fine silty sand, followed by 3 m of silty coarse sand and gravel. The pile settled about 8 mm under a static load of 1112 kN but there was no further settlement under vibrations with a 534 kN load. Dodge and Swiger concluded that the superior performance of the pedestal pile was due to the increased end area reducing the bearing pressure at the toe as compared to the straight-sided piles, or to the increased compaction of the sand caused by forming the pedestal, or to both of these causes. However, they were of the opinion that any type of pile bearing on the sand stratum would be liable to settlement under long-continuing vibratory loads. Consequently, the foundations of precision machine tools, turbine test platforms, and heavy crane columns were carried by long steel piles driven through the sands on to rock or hardpan. Pedestal piles bearing on the sand were used for the office buildings, some machine tools, and lightly loaded crane columns.

## FOUNDATIONS OF GEAR-CUTTING ESTABLISHMENT, CLYDEBANK

A similar problem to the Schenectady factory was given by the foundations of the gear-cutting establishment at John Brown & Co.'s shipyard at Clydebank. The machines to be installed comprised a 216 in. shaving machine, a 216 in. hobbing machine, a 100 in. shaving machine, and a 100 in. hobbing machine, together with smaller gear grinding, shaving, and meshing machines. The 216 in. machines were designed to handle gear wheels up to 130 tonne in mass. The machines were set to operate to an accuracy of 0·008 mm and so sensitive were they to atmospheric conditions that each machine was installed in a separate enclosure controlled to constant temperature and humidity. Small settlements would have been detrimental to their proper functioning and the vibration problems were complicated by the proximity of other machinery installations in the shipyard and traffic vibrations from the nearby Glasgow–Dumbarton road. The soil conditions comprised about 2·7 m of loose fill and soft clay overlying 15 m of loose to medium-dense sand followed by stiff boulder clay. To minimize the effect of vibrations from surrounding sources it was decided to construct each machine on a separate massive 3·7 m deep concrete base and all the bases were to be enclosed in a reinforced concrete basement structure. The bases were isolated from each other and from the basement by an air-gap at least 0·46 m wide (Figs. 7.32 and 7.33).

It was necessary to support the basement structure on pile foundations, since the settlements under the dead load of the machinery and bases and additional settlements caused by vibration from the machines themselves would have been excessive due to the looseness of the upper layers of the sand stratum. It was thought undesirable to terminate the piles in the sand because of the likely long-term settlement under vibration loads transmitted to it by the piles. Accordingly, 15 m long steel box piles were driven open-ended through the sand to a satisfactory set in the stiff boulder clay. This type of pile was selected for its penetrating ability and also the sand inside the piles could, if necessary, have been cleared out and driving facilitated by jetting from within the pile, if refusal had been met within the sand stratum. However, by using a double-acting steam hammer for driving, all the piles reached the boulder clay without difficulty or recourse to jetting.

Because of limitations of headroom, the same type of pile could not be used for the foundations of the building enclosing the plant. The building columns also carried a heavy overhead travelling crane. For these foundations a driven and cast-in-place concrete pile with an enlarged base (Franki pile) was adopted. These piles were driven to a penetration of about 4·6 m into the sand stratum. Experiences elsewhere on the shipyard had shown that these piles could carry moderate loadings, including loads from travelling cranes, in similar soil conditions and without appreciable settlement. Also, vibrations caused in driving these piles did not result in settlement of closely

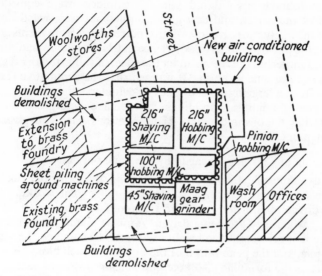

FIG. 7.32. LAYOUT OF GEAR-CUTTING MACHINERY, JOHN BROWN & CO., CLYDEBANK

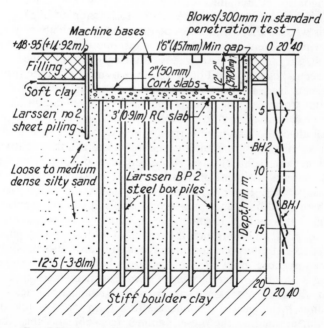

FIG. 7.33. SECTION THROUGH MACHINERY FOUNDATIONS

431

adjacent foundations. Bored piles or cylinders were considered instead of the driven and cast-in-place piles but were ruled out in view of the likely excessive loss of ground resulting from forming the hole for the pile or cylinder. Experience in trial boreholes had shown that sand surged up the casing under the effect of sub-artesian pressure of water in the sand stratum. It was felt that the cumulative loss of ground from a large number of piles or cylinders might have caused settlement of adjoining buildings. A detailed description of the gear-cutting establishment and its foundations has been given by McLaughlin.[7.38]

### Calculation of Carrying Capacity by Dynamic Formulae

All dynamic pile formulae are based on the principle that the resistance of piles to further penetration under their working load has a direct relationship to their resistance to the impact of the hammer when they are being driven. Thus, dynamic formulae take into account the weight and height of drop of the hammer, the weight of the pile, and the penetration of the pile under each blow. Refined variants of the formulae also take into account losses of energy due to elastic compression of the pile, the helmet, the packing, the ground surrounding the pile, and losses due to the inertia of the pile. The protagonists of dynamic formulae claim that they have a sound theoretical basis since they are related to Newtonian impact theory. If this were so there would not be the great multiplicity of formulae all giving different answers for the same conditions and it would not be necessary to introduce so many empirical constants. The physical characteristics of the soil do not appear in most dynamic formulae. This can lead to dangerous misinterpretation of the results of dynamic formulae calculations since they represent conditions at the time of driving. They do not take into account the soil conditions which affect the long-term carrying capacity and settlement of piles, such as effects of remoulding and re-consolidation, negative skin friction, and group effects. For example, a dynamic pile formula might show a low value of resistance for a long pile driven deep into a sensitive clay. However, tests have shown that the carrying capacity in these conditions increases progressively for some months after driving. It is unusual to undertake re-driving tests a month after first driving piles, and even then the results of re-driving tests might not be capable of interpretation since the driving resistance again falls to a low value after only a few blows of the hammer. The time effects on piles driven into fine silty sands have been mentioned on page 384. Again, these are not taken into account by dynamic formulae. Finally, dynamic formulae are inapplicable to certain types of pile driving equipment such as the diesel hammer (p. 465) and the vibratory pile driver (p. 469). In fact, obsession with dynamic formulae may have inhibited the development of these efficient forms of pile driving.

Consideration of the resistance to the driving of piles is of importance in ground conditions where there may be a risk of breakage during driving. Using the procedure described by Smith,[7.39] it is possible to calculate the maximum height of drop for a given weight of hammer to avoid overstressing the pile. This procedure is based on the stress-wave theory.

It must not be thought that driving resistance observations should not be made on test piles and permanent piles. It is most important that records of blows per 0·2 or 0·5 m of penetration should be kept for *every pile* driven. These records are a valuable check on the designer's assumption of the sequence of the soil strata and they ensure that a bearing stratum of satisfactory resistance has been reached. The driving resistance diagrams should be compared with any available records of static or dynamic penetration tests or shear strength–depth diagrams.

PROCEDURE IN CORRELATING STATIC METHODS OF CALCULATING PILE RESISTANCE WITH DRIVING RECORDS

The following steps should be followed at the design test piling and permanent piling stages—

1. DESIGN STAGE. Calculate the ultimate carrying capacity of the piles or pile group by static methods based on soil conditions as found by borings and laboratory tests, taking into account time-effects, group-effects, and long-term settlement.

2. TEST PILING STAGE. Test piles may be driven and loaded before full-scale construction commences on a site, or the first of the permanent piles may be used as test piles and their length or working load modified in the light of the test results. The driving equipment used for the test piles should be the same as that proposed for the permanent piles. The driving resistance in blows per 0·2 to 0·5 m should be obtained throughout the full depth of penetration and the results should then be checked with records of adjacent boreholes. This will ensure that the required design depth of penetration into the main bearing stratum has been achieved. The stiffness or density of the bearing stratum can also be related to the driving resistance at any given depth.

Loading tests are always justifiable if the number of piles to be driven is large, but the relatively high cost may not be justified for a small number of piles. If possible, test piles should be loaded to failure so that the actual safety factor of the working load may be established. The procedure for making pile driving and loading tests is given on pages 474 to 479. Pile loading tests are not required when piles are driven to refusal on to rock or other hard strata, unless the working loads are to be exceptionally heavy and approach the ultimate bearing capacity of the rock or unless the pile itself is suspected to be in a defective condition.

As a result of loading tests the engineer may decide to reduce or increase the depth of penetration of the pile into the bearing stratum.

3. CONSTRUCTION STAGE. Unless piles are driven to refusal on a hard stratum the driving resistance for the full depth of penetration should be measured on all the permanent piles to check possible changes in level or characteristics of the bearing stratum. The measured driving resistances should be compared to those obtained for the test pile. If they are appreciably lower the piles should be driven deeper until the driving resistances reach the values obtained for the test pile.

## EXAMPLES ON CHAPTER 7

### EXAMPLE 7.1

An isolated 350 × 350 mm reinforced concrete pile in a jetty structure is required to carry a maximum compression load of 400 kN and a net uplift load of 320 kN. The soil consists of a loose to medium-dense saturated fine sand (average $N = 15$ blows per 0·3 m) extending to a depth of 9 m below sea bed followed by dense sand and gravel (average $N = 40$ blows per 0·3 m). Determine the required depth of penetration of the pile. No erosion is expected.

Volume displacement of pile $= V = 0·35^2 \times 1 = 0·122$ m$^3$/m.

From sea bed to 9 m penetration:

For $N$ value of 15, $\phi = 31°$ (from Fig. 1.14)

From Fig. 7.5 (a), $\delta/\phi = 0·85$, giving $\delta = 0·85 \times 31° = 26°$.

Interpolating between Figs. 7.5 (c) and (d), for $V = 0·122$, $\phi = 31°$ and $\omega = 0°$, $K_\delta = 1·35$.

From Fig. 7.5 (f), for $\delta = 0·85$, correction factor for $K_\delta = 0·95$.

Therefore corrected $K_\delta = 0·95 \times 1·35 = 1·3$.

From equation 7.5, total skin friction from sea bed to 9 m

$= 1·3 \times \frac{1}{2} (0 + 9) \times (1·75 - 1) \times \sin 26°$
$\qquad\qquad\qquad\qquad\qquad \times 4 \times 0·35 \times 9 \times 9·807$ kN

$= 238$ kN

It will be desirable to take a safety factor of 1·5 against failure in uplift because of the possible reduced skin friction in uplift resistance.

Therefore, required ultimate uplift load = 800 kN.

It will be necessary to drive the pile into the dense sand and gravel to a sufficient depth to mobilize an ultimate uplift resistance of $800 - 238 = 562$ kN.

From 9 to 10 m below sea bed—

For $N$ value of 40, $\phi = 38\cdot5°$

From Fig. 7.5 (*a*), $\delta = 0\cdot85 \times 38\cdot5 = 33°$.

Interpolating between Figs. 7.5 (*d*) and (*e*), we get $K_\delta = 2\cdot5$.

From Fig. 7.5 (*f*), correction factor for $K_\delta = 0\cdot9$.

Therefore, corrected $K_\delta = 0\cdot9 \times 2\cdot5 = 2\cdot2$.

Therefore, unit skin friction from 9 to 10 m

$$= 2\cdot2 \times \tfrac{1}{2}(9 + 10) \times (2\cdot0 - 1\cdot0) \times \sin 33° \times 9\cdot807$$
$$= 111\cdot6 \text{ kN/m}^2$$

Ultimate skin friction per m $= 4 \times 0\cdot35 \times 111\cdot6$

$$= 156 \text{ kN/m}$$

Therefore, required penetration into dense sand and gravel $= 562/156$ $= 3\cdot6$ m.

Calculating the end resistance of the pile at 12·6 m depth below sea bed—

For $\phi = 38\cdot5°$, Fig. 7.4 gives $N_q = 115$.

From equation 7.4 (base resistance only)

$$Q'_b = A_b p_d N_q = 0\cdot35^2 \times (9 \times 0\cdot75 + 3\cdot6 \times 1\cdot0) \times 115 \times 9\cdot807$$
$$= 1430 \text{ kN}$$

Therefore total pile resistance $= 1430 + 800 = 2230$ kN

Factor of safety on compression load $= \dfrac{2230}{400} = 5\cdot5$

which is ample, and indicates that the required penetration depth of the pile is governed by considerations of uplift resistance.

EXAMPLE 7.2

A step-tapered steel pile having a tip diameter of 200 mm and a diameter at sea bed level of 400 mm is driven into the same soil strata as given in Example 1. Calculate the ultimate resistance of the pile driven to 13 m below sea-bed level.

For the given taper, tan $\omega = 0.0088$.

At a depth of 9 m, $V = \dfrac{\pi}{4} \times (0.26)^2 \times 1 = 0.053 \text{ m}^3/\text{m}$.

From Fig. 7.5 (a), $\delta/\phi = 0.75$, giving $\delta = 0.75 \times 31° = 23°$.

Interpolating between Figs. 7.5 (c) and (d), for $V = 0.053$, $\phi = 31°$ and tan $\omega = 0.0088$, $K_\delta = 3.3$.

From Fig. 7.5 (f), corrected $K_\delta = 0.9 \times 3.3 = 3.0$.

Therefore total skin friction from 0 to 9 m

$= 3.0 \times \frac{1}{2}(0 + 9) \times 0.75 \times \sin 23° \times \pi \times 0.33 \times 9 \times 9.807$

$= 362 \text{ kN}$

At a depth of 13 m $V = \dfrac{\pi}{4} \times (0.20)^2 \times 1 = 0.031 \text{ m}^3/\text{m}$

From Fig. 7.5 (a), $\delta/\phi = 0.6$, giving $\delta = 0.6 \times 38.5° = 23.1°$.

Interpolating between Figs 7.5 (d) and (e), we get $K_\delta = 14$.

From Fig. 7.5 (f), corrected $K_\delta = 0.7 \times 14 = 9.8$.

Therefore total skin friction from 9 to 13 m depth

$= 9.8 \times \frac{1}{2}(9 + 13) \times 1.0 \times 9.807 \times \sin 23.1° \times \pi \times 0.231 \times 4$

$= 1204 \text{ kN}$.

(This gives a unit skin friction higher than 110 kN/m², but high values are possible with tapered piles.)

From equation 7.4 (base resistance only)

$Q'_b = A_b p_a N_q = \dfrac{\pi}{4} \times 0.20^2 \times (9 \times 0.75 + 4.0 \times 1.0) \times 9.807 \times 115$

$= 381 \text{ kN}$.

Ultimate pile resistance $= 362 + 1204 + 381 = \underline{\underline{1947 \text{ kN}}}$

EXAMPLE 7.3

A borehole and static cone penetration test gave the results shown in Fig. 7.34. An isolated B.S.P. cased pile is required to carry a safe working load of 500 kN in compression. Determine the required diameter and penetration of the pile.

We will use the method of Van der Veen (p. 382), which requires a safety factor of 2·5 to ensure that settlements are kept within tolerable limits.

Therefore required ultimate pile resistance $= 50 \times 2\cdot5 = 125$ tons

From Table 8.7, a B.S.P. cased pile of 16·288 in. o.d. is required to carry a working load of 50 tons without overstressing the concrete filling to the casing tube. If as a first step the pile is regarded as wholly end-bearing—

$$\text{Ultimate end bearing pressure} = \frac{1250}{\frac{\pi}{4} \times 0\cdot414^2} = 9300 \text{ kN/m}^2$$

$$= 94\cdot8 \text{ kg/cm}^2$$

It will be seen from Fig. 7.34 that we cannot get this end resistance in the loose sand from 0 to 11·6 m below ground level. It will be necessary to drive the pile about 1·5 m into the dense sand layer to ensure that the pile has been properly seated in this layer. From Fig. 7.34, the average cone resistance over a distance of 3 pile diameters above the pile point and one diameter below the point is 120 kg/cm².

Therefore ultimate end bearing resistance of pile

$$= \frac{\pi}{4} \times 0\cdot414^2 \times 120 \times \frac{1}{0\cdot0102}$$

$$= 1584 \text{ kN}$$

From equation 7.6, skin friction from 0 to 11·6 m

$$= \frac{\text{average cone resistance}}{2} \text{ kN/m}^2$$

$$= \frac{40}{2} \text{ kN/m}^2 \text{ (from Fig. 7.34)}$$

Therefore total skin friction from 0 to 11·6 m

$$= \pi \times 0\cdot414 \times 11\cdot6 \times \frac{40}{2} = 302 \text{ kN}$$

The average cone resistance from 11·6 to 13·1 m is 120 kg/cm²

$$\text{Therefore total skin friction} = \pi \times 0\cdot414 \times 1\cdot5 \times \frac{120}{2}$$

$$= 117 \text{ kN,}$$

Therefore total ultimate resistance on pile = 1584 + 302 + 117
$$= 2003 \text{ kN}$$

Safety factor $= \dfrac{2003}{500} = 4 \cdot 0$

This is higher than necessary but it will not be possible to terminate the pile at an appreciably higher level. However, if the driving

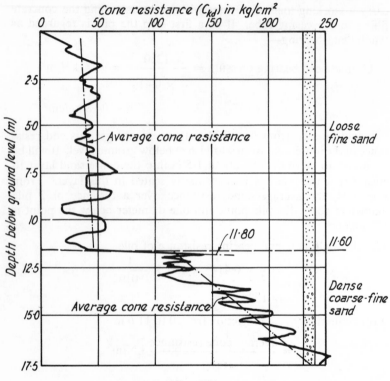

Fig. 7.34

records indicated refusal or near refusal of further driving at say 12·5 m depth this could be accepted.

EXAMPLE 7.4

Determine the required penetration of a 1 m diameter steel pile driven with a closed end into the stratum of dense sand shown in Fig. 7.34 to obtain a bearing resistance on the end of the pile equal to the cone resistance.

Using De Beer's graphical method described on page 384, it will be seen from Fig. 7.34 that the cone develops its full resistance from the "surface" condition to the fully developed condition of 140 kg/cm² from 11·6 m to 11·8 m below ground level, i.e. a vertical depth of 0·2 m.

Then the vertical depth below the top of the dense stratum to obtain an ultimate resistance on a 1 m pile at least equal to 140 kg/cm² is 1·0/0·036 × 0·2 = 5·55 m or 17·15 m below ground level. At this depth the average cone resistance has increased to 250 kg/cm², or 24 510 kN/m². Using the latter value, the ultimate carrying capacity of the pile, assuming it to be virtually end bearing is $\frac{1}{4}\pi$ × 1·0² × 24 510 = 19 300 kN.

A safety factor of $2\frac{1}{2}$ gives an allowable load of 7720 kN on the pile. For a safe working stress of 210 N/mm² on the steel, the required wall thickness is 12 mm.

EXAMPLE 7.5

A jetty is sited on 4·5 m of very soft clayey silt overlying stiff to very stiff clay. Tests on undisturbed samples gave the shear strength/depth relationship shown in Fig. 7.35. For structural reasons it is

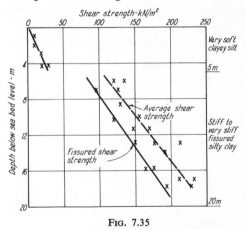

FIG. 7.35

desired to use 500 mm steel tube piles. Determine the required penetration to carry a safe working load of 400 kN.

Because of lateral movements in the jetty structure due to berthing forces, wind and wave action, it will be advisable to ignore the skin friction in the very soft clayey silt. Take as a first trial a penetration length of 13 m below sea bed level. From Fig. 7.35, the average shear strength from 5 to 13 m = 140 kN/m². Fissured shear strength at 13 m = 145 kN/m².

It will be seen from Fig. 7.10 that the adhesion factor corresponding to an average shear strength of 140 kN/m², soft clay over stiff clay,

and $\dfrac{L}{B} = \dfrac{8}{0\cdot5} = 16$ is 0·50.

Therefore, from equation 7.9, total skin friction on portion of shaft in stiff clay is

$$0\cdot50 \times 140 \times 8 \times \pi \times 0\cdot5 = 880 \text{ kN}$$

From equation 7.8, net end resistance in fissured stiff clay is

$$9 \times 145 \times \tfrac{1}{4}\pi \times 0\cdot5^2 = 256 \text{ kN}$$

Therefore total pile resistance = 880 + 256 = 1136 kN

Safety factor on working load of 400 kN is 1136/400 = 2.8

This is rather higher than necessary, a safety factor of 2·5 would have been adequate, but before adopting a lesser penetration we must check the safety factor on the lower range of shear strength.

From equation 7.11, and taking the average lowest shear strength along the pile shaft as 110 kN/m²

$$\text{Allowable pile load} = \frac{256}{3} + \frac{0\cdot52 \times 110 \times 8 \times \pi \times 0\cdot5}{1\cdot5}$$
$$= 564 \text{ kN}$$

This is well in excess of the required safe working load, therefore we could consider reducing the penetration below sea bed to about 7 m to maintain a safety factor of at least 2·5 on the combined end and skin friction resistance, subject to a loading test.

### Example 7.6

A precast concrete pile 350 mm square is to be driven into firm, stiff fissured clay. The shear strength/depth relationship is shown in Fig. 7.36. Determine the required penetration of the pile to carry a safe working load of 600 kN.

Taking a trial penetration of 12 m below ground level—

Average shear strength from 0 to 12 m = 100 kN/m²
Fissured shear strength at 12 m      = 110 kN/m²

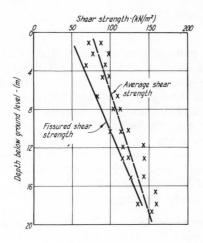

Fig. 7.36

It will be seen from Fig. 7.10 that for no different overlying strata the adhesion factor for an average shear strength of 100 kN/m² and $\dfrac{L}{B} = \dfrac{12}{0\cdot35} = 34$ is 0·8. Therefore, from equation 7·9

Total skin friction on pile shaft is

$$0\cdot8 \times 100 \times 12 \times 4 \times 0\cdot35 = 1344 \text{ kN}$$

From equation 7·8, net end resistance on fissured clay is

$$9 \times 110 \times 0\cdot35^2 = 121 \text{ kN}$$

Therefore, total pile resistance = 1344 + 121 = 1465 kN

The safety factor on a working load of 600 kN is 1465/600 = 2·4, which is satisfactory.

Checking safety factors for possible lower skin friction values and using the cohesion factor corresponding to an average fissured shear strength of 77 kN/m² we get, from equation 7.11,

$$\text{Allowable pile load} = \frac{121}{3} + \frac{0.9 \times 77 \times 12 \times 4 \times 0.35}{1.5}$$
$$= 40 + 776 = 816 \text{ kN, which is satisfactory.}$$

Therefore a penetration of 12 m will be satisfactory.

### EXAMPLE 7.7

A multi-storey building is to be constructed on a stiff to very stiff fissured clay. The shear strength/depth relationship for the full depth of the clay can be taken as being the same as that shown in Fig. 7.35, assuming that the average shear strength curve for the stiff to very stiff clay extends up to ground level. Settlement calculations for the whole pile group beneath the building show that the piles must be taken to a depth of at least 15 m below ground level to keep consolidation settlements within tolerable limits. Determine the required dimensions of a large-diameter bored and cast-in-place pile to carry a column load of 2500 kN and make a preliminary estimate of the elastic settlement at the working load.

Taking an overall load factor of 2, then the required ultimate pile load is 5000 kN. As a first trial take a shaft diameter of 1·0 m and a base diameter of 1·8 m. Because the piles are under-reamed the adhesion factor should not exceed 0·3. We must also deduct 3 m from the overall pile length to allow for the possible loss of adhesion over the under-reamed length and for two shaft diameters above (p. 396).

$$\text{Ultimate shaft load} = 0.3 \times 112 \times 12 \times \pi \times 1.0$$
$$= 1267 \text{ kN}$$

The fissured shear strength at 15 m depth is 162 kN/m².

$$\text{Ultimate base resistance} = 9 \times 162 \times \frac{\pi}{4} \times 1.8^2$$
$$= 3710 \text{ kN}$$

Therefore total pile resistance = 1267 + 3710 = 4967 kN.

This nearly enough satisfies the criterion of an overall load factor of 2 and satisfies the criterion of Burland, Butler and Dunican that the working load should be less than ultimate shaft load + ⅓ ultimate base load which in our case is equal to 1267 + 1240 = 2507 kN.

At the working load, the load on the base of the pile is 2500 − 1267 = 1233 kN. Therefore the pressure on the 1·8 m diameter base is

484 kN/m². From equation 7·12, a preliminary estimate of the immediate (elastic) settlement is

$$\rho_i = 0{\cdot}02 \times 1{\cdot}8 \times 1000 \times \frac{484}{9 \times 162}$$
$$= 12 \text{ mm}$$

This is well within acceptable limits, and on this evidence it would be unnecessary to make plate bearing tests in the pile boreholes to obtain a closer estimate of settlements.

EXAMPLE 7.8

Bored piles are required to support a wall footing carrying a uniformly distributed load of 160 kN per metre run. The soil conditions below ground level consist of 3·7 m of recently placed loose ash fill overlying medium dense angular well graded sand ($N = 25$ blows per 0·3 m). The density of the ash fill is 1·1 Mg/m³. No ground-water level was met in 20 m deep boreholes. Design suitable piled foundations.

It will be reasonable to place the piles in pairs with each pair at 3 m centres giving a working load on each pile of 240 kN.

The piles are too widely spaced for them to act as a group, so it is only necessary to consider the carrying capacity of a single pile. Since the ash fill is loose it is likely to consolidate under its own weight, thus causing drag-down on the pile shaft. Because the skin friction is likely to be small in relation to the end-bearing resistance of the piles it will be sufficiently accurate to use the simpler equation 7.3 which gives conservative values, rather than the more complex Nordlund method.

From equation 7.3 unit skin friction just below top of sandy stratum at 3·7 m depth

$$= \bar{K}_s \gamma d \tan \delta$$

Since withdrawal of the pile tube is likely to loosen the sand we must take from Table 7.1, for loose conditions,

$\bar{K}_s = 1$, $\phi = 33°$, and $\delta = 0{\cdot}75 \times 33° = 24{\cdot}75°$

Therefore, unit skin friction in sand at base of fill

$$= 1 \times 1{\cdot}1 \times 9{\cdot}807 \times 3{\cdot}7 \times \tan 24{\cdot}75°$$
$$= 18{\cdot}4 \text{ kN/m}^2$$

If we assume piles to be 9 m long,

Unit skin friction at toe of piles
$$= 1 \times (1{\cdot}1 \times 3{\cdot}7 + 1{\cdot}9 \times 5{\cdot}3) \times 9{\cdot}807 \times \tan 24{\cdot}75°$$
$$= 63{\cdot}9 \text{ kN/m}^2$$

Assuming 350 mm diameter piles will be required,

Total skin friction in sand

$$= \frac{(18\cdot4 + 63\cdot9)}{2} \times 5\cdot3 \times \pi \times 0\cdot35$$
$$= 240 \text{ kN}$$

We must assume that the boring will loosen the sand somewhat around the pile toe giving $\phi$ say 33°, for which $N_q = 35$ (from curve for $D/B = 20$ in Fig. 7.4).

Therefore from equation 7.4

Total resistance of 350 mm pile

$$= \frac{\pi \times 0\cdot35^2}{4} (1\cdot1 \times 3\cdot7 + 1\cdot9 \times 5\cdot3) \times 9\cdot807 \times 35 + 240$$
$$= 467 + 240$$
$$= 707$$

Because the fill has recently been placed it will still be settling under its own weight at the time the piles are required to carry the wall loading. Therefore negative skin friction must be added to the pile loads. Because the sand beneath the pile toe is incompressible relative to the fill (i.e. assuming that installation of the pile has not loosened the soil beneath the toe) the distribution of negative skin friction on the pile shaft will be roughly the same as that shown in Fig. 7.14 (c). The peak value of skin friction at the base of the fill will be roughly equal to that in the sand at this level.

Therefore if we assume from Fig. 7.14 (c) that the negative skin friction acts over the upper 3.3 m of the shaft only then, at 3.3 m, skin

friction $= \dfrac{3\cdot3}{3\cdot7} \times 18\cdot4 = 16\cdot4$ kN/m² and at ground level it is zero.

Total negative skin friction on upper 3.3 m of pile shaft

$$= \frac{(0 + 16\cdot4)}{2} \times \pi \times 0\cdot35 \times 3\cdot3 = 30 \text{ kN}$$

Safety factor on pile $= \dfrac{707}{240 + 30} = 2\cdot6$

This is just above to the desirable safety factor of 2.5.

Therefore, we can support the walls on pairs of 350 mm piles at 3 m centres. The piles can be spaced at two diameters centre to centre, i.e. at 700 mm centres, requiring a pile cap 1360 by 660 by 500 mm deep.

EXAMPLE 7.9

Bored piles are required to carry a house foundation on a site where stiff fissured clay is affected by seasonal swell and shrinkage movements to a depth of 1·5 m below ground level. The layout of the walls requires a pile spacing of 1·5 m centres when the working load on a single pile beneath the wall will not exceed 65 kN. Below the weathered crust the shear strength of the stiff clay increases from 50 kN/m² at 1·5 m to 200 kN/m² at 10 m (average figures). Determine the required diameter and depth of penetration of the piles.

It will be desirable to keep the pile length within the depth range of a light mechanical auger, i.e. they should not be more than 6 m long. The adhesion in the top 1·5 m from ground level must be ignored since soil shrinkage may cause all adhesion to be lost. Since the piles are relatively short and within the weathered desiccated zone it will be advisable to take only 0·3 × average shear strength in adhesion (p. 393).

For a 350 mm pile 4·5 m long—

Shear strength at 4·5 m depth $= 103$ kN/m²

Average shear strength $= \dfrac{50 + 103}{2} = 76\cdot5$ kN/m²

Total adhesion $= 0\cdot3 \times 76\cdot5 \times \pi \times 0\cdot35 \times 3$

$= 76$ kN

Total end resistance $= 9 \times 103 \times \dfrac{\pi}{4} \times 0\cdot35^2$

$= 89$ kN

Total pile resistance $= 165$ kN

Safety factor $= \dfrac{165}{65} = 2\cdot5$ which is satisfactory.

The real safety factor might be a little lower than this since in calculating the end resistance we took a bearing capacity factor of 9 on the *average* shear strength. Strictly, this factor should be used only on the fissured strength.

EXAMPLE 7.10

A structure weighing (inclusive of the base slab) 30 000 kN has base dimensions of 10 m square. It is to be constructed on a site where boreholes show firm intact clay (average cohesion at 1·5 m below ground level = 40 kN/m²) progressively increasing in shear strength to 240 kN/m² at a depth of 30 m. Design suitable foundations.

From Fig. 2.11 (*d*) the ultimate bearing capacity of the firm clay for a foundation 10 m square by say 1·25 m deep is 6·5 × 40 = 260 kN/m².

This is less than the bearing pressure of $\dfrac{30\,000}{10 \times 10}$ = 300 kN/m². It will

be uneconomical from the structural aspect to increase the size of the foundation, and it will be necessary to take the foundation to a depth of about 15 m before a safety factor of 3 is obtained for a foundation 10 m square. It is clearly a case for piling the foundation. Adopting a pile spacing of 1·2 m centres as a first estimate, we can obtain a pile group 8 piles square, i.e. a total of 64 piles giving a working load of 469 kN per pile. It will be desirable to use driven and cast-in-place piles with an enlarged end to take advantage of their higher end resistance since there is no really good bearing stratum of rock or dense gravel within an economical piling depth.

Assume a shaft diameter of 450 mm and an enlarged end 750 mm diameter.

$$\text{End resistance of piles 18 m long} = 9 \times 160 \times \frac{\pi}{4} \times 0 \cdot 75^2$$

$$= 636 \text{ kN}$$

The pile cap will be about 1·25 m thick giving a shaft length above the enlarged end of

$$18 - (1 \cdot 25 + 0 \cdot 75) = 16 \text{ m}$$

The average shear strength along the shaft is 92 kN/m². We do not know the relationship between shear strength and skin friction for driven and cast-in-place piles but it will certainly not be less than that for bored piles for which skin friction = 0·45 × 92 = 41·4 kN/m². Therefore,

Total skin friction on pile shaft

$$= \pi \times 0 \cdot 45 \times 16 \times 41 \cdot 4 = 936 \text{ kN}$$

Total ultimate carrying capacity of a single pile

$$= 636 + 936 = 1\ 572\ \text{kN}$$

$$\text{Safety factor} = \frac{1572}{469} = 3 \cdot 35$$

This is somewhat higher than would be required for single piles but we must consider the group effect. Since the piles are at a greater spacing than $2\frac{1}{4}$ diameters, block failure will not occur.

It will be advisable to check the settlement of the pile group by the approximate method (p. 137). From the aspect of settlement the group will behave as a virtual raft foundation at a depth of $\frac{2}{3} \times 16 \cdot 75 = 11 \cdot 2$ m below underside of pile cap. Allowing a spread of load of 1 in 4 the virtual raft foundation is 14 m square. From Table 1.3 the $m_v$ for the very stiff clay below pile base level will be about $0 \cdot 05$ m$^2$/MN. Thus from equation 2.33,

$$\text{Settlement} = 0 \cdot 05 \times 0 \cdot 55 \times \frac{30}{14 \times 14} \times 1 \cdot 5 \times 14 \times 1000$$

$$= 88\ \text{mm}$$

If settlements of this order of magnitude are undesirable it would be advisable to make a more detailed settlement analysis since the approximate method gives only a very rough indication.

The alternative of large diameter under-reamed bored piles could be considered for this structure. Taking three rows of three piles at say 4·5 m centres both ways, the working load on each pile will be $\frac{30\ 000}{9} = 3333\ \text{kN}$.

Take a 1·2 m diameter shaft under-reamed to, say, a 3 m diameter base at a depth of 15 m below ground level.

Shear strength of clay at 15 m $= 135$ kN/m$^2$

End resistance of base of piles $= 9 \times 135 \times \dfrac{\pi}{4} \times 3^2$

$$= 8588\ \text{kN}$$

In considering the shaft adhesion on the piles, we shall have to neglect any adhesion over the sloping portion, i.e. for a depth of 1·8 m at 2:1 slope, and for a distance up the pile shaft at least equal to twice the shaft diameter for the reasons given on page 396. Thus we must only consider shaft adhesion over a length equal to

$$15 - (1 \cdot 8 + 2 \cdot 4 + 1 \cdot 25) = 9 \cdot 55\ \text{m}$$

Average shear strength along shaft = 78 kN/m²

Unit adhesion on shaft          = 0·30 × 78 = 23·4 kN/m²

Total adhesion                  = 23·4 × $\pi$ × 1·2 × 9·55

                                = 842 kN

Total ultimate resistance of pile   = 8589 + 842

                                = 9431 kN

Safety factor                   = $\dfrac{9431}{3333}$ = 2·8

which is satisfactory. The criterion (p. 396) that the working load should not be greater than the ultimate shaft load + $\frac{1}{3}$ ultimate base load is also satisfied.


EXAMPLE 7.11

A bridge pier imposing a total load of 22 000 kN has plan dimensions at ground level of 18 by 4·5 m. It is sited on 7·5 m of recently placed loose sand filling ($N$ = 9 blows per 0·3 m) overlying 4·5 m of peaty soft clay ($c$ = 24 kN/m²) followed by stiff clay ($c$ = 60 kN/m² at 12 m below ground level increasing to 300 kN/m² at 25 m below ground level). Ground water level is 0·6 m below ground level.

This is obviously a case for piling but because of the "squeezing" ground from 7·5 to 12 m below ground level and the overlying loose water-bearing sand, this is not a clear case for an in-situ type pile. The clay below 12 m is not particularly stiff; therefore it will be desirable to use a pile of fairly large diameter to get the most out of the ground in end resistance and adhesion. A 508 mm o.d. West's Shell pile (p. 520) has a nominal maximum working load of 800 to 1000 kN. We can space the piles at $\pi$ × 0·51 = 1·6 m centre to centre both ways, which permits a total of 13 × 4 = 52 piles beneath the 18 by 4·5 m base. The pile cap will be 20 m by 5·8 m by 1·2 m thick. It will be desirable to avoid excavating below the water table so we will allow the pile cap to project 0·6 m above ground level and we shall have to add the weight of the cap to the working load on the piles.

Calculating total structural load on piles—

Working load from bridge pier = $\dfrac{22\ 000}{52}$ = 423 kN

$$\text{Load from pile cap} = \frac{20 \times 5 \cdot 8 \times 1 \cdot 2 \times 2 \cdot 4 \times 9 \cdot 807}{52} = 63 \text{ kN}$$

per pile

Weight of soil displaced by pile cap

$$= \frac{20 \times 5 \cdot 8 \times 0 \cdot 6 \times 1 \cdot 6 \times 9 \cdot 807}{52} = 21 \text{ kN}$$

Net working load on top of pile shaft

$$= 423 + (63 - 21) = 465 \text{ kN}$$

Although the sand-fill is recently placed it will have consolidated under its own weight, but it will be causing consolidation of the underlying soft peaty clay. Therefore there will be negative skin friction both from the sand filling and from the soft clay. Because the compression of the soft clay is large relative to the yielding of the pile toe, the negative skin friction from the sand will act over the full depth of the layer, and it will be sufficiently accurate to assume that it acts over the full depth of the soft clay layer also. We must therefore add the total weight of these two layers, which is enclosed by the perimeter of the pile group.

Gross weight of soil enclosed by pile group

$$= 19 \cdot 71 \times 5 \cdot 21 \times 9 \cdot 807 \, (6 \cdot 9 \times 0 \cdot 65 + 4 \cdot 5 \times 0 \cdot 5) = 6778 \text{ kN}$$

Deduct weight of soil displaced by piles in group

$$= 52 \times \frac{\pi}{4} \times 0 \cdot 508^2 \times 9 \cdot 807 \, (6 \cdot 9 \times 0 \cdot 65 + 4 \cdot 5 \times 0 \cdot 5) = 696 \text{ kN}$$

Net weight causing dragdown $= 6082$ kN

Weight of pile shaft in fill and clay $= 54$ kN

Therefore,

Total load on pile group $= 52 \times (465 + 54) + 6082$
$= 33\,070$ kN

From equation 7.19, dragdown load will not exceed

$$Q_2 = 52 \times 465 + 52 \times \pi \times 0 \cdot 508 \times (6 \cdot 9 \times 10 + 4 \cdot 5 \times 24)$$
$$= 38\,869 \text{ kN plus weight of piles}$$

Total load on pile shaft at surface of stiff clay stratum—

$$= \frac{33\ 070}{52} = 636 \text{ kN}$$

Calculate the ultimate carrying capacity of a 508 mm pile driven to 20 m below ground level, i.e. to penetration of 8 m into stiff clay— Shear strength at 20 m below ground level = 208 kN/m²

Average shear strength along pile shaft
$$= \frac{60 + 208}{2}$$
$$= 134 \text{ kN/m}^2$$

End resistance of pile $= 9 \times 208 \times \frac{\pi}{4} \times 0\cdot508^2 = 379 \text{ kN}$

From Fig. 7.10,

Shaft skin friction for $c$ of 134 kN/m² and $L/B = 20$ and soft clay overburden $= 0\cdot65 \times 134 = 87 \text{ kN/m}^2$

Total shaft skin friction $= \pi \times 0\cdot508 \times 8 \times 87 = 1111 \text{ kN}$

Ultimate carrying capacity of pile $= 379 + 1111 = 1490 \text{ kN}$

Safety factor on structural load
$$= \frac{1490}{465} = \underline{\underline{3\cdot2}}$$

Safety factor on total load
$$= \frac{1\ 490 \times 52}{33\ 070} = \underline{\underline{2\cdot3}}$$

The above safety factors should be satisfactory since the pile group is relatively narrow and the shear strength of the soil is increasing rapidly below the base of the piles; therefore the settlement of the group should be quite small.

However, we must consider the possibility of block failure of the group. The ultimate carrying capacity of a pile group considered as a block foundation is given by equation 7.14, namely—

$$Q_u = 2D(B + L)\bar{c} + 1\cdot3cN_c \times B \times L$$
$$= 2 \times 8(19\cdot71 + 5\cdot21) \times 134 + 1\cdot3 \times 208$$
$$\times 9 \times 19\cdot71 \times 5\cdot21$$
$$= 303 \text{ MN approx.}$$

Safety factor against block failure $= \frac{303}{33} = 9\cdot2$ which is amply safe.

EXAMPLE 7.12

A piled trestle shown in Fig. 7·37 consists of four vertical piles surmounted by a 1·200 m thick pile cap. It carries a horizontal load

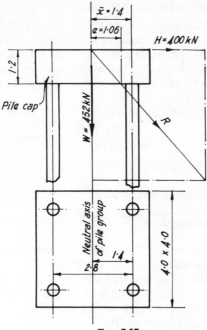

FIG. 7.37

applied to the surface of the cap of 400 kN. Determine the loads on the piles. For a pile cap 4·00 m square—

Weight of pile cap = 4 × 4 × 1·2 × 9·807 × 2·4

$$= 452 \text{ kN}$$

Resultant of vertical load of pile cap and horizontal load cuts the underside of the pile cap at a point 1·06 m from centre of cap. From equation 7.8,

Vertical component of load on piles

$$= \frac{452}{4} \pm \frac{452 \times 1 \cdot 06 \times 1 \cdot 4}{4 \times 1 \cdot 4^2}$$

$$= 198 \text{ kN maximum and } 28 \text{ kN minimum}$$

Any tendency to uplift will be counterbalanced by the weight of the pile and the skin friction in the ground.

EXAMPLE 7.13

A steel jetty pile of hollow tubular section driven through 5·500 m of soft silt on to hard fissured and broken rock carries an uplift load of 250 kN. Design a suitable anchorage.

We cannot obtain any uplift resistance from the soft silt; therefore we shall have to provide a positive anchorage to the rock. Since the pile is a hollow section we can drill into the rock through the bottom of the pile and provide a steel rod anchor bolt grouted into the rock. The bolt should be of deformed section and provided with an end washer. Thus,

Required cross-sectional area of rod for 125 kN/m² safe stress

$$= \frac{250 \times 1\,000}{125} = 2000 \text{ mm}^2$$

Therefore a 50 mm diameter bar will be satisfactory. (Area = 1963 mm²).

For allowable steel-to-grout bond stress of 0·7 N/mm² (p. 423),

$$\text{Required bond length} = \frac{250 \times 1000}{\pi \times 50 \times 0·7 \times 1000} = 2·27 \text{ m}$$

The grout-to-rock bond will not require a greater bond length.

Since the rock is fissured and broken it is possible that failure would occur due to uplift of an inverted cone of rock with a half angle of say 30°. Taking the submerged density of the rock to be 1·60 Mg/m³, a 3·90 m deep cone has a weight of 258 kN. This gives a safety factor of greater than one against uplift.

Therefore the required length of rod is governed by the depth of 3·90 m required to prevent lifting the rock.

If the length of rod carried up into the pile is set in concrete having a works cube strength of 20 N/mm² clause 303 (*e*) of *CP 114* gives—

$$\text{Required length} = \frac{\text{Bar diameter} \times \text{Tensile stress in bar}}{4 \times \text{Permissible average bond stress}}$$

$$\frac{50 \times 125}{4 \times 0·80 \times 1000} = 1·953 \text{ m, say } 2·000 \text{ m}$$

REFERENCES

7.1 BROMS, B., Methods of calculating the ultimate bearing capacity of piles, a summary, *Sols-Soils*, **5**, 18–19, pp. 21–31 (1966).

7.2 VESIC, A. S., Tests on Instrumented Piles, Ogeechee River Site, *J. Soil Mech. and Found. Div.*, *Amer. Soc. Civ. Eng.*, **96**, SM2, (1966).

7.3 NORDLUND, R. L., Bearing capacity of piles in cohesionless soils, *Proc. Amer. Soc. Civ. Eng.*, SM3, pp. 1–35 (May, 1963).

7.4   VESIC, A. S., Investigations of bearing capacity of piles in sand, *Duke University (U.S.A.) Soil Mech. Lab. Publ.* No. 3 (1964).

7.5   BEREZANTSEV, V. G., Load-bearing capacity and deformation of piled foundations, *Proc. 5th Int. Conf. Soil Mech.*, **2**, pp. 11–12 (Paris, 1961).

7.6   VAN DER VEEN, C., The bearing capacity of a pile predetermined by a cone penetration test, *Proc. 4th Int. Conf. Soil Mech.*, **2**, pp.72–75 (London, 1957).

7.7   MEYERHOF, G. G., Penetration tests and bearing capacity of cohesionless soils, *Proc. Amer. Soc. Civ. Eng.*, **82**, SMI (Jan., 1965).

7.8   DE BEER, E., The influence of the transverse dimensions of a pile on the point resistance, *De Ingenieur*, Nos 3 and 5 (1965); *Bouw en Waterbouwkunde* Nos 1 and 2 (1965).

7.9   *Soil Mechanics in Engineering Practice*, p. 530.

7.10   FELD, J., Discussion on session 6, *Proc. 4th Int. Conf. Soil Mech.*, **3**, p. 181 (London, 1957).

7.11   FELLENIUS, B., Results of tests on piles at Gothenburg Railway Station, *Bull. No. 5, Geotech. Dept., Sw. State R.* (1955).

7.12   SEED, H. B. and REESE, L. C., The action of soft clay along friction piles, *Proc. Amer. Soc. Civ. Eng.*, **81**, p. 842 (1955).

7.13   EIDE, O., HUTCHINSON, J. N. and LANDVA, A., Short- and long-term test loading of a friction pile in clay, *Proc. 5th Int. Conf. Soil Mech.*, **2**, pp. 45–53 (Paris, 1961).

7.14   TOMLINSON, M. J., The adhesion of piles in stiff clay, *Research Report No. 26, Constr. Ind. Res. and Inf. Assoc.*, London (1970).

7.15   TOMLINSON, M. J., Some effects of pile driving on skin friction, *Proc. Conf. on Behaviour of Piles, Inst. Civ. Eng.* (London, 1971).

7.16   WOODWARD, R. J., LUNDGREN, R. and BOITANO, J. D., Pile loading tests in stiff clays, *Proc. 5th Int. Conf. Soil Mech.*, **2**, pp. 177–184 (Paris, 1961).

7.17   NORDLUND, R. L., Some experiences with the driving and loading of heavy large-diameter piles in stiff clays, *Proc. 1st Pan-Amer. Congr. Soil Mech. and Foundn. (Mexico City*, 1959), **1**, pp. 349–369.

7.18   MEYERHOF, G. G. and MURDOCK, L. J., An investigation of the bearing capacity of some bored and driven piles in London Clay, *Géotechnique*, **3**, No. 7, pp. 267–282 (Sept., 1953).

7.19   BALLISAGER, C. C., Bearing capacity of piles in Aarhus Septarian Clay, *Danish Geotech. Inst. Bull.*, No. 7, pp. 14–19 (1959).

7.20   SKEMPTON, A. W., Cast-*in-situ* bored piles in London Clay, *Geotechnique*, **9**, No. 4, pp. 153–173 (Dec., 1959).

7.21   Symposium on Large Bored Piles, Institution of Civil Engineers, Reinforced Concr. Assoc., London, 1966.

7.22   JOHANNESSEN, I. J. and BJERRUM, L., Measurement of the compression of a steel pile to rock due to settlement of the surrounding clay, *Proc. 6th Int. Conf. Soil Mech.*, **2**, pp. 261–264 (Montreal, 1961).

7.23   CLAESSEN, A. I. M. and HORVAT, E., Reducing negative skin friction with bitumen slip layers, *Proc. Amer. Soc. Civ. Eng.*, **100**, GT8, pp. 925–944 (Aug., 1974).

7.24 HORN, H. M. and LAMBE, T. W., Settlement of buildings on the MIT campus, *Proc. Amer. Soc. Civ. Eng.*, **90**, No. SM5, pp. 181–195 (Sept., 1964).

7.25 KEZDI, A., Bearing capacity of piles and pile groups, *Proc. 4th Int. Conf. Soil Mech.*, **2**, pp. 46–51 (London, 1957).

7.26 VESIC, A., Discussion on deep foundations, *Proc. 6th Int. Conf. Soil Mech.*, **3**, pp. 509–611 (Montreal, 1965).

7.27 SKEMPTON, A. W., YASSIN, A. A., and GIBSON, R. E., Théorie de la force portante des pieux dans le sable, *Ann. Inst. Tech. Batim*, **6**, pp. 285–290 (March–April, 1953).

7.28 DA COSTA NUNES, A. J. and VARGAS, M., Computed bearing capacity of piles in residual soils compared with laboratory and load tests, *Proc. 3rd. Int. Conf. Soil Mech.*, **2**, pp. 75–79 (Zürich, 1953).

7.29 FULLER, F. M. and COUPER, J. N. C., The reconstruction of Deptford Creek Bridge, *Proc. Inst. C.E.*, **4**, Pt. 3, pp. 314–364 (Aug., 1955).

7.30 WHITAKER, T., Experiments with model piles in groups, *Geotechnique*, **7**, No. 4, pp. 147–167 (Dec., 1957).

7.31 CLARKE, N. W. B. and WATSON, J. E., Settlement records and loading data for various buildings erected by the Public Works Department Municipal Council, Shanghai, *Proc. 1st Int. Conf. Soil Mech.*, **2**, p. 174 (Sect. F., Paper 12 (1936).

7.32 ZEEVAERT, L., Compensated friction pile foundation to reduce settlement of buildings on the highly compressible volcanic clay of Mexico City, *Proc. 4th Int. Conf. Soil. Mech*, **2**, pp. 81–86 (London, 1957).

7.33 TOMI INSON, M. J. and HOLT, J. B., The foundations of the Bank of China Building, Hong Kong, *Proc. 3rd Int. Conf. Soil Mech.*, **1**, pp. 466–472 (Zürich, 1953).

7.34 MEYERHOF, G. G. and ADAMS, J. I., The ultimate uplift capacity of foundations, *Can. Geotech. J.*, **5**, 4, pp. 225–244 (Nov., 1968).

7.35 BROMS, B., The lateral resistance of piles in cohesive soils, *Proc. Amer. Soc. Civ. Eng.*, **90**, SM2, pp. 27–63 (Mar., 1964); The lateral resistance of piles in cohesionless soils, *Proc. Amer. Soc. Civ. Eng.*, **90**, SM3, pp. 123–156 (May, 1964); Design of laterally loaded piles, *Proc. Amer. Soc. Civ. Eng.*, **91**, SM3, pp. 79–99 (May, 1965).

7.36 BOWLES, J. E., *Foundation design and analysis*, McGraw-Hill, New York, pp. 543–557 (1968).

7.37 DODGE, C. F. and SWIGER, W. F., Vibration testing of friction piles, *Eng. News. Rec.*, pp. 717–720 (13th May, 1948).

7.38 McLAUGHLIN, W., The new gear-cutting establishment at Clydebank, *Trans. N.E. Coast Inst. Eng. & Shipbuilders*, **71**, pp. 319–362 (1954–1955).

7.39 SMITH, E. A. L., Pile driving analysis by the wave equation, *Proc. Amer. Soc. Civ. Eng.*, **86**, SM 4, pp. 35–61 (1960).

# 8

# Piled Foundations–2
# Structural Design and Construction
# Methods

THE structural features and methods of constructing piles will be described in this chapter. The following types will be considered—

*Driven Piles*

Timber (round or square sections)
Precast concrete (solid or hollow sections)
Prestressed concrete (solid or hollow sections)
Steel H-beam, box and tube

*Driven and Cast-in-Place Piles*

Withdrawable steel drive tube, end closed by concrete plug (Franki, Dowsett).
Withdrawable steel drive tube, end closed by detachable point (Alpha, Delta, G.K.N., Simplex, Vibro, Western).
Steel shells driven by withdrawable mandrel or drive tube (Raymond "taper" or "step-taper," Western "button-bottom").
Precast concrete shells driven by withdrawable mandrel (Wests).

*Screw Piles and Screw Cylinders*

*Bored Piles*

Continuous bored

Augered

Large-diameter under-reamed

Types incorporating precast concrete units

Drilled-in tubes

*Composite Piles*

The above list might at first sight present rather a bewildering choice to the engineer. However, in practice it is found that three main factors—location and type of structure; ground conditions; and durability—will narrow the choice to not more than one or two basic types. The final selection is then made from considerations of overall cost.

Dealing with the first factor, *location and type of structure*, the driven pile or the driven and cast-in-place pile in which the shell remains in position are the most favoured for works over water such as piles in wharf structures or jetties. Structures on land present a wide choice of pile type, and driven and cast-in-place types are usually the cheapest for moderate loadings and unhampered site conditions. However, the proximity of existing buildings will often necessitate the selection of a type which can be installed without ground heave or vibration, e.g. some form of bored and cast-in-place pile. Jacked piles are suitable types for underpinning existing structures. Large-diameter bored piles are normally the most economical type for very heavy structures, especially in ground which can be drilled by power augers.

The *ground conditions* influence both the choice of pile type and the technique for installing piles. For example, driven piles cannot be used economically in ground containing boulders and where ground heave would be detrimental. On the other hand, driven piles are preferred for loose water-bearing sands and gravels where compaction due to driving can develop the full potential bearing capacity of these soils. Steel H-piles, having a low ground displacement, are suitable for conditions where deep penetration is required in sands and gravels. Stiff clays favour the adoption of bored and under-reamed types. Under-reamed bases cannot be formed in cohesionless soils.

*Durability* often affects the selection of pile type. For piles driven in marine conditions, precast concrete piles may be preferred to steel piles from the aspect of resistance to corrosion. Timber piles may be rejected for marine conditions because of the risk of attack by destructive mollusc-type borers. Where soils contain sulphates or other deleterious substances, piles incorporating high-quality precast concrete units are preferable to piles formed by placing concrete in situ in conditions where placing difficulties, such as the presence of ground water, may result in the concrete not being thoroughly compacted.

Having selected one or two basic types from consideration of the above factors, the final choice is made from considerations of *cost*. This does not necessarily mean the lowest quoted price per metre run of pile. The engineer must assess the overall cost of the piling work. He must take into consideration resources of the piling contractor to achieve the speed of operations required by his construction programme; the possibility of having to take piles to a greater depth than envisaged in the piling contractor's quotation; the experience of the piling contractor in overcoming possible difficult conditions; the cost of an extensive test loading programme on sites where the engineer has insufficient experience of the behaviour of piles of the selected type in the particular ground conditions; the cost of routine check loading tests; the cost of the engineer's supervision of pile installation and test loading; and the cost of the contractor's site organization and overheads which is incurred between the time of initial site clearance and the time when he can proceed with the superstructure.

The above factors will be discussed in greater detail in the following pages in the course of describing the various types of pile. However, it will be advantageous first to describe the equipment used for pile driving, methods of driving piles, including special methods for overcoming difficult conditions, observations of driving resistance, and test loading. All these are common to most forms of driven piles.

## Pile Driving Equipment

### PILE FRAMES

Nowadays, pile frames are usually mounted on standard tracked crane base machines for mobility on land sites (Fig. 8.1) or on framed bases for mounting on stagings or pontoons for marine construction (Plate VIII). Both types are capable of full rotation and backward or forward raking (Plate VIII). Light and easily transportable mast-type frames of tubular construction are also manufactured (Fig. 8.2).

All types of pile frames consist essentially of *leaders* which are a pair of steel members extending for the full height of the frame and

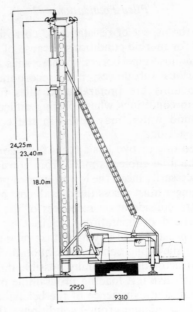

24,25 m
23.40 m
18.0 m
2950
9310

FIG. 8.1. THE AKERMANS M14-5P PILE FRAME

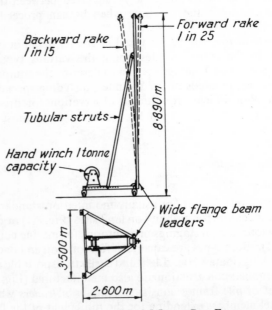

Forward rake
1 in 25

Backward rake
1 in 15

Tubular struts

8·890 m

Hand winch 1 tonne
capacity

Wide flange beam
leaders

3·500 m
2·600 m

FIG. 8.2. DELMAG G.L. 8·5 LIGHT PILE FRAME

which guide the hammer and the pile as it is driven into the ground, of the structural framework which supports the leaders, and of the base frame. Where long'piles have to be driven the leaders can be extended at the top by a telescopic boom. Where the pile frame is mounted on an elevated platform or on a floating pontoon or other vessel, *extension leaders* can be bolted on to the bottom of the frame.

In the simpler types of pile frame the structural framework forms a rigid bracing between the leaders and the base frame but in the case of universal frames screw-operated telescoping gear or hydraulic rams are provided to rake the leaders backwards or forwards. The frames may be fitted with only a single sheave at the top which is used to raise the hammer and pile or to operate a drop hammer in the leaders; or a treble sheave may be fitted of which the centre sheave is used for raising the hammer and the two outer sheaves for the pile.

The base frame may be mounted on swivel wheels fitted with self-contained jacking screws for levelling the frame or it may be carried on steel rollers. The rollers run on steel girders or long timbers and the frame is moved along by winching from a dead man set on the roller track, or by turning the rollers by a tommy-bar placed in holes at the ends of the rollers. Movement parallel to the rollers is achieved by winding in a wire rope terminating in hooks on the ends of the rollers; the frame then skids in either direction along the rollers. The leaders of the larger types of pile frame can be moved in any direction by a power unit, thus permitting a number of piles in a group to be driven without moving the undercarriage.

It is important to ensure that the pile frame remains in its correct position throughout the driving of a pile. If it is allowed to move laterally or out of plumb, this may result in eccentric blows of the hammer with consequent risk of breakage and driving out of line. It is particularly necessary to check the alignment of the frame when driving raking piles. If settlement of the frame occurs during driving, the weight of the frame may be transmitted to a partly driven pile. These conditions give rise to a serious risk of pile breakage.

PILING WINCHES

The piling winch is mounted on the base. Winches may be powered by steam, diesel or petrol engines, or electric motors. Steam-powered winches are commonly used where steam is also used for the piling hammer. Diesel or petrol engines, or (less commonly) electric motors, are used in conjunction with drop-hammers or where compressed air is used to operate the hammers. With the heavier steam-operated plant it is the usual practice to mount the steam boiler on the pile frame.

Light winches may only have a single drum but double- and triple-drum winches which can raise hammer and pile separately are more useful where speed of handling and driving is desirable. The winches may be fitted with reversing gear so that in addition to their main purpose of lifting the hammer and pile, they can also carry out the auxiliary function of operating the raking, rotating, and travelling gear.

The reader is referred to handbooks of manufacturers of piling equipment, such as that of B.S.P. International Foundations Ltd., for tables giving particulars of dimensions and capacities of frames, winches, and boilers for given sizes of pile and hammer.

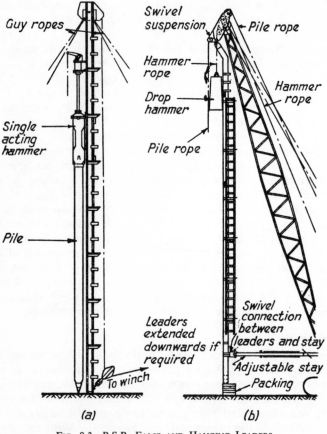

FIG. 8.3. B.S.P. FALSE AND HANGING LEADERS
(a) Guyed false leaders.
(b) Hanging leaders for excavator.

## FALSE AND HANGING LEADERS

For jobs where it is inconvenient or uneconomical to use a pile frame—for example, where piles have to be driven within a deep trench, or for test piling work where only two or three piles may be driven—false leaders are a useful expedient. They consist of a pair of leaders similar to those used on a pile frame, braced together with short connexions, or forming part of a tubular mast. They are held in a vertical or raking position by guy-ropes (Fig. 8.3 (*a*)). Similar leaders can also be designed for suspension from the jib of a crane or excavator when they are referred to as hanging leaders (Fig. 8.3 (*b*)) supplemented as necessary by guy-ropes. A steel strut, capable of adjustment in length, forms a rigid attachment from the foot of the leaders to the bed-frame of the excavator or crane.

Where guyed leaders are used, the pile and hammer are lifted by an independent powered winch. Where leaders are suspended from an excavator or crane, the winch units of these machines are used and

separate drums can be employed for the pile and hammer. Steam or compressed air for hammer operation are supplied by a separate unit, or drop hammers may be used with a friction winch. Guyed or hanging leaders should preferably be used in conjunction with single- or double-acting hammers since the flexure caused by a drop-hammer may result in eccentric blows and fracture of long concrete piles.

## HAMMER GUIDES

In situations where it is desirable to dispense wholly with piling frames or false leaders, hammer guides (or rope-suspended leaders) can be attached to the piles, and the latter are guided by timber or steel frameworks. An example of a guide for a diesel hammer is shown in Fig. 8.4. These methods have the advantage of economy in plant and the piles may be driven to a very flat angle of rake.

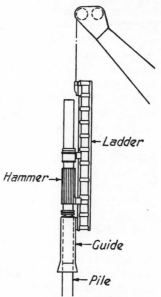

FIG. 8.4. HAMMER GUIDE AND ROPE-SUSPENDED LEADERS FOR DELMAG DIESEL PILE HAMMER

However, an independent crane is necessary for pitching the pile and setting the guide and hammer. The guides for the piles have to be well constructed and rigidly secured against movement, especially for raking piles. Because of the eccentricity of thrust on the hammer guides, severe stresses and fatigue are set up in the guides and breakages of parts may be frequent. Hammer guides were used for driving the foundation piles of the Hindiya Bridge and frequent breakages were experienced until the single-acting hammer was replaced by a double-acting hammer.[8.1]

## PILING HAMMERS

The simplest form of hammer is the *drop-hammer* which is used in conjunction with light frames and for test piling where it may be uneconomical to bring a steam boiler or compressor on to a site to drive only three or four test piles. Drop hammers are solid masses of cast iron trom 1000 to 5000 kg mass fitted with a lifting eye and lugs for sliding in the leaders. They have the disadvantage that it is not easy to control the height of drop with any accuracy and there is the danger that the operator will use too great a drop when driving becomes difficult, with consequent greatly increased risk of damage to the pile.

*Single-acting Steam or Compressed-air Hammers* comprise a massive weight in the form of a cylinder. Steam or compressed air admitted to the cylinder raises it up the fixed piston rod. At the top of the stroke, or at a lesser height which can be controlled by the operator, the steam is cut off and the cylinder falls freely on to the pile helmet (Fig. 8.5). The steam is admitted to the cylinder through the piston rod, the upper part of which is hollow. A valve at the top of the rod is opened by pulling on a rope attached to the lever. Releasing the rope closes the valve. Thus, the height of drop and frequency of each individual stroke is controlled by the operator. The maximum height of drop is usually about 1·37 m and the hammer can be operated at a rate of up to about 45 strokes per minute.

A useful rule to determine a suitable weight of drop-hammer or single-acting hammer is to select a hammer weighing approximately the same as the pile. This will not be possible in the case of the heavier reinforced concrete piles when the hammer is more likely to be half of the weight of the pile. However, it should not weigh less than a third of the pile. In order to avoid damage to the pile, the height of drop should be limited to 1·2 m. Concrete piles are especially liable to be shattered by a blow from too great a height. A blow delivered by a heavy hammer with a short drop is much more effective and much less damaging to the pile than a blow from a light hammer with a long drop, particularly in stiff clay soils. Special care is needed when seating a pile on to a hard bearing stratum such as rock, especially on to a steeply sloping rock surface. B.S.P. single-acting hammers are made with cylinder mass varying from 2500 to 15 000 kg. The largest hammers are used for driving steel tube piles in marine structures. The world's largest is the Menck MRBS 7000 with a ram mass of 70 tonne.

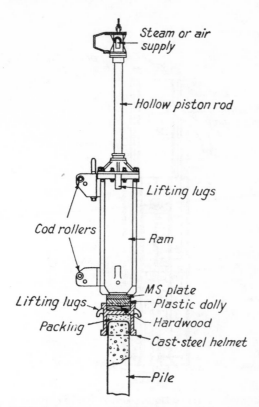

FIG. 8.5. B.S.P. SINGLE-ACTING HAMMER DRIVING PILE WITH CAST-STEEL HELMET AND PLASTIC DOLLY

*McKiernan–Terry and B.S.P. Double-acting Pile Hammers* are used mainly for sheet pile driving (Fig. 8.6), and are designed to impart a rapid succession of blows to the pile. The rate of driving ranges from 500 blows per minute for the light types, to 95 blows per minute for the heaviest types. B.S.P. hammers are divided into three groups: *Light* hammers, size 200 and 300, are used for driving timber runners, trench sheeting or light section sheet piling; *Medium* hammers, 500 N, 600 N and 700 N, for most sizes of steel sheet piling; and *Heavy* hammers, sizes, 900, 1000 and 1100, for driving the heaviest section sheet piling in hard ground and for timber, concrete, or steel bearing piles. Menck automatic piling hammers cover a wide range varying from SB 80 (270 kg ram mass) up to the SB 400 (1300 kg ram mass).

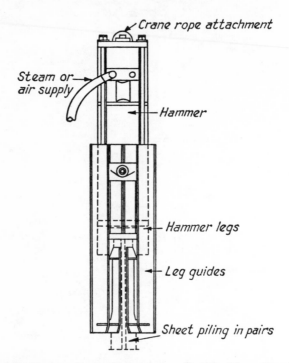

FIG. 8.6. McKiernan–Terry Double-acting Hammer (Heavy Duty) with Leg-guides for driving Sheet Piling

Double-acting hammers can be driven by steam or compressed air. The former is most usually employed since the volume of air required, except for the lighter types, is beyond the capacity of the normal range of portable air compressors. A piling frame is not required with this type of hammer which can be attached to the top of the pile by leg-guides, the pile being guided by a timber framework. When used with a pile frame, back guides are bolted to the hammer to engage with the leaders, and only short leg guides are used to prevent the hammer from moving relatively to the top of the pile. The heavy-duty hammers can drive under water to depths of 25 m.

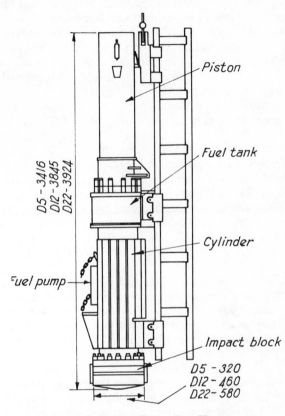

FIG. 8.7. DELMAG DIESEL PILE HAMMER

Care is needed in their maintenance and lubrication and during driving they must be kept in alignment with the pile and prevented from bouncing. *Double-acting* hammers can be fitted with a chisel point for demolition and rock breaking or with jaws for extracting piling.

*Diesel pile hammers* provide an efficient means of pile driving in favourable ground conditions but they are not effective for all types of ground. With this type of hammer (Fig. 8.7) the falling ram compresses the air in the cylinder and the impact atomizes a pool of diesel oil lying at the concave end of the cylinder. The atomized fuel ignites with the compressed air and the resulting explosion imparts an additional "kick" to the pile, which is already moving downwards under the impact of the ram. The explosion also raises the ram ready for the next downstroke. Burnt gases are scavenged from the cylinder on the upstroke of the ram. The blow, being sustained, is more efficient than the simple impact of the conventional hammer. These hammers can be economical as they dispense with steam or compressed air plant and are entirely self-contained. Diesel hammers are ineffective in soft or yielding soils when the impact of the blow in insufficient, to atomize the fuel. The largest of the various makes of diesel hammer are the Koehring-MKT DE40 (1814 kg), the B.S.P. DE50B (2260 kg), the Delmag D55 (5400 kg) and the Kobe K150 (15 000 kg). The ram mass being given in each case.

These hammers may also cause breakage of precast concrete piles where sharply resistant layers are encountered while driving through soft ground. The Link-Belt diesel hammer is provided with a means of controlling the energy of the blow by varying the amount of diesel fuel injected. With other types the energy cannot be varied. Thus when a resistant layer is met the "kick" of the explosion will result in a sharper impact on the pile and the possibility of a fracture.

Makers of double-acting and diesel hammers publish figures of rated energy per blow for comparison with drop hammers and for use in dynamic pile formulae. However, it is doubtful whether these figures provide a sound basis for comparison. Measurements of energy of blow were made by means of load cells in a detailed study of pile hammer performance undertaken by the Michigan State Highway Commission.[8.2] It was found that the energy of blow delivered to the pile depended on the type of packing and its condition; on the pile length, rigidity and mass, and on the ground conditions. The energy was determined from the summation of the increments of force, measured from the load cell, multiplied by the simultaneous increments of displacement of the pile head during a single hammer blow. In the case of several types of hammer this was less than half of the manufacturer's maximum rating.

### HELMET, DRIVING CAP, DOLLY, AND PACKING

A cast steel helmet is placed over the top of a concrete pile (Fig. 8.5), its purpose being to hold the resilient dolly and packing which are interposed between the hammer and the pile to prevent shattering of the latter at the head. The helmet should fit loosely around the pile, so that the latter can rotate slightly without binding on the helmet. Longer dollies or "followers" are used when driving piles below the level of the bottom of the leaders.

The dolly is placed in a square recess in the top of the helmet. It is square at the base and rounded at the top. Elm dollies are used for easy to moderate driving, and for hard driving a hardwood, such as oak, greenheart or pynkado, is used. Plastic dollies can withstand much heavier driving than timber dollies. They comprise a sandwich construction of a layer of resin-bonded laminated fibre between an upper metal plate and a hardwood base. In moderately hard driving conditions, plastic dollies will last for several hundred piles. In severe driving conditions at Uskmouth Power Station, described by Williams,[8.3] elm dollies for 406 by 406 mm and 457 by 457 mm concrete piles only lasted for very few piles, and in the worst cases they were useless after only one pile had been driven. Resin-bonded laminated timber dollies of ninety-two plies and nearly 100 mm in thickness lasted on average for seven piles, and the best types were a Bakelite-type plastic reinforced with cotton fibre used in conjunction with a top steel plate and a 50 mm pad of elm underneath. These composite plastic dollies were used up to forty times.

Packing is placed between the helmet and the top of the pile to cushion the blow between the two. Various types of materials are used, including hessian sacking, thin timber sheets, coconut matting, and wallboard. Asbestos fibre can withstand many thousands of blows without losing its stiffness and this material does not char under long periods of hard driving. In the conditions at Uskmouth, described by Williams, up to 125 mm of sawdust was contained in jute sandbags and covered with two dry cement sacks placed at right angles over the head of the pile. This proved to be the best type of packing for the conditions.

Driving caps are used to protect the heads of steel bearing piles. They are specially shaped to receive the particular type of pile to be driven and are fitted with a recess for a hardwood dolly and with steel wedges to keep the caps tight on the pile. If the caps are allowed to work loose they will damage the pile head.

Generally, great care is needed in the selection of materials and thicknesses for dollies and packings, since lack of resilience will lead to excessive damage to the pile head or, in severe cases, to breakage of the hammer.

### Jetting Piles

Water jetting may be used to aid the penetration of a pile into a sand or sandy gravel stratum. Jetting is ineffective in firm to stiff clays or any soil containing much coarse gravel, cobbles, or boulders. If the piling scheme is planned on the assumption that jetting will be used, it is preferable to cast a central jet pipe, say a 50 or 75 mm pipe terminating in a tapered nozzle into the pile (Fig. 8.8). Elaborate forms of built-in jetting nozzles are sometimes used, including separate nozzles leading upwards at an angle and emerging at the sides of the pile as well as the central downward hole. However, it is doubtful if these are much more effective than the single nozzle-ended vertical pipe.

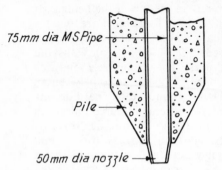

FIG. 8.8. PILE WITH CENTRAL JET PIPE

The jet pipe is led out of the side of the pile and connected by flexible armoured hose to the jetting pump. The pile should be gently "dollied" up and down on the winch. If it is rammed hard down, the nozzle is likely to be blocked by soil wedging into the tapered part. Jetting should be cut off at least 1 m above the predicted founding level and the pile driven down by hammer until the required driving resistance is achieved.

If the jetting is only required to aid penetration of an occasional pile which "hangs-up" in driving, a separate jet pipe is used. This is worked up and down close to the side of the pile. An angled jet may be used to ensure that the wash water flows to the pile point. In difficult conditions, two or more jet pipes may be used for a single pile. Tube or box piles driven open-ended can be jetted from within the pile, and steel H-beam piles can be jetted by sinking the jet pipe down the space between the web and flanges.

An adequate quantity of water is essential for jetting. Suitable quantities of water for jetting a 250 to 350 mm pile are—

| Fine sands | 15 to 25 l/s |
| Coarse sands | 25 to 40 l/s |
| Sandy gravels | 45 to 600 l/s |

A pressure of at least 5 bar or more is required. It is sometimes a difficult problem to dispose of the large quantities of water and sand flowing at ground level from around the piles, and great care is needed when jetting near existing foundations or near piles driven to depths shallower than the jetting levels. The escaping water may undermine the pile frame, causing its collapse. Jetting through sands may be impossible if the sandy strata are overlain by clays which prevent escape of the jetting water.

## Pile Driving by Vibration

Vibratory methods of driving sheet piles or bearing piles are best suited to sandy or gravelly soils. Pile driving vibrators consist of pairs of exciters mounted on the vibrator unit, the motors of each pair rotating in opposite directions. The amplitude of vibrations is sufficient to break down the skin friction on the sides of the pile. Characteristics of some typical pile driving vibrators are—

| Type | Minimum power supply (kVA) | Frequency of exciter (Hz) | Mass of vibrator (kg) |
|---|---|---|---|
| Bodine | 740 | up to 135 | 10 000 |
| BSP VF 55 | 179 | 10–120 | 3 800 |
| Koehring-MKT V14 | 104 | 24–31 | 5 000 |
| Menck 44–15/30 | 250 | 25–50 | 9 600 |
| Muller MS 120 | 400 | 17–36 | 9 600 |
| Schenk DR 60 | 250 | 17–39 | 7 200 |
| Tomen VM2–5000 | 90 | 18–30 | 4 887 |
| Vibro-Mac 12 | 220 | 10–16 | 6 100 |

Vibrators will drive steel piles through loose to medium-dense sands and gravels with comparative ease but there are likely to be difficulties with dense sands, where the energy may be insufficient to displace the material to permit entry of the pile. Vibrators are little used in stiff clays, although the Bodine Resonant Driver, has been used for driving tube piles in clay.

Vibrators can also be used for extracting piles and are frequently used in connexion with large-diameter bored and cast-in-place piling work for sinking and extracting the pile casings.

## Pile Driving over Water

Piles for jetty or wharf structures built over water can be driven from specially designed pile frames cantilevered out from the permanent piles already driven (Fig. 8.9), from ordinary pile frames operating from temporary piled trestles, or from floating plant. The first-mentioned method has the advantage of being independent of weather conditions but progress is limited to the output of a single pile frame on narrow structures, and the method cannot be used economically where bents of heavy piles are to be driven at widely spaced centres, i.e. there is a limiting distance over which a heavy frame can be designed to cantilever. Pile driving from temporary falsework trestles may be economical for wharves where piles have to

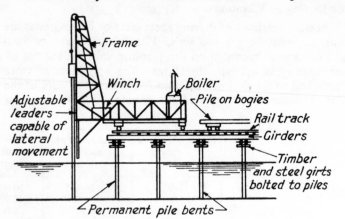

FIG. 8.9. PILE DRIVING OVER WATER WITH CANTILEVER FRAME

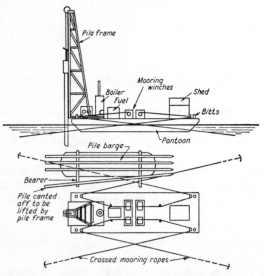

FIG. 8.10. PILE DRIVING FROM PONTOON

be driven at fairly close spacing, a large number of them being in relatively shallow water on the inshore side of the wharf. The method is rarely economical for use in deep water a long distance from the shore, since the floating plant necessary for driving temporary piles might just as well be used for the permanent work.

Floating pile-driving plant normally consists of a pile frame erected on one end of a rectangular steel pontoon (Fig. 8.10), although ordinary barges can be used for light pile frames. Piling pontoons are provided with four powered winches or two centrally placed double-drum winches for warping them into position and a very close adjustment of position can be achieved. The cells of the pontoons are ballasted, usually with water, to counteract the weight of the frame and to give the vessel the necessary stability. Piles are brought by barge alongside the pontoon and one end is lifted by the sheaves on top of the frame; the other end is canted off the deck of the barge, allowing the pile to swing freely into a vertical position from where it is adjusted to the correct height in the leaders.

Single- or double-acting hammers are preferable to drop hammers when operating from floating plant in unsheltered waters, since the blows can be controlled with greater accuracy and there is less risk of damage to the pile.

## Pile Driving through Difficult Ground

Driving piles through some types of ground, such as beds of boulders or filling containing obstructions such as large masses of old brickwork or concrete, is impossible unless special methods are used. These methods include boring a hole of sufficient diameter through the difficult ground to receive the pile. In loose ground the hole may have to be cased which sometimes leads to difficulties with extraction of the casing. Another method is to drive a heavy steel spud or joist section through the ground and to drive the pile through the loosened soil left after withdrawing the spud. This method again is liable to result in extraction difficulties and possible overstraining of the pile frame if attempts are made to extract the spud by the piling winch. In ground containing boulders, a jackhammer or rotary diamond core drills may be used to drill into boulders which are broken up by firing small explosive charges lowered down the drill holes.

The Western Foundation Corporation of U.S.A. has used a hollow box-shaped steel casing which is driven through the ground with its lower end closed by two steel flaps. After the obstructions are passed an H-pile is dropped down the hollow casing, the flaps are forced open as the pile is driven, and, after completion of driving, the special section is extracted for re-use. This device can also be used for driving piles which are too long for the pile frame. By dropping the piles into the casing, the pile head is brought down to a level at which it and the hammer can be accommodated within the leaders.

On sites where it is important to avoid noise and vibration, mechanical augers have been used to bore uncased holes to receive piles which are dropped down the hole and then driven a short distance to their required bearing level. This method would only be used where cast-in-situ piles are unsuitable because of ground or structural conditions.

### Test Piling

INSTALLING TEST PILES

Wherever possible, test piles should be of the same type and dimensions as the permanent piles which are intended to be used. This is the only way to ensure that the designed penetration will be attained and that the designer's estimate of the safe working load can be checked when the piles are subjected to test loading. Careful records should be kept of all stages of installation. The following information should be recorded—

> Contract (title and address).
> Principal dates (installation, concreting, driving, loading etc.).
> Size, type, length (as pitched and as driven), and identification no. of pile.
> Age of pile (if concrete).
> Reinforcement details.
> Weight of pile (tons).
> Weight of helmet, dolly and anvil (tons).
> Type of hammer.
> Serial no. of hammer.
> Mass of pile (kg).
> Mass of helmet, dolly and anvil (kg).
> Type of hammer.
> Serial no. of hammer.
> Mass of ram.
> Condition of packing and dolly before driving.
> Condition of packing and dolly after driving.
> Condition of pile head and dolly after driving.
> Ground level above datum.
> Reduced level of pile toe.
> Reference to nearest borehole or other soil information.
> Co-ordinates of axis of pile after completion of driving.
> Observations of ground heave or subsidence around pile.
> Condition of pile and shoe (if extracted).
> Method of load testing.

The records during the actual driving should be entered on a table of the type shown in Table 8.1.

**Table 8.1**
**FORM OF TEST PILE DRIVING RECORD**

| Time (hr) | Penetration below ground level (m) | No. of blows per 0·5 m | Set in mm per blow | Actual stroke of ram (m) | Measured temporary compression* | | Remarks |
|---|---|---|---|---|---|---|---|
| | | | | | Amount (mm) | Distance from top of pile (m) | |
| | | | | | | | |

* Only if required in connexion with dynamic formula calculations.

To obtain the above records, the pile should be marked off in half metres from the toe. The driving resistance in blows /0·5 m or 0·2 m is recorded for the full depth driven, note being made of the depth to which the pile falls under its own weight or the weight of the pile and hammer. Measurements of the set in mm per blow need only be made when the temporary compression is being recorded and at the final stages of driving. The temporary compression is measured by clamping a piece of card or graph paper on to the pile and ruling a line across the paper on a horizontal straight-edge placed just clear of the paper (Fig. 8.11 (*a*)). The vertical and horizontal movements of the pile produce a pattern in the pencil stroke at each blow of the hammer as shown in Fig. 8.11 (*b*), from which the temporary compression may be measured directly. Measurements of temporary compression are made at several stages after the pile has entered the stratum within which the pile may be expected to take up its bearing.

Where piles are driven into sands, silts, or clays, the re-driving characteristics should be observed. Re-driving may be started after a few hours in the case of sands, after twelve hours for silts, and after twenty-four hours or more for clays. The re-driving should continue until the resistance is similar to that previously recorded and the final set and temporary compression should again be measured. After completion of all driving tests the data should be presented in the form of a chart (Fig. 8.12).

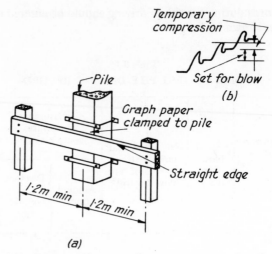

FIG. 8.11. READING TEMPORARY COMPRESSION DURING PILE DRIVING
(*a*) Apparatus for taking readings on pile.
(*b*) Diagram of set and temporary compression.

TEST LOADING

Two types of test loading can be performed on piles. These are the constant rate of penetration (C.R.P.) test and the maintained load test. In the latter type the loads are applied in increments.

In the *C.R.P. test* the pile is jacked into the soil, the load being adjusted to give a constant rate of downward movement to the pile, which is maintained until failure point is reached. Failure is defined either as the load at which the pile continues to move downward without further increase in load, or the load at which the penetration reaches a value equal to one-tenth of the diameter of the pile at the base. A penetration rate of 0·8 mm per minute is suitable for friction piles in clay, for which the total penetration to reach failure is likely to be less than 25 mm. Considerably larger movements possibly as much as one-tenth of the base diameter will be required for end-bearing piles, and a jacking rate of 1·5 mm per minute is suitable. Whitaker[8.4] states that the results will not be altered significantly if the above rates are halved or doubled.

The C.R.P. test has the advantage that it is rapidly performed, and is thus useful for preliminary test piling when failure loads are unknown, and when the design is based on a factor of safety against ultimate failure, it is desirable to know the real safety factor. However, the method has the disadvantage that it does not give the elastic settlement under the working load (i.e. total settlement less the permanent set) which is of significance in determining whether or not there has been plastic yield of the soil at the working load. Also it has the very considerable drawback of requiring very heavy kentledge or anchored loads when large-diameter piles are loaded to failure. For this reason the author considers that the C.R.P. test is

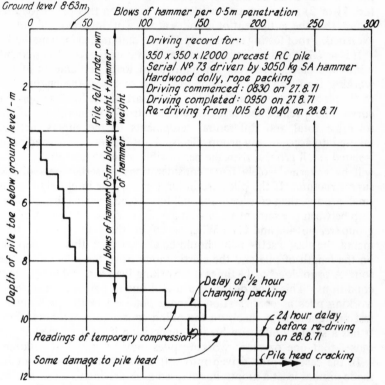

FIG. 8.12. TYPICAL RECORD OF DRIVING RESISTANCE OF TEST PILE

best suited to the research type of investigation where fundamental pile behaviour is being studied.

In the case of ground conditions where there is a reasonable amount of experience to guide the engineer on pile-carrying capacity and where pile lengths and diameters can be predicted with some degree of confidence, then a *proof load test* is all that is required. If a pile is considered in relation to its true function, i.e to support the superstructure, all that the structural engineer needs to do is to satisfy himself that the settlement under the working load will not exceed a value which can be tolerated by the superstructure. The pile failure load has no direct bearing on the structural design. However, because of the natural variation in ground conditions, a test at the working load is insufficient. A test on one pile might just satisfy the settlement criterion, but the same load applied to an adjacent *untested* pile might cause excessive settlement. Therefore the test load must be carried to some multiple of the working load (i.e. $1\frac{1}{2}$ or 2) and a limiting settlement placed on this proof load to ensure that the settlement of all piles at the working load will not be exceeded. Proof testing is normally done by maintained load methods.

It is usual to specify limiting total and residual (i.e. total settlement minus the elastic recovery on removal of load) settlements at the working load and at the proof load. In this way the engineer is really placing a lower limit on the early part of the load–settlement curve. The specified values are determined from considerations of the tolerable total and differential settlements of the superstructure, taking into account any group effects. Thus if piles are isolated or in isolated small groups, then the permissible settlement of the test pile will be governed solely from considerations of settlements of the superstructure. If the piles are in large groups or in closely spaced small groups, then consideration will have to be given to the relationship between the settlement of a single pile and the settlement of the group (*see* pp. 408 and 411). When specifying the limiting *total* settlements, the elastic settlement should be allowed for; this will depend on the length of pile and the elastic modulus of the pile and of the soil. A proof load of $1\frac{1}{2}$ times the working load is suitable for most conditions. This type of test is a useful one to perform on selected working piles as confirmation of data obtained in the preliminary test piling and as a check on the piling contractor's workmanship. It has a salutary effect on his job supervision if he is warned at the outset that one or more working piles may be tested at random.

In the case of piles driven into soft clays the test should not be made until at least a month has elapsed after driving to allow for the effects of increase in carrying capacity with time (*see* p. 387).

It is preferable to load the pile by jacking against a platform loaded with kentledge, rather than by balancing the load on top of the pile. With the latter method there is a risk of a serious accident due to tilting of the platform or collapse of the pile shaft. The load on the pile should be measured directly by a pressure capsule or proving ring interposed between the pile head and jack or between the jack and the platform. It is unwise to rely on the reading of the pressure gauge on the hydraulic jack, although this gauge can be used to give the increments of loading. Settlements of the pile are recorded by dial or vernier pointer gauges resting on an arm clamped to the pile head, the gauges being carried by beams or scaffolding supported well clear of the pile and platform supports (Fig. 8.13). In the case of maintained loading, the load should be applied in increments of about one-sixth of the ultimate load or maximum test load. The settlements should be measured to 0·25 mm during and after application of the

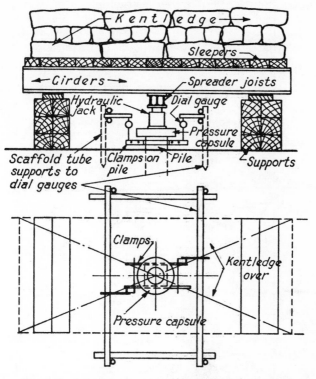

FIG. 8.13. ARRANGEMENT OF LOADING TEST RIG FOR PILES

increment and the next increment should not be applied until the rate of settlement has decreased to 0·1 mm in 20 min. After reaching failure or proof load, the load should be removed in decrements of one-sixth of the total load and the recovery measured. Again the decrement should not be made until the recovery rate has decreased 0·1 mm in 20 min. It is sometimes the practice to unload the pile after reaching various stages in the loading. It is always good practice to unload the pile after reaching the design working load, and it is desirable to hold the working load (and the proof load if not loaded to failure) for a period of twenty-four hours. Typical load–settlement and time–settlement curves are shown in Fig. 8.14.

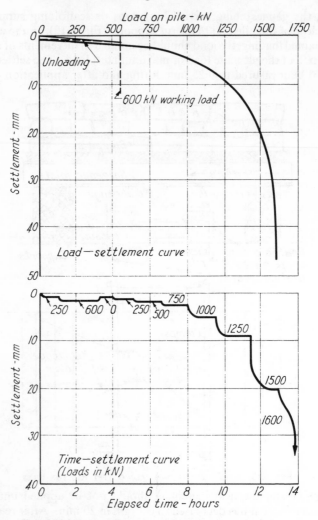

FIG. 8.14. TYPICAL RESULTS OF LOADING TEST ON A PILE

## PROGRAMME FOR TEST PILING

On large piling projects it may be worthwhile to undertake a programme of C.R.P. test piling involving different types, sizes, and lengths of pile, and observing ultimate loads for the various types and for increasing depths of penetration into the bearing stratum. In piling problems involving piling through fill or other compressible strata where "negative skin friction" may be an important factor in the design, the test piles can be driven through a casing bored through the compressible layers. This will give the carrying capacity of the pile within the bearing stratum only.

If proof test loads are made on permanent piles driven in a group, the adjacent piles can be used as resistance for the test load. Special tension members must be cast into the body of the anchor piles and yokes fitted to these members to carry the ends of a girder spanning between adjacent piles (Fig. 8.15). This procedure may be

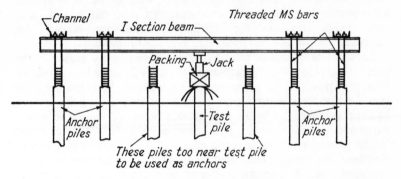

FIG. 8.15. USE OF PERMANENT PILES AS ANCHORAGE FOR LOADING TEST

economical at the preliminary test piling stage. In favourable ground the required depth of anchor piles can be much shortened by under-reaming them (*see* p. 529).

## TYPES OF DRIVEN PILES

In the following descriptions of the various types of pile, the maximum carrying capacity in most cases refers to the carrying capacity of the material of the pile considered as a short column. Where piles are required to act as long columns, the appropriate reduction factors should be applied (*see* p. 420).

### Timber Piles

Timber piles are frequently used in North America, China, and Scandinavia in the form of trimmed tree trunks, driven butt uppermost. When used in foundation work their lightness gives buoyancy to the foundation. Their lightness, flexibility, and resistance to shock makes timber piles very suitable for temporary works, and in Great Britain their use is generally confined to this purpose.

If timber piles are kept permanently wet or permanently dry, i.e. driven wholly below or wholly above water level, they can have a very long life. However, they are liable to decay in the zone of a fluctuating water table. Also in the case of marine or river structures, the immersed portions of the piles are liable to severe attack by marine organisms. Timber piles are also liable to attack above the water level by fungi and ants or other wood-destroying insects. Care in selection and treatment of timber can prevent or minimize attack. Suitable types of timber for exposed wet and dry situations are northern pine, Kauri pine, larch, oak, Bermuda and Lebanon cedar, hornbeam, yew, teak, greenheart, and jarrah. For wholly wet situations, alder, beech, elm, northern pine, larch, oak, and teak are suitable, and for wholly dry conditions, Norway fir, American yellow and red pine, ash, and walnut are used.

Those parts of timber piles which are permanently buried in the ground and below the lowest ground water level can be left untreated. Wherever possible, the concrete pile caps should be taken down so that their undersides are below ground water level, and the portion of the pile embedded in the caps should be cut off square to sound wood and liberally coated with creosote or other preservative. If the lowest ground water table is too deep to take the pile caps down to that level the portion subjected to fluctuating water level or damp conditions can be preserved against decay to a limited extent by pressure-treatment with a preservative.

When assessing the depth below ground level requiring concrete or creosote protection, due account should be taken of the possible lowering of the ground water table by future drainage schemes.

Further information on the behaviour of timber in foundations and methods of preservation are given on pages 749 to 752.

The British Standard Code of Practice CP 2004 recommends that timber of stress grade 50 or better will be suitable for piling. Working stresses in compression should not exceed those tabulated in CP 112 for compression parallel to the grain for the green timber. In calculating working stresses, the slenderness ratio and bending stresses due to transverse loading and eccentric loading should be allowed for.

The *New York Foundation Code* permits a safe working stress of 5·9 N/mm² on the net area of cedar, Norway pine, spruce and similar woods; and 8·3 N/mm² on the net area of Douglas fir, oak, southern pine and woods of similar strength.

Mohr[8.5] has suggested that working loads on timber piles should be restricted to 100 to 250 kN in order to avoid unseen damage to the buried portions of the pile as a result of hard driving to achieve high carrying capacity. He shows pictures of timber piles which have become "broomed" into large masses of loose wood fibres as a result of excessive zeal in hard driving to reach a specified "set" or to break through a shallow hard layer.

Where end-bearing piles are driven into dense or hard materials a shoe is required to prevent splitting or "brooming" of the pile point. A typical shoe for timber piles is shown in Fig. 8.16. A shoe is not required where piles are driven wholly in soft ground.

It is usual in British practice to provide a steel hoop around the

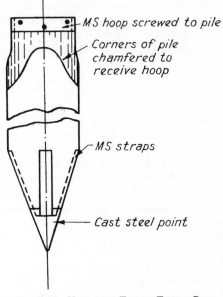

MS hoop screwed to pile

Corners of pile chamfered to receive hoop

MS straps

Cast steel point

FIG. 8.16. HEAD AND TOE OF TIMBER PILE

head of the pile to prevent damage during driving. The head of a square pile is chamfered to take the hoop as shown in Fig. 8.16. Damage at the head can be reduced by using the heaviest practicable hammer. In difficult driving conditions, jetting or pre-boring a hole for the pile should be adopted rather than risking undetected splitting or breakage of piles below ground level. Hartford[8.6] recommends a cast steel cap block weighing about one-fifth of the weight of the hammer as a better form of protection than the steel hoop. The block should be deeply recessed to allow it to fit well down over the head of the pile and to allow space for the insertion of hardwood packing. The recess should be tapered for easy placing and removal of the block. Some specifications forbid the use of hooks or spikes for handling creosoted timber piles, but Hartford is of the opinion that scoring or gouging of a pile by stones during driving has a more severe effect on the pile than any handling at the surface.

Piles are generally in 6 to 12 m lengths but they may be spliced if longer lengths are required. Splices may be made in a similar manner to that shown in Fig. 8.39. If the splices are made before the piles are lifted and driven, it is preferable to avoid a splice near the middle of the pile since sagging and distortion are at a maximum at this point when the pile is being lifted from a horizontal position. The butting surfaces of piles at the splices should be cut truly square to ensure even contact over the whole area of cross-section.

### Precast Concrete Piles

Precast concrete piles were, in the years preceding the 1939–45 war, the commonest type of driven pile. However, as a result of the post-war shortage of reinforcing steel, precast concrete piles (which require a considerable quantity of reinforcement) became supplanted to a considerable extent by driven and cast-in-place piles or prestressed concrete piles. Both of the latter types require much less steel than the precast concrete pile. However, precast concrete piles are still widely used for structures such as wharves or jetties where the pile is required to be carried above soil level in the form of a structural column. They are also used in soil conditions which may be unfavourable to cast-in-place piles, and in conditions where a high resistance to lateral forces is required; for example, in foundations to crane gantries or heavy reciprocating machinery or as anchor piles to the ties of retaining walls.

Precast concrete piles are normally of square section for short and moderate lengths, but hexagonal, octagonal, or circular piles are usually preferred for long lengths. If soil conditions require a large cross-sectional area, precast concrete tubes are used. They are driven hollow to save weight in handling and can be filled with concrete after driving. To avoid excessive whippiness in handling and driving, the usually accepted maximum lengths for various square-section piles are—

| Pile size (mm square) | Maximum length (m) |
|---|---|
| 250 | 12 |
| 300 | 15 |
| 350 | 18 |
| 400 | 21 |
| 450 | 24 |

## DESIGN OF PRECAST CONCRETE PILES

The structural design of precast concrete piles is governed by the need to give adequate strength against the stresses caused by lifting and handling the piles and subsequently by the driving of the piles. Once the piles are driven to their final position the stresses caused by foundation loading are likely to be much lower than those induced by handling and driving.

The design of piles to resist driving stresses has been greatly influenced by the researches of Glanville, Grime, and Davies[8.7] at the Building Research Station. They embedded stress-recorders in piles to measure the magnitude and velocity of the stress-wave, which after each blow travels from the head of the pile to the toe where it is partly reflected to return to the head. The researches showed that the stresses produced in a pile by the hammer blows far exceed those given by the driving resistance (calculated by a dynamic formula) divided by the cross-sectional area of the pile. The driving stresses were found to depend almost wholly on the fall of the hammer and the nature of the packing between the helmet and the pile. They made the following recommendations for the provision of reinforcement—

(*a*) The quantity of longitudinal steel should be proportional to the stresses arising in lifting and handling (the researches showed that the proportion of main steel did not seem to have any effect on the resistance to driving stresses).

(*b*) The quantity of transverse reinforcement, where hard driving is expected, should not be less than 0·4 per cent of the gross concrete volume.

(*c*) The proportion of link steel in the head of the pile should be 1·0 per cent.

The *Code of Practice for Foundations* (*CP 2004*) states—

"The lateral reinforcement is of particular importance in resisting driving stresses and should be in the form of hoops or links and of diameter not less than 6 mm ($\frac{1}{4}$ in.). For a distance of about three times the width from each end of the pile, the volume of lateral reinforcement should be not less than 0·6 per cent of the gross volume.

In the body of the pile the lateral reinforcement should be not less than 0·2 per cent, spaced at not more than half the width of the pile. The transition between the close spacing near the ends and the maximum spacing should be made gradually over a length equal to three times the width.

"The cover over all reinforcement, including binding wire, should not be less than 40 mm ($1\frac{1}{2}$ in.) of concrete but where the piles are exposed to sea water or other corrosive influences, the cover should be nowhere less than 50 mm (2 in.). The hoops and links should fit tightly against the longitudinal bars and be bound to them by welding or soft iron wire, the free ends of which should be turned into the interior of the pile. The longitudinal bars may be held apart by spreader forks not more than 1·5 m (5 ft.) apart.''

It should be noted that the percentage of lateral reinforcement in the form of links or ties in the head and body of the pile as recommended by the *Code* is only about half the quantity recommended by Glanville, Grime, and Davies. However, the latter recommendations were made for hard driving conditions, whereas the figures given in the *Code* are minimum values for easy driving conditions.

In a comprehensive review of current practice in reinforced concrete pile design, Saurin[8.8] listed bending moments for a variety of conditions of support in lifting and handling a pile of weight $W$ and length $L$ as follows—

| Condition | Maximum static bending moment |
|---|---|
| (a) Lifting by two points $\frac{1}{5} \times L$ from either end. | $\pm \dfrac{WL}{50}$ |
| (b) Lifting by two points $\frac{1}{4} \times L$ from either end. | $- \dfrac{WL}{32}$ |
| (c) Pitching by one point $\frac{3}{10} \times L$ from the head. | $\pm \dfrac{WL}{22}$ |
| (d) Pitching by one point $\frac{1}{3} \times L$ from the head. | $- \dfrac{WL}{18}$ |
| (e) Pitching by one point $\frac{1}{4} \times L$ from the head. | $+ \dfrac{WL}{18}$ |
| (f) Pitching by one point $\frac{1}{5} \times L$ from the head. | $+ \dfrac{WL}{14}$ |

| Condition | Maximum static bending moment |
|---|---|
| (g) Pitching by one end. | $+ \dfrac{WL}{8}$ |
| (h) Balancing by the centre. | $- \dfrac{WL}{8}$ |

The above conditions are illustrated in Fig. 8.17 (*a*) to (*h*).

Saurin recommended designing the longitudinal reinforcement for a maximum static bending moment of $\pm \dfrac{WL}{18}$. This will permit lifting by a point between one-third and one-quarter of the length of the pile from the end. The bending moment produced by lifting at the one-fifth or one-quarter points is comparatively small; this is advantageous since piles are commonly lifted from their casting bed to the stacking area at an early age and before the concrete has reached its design strength.

If a safety factor of 2·25 on the yield strength of the steel is accepted, the ultimate moment of resistance of the pile section designed on a bending moment of $\frac{WL}{18}$ is $\frac{WL}{18} \times 2·25$ which is equal to $\frac{WL}{8}$. Thus the ultimate moment of resistance is equal to the

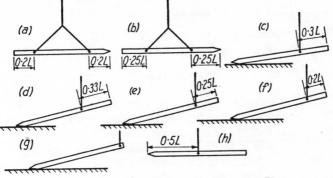

Fig. 8.17. Methods of Lifting and Pitching Piles

bending moment given by supporting the pile at its two ends. Saurin therefore gave the following design criterion—

"A pile shall be considered suitably reinforced against bending stresses if the ultimate moment of resistance of its section is equal to the maximum bending moment produced when the pile is supported horizontally by its two ends."

Using this criterion and Evans' equation[8.9] for calculating the ultimate strength of reinforced concrete sections by plastic yield theories, Saurin prepared design tables for square section piles which have been modified for metric units in Table 8.2. A cover of 37·5 mm to the main bars was assumed. Evans' equation is—

Ultimate moment of resistance

$$= M = bd^2pt_y \left(1 - \frac{0·6\,pt_y}{u}\right) . \qquad . \qquad . (8.1)$$

where $b$ = breadth of pile

$d$ = effective depth of pile

$p$ = ratio of tension reinforcement $= \dfrac{A_s}{bd}$

$t_y$ = yield point of reinforcement

$u$ = crushing strength of concrete.

**Table 8.2**

### MAXIMUM PILE LENGTHS FOR GIVEN REINFORCEMENT

| Bar diameter (mm) | 300 mm pile (m) | 350 mm pile (m) | 380 mm pile (m) | 400 mm pile (m) |
|---|---|---|---|---|
| 20 | 11·5 | 11.0 | — | — |
| 25 | 13·5 | 13·0 | — | — |
| 32 | 17·0 | 16·5 | 16·0 | 15·5 |
| 40 | — | — | 20·5 | 20·0 |

The maximum pile length in Table 8.2 was calculated for $t_y = 262$ N/mm² and $u = 27$ N/mm² from the equation—

$$\text{Maximum length } L = \frac{8M}{W} \quad . \quad . \quad . \quad (8.2)$$

The minimum diameter of reinforcing bar shown in Table 8·2 is 20 mm. Piles shorter than the maximum length of 11 mm given in the table can be lifted by the toggle bolt hole which is normally provided at a point 1200 mm from the head, but when such piles approach a length of 11 m, it is advisable to check that the design bending moments are not exceeded by lifting from this hole.

Design tables for transverse reinforcement suitable for moderately hard driving are given by Saurin as shown in Table 8.3 (modified for metric units).

**Table 8.3**

### DESIGN TABLE FOR TRANSVERSE REINFORCEMENT IN BODY OF PILE

| Size of pile (mm²) | Diameter of links (mm) | Spacing (mm) |
|---|---|---|
| 300 | 6 | 150 |
| 350 | { 6 | 150 |
|  | { 8 | 250 |
| 380 | { 6 | 140 |
|  | { 8 | 210 |
| 400 | { 6 | 125 |
|  | { 8 | 200 |

*Notes.* This table assumes ordinary single links and 40 mm of concrete cover on the main bars. No change will be necessary if 50 mm of cover is used. The proportion of link steel to gross concrete volume is approximately 0·2 per cent.

The percentage of transverse steel shown in Table 8.3 is about 0·2 per cent. Although Glanville, Grime, and Davies recommended up to 0·4 per cent for hard driving, Saurin remarked that transverse reinforcement even lighter than 0·2 per cent had withstood very hard driving indeed.

Saurin's design table for head and toe reinforcement is given in Table 8.4.

Table 8.4

**DESIGN TABLE FOR REINFORCEMENT OF HEAD AND TOE OF PILE**

| Pile-diameters from head | Link steel | Helix | Percentage on gross concrete volume |
|---|---|---|---|
| 1 | one-third normal spacing | Pitch equal to normal link spacing | 1·0 |
| 2 | | | |
| 3 | one-half normal spacing | — | 0·4 |
| 4 | | | |
| 5 | two-thirds normal spacing | — | 0·3 |
| 6 | normal spacing | — | 0·2 |

*Notes.* Diameter of helix steel to be same as that of link steel. At the toe a similar arrangement is required but no helix is necessary.

Where driving conditions are moderately hard to hard a spiral or helix has been found advantageous. The helix is normally placed inside the main bars but Saurin remarks it is best placed outside them. The reduction in concrete cover over the helix is not detrimental since this part of the pile is normally broken down for bonding into the pile cap.

Typical details of reinforcement in precast concrete piles are shown in Fig. 8.18 (*a*) and (*b*). The 787 mm octagonal pile shown in Fig. 8.18 (*b*) was designed by the author's firm for the Irish Refining Company's Marine Terminal at Cork, Eire.

PILE SHOES

Where piles are driven wholly in soft soils no shoe need be provided. The ends of the piles are usually cast in the shape of a blunt point as shown in Fig. 8.19 (*a*). A sharper point (Fig. 8.19 (*b*)) is preferred for driving into hard clays or compact sands and gravels. The metal drive shoe commonly seen on concrete piles whether driven in soft or hard conditions is based on a design used to stop timber piles from splitting or brooming, and in soft conditions

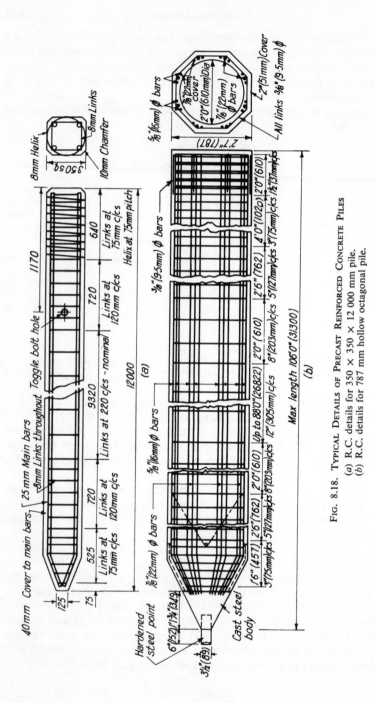

FIG. 8.18. TYPICAL DETAILS OF PRECAST REINFORCED CONCRETE PILES
(a) R.C. details for 350 × 350 × 12 000 mm pile.
(b) R.C. details for 787 mm hollow octagonal pile.

no metal shoe of any kind is required. Where the piles are to be driven into soil containing large cobbles or boulders, a shoe as shown in Fig. 8.19 (c) is needed to split the boulders or to prevent breaking of the toe when the pile pushes large cobbles or boulders to one side. The area of the top of the metal shoe in contact with the concrete of the pile should be large enough to ensure that the compressive stress on the concrete is within the safe limits.

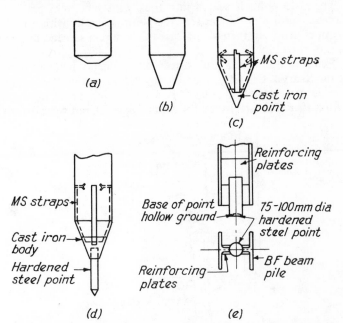

FIG. 8.19. TYPES OF PILE TOES FOR VARIOUS GROUND CONDITIONS

    (a) Soft ground.
    (b) Stiff to hard clay, compact sands and gravels.
    (c) Ground containing cobbles or boulders.
    (d) Rock point for penetrating level bedrock surface.
    (e) Oslo point used on sloping bedrock surface.

Where piles are required to penetrate rock, to obtain lateral resistance for example, a special rock point as shown in Fig. 8.19 (d) is used. Where piles are driven on to hard rock, the "Oslo Point" (Fig. 8.19 (e)) is recommended. This design is particularly suited to driving on to a sloping rock surface when, under careful blows of a heavy hammer with a short drop, the sharp edge of the hollow ground point will bite into the rock so preventing the point from slipping down the rock surface. The researches leading to the development of the Oslo point are described by Bjerrum.[8.10] The author's firm used this type for the octagonal piles as shown in Fig. 8.18 (*b*). A hardened steel to BS 970:EN24 was used for the 88 mm diameter point which was embedded in a chilled cast-iron shoe. The point was machined concave to 12 mm depth. The Brinell hardness of the steel was 400 to 600. It was found that careful flame treatment of the point was necessary after casting it into the shoe since the latter operation resulted in a loss of hardness of the steel.

The Oslo point is seated into rock with very light blows of the hammer until it is evident that the point is wholly within rock; the hammer drop can then be increased to ensure a satisfactory penetration of the point.

Reinforced concrete piles driven on to steeply inclined hard rock at the Skarvik Oil Jetty, Gothenburg,[8.11] were dowelled to the rock by steel rods set in drill holes. The 450 mm square piles were provided with a structural steel shoe shown in Fig. 8.20 and were driven until

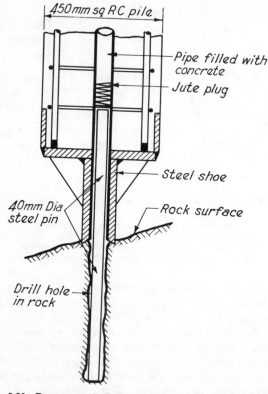

FIG. 8.20. DOWELLING R.C. PILES TO ROCK, SKARVIK OIL JETTY, GOTHENBURG

the shoe was just bearing on the rock. A hole was then drilled into the rock, the drill rods passing through a hole cast in the centre of the pile. The dowel in the form of a 40 mm steel pin was then lowered into the drill hole and the hole in the pile was finally filled with concrete.

Precast concrete piles cannot be expected to split large boulders when the boulders are in contact with one another or are embedded in hard or compact soil. In these cases, special precautions are taken in driving as described on page 471.

## CONCRETE FOR PILES

It is the usual practice in Britain to limit the stresses in the pile due to working loads and to handling and pitching to the maximum working stresses permitted by *C.P 114*. Considerably higher stresses may occur during driving. For this reason *CP 2004* recommends for hard and very hard driving conditions for all piles and for piles in marine works concrete mix with a minimum cement content of 400 kg/m$^3$ (works cube strength 25 N/mm$^2$ at 28 days), but for normal and easy driving conditions a cement content of 300 kg/m$^3$ (works cube strength 20 N/mm$^2$) can be used. Where hard driving is expected it may be advantageous to adopt even richer mixes in the head and toe of the pile, say of the order of 600 kg/m$^3$ minimum cement content. The design values selected for the average compressive stress on the piles due to their working loads are subject to the reduction factors given in Table 7.3 (p. 421) when piles act as columns.

Portland cement should normally be used for piles. High alumina cement concrete is advantageous from the point of view of early release from the formwork and a reduced curing period, but there is evidence of a substantial retrogression in strength of high alumina cement concrete during or subsequent to the curing period. There is no evidence of retrogression in strength of concrete made with sulphate-resisting or supersulphate cement after it is exposed, even to tropical sun temperatures (*see* p. 757).

## CASTING

Piles may be cast directly on to a concrete bed or bottom forms may be used laid on rigid timber bearers. The casting bed should be laid on sufficient depth of well-compacted hard filling to prevent settlement of the bed under the weight of the pile. This is particularly necessary when piles are cast in tiers, one on top of another. Side formwork should be provided in greater numbers than bottom forms since the side units can be struck at an earlier age. After fixing and oiling of the shutters, the pre-assembled reinforcing cage is lowered into the mould and supported by wire ties from cross-bolts as shown in Fig. 8.21. Sufficient ties should be provided to prevent sagging of the steel. If sagging occurs the cover to the bars will be reduced with consequent rusting of the steel and spalling of the concrete. Pile heads must be cast truly square to the axis.

Lifting and toggle bolt holes are formed by inserting short lengths of steel tube. The concrete is compacted by small diameter poker vibrators which should be inserted and withdrawn for short periods and at close-spaced intervals. The concrete between the bars and the

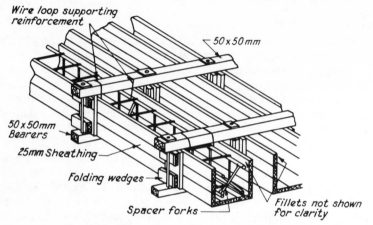

FIG. 8.21. FORMWORK FOR PRECAST CONCRETE PILES

forms should be "sliced" or "spaded" to avoid honeycombed patches on the face. Special care should be taken in working concrete against the upper sloping faces of hexagonal or octagonal piles. Equal care should be taken in the treatment of the exposed face by means of a wood float. The forms should be slightly overfilled so that the concrete is pressed down by the float so compacting it and ensuring a dense close-knit surface.

The side forms should be removed as soon as is practicable and the piles kept continuously wet for four days in normal (10°C) air temperature conditions. This wet curing process should be continued until the concrete is hard enough for the piles to be lifted and transported to the stacking area. At some stage after casting, the piles should be clearly marked with a reference number, their length, and the date of casting. This will ensure that the correct piles are used for the particular location and will be a safeguard against driving too soon after casting. The allowable time between casting, lifting, and driving may be assessed by crushing tests on concrete cubes made at the same time as the piles are cast. The cubes should be cured and stored under the same conditions as the piles so that the strengths can be compared. Where piles are cast on a concrete bed, they should be slightly canted by bar and wedges before being lifted. This allows air to get beneath the pile, thus releasing suction between the pile and the bed.

Supports between piles in the stacks should be placed at the predetermined lifting-hole positions to ensure that the design bending moments are not exceeded. Fig. 8.22 shows how excessive

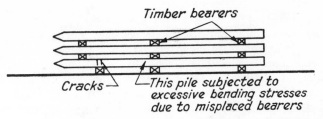

FIG. 8.22. OVERSTRESSING IN PILE DUE TO CARELESS STACKING

bending moments can result from carelessly placed packing. The stack should be arranged to allow air to circulate freely around the piles. The piles in the stack should be protected from over-rapid drying in hot weather by covering with tarpaulins or other forms of sheeting.

It is sometimes the practice to cast piles on to a concrete bed at a spacing, centre to centre, of twice their width. Then after striking the side forms, piles are cast in the spaces between, followed by another layer on top of the first and so on. This procedure saves space in the casting area, but has the disadvantage that the strongest piles are at the bottom of the stack, and none can be moved until the topmost pile is strong enough for handling.

Before being driven, the piles should be carefully inspected to ensure that they are free from any cracks. Fine transverse cracks can result from careless handling or lifting when they are of an immature age. Such cracks may lead to corrosion of the reinforcement especially if the piles are in exposed situations, for example in marine structures.

## STRIPPING PILE HEADS

After driving the pile to the desired level, it is usual to strip the pile head to expose the reinforcement which is then bonded into the pile cap. Pneumatic jackhammers are the most practical tools for this job. No method should be used which results in cracking or shattering of the concrete below the level of the underside of the pile cap.

If the pile has refused further driving at too high a level it will be necessary to cut off the surplus length. This can be done by breaking off the corners to expose the reinforcement which is cut through by hacksaw or burning. The pile can then be broken at this point by pulling it over with ropes attached to the head. The concrete should then be broken away for sufficient depth below the cut to expose the reinforcement for bonding into the pile cap.

Splicing Piles

If piles are required to be driven deeper than anticipated it may be necessary to extend them by splicing the reinforcement and casting on an additional length. The concrete in the head of the pile already driven should be broken away to expose the reinforcement for a distance of forty times the diameter of the longitudinal bars. The reinforcing cage for the extension length is then set in position and the bars welded at the joints or lapped for the full forty diameters; after which formwork is assembled in alignment with the pile already in the ground and the extension is then concreted.

**Jointed Precast Concrete Piles**

One of the principal disadvantages of the conventional precast concrete pile is that it cannot readily be extended. Thus if the bearing stratum lies locally at depths greater than indicated by borings, delays will occur while pile heads are stripped down and additional lengths cast on and allowed to mature. Furthermore, if the bearing stratum is shallower than anticipated the cut-off length of pile is wasted. This disadvantage can be overcome by using short precast concrete units which are assembled and locked together before driving the complete pile. Additional lengths can be added as required or lengths left projecting from the ground can be removed.

The Swedish "Herkules" pile was developed to meet these requirements. It consists of hexagonal precast concrete units with bayonet-type joints. The latter are stated to be capable of resisting the same compression, tension and bending stresses as the body of the pile. Other jointed precast concrete piles of square section are the West's "Hardrive" and F.C. Piling Co. "Balken" pile.

**Prestressed Concrete Piles**

Because of the savings in reinforcement and lighter weights for handling (given by a smaller cross-section), prestressed concrete piles have been used to an increasing extent in the last 15 years. In Great Britain, they have largely supplanted ordinary precast concrete piles on sites where long lengths are required. The savings in reinforcement are given by the use of high tensile steel wires. The prestressing of the piles requires high quality concrete, which in turn gives good resistance to driving stresses. As in the case of ordinary precast concrete piles, the longitudinal reinforcement is designed to resist stresses in lifting and handling, and no additional reinforcement, other than link steel, is required to resist driving stresses. Also, the pile is stressed to prevent the development of hair cracks during handling. This, together with the high quality concrete, gives a prestressed concrete pile a good durability in corrosive soils or in marine work. The manufacturers of prestressed piles claim an advantage in that a smaller cross-section is possible than with

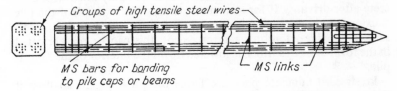

FIG. 8.23. TYPICAL ARRANGEMENT OF PRESTRESSED CONCRETE PILE

ordinary precast piles. This is not necessarily advantageous since a large cross-section may be necessary to develop the required end-bearing and shaft friction.

Prestressed concrete piles are usually made by the pre-tensioning process, i.e. the wires are placed in the moulds and stressed by jacking the ends of the wires against an abutment, after which the concrete is placed and vibrated into the moulds. After the concrete has reached the required compressive strength, the ends of the wires projecting from the concrete are cut off and the stress is transferred to the pile. The pile is then lifted and transferred to the stacking area. Piles are usually made in solid square sections up to 400 mm square. Piles larger than 500 mm are more economically made with a hollow core.

Manufacturers normally supply these piles to customers' individual designs, such as that shown in Fig. 8.23.

Another method of prestressing concrete piles is post-tensioning. This is generally used for special types such as large cylindrical sections. The precast units have holes cored longitudinally through them. After the curing and hardening period, the units are placed end to end so that the cored holes match up to give a continuous duct down the full length of the assembly. Prestressing wires or cables are threaded through the ducts and tensioned by jacking, after which the ducts are grouted under pressure, the jacks released, and the pile is then ready for lifting and stacking. By such methods, large-diameter hollow cylindrical sections can be made up in long lengths. The lengths can be readily adjusted by adding on or taking away one or more sections, although once the assemblies have been stressed and grouted-up the lengths cannot be adjusted.

Prestressed concrete piles are handled and driven in a similar manner to ordinary precast concrete piles. Since the wires are fully bonded to the concrete by the grout, there is no objection to breaking down the head for bonding into a pile cap or for splicing on an additional length in ordinary reinforced concrete. However, care is necessary in this operation because of the stress present in the wires. Hollow prestressed concrete piles are usually filled with concrete after driving. If for structural reasons (for example if the pile is extended above ground level in the form of a column), it is necessary to provide additional reinforcement, this can be prefabricated in the form of a cage which is lowered down the interior of the hollow pile.

Prestressed concrete piles are liable to cracking and spalling if they are not handled and driven carefully.

In addition to precautions in cushioning the head and avoiding high-velocity impact, the Prestressed Concrete Institute[8.12] recommend the following precautions—

"1. Ensure that the pile driving helmet or cap fits loosely around pile top so that the pile may rotate slightly without binding within the driving head.

2. Ensure that the pile is reasonably straight and not cambered because of uneven prestress or poor concrete placement during casting. Improper storage, handling, or hauling of piling can also cause excessive camber and even cracking. Care should be taken to support or pick up piling at the prescribed points. High flexural stresses may result during driving of a crooked pile.

3. Ensure that the top of the pile is reasonably square or perpendicular to the longitudinal axis of the pile.

4. Cut ends of prestressing or reinforcing steel flush with the end of the pile head to prevent their direct loading by the ram stroke.

5. A reasonable amount of spiral reinforcing is needed at the pile head and tip.

6. Use adequate amount of residual prestress in prestressed piles to resist reflected tensile stresses. The amounts of prestress required depend on the driving equipment, length of pile, and soil conditions as previously discussed. In general, longer piles (and batter piles) should have more prestress than shorter piles. Some experiences are as follows:

(*a*) short piles have been successfully driven with from 350 to 400 psi (2·4 to 2·75 N/mm²) prestress,

    (*b*) the Joint AASHO–PCI Committee on Bridges and Struc tures specify a minimum of 700 psi (4·8 N/mm²) after losses,

    (*c*) on certain occasions from 1000 to 1200 psi (6·9 to 8·3 N/mm²) have been used on long piles and batter piles.

7. Chamfer top and bottom edges and corners of piles."

There is a tendency among some manufacturers to provide too little transverse reinforcement in the heads of piles, with consequent crumbling during hard driving. Dean[8.13] gives an account of his experiences with prestressed concrete piles in Florida. He states that the initial stress in the concrete at transfer of prestress should be 5·5 N/mm²; this is because the rebound in driving the piles, particularly when driving in plastic materials, sets up tensile or shearing forces in the piles sufficient to destroy them when only 2·75 N/mm² stress was used. Piles stressed to 5·5 N/mm² appeared to be almost indestructible with normal driving equipment.

Dean states that prestressed concrete piles have a disadvantage if they require to be lengthened. Ordinary precast concrete piles have about 2 per cent longitudinal steel which is sufficient for splicing by lapping or welding. Prestressed piles, however, have only 0·5 to 1 per cent steel which is insufficient for splicing on to a normal reinforced concrete extension. If piles have to be lengthened the bars in the new length must be wired to the cables and holes drilled into the pile for additional bars. Dean states that it is preferable to pull the pile and substitute a longer one. Some manufacturers provide a few longitudinal mild steel bars in the head for splicing or bonding into a pile cap. Prestressed piles reinforced with Lee-McCall high tensile steel bars can be lengthened by means of special couplers screwed on to the ends of the bars. This permits the extension to be post-tensioned. The requirements for prestressing are set out in considerable detail in British Standard *CP 2004* (Clause 7.4.3.).

Gardner and New[8.14] in a review of British practice in prestressed concrete pile design quote a minimum prestress of 500 lb/in.² (3·4 N/mm²). They give a method of lengthening piles carrying only a direct load as follows—

"(*a*) The top of the pile is cleaned and moistened and covered with a layer of earth-dry sand–cement mortar of ½ in. (12 mm) minimum thickness, pressed into shape by hand.

"(*b*) A sleeve consisting of welded mild-steel plates, ⅜ in. (9·5 mm) thick, and of length four times the pile width, with a central diaphragm, is placed on the top of the pile with the diaphragm bedded on the mortar. A $\frac{1}{2}$ in. (12 mm) minimum layer of the same mortar is placed inside the sleeve evenly over the diaphragm and well tamped with a timber punner.

"(c) A further length of special prestressed pile with two square ends, complete with lifting holes and extra stirrups at each end, is then introduced into the open-ended sleeve bearing on the dry mortar layer. Driving is then continued immediately without waiting for any set to take place in the mortar."

Gardner and New add that the head must be dressed back reasonably square if it has been damaged during driving. If the extension piece exceeds 3 m in length it will be necessary to stiffen the sleeve by welding angles to each corner.

A notable example of the employment of prestressed concrete piles in Great Britain is in the foundations of the Esso Marine Terminal at Milford Haven.[8.15] The 1070 m long approach jetty and the four-berth pierhead were carried by 915 hollow cylindrical prestressed piles 698 and 589 mm outside diameter with a 75 mm wall thickness. The piles were up to 43 m long and weighed up to 18 tonne each. They were cast by a pre-tensioning method, up to five piles being constructed simultaneously on a 152 m length of casting bed. The 7 mm prestressing wires were each tensioned to 31·3 kN. The internal formwork for the piles consisted of lightly stressed wires over which was wrapped tarred building paper. The wires were kept in position by diaphragm spacers of weak concrete. The spacers or "biscuits" were broken by pulling a "go-devil" through the pile, after which the wires were pulled out by a tractor. The concrete mix adopted was designed to achieve a minimum compressive strength of 51·7 N/mm² at 28 days. The piles were driven by a pile frame mounted on a converted tank landing craft using a 10-tonne B.S.P. hammer. As many as seven or eight piles were driven in a day by the contractors John Mowlem and Co. who where responsible for the detailed designs of the structure.

### Steel Piles

Although steel piles have their widest use in the form of sheet piling, they are used to a considerable extent as bearing piles in foundations. They have the following advantages over other types—

(a) If driven on to a hard stratum they have a high carrying capacity.

(b) They can withstand hard driving without shattering; if the pile head buckles during hard driving it can readily be cut down and re-shaped for further driving.

(*c*) If required they can be designed to give relatively small displacement of the soil into which they are driven.

(*d*) They can readily be lengthened (without much delay to driving) by welding on additional lengths, thus permitting deep penetrations to be achieved without the need for a tall pile frame.

(*e*) They can be readily cut down if not driven to their full penetration and the cut-off portions have value as scrap.

(*f*) They can be roughly handled without damage.

(*g*) They have a good resistance to lateral forces and buckling.

Steel piles are used in marine structures where their resilience and column strength are advantageous in resisting impact forces from the berthing of ships.

Corrosion need not be a drawback to the use of steel bearing piles. Methods of protection of steel piles against corrosion are described in Chapter 13.

Working stresses should be appropriate to the grade of steel (in British practice to BS 4360 grades 43A, 50B). The values adopted should allow for the higher stresses that occur whilst the piles are being driven to the required ultimate bearing resistance and also for the additional driving stresses at the head and possibly at the toe of the pile. A steel suitable for marine structures where piles are subjected to high impact forces from ships or waves in low temperature conditions is a high tensile alloy steel conforming to Grades 55C or E of BS 4360.

Working stresses are subject to the reduction factors given in Table 7.3 (p. 421). Where steel tube or box piles are filled with concrete (minimum cement content 300 kg/m³) the load is shared between the concrete and the steel. The working stress in the concrete should not exceed the value normally used for precast concrete piles.

The *New York Foundation Code* permits an allowable stress of 248 N/mm² but places a maximum limit on the working load to prevent excessive driving stresses.

The three main types of steel pile in general use are—

(*a*) H-beam piles
(*b*) Box piles
(*c*) Tube piles.

## DETAILS OF H-BEAM AND BOX PILES

H-beam piles are usually in the form of wide-flange sections. In Great Britain they are rolled in accordance with B.S. 2566. Although a wide range of broad-flanged beams are rolled only the sections generally used for piling work are shown in Table 8.5.

Since they do not cause large displacement of the soil, H-beam piles are useful where upheaval of the surrounding ground would damage adjoining property, or where deep penetration is required through loose or medium dense sands. In the latter case, the sand around the piles is not consolidated to any appreciable distance from them, thus facilitating driving large groups of piles without the need for hard driving and consequent vibrations which might cause settlement of adjacent property founded on the sand. Deep scour was considered likely between the piers of the Tay Road Bridge in Scotland To achieve the required deep penetration of piles supporting the piers, an H-section was selected. Test piles of 305 by 305 mm section were driven by diesel hammer to depths of up to 49 m in medium-dense sands, gravels, and cobbles. If strengthened by welding on stiffening plates, the H-section is a useful means of punching through thin layers of rock or boulders. It might be expected that the H-beam pile would have a better penetrating ability than steel box or tube piles. However, experiences in driving the two types at the oil loading jetties at Mina-al-Ahmadi, Persian Gulf, showed that both 370 by 346 mm by 109 kg/m H-beams and Rendhex No. 4 box piles could be driven without undue difficulty through hard shelly conglomerate caprock on the sea bed. The rock layer was up to 2 m thick and was underlain by loose shelly sand. The 30 m long H-beam piles required up to 100 blows per 300 mm of a 2270 kg hammer falling 1·6 m to break through the 0·9 to 1·2 m thick caprock. The Rendhex piles took up to 60 blows per 300 mm of the Delmag D.22 hammer to penetrate 1·5 m of the same type of rock.

A disadvantage of the H-beam pile is the tendency to bend on the weak axis during driving. Thus if piles are driven to a deep penetration, a considerable curvature may result. Measurements of curvature made at Lambton, Ontario[8.16] on 310 and 352 mm H-beam piles driven through 46 m of clay into shale showed up to 1·8 or 2 m deflexion from the vertical with a minimum radius of curvature of 52 m. It was evident from these measurements that the safe working stresses in the steel were exceeded before the piles were subjected to superimposed load. The piles failed under test load. This was thought to be due to plastic deformation of the pile shaft in the region of the maximum curvature. Similar bending has been observed by Bjerrum[8.10] in H-piles in Norway. He states that any driven H-pile having a radius of curvature of less than 370 m after driving should be rejected. In this respect the steel tube pile filled with concrete after driving has an advantage since the concrete is not stressed until the superimposed load is applied to the pile.

The low resistance to penetration of the H-beam pile in loose sandy soils may be a disadvantage in circumstances where high

### Table 8.5
### TYPES, DIMENSIONS, AND PROPERTIES OF STEEL H-BEAM PILES

British Steel Corporation Universal Bearing Piles, and United States Steel CBP Bearing Piles.

| Serial size mm | Weight per m kg | Depth D mm | Width B mm | Thickness of web and flange $t$ mm | Area of section cm² | Moment of inertia | | Radius of gyration | | Modulus of section | | U.S. steel section index |
|---|---|---|---|---|---|---|---|---|---|---|---|---|
| | | | | | | $XX$ axis cm⁴ | $YY$ axis cm⁴ | $XX$ axis mm | $YY$ axis mm | $XX$ axis cm³ | $YY$ axis cm³ × 10³ | |
| 356 × 368 | 174 | 362 | 378 | 20·4 | 222·2 | 51134 | 18444 | 152 | 91·1 | 2829 | 976 | CBP 145 |
| | 152 | 356 | 376 | 17·9 | 193·6 | 43916 | 15799 | 151 | 90·3 | 2464 | 841 | |
| | 133 | 352 | 373 | 15·6 | 169·0 | 37840 | 13576 | 150 | 89·6 | 2150 | 727 | |
| | 109 | 346 | 370 | 12·9 | 138·4 | 30515 | 10901 | 148 | 88·7 | 1762 | 588 | |
| 305 × 305 | 223 | 338 | 325 | 30·5 | 285·0 | 52817 | 17570 | 136 | 78·0 | 3126 | 1080 | CBP 124 |
| | 186 | 328 | 320 | 25·7 | 237·0 | 42625 | 14108 | 134 | 77·0 | 2597 | 881 | |
| | 149 | 318 | 315 | 20·6 | 190·0 | 33040 | 10869 | 132 | 76·0 | 2075 | 689 | |
| | 126 | 313 | 313 | 17·8 | 161·0 | 27526 | 9013 | 131 | 75·0 | 1763 | 577 | |
| | 110 | 308 | 310 | 15·4 | 140·4 | 23580 | 7689 | 130 | 74·0 | 1532 | 496 | |
| | 95 | 304 | 308 | 13·4 | 121·0 | 20111 | 6529 | 129 | 73·0 | 1324 | 424 | |
| | 88 | 302 | 307 | 12·3 | 112·0 | 18402 | 5959 | 128 | 73·0 | 1220 | 388 | |
| | 79 | 299 | 306 | 11·1 | 100·4 | 16400 | 5292 | 128 | 72·6 | 1096 | 346 | |

**Table 8.5** (*cont.*)

| Serial size | Weight per m | Depth D | Width B | Thickness of web and flange t | Area of section | Moment of inertia | | Radius of gyration | | Modulus of section | | U.S. steel section index |
|---|---|---|---|---|---|---|---|---|---|---|---|---|
| | | | | | | XX axis | YY axis | XX axis | YY axis | XX axis | YY axis | |
| mm | kg | mm | mm | mm | cm² | cm⁴ | cm⁴ | mm | mm | cm³ | cm³ × 10³ | |
| 254 × 254 | 85 | 254 | 260 | 14·3 | 108·1 | 12264 | 4188 | 107 | 62·2 | 965 | 323 | CBP 103 |
| | 63 | 247 | 256 | 10·6 | 79·7 | 8775 | 2971 | 105 | 61·1 | 711 | 232 | |
| | 71 | 250 | 257 | 12·1 | 91·0 | 10153 | 3451 | 106 | 61·0 | 813 | 268 | |
| 203 × 203 | 54 | 204 | 207 | 11·3 | 68·4 | 4987 | 1683 | 85·4 | 49·6 | 489 | 162 | CBP 83 |
| | 45 | 200 | 205 | 9·5 | 57·0 | 4079 | 1539 | 84·6 | 49·0 | 408 | 133 | |

shaft friction and end-bearing resistance is required at an economical depth of penetration. Since little consolidation of the sand is effected around and beneath an H-beam pile the shaft friction is relatively low and the pile may not achieve satisfactory resistance until driven to a dense sand stratum or other resistant material. A box pile, on the other hand, displaces a large volume of soil and the frictional resistance and end resistance is rapidly built up. When box piles are driven into clays, they can be driven open-ended since a plug of clay is taken down with the pile and forms a hard compact mass with an end resistance equal to the gross cross-sectional area of the end of the pile. A similar plug of clay is formed within the flanges of H-beam piles. However it is necessary to check by calculation that there is adequate skin frictional resistance on the interior of the hollow pile or within the flanges of the H-pile to yielding of the soil plug at the designed base load on the pile. In the case of granular soils or weak rocks shattered by pile driving, the skin friction mobilized on the interior of hollow piles or within H-pile flanges will not be sufficient to build up any useful resistance in the form of a plug at the pile toe. Therefore the base resistance of tube or box piles and H-piles in granular soils or rocks should be calculated only on the net cross-sectional area of the steel. The skin frictional resistance of clays to H-piles was discussed on p. 392. In granular soils the skin friction on hollow piles or H-piles can be calculated on all steel surfaces provided that this can be checked by measuring the length of soil plug after driving. The interior skin friction must not exceed the plug weight.

In Germany special types of steel H-beam piles are manufactured which are capable of being welded or coupled together to increase their end bearing area or resistance to lateral loads. Schenck[8.17] has described the use at Bremen and Bremerhaven of "winged piles" consisting of short lengths of steel H-beams welded to the bottom of the Peine (a wide-flanged beam) pile or to H-beam piles made up from Larssen trough sections. These "winged piles" are specifically designed to give a high end resistance for a limited penetration into a bearing stratum of sand.

FILLING BOX AND TUBE PILES WITH CONCRETE

If driving conditions permit, it is preferable to drive box or tube piles with a closed end since this avoids splitting or enlargement of the ends. Alternatively they may be driven open-ended and if required they can then be cleaned-out for their full depth and hearted with concrete. If long piles are driven by welding on successive lengths, a convenient method is to drive the first length open-ended,

Table 8.6

## TYPES AND DIMENSIONS OF STEEL BOX PILES (see p. 509)

(a) Larssen Box Piles

| Section no. | B mm | H mm | d mm | Weight including welds kg/m | Section modulus cm³ XX axis | Section modulus cm³ YY axis | Moment of inertia cm⁴ XX axis | Moment of inertia cm⁴ YY axis | Least radius of gyration mm | Perimeter mm approx. | Cross sectional area cm² Steel only | Cross sectional area cm² Whole pile |
|---|---|---|---|---|---|---|---|---|---|---|---|---|
| BP. 1A | 432 | 167 | 7·2 | 67·3 | 420 | 840 | 3 492 | 18 142 | 63·6 | 1120 | 85·8 | 596·6 |
| BP. 1B | 432 | 214 | 7·1 | 71·3 | 565 | 891 | 6 048 | 19 246 | 75·9 | 1220 | 91·3 | 774·2 |
| BP. 1GB | 432 | 165 | 8·1 | 72·3 | 457 | 980 | 3 775 | 19 614 | 64·0 | 1220 | 92·1 | 619·4 |
| BP. 1U | 432 | 165 | 9·4 | 84·8 | 533 | 1087 | 4 400 | 23 620 | 64·0 | 1220 | 108·3 | 619·4 |
| BP. 2 | 438 | 240 | 10·2 | 97·6 | 850 | 1177 | 10 198 | 25 777 | 90·7 | 1240 | 124·4 | 858·1 |
| BP. 2B | 436 | 314 | 8·6 | 93·4 | 982 | 1201 | 15 430 | 26 156 | 105·7 | 1400 | 119·1 | 1077·4 |
| BP. 2N | 436 | 314 | 9·5 | 97·6 | 1068 | 1224 | 16 791 | 26 672 | 116·1 | 1420 | 124·4 | 1083·8 |
| BP. 3 | 438 | 289 | 14·2 | 124·0 | 1332 | 1358 | 19 251 | 29 761 | 110·5 | 1320 | 158·1 | 1019·4 |
| BP. 3B | 438 | 343 | 13·5 | 124·1 | 1526 | 1380 | 26 152 | 30 218 | 127·5 | 1420 | 158·2 | 1161·3 |
| BP. 3/20 | 544 | 390 | 11·7 | 139·1 | 1991 | 2089 | 38 789 | 56 807 | 127·8 | 1650 | 177·4 | 1580·6 |
| BP. 4A | 436 | 429 | 15·7 | 148·0 | 2217 | 1645 | 47 529 | 35 833 | 137·7 | 1600 | 188·8 | 1412·9 |
| BP. 4B | 467 | 394 | 15·5 | 168·9 | 2270 | 2078 | 44 682 | 47 500 | 145·8 | 1550 | 215·2 | 1432·3 |
| BP. 4/20 | 543 | 427 | 14·3 | 165·0 | 2661 | 2366 | 56 828 | 64 316 | 164·6 | 1780 | 210·4 | 1855·4 |
| BP. 5 | 467 | 394 | 22·1 | 200·0 | 2973 | 2252 | 58 501 | 51 471 | 142·2 | 1550 | 255·0 | 1432·3 |
| BP. 6 | 464 | 502 | 22·1 | 243·6 | 4215 | 2912 | 105 731 | 67 563 | 147·6 | 2080 | 310·6 | 1793·5 |
| BP. 10B/20 | 541 | 215 | 12·7 | 132·7 | 980 | 1844 | 10 547 | 49 906 | 78·7 | 1320 | 170·3 | 922·5 |

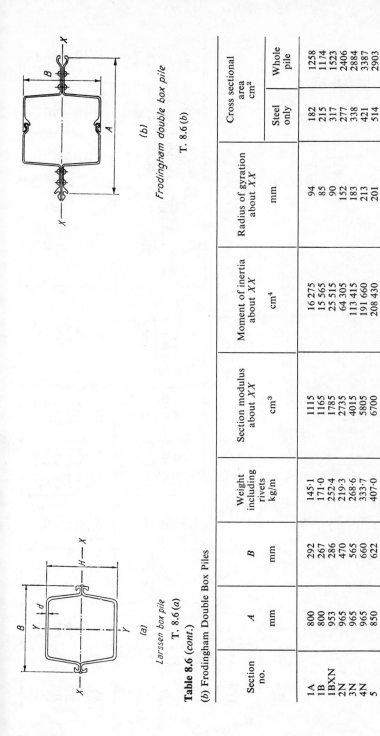

(a)

Larssen box pile

T. 8.6 (a)

(b)

Frodingham double box pile

T. 8.6 (b)

**Table 8.6** (cont.)

(b) Frodingham Double Box Piles

| Section no. | A mm | B mm | Weight including rivets kg/m | Section modulus about XX cm³ | Moment of inertia about XX cm⁴ | Radius of gyration about XX mm | Cross sectional area cm² | |
|---|---|---|---|---|---|---|---|---|
| | | | | | | | Steel only | Whole pile |
| 1A | 800 | 292 | 145·1 | 1115 | 16 275 | 94 | 182 | 1258 |
| 1B | 800 | 267 | 171·0 | 1165 | 15 565 | 85 | 215 | 1174 |
| 1BXN | 953 | 286 | 252·4 | 1785 | 25 515 | 90 | 317 | 1523 |
| 2N | 965 | 470 | 219·3 | 2735 | 64 305 | 152 | 277 | 2406 |
| 3N | 965 | 565 | 268·6 | 4015 | 113 415 | 183 | 338 | 2884 |
| 4N | 965 | 660 | 333·7 | 5805 | 191 660 | 213 | 421 | 3387 |
| 5 | 850 | 622 | 407·0 | 6700 | 208 430 | 201 | 514 | 2903 |

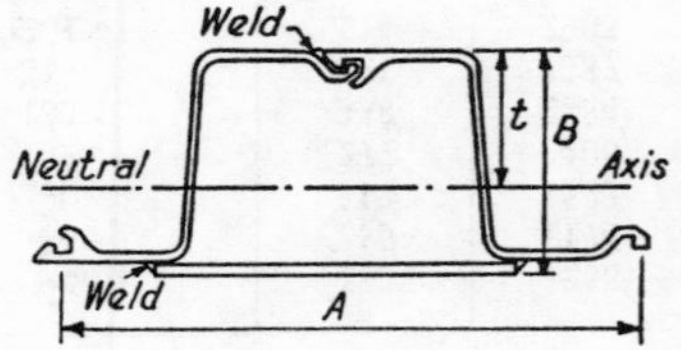

(c)

Frodingham plated box pile

T. 8.6(c)

**Table 8.6** (*cont.*)

(c) Frodingham Plated Box Piles

| Section no. | A mm | B mm | t mm | Size of standard plate mm | Weight including welds kg/m | Minimum section modulus about neutral axis cm³ | Moment of inertia about neutral axis cm⁴ | Radius of gyration about neutral axis mm | Cross sectional area cm² | |
|---|---|---|---|---|---|---|---|---|---|---|
| | | | | | | | | | Steel only | Whole pile |
| 1A | 800 | 156 | 100 | 508 × 10 | 109·2 | 520 | 5 200 | 61 | 139 | 677 |
| 1B | 800 | 144 | 93 | 558 × 11 | 132·9 | 540 | 5 035 | 55 | 170 | 652 |
| 1BXN | 953 | 157 | 102 | 711 × 14 | 203·9 | 830 | 8 490 | 57 | 259 | 858 |
| 2N | 965 | 248 | 164 | 660 × 13 | 174·2 | 1280 | 21 060 | 97 | 222 | 1290 |
| 3N | 965 | 297 | 195 | 660 × 14 | 206·3 | 1870 | 36 375 | 118 | 263 | 1548 |
| 4N | 965 | 346 | 223 | 660 × 16 | 247·1 | 2705 | 59 475 | 137 | 315 | 1813 |
| 5 | 850 | 330 | 202 | 533 × 19 | 281·2 | 3055 | 61 805 | 131 | 359 | 1555 |

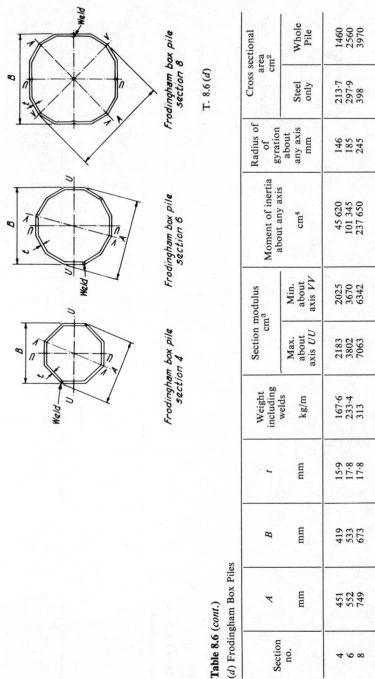

Frodingham box pile
section 8

Frodingham box pile
section 6

Frodingham box pile
section 4

T. 8.6 (d)

**Table 8.6** (cont.)

(d) Frodingham Box Piles

| Section no. | A mm | B mm | t mm | Weight including welds kg/m | Section modulus cm³ | | Moment of inertia about any axis cm⁴ | Radius of of gyration about any axis mm | Cross sectional area cm² | |
|---|---|---|---|---|---|---|---|---|---|---|
| | | | | | Max. about axis $UU$ | Min. about axis $VV$ | | | Steel only | Whole Pile |
| 4 | 451 | 419 | 15·9 | 167·6 | 2183 | 2025 | 45 620 | 146 | 213·7 | 1460 |
| 6 | 552 | 533 | 17·8 | 233·4 | 3802 | 3670 | 101 345 | 185 | 297·9 | 2560 |
| 8 | 749 | 673 | 17·8 | 313 | 7063 | 6342 | 237 650 | 245 | 398 | 3970 |

**Table 8.6** (*cont.*)

(*e*) Rendhex Box Piles:

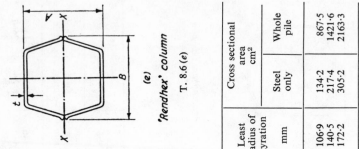

(*e*)
'Rendhex' column

T. 8.6 (*e*)

| Section no. | A | B | t | Weight including welds | Section modulus cm³ | | Moment of inertia cm⁴ | | Least radius of gyration | Cross sectional area cm² | |
|---|---|---|---|---|---|---|---|---|---|---|---|
| | mm | mm | mm | kg/m | XX axis | YY axis | XX axis | YY axis | mm | Steel only | Whole pile |
| 3 | 330·2 | 327·0 | 12·7 | 105·7 | 1180 | 995 | 19 488 | 15 445 | 106·9 | 134·2 | 867·5 |
| 4 | 406·4 | 414·3 | 15·9 | 171·4 | 2466 | 2083 | 50 110 | 43 142 | 140·5 | 217·4 | 1421·6 |
| 6 | 508·0 | 508·0 | 17·8 | 240·3 | 4356 | 3572 | 110 622 | 90 728 | 172·2 | 305·2 | 2163·3 |

then to provide the next or next-but-one length with a diaphragm so that the upper part of the pile, which may be subject to corrosion, remains empty and clean for hearting with concrete. In calculating the stresses on the cross-section resulting from the working load, the strength of the hearting material can be taken into consideration, but the cross-sectional area of steel in a hollow pile is likely to be governed by driving stresses rather than by the compressive stress set up by the working load.

The "pre-packed" system is a suitable method for hearting hollow piles, particularly if they become filled with water. A small-diameter pipe is first lowered down the interior of the pile and surrounded by

Details of steel box piles rolled and fabricated in Great Britain as given in the manufacturers' handbooks are shown in Table 8.6. The Larssen box pile and the Frodingham double box and plated box piles are suitable for incorporation in a sheet pile wall.

Simple rectangular box piles can be made up by welding flat steel plates. Piles of this type were used by the author's firm for the approaches to the Regent Oil jetty in Milford Haven. Piles of 692 by 457 mm overall section were made up from 16 mm mild steel plate. The large section was required to resist flexural stresses set up by expansion and contraction of the multiple oil pipelines carried by the approach trestle.

M.V. piles are small square box-section steel piles driven with an enlarged shoe and subsequently grouted to fill the space between the shaft and the soil. They are frequently used as anchor piles to resist tension loads.

## Tube Piles

Steel tube piles incorporating high tensile tubes are used for marine structures where high lateral forces due to the berthing impact of ships and to wave action must be resisted. Due to their circular section these tubular piles offer less resistance to waves and currents than the rectangular H-section piles. Also the use of high tensile steel gives economy in weight of material and hence reduced shipping and handling costs. The piles can be made in three parts: the upper part and lower part in mild steel, and the centre part in high tensile steel. This confines the more expensive high tensile steel to the highly stressed zone in the region of the sea-bed and facilitates welding of bracing steelwork to the upper section.

The piles can be installed by driving or by drilling them into the sea-bed. The latter method was used by the author's firm for the construction of two oil tanker jetties in Milford Haven. In the case of the Regent Oil jetty the cylinders were drilled into the siltstone on the sea bed by means of a large rotary table. This was mounted on a De Long spud pontoon, which was subsequently incorporated in the permanent structure. The largest cylinders were used for the mooring dolphins. They were 1308 mm internal diameter and up to 39 m long, and were drilled 10·7 m into rock. After reaching their final level they were plugged with 2 to 4 m of concrete and then the space between the cylinders and the rock was grouted with cement. High tensile steel was used for the cylinders. A similar method was used for drilling large-diameter high tensile steel cylinders into the marly limestone below the sea bed for the Abu Dhabi Marine Areas Ltd. tanker loading facilities at Das Island in the Persian Gulf. Large-diameter cylinders for marine structures can also be installed by methods used for sinking large-diameter piles on land as described on pages 527 to 529.

Steel tube piles are widely used in U.S.A., sometimes in the form of ordinary pipe-sections filled with concrete, and also in the form of specially designed fluted sections (to give rigidity for handling and driving) which are driven to the full depth by ordinary pile hammer and then filled with concrete. The Union "monotube" pile is a tapered fluted steel section used in U.S.A. These piles with a tip diameter of 203 mm and butt diameters of 305, 355, 406, or 457 mm are provided in various gauges of steel depending on the driving conditions. They are driven without a mandrel. The upper part of the pile has parallel sides and the lower part is tapered.

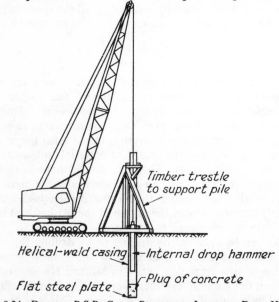

Fig. 8.24. Driving B.S.P. Cased Piles with Internal Drop Hammer

Another form of steel pile is the light tapered sheet steel casing driven by means of a mandrel which is subsequently withdrawn and the space filled with concrete. This type is described on page 519.

The B.S.P. cased pile is a spirally welded mild-steel tube driven with a closed end either by a single- or double-acting hammer working on top of the pile or by an internal drop hammer delivering its blow on to a plug of concrete placed in the bottom of the pile (Fig. 8.24). The standard casings are supplied with internal diameters ranging from 254 to 813 mm in increments of 51 mm. B.S.P. International Foundations Ltd. give design data for typical casings to carry a range of working loads as shown in Table 8.7.

**Table 8.7**

**TYPICAL CASING SIZES FOR B.S.P. CASED PILES**

| Working load (kN) | Inside dia. of casing (mm) | Casing thickness (s.w.g.) (mm) | Welded flat plate shoe thickness (mm) | Weight of standard internal drop hammer (kg) |
|---|---|---|---|---|
| 150 | 254 | 10 s.w.g. (3·25 mm) | 9·5 | 760 |
| 250/350 | 305 | 10 s.w.g. (3·25 mm) | 9·5 | 1270 |
| 400 | 356 | 10 s.w.g. (3·25 mm) | 12·7 | 2030 |
| 500 | 406 | 9 s.w.g. (3·66 mm) | 12·7 | 2540 |
| 650 | 457 | 8 s.w.g. (4·06 mm) | 15·9 | 3050 |
| 800 | 508 | 7 s.w.g. (4·47 mm) | 15·9 | 4060 |

## TYPES OF DRIVEN AND CAST-IN-PLACE PILES

### Franki Piles

The Franki pile is a form of driven and cast-in-place displacement pile which is widely used throughout the world. The stages in forming the pile are shown in Fig. 8.25 (*a*) to (*d*). The pile tube is first pitched in a shallow excavation. A plug of gravel or lean concrete is then placed in the bottom of the tube and compacted with a heavy steel rammer (*a*). As the plug is rammed it is forced down into the soil and the tube is allowed to follow down with the plug (*b*). Driving continues until the bearing stratum is reached, when the tube is prevented from sinking further and the concrete is hammered out to form a bulb (*c*). A reinforcing cage is then lowered down the tube and the pile shaft concreted. The tube is withdrawn in stages as the concrete is placed and rammed (*d*).

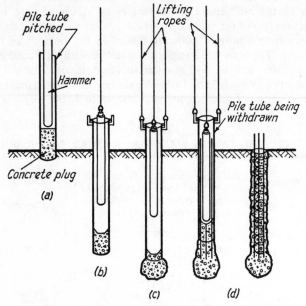

FIG. 8.25. STAGES IN FORMING A FRANKI PILE

The advantages of the Franki pile are—

(*a*) The enlarged end gives a higher end resistance than the conventional straight-sided pile.

(*b*) The action of hammering out the bulb in a sandy soil compacts the soil for several bulb diameters around and below the pile, thus increasing the end resistance.

(*c*) When forming the bulb in a clay soil, water expelled from the clay is absorbed by the dry concrete of the bulb, thus consolidating and strengthening the clay around the bulb.

(*d*) Ramming the concrete against the soil in forming the shaft compacts the soil and increases the shaft friction or adhesion.

(*e*) The dry concrete plug is watertight, so keeping the driving tube free from water or slurry.

(*f*) Because the hammer blow is made directly on the plug there is less surface vibration than with ordinary forms of driven piles.

The disadvantages of the Franki pile are not peculiar to this type but are found in most forms of driven and cast-in-place piles. With the employment of correct techniques the disadvantages can, in most cases, be overcome, but the engineer should be aware of the possibility of their occurrence. They are listed as follows—

(a) When piles are driven in large groups, the soundness of partly hardened concrete in already driven piles may be impaired by heaving or lateral displacement of the ground due to driving adjacent piles.

(b) Severe cases of ground heave in a clay soil may cause failure in tension of pile already driven.

(c) If concreting the pile shaft is carelessly done "waisting" or "necking" of the pile shaft may occur in soft clays or peat. (This can be overcome by placing the concrete in a permanent metal sleeve.)

(d) Water under pressure may pipe up the side of the pile shaft washing away cement from unset concrete and causing reduction in pile diameter.

Moderately deep penetration of Franki piles can be facilitated by first boring the upper part of the shaft before placing the plug then driving the tube and plug in the usual way, but Franki piles cannot be driven to very great depths. Typical working loads are—

| Nominal shaft diameter (mm) | Nominal maximum working load (kN) |
|---|---|
| 330–355 | 350 |
| 355–381 | 500 |
| 406–457 | 700 |
| 457–508 | 900 |
| 508–558 | 1100 |
| 584–635 | 1400 |

The Franki Pile Co. usually arrive at the required lengths of their piles from observations of the resistance to driving of the tube and concrete plug. It is possible for the engineer to make approximate estimates of the carrying capacity of Franki piles using "static" methods with an assumed bulb diameter. However, the effects of tube driving and withdrawal on skin friction are uncertain in this type of pile, and the size of the bulb cannot be predicted accurately. Therefore, the engineer's calculations can only give an approximate guide to carrying capacity and it is advisable to carry out loading tests on full-scale piles to check the estimate of capacity. It is usual for the engineer, when using these and other proprietary types of pile, to be guided by the piling contractor on the required shaft diameter and length. However, it is essential for the piling contractor to be provided with accurate information on the soil conditions, including data on the shear strength of cohesive soils and the relative density of cohesionless soils. The engineer should also specify the minimum compressive strength and minimum cement content of the concrete.

The *Dowsett* pile is very similar in type and installation method to the Franki pile. Dowsett piles have 432 and 483 mm nominal shaft diameters with working loads similar to the corresponding Franki piles.

## Vibro Piles

Vibro piles are formed by driving a steel tube into the ground by the blows of a 2030 to 4060 kg hammer. The tube is provided with a loose conical cast-iron shoe which keeps the tube closed until it is driven to the required depth. A steel reinforcing cage is then lowered into position and the tube is filled with concrete up to pile cap level. Extracting links are then fitted to the tube and connected to the hammer which makes alternate upward and downward blows on the tube. On the upward blow the tube is extracted for a short distance and the concrete slumps outwards against the walls of the hole. On the downward blow given to the tube the mass of concrete contained

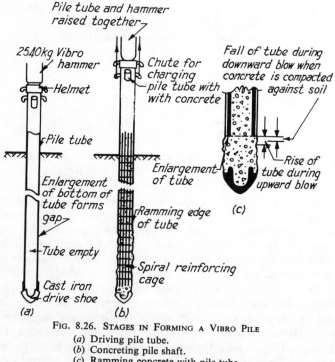

FIG. 8.26. STAGES IN FORMING A VIBRO PILE
(a) Driving pile tube.
(b) Concreting pile shaft.
(c) Ramming concrete with pile tube.

in the tube moves downwards, thus compacting the concrete below the tube and forcing it into closer contact with the soil. The extracting and tamping blows are performed in rapid succession to keep the concrete "alive," thus preventing it from rising with the tube and lifting the reinforcement. Stages in forming the pile are shown in Fig. 8.26 (*a*) to (*c*).

Vibro piles are installed in five sizes—

| Nominal shaft diameter (mm) | Nominal maximum working load (kN) |
|:---:|:---:|
| 343 | 450 |
| 380 | 600 |
| 432 | 750 |
| 482 | 960 |
| 534 | 1100 |

As in the case of Franki piles it is difficult to make close estimates of the carrying capacity of Vibro piles by "static" methods because of uncertainties in the value of shaft friction and in the size of any enlargement at the bottom of the pile.

The disadvantages of the Vibro pile are similar to those listed for the Franki pile.

### Simplex, Delta and G.K.N. Piles

Piles of the above types are formed by driving a steel tube with a detachable cast-iron shoe in a similar manner to the Vibro pile. The tube is extracted by wire ropes connected to the piling winch while the concrete is being rammed by a falling rammer working inside the reinforcing cage. Alternatively the pile tube can be filled completely with high slump concrete before it is extracted.

### Alpha Piles

A steel tube closed with a detachable cast-iron shoe is driven to the desired level. A concrete-filled mandrel is driven inside the tube (Fig. 8.27 (*a*)). When the tube has been fully driven the mandrel is raised to allow some concrete to slump down in the tube (*b*). The concrete is replenished in the mandrel and the latter is driven down as the tube is raised. Driving the mandrel forces out the concrete to give a bulb (*c*). After the bulb is completed, the mandrel is raised and replenished with concrete in stages. At each stage the concrete in the pile shaft is pressed against the soil by the dead weight of the hammer on the mandrel (*d*). The tube and mandrel are finally drawn clear of the ground and the pile is completed. The flanged lower end of the mandrel is provided with circumferential holes through which the

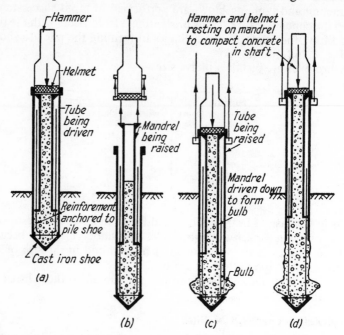

FIG. 8.27. STAGES IN FORMING AN ALPHA PILE

reinforcing bars are passed. This serves to locate the bars and preserve the correct cover of concrete. Alpha piles are provided in the following sizes—

| Nominal shaft diameter (mm) | Shoe diameter (mm) | Nominal maximum working load (kN) |
|---|---|---|
| 400 | 394 | 500 |
| 450 | 444 | 700 |
| 500 | 495 | 1000 |

### Western "Button-Bottom" Piles

This type of pile is used widely in the U.S.A., Mexico, and Canada. The operations in driving the piles are shown in Fig. 8.28 (a) to (c) as follows—

1. A 432 mm diameter precast concrete point is driven into the ground on the end of a steel tube (*a*).

2. After reaching the prescribed level, a spirally corrugated steel shell is lowered into the tube and locked into the point at the bottom (*b*).

3. The steel shell is filled with concrete, with or without a reinforcing cage, and the driving tube is withdrawn (*c*).

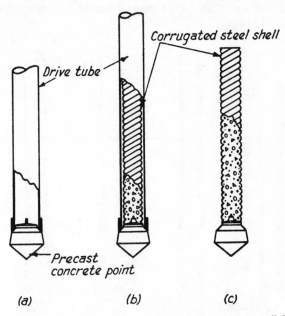

FIG. 8.28. STAGES IN FORMING A WESTERN "BUTTON-BOTTOM" PILE

The corrugated steel shell is advantageous when piles in soft "squeezing" ground are to be formed. Also, when piles are driven in a large group, heaving of the soil cannot cause the pile shaft to fail in tension; therefore no reinforcement need be provided against uplift by ground heave. The designers claim that the corrugated steel shell adds to the skin friction on the shaft. However, since a void is formed around the shell when the driving tube is withdrawn, it must be filled by soil falling inwards. Thus, in a stiff clay or dense sand, it must be expected that the shaft friction or adhesion will be lower than that developed by a pile in which the concrete is tamped in direct contact against the soil. For this reason the button-bottom pile must be regarded mainly as an end-bearing pile.

### Western Pedestal Pile

This is similar in principle to the button-bottom pile except that provision is made for an enlarged base. The procedure is illustrated in Fig. 8.29 (*a*) to (*d*) as follows—

1. The drive tube fitted with the standard button-bottom is driven to the required level (*a*).
2. A charge of concrete is placed in the drive tube.
3. A solid core is set on top of the concrete and the casing extracted for a short distance (*b*).

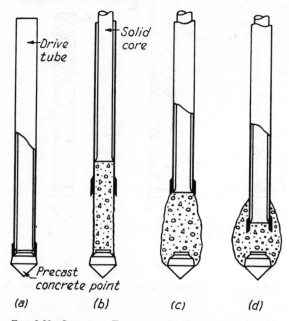

FIG. 8.29. STAGES IN FORMING A WESTERN PEDESTAL PILE

4. The core is hammered to force out the concrete, thus forming an enlargement above and around the button (*c*).
5. The drive tube and core are driven together into the enlargement thus giving further compaction and enlargement (*d*).
6. The pile shaft is concreted and the drive tube withdrawn. The core is held in place on top of the concrete as the tube is withdrawn in order to prevent the concrete from rising with the tube.

In soft ground, a corrugated steel shell is placed inside the drive tube before the shaft is concreted.

The pedestal pile has all the advantages of the button-bottom pile, with the added advantages of the enlarged end and of concrete placed in direct contact with the soil which increases the shaft friction, except where soft soil conditions require a steel shell.

### Steel Shell Piles driven with Mandrel (Raymond Piles)

These types are installed by the Raymond Concrete Pile Co. and they are known as the Raymond Taper or Step-Taper piles. The steel shells of the taper piles are in 1·2 and 2·4 m long spirally reinforced light steel sections. The tapered sections decrease uniformly in diameter by 1 mm per 48 mm of length to a maximum length of 11·3 m where the tip diameter is 203 mm. Step-tapered piles are formed from 1·2 m and 2·4 m long straight-sided sections of spirally corrugated

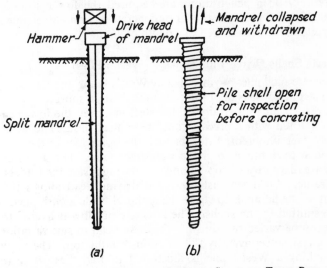

FIG. 8.30. STAGES IN FORMING A RAYMOND STANDARD TAPER PILE

steel. Each successive length decreases in diameter by 25 mm in 2·44 mm to a minimum diameter of 216 mm. Step-tapered piles can be driven to a maximum depth of 24 m. The 24 m pile has a tip diameter of 216 mm and a butt diameter of 438 mm. The procedure in driving tapered piles is illustrated in Fig. 8.30 (*a*) and (*b*) as follows—

1. The steel shells are assembled to the required length over the tapered steel mandrel which is expanded to grip the shells.

2. The mandrel and shells are lifted into the leaders of a pile frame and then driven to the required level by single- or double-acting hammer (*a*).

3. The mandrel is contracted and withdrawn and the interior of the pile inspected.

4. The shell is concreted with or without a reinforcing cage (*b*).

A somewhat similar procedure is used for driving step-taper piles. Conditions for concreting the Raymond pile are good in that the joints in the shells are screwed and sealed to make them watertight and the alignment of the shells can be inspected before the concrete is placed. The shells give resistance against squeezing ground and against failure of the shaft in tension due to ground heave when driving piles in large groups.

Raymond piles have been used in many parts of the world. They are adaptable to varying soil conditions since sections can be added or taken away as required to suit varying depths of penetration. Where very deep penetrations are required the lower section can consist of a steel pipe or a timber or concrete section. Steel pipe step-taper piles have been driven to a depth of 46 m.

### Concrete Shells Driven with Mandrel (West's Piles)

Concrete shell piles are installed by West's Piling and Construction Co. The pile consists of precast concrete shells in short lengths which are threaded on to a straight-sided steel mandrel, the lower end of which is fitted with a precast concrete conical shoe. The shells are joined by circumferential steel bands; the inside face of these can be painted with bitumen to give a watertight joint. The mandrel and shells are driven by a drop hammer operating inside the leaders of a pile frame. An ingeniously designed driving head allows the full weight of the hammer to strike the mandrel while a cushioned blow is transmitted to the shells. The intensity of blow delivered to the shells can be varied by adjusting the drive head to suit variations in driving resistance given by skin friction or adhesion. The sequence in installing a West's pile is illustrated in Fig. 8.31 (*a*) to (*c*) as follows—

1. The concrete shoe is set in a shallow hole and the mandrel is lowered on to the shoe (*a*).

2. The concrete shells are threaded on to the mandrel.

3. The pile is driven to the required level (*b*).

4. The mandrel is withdrawn and any surplus shells removed.

5. The interior of the pile is inspected, a steel reinforcing cage set in position, and the interior of the shells is filled with concrete (*c*).

The West's pile has the advantage that the length can be readily adjusted to suit varying ground conditions by adding or taking away the shells. The longest pile driven has been 32 m. The West's

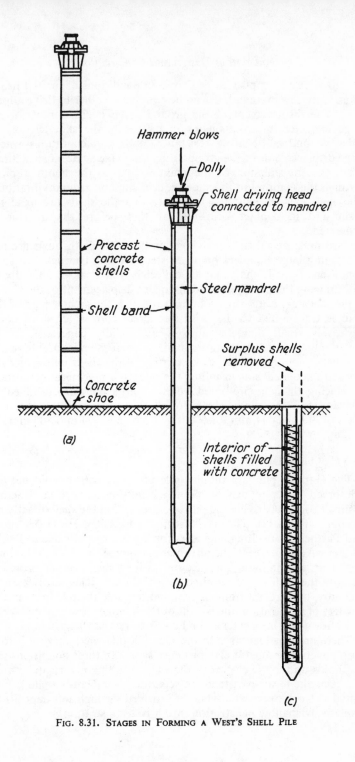

Hammer blows

Dolly

Shell driving head
connected to mandrel

Precast
concrete
shells

Steel mandrel

Shell band

Surplus shells
removed

Concrete
shoe

Interior of
shells filled
with concrete

(a)

(b)

(c)

FIG. 8.31. STAGES IN FORMING A WEST'S SHELL PILE

system allows long piles to be driven in conditions of limited head-room since several mandrels can be coupled together to drive a long pile.  The displacement of the ground given by its comparatively large diameter is advantageous in increasing the skin friction or adhesion and end-bearing resistance, except in conditions where large displacements of the ground might damage adjacent structures. Also, the transmission of the main weight of the hammer blow through the mandrel to the shoe reduces shallow ground vibrations. The shaft can be inspected to ensure that the shells are in align-ment and in contact with one another before the interior is concreted.

Care must be taken in driving this type of pile through ground containing large boulders or on to steep sloping bedrock.  In such conditions the pile shaft may be deflected which causes difficulty in withdrawing the mandrel and consequent displacement of the shells. If the shells are not properly butting together the greater part of the load is transmitted to the in-situ concrete core which is of com-paratively small diameter and, if not solidly concreted, might collapse under a heavy working load.  Also, if the piles are driven in groups, ground heave may cause parting of the shells unless precau-tions are taken such as installing the piles in a predetermined order, or placing them in pre-bored holes.  West's piles are installed in 508 and 533 ext. diam. shells for working loads in the range of 750 to 1200 kN, 444 mm for 500 to 800 kN, and 381 and 406 mm for loading up to 650 kN.

### The Gambia Pile

The Gambia pile is a tubular pile provided with a solid heavily reinforced concrete driving point.  The single- or double-acting hammer used for driving the pile operates within the shell directly on the point (Fig. 8.32).  The pile illustrated was designed by G. Maunsell and Partners, consulting engineers for the Narrows Bridge at Perth, Western Australia.[8.18]  The advantages claimed for the Gambia pile are: first, ease in handling since only a light shell need be provided because the shell is not required to withstand driving stresses; and secondly, only a light frame is required to guide the pile in its initial few feet of penetration, the weight of the hammer being taken by the pile after it has been pitched and come to rest in the ground.

There are disadvantages in the Gambia pile when driving it to a deep penetration in stiff clay or dense sand.  In these conditions the soil holds up the upper part of the shaft resulting in circumferential cracks as the lower part tends to separate.  The Gambia pile is best suited to work over water where it is driven through soft deposits to a relatively shallow penetration into a bearing stratum.

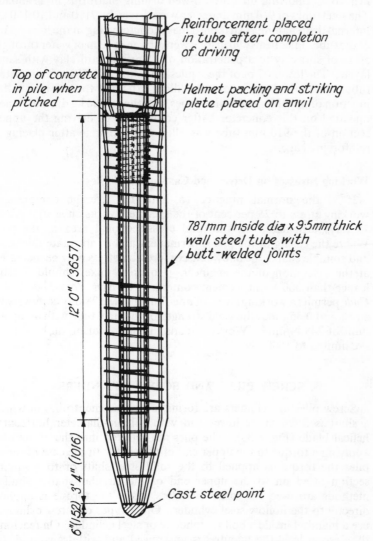

Reinforcement placed
in tube after completion
of driving

Top of concrete
in pile when
pitched

Helmet packing and striking
plate placed on anvil

787mm Inside dia x 9·5mm thick
wall steel tube with
butt-welded joints

12' 0" (3657)

3' 4" (1016)

6"(152)

Cast steel point

FIG. 8.32 TOE OF GAMBIA PILE, NARROWS BRIDGE, PERTH

A simplified version of the Gambia pile was used by the author's firm for supporting offshore oil-well drilling platforms in Trinidad. The steel tubes of 914 mm diameter were driven by 7110 and 10 160 kg internal drop hammers striking a mass concrete plug in the lower part of the tube. Piles nearly 90 m long were driven in 10 m of water through 50 m of soft clay to a penetration of 21 m into stiff clay with sand layers. The lower 27 m of these piles consisted of a 610 mm diameter tube. The initial mass concrete filling extended to 2 m above the junction of the 910 and 610 mm tubes, and the 10 160 kg drop hammer operated on this concrete. After completion of driving the upper section of the 910 mm tube was filled with concrete after placing a reinforcing cage.

## Working Stresses on Driven and Cast-in-Place Piles

It is the normal practice to limit the average compressive working stress to 25 per cent of the specified works cube strength at 28 days, calculated on the total cross-sectional area of the pile. Where the casing of the pile is permanent and of adequate thickness and suitable shape, the allowable compressive stress may be increased at the discretion of the engineer. Concrete mixes should not be leaner than 300 kg/m³ cement content. The *New York Foundation Code* permits a working stress of one-fourth of the 28-day compressive stress and 0·35 times the yield strength of the steel tube with an upper limit of 248 N/mm². Working loads for piles bearing on hard rock are limited to 1500 kN.

## SCREW PILES AND SCREW CYLINDERS

Screw piles or cylinders are forms of displacement piles in which a shaft is fitted at its lower end with a large-diameter horizontal helical blade (Fig. 8.33). The piles are screwed into the ground by applying a torque to the upper end of the shaft. In the case of screw piles the torque is applied to the solid steel shaft or to a square section fitted on to the upper end of the circular shaft. Similar methods are used for screw cylinders where the torque is applied directly to the hollow steel cylinder. Other types of screw cylinders use a mandrel inside a hollow concrete or steel cylinder. On reaching the desired level the mandrel is unscrewed and withdrawn and the interior of the cylinder filled with concrete.

Because of the slowness and difficult problems associated with their installation screw piles are uneconomical for their main employment in marine structures when compared with large diameter steel tube piles installed by driving or drilling-in methods. For this reason the large diameter screw pile or Screwcrete cylinders are virtually obsolete.

Forms of screw piles are used for land foundation work in Belgium and Holland. The *Fundex* pile has a helically-screwed point on to which is locked a steel drive tube by a bayonet joint. The tube is rotated to screw down the pile and is simultaneously thrust down by hydraulic rams on reaching founding level, reinforcement and concrete are placed in the tube which is then unlocked and extracted. The *Tubex* pile is similar in principle but the steel drive tube remains in position.

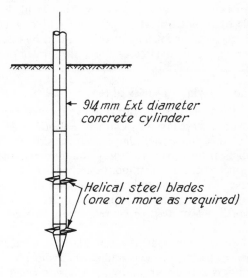

*914 mm Ext. diameter concrete cylinder*

*Helical steel blades (one or more as required)*

Fig. 8.33. A Screwcrete Cylinder

**Installation**

The simplest method of installing screw piles employs a capstan head fitted to the upper end of the shaft. Torque is applied to the capstan manually or by rope to a powered winch. Braithwaite & Co. the original specialist contractor for these piles employed electric screwing capstans operating within a specially designed head frame. Screw cylinders may be used with closed ends (bullet-pointed) or with open ends. The latter type is used in difficult sinking conditions when water jetting is used to loosen the soil below the blade and an air-lift ejector is also used within the hollow cylinder to remove soil from below its base.

Screw piles are best suited to conditions where they can be sunk through soft clays or silts to a very limited penetration into firm to stiff clays or medium-dense to dense sands. In view of their large end diameter the penetration into the bearing stratum need be only very small before they achieve the desired carrying capacity. Screw piles and cylinders are also useful in conditions where no suitable bearing stratum for ordinary piles exists within reasonable depth. Screw piles used in these conditions have been described by Morgan.[8.19] Although they can achieve a relatively high carrying capacity at a depth of penetration much shorter than a conventional pile, the soil beneath a group of screw piles is likely to be more compressible than that beneath a group of long conventional piles. Some additional settlement may also be caused by disturbance of a soft sensitive clay below the blades due to the screwing action.

### Calculation of Carrying Capacity of Screw Piles

Methods of calculating the carrying capacity of screw piles and Screwcrete cylinders are given by Guthlac Wilson.[8.20] However, since publication of this paper there have been considerable advances in the theory of bearing capacity of deep foundations, and the author recommends using the static methods described in Chapter 7. Guthlac Wilson's paper includes a number of examples of test loadings and settlement observations on screw piles in different soil conditions, which are worthy of study if screw piles are proposed for use on a project.

In using "static" methods the full blade diameter is taken in calculating end resistance. The undisturbed shear strength of the soil is used unless it is disturbed by screwing or water jetting when lower values should be used. The factor of nine times the shear strength for calculating end resistance should only be used if the blade is screwed a minimum distance of $1\frac{1}{2}$ blade diameters into the bearing stratum. For lesser depths of penetration, the factors shown in Fig. 2.11 (p. 90) should be used.

The skin friction on the shaft may be taken into account if the piles are screwed into uniform deposits of soil. However, low unit values should be used since the soils will have been completely disturbed by the passage of the blade. Where screw piles are terminated in a stiff or dense stratum overlain by soft compressible soils, the skin friction in the latter should not be taken into account in evaluating the carrying capacity, due to the effect of negative skin friction.

## TYPES OF BORED PILES

**Augered Piles**

There are two types of augered piles, the hand and the mechanical.

### HAND AUGER

The simplest method of constructing bored and cast-in-place piles is to sink an unlined hole by an auger to the required depth and then to fill the hole with concrete. No reinforcement is used except for dowel bars which are set in the tops of the piles to bond into the reinforcement of pile caps or capping beams. Simple piles of this type are used for light loadings, for example in house foundations or beneath columns in light single-storey framed buildings. Reinforcement is only required if the piles have to withstand bending moments or lateral forces or if the uplift from swelling soil is an appreciable factor.

Hand auger boring without casing can only be used in soils which are self-supporting, for example firm to stiff clays and silts or cohesive sands or clayey gravels above the water table. For economic reasons, hand auger holes for piling work are usually restricted to not more than 350 mm diameter up to a depth of 4·5 m.

### MECHANICAL AUGER (OR BUCKET AUGER) RIGS

For piles of larger diameter or for depths greater than 4·5 m it is necessary to use a mechanical auger. The large spiral auger or bucket auger rotary drilling machines which have been developed over the years for installing large diameter bored piles have been brought to a stage of high efficiency and they are capable of dealing with a wide range of soil types and can drill in weak rocks. The use of a bentonite slurry in conjunction with bucket auger drilling can eliminate some of the difficulties involved in drilling in soft silts and clays and loose granular soils without continuous support by casing tubes. Auger machines mounted on lorries or crane base machines when fitted with triple-telescoping "Kelly" tubes can drill to depths up to 45 m. The largest machines can drill pile shafts with diameters up to 2·13 m and with under-reaming tools can form enlarged bases with diameters up to 7·3 m. The Highway auger of the type shown in Plate IX can drill holes up to 1370 mm in diameter to depths up to 12·5 m.

The Calweld drill (Plate X) employs a rotating bucket with a hinged bottom flap. The bucket can be swung clear of the mast to allow the contents to be dumped directly in a lorry or hopper.

For successful operation of rotary auger or bucket type machines the soil must be reasonably free of tree roots, cobbles and boulders, and it must be self-supporting with or without bentonite slurry since mechanical augers can only operate in uncased holes. If the ground is liable to cave in, the usual practice is to place a length of casing into the augered hole by means of a crane or by the mast of the machine. The bottom of the kelly can then be locked to the top of the casing to turn and push it into the ground, so giving a seal against the entry of water. A smaller sized auger plate is then used inside the casing for the lower part of the hole. If need be a further length of casing can be used by telescoping it inside the length already set.

CONTINUOUS FLIGHT AUGER RIGS

The Dowsett "Prepakt" pile (installed under licence by Intrusion Prepakt Inc.) employs a continuous flight auger to drill the pile borehole. In stable soils the auger is withdrawn after completion of drilling, a flexible hose is lowered to the base of the hole and a sand–cement mortar is pumped down the hose to form the pile shaft. In weak unstable soils the mortar is pumped down the hollow stem of the auger while it is still rotating. The "Prepakt" pile can be installed with little noise and vibration and is a useful type for work close to existing structures.

### Bored Piles (Boring by Percussion or Grab Type Rigs)

In ground where hand or mechanical augering is impossible, e.g. in water-bearing sands or gravels, stony or bouldery clays, or very soft clays and silts, it is the usual practice to sink the hole for small and medium diameter bored and cast-in-place piles by a conventional boring rig. A common type of rig for small-diameter piles is similar to that used for exploratory borings (Plate I). Specially designed rigs are used for large-diameter piles.

GRAB-TYPE BORED PILING RIGS

Specially designed borings rigs for large-diameter bored piles using grabbing methods include the Benoto machine (Plate XI), the Bade machine, the Hochstrasser–Weise and the "turn-grab." In these types the casing is given a continuous semi-rotary motion to keep it sinking as the borehole is advanced. Various types of grab are provided for different soil conditions. The casing may be provided with welded joints and left in position or with bolted joints and withdrawn while the shaft is concreted. The Benoto EDF 55 rig normally sinks holes up to 1 m in diameter to a depth of 30 m. The "turn-grab" machine employs 1270 mm diameter standard casing and can drill to a depth of 30 m.

Although they can be used in all types of soil, grab types of boring rigs are best suited to difficult soils such as coarse gravel and cobbles, boulder clays, marls, or thinly bedded shales and clays. The spiral auger or bucket-type rigs can usually work faster than the grab types in firm to stiff clays and uniform sands.

## Under-reamed Bored Piles

The construction of very tall buildings of twenty storeys or more on London Clay created a demand for large-diameter piles with or without enlarged or "belled-out" bases. The various aspects of design, construction, testing, and economics of large-diameter bored piles were discussed in a symposium held at the Institution of Civil Engineers in 1966.[7.21] The following remarks on the construction of foundations of this type include much useful and practical information from the paper by Palmer and Holland in this symposium.

The savings in cost given by under-reamed piles are mainly due to savings in material excavated from the pile borehole, and in concrete used to replace the excavated material. However, in difficult ground such as boulder clays containing lenses of silt or sand, or in any cohesionless soil, it is practically impossible to form an under-ream. Also, because of the longer time taken to form an under-ream by mechanical means or hand excavation compared with the time taken to drill the straight-sided pile, the economic advantages of the under-reamed pile are somewhat marginal even in favourable ground such as London Clay.

Excavation for the under-ream is achieved by a belling bucket rotated by the drill rods or "kelly." Two types of belling bucket are used. The one generally favoured has arms which are hinged at the top of the bucket (Fig. 8.34) and are actuated by the drill rods or kelly. The arms are provided with cutting teeth and the excavated soil is removed by the bucket. This type cuts to a conical shape, which is an advantage in maintaining stability in fissured soils, and also the arms are forced back into the bucket when it is raised from the hole. The second type (Fig. 8.35) has arms hinged at the bottom of the bucket. This type has the advantage of being capable of cutting a larger bell than the top-hinged type and because the cutting action is always on the base of the hole, it produces a cleaner base with less loose and softened material. However, the hemispherical upper surface of the bell is less stable than the conical surface and the bottom-hinged arms have a tendency to jam in the hole when raising the bucket.

Belling buckets normally cut to base diameters up to 3700 mm, although diameters of as much as 7300 mm are possible with special equipment. It is not usually practicable to form bells on piles having shafts of less than 762 mm diameter. Although the base of a mechanically under-reamed pile can be cleaned by specially designed mechanical tools, this is a somewhat tedious operation and it is generally preferable to clean out the base by hand, when all soil crumbs and softened material are removed.

Enlarged bases can be formed in stable and relatively dry soils or rocks by hand excavation. This requires some form of support of the roof of the bell to ensure the safety of the workmen. One method of support which has been used is in the form of a "spider" consisting of a number of hinged steel ribs. The assembly is lowered

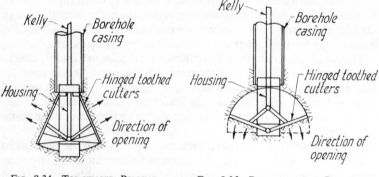

FIG. 8.34. TOP-HINGED BELLING-
BUCKET

FIG. 8.35. BOTTOM-HINGED BELLING-
BUCKET

down the borehole and the ribs are then expanded to force them into contact with the roof of the bell. If very large base areas are required, tunnels can be driven to connect the bells, and the whole base area can then be filled with concrete which is suitably reinforced to achieve the required beam action.

It is often impossible to predict from ordinary site investigation boreholes all the difficulties which may be encountered in attempting to form under-reamed bases on large-diameter piles. For this reason, the author's firm frequently adopts the practice of including an item in its piling contracts for drilling a trial pile borehole in advance of the main piling contract. This item can be expensive as the selected piling contractor must bring his men and equipment on to the site and take them away again, but this procedure can often save a considerable amount of money at the main piling stage since difficulties can be foreseen, any modifications to the pile design can be made, and if necessary the idea of under-reaming the piles can be abandoned in favour of adopting deeper straight-sided piles. Test loading to check design assumptions can also be made at this preliminary trial stage.

## PRECAUTIONS IN CONSTRUCTING LARGE-DIAMETER PILING

It is desirable to make a close inspection of the base of all boreholes with or without bells to ensure that they are clean and free from softened material and that the walls of the shafts are in a stable condition. Large-diameter bored piles are frequently used on a "one column—one pile" basis, and it is unusual to provide more than three piles to a column. In these conditions failure even of a single pile due to faulty construction methods would have disastrous consequences. Therefore, during the site supervision of piling contracts the engineer should treat each pile in the same way as he would an ordinary pad foundation, i.e. the piling contractor must not be permitted to place concrete until the resident engineer or clerk of works has satisfied himself that the soil is not weaker than that taken as the basis for pile design and that the hole is in a fit condition to receive concrete.

The following precautions are recommended in the construction and subsequent inspection of large-diameter piles—

1. The pile shaft should be supported by casing through soft or loose soils to prevent the walls of the shaft from collapsing. (This casing can be extracted after concreting the shaft.)

2. Casing should be provided to seal off water-bearing soil layers. Any soil adhering to the inside of the casing should be cleaned off before inserting the casing in the borehole, and again before placing concrete. The casing should be drilled into an impervious soil layer beneath the water-bearing layer to a sufficient depth to maintain the seal until the remainder of the borehole is completed, and until the concrete is brought up above ground-water level.

3. Soil or rock cuttings removed from the pile borehole should be compared with the descriptions stated on the site investigation borehole records.

4. Shear-strength tests should be made on undisturbed soil samples taken from the bottom of selected piles as a check on the design data.

5. Boreholes for shallow piles, if too small to enable a man to go down and inspect the base, should be inspected by shining a light down the shaft. Any loose crumbs or lumps of soil should be cleaned out before concrete is placed.

6. All deep pile holes should be plumbed to the bottom immediately before concreting by lowering a "cage" to the full depth. The plumbed depth should be compared to the depth accurately measured immediately after completion of drilling. This check will ensure that no soil has collapsed into the borehole.

7. All piles having a shaft large enough to admit a man should be

inspected immediately before placing concrete. Any loose soil adhering to the casing or borehole walls should be removed. Any loose fallen material, or soil softened by trampling on the base, should be cleared out. If necessary, this should be done in small areas, each area being protected in turn by a layer of dry concrete. Any accumulations of water should be pumped or baled out before placing the sealing concrete or first lift of the base concrete. If the inflow of water is such that cement would be washed from the unset concrete or instability caused to the soil beneath the base, then attempts to concrete the pile "in the dry" should be abandoned and underwater methods should be resorted to as described on page 534.

8. The time interval between completion of boring and placing concrete should be as short as possible, and in any case should not be longer than six hours.

9. If men are required to work at the base of piles, a loosely fitting safety casing should be suspended in the shaft to protect the men from material falling from the sides of the shaft. The method of suspension must be absolutely secure, as slipping might easily kill a man working in an enlarged base. The top of the casing should project above ground level as a safeguard against tools or stones being accidently kicked down the hole.

10. Men working down the holes should wear safety helmets and harness. The latter is required to enable them to be lifted out quickly should they be injured or overcome by gas.

11. While men are working down the hole a "top man" should always be in attendance to ensure that no tools or objects are lying near the hole, and that any tools required for use are properly secured before being lowered down the hole. The top of the hole should be covered while it is left unattended.

12. Safety lamps and other gas-detecting devices should be kept at hand and in proper working order.

13. Frequent tests for gas should be made in filled ground or where pile boreholes pass through beds or peat of organic clays or when working on sites where old gas mains may be encountered.

14. All work should conform to the requirements of British Standard CP 2011 (safety precautions in the construction of large diameter bore holes for piling and other purposes).

CONCRETING BORED PILES

In dry boreholes, or in holes where water can be removed by baling the piles are concreted by the simple method of tipping a reasonably workable mix (not leaner than 300 kg cement per cubic metre of concrete) down the borehole from a barrow or dumper. A hopper is provided at the mouth of the hole to receive the charge of concrete and to prevent contamination with earth and vegetable matter on the ground surface. Before any concrete is placed, the hole should be baled dry of water and loose or softened soil should be cleaned out and the bottom of the hole rammed. If the bottom of the hole is wet, a layer of dry concrete should first be placed and well rammed. Then the concrete can be placed using a readily workable mix (75 to 100 mm slump), which is self-compacting but does not segregate.

There are a number of practical difficulties in concreting bored piles in water-bearing soils, in squeezing ground, or a combination of the two. The difficulties are aggravated if a reinforcing cage is provided. If the bottom of the casing is lifted above the concrete while the shaft is concreted and the casing is withdrawn in successive lifts, then water may surge into the hole and weaken the concrete. Also, any water which is carried up the pile shaft in the form of laitance will have a serious weakening effect on the concrete. Sand or soft clay is liable to squeeze in and cause "waisting" or "necking." If on the other hand the concrete is kept high in the casing, then ramming may compact the concrete inside the casing. Lifting the casing will then lift the concrete inside it and, if a reinforcing cage is provided, the lower part of the pile will also be lifted. There is no simple remedy for such a mishap. The only thing to do is to remove all concrete and reinforcement, clean out the hole and start again. In these conditions concreting a pile demands the greatest of care. The concrete should be rich and easily workable.

The main difficulty in concreting bored piles occurs in water-bearing ground when the hole cannot be baled or pumped dry before placing the concrete. In these conditions the hole must be lined with casing throughout its depth and a plug of concrete should then be deposited under water in the base of the hole by tremie pipe. As soon as the concrete has hardened sufficiently, the hole should be pumped free of water. The casing should then be gently turned and lifted slightly to free it from the plug. The remainder of the concreting in the shaft should be placed "in the dry" up to the surface. The casing should then be lifted entirely from the borehole (a casing vibrator is a useful device to assist the lifting), additional concrete being placed as necessary after the concrete has slumped to fill the void left by withdrawing the casing.

If the ground water is under a high pressure it may not be possible to turn and lift the casing without inflow of water between the concrete plug and the inside of the casing. If this should take place the inflow should be stemmed by caulking and further attempts to free the casing should be abandoned. Instead, the casing should be cut by oxy-acetylene just above the plug, any inflow through the flame-cut space being stopped by caulking. Then the shaft should be concreted as before and the casing then raised, leaving the portion around the plug permanently in place. Consideration may be given to placing the sealing plug in a plastic bag instead of using a tremie pipe.

As an alternative to plugging the base of the pile and then concreting in the dry, the entire shaft may be concreted under water using a tremie pipe. This method would, in any case, be necessary where the pile hole is too small to enable a man to go down to carry out caulking or cutting operations as previously described. The author prefers concreting in the dry wherever possible since it is impossible to avoid some laitance forming when concreting through a tremie pipe. If the laitance layer becomes excessively thick the concrete will be seriously weakened. Concrete placed through a tremie pipe should be easily workable (125 to 175 mm slump) and should have a minimum cement content of 400 kg/m$^3$. A retarder should be used if there is a risk of the concrete setting before the casing is lifted out of the hole.

It will be noted that no mention has been made of placing concrete by means of a bottom-opening bucket. From personal experience and from several examples given in technical literature, the author is convinced that the use of such a device is unsound practice. When placing concrete in a deep borehole a crane operator does not have sufficient sensitivity in the "feel" of the bucket to be sure that he is opening it just beneath the surface of the concrete. The bucket may lodge on the reinforcing cage at a higher level and it will then be opened to allow concrete to fall through the water; if it is lowered to too great a depth into fluid concrete there will be surging and mixing of the concrete with water as the bucket is withdrawn. The result of mishandling of a bottom-opening bucket is the formation of layers of laitance and honeycombed concrete. Nothing can be done with the defective concrete. Attempts to grout honeycombed concrete have failed because it is impossible to build up pressure in the honeycombed layer. The grout merely finds an easy way to the surface up the side of the pile.

It is sometimes the practice to use bentonite mud instead of casing to support the walls of a pile borehole and then to place concrete beneath the bentonite by means of a tremie pipe. However, it is necessary to keep an adequate head of concrete in the tremie pipe and to keep it moving continuously in order to overcome the pressure of the high density thixotropic bentonite fluid which is displaced by the outflowing concrete. Difficulties in placing concrete by tremie pipe beneath bentonite were experienced in the 18–21 m deep piled foundations of Wuya Bridge, Nigeria.[8.21] On this site a mud density of 1600 kg/m$^3$ was required to prevent collapsing of the soil, and the mud formed a gel due to the high ground temperatures. The concrete jammed in the tremie pipe, especially when filling was suspended to remove sections of pipe. The method finally adopted was to use a highly workable concrete with a plasticizer and retarder, and to withdraw the tremie pipe as a single unit without breaking joints.

When ground water is present in fissured rock strata, trouble may be experienced as a result of surging of this water whereby the cement is washed out of unset concrete in the pile boreholes. This surging may be due to boring operations in piles adjacent to those already concreted. If this cause is suspected the boring operations must stop until the concrete has hardened sufficiently, or the boring of all piles in a group must be completed before concrete is allowed to be placed.

Concreting of bored piles under water by the "prepacked" or "pre-placed" method is not recommended because of the likely contamination of the pre-placed aggregate by silt or clay suspended in the water.

**Pressure Piles**

Pressure piles are a proprietary form of bored piling in which compressed air is used to compact the concrete in the pile shaft. The cased borehole is sunk by normal boring methods using a rig powered by compressed air. When founding level is reached a charge of concrete is placed at the bottom of the borehole. A pressure cap is then screwed on to the top of the casing through which compressed air is admitted. This compacts the concrete in the casing and in some conditions may give an enlarged end. The casing is also lifted by the compressed air and assisted by the winch. The cap is removed, the top length of casing unscrewed, another charge of concrete is placed, and the cycle repeated until the whole shaft has been concreted.

When ground water is present an airlock is screwed to the top of the casing. Compressed air is admitted through the lock, and drives out the ground water and compacts the soil at the bottom of the borehole which may have become loosened by surging during sinking the borehole (Fig. 8.36). The bottom door of the airlock is closed to allow a charge of concrete to be placed in the airlock. The airlock door is then closed, the bottom door opened, and the concrete dropped to the bottom. The casing is then permitted to lift and the cycle is repeated until sufficient concrete has been placed to prevent upward seepage of water into the casing.

Pressure piles are installed by the Pressure Piling Company using nominal shaft diameters of 340 mm and 430 mm for working loads up to 300 and 450 kN respectively. Higher working loads can be used if the piles are bearing on a solid stratum. The process has the advantage of preventing the risk of "necking" or "waisting" of the pile shaft due to squeezing ground. No ramming or vibration is used

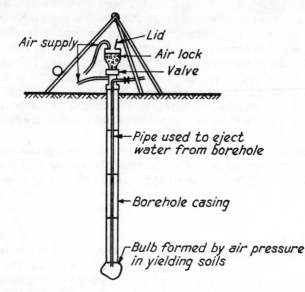

FIG. 8.36. CONCRETING PRESSURE PILE IN WATER-BEARING GROUND

and this may be advantageous when working alongside existing structures. Pressure piles are frequently used in underpinning work.

### Prestcore Piles

These are a proprietary form of bored pile in which precast concrete cylindrical units are lowered down a borehole. The procedure is as follows—

1. The cased borehole is sunk by normal boring methods to the desired level and a charge of concrete is placed at the bottom of the casing (Fig. 8.37 (*a*)).

2. Cylindrical precast concrete units having a central hole and small peripheral holes are threaded on to a steel pipe and lowered down the borehole. Reinforcing rods are also threaded through the peripheral holes (*b*).

3. The casing is partially lifted by jacking-off the top unit. This beds down all the units and forces the bottom in-situ concrete downwards and outwards. In soft ground the concrete tends to form an enlarged end (*c*).

4. A grout head is then screwed on to the casing and cement grout under pressure is introduced through the central pipe. The grout forces its way between the precast concrete units and the soil and

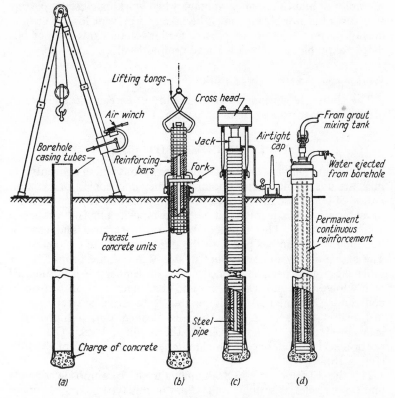

Fig. 8.37. Stages in Forming a Prestcore Pile

fills the holes containing the reinforcing rods. Ground water is expelled by the rising column of grout (*d*).

5. Grouting is continued as the casing is extracted and the grout fills the space between the outer face of the units and the soil.

Prestcore piles are installed by various firms under licence from B.S.P. International Foundations Ltd. The units are supplied in nominal diameters of 350, 460 and 660 mm for working loads of up to 400, 600, and 1000 kN respectively, depending on the ground conditions.

The precast concrete units are advantageous in squeezing ground and in ground containing aggressive chemicals. In the latter conditions it can be ensured that high quality concrete is used, with special cements as necessary (*see* Chapter 13). No ramming or vibration is employed and this is an advantage when working close to existing structures but precautions must be taken to prevent loss of ground during boring. The use of precast sections makes this type of pile more adaptable to extension above ground level.

**Working Stresses for Bored Piles**

The allowable working stresses should not exceed those given for driven and cast-in-place piles on page 524.

## TYPES OF COMPOSITE PILES

Composite piles are used in ground conditions where conventional piles are unsuitable or uneconomical. They may consist of a combination of bored and driven piles, or driven piles embodying two types of material. A frequently used type of composite pile is the concrete and timber pile. This type combines the cheapness and ease of handling of the timber pile with the durability of the concrete pile. The susceptibility of the former to decay above the ground water table has already been mentioned. Thus the timber pile is terminated below lowest ground water level and the upper portion formed in concrete. One method of doing this is to drive a steel tube to just below water level. The tube is cleaned out, a timber pile is lowered down it and driven to the required level. The upper portion is then concreted with simultaneous withdrawal of the tube (Fig. 8.38).

It is the usual practice in Scandinavia to drive composite concrete and timber piles as a single unit. Piles of this type having an upper 460 mm square reinforced concrete section 17·7 m long and lower timber sections 5 to 26 m long were driven at the site of the Skarvik Oil Jetty, Gothenburg.[8.11] The timber sections were first driven until the head was a few metres above the ground. The concrete section was then hung in the leaders and lowered down until the sleeve at the bottom of the concrete section was pressed down over the prepared head of the timber pile. The sleeved joint is shown in Fig. 8.39. The tarred sleeve was heated to reduce the friction between it and the timber. The shorter timber piles could not be driven far enough for them to remain fixed in position in the ground while the joint was made. For these cases, the contractors, Messrs. Christiani and Nielsen, devised a split pipe cage which held the timber pile while the concrete pile was brought into the leaders. The timber section was then drawn up into contact with the sleeve by raising the cage from the piling winch. The cage was finally opened and removed.

Another method of composite piling is to use a hollow precast concrete driven section which remains in position after a timber pile has been driven down the interior to the required penetration.

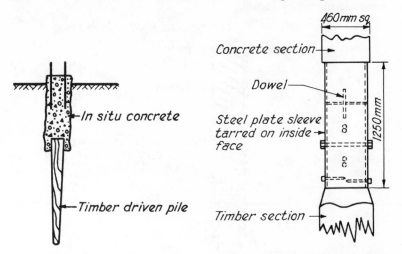

FIG. 8.38. COMPOSITE TIMBER AND          FIG. 8.39. SLEEVED JOINT IN COMPOSITE
       CONCRETE PILE                      CONCRETE AND TIMBER PILE AT SKARVIK
                                             OIL JETTY, GOTHENBURG[8.12]

Composite steel H-beam and concrete piles can be driven in a similar manner to concrete and timber piles. The concrete portion is used in the zone above and immediately below ground level which is most susceptible to corrosion. The design of such composite piles should provide a rigid connexion between the two components.

Composite piles were used where deep penetration was required in difficult ground conditions for the foundation of Hindiya Bridge over the Euphrates River in Iraq.[8.1] Steel tubes about 12 m long by 500 mm outside diameter were driven through soft to stiff clays followed by stiff clays and sands using a 9B₃ McKiernan–Terry double-acting hammer. The inside of the tube was cleaned out by jetting and a 305 by 305 mm by 122 kg/m steel H-beam pile was lowered down the tube and driven a further 10 to 12 m. After trial and error the practice of cleaning out the tube was to use a jet pipe to clean out the upper soft clays in entirety. The jetting did not remove the very stiff clay in the lower part of the tube except that it formed a hole of about 150 mm diameter. Driving the H-beam pile through the tube broke up the stiff clay, thus facilitating its later removal by jetting. The spaces between the tube and the H-beam were filled with concrete using a 150 mm diameter bottom-opening skip to form an underwater plug at the bottom of the tube. After the plug had hardened, the water was pumped out and the remaining length was filled with concrete placed by shovel.

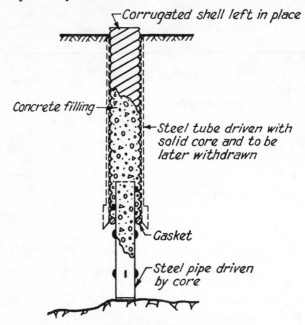

FIG. 8.40. WESTERN PROJECTILE PILE

The 9B$_3$ hammer was found to be more effective in pile driving than the 4060 kg single-acting steam hammer which was used in the early stages.

The Western Foundation Corporation of U.S.A. have devised various proprietary forms of composite piling. Their "projectile" pile is shown in Fig. 8.40. The heavy casing is first driven to the required penetration using a core to keep the end of the tube closed. The core is removed and a projectile section consisting of a length of steel tube with a closed end is inserted and driven, using the core as a follower. The core is again withdrawn and a corrugated steel shell is lowered down the casing and locked on to the pipe by means of a projection on the latter, which locks on to the corrugations of the shell. A gasket fitted to the top of the pipe prevents mud or water entering the space between the pipe and the shell. Concrete is then placed in the pipe and the shell, and the outer drive casing is with-drawn. H-beams or timber piles may be used as "projectiles" instead of pipes.

## THE DESIGN OF PILE CAPS AND CAPPING BEAMS

### Pile Caps

It is impossible to ensure that piles are driven or bored truly vertical or exactly to the prescribed rake; therefore pile caps should be of ample dimensions to allow them to accommodate piles which may be a few inches out of their intended position in any direction.

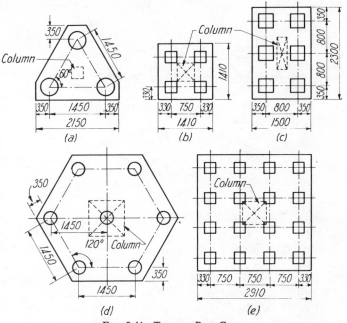

FIG. 8.41. TYPICAL PILE CAPS

    (*a*) Cap for three 450 mm diameter friction piles.
    (*b*) Cap for four 350 mm square end-bearing piles.
    (*c*) Cap for six 400 mm square end-bearing piles.
    (*d*) Cap for seven 450 mm diameter friction piles.
    (*e*) Cap for sixteen 350 mm square end-bearing piles.

This can be done by extending the pile cap for a distance of 100 to 150 mm outside the outer faces of the piles in the group. The pile cap should be deep enough to ensure full transfer of the load from the column to the cap in punching shear and from the cap to the piles.

In an isolated pile group, the pile cap must include at least three piles to ensure stability against lateral forces. A pile cap for only two piles should be connected by tie beams to adjacent caps. Typical designs of pile caps for various numbers of piles are shown in Fig. 8.41 (*a*) to (*e*).

The minimum spacing of piles in a group has been referred to on pages 408 and 410. Using this or a greater spacing the piles should be

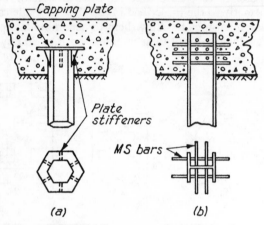

FIG. 8.42. CAPPING FOR STEEL PILES
(*a*) Capping for hexagonal pile.
(*b*) Capping for H-beam pile.

arranged so that the centroid of the group coincides with the line of action of the load. This ensures that all piles carry an equal load and so avoids tilting of the group if they are bearing on compressible strata.

The heads of reinforced concrete piles should be stripped down and the projecting reinforcement bonded into the pile cap to give the required bond length. Research by the Ohio Department of Highways[8.22] showed that if the concrete cap is of adequate size and arrangement and properly reinforced for the pile reactions, there is no need to provide a bearing plate or other load transfer device at the head of a steel H-pile. However, in the case of slender steel piles, the depth of the pile cap required for resistance to punching shear may be uneconomically large. Savings in the depth of the pile cap can be achieved by welding or riveting projections to the head of the steel pile to give increased area in bearing. Load transfer devices used for the heads of Rendhex steel box piles and H-beam piles are shown in Fig. 8.42 (*a*) and (*b*).

The depth of pile cap required for timber piles is very often dictated by the need to carry concrete protection to the timber below the lowest ground water level.

For small pile caps and relatively large column bases the column load may be partly transferred directly to the piles. The part directly transferred by overlapping in a four-pile group is shown in the shaded areas in Fig. 8.43. In these conditions shear forces are negligible and only bending moments need be calculated. On the

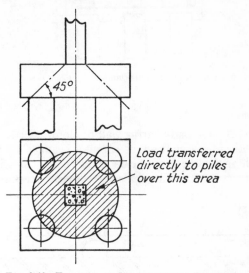

FIG. 8.43. TRANSFER OF LOAD THROUGH PILE CAP

other hand, single column loads on large pile groups with widely spaced piles can cause considerable shear forces and bending moments, requiring a system of links or bent-up bars and top and bottom horizontal reinforcement in two layers. A typical arrangement of reinforcement for a small pile group is shown in Fig. 8.44. A minimum cover of 40 mm should be provided to the reinforcement in the pile cap.

Where a column is carried by a single large-diameter pile, there is no need to provide a cap. In the case of reinforced concrete columns, starter bars can be cast into the head of the pile or pockets can be left for the holding-down bolts of steel columns.

The design of reinforcement is highly indeterminate because of relative movements between piles, inequalities of load transfer, and the rigidity of the pile cap. The reader is referred to textbooks on reinforced concrete for empirical methods of designing reinforcement, or to handbooks of piling firms for standard designs for various column loads and pile arrangements.

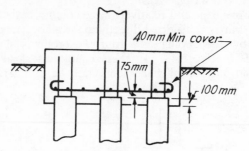

FIG. 8.44. ARRANGEMENT OF REINFORCEMENT IN RECTANGULAR PILE CAP

**Capping Beams**

Piles supporting a load-bearing wall or close-spaced columns may be tied together by a continuous capping beam. The piles can be staggered along the line of the beam to take care of small eccentricity of loading (Fig. 8.45). Where piles are used to support light struc-

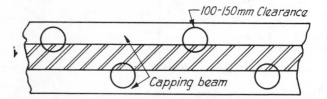

FIG. 8.45. PILES SUPPORTING LOAD-BEARING WALLS

tures with load-bearing walls the piles may be placed at a wide spacing beneath the centre of the wall (Fig. 8.46).

Investigations at the Building Research Station have shown that load-bearing walls themselves act as beams spanning between piles. It is therefore possible to design the capping beams for lower bending moments than those given by conventional design which assumes that the whole of the load in a triangle of the wall above the beam is carried by the beam. The bending moment at the centre of a simply supported beam is $\frac{WL}{8}$, where $W$ is the weight of the triangle of brickwork above the beam. The Building Research Station[8.23] recommends a minimum bending moment of $\dfrac{WL}{100}$, where full composite action takes place and $W$ is the weight of the *rectangle* of brickwork above the beam plus any superimposed loads. It is stated that these "equivalent bending moments" show considerable saving over conventional design methods but the depth of beam to span ratio must be kept between one-fifteenth and one-twentieth. However with a heavily loaded wall only

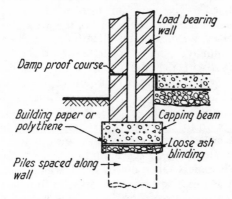

FIG. 8.46. SINGLE ROW OF PILES SUPPORTING LIGHT BUILDING

a small degree of composite action is allowed and it may be necessary to use a beam deeper than $L/15$. With considerable composite action (bending moments $WL/40$ or less) the reinforcement should be calculated for a beam depth of $L/15$ even if a deeper beam is required for practical reasons. A cover of 25 mm is recommended (40 mm would be preferable for good quality work). The top steel should be placed 25 mm below the upper surface of the concrete immediately over the pile heads and should extend on each side of the pile as far as the quarter-span points. If a door is situated at the end of a span, shear reinforcement is necessary.

The design method assumes that the ground floor is carried by the soil independently of the capping beam. If a suspended floor slab is required the beam should be designed by conventional methods. Where the piles are provided as a safeguard against swelling and shrinkage of clay soils, the capping beams should be placed on 50 to 75 mm of loose ashes or clinker covered with building paper or on a layer of perforated polystyrene. The purpose of this layer is to absorb some of the upthrust on the underside of the capping beam from the swelling of the soil. A suspended floor slab is recommended for all cases where piles are required for swelling soil conditions.

## THE ECONOMICS OF PILED FOUNDATIONS

The engineer is frequently faced with marginal conditions when there appears to be little to choose between piling and taking conventional strip or pad foundations down to a somewhat greater depth to reach soil of satisfactory bearing capacity. For any given site there must be one particular level below which it is cheaper to pile than to adopt deep strip or pad foundations, and the engineer must make his choice on the basis of fairly detailed estimates of cost. The following notes are intended to give some information to the engineer on the various factors which influence the cost of the work.

In the first place, it is not simply a matter of adding up the cost of $x$ m³ of excavation and $y$ m³ of concrete for a deep pad foundation and comparing it with the cost of $z$ m of piling to carry the same working load. Pile foundations require a cap or a capping beam. The minimum thickness of a cap for a pair of piles is about 450 mm and caps for four piles may have to be 600 to 1200 mm thick, and the plan dimensions up to 2100 mm square for 550 mm diameter piles. It may also be necessary to connect pile caps together by tie beams in two or more directions. Excavation in pile caps, capping beams, and tie beams is mainly taken out by hand, which costs about three times as much as machine excavation in strip foundations or twice as much as machine excavation in column bases of fairly large dimensions. Also, piled foundations involve structural design and a higher degree of supervision over their construction. Thus the costs of excavation and concrete in pile caps and capping beams together with the costs of piling and of design and supervision weigh heavily against piled foundations. In fact, in dry soil conditions where advantage can be taken of the low cost of mechanical excavation in bulk, the total cost of excavating to a depth of as much as 4·5 m, constructing column bases in mass concrete up to ground level, and backfilling the soil around the bases, is cheaper than the cost of providing the equivalent number of 8 m long piles, together with the pile caps and capping beams, to carry the same working load. This cost comparison was made for a typical multi-storey block of dwellings. On the other hand for small-scale work, say for individual houses where excavation is taken out by hand and conditions are suitable for the cheap, uncased, mechanically augered piles, a cost analysis by the Building Research Station showed that the bored pile foundation was cheaper than 0·6 m wide by 1·2 m deep conventional brick footings in hand-dug trenches, but not cheaper than mechanically excavated narrow strip foundations (*see* p. 214).

When excavation must be taken down into water-bearing sands and gravels the economics may swing in favour of piled foundations since the cost of hand excavation in these conditions may be two or three times greater than hand excavation in dry ground. Take as an example a marginal case of a column carrying a load of 2000 kN on very loose sand overlying dense sand at a depth of 1·5 m. The water table is 1 m below ground level. The settlement for foundations on the loose sand would be excessive so it will be necessary to take pad foundations down to the dense sand where we can use a safe bearing pressure of say 250 kN/m², which will require pad foundations 2·8 m square by 1·5 m deep. Assuming a large number of these bases, the excavation can be taken out mainly by machine but below the water table the excavation will have to be taken out largely by hand with close timbering and pumping. The rough cost of a single pad foundation calculated on 1974 prices will be—

|  | £ |
|---|---|
| Excavation: 24 m³ @ £0·90 . . . . . . . . | 21·60 |
| Extra over for excavation in water-bearing sand 4·50 m³ @ £4·30 . | 19·35 |
| Carting away surplus soil: 11·76 m³ @ £0·44 . . . . . | 5·17 |
| Formwork: 16·80 m² @ £3·80 . . . . . . . | 63·84 |
| Mass concrete: 11·76 m³ @ £7·50 . . . . . . | 88·20 |
| Close timbering and pumping, say . . . . . . . | 65·00 |
| Return fill and ram soil around completed bases: 12·24 m³ @ £1·00 . | 12·24 |
| | |
| Total cost of one pad foundation . . . . . . . | 275·40 |

The alternative of a piled foundation will require, say, four piles taken down to a depth of 4·5 m below ground level each carrying a 500 kN working load. The pile cap will probably be 1·60 m square by 0·80 m deep, i.e. it can be constructed wholly above ground water level. It will be necessary to provide a richer structural concrete and reinforcement in the pile cap. Excavation will be entirely by hand. The cost of a single foundation will be roughly as follows—

|  | £ |
|---|---|
| Excavation, say 4.0 m³ @ £2·50 . . . . . . . | 10·00 |
| Cart surplus to tip: 2·0 m³ @ £0·55 . . . . . . | 1·10 |
| Formwork: 5·12 m³ @ £4·60 . . . . . . . . | 23·55 |
| Concrete: 2·05 m³ @ £7·80 . . . . . . . . | 15·99 |
| Supply, bend and fix reinforcement: 200 kg @ £0·14 . . . | 28·00 |
| Return fill and ram soil around pile cap, say: 2.0 m³ @ £1·20 . . | 2·40 |
| 4 no. × 3·70 m long piles: @ £6·50/m . . . . . . | 96·20 |
| Strip heads of 4 no. piles to expose reinforcement and tie in to pile cap | |
|     steel = 4 no. × £2·00 . . . . . . . . | 8·00 |
| | |
| Total cost of one piled foundation . . . . . . . | 185·24 |

Thus, the piled foundation is appreciably cheaper, the saving being accounted for almost wholly by the cost of timbering and pumping.

Another justification for piled foundations on structural and economic grounds occurs in highly variable soil conditions such as random pockets or lenses of soft silt and clay in sandy glacial deposits. Ideally the foundation should be designed for the particular conditions at any given point of loading, i.e. adopting high bearing pressures with small pad foundations in areas of compact sands and low bearing pressures with large individual or combined pad foundations for the softer and more compressible soils. However, this procedure would require a very detailed soil investigation at a correspondingly high cost, or else the foundations could be designed individually as the soil conditions were recorded during the excavation work. The latter would not permit any advance design or job planning and would lead to delays due to ordering and cutting reinforcement or fabricating formwork. By adopting piled foundations for all column bases or load-bearing walls whether in good ground or bad, the job can be designed and planned well in advance of construction, which will proceed without delay, and by using some form of in-situ pile the length of the pile can be varied to suit the varying soil conditions rather than by increasing or decreasing the number of piles. Settlements will be of a very small order if the piles in the bad ground conditions have an adequate safety factor; thus relative settlements between columns will be negligible. It would be difficult to achieve this with pad foundations of varying size and bearing pressure.

### The Choice of Type of Pile

Having decided that piling is necessary, the engineer must make a choice from a variety of types and sizes. It has already been noted that there is usually only one type of pile which is satisfactory for any particular site conditions. The following notes will summarize the detailed descriptions already given of the various types of pile and their particular application.

### Driven Piles

*Advantages*

1. Material of pile can be inspected before it goes into the ground.
2. Stable in "squeezing" ground.
3. Not damaged by ground heave when driving adjacent piles.
4. Construction procedure unaffected by ground water.
5. Can be readily carried above ground level, especially in marine structures.
6. Can be driven in very long lengths.

*Disadvantages*

1. Cannot be readily varied in length to suit varying level of bearing stratum.

2. May break during hard driving causing delays and replacement charges, or worse still may suffer major unseen damage in hard driving conditions.

3. Uneconomical if amount of material in pile is governed by handling and driving stresses rather than by stresses from permanent loading.

4. Noise and vibration during driving may cause nuisance or damage.

5. Displacement of soil during driving piles in groups may damage adjacent structures or cause lifting by ground heave of adjacent piles.

6. Cannot be driven in very large diameters.

7. End enlargements usually impracticable.

8. Cannot be driven in conditions of low headroom.

## DRIVEN AND CAST-IN-PLACE PILES

*Advantages*

1. Length can be readily adjusted to suit varying level of bearing stratum.

2. Tube is driven with a closed end, thus excluding ground water.

3. Possible to form an enlarged end in most types.

4. Material in pile is not determined from handling or driving stresses.

5. Noise and vibration can be reduced in some types.

*Disadvantages*

1. "Necking" or "waisting" may occur in squeezing ground unless great care is taken when concreting shaft.

2. Concrete shaft may be weakened if strong artesian water-flow pipes up outside of shaft.

3. Concrete cannot be inspected after completion.

4. Limitations on length of driving in most types.

5. Displacement of ground may damage "green" concrete of adjacent piles, or cause lifting by ground heave of adjacent piles.

6. Noise, vibration, and ground displacement may cause a nuisance or damage adjacent structures.

7. Cannot be used in river or marine structures without special adaptation.

8. Cannot be driven in very large diameters.

9. Very large end bulbs cannot be made.

10. Cannot be driven in conditions of very low headroom.

## BORED AND CAST-IN-PLACE PILES

### Advantages

1. Length can be readily varied to suit varying ground conditions.
2. Soil removed in boring can be inspected and if necessary sampled or in-situ tests made.
3. Can be installed in very large diameters.
4. End enlargements up to two or three diameters are possible in clays.
5. Material of pile is not dependent on handling or driving conditions.
6. Can be installed in very long lengths.
7. Can be installed without appreciable noise or vibration.
8. Can be installed in conditions of very low headroom.
9. No risk of ground heave.

### Disadvantages

1. Susceptible to "waisting" or "necking" in "squeezing" ground.
2. Difficult to make a satisfactory job of concreting if pile tube is filled with water unless compressed air is used with air lock.
3. Concrete is not placed under ideal conditions and cannot be subsequently inspected.
4. Water under artesian pressure may pipe up pile shaft washing out cement.
5. Enlarged ends cannot be formed in cohesionless materials.
6. Cannot be readily extended above ground level especially in river and marine structures.
7. Boring methods may loosen sandy or gravelly soils.
8. Sinking piles in groups may cause loss of ground in cohesionless soils, leading to settlement of adjacent structures.
9. May be impossible to install in some conditions due to "piping" or "boiling" of very soft or loose materials up the tube.

## CHOICE BETWEEN TYPES OF PILE IN EACH CATEGORY

### DRIVEN PILES

*Timber*—Suitable for light loads or temporary works. Unsuitable for heavy loads. Subject to decay due to fluctuating water table. Liable to unseen splitting or brooming if driven too heavily.

*Concrete*—Suitable for all ranges of loading. Concrete can be designed to suit corrosive soil conditions. Readily adaptable to various sizes and shapes. Disadvantages: additional reinforcement must be provided for handling and driving stresses; cannot be readily cut down or extended; liable to unseen damage under heavy driving; delay between casting and driving.

*Steel*—Suitable for all ranges of loading. Can be readily cut down or extended. Cut-off portions have scrap value and they can be used for extending other piles. Can be driven hard without damage. Can be driven in very long lengths by welding on additional lengths. Some types have small ground displacement. Structural steel bracing can be readily welded or bolted on. Resilience makes it suitable for jetty or dolphin structures. Disadvantages: subject to corrosion in marine structures and requires elaborate paint treatment and/or cathodic protection; long and slender piles liable to go off line during driving.

DRIVEN AND CAST-IN-PLACE PILES. The author finds it difficult for obvious reasons to make comparisons between proprietary types of pile but in general it may be said that the types which have a withdrawable tube are cheaper than those where a steel or concrete tube or shells are left in the ground for subsequent hearting with concrete. However, the latter types are a sounder form of construction for "squeezing" soils or water-bearing sands or where re-driving is necessary following ground heave. The types in which the hammer acts on the plug of concrete or shoe at the bottom of the pile are likely to cause much less noise and vibration than those in which the hammer acts on top of the tube. Generally, the recommended procedure is to approach several proprietary piling firms for quotations and let the issue be decided on the basis of costs. Reputable piling firms will not hesitate to say that their piles are unsuitable for particular ground conditions.

BORED AND CAST-IN-PLACE PILES. The cheapest forms are the simple, mechanically augered piles sunk without any casing. However, they are only suitable for reasonably firm to stiff cohesive soils. The cost more than doubles when casing has to be installed and withdrawn and the slower conventional boring methods must be used.

The enlarged base has advantages in permitting shorter piles, so bringing them within the depth range of a particular type of mechanical rig. However, enlarged bases to bored piles cannot be contemplated in sands or gravels.

Although compressed-air methods of concreting can be used in water bearing soils where there is a risk of water carrying sand or silt into the partially completed shaft, or where water under artesian pressure may wash the cement out of the concrete, the use of drilling under bentonite slurry has largely supplanted such techniques.

Very often headroom conditions decide the type of pile.

## REFERENCES

8.1    SWANSBOURNE, J. F. C., The design and construction of Hindiya Bridge, *Proc. Inst. C.E.*, **8**, pp. 1–16 (Sept., 1957).

8.2    *A Performance Investigation of Pile Driving Hammers and Piles*, Lansing, Michigan State Highway Commission (Mar., 1965).

8.3    WILLIAMS, N. S., Contribution to discussion on "Pile driving in difficult conditions," *Inst. C.E. Works Constr. Div.* (1951).

8.4    WHITAKER, T., The constant rate of penetration test for the determination of the ultimate bearing capacity of a pile, *Proc. Inst. C.E.*, **26**, pp. 119–123 (Sept., 1963).

8.5    MOHR, H. A., Wood piles, *J. Bost. Soc. C.E.*, **46**, No. 2, pp. 132–161 (1959).

8.6    HARTFORD, F. D., Notes on driving timber piles, *Eng. News Rec.*, pp. 83–85 (29th Nov., 1945).

8.7    GLANVILLE, W. H., GRIME, G., and DAVIES, W. W., The behaviour of reinforced concrete piles during driving, *J. Inst. C.E.*, **1**, p. 150 (Dec., 1935).

8.8    SAURIN, B. F., The design of reinforced concrete piles with special reference to the reinforcement, *J. Inst. C.E.*, **32**, No. 5, pp. 80–109 (March, 1949).

8.9    EVANS, R. H., The plastic theories for the ultimate strength of reinforced concrete beams, *J. Inst. C.E.*, **21**, No. 2, pp. 98–121 (Dec., 1943).

8.10   BJERRUM, L., Norwegian experiences with steel piles to rock, *Geotechnique*, **7**, No. 2, pp. 73–96 (June, 1957).

8.11.   Skarvik Oil Jetty, Gothenburg, *Dock and Harbour Authority*, p. 37 (May, 1958).

8.12   HIRSCH, T. J., Recommended practices for driving prestressed concrete piling, *J. Prestressed Conc. Inst.*, **2**, No. 4, pp. 18–27 (Aug., 1966).

8.13   DEAN, W. E., Prestressed concrete—difficulties overcome in Florida Bridge practice, *Civ. Eng.* (*U.S.A.*) **27**, pp. 61–63 (June, 1957).

8.14   GARDNER, S. V. and NEW, D. H., Some experiences with prestressed concrete piles, *Proc. Inst. C.E.*, **18**, pp. 43–66 (Jan., 1961).

8.15   Building Esso Refinery at Milford Haven, *Engineering*, **188**, No. 4877, p. 315, and No. 4878, pp. 346–347.

8.16   HANNA, T. H., Behaviour of long H-section piles during driving and under load, *Ontario Hydro Res. Quarterly*, **18**, No. 1, pp. 17–25 (1966).

8.17   SCHENCK, W., The driven pile, *D.S.I.R. Library Communications No. 962* (London, H.M.S.O., April, 1960).

8.18.   BAXTER, J. W., BIRKETT, E. M., and GIFFORD, E. W. H., The Narrows Bridge, Perth, Western Australia, *Proc. Inst. C.E.*, **20**, pp. 39–84 (September, 1961).

8.19   MORGAN, H. D., The design of wharves on soft ground, 1943–44: *J. Inst. C.E.*, **22**, No. 5, pp. 5–45 (March, 1944).

8.20   WILSON, G., The bearing capacity of screw piles and screwcrete cylinders, *J. Inst. C.E.*, **34**, No. 5, pp. 4–93 (1949–50: March, 1950).

8.21 SAMUEL, R. H., The construction of Wuya Bridge, Nigeria, *Proc. Inst. C.E.*, **33**, pp. 353–380 (Mar., 1966).

8.22 Investigation of the strength of the connexion between a concrete cap and the embedded end of a steel H-pile, *Research Report No. 1* (State of Ohio Department of Highways, Dec., 1947).

8.23 WOOD, R. H. and SIMMS, L. G. A tentative design method for the composite action of heavily loaded brick panel walls supported on reinforced concrete beams, *B.R.E. Current* Paper 26/69, H.M.S.O. (July 1969).

# 9

# Foundation Construction

PRESENT day foundation construction methods involve a high degree of mechanization. Optimum working speeds of plant are achieved only in clear working conditions giving maximum mobility for the plant and vehicles. Therefore, an efficient and well-maintained system of temporary roads should be provided on extensive sites in order to achieve and maintain a rapid tempo of construction in all weathers. Equally important is attention to site drainage to give dry working conditions and to avoid unnecessary pumping.

## SITE PREPARATION

### Temporary Roads

The form of construction of temporary roads depends, of course, on the subgrade soil conditions. On well-drained sandy or gravelly soils, no construction will be necessary other than grading to levels and rolling to give a good running surface. Sandy surfaces are liable to rutting in very dry weather or during heavy rain. If required, increased stability can be obtained by rolling in stone or clinker or by laying some form of prefabricated metal tracking, such as Sommerfield track. Stabilization with cement can be considered for important temporary roads carrying heavy traffic over an extended period. On a sandy soil an addition of about 7 to 10 per cent of cement gives a satisfactory base. For a well-graded gravel the cement content can be as low as 4 or 5 per cent.

All forms of construction traffic can run on a clayey or silty soil when it is dry. Thus, if it is certain that all construction requiring transport over the site can be completed in the dry season, site roads are unnecessary. However, if the construction programme requires work to continue through the winter and in all periods of rainy weather, then some substantial form of temporary road construction is absolutely essential. It is also important to construct these temporary roads *before the onset of wet weather*. All too often it happens that no thought is given to the need for site roads while traffic is running unhampered over the dry sunbaked clay. Then the rains start and, within a day or two, deep wheel ruts start to form. The churned-up area gets wider and wider as drivers seek fresh routes on undisturbed ground, until eventually the whole site is a morass. Water lies in ruts, and thus aggravates the softening and slows down the drying. Drastic measures are taken when the vehicles are floundering to a standstill all over the site. Lorry loads of broken bricks and concrete are tipped on the site and bulldozed out to form a road. Half of this material is "lost" as it sinks into the liquid mud and the remainder continues to sink down as mud is squeezed up between the interstices of the stones under the weight of vehicles. Eventually, some 1 to 1·5 m thickness of material has to be spread before a rough and wavy-surfaced road is obtained. This description is in no way exaggerated. It is inevitable when construction of site roads is left too late. It is also a false economy to make the site roads too narrow. On narrow roads passing vehicles are forced to run off the road, when near-side wheels become bogged and the haunches of the road are broken down.

By constructing the roads before the onset of the wet weather, advantage can be taken of the high bearing value of the dry clay to economize in thickness of road material, although some allowance must be made for softening of the subgrade due to limited percolation of water through the surfacing. The cost of providing an impervious tar or bitumen surfacing to temporary roads cannot usually be justified, and in any case such surfacings are liable to disruption by tracked vehicles.

Excavation and earth-moving can be troublesome on chalk or marl sites. In dry weather vehicles can run anywhere but dust is a nuisance with heavy traffic. In rainy weather the chalk or marl surface becomes highly greasy and it is necessary to blind the surface with ashes or gravel to prevent vehicles from skidding.

It is always helpful to maintain good relations with the local authority, police, and public, by providing proper tyre washing or road brushing facilities if earthmoving vehicles have to run on the public roads. It is even worth while considering the construction of a temporary bridge if vehicles merely have to cross a public highway on a long-term project. By this means there will be no hold-up in having to clean vehicle wheels, accidents will be avoided, and vehicles need not be licensed to travel on the highway.

### Site Drainage

Much can be done to improve working conditions in wet weather by attention to the surface and subsoil water drainage. This is imperative for construction in tropical or sub-tropical climates where heavy rainstorms can cause rapid flooding or erosion of a site with consequent damage to partly constructed works. If temporary roads cross ditches, these should be piped beneath the roads and any ditches running towards the working area should be diverted. Any existing subsoil drains which may be exposed by excavations should be carefully inspected. If they appear to be "live" they should be intercepted by a cross drain and led to the nearest ditch or surface-water sewer. It is highly wasteful to pump surface water from excavations which might be prevented from entering the excavation by a few well-placed cut-off ditches or stone-filled drains.

### Site Preparation in Built-up Areas

Site preparation in built-up areas should include tracing and clear marking of existing underground telephone and power cables, gas and water mains, and sewers. This is important since many fatal accidents have been caused by men or machines striking electric cables and gas mains, and the cost of repairing trunk telephone cables can run into a thousand pounds or more. The bursting of a water main can be disastrous to a partly completed excavation if flooding causes collapse of the sides. Safety precautions should be taken in consultation with the supply authorities wherever site roads or tracks are crossed by overhead cables.

If deep excavations, blasting, or pile driving are to be carried out near existing structures, careful inspections should be made jointly with the property owners to determine whether there are any signs of cracking or settlement. Any cracks should be photographed and marked with tell-tales. During the progress of the work, periodic levels should be taken on nearby buildings and measurements made of the widths of cracks at tell-tale positions as a check on possible movement. It is surprising how often property owners are quite unaware that their buildings are cracked and in all good faith make claims against the contractor if their property is shaken by blasting or pile driving.

## EXCAVATION METHODS

**Bulk Excavation**

The choice of plant for bulk excavation is largely determined by the quantity and by the length of haul to the disposal point. If the tip area is close to the excavation, say within 100 m, then the earth can be moved by *bulldozer* or *angledozer*.* Longer hauls (say 100 to 600 m) require crawler or rubber-tyred tractor-drawn *scrapers*. For even longer hauls beyond about 600 to 800 m, then the faster-moving rubber-tyred tractors are required for hauling the scrapers. However, the size and depth of the excavation and the soil conditions must be favourable for economical use of scrapers; they are unsuitable for deep excavations covering a small area since the ramp roads enabling the scrapers to climb in and out of the cut cannot be conveniently arranged. There must also be room for the scraper to turn in the cut. These machines are best suited to fairly large areas of shallow excavation. They can excavate all soil types except soft clays and silts. Soft or laminated rocks, such as shales or marl, can be dealt with if loosened by a ripper or rooter. Scrapers are unsuitable for haulage over public roads.

If the haul distance for the excavated material exceeds about 800 to 1000 m, then excavators loading into lorries or trailer wagons are required. Types of mechanical excavator available include the face shovel, backacter (backhoe), dragline, drag-scraper, grab, and loading shovel.

*Loading shovels* are suitable only for shallow cuts up to a few metres deep since the method of filling the bucket is not so efficient as other types, and loading lorries requires the bucket arm to be raised thus slowing the loading cycle. Loading shovels mounted on rubber-tyred or crawler tractors are a convenient and almost universal method for shallow excavation in fairly small areas, and also in deep excavations for operating beneath the bracing frames.

*The face shovel* is the most efficient type of excavator for large quantities of bulk excavation. The height of the face is limited only by the size of the machine but it is uneconomical for face heights lower than about 1 m. The important feature of a face shovel from the aspect of foundation excavation is that it must stand at excavation level and feed into lorries also standing at the same level. This requires a ramp road to enable the machine to dig its way into the excavation and to climb out again. For this reason face shovels are unlikely to be suitable for deep excavations in confined areas where there is no room to form the ramp road.

---

* The types of mechanical plant available for earthmoving are too many and diverse for detailed description and illustration in this book. The reader is referred to current manufacturers' catalogues for detailed descriptions.

*Backacters* are rather less efficient in excavating than face shovels and their excavation depth is limited by the length of jib and bucket arm. However, they are very suitable machines for deep excavation in small areas such as for column bases or for trench excavations. They also have the advantage of operating from ground level thus avoiding the need for ramp roads.

*Draglines* also have the advantage of working from ground level, and their excavation depth is limited only by the amount of wire rope that can be wound on the bucket-rope drum. Long jib machines can also dispose of the material in large piles adjacent to the cut; thus they are useful for sites where most of the excavation is to be returned around the completed foundations. They have the disadvantage that they cannot cut to a vertical face on all sides of the excavation and, because of the swinging bucket, the time of loading vehicles is slightly slower than with rigid bucket arm types.

*Grabs* (clam-shell buckets) suspended from mobile or derrick cranes or from excavator-type cranes are rather slow in operation due to the time required to close the grab and wind it into and out of the excavation. However, they are the most suitable type of excavator for deep excavations in small areas and are the only type of mechanical excavator suitable for working in timbered shafts and trenches. The depth of excavation is only limited by the capacity of the winding rope drum. Different types of grab are available for different materials.

*Drag-scrapers*, or cable scrapers, consist of a scraper bucket travelling on a rope suspended between a fixed tower and a travelling tower or between two travelling towers. The loaded bucket is tipped either into vehicles or a conveyor belt or on to a pile near the winding tower. These machines are essentially used for excavating in large areas on soft ground or below water where tracked machines or vehicles cannot operate. They would not be considered for normal excavation work.

*Belt conveyors* are a useful means of transporting excavated material across ground impassable to vehicles or over water. The excavator loads into a hopper with a belt feeder beneath the hopper regulating the discharge on to the belt. The length of haul by belt conveyor is more or less unlimited and they can be set up on travelling carriages to move with the excavator.

Mechanical excavators of the face shovel type are readily convertible to grab crane, dragline, or backacter, and an excavation job could thus be tackled in a number of different ways using the same machine. Thus it would work as a backacter or grab to dig foundation trenches for the retaining walls of a basement and convert to a face shovel for the bulk excavation in the dumpling. A loading shovel could carry out shallow excavation to floor level of, say, a steel-framed factory building and convert to a backacter to dig the column bases.

Mechanical excavators can excavate sands, gravels, and clays, and also soft or laminated rocks such as marl, chalk, and shale without the need for explosives.

### Rock Excavation

The use of explosives to break up the rock in advance of mechanical excavation is necessary in all but the softest rocks such as weathered marls, chalk, and shales. Explosives are sometimes necessary in shales to loosen the layers, especially if, as is often the case, they are interbedded with sandstones and siltstones. However, the use of explosives involves noise and vibration and the risk of annoyance to the public and possible damage to property. Much can be done to minimize blasting vibrations by limiting the weight of charges and the use of delay detonators. Expert advice from manufacturers of explosives should be sought on these aspects of the work.

There are two methods of drilling and blasting which can be adopted for the scale of excavations involved in foundation work. These are—

(a) Benching
(b) Wellhole blasting.

Method (a) is applicable to most foundation excavations. Method (b) is for large-scale rock removal such as general levelling over a large site. In the benching method the face is taken back in a series of steps or benches. The maximum height of bench worked is usually limited to 10 m. Excavators work on the benches loading spoil into lorries or other haulage equipment. Holes are drilled by hand-held jackhammers for small-scale work or tripod or wagon-mounted jackhammer drills for work involving large numbers of holes. Using typical charges for the spacings and burdens (i.e. horizontal distance from face to drill hole) shown in Table 9.1, average yields of 10 000 to 15 000 kg of rock per kg of explosive can be expected. The most suitable type of explosive for general work is Polar Ammon Gelignite "B."

Wellhole blasting involves the drilling of comparatively large diameter holes at a wide spacing. The large well drills used are more expensive to hire and maintain than the smaller jackhammer drills. They are particularly suited to limestone, shales, and marls, but not for highly abrasive igneous rocks where the wear and tear on drill bits increases the cost of drilling. For wellhole blasting to be economical the face should be at least 10 m high, the usual heights being

**Table 9.1**

**HOLE PLACING FOR BENCHING**

| Depth of hole m | Spacing m | Burden m | Charges kg |
|---|---|---|---|
| 1·000 | 1·000 | 0·600 | 0·1–0·2 |
| 1·200 | 1·200 | 0·800 | 0·2–0·4 |
| 1·500 | 1·500 | 0·900 | 0·4–0·7 |
| 1·800 | 1·500 | 1·200 | 0·7–0·9 |
| 2·400 | 1·800 | 1·500 | 1·3–1·8 |
| 3·000 | 2·000 | 1·700 | 2·3–2·7 |
| 3·600 | 2·400 | 1·800 | 3·6–4·0 |
| 6·000 | 3·000 | 3·000 | 11·0 |
| 9·000 | 3·600 | 4·500 | 30 |

15 to 25 m. The spacing of the holes should be roughly equal to the burden. The hole diameters used are 40 to 250 mm, usually 150 mm. The yield of the explosive charges loaded into the holes varies from 8000 kg of rock to 1 kg of explosive up to 15 000 kg to the kilogram in favourable conditions. Wellhole blasting produces good fragmentation so reducing the amount of secondary blasting to break down boulders. If delay detonators are used the ground vibrations are not large. However, it is only on the largest foundation excavation jobs that wellhole blasting can be considered instead of drilling and benching with jackhammer drills.

If the proximity of buildings prohibits the use of conventional explosives, then there is no alternative to breaking up the rock piecemeal by hand-held pneumatic breakers or lorry mounted dieselpowered breakers, although the use of "Cardox" (liquid carbon dioxide in a steel tube) provides a method of blasting with a minimum of noise and vibration.[9.1] Compressed air or diesel breakers inevitably cause noise and vibration, and if these must be avoided at all costs it will be necessary to resort to special methods of loosening the rock. These include freezing water in drill holes by liquid oxygen or the use of hydraulic burster cartridges. Holes for these methods can be drilled without much noise or vibration by rotary diamond core drills or, if no noise at all can be permitted, by the oxygen lance method. In the latter method drilling rates up to 9 m per hour to a depth of 36 m have been obtained in granite. The size of the hole is 150 to 250 mm diameter. However, all these special methods are necessarily costly and are only considered in special circumstances.

## Stability of Slopes to Open Excavations

Two main considerations govern the determination of stable slopes for open excavations. The first of these, as would be expected, is the type of soil. The second is the permissible degree of risk of slipping. For example, if important property is close to the top of an excavation there must be no risk of a slip, and a high safety factor must be adopted. Similarly, there must be an adequate safety factor if a slip could damage a partly completed basement retaining wall or undermine a sewer or water main. On the other hand, if slipping causes no damage to existing or new structures and if excavation plant is on hand to clear away slipped material, then it is justifiable to take some risks in the interests of economy in the total quantity of excavation, provided of course that there will be no danger to workmen. This latter factor is important in narrow excavations and will be discussed in greater detail under "Trench Excavations."

### SLOPE STABILITY IN COHESIVE SOILS

It can be shown theoretically[9.2] that an open excavation in a normally consolidated clay soil will stand vertically without support provided that the height of the face does not exceed the critical height $(H_c)$ where—

$$H_c = \frac{4\bar{c}}{\gamma \times 9 \cdot 807} \qquad . \qquad . \qquad . \qquad . \qquad . \qquad . \qquad (9.1)$$

and $\qquad \bar{c} = $ cohesion of clay

$\qquad \gamma = $ density of clay (mass per unit volume)

Values of $H_c$ for clays of various consistencies are—

|  | Very soft | Soft | Firm |
|---|---|---|---|
| Cohesion (kN/m²) | 0–17·5 | 17·5–35·0 | 35·0–70·0 |
| Critical height (m) | 4 | 4–8 | 8–16 |

However, the above theoretical method cannot be unreservedly adopted because of changes in the stability of the ground with the passage of time as a result of changes in pore-water pressure behind the face on release of lateral pressure. This is particularly important in stiff fissured clays, the stability of which may be provided by negative pore-water pressures which serve to keep the fissures tightly closed when the mass of clay remains undisturbed. However, on removal of lateral pressure by excavation the change from negative to positive pore pressures may take place in days or hours, and instead of the clay being held together at the fissures it is liable to slide in a mass of small fragments falling from the face or in the form of a massive bodily slip along a well-defined fissure plane. In soft or firm normally consolidated clays (which are generally unfissured), long-term drying will open up cracks in the soil. Water getting into these at times of subsequent rain is liable to force off a mass of clay from the face. Thus, the critical heights *for normally consolidated clays* shown above should only be provided where major slips are not liable to cause serious damage to temporary or permanent work or danger to workmen. It is generally safe to work to the lower ranges of critical heights in wide excavations without entailing risk to workmen.

If the depth of the excavation exceeds the critical height then cutting back to a safe slope will be necessary. In the case of *normally consolidated soft to firm clays* the required slope for a given safety factor can be determined with fair accuracy by the normal slip circle analysis, provided that there is reasonably adequate information on the shear strength of the soil. The safety factor depends on the risk involved in a major slip. If this would not cause damage to property or risks to life, then a low safety factor, say 1·2 to 1·3, is suitable. If it is essential to avoid any risk of slipping then a safety factor of 2 to 3 would be required. It must be remembered that a rotational slip involves the movement of a considerable body of earth accompanied by upheaval at the toe. Therefore, in deep excavations the trouble and expense in clearing a large mass of slipped earth must be kept in mind when assessing the safety factor. The risks of slipping are greatly increased if spoil is tipped close to the top of the slope. The stability analysis should take account of this possibility and, if necessary, the spoil tip must be moved back to a safe distance beyond the top of the slope.

*Stiff boulder clays* will stand vertically over long periods with only minor falls from the face as a result of frost damage or erosion from sandy lenses in the clay. The main risk of instability of boulder clay slopes lies in the possibility of lenses or pockets of water-bearing sand and gravel in the clay.

The excavation for a dry dock at South Shields, described by Stott and Ramage,[9.3] was an excellent example of how a stiff boulder clay (average shear strength 120 kN/m$^2$) can stand at a very steep slope. The 12 m deep excavation was cut with nearly vertical sides, and the face at any point remained unsupported for periods of up to six months while precast concrete buttresses were propped against the face and in-situ concrete panel walls were cast between them (Plate XIII). There is no doubt that this construction method gave a very considerable saving in money over the conventional method of constructing dock walls in a timbered trench.

*Stiff fissured clays* can give difficult problems in slope stability.

Because of the unpredictable effect of pore-pressure changes on removal of overburden pressure, the safe slopes over the normal construction period for foundation excavations cannot be calculated from a knowledge of the shear strength of the soil. Some observations collected by the author on the stability of excavation slopes in London Clay are shown in Table 9.2. Slips in an unstable slope in this type of clay take the form of a bodily collapse of a large mass of earth or minor falls caused by slipping or crumbling along a well-defined fissure plane (Plate XII). If there are no risks to structures or property above the crest of the slopes they can be excavated at 1 in ½. This batter will not by any means ensure freedom from slipping but the mass of the slips should be small enough to avoid undue trouble in clearing them or to avoid damage to partly completed structures. If slipping is likely to undermine structures or to give risks to life, then a slope of 1 in 2 or 2½ must be provided or else the face must be strutted.

SLOPE STABILITY IN COHESIONLESS OR PARTLY COHESIVE SOILS

Dry *sands and gravels* can stand at slopes equal to their natural angle of repose no matter what the depth. Values of the angle of repose quoted by Terzaghi and Peck are as follows—

|  | Angles of repose for dry sands | |
| --- | --- | --- |
|  | Round grains uniform | Angular grains well-graded |
| Loose | 28·5° | 34° |
| Dense | 33·0° | 46° |

Damp sands and sandy gravels possess some cohesion and can stand vertically for some time. It is usual to excavate these materials to a steep batter for construction periods of up to a few weeks. A 5 m deep excavation for a basement structure in Hammersmith is shown in Plate XIV. Pumping from a sump at the base of the lift well kept the water table (normally standing 4·4 m below ground level) in the region of the toe of the slopes, so preventing erosion. *Water-bearing sands* are very troublesome in open excavations; if they are cut steeply, seepage of water from the face will result in erosion at the toe followed by collapse of the upper part of the face until a stable angle of 15° to 20° is eventually reached (Plate XV). Further information on the measures to avoid instability of slopes in water-bearing ground is given in Chapter 11.

Water-bearing sandy soils are particularly troublesome when

**Table 9.2**

**STABILITY OF EXCAVATIONS AT THE CONSTRUCTION STAGE IN LONDON CLAY**

| Site | Total height (m) | Slope vert : horiz | Stability conditions | Reference |
|------|------------------|--------------------|----------------------|-----------|
| Northolt, Middx. | 2·4 | 1 : 1 | Wholly in brown London Clay; unstable | |
| Isleworth, Middx. | 3·7– 4·3 | 1 : ½ | Wholly in stiff blue London Clay; stable except for minor shallow slips five months after excavation | |
| Muswell Hill, London | 6·1 | Vertical | Wholly in brown London Clay; slipped six weeks after excavation | Tomlinson (1955)[9.4] |
| Mill Lane, London | 6·1 | 1 : ½ | Wholly in stiff London Clay; slipping arrested by covering slopes and 1–2 m back from crest with tarpaulins | Serota (1955)[9.5] |
| Bradwell-on-Sea, Essex | 7·0 | 1 : ½ | Wholly in brown London Clay; stable four months after excavation | Meigh (1957)[9.6] |
| Paddington | 7·6 | Vertical | Wholly in London Clay; stable | Skempton (1955)[9.7] |
| London Airport | 7·6– 9·1 | 1 : 1½ | 3·6–4·6 m gravel overlying stiff blue London Clay; extensive slipping about six weeks after excavation | Tomlinson (1955)[9.4] |
| Euston | 9·1 | Vertical | Wholly in London Clay; stable | Skempton (1955)[9.7] |
| Bradwell-on-Sea, Essex | 13·7 | 1 : 1 in overburden 1 : ½ in London Clay | 2·4 m fill, 2·7 m marsh clay, 7·3 m brown London Clay, 1·2 m blue London Clay, slipped nineteen days after excavation | Meigh (1957)[9.7] |
| Bradwell-on-Sea, Essex | 14·8 | 1 : 1 in overburden 1 : ½ in London Clay | 3·5 m fill, 2·7 m marsh clay, 7·3 m brown London Clay; 1·2 m blue London Clay; slipped one day after excavation | Meigh (1957)[9.6] |

interbedded with thin layers of silt or clay. This type of ground is not uncommon in glacial deposits. The silt or silty sand is liable to bleed from the face causing undermining and collapse of the more stable layers (Plate XVI). Because of the impermeable layers it may not be possible to use a ground water lowering system; sheet piling to exclude ground water is often the only answer in this type of ground.

*Dry silt* will stand unsupported vertically, especially if it is slightly cemented. For example, loess soils found in U.S.A., U.S.S.R. and Middle Eastern countries are slightly cemented silts which can stand vertically to heights of more than 15 m. Indeed, excavations in such soils should preferably be cut vertically to avoid severe erosion due to water flowing over them. Uncemented dry silt is liable to flow like a liquid when subjected to vibrations and *wet silt* is one of the most troublesome materials which can be met in excavations. Seepage of water from a steeply cut face in silt causes the material to flow outwards from the toe at a very flat gradient; this is followed by slumping of the upper part and the whole face is progressively undermined until it eventually attains an overall stable angle.

SLOPE STABILITY IN ROCKS

It must not be taken for granted that rock excavations will stand with vertical slopes without trouble. Their stability depends on the angle of the bedding planes and the degree of shattering of an unsound rock. For example, dangerously unstable conditions can occur if bedding planes slope steeply towards an excavation (Fig. 9.1 (a)), especially if there is ground water present causing lubrication along the bedding planes. Stable conditions are assured only when the bedding planes are near the horizontal or slope away from the excavation (Fig. 9.1 (b)). Shattered rocks consisting of a large mass of loose fragments are liable to fall from a steeply cut face causing undermining and major collapse of overlying sound rock (Fig. 9.1 (c)).

Unstable rock conditions were met in excavations for Stockholm's Underground Railway[9.8] where extensive fissures in the rock were filled with sand and clay. To prevent the rock slipping towards the excavation, prestressed anchor bolts were grouted into holes drilled deep into sound rock below excavation level (Fig. 9.2). Rock bolts can be of considerable help in preventing massive falls from a steeply cut rock face as well as in their normal application to support roofs of tunnels in rock. Three main types of rock bolts are available. In one type the end of a solid rod terminates in a split wedge which is forced against the walls of the drill hole by pulling on the bolt. This has the added advantage of giving a positive test on the holding power of the bolt. The second type consists of a perforated split sleeve around the solid section bolt. The sleeve is lightly packed with a mixture of cement and iron filings, the two halves are wired together and it is pushed into the drill hole. The bolt is then driven down into the sleeve. This forces the two halves apart and against the walls of the hole and the cement is also forced through the perforations in tight contact with the rock. The third type employs a hollow rod

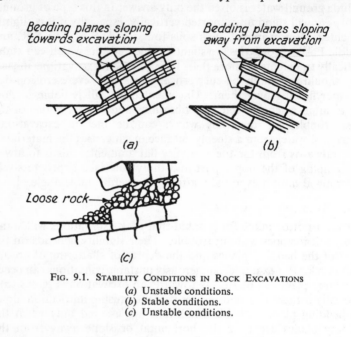

FIG. 9.1. STABILITY CONDITIONS IN ROCK EXCAVATIONS
(*a*) Unstable conditions.
(*b*) Stable conditions.
(*c*) Unstable conditions.

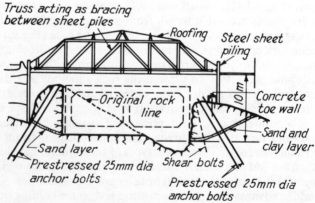

FIG. 9.2. ROCK BOLTING IN EXCAVATION FOR UNDERGROUND RAILWAY, STOCKHOLM[9.8]

with a wedge anchorage at the end. Grout is injected around the rod and flows back down the hollow space towards the outer end. Grout issuing from the latter indicates that injection is complete. Scrap hollow drill rods can also be used for grouted anchors. Grouting of rock bolts provides a more durable anchorage with less risk of slipping than ungrouted solid rods, which rely for anchorage solely on the friction on the wedge. Long-term creep of the rock stressed by the wedge can cause relaxation of the anchorage. Retightening is then required to restore the original value. Washer plates, light steel sections or steel mesh are used between the bolts to support the rock face. The type of supporting medium depends on the closeness of the joints in the rock.

Marl or chalk can stand vertically to a considerable height but are liable to long-term disintegration of the face by frost. The falls caused by frost action from a vertical face in chalk may be fairly extensive but a 60° slope will remain generally stable for many years, although there will be a gradual accumulation of debris at the toe. A 45° slope in chalk will be virtually trouble-free, especially if it can be covered with turf to bind the surface and prevent erosion of frost-loosened material.

Excavation in scree or boulder debris can be very difficult and adequate slopes must be given in order to avoid dangerous slides of boulders.

Further information on the stability of slopes in various types of rock formations is given in *CP 2003*. This *Code*[9.9] gives much useful information on excavation methods and timbering.

### Trench Excavation

An important factor in trench excavations for strip foundations or for retaining walls to basements is the stability against collapse of the trench sides. Such a collapse in a deep and narrow trench would be very likely to kill anyone unlucky enough to be buried by the fall. In Britain there is no definite requirement in the Factories Acts to timber trenches in all circumstances.

Regulation 8 (i) of "The Construction (General Provisions) Regulations, 1961," states—

"An adequate supply of timber of suitable quality or other suitable support shall where necessary be provided and used to prevent, so far as is reasonably practicable and as early as is practicable in the course of the work, danger to any person from a fall or dislodgement of earth, rock or other material forming the side or roof of or adjacent to any excavation, shaft, earthwork or tunnel:

"Provided that this Regulation shall not apply—

(*a*) to any excavation, shaft or earthwork, where, having regard to the nature and slope of the sides of the excavation, shaft or earthwork and other circumstances, no fall or dislodgement of earth or other material so as to bury or trap a person employed or so as to strike a person employed from a height of more than four feet (1·219 m) is unable to occur; or

(*b*) in relation to a person actually engaged in timbering or other work which is being carried out for the purpose of compliance with this Regulation, if appropriate precautions are taken to ensure his safety as far as circumstances permit."

Thus, the decision whether or not to timber a trench, or the amount of support that is necessary, rests with the engineer. The usually accepted procedure is to provide some form of timbering, no matter what the soil conditions, whenever the trench is of such a depth that a collapse will cause death or injury to workmen. This usually requires support to the sides of all trenches deeper than 1·2 m. Having decided to timber the trench, considerable judgment is then required on the amount of sheeting and strutting necessary. This aspect will be discussed in the next section of the chapter.

Mechanical excavation for trenches is carried out by backacter (backhoe) or dragline excavators, or by grabbing. Small hydraulically operated tractor-mounted backacters are used for narrow and shallow trench excavations. Dragline excavators can dig to any width and their excavating depth is only limited by the length of cable that can be accommodated by the winding drum. However, because of their mode of digging they cannot be used to excavate in trenches where timbering must be kept close to the working face. In these conditions grabbing is the only practicable method. The operator of the grab excavator can drop the bucket between the struts and waling of the trench timbering thus allowing deeper sets of bracing frames to be placed as the excavation is taken progressively deeper.

The choice between excavating a trench with vertical sides supported by timbering or with untimbered sloping sides is generally a matter of economics. However, there are circumstances where timbered trenches are unavoidable, such as in a restricted working area where space is not available for a wide trench, or in water-bearing sands which would cause slumping-in of the trench sides to a very flat angle of repose. The untimbered trench has the advantage of a clear working space unhampered by struts, but a deep untimbered trench requires the slopes to be cut well back to ensure the safety of the workmen, and the cost of this extra excavation together with the additional cost of carefully replacing and ramming the backfilling might well outweigh the cost of timbering a vertical-sided trench to the same depth.

### SUPPORT OF EXCAVATIONS BY TIMBERING AND SHEET PILING

The design of temporary supports to the sides of excavations is governed by the soil and ground water conditions, and by the depth and width of the excavated area. In water-bearing sands and silts continuous support will have to be given to the face by means of timber *runners* or *poling boards* or by steel *trench sheets* or *sheet piling*. With each of these methods it is necessary to drive the face support ahead of the excavation. Firm to stiff clays, compact dry or clay-bound gravels, compact or cemented sands, shales and stratified rocks can stand unsupported for varying lengths of time. Therefore, in these types of ground it is only necessary to provide timbering at an open spacing sufficient to withstand inward yielding of the mass of ground behind the face, and to avoid the risk of collapse of the sides due to, say, opening of fissures in a stiff clay or weakening along the bedding planes of a dipping rock stratum.

Wide excavations require heavier bracing to the frames of *walings* and *struts* than do narrow trenches or small shafts, and in the case of very wide excavations it will be necessary to support the face by *raking struts* or *shores*, or to tie it back by *ground anchors*.

Design of timbering schemes in advance of construction and the ordering of only sufficient timber for the work (as far as possible pre-cut to the designed lengths) will ensure safety in construction and will avoid waste and excessive cutting of the timbers. It must also be noted that a good design of a timbering scheme is one which permits easy *striking*. A design which necessitates cutting or smashing up of valuable timber in heavy walings and struts in order to remove them on completion of the temporary work is thoroughly wasteful. Considerations of safety in restricted conditions also require ease of striking.

### Support of Excavations in Loose Sands and Gravels, and Soft Clays and Silts

In these ground conditions it is necessary to provide continuous support to the face by *close timbering* and it is also necessary to place the timbering in position as quickly as possible in order to avoid the sides slumping in. The close support can be provided either in the form of *runners, poling boards,* or *sheet piles* driven ahead of the excavation, or by placing horizontal *laggings* or *sheeting* behind *soldier piles* driven in advance of excavation.

TIMBERING WITH RUNNERS

The procedure in installing timber runners is shown in Fig. 9.3 (*a*) to (*d*). A shallow excavation is first taken out and guide walings and struts are placed (*a*). The walings are temporarily blocked off the face by short boards (uprights) placed behind them. These enable the struts to be tightened and cleats or lip blocks are nailed or bolted to the ends of the struts. These are an important detail since they prevent the struts from falling if they work loose due to shrinkage of the timber or distortion of the walings. The struts are tightened by cutting them slightly too long and then driving one end with the other held in position, until they are at right angles to the waling. Heavy struts are tightened by folding wedges at one or both ends, or by jacking. Timber runners are then pitched behind the walings. They are usually 175 by 38 mm or 175 by 50 mm boards in lengths of up to 4·8 m. In clays their lower ends are sharpened with the bevel towards the face. This keeps them hard against the face as they are driven down. However, sharpening is not advisable in gravels because of the risk of splitting or "brooming" as they are driven down. Steel trench sheets (Fig. 9.19) can be used instead of timber. To facilitate pitching and driving long runners, an external guide waling is placed about 1 m above ground level. This can conveniently form part of a trestle used by workmen in driving down the runners by a heavy maul. A wedge or "page" is placed between the runners and the waling to allow the runners to be driven down and then tightened against the face of the excavation one at a time. When the excavation reaches the level of the second bracing frame the walings are threaded through the struts of the top frame and then set in position. Longer uprights are set between the walings enabling the struts to be tightened against the face. Puncheons are placed between walings to support the top frame and lacing boards are nailed vertically between pairs of struts (*b*). The purpose of the lacing boards is to brace the two frames together, so preventing distortion resulting from uneven ground movements on either side of the excavation, and also to act as a safeguard against buckets or skips catching and lifting the struts as they are lifted out by crane. The excavation may then be taken deeper and, if necessary, a third frame is set and further puncheons and lacings are fixed between the second and third frames. The bottom frame is supported by puncheons on footblocks on the bottom of the excavation.

If the excavation has to be taken deeper than the runners, which are not usually more than 4·8 m long, a second setting of runners is placed within the walings of the top setting and an inner guide waling is also placed (*c*). These runners are then driven down in a similar

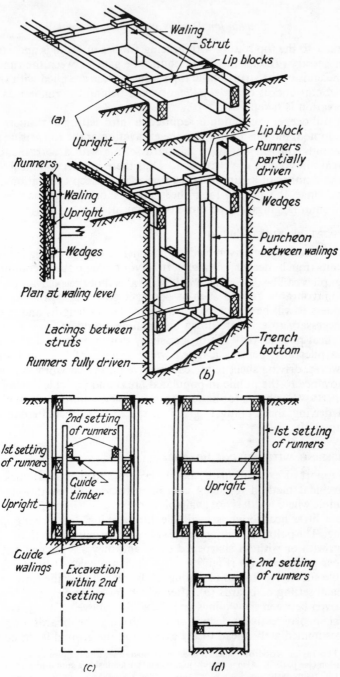

FIG. 9.3. SUPPORT OF EXCAVATION IN LOOSE SOIL WITH RUNNERS

(a) First-stage excavation.    (c) Pitching second set of runners.
(b) Second-stage excavation.    (d) Completed excavation.

manner to the top setting with bracing frames of walings and struts as necessary (*d*). There will, of course, be gaps between the runners at the ends of the struts of the top setting; these are filled with short horizontal boards or *cross poling*, tucked behind the runners as the excavation is taken down.

If still deeper excavation is required, a third setting of runners can be adopted, but this means that the excavation at the top setting will be about 1 m wider than at the third setting with a corresponding increase in volume of excavation. Thus there is an economical limit to the number of settings that can be used in deep excavations; at some stage the use of long sheet piles, short poling boards, or horizontal laggings will be more economical.

### SUPPORT BY SHEET PILING

Steel sheet piling driven by drop hammer or double-acting hammer permits much deeper settings. In favourable ground conditions sheet piles can be driven in 15 m lengths ahead of the excavation, but in unfavourable ground such as compact gravel or soil containing boulders it will be preferable to drive in shorter lengths and it may be necessary to excavate down and remove boulders from beneath the sheet piles as they are progressively driven deeper. The use of sheet piles also permits a much wider spacing of bracing frames. However, driving sheet piling can involve noise and vibration* with annoyance to the public in populated areas and possible damage to property. Further information on available sections and handling and driving sheet piling is given in the section on cofferdams in Chapter 10.

### TIMBERING WITH POLING BOARDS

Support of excavations by poling boards and tucking frames is a convenient method for deep cuts in restricted site conditions, for example where width is not available for several settings of runners or where little headroom is available for pitching and driving sheet piling. The poling boards are quite short, not usually more than 1·2 m long, with or without sharpened ends, and they are pitched outside timber guide walings (Fig. 9.4 (*a*)). They are splayed outwards to enable successive frames of walings to be placed near the lower ends of each setting of boards (*b*), after which the next setting of boards is driven between the walings and the setting above. The excavation is taken progressively deeper and by driving the boards in short stages immediately ahead of the excavation the ground is supported

---

* The Taylor-Woodrow "silent" pile driver operates without noise or appreciable vibration (*see* p. 636). Also a drop hammer can be used inside a sound-absorbent box ("Hush" piling system).

at all times (*b*). Before the next setting of boards is placed the space to be occupied by them is filled temporarily by a tucking board. After completion of driving a setting of boards, the tucking board is replaced as shown in (*b*).

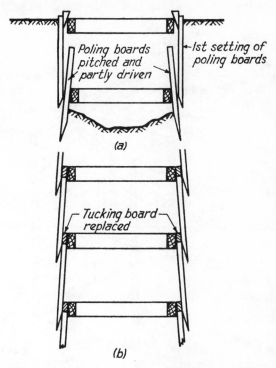

Fig. 9.4. Support of Deep Excavation in Loose Soil with Poling Boards and Tucking Frames

## HORIZONTAL TIMBERING

The other method mentioned above is to support the ground by horizontal laggings between soldier piles. This method is normally applied to deep excavations. The soldier piles are usually rolled-steel broad-flanged beams driven before excavating from ground level to a level 1 to 2 m below the bottom of the excavation. As the excavation is taken down timber polings are inserted horizontally between the flanges of the piles (Fig. 9.5) and held against the face by wedges. It is necessary to expose the ground over a depth of two or three boards to provide enough space to slip one board between the flanges. Driving the soldier piles, which are usually some 3 to 4 m apart, involves considerably less *duration* of vibrations than driving steel sheet piling. In water-bearing ground it is important to leave narrow gaps or louvres between the boards to allow drainage, so avoiding build-up of hydrostatic pressure behind the timbering. Where inflowing water causes erosion in the soil it can be checked by

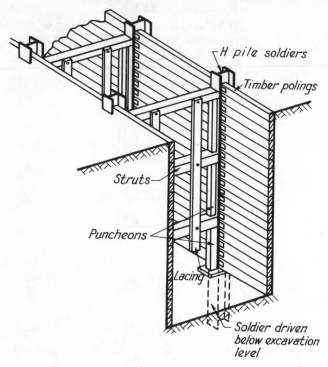

FIG. 9.5. SUPPORT BY SOLDIER PILES AND HORIZONTAL SHEETING

temporary earth banking and ditches to lengthen the seepage path (Fig. 9.6). The soldier pile method can also be used in conjunction with vertical runners as shown in Fig. 9.7. A waling is placed to span between the soldiers and the runners pitched behind. Further walings are set as the excavation progresses deeper. Where it is essential to avoid noise or vibration the soldiers can be set in pre-bored holes.

Horizontal timber sheeting can also be used in shallow excavations when short vertical walings are used to support the ends of the planks.

### Support of Excavations in Stiff Clays, Compact or Cohesive Dry Sands, or Weak Rock Strata

These materials can usually be relied upon to stand unsupported for a varying length of time but support is eventually needed to prevent yielding and settlement of the adjacent ground surface or to ensure the safety of workmen. Their ability to stand for a time without support greatly simplifies procedure in timbering. In trench excavations one of the simplest forms is the *open timbering* shown in Fig. 9.8.

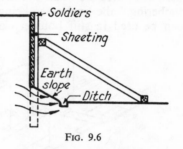

FIG. 9.6

After reaching the bottom of the excavation, 50 to 100 mm boards are placed against the face at each end of the walings. The walings are then placed and strutted across, further boards being placed at each intermediate strut position, and, if necessary, at intermediate positions between struts. If necessary, additional packing

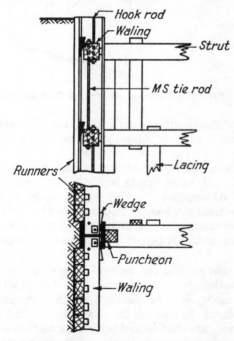

FIG. 9.7. SUPPORT BY SOLDIER BEAMS WITH RUNNERS

timbers are placed behind the boards if the face has been cut to an irregular line. If the boards are at 2 m centres the system is known as "open timbering" and for this spacing the walings can be omitted, each pair of boards being individually strutted by "pinchers." Boards at 1 m centres are "half timbering" and at 0·5 m centres "quarter timbering," the final stage being close timbering. Open timbering can be used in stiff boulder clays or sound rocky ground. Half

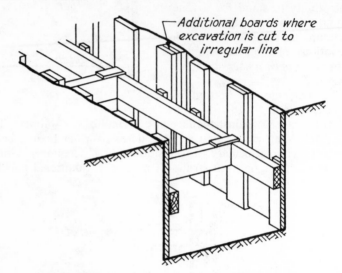

Additional boards where excavation is cut to irregular line

FIG. 9.8. OPEN TIMBERING IN STIFF OR COMPACT SOILS

timbering is suitable in stiff fissured clays or compact, cohesive sandy or gravelly soils, and close timbering in dry sands and gravels or crumbly shales.

In deep excavations several settings of boards can be used (Fig. 9.9). This method, using centre walings, is known as the *middle board system*. Alternatively, tucking frames can be used (Fig. 9.10). The walings overlap the ends of abutting boards. After bottoming a length of excavation, the boards are tucked behind the waling last set and another waling is placed and strutted at the bottom of the excavation.

The soldier pile method can be used in good ground but instead of driving the piles ahead of the excavation short soldiers, say 1 to 2 m long, are used. After bottoming a length of the excavation the soldiers are placed, packed off the face, and strutted across. The horizontal boards are then tucked behind the soldiers and tightened against the face by wedges. In this method square timbers are generally used for the soldiers in preference to steel sections. Single struts are used at the centres of the soldiers (Fig. 9.11) unless the latter are long when two struts might be needed across each opposite pair.

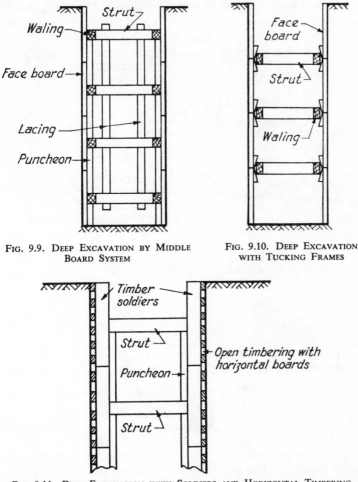

FIG. 9.9. DEEP EXCAVATION BY MIDDLE BOARD SYSTEM

FIG. 9.10. DEEP EXCAVATION WITH TUCKING FRAMES

FIG. 9.11. DEEP EXCAVATION WITH SOLDIERS AND HORIZONTAL TIMBERING

## Timbering in Shafts

A system of strutting different to that described above is used in timbering shafts for piers.

In the case of small shafts (Fig. 9.12 (*a*)) no struts are needed since the ends of the walings are self-supporting where they are "caught" by the walings or liners on the adjacent sides. The arrangement of struts for a large square shaft (*b*) is convenient, as the centre is left clear for hoisting materials by crane. In the case of rectangular shafts cross struts may be necessary (*c*). The striking piece at the end of one of the walings will be noted. This is provided because in a

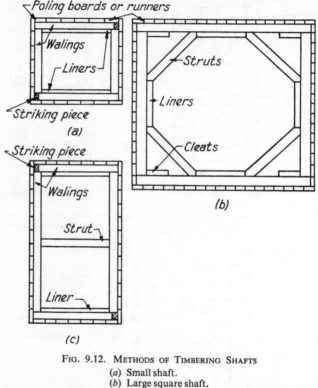

FIG. 9.12. METHODS OF TIMBERING SHAFTS

(*a*) Small shaft.
(*b*) Large square shaft.
(*c*) Rectangular shaft.

small excavation in swelling ground the walings can become tightly locked together. The provision of a striking piece, i.e. a piece of softwood which is readily prised out by crowbar, avoids the necessity of smashing a waling to pieces to release it.

## Support of Excavations in Variable Ground

It is quite the usual practice to vary the type of support for varying soil conditions in a given excavation. For example, Fig. 9.13 shows a method of timbering suitable for a site where loose or water-bearing sands and gravels or soft clays overlie stiff or compact material. The upper part of the excavation is supported by timber runners. On reaching the stiff stratum the support can be changed to open timbering by the "middle board" method. A "garland drain" is placed at the base of the water-bearing stratum to intercept water seeping through the close timbering, so preventing it from accumulating at the bottom of the excavation in the stiff stratum.

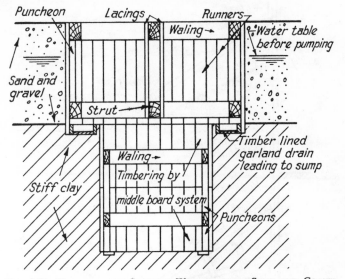

FIG. 9.13. TIMBERING FOR SHAFT IN WATER-BEARING SAND AND GRAVEL OVERLYING STIFF CLAY

The reverse method of support would be used in the case of, say, a stiff clay stratum overlying loose sand. Open timbering by the middle board system would be set in the stiff material; runners would then be pitched inside the walings of the upper settings and driven down with the deepening of the excavation into the loose material.

### Support of Large Excavations

Very large excavations can be supported by systems of raking shores. In soft or loose soils sheet piling can be pre-driven and the excavation is taken down leaving a sloping face to support the sheet piles. The top waling is then placed and raking shores are fixed (Fig. 9.14 (a)). The excavation is then taken deeper and a second and, if necessary, a third waling is fixed and shored up (Fig. 9.14 (b)). The walings are held up by puncheons in the usual way and by hangers from the top of the sheet piling. The raking shores are braced by lacing timbers bolted on and the feet of the shores bear on king piles, on the partly completed concrete floor of the excavation or on a timber or steel beam sill held by pins cast into a concrete floor. As an alternative to sheet piling, timber runners can be driven in one or

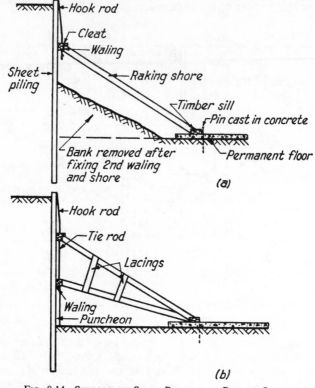

FIG. 9.14. SUPPORT BY SHEET PILING AND RAKING SHORES
(a) First-stage excavation.
(b) Second-stage excavation.

more settings behind walings in a similar manner to that described for trench excavations (Fig. 9.15). The method using soldier piles and laggings can also be used with raking shores (Fig. 9.16). For supporting the face of wide excavations in good ground, i.e. stiff clays, compact and cohesive sands, gravels, etc., raking shores can be used in conjunction with open timbering by the middle board system with tucking frames or with short soldiers. The layout of raking shores at the corners of excavations may become rather congested.

A suitable arrangement to give improved working space is shown in Fig. 9.16.

The methods of using raking shores, described above, have disadvantages. The shores obstruct the working area on the floor of the excavation; a flat angle is required to prevent them from sliding up on the walings or forcing up the walings; and rigid support to the lower ends is needed to avoid yielding. If the excavation is not too

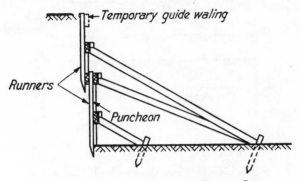

FIG. 9.15. SUPPORT BY RUNNERS AND RAKING SHORES

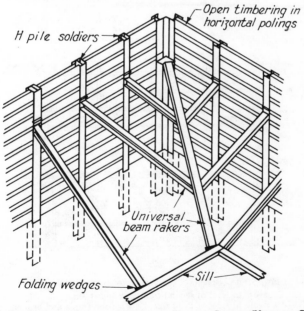

FIG. 9.16. SUPPORT BY SOLDIER PILES AND RAKING SHORES (VIEW AT CORNER OF EXCAVATION)

wide it is usually preferable to carry the struts right across. Careful design with transverse or diagonal strutting is necessary in order to prevent buckling of long struts, but at the same time the working space within the bracing frames should be as roomy as possible to avoid undue hindrance to construction operations.

A typical sequence of operations is shown in Fig. 9.17 (*a*) to (*d*).

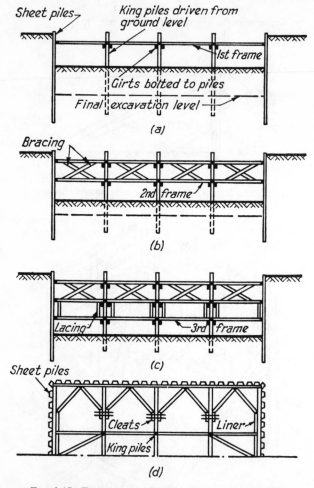

FIG. 9.17. TIMBERING TO DEEP AND WIDE EXCAVATION

(*a*) Excavate to level of second frame, fix top frame.
(*b*) Excavate to level of third frame, fix second frame and bracing.
(*c*) Excavate to final level, third frame fixed.
(*d*) Half plan of timbering.

The king piles, which may be Universal beams or box piles, are driven at the positions of joints in the struts and serve to support the bracing frames (Fig. 9.18). They have a vital function in restraining the struts from buckling in a vertical direction, and they must be driven deep enough into the soil to develop satisfactory resistance to com-

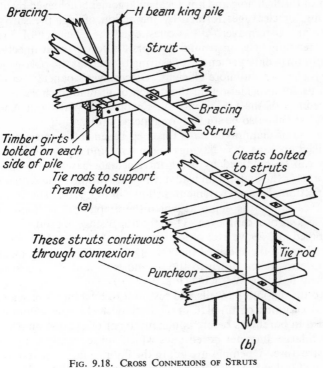

FIG. 9.18. CROSS CONNEXIONS OF STRUTS
(a) Connexion with king pile.
(b) Connexion without king pile.

pressive or uplift forces, especially when only a single bracing frame is provided. Typical details at junctions of struts are shown in Fig. 9.18 (a) and (b).

The use of tied back anchorages instead of strutting or raking shores to support the sides of wide excavations has the considerable advantage of providing a completely clear working area. The higher cost of anchors compared with shoring is counterbalanced by the reduced cost of excavation. Ground anchors are installed by drilling holes at a downward inclination to obtain a grouted bond length beyond the zones of potential slipping or yielding of the tied-back mass of soil. The bond length depends on the friction developed between the grouted annulus around the anchor and the surrounding soil. High ultimate resistances of the order of 400 to 1800 kN are obtainable in cohesionless soils, the highest range being in very dense sandy gravels. Lower values are obtained in cohesive soils, depending on the diameter of the drill hole and any local enlargements achieved by under-reaming, or cleavages formed by the action of high pressure grout injections. Ostermayer[9.9a] has questioned the efficiency of forming under-reaming bells on ground anchors and claims that injection of grout to form enlargements by fissuring the clay at the post-grouting stage is cheaper and more efficient. Ostermayer's paper[9.9a] contains much useful information on the design of ground anchors, and the Proceedings of the Conference on Diaphragm Walls and Anchorages[5.10] should also be studied for general information.

The use of diaphragm walls for deep basement construction was described on page 285. Savings in construction costs and improved safety can be obtained by using intermediate basement floors and supports for the diaphragm wall during excavation. The sequence of construction of a deep basement is shown in Fig. 9.19. The first stage is to excavate to the depth at which the diaphragm wall can stand safely as a vertical cantilever. Then the upper stage of ground anchors is installed just above excavation level (Fig. 9.19 (a)). After stressing the anchors to the specified increment above the working load, the excavation is taken down to the second level and the intermediate basement floor is constructed (Fig. 9.19 (b)). The floor acts as a rigid strut to the diaphragm walls and restraint to buckling is provided by vertical columns of tubular or H-section steel. The columns are installed in boreholes before commencement of excavation and they bear on large diameter bored piles which subsequently support the superstructure. Openings are left in the floor to facilitate removal of excavated soil at the third stage of excavation beneath the floor. The second level of ground anchors are installed at this stage (Fig. 9.19 (c)) followed by the final excavation to the bottom of the lowest basement floor which is then concreted to form the lowest level of permanent strutting and the ground floor is constructed. The stressing heads of the ground anchors can then be removed to permit construction of the interior facing wall. The steel columns are removed or encased in concrete and openings filled in to complete the basement construction (Fig. 9.19 (d)).

Deep excavations of this type cannot be undertaken without some inward yielding with corresponding settlement of the ground surface. Movement takes place at the various stages shown in Fig. 9.19 from the following causes—

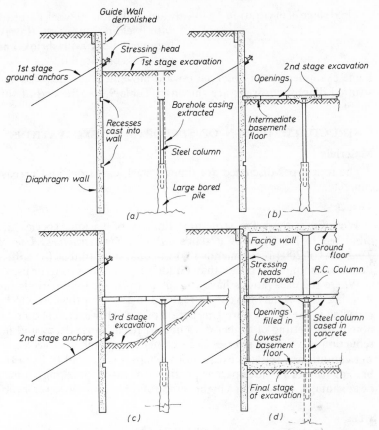

FIG. 9.19. SEQUENCE OF CONSTRUCTION OF DEEP BASEMENT WITH SUPPORT
BY ANCHORED DIAPHRAGM WALL

| 1st stage excavation | — ⎱ inward deflexion of wall as canti- |
|---|---|
| Drilling and grouting anchors | — ⎰ lever |
| Stressing anchors | —some reverse deflexion |
| 2nd stage excavation | —inward deflexion of wall as a beam with yielding supports |
| 3rd stage excavation | —inward deflexion of wall as beam (intermediate basement floor will shrink and compress elastically) |
| Drilling and grouting 2nd level of anchors | —inward deflexion of wall as beam with yielding supports |
| Stressing anchors | —some reverse deflexion |

Final stage of excavation          —inward deflexion of wall as beam
                                    with yielding supports (lowest
                                    basement floor will shrink and
                                    compress elastically)

Some examples of the observed inward movement of anchored and
strutted diaphragm walls are shown in Table 9.3 at the end of this
chapter.

## STRUCTURAL DESIGN OF SUPPORTS TO EXCAVATIONS

### Materials

The four types discussed are timber, steel, cast iron, and precast
concrete.

### TIMBER

Working stresses for structural timbers of various species are
tabulated in BS Code of Practice *CP 112, The Structural Use of
Timber.* CP 2004 recommends that the quality of timber for cofferdam work should not be less than Grade 50 (green stresses to be used).

Where the excavations have to remain open for long periods the
working stresses may have to be reduced to allow for the decay to be
expected in the timber during its period of use. However, it should be
noted that wetting of timber does not, by itself, cause decay and no
reduction in working stresses need be made for timber subjected to
wet conditions. In deep excavations where it is desired to keep the
bracing frames as wide apart as possible (for ease in working), it may
be advantageous to adopt a higher grade of timber for the lower levels.

### STEEL

Steel trench sheets can be used as runners or poling boards.

Steel is also used for struts in the form of light adjustable units for
trench work or for raking shores and also for walings and struts in
deep excavations, either in the form of heavy Universal beams or
compound girders, or of lighter trussed sections built up from angles
or channel. Structural design methods generally conform to design
procedures used in building work but it is usual to allow a discretionary
increase of up to 25 per cent in working stresses for temporary work.
Steel bracing is mainly used in conjunction with steel sheet piling
where it is desired to utilize a high proportion of the flexural strength
of the sheet piling by means of a wide spacing of the frames (*see* p. 628).

### PRECAST AND CAST-IN-SITU CONCRETE

Precast concrete is used in the form of planks for sheeting excavations where the support has to be left permanently in place. Precast

concrete can also be used for walings and struts, and on sites where
sheet piles are required to be left permanently in place they are often
constructed in reinforced concrete cast in-situ. A discretionary
increase of $33\frac{1}{2}$ per cent in the working stresses over those normally
used in structural design is permitted for temporary work in precast
concrete but no increase is usually allowed for cast-in-situ concrete,
and even lower stresses may have to be used for work constructed in
adverse conditions.

Tubular steel struts were used in conjunction with reinforced
concrete walings to support the 26 m wide by 13 m deep excavation
for the southern approach to the River Ij tunnel in Amsterdam
constructed in 1963–4 (Fig. 9.20). In plan, the sheet piling formed a

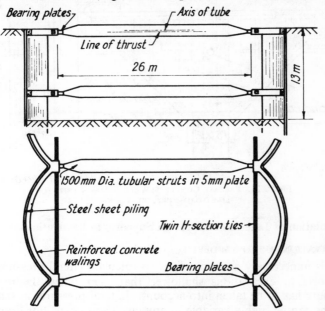

FIG. 9.20. SUPPORT OF EXCAVATIONS FOR RIVER IJ TUNNEL, AMSTERDAM

series of arches with chord lengths of 12 to 18 m. Each arch was
supported by massive reinforced concrete arch walings at two levels.
Steel H-sections were provided along the chords to resist longitudinal
forces. The ends of adjacent walings formed a massive concrete
thrust block fitted with bearing plates to receive the cone-shaped
ends of the 1500 mm diameter tubular steel struts. The tubes were of
welded plate construction without internal stiffening. They were
designed to resist a thrust of 1000 kN.

An interesting feature of the design was the placing of the cone-ends eccentrically to the axis of the tube. The eccentric thrust so provided neutralised the bending stresses set up by the 5 to 6 tonne mass of the strut and ensured that the whole cross-section was more or less equally stressed in compression.

Precast bracing units consisting of centrally supported short walings were used by Edmund Nuttall Ltd. in sheet piled excavations for the approaches to the Dartford–Purfleet Tunnel[9,10] (Fig. 9.21).

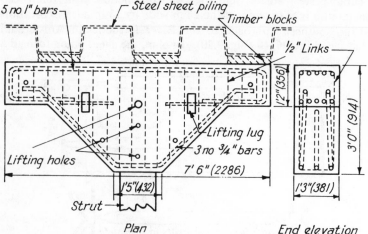

Plan                    End elevation

FIG. 9.21. PRECAST CONCRETE WALING UNITS USED FOR
DARTFORD–PURFLEET TUNNEL

### Calculation of Lateral Pressures on Supports to Excavations

EXCAVATIONS UP TO 6 M DEPTH

It is unnecessary and unrealistic to calculate lateral pressures on supports to excavations shallower than 6 m unless hydrostatic pressure has to be taken into account. Lateral pressures at shallow depths can be highly variable in any given soil type. For example, a clay will shrink away from behind the timbering in dry weather, sometimes forming a wide gap down which crumbs of dry clay may fall. The onset of wet weather causes the clay to swell and, if the gap has become filled with clay debris, the swelling forces on the timbering may be high enough to cause crushing or buckling of the struts. In stiff or compact soil higher stresses can be caused in struts and walings by hard driving of folding wedges at the ends of struts than from earth pressure. Again, if dry timber is used to support an excavation in water-bearing ground, the seepage through the runners on to the walings and struts, and the effects of rain falling on to the struts, can cause heavy stresses in the timbers due to swelling of the dry timber. Expansion of soil at times of hard frost can also cause heavy loads on timbering.

Therefore, the usual method of designing timbering by rule of thumb for shallow excavations is fully justified. The sizes of timbers given by such methods have been based on centuries of experience and take into account the desirability of re-using the timber as many times as possible, the requirement of withstanding stresses due to swelling of dry timber, and the necessity or otherwise of driving wedges tightly at the ends of the struts (or of jacking the ends of the struts) to prevent yielding of the sides of the excavation. They bear little or no relationship to the stresses arising from earth pressure. The reader may have noticed that the sizes of timbers used in the shallower excavations are more or less the same on any job no matter what the type of soil or even the depth of excavation.

If steel struts and walings are used, the stresses in them may be more representative of earth pressure than with timber members. However, the usual procedure is to use the struts to apply pressure *to the ground* by wedging or jacking rather than to allow earth pressure to come on to the supports. The jacking and wedging forces depend on the extent to which it is desired to prestress the ground to prevent yielding. An example of the forces required to prestress the ground to prevent settlement is given by the 10 to 12 m deep excavation for London's Hyde Park Underpass,[9.11] which was taken out within 1 m of the foundations of St. George's Hospital. As a precaution against yielding and settlement, the 9 m long steel walings were set at three levels, each waling having three struts (twin 356 × 406 mm beams). Total loads jacked into each waling frame were 837 kN, 3198 kN and 4065 kN respectively for the three levels, i.e. a total jacking load of 8700 kN for about 100 m² of excavated face. The measured settlement of the hospital wall was less than 3 mm.

Runners or poling boards are usually 38 mm thick, or 50 mm thick if many re-uses are desired. They can be as thin as 20 mm but timber as light as this cannot withstand repeated driving and is liable to split and disintegrate with rough handling. The thickness of runners and poling boards also depends to some extent on the spacing of walings. Boards 38 to 50 mm thick are suitable for walings at not more than 1·2 m centres. For wider spacings up to 2·4 m centres it would be necessary to use 75 to 100 mm planks. Walings for trenches or shafts up to 1·5 m deep need not be larger than 225 × 75 mm. This size can also be used for deeper excavations, say to 6 to 10 m, provided that they are not spaced at more than 1 m centres with struts at 1·5 to 2 m centres.

Deep excavations with a wide spacing of walings and struts require heavier members than 225 × 75 mm timbers. For walings at 1 to 1·2 m centres, 250 × 100 mm timbers are used; for wide spacings up to 2 m centres it is possible to use 300 × 150 mm walings in good ground. Loose or swelling ground would require 300 × 300 mm walings for a spacing of 2 m centres. Heavier timbers than 300 × 300 mm are unusual in excavation work due to the difficulty of obtaining larger sizes, though 350 × 350 mm baulks are occasionally used where heavy loads have to be carried; the usual procedure is to place 300 × 300 mm in pairs, spiked or bolted together.

Strut sizes for excavations to a depth of about 6 m are again only nominal and calculated on "rule of thumb" procedures. One such rule which is applicable to square struts for excavations from 1·2 to 3 m wide is—

$$\text{strut thickness (mm)} = 80 \times \text{trench width (m)} \quad . \quad (9.2)$$

It is convenient practice, though not always employed, to use struts of the same depth as the walings and often of the same scantling in order to avoid too many sizes of timber on the same job. Thus, 225 × 75 mm struts are used with 225 × 75 mm walings, 300 × 150 mm struts with 300 × 150 mm walings, and so on. The spacings of struts are governed by the lengths of the walings. Thus, 225 × 75 mm walings are usually supplied in 3600 to 4800 mm lengths. Three struts is a convenient number for a pair of 3600 mm walings, giving a spacing of 3400 mm for the three struts, with the pair at the abutting ends of walings at about 200 mm centres (Fig. 9.22). Heavier timbers,

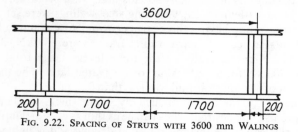

Fig. 9.22. Spacing of Struts with 3600 mm Walings

for example 300 × 150, 225 × 225, and 300 × 300 mm, can be obtained up to 6·3 m long or even longer by special order. However, it is often convenient to work with much shorter lengths because of the difficulty in threading long walings for lower settings through the previously set frames. Also, short walings are preferred for convenience in striking timbering before backfilling deep excavations, when the lower frames have to be struck first and threaded back through the upper frames with the added obstruction of the completed foundation structure within the excavation.

Structural steelwork is not often used for framing in excavations shallower than 6 m, except in wide excavations where the buckling stresses caused in long struts may be too much for timber, or in cofferdams where hydrostatic pressure has to be allowed for.

## EXCAVATIONS DEEPER THAN 6 M

Economies in material can be achieved by calculating earth pressures in excavations deeper than 6 m. It is not necessary to do this in all cases. Long experience of timbering in known ground conditions is often the best guide. But where deep excavations have to be carried out in soil conditions of which the engineer has no previous experience to guide him or where a different system of ground support is employed to that usually adopted for the locality, then it will be advisable to calculate earth pressures based on information provided by borings and laboratory tests on soil samples. Earth pressure calculations also make possible an economical spacing of walings and struts and permit the development of the full flexural strength of the various components including the sheeting members.

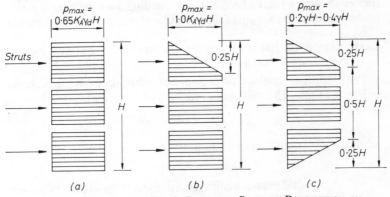

FIG. 9.23. TERZAGHI AND PECK'S RULES FOR PRESSURE DISTRIBUTION ON STRUTTED EXCAVATIONS

(*a*) Sands.       (*b*) Soft to firm clays.       (*c*) Stiff fissured clays.

The method of earth pressure calculation in general use for excavation supports has been developed by Terzaghi based on observations of actual loads in struts in full-scale excavations in sand in Berlin (Spilker, 1937)[9.12] and in soft clay in Chicago (Peck, 1943).[9.13] Terzaghi and Peck's empirical design procedure is described in *Soil Mechanics in Engineering Practice*.[9.14] Fig. 9.23 shows their rules for calculating the pressure distribution in sands and clays.

It is important to recognize the difference between the pressure distribution on a retaining wall and on a strutted excavation. A retaining wall acts as a structural unit and fails as a unit whereas a strutted excavation has some flexibility, and local concentrations of earth pressure can cause high loads on individual bracing members. If one strut fails it will immediately throw increased loads on to the adjoining members, thus initiating a general collapse of the system. Hence the trapezoidal distribution of Terzaghi and Peck was intended to be an *envelope* covering the maximum strut loads likely to occur at any level rather than representing the average strut loads.

Studies of earth pressure in soft clay at Shellhaven by Skempton and Ward[9.15] illustrated the effects on the strut loads of pile driving into a soft clay. The pile driving lowered the shear strength of the sensitive clay resulting in a 60 per cent increase in the strut loads in the lowest frame. The effects of frost in Norwegian stiff clay on strut loads were measured by Di Biagio and Bjerrum.[9.16] They caused a fivefold increase in strut loading in a 4 m deep excavation accompanied by buckling of walings and struts, necessitating the installation of additional timber bracing frames. The subsequent thaw was accompanied by a large reduction in strut loads. The two upper frames showed a marked reduction in loading over the winter period probably due to expansion of the ground surface adjacent to the trench.

## CALCULATION OF EARTH PRESSURE ON STRUTTED EXCAVATIONS IN COHESIONLESS SOILS

The empirical envelope of pressure distribution in sands is shown in Fig. 9.23 (*a*). The maximum intensity of pressure is given by—

$$p_{max} = 0 \cdot 65 K_a \gamma_d H \qquad . \qquad . \qquad . \qquad (9.3)$$

where $K_a$ = coefficient of earth pressure = $\dfrac{P_a}{\dfrac{\gamma_d H^2}{2}}$

$P_a$ = total pressure calculated as for a retaining wall with zero wall friction
$\gamma_d$ = bulk density of the soil
$H$ = depth of excavation.

The value of $K_a$ varies with the angle of shearing resistance of the soil, and values are given in Appendix A together with typical values for the bulk density of various materials.

It should be emphasized that the empirical rules for the calculation of earth pressures are based on *dry* or *drained* soils. Hydrostatic pressure cannot be redistributed and it must be allowed for in full with the normal triangular distribution associated with hydrostatic pressure. Methods of calculation in such cases are described on page 627.

CALCULATION OF EARTH PRESSURE IN STRUTTED EXCAVATIONS
SOFT TO FIRM COHESIVE SOILS

The trapezoidal envelope of earth pressure in strutted excavations in cohesive soils is shown in Fig. 9.23 (*b*). The maximum intensity of pressure is given by the formula—

$$p_{max} = 1 \cdot 0 K_A \gamma H \qquad . \qquad . \qquad . \qquad (9.4)$$

where $K_A = 1 - \dfrac{m 4 \bar{c}}{\gamma H}$

$\gamma$ = density of the soil
$H$ = depth of cut
$\bar{c}$ = average cohesion of clay
$m$ = a coefficient.

This pressure distribution was derived empirically by Peck for soft to medium clays, and Terzaghi and Peck state that in adopting values of cohesion of the clay from field and laboratory test data the *lowest average* shear strength from any one of the borings should be taken. In the case of soft sensitive clays due allowance should be made for loss in shear strength due to remoulding or disturbance of such soils. The coefficient $m$ can be taken as unity for most soft to firm clays, but observations in soft clays at Oslo indicated a value of 0·4 where $\gamma H / c$ is greater than 4.

CALCULATION OF EARTH PRESSURE IN STRUTTED EXCAVATIONS IN
STIFF FISSURED CLAY

The pressure distribution of Terzaghi and Peck is shown in Fig. 9.23 (*c*). The maximum pressure is given by—

$$p_{max} = 0 \cdot 2 \gamma H \text{ to } 0 \cdot 4 \gamma H \qquad . \qquad . \qquad . \qquad (9.5)$$

The lowest range is applicable to excavations which remain open only for a very short period of time.

Measurements in a 4 m deep trench in Oslo by Di Biagio and Bjerrum[9.16] before the onset of winter frosts showed loads of up to 20 kN per strut, with strut spacings of 0·66 m vertically and 1 m horizontally, corresponding to earth pressures of up to 75 kN/m². Measurements made on the basis of the load required to produce a given degree of indentation of struts into walings indicated earth pressures of the order of 100 kN/m² in a 18 m deep excavation in stiff London Clay at Isleworth.[9.17] The deeper part of the excavation in

London Clay was supported by 300 × 300 mm walings at 1·5 m centres with 300 × 300 mm struts at 2·4 m centres. The indentation measurements suggested strut loads of the order of 350 to 400 kN.

A reappraisal of the Oslo work by Bjerrum and Kirkedam[9.18] gives an explanation of the measured strut loads and a method of calculation of earth pressures on the basis of an effective stress analysis using values of $c'$ and $\phi'$ obtained from drained triaxial compression tests. Their analysis introduced the concept of increasing earth pressure with increasing time as a result of progressive softening along fissure planes. Thus the measurements of Di Biagio and Bjerrum at Oslo showed the following increase in pressure with time—

| Date | Average pressure (kN/m²) |
|---|---|
| 20.9.55 | 25 |
| 7.10.55 | 35 |
| 21.10.55 | 45 |
| 27.10.55 | 45 |
| 15.11.55 | 75 |

The above measurements suggest an immediate opening of fissures during excavation, but initially resistance to sliding of the wedge, shown in Fig. 9.24, is given by the full cohesion of the clay. Progressive softening along fissure planes increases the pressure from the sliding wedge until eventually (two months in the Oslo case) the cohesion is reduced to zero and the earth pressure can be determined by an effective stress analysis using $c' = 0$ and $\phi'$ at the value given by the drained triaxial test.

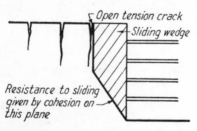

FIG. 9.24. PRESSURE ON TIMBERING IN STIFF CLAY (BJERRUM AND KIRKEDAM[9.18])

Further work needs to be done before the Norwegian investigations can be used for practical calculations of earth pressure on strutted excavations in stiff clays. In the meantime the author can only recommend "rule of thumb" procedures based on known good practice in the particular locality. The timbering scheme shown in Fig. 9.25 would appear to be general practice for timbered excavations in open ground in stiff London Clay. Heavier timbering would be necessary if it was desired to put heavy loads into the struts by wedging or jacking to minimize yielding.

WATER PRESSURE ON SHEET PILED EXCAVATIONS IN CLAY

Because borings show no water present in a clay soil it must not be assumed that hydrostatic pressure cannot build up outside a sheet piled excavation in clay. For example, if the sheet piles are driven

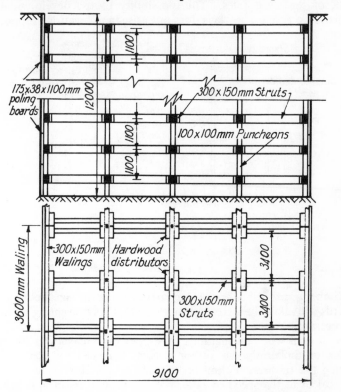

FIG. 9.25. TIMBERING TO 12 m DEEP EXCAVATION IN STIFF LONDON CLAY

completely through the clay stratum into a water-bearing sand layer, the water may creep up from this layer into the slight gap which is always likely to be present between the sheet piles and the clay in the region of the interlocks. The water pressure in this gap may then force back the clay sufficiently to cause water pressure over a wide area of the sheet piling at the sub-artesian pressure within the sand layer (Fig. 9.26 (*a*)). Another possible source of water developing pressure is seepage down the back of the piling from ponded surface water (Fig. 9.26 (*b*)). A route for such seepage is the enlarged hole formed by whip in long sheet piles during driving or shrinkage of the clay away from the sheet piles in dry weather. This entry of water can be prevented by keeping the clay well rammed against the back of the piling. Some stiff fissured clays contain water under pressure in random fissures or pockets. If such fissures are intersected by sheet piles they form a route for water to find its way to the back of the sheet piles. This possibility of the development of hydrostatic pressure in clays does not arise in excavations supported

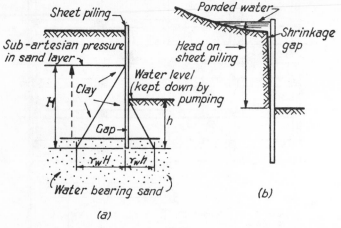

(a)

(b)

Fig. 9.26

by timber or precast concrete face boards where the gaps between the boards will allow the water to leak through, thus preventing build-up of pressure.

As a final word on methods of supporting excavations by sheet piling or timbering, the author stresses the need for accuracy in setting the timbers. Poling boards or runners should be set truly vertical or at the specified rake, walings should be set horizontally using a spirit level and struts should be truly horizontal and at right angles to the walings, and also vertically over one another. This need for accuracy is not merely a whim of the old school of timbermen, it plays a vital part in the early detection of dangerous ground movements. Thus if walings are bulging or struts bowing at a particular place, the movement can be readily seen if the struts and walings have been placed in truly vertical planes in the first instance. Any tendencies to bodily ground movements resulting in displacement of one side of the excavation relative to the other will also be noticed if the bracing frames show signs of racking.

## Overall Stability of Strutted Excavations

In all types of ground except massive rock some inward yielding of the sides of a strutted excavation will take place no matter how carefully the timbering is done. The yielding is accompanied by settlement of the ground surface near the excavation. The magnitude of the yielding and its accompanying settlement depends on the type of ground and the care with which the ground is supported. In soft silts and clays there is the additional risk of upward heaving of the

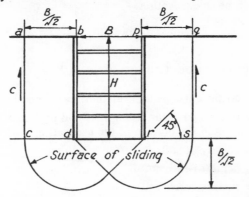

Fig. 9.27. Stability of Excavations in Clay (after Terzaghi and Peck[9.19])

bottom of the excavation accompanied by major settlement of the ground surface. Terzaghi and Peck[9.19] have analysed the mechanics of bottom heave in a soft clay as illustrated in Fig. 9.27.

The two strips *cd* and *rs* at the level of the bottom of the excavation carry a surcharge equal to the weight of the mass of clay enclosed by the rectangles *abcd* and *pqrs*. Therefore, if the bearing pressures imposed by these masses of soil exceed the bearing capacity of the soil at the level of *cd* and *rs*, the soil will fail as in a strip foundation along a curved surface of sliding as shown in the figure. Terzaghi and Peck show by calculation that the widths *cd* and *rs* are equal to $\dfrac{B}{\sqrt{2}}$, and if the cohesion between the soil and the timbering is neglected the downward movement of the rectangles is resisted only by the cohesion *cH* along the sides *ac* and *qs*. Therefore the total load on the strips *cd* and *rs* is given by—

$$P = \tfrac{1}{2}\sqrt{2}B\gamma H - cH$$

and the intensity of pressure on the strips is given by—

$$p = \gamma H - \frac{\sqrt{2}cH}{B} \qquad . \qquad . \qquad . \quad (9.6)$$

Since failure by heaving is disastrous to construction operations, the safety factor against this happening should be at least 1·5. The ultimate bearing capacity of the soil at the strip *cd* and *rs* is 5·7 × *c*. Therefore, for a safety factor of 1·5, the intensity of pressure on the strips should not be less than $\dfrac{5·7c}{1·5} = 3·8c$.

The mechanics of bottom heave have been given further study by Bjerrum and Eide[9.20] who derived the following formula for the critical depth of an excavation—

$$\text{Critical depth} = D_c = \frac{N_c s}{\gamma} \qquad . \qquad . \qquad . \quad (9.7)$$

$$\text{Factor of safety against bottom heave} = F = \frac{N_c \times s}{\gamma D + P} \quad . \quad (9.8)$$

where $N_c$ = coefficient depending on the dimensions of the excavation

$s$ = undrained shear strength of soil in a zone immediately around the bottom of the excavation

$\gamma$ = density of soil

$D$ = depth of excavation

$P$ = surface surcharge.

Values of $N_c$, as given by Bjerrum and Eide, are shown in Fig. 9.28.

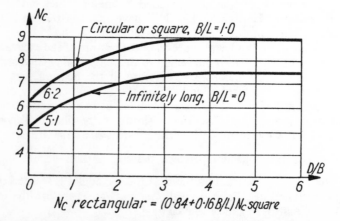

FIG. 9.28. CRITICAL DEPTH OF EXCAVATIONS IN CLAY (BJERRUM AND EIDE[9.20])

Four cases of inward yielding and bottom heave of sheet piled excavations in a soft sensitive clay at Tilbury, Essex, have been analysed by Ward.[9.21] In these cases the tops of the sheet piles came in, or if a top frame was fixed in time to stop this movement, the bottom heaved and the top frame was displaced. A typical case of a 4·6 m deep excavation is shown in Fig. 9.29. The piling on one side moved outwards and away from the top frame of timbering and rose *above* its original level. A gap was formed between the clay and the back of the sheet piling (which remained straight) and the bottom heaved. Ward concluded from this investigation that in a deep deposit of normally consolidated clay the uppermost frame of struts should be placed across a cofferdam before the depth of excavation reaches a value

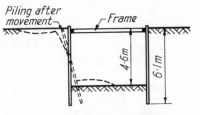

given by $D_c = \dfrac{4s}{\gamma}$.

Ward also made the important point that inward yielding and bottom heave appeared to be quite unrelated to the length of the sheet piling and to the materials into which the sheet piles were driven. In one of

FIG. 9.29. MOVEMENT OF SHEET PILED EXCAVATIONS AT TILBURY POWER STATION (WARD[9.21])

his cases where heave and yielding occurred at an excavation depth of only 1·8 to 2·1 m the sheet piles were over 21 m long and were driven into sandy gravel or chalk. The type of inward yielding described by Ward is a form of shear failure of the soil and should not be confused with the smaller scale yielding resulting from soil swelling. Bjerrum and Eide state that "experience cannot yet indicate exactly how much the danger of a base failure is reduced if sheet piles are driven below the bottom of an excavation. The stabilizing effect of sheet piling seems, however, to be small for the cases where the shear strength of the clay does not increase with depth."

Base failure of cofferdams or deep excavations due to "piping" or "boiling" of ground water and water under artesian pressure beneath excavations is described on page 631.

The problems of inward yielding of the supported sides of strutted or anchored excavations and the accompanying settlement of the ground surface has been mentioned in the preceding pages of this Chapter and also in Chapter 5. This subject was reviewed comprehensively by Peck[9.22] who stated that the amount of yielding for any given depth of excavation is a function of the characteristics of the supported soil and not of the stiffness of the supports. Steel structural members, even of heavy section, are not stiff enough to reduce yielding by any significant amount. Yielding also takes place with cast-in-place concrete diaphragm walls but to a somewhat lesser extent than with steel or timber bracing to conventional sheeting.

Settlements close to excavations in dense cohesionless soils are negligible, and settlements of the order of 0·5 per cent of the excavated depths can occur in loose sands and gravels. The greatest movements occur with excavations in soft to firm plastic clays. Peck[9.22] summarized the results of a number of excavations in these soils in the graphical form shown in Fig. 9.30. When deep excavations are made in stiff over-consolidated clays, it is likely that elastic heave due to

Table 9.3

OBSERVATIONS OF MAXIMUM INWARD DEFLEXION OF SIDES OF DEEP EXCAVATIONS

| Location | Method of support | Excava- tion depth (m) | Max. inward deflexion (mm) | Deflexion / depth × 100 | Soil type | Ref. |
|---|---|---|---|---|---|---|
| Chicago | Sheet piling, strutted | 11·4 | 58 | 0·51 | Soft clay | 9·13 |
| Oslo, Vaterland Subway | Sheet piling, strutted | 9 | 23 | 0·25 | Soft clay | |
| St. Louis | Sheet piling, strutted | 11·4 | 13 | 0·11 | Firm to stiff clay | 9·23 |
| North London | Sheet piling, strutted | 11·5 | 25 | 0·22 | Stiff clay | |
| Moorgate, London | Diaphragm wall, strutted | 18 | 57 | 0·32 | Stiff clay | 9·24 |
| South Africa | Diaphragm wall, anchored | 14·7 | 76 | 0·52 | Firm, fissured clay | 5·10 |
| South Africa | Diaphragm wall, anchored | 14·7 | 38 | 0·26 | Firm fissured clay | 5·10 |
| South Africa | Diaphragm wall, anchored | 22·9 | 38 | 0·16 | Firm fissured clay | 5·10 |
| South Africa | Diaphragm wall, anchored | 14·7 | 19 | 0·13 | Very stiff fis- sured clay | 5·10 |
| South Africa | Diaphragm wall, anchored | 18·3 | 25 | 0·14 | Weak jointed rock | 5·10 |
| Buffalo, N.Y. | Timber sheeting tied back | 6·4 | 10 | 0·16 | 5·4 m loose sand over dense sand and gravel | |
| Buffalo, N.Y. | Timber sheeting tied back | 11·2 | 53 | 0·47 | 5·4 m loose sand over dense sand and gravel | |
| Bloomsbury, London | Diaphragm wall, strutted | 16 | 12 | 0·07 | Gravel over London clay | 5·10 |
| Westminster Palace Yard | Diaphragm wall, strutted | 12 | 20 | 0·17 | Gravel over London clay | 5·10 |
| Zurich | Diaphragm wall, strutted | 20 | 36 | 0·18 | Lake deposits and glacial moraine | 9·25 |
| New York, World Trade Centre | Diaphragm wall, anchored | 17·7 | 66 | 0·37 | Sand | 5·10 |
| London, Guildhall | Diaphragm wall, anchored | 9·7 | 10 | 0·10 | Gravel over stiff clay | 5·10 |
| London, Bloomsbury | Diaphragm wall, anchored | 10 | 4 | 0·04 | Gravel over stiff clay | 5·10 |
| London, Victoria St. | Diaphragm wall, anchored | 8 | 3 | 0·04 | Gravel over stiff clay | 5·10 |
| London, Vauxhall | Diaphragm wall, anchored | 14·5 | 22 | 0·15 | Gravel over stiff clay | 5·10 |

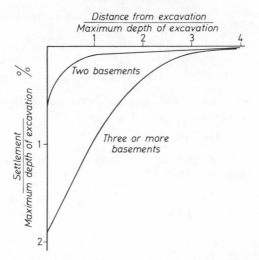

FIG. 9.30 RELATIONSHIP BETWEEN EXCAVATION DEPTH AND SETTLEMENT OF GROUND SURFACE FOR EXCAVATIONS IN SOFT TO FIRM CLAYS (AFTER PECK[9.22])

removal of overburden pressure will cause uplift of the base and sides of the cut, rather than causing settlement at the excavation stage.

The published and unpublished results of observations of inward yielding of deep excavations are summarized by the Author in Table 9.3. These generally confirm the conclusions made in Peck's review.

## EXAMPLES ON CHAPTER 9

### EXAMPLE 9.1

Design the supports for a 31·6 m long by 4·5 m wide by 12 m deep excavation in a fairly compact fine to medium dry sand.

To give clearance to the permanent structure shown dotted in Fig. 9.32 the bottom frames must be set 2·35 m clear above the base of the excavation. If we assume 300 mm deep timbers the centre of the bottom frame will be 9·5 m below ground level. A convenient spacing for the remaining frames will be 1·8 m centres requiring frames at depths of 0·5 m, 2·3 m, 4·1 m, 7·7 m, and 9·5 m below ground level. This will suit the trapezoidal pressure distribution satisfactorily. There will be little, if any, loading on the top frame, but we require one to act as a guide waling. Sheet piling will be preferable to timber runners to save in width of excavation at the top, since at least three settings of timber runners would be needed. It will also be possible to drive 14 m to 16 m long sheet piles for their full length into this ground.

Calculation of the pressure on 2nd and 6th frames—

Assume $\phi = 35°$ for a fairly compact sand

giving $K_a = 0.27$ from Appendix A for $\delta = 0$

also take $\gamma_d = 1.90$ Mg/m³

Therefore maximum intensity of pressure on sheet piling =
$$p_a = 0.65 \times 0.27 \times 1.90 \times 9.807 \times 12$$
$$= 39.2$$

For frames spaced at 1·8 m centres and assuming the sheet piling to be simply supported at the walings—

$$\text{Bending moment on sheet piling} = \frac{39\ 200 \times 1.8^2 \times 10^3}{8} \text{ Nmm per}$$

metre run of trench.

Required section modulus for safe stress in the steel of 165 N/mm² is given by—

$$Z_p = \frac{39\ 200 \times 1.8^2 \times 10^3}{8 \times 165} = 96 \times 10^3 \text{ mm}^3$$

This value of $Z_p$ would require sheet piling of only a light type, for example Larssen 1GB ($Z_p = 419$ cm³) or Frodingham 1A ($Z_p = 563$ cm³). However, such light types would buckle when driven in 14 m lengths. Contractors do not usually stock sheet piles much lighter than Larssen No. 2, since this and heavier sections are adaptable to a wide range of conditions and so can be re-used many times. We will therefore assume Larssen No. 2 ($Z_p = 850$ cm³) or Frodingham 2 ($Z_p = 996$ cm³). In any case these or heavier sections are needed to stand up to fairly hard driving conditions.

To develop the full flexural strength of a sheet pile of this section, it would be necessary to space the walings wider than 1·8 m, with correspondingly increased loads on walings and struts. However, the following calculations will show that the heaviest timbers normally available (i.e. 300 × 300 mm) cannot be spaced further apart than 1·8 m centres, and it will not be economical to order and fabricate steel walings and struts for a relatively small and "one-off" job. The provision of steel bracing frames would be justified only for a long length of excavation or for a number of repetitions of the same size of excavation. They could also be considered on a hired basis.

Allowing seven 4·5 m walings on each side of the trench, three struts can be provided to each waling, say, at 2 m centres with the end of the waling cantilevering 0·25 m beyond the centre of the last strut.

The loads transmitted by the sheet piling to the walings must be regarded as a series of point loads (*see* p. 630). Thus, for Larssen No. 2 piling, the troughs are at 400 mm centres, and it is possible for four $39\cdot2 \times 0\cdot4 \times 1\cdot8$ kN point loads to be applied to the 2 m span between struts. This gives a bending moment on walings, assuming them to be simply supported between struts, of 34 kN/m.

The moment of resistance of a $300 \times 300$ mm timber waling is $55\cdot7$ kNm for a maximum fibre stress (in bending) of $12\cdot4$ N/mm². If the struts and walings are drawn to scale at the spacings assumed above, it will be seen that the $4\cdot5$ m long walings can be threaded through the struts of each successive frame.

Calculating the load on the struts—

Maximum load on any strut $= 39\cdot2 \times 1\cdot8 \times 2\cdot0 = 141$ kN

The effective length of the struts between walings is $3\cdot9$ m. Assuming $300 \times 150$ mm struts—

$$\frac{\text{Effective length}}{\text{Least radius of gyration}} = \frac{3\cdot9}{\sqrt{\left(\dfrac{1}{12} \times \dfrac{0\cdot3 \times 0\cdot15^3}{0\cdot3 \times 0\cdot15}\right)}} = 90$$

The reduction coefficient from Table 7·2 is $0\cdot41$. Therefore, for a basic working compressive stress of $10\cdot3$ N/mm² for compression—

Safe stress $= 0\cdot41 \times 10\cdot3 = 4\cdot21$ N/mm²

$$\text{Actual stress on } 300 \times 150 \text{ mm strut} = \frac{141 \times 10^3}{300 \times 150}$$
$$= 3\cdot1 \text{ N/mm}^2$$

which is within safe limits.

The compressive stress on the waling perpendicular to the grain from the strut load is $\dfrac{300 \times 150}{141 \times 10^3} = 3\cdot1$ N/mm² which is within the allowable value of $4\cdot1$ N/mm.² Therefore it is only necessary to provide hardwood folding wedges at one end of the struts to allow them to be tightened. The shear force on the waling at each side of the struts is $39\cdot2 \times 1\cdot8 \times 1\cdot850 = 130$ kN. The shear stress at these positions is $\dfrac{130 \times 10^3}{2 \times 300 \times 300} = 0\cdot7$ N/mm² which is satisfactory. The completed timbering is shown in Fig. 9.32.

## EXAMPLE 9.2

As an example of the calculations for the design of supports to excavations in clays, we can take the trench used in the previous example. The average shear strength of the firm clay is 43 kN/m². We can assume an in-situ density of 1·75 Mg/m³ and take m = 1.

Maximum intensity of pressure = $1·75 \times 9·807 \times 12 - 4 \times 43$ = 33·2 kN/m².

The clay is strong enough to stand unsupported for 2 m or more before the face boards are set. Therefore, we can take, say 1·2 m long boards supported by 250 mm deep walings at their centres using the "middle board" system of timbering.

Thus for a spacing of walings at 1·2 m centres, and assuming the boards to cantilever from the centre of the walings,

$$\text{Max. bending moment on board} = \frac{33·2 \times 10^3 \times 0·6^2}{2}$$

$$= 6000 \text{ Nm per m run}$$

Moment of resistance of 75 mm thick poling boards for 12·4 N/mm² fibre stress

$$= 12·4 \times \frac{1}{12} \times 1000 \times 75^3 \times \frac{2}{75}$$

$$= 11\ 600 \text{ Nm per m run.}$$

Considering next the loads on the walings, in view of their close spacing it will be necessary to use a fairly short length, say 4 m with three struts to a waling giving a span between struts of 1·7 m.

$$\text{Bending moment on waling} = \frac{33·2 \times 1·2 \times 1·7^2}{8}$$

$$= 14·4 \text{ kNm.}$$

The moment of resistance of a $250 \times 250$ mm timber is 32·3 kNm which is satisfactory.

Load on struts for 1·7 m spacing = $33·2 \times 1·7 \times 1·2 = 67·8$ kN.

The effective length of the struts between $250 \times 250$ mm walings is 4 m. To facilitate the connection of the struts to the walings the same depth of timber should be used. Use two 250 mm by 100 mm members bolted together for the strut at the centre of each waling, and one 250 mm by 100 mm for the less heavily loaded struts at each end of the walings.

For $250 \text{ mm} \times 200 \text{ mm}$ struts—

$$\frac{\text{Effective length}}{\text{Least radius of gyration}} = \frac{4}{\sqrt{\left(\dfrac{1}{12} \times \dfrac{0·25 \times 0·20^3}{0·25 \times 0·20}\right)}} = 69$$

The reduction coefficient from Table 7.2 is 0·62, therefore the safe working stress for basic stress of 10·3 N/mm² in compression using

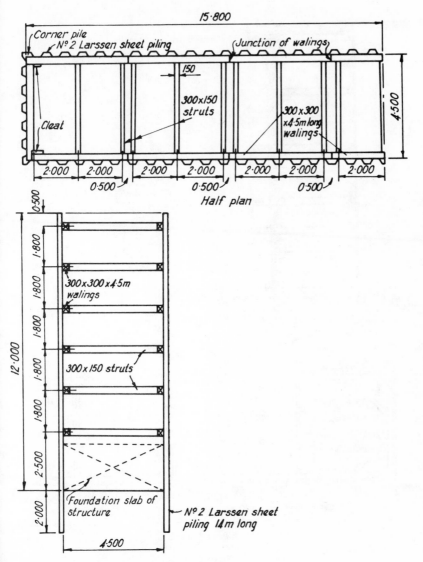

Half plan

Cross section of trench

FIG. 9.32

605

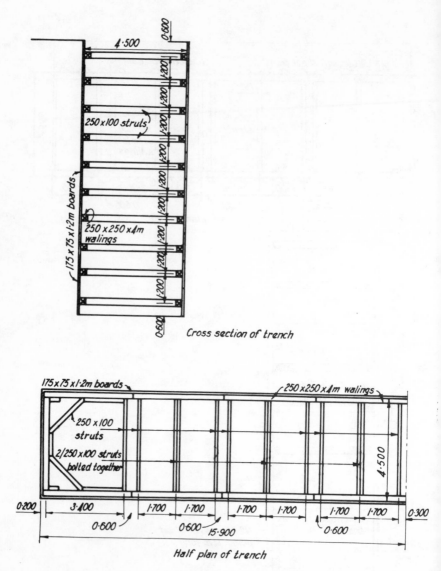

Cross section of trench

Half plan of trench

FIG. 9.33

*Note:* All details of timbering, including puncheons, tie rods, etc., have not been shown.

Douglas fir timber $= 0.62 \times 10.3 = 6.40 \text{ N/mm}^2$.

Actual stress on strut $= \dfrac{67.8 \times 10^3}{250 \times 200} = 1.35 \text{ N/mm}^2$.

This stress is within safe limits.

The crushing stress perpendicular to the grain on the walings is within safe limits and therefore a spreader is not needed. The arrangement of the timbering is shown in Fig. 9.33.

## REFERENCES

9.1 DAVIES, B. and HAWKES, I., The mechanics of blasting strata using the Cardox and air blasting systems, *Colliery Engineering*, pp. 461–467 (Nov., 1964).

9.2 *Soil Mechanics in Engineering Practice*, pp. 236–237.

9.3 STOTT, P. F. and RAMAGE, L. M., The design and construction of a dry dock at South Shields for Messrs. Brigham and Cowan Ltd., *Proc. Inst. C.E.*, **8**, pp. 161–188 (Oct., 1957).

9.4 TOMLINSON, M. J., *European Conference on the Stability of Earth Slopes, Roy. Sw. Geotech. Inst., Stockholm* (Discussion), Vol. 3, pp. 119–120 (Sept., 1954).

9.5 SEROTA, S., *European Conf. on the Stability of Earth Slopes, Roy. Sw. Geotech. Inst., Stockholm* (Discussion), Vol. 3, pp. 121–122(Sept., 1954).

9.6 MEIGH, A. C., Discussion on Session 9, *Proc. 4th Int. Conf. Soil Mech. London*, **3**, pp. 255–256 (1957).

9.7 SKEMPTON, A. W., *European Conference on the Stability of earth slopes, Roy. Sw. Geotech. Inst., Stockholm* (Discussion), Vol. 3, pp. 113–119 and 120–121 (Sept., 1954).

9.8 Subway for Stockholm built in unusual cofferdams, *Eng. News Rec.*, **159**, No. 12, pp. 52–57 (Sept., 1957).

9.9 British Standard Code of Practice *CP 2003*:1959, *Earthworks* (London, B.S.I).

9.9a OSTERMEYER, H., Construction, carrying behaviour and creep characteristics of ground anchors, *Proc. Conf. on Diaphragm Walls and Anchorages*, Inst. Civ. Eng. (London, 1974).

9.10 KELL, J., The Dartford Tunnel, *Proc. Inst. C.E.*, **24**, pp. 359–372 (Mar., 1963).

9.11 GRANTER, E., Park Lane improvement scheme: design and construction, *Proc. Inst. C.E.*, **29**, pp. 293–318 (Oct., 1964).

9.12 SPILKER, A., Mitteilung über die Messung der Kräfte in einer Baugrubenaussteifung, *Bautechnik*, **15**, p. 16 (1937).

9.13 PECK, R. B., Earth pressure measurement in open cuts, Chicago subway, *Trans. A.S.C.E.*, **108**, pp. 1008–1036 (1943).

9.14 *Soil Mechanics in Engineering Practice*, pp. 394–413.

9.15 SKEMPTON, A. W. and WARD, W. H., Investigations concerning a deep cofferdam in the Thames Estuary clay at Shellhaven. *Geotechnique*, **3**, No. 3, pp. 119–139 (Sept,. 1952).

9.16 DI BIAGIO, E. and BJERRUM, L., Earth pressure measurements in a trench excavated in stiff marine clay, *Proc. 4th Int. Conf. Soil Mech*, **2**, pp. 196–202 (London, 1957)

9.17 WATSON, D. M., West Middlesex main drainage, *J. Inst. C.E.*, **5**, No. 6, pp. 463–617 (1936–37: April, 1937).

9.18 BJERRUM, L. and KIRKEDAM, R., Some notes on earth pressures in stiff fissured clay, *Publication No. 33, Norwegian Geotech. Inst., Oslo*, pp. 39–44 (1960).

9.19 *Soil Mechanics in Engineering Practice*, pp. 265–266.

9.20 BJERRUM, L. and EIDE, O., Stability of strutted excavations in clay, *Geotechnique*, **6**, No. 1, pp. 32–47 (March, 1956).

9.21 WARD, W. H., Experiences with some sheet pile cofferdams at Tilbury, *Geotechnique*, **5**, No. 4, p. 327 (Dec., 1955).

9.22 PECK, R. B., Deep excavations and tunnelling in soft ground, *Proc. 7th Int. Conf. Soil Mech.*, State-of-the-Art, pp. 225–290 (Mexico, 1969).

9.23 NORWEGIAN GEOTECHNICAL INSTITUTE, Measurements at a strutted excavation, *NGI Technical reports*, Nos. 1–9, 1962–66.

9.24 COLE, K. W. and BURLAND, J. B., Observations of retaining wall movements associated with a large excavation, *Proc. 5th European Conf. Soil Mech.*, **I**, pp. 445–453 (1972).

9.25 HUDER, J., Deep braced excavation with high ground water level, *Proc. 7th Int. Conf. Soil Mech.*, **2**, pp. 443–448 (Mexico, 1969).

# 10

# Cofferdams

A COFFERDAM is essentially a temporary structure designed to support the ground and to exclude water from an excavation—either ground water or water lying above ground level. A sheet piled excavation in dry ground is not a cofferdam. It should also be noted that a cofferdam does not necessarily exclude all water and it is usually uneconomical to design cofferdams to do so.

Although steel sheet piling is widely used for cofferdams because of its watertightness and structural strength, it is by no means the only material, and a wide variety of types is available. Some of these are—

1. Earth embankments
2. Rockfill embankments
3. Sandbag embankments
4. Single-wall timber sheet piling
5. Double-wall timber sheet piling
6. Flexible sheeting on timber framing
7. Rock or earth-filled timber cribs
8. Single-wall steel sheet piling
9. Double-wall steel sheet piling
10. Cellular steel sheet piling
11. Bored cast-in-situ piling
12. Precast concrete blockwork
13. Precast concrete frame units
14. Structural steel cylinders and shells (movable cofferdams).

The choice of type depends on the site conditions, for example depth of water, depth and size of excavation, soil types, velocity of flow in waterway, tide levels, and the risk of damage by floating debris or ice. The choice depends also on the availability and ease of transport to the site of heavy construction plant and such materials as timber and sheet piling. Thus, earthfill cofferdams are suitable for low heads of water in still or sluggishly moving water. Single-wall sheet pile cofferdams are suitable for narrow excavations and restricted site areas where cross bracing can be used, and double wall cofferdams or cellular sheet piling for wide excavations where self-supporting dams are required. Rock or earth-filled timber cribs would be suitable for a remote site in undeveloped territory where heavy timber in log form is available, and the cost of importing and transporting steel sheet piling and the necessary plant to handle and drive it might be prohibitively high. The foundation soil conditions are an important factor in the choice of cofferdam types. Thus, a heavy earth-filled crib or cellular cofferdam could not be carried by deep deposits of soft clay, and single-wall timber or steel sheet piling would be required in these conditions. Single-wall timber sheet pile cofferdams would be inadvisable for work required to remain in use for long periods in water infested with marine borers.

The design of cofferdams which obstruct, wholly or partly, the flow of rivers must take into account hydraulic problems such as bed erosion and overtopping. These problems can often be solved with the aid of scale models employing an erodible bed to enable the scour tendencies to be studied. The book on cofferdams by White and Prentis[10.1] gives an excellent account of the theoretical and practical considerations involved in the design and construction of large river cofferdams. The authors have a wide range of experience of this type of work and their account of practical difficulties and cofferdam failures is especially interesting and informative.

Generally, the choice of cofferdam type and the detailed designs should be based on a thorough knowledge of the soil conditions by an adequate number of borings and on a careful study of available materials and statistics of the flows and hydrographs of the waterway.

### Earthfill Cofferdams

Cofferdams formed by an embankment or dyke of earth are suitable for sluggish rivers, lakes or other sheltered waters not subject to high velocity flow or wave action. Fast flowing water causes severe erosion of earth embankments and the cost of protection by stone or other types of blanketing may not be justifiable if other forms of construction are available. Earthfill dams are usually restricted to low or moderate heads of water. The type of soil to be used depends on availability and the site conditions. For example, clay fill is unsuitable if the bank has to be formed by dumping material under water, when the clay would soften and stable slopes could not be achieved. However, clay fill is very satisfactory if the bank can be constructed in the dry, say, at a low-water season of river flow. If the clay is excavated in a fairly dry condition and is spread and rolled in thin layers, an embankment of considerable stability and watertightness can be obtained. Sand is generally the

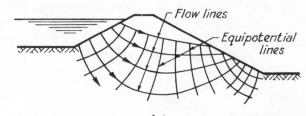

*(a)*

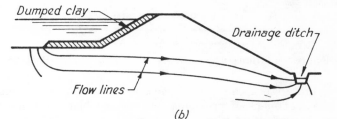

*(b)*

Fig. 10.1

(a) Seepage through permeable embankment.
(b) Controlling seepage by clay blanket and toe drainage.

best material for earthfill cofferdams constructed "in the wet." Embankments of sand or gravelly sand fill can be formed by dumping from barges, by pumping from a suction dredger, or by end tipping from the shore. Consideration can be given to composite construction such as a clay core with sand fill on both sides.

The possibility of erosion due to seepage from the inside slopes is liable to occur in sand fill embankments. The flow lines of seepage through permeable material are illustrated in Fig. 10.1 (a). They emerge on the inside face in a concentrated pattern and it is necessary to provide a drainage ditch at this point to collect the seepage and convey it to a pumping sump. Unstable conditions caused by "boils" or erosion of the sand due to excessive velocity in the outflowing water will occur if the hydraulic gradient, i.e. the head of water divided by the length of the seepage path, exceeds unity. The hydraulic gradient can be determined by drawing a flow net (Fig. 10.1 (*a*)). If there is no safety factor against erosion, the seepage path must be lengthened by flattening the inside slope or by blanketing the outside face and bed with clay (Fig. 10.1 (*b*)). Precautions to be observed in maintaining the inside slopes and in designing drainage ditches, filters, and pumping sumps are described in Chapter 11.

Protection against wave action and erosion by flowing water can be obtained by blanketing the slopes with material such as large

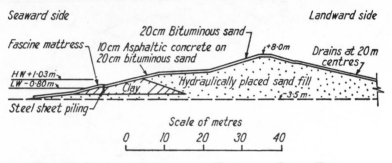

FIG. 10.2. EARTHFILL COFFERDAM FOR HARINGVLIET SLUICE, HOLLAND

gravel, broken rock, canvas tarpaulins, or willow or nylon mattresses, but the economics of providing and placing blanketing material rather than adopting a type of cofferdam not affected by erosion must be considered. Erosion of the top and inside face by over-topping is sometimes a cause of failure. The alternative to blanketing the inside slopes is to provide sluices through the embankments of sufficient capacity to allow rapid flooding of the cofferdam if a sudden rise in outside level threatens to overtop it.

An earthfill cofferdam consisting of an embankment formed by pumped sand with a clay core was used for the Haringvliet Sluice forming part of Holland's Delta Plan (Packshaw[10.2]). Protection against wave action and tidal scour below low water was given by a fascine mattress, and protection against wave action above high water by a layer of asphaltic concrete, as shown in Fig. 10.2.

If earthfill cofferdams are to be built across a flowing waterway, there may be difficulties in the "closure" of an earth embankment as the velocity of flow through the gradually narrowing gap may be sufficient to carry away the filling as it is being placed. These conditions can also occur if embankments are constructed in tidal waters, when the water rushing in and out of the "tidal compartment" will cause erosion through the gap between the ends of a partly completed embankment. It may be necessary to drive sheet piles into the ends of the bank at the closure section and to complete the closure by sheet piling only, or to adopt such expedients as sinking barges or caissons in the gap. It is important to keep a careful watch on the state of earthfill cofferdams during the whole period they are in operation. Any cracks should be made good and seepages of water dealt with by stone-filled or piped drains.

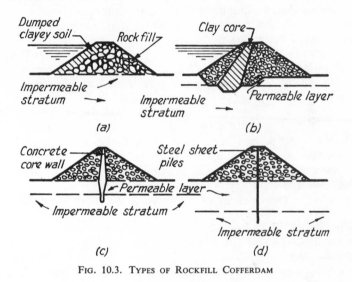

FIG. 10.3. TYPES OF ROCKFILL COFFERDAM

## Rockfill Cofferdams

Rockfill embankments for cofferdams are similar in construction to earthfill dams but because of the inherent stability of the material they can be formed with steeper slopes than earthfill dams. In fact, slopes equal to the natural angle of repose of tipped rock (about 1 in $1\frac{1}{2}$) can be used and even steeper slopes of up to 1 in $1\frac{1}{4}$ may be adopted if the rock on the face is handpacked to the required profile. Rockfill dams have the disadvantage of not being impervious. In the case of low height dams sufficient watertightness can be achieved by dumping ashes or loamy soil on to the outer face. Seepage will carry this material into the interstices of the rock and a fair degree of watertightness will gradually be attained (Fig. 10.3 (*a*)). A more positive form of cut-off is required for high heads of water; this can be achieved by a clay or concrete core wall (Fig. 10.3 (*b*) and (*c*)) or by sheet piling. The clay or concrete wall type of cut-off is usually restricted to cofferdams built in the dry. For construction under water a sheet pile wall can be built out from the bank using guide walings supported by a piled trestle. Rockfill can then be end-tipped out from the bank on both sides of the sheet piling (Fig. 10.3 (*d*)).

For rockfill cofferdams constructed in the dry the provision of a sloping watertight core or cut-off has certain advantages. For example, the rockfill of a dam with a sloping clay core as shown in Fig. 10.3 (*b*) can be built up in weather unfavourable to placing and rolling clay, leaving the clay to be brought up in better weather periods. With this type of construction it is necessary to have a reasonably high stability in the clay by using, say, a well-compacted and fairly dry lean clay such as boulder clay in order to avoid a slip developing through the clay layer. It is also necessary to protect the outside face of a clay core against wave action by blanketing with rockfill.

### Timber Sheet Pile Cofferdams

Timber sheet piling was extensively used for cofferdam work in the nineteenth century but it has been gradually replaced by steel piling. However, where timber is readily available it can still be used with advantage and economy in low head dams.

Fowler[10.3] gives details of eight types of timber sheet piles, as shown in Figs. 10.4 (*a*) to (*g*). He gives the following "rule of thumb" for the spacing of walings: 75 mm planks require walings every 1·8 m for less than 1·5 m head of water, or every 0·9 m for 6·4 m head; 100 mm planks require walings every 2 m for 2·7 m head and every 1·5 m for 5·4 m head; 225 mm planks require walings every 2·7 m for 6 m head. Timber sheet piling of the Wakefield pattern (Fig. 10.4 (*g*)) is used extensively in Mexico City and in Canada where timber is readily available. Timber sheet piling was also used extensively for the Stockholm Underground Railway extensions constructed in 1953–57 where the depth of water was less than 3·6 m and where there was only a small thickness of overburden to rock. The cofferdam was constructed by driving a row of H-beam king piles on each side of the excavation. The piles were supported on their outer face by raking steel H-beam struts. Timber walings were fixed at two levels between flanges of the king piles, and 75 mm tongue-and-groove timber sheet piles were driven in front of these walings through the thin overburden of sand and gravel to bedrock. The thrust transferred from the walings to the king piles was carried by steel trusses spanning across the excavation. These trusses also served as a working platform for plant and materials and to support the sheet steel cover over the whole of the cut-and-cover excavation.

This allowed work to continue in severe winter conditions. Soil was tipped in front of the sheet piles to increase the watertightness. The arrangement of the timber piled cofferdam and supporting truss is shown in Fig. 10.5.

Where timber sheet pile dams are required to retain high heads of water it is the usual practice to use a double wall and to fill the space

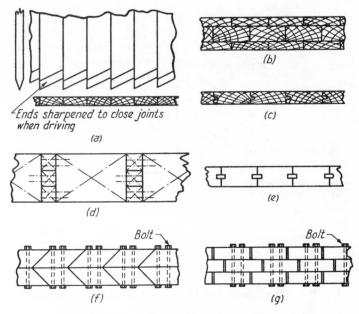

FIG. 10.4. TYPES OF TIMBER SHEET PILING (FOWLER[10.3])

(*a*) Plain butt-jointed sheeting.
(*b*) Lapped butt-joint.
(*c*) Tongue and groove joint.
(*d*) Joint formed by nailing or spiking strips to sheet piles.
(*e*) Keyed joint with keys inserted and driven after driving piles.
(*f*) Birdsmouth joint formed by bolting together double-bevelled planks.
(*g*) Wakefield sheet piling.

between the two with puddled clay. This type of construction was commonplace before the advent of steel sheet piling and the older engineering journals contain many examples of this type of work.

The main disadvantage of timber sheet pile dams is their limited depth of cut-off since the piles cannot be driven deeply into granular soils or stiff clays without risk of splitting or "brooming." They are most useful for low heads of water and for cofferdams founded on an irregular bedrock surface.

## Timber Cribwork Dams

Cribwork dams are usually constructed in the form of preassembled timber cribs which are lifted by crane or floated into position and sunk on to the river bed. Stone filling is then placed in the crib to give stability and steel sheet piling or other forms of sheeting are

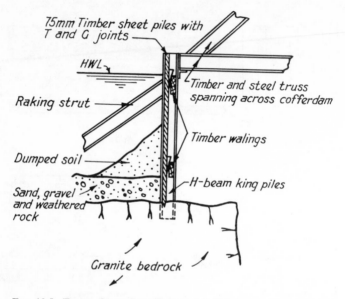

FIG. 10.5. TIMBER SHEET PILE COFFERDAM, STOCKHOLM UNDERGROUND RAILWAY

driven on the outer face to give watertightness. They are essentially free-standing dams used for wide excavations and are suitable for irregular and rocky river bottoms where the cribs can be carefully "tailored" to suit the river-bed profile. It is essential that they are placed on a foundation of adequate bearing capacity to resist the heavy weight of contained rockfill and the bearing pressures caused by the water and earth pressure. This form of construction also facilitates closure in fast-flowing water, where the cribs can first be placed and filled with rock and the flow allowed to pass between them. The gaps between cribs can then be filled with sheet piling or horizontal timber stoplogs.

The arrangement of the timber crib cofferdams used for the Ripon Falls Weir[10.4] is shown in Fig. 10.6.

The cribs were 12·5 m by 4·9 m in plan and spaced at 9·75 m centres.

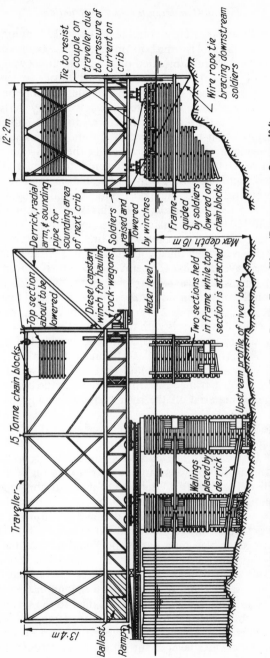

Fig. 10.6. Constructing Cribwork Dams for Ripon Falls Weir (Bertlin and Olivier[10.4])

They were built up from eucalyptus poles up to 12·5 m long with a butt diameter of 250 mm for the bottom poles and 200 mm for the top poles. The cribs were prefabricated on land in sections weighing not more than 45 tonne. The sections were carried out by suspending them from a steel-framed cantilevered traveller running on rails on the cribs already placed, and were then lowered by vertical steel guides. As soon as the first unit had been lowered sufficiently to relieve the suspension tackle of weight by its buoyancy, a further section was brought out and lowered on to the partly sunk bottom unit. The two sections were then lowered together and a third section added, until the whole crib unit rested on the river bottom. The cribs were restrained in a horizontal direction by wire rope tackle anchored to the traveller. In this way the complete crib weighing up to 120 tonne was placed by a comparatively light traveller unit. The time taken to erect the whole unit was about eight to ten days. The cribs were then filled with rock and concrete bearing pads placed for the traveller rails. The traveller was then moved forward for the next unit which was constructed in the same manner. The facing wall on the upstream side of the cribs was formed by two rows of Krupp K111 sheet piling 2·1 m apart supported by steel beams between the cribs at two levels with the space between the rows partly filled with murram (a lateritic soil). It was originally intended to have only a single row of sheet piles with an earth bank in front as a bottom seal. However, it was found that a second wall had to be driven in front to give protection from currents to the divers engaged in clearing loose material off the river bed and placing the murram seal.

White and Prentis[10.1] give a detailed description of the Ohio River type of articulated timber cofferdam which was designed for use in the river of that name. The dam consists of two rows of timber sheeting with earthfill between and earth banking on both sides to give it stability (Fig. 10.7 (*a*)). Because of its width this type of dam is stable against seepage when constructed on a permeable bottom as well as on a rock foundation. The distinctive feature of the Ohio dam is its articulated construction in the form of a continuous linked framework preassembled on a barge and "paid-out" as the barge is towed along the line of the dam (Fig. 10.7 (*b*)). The framework is tailored to suit the profile of the river bed as determined by close-spaced soundings. A gang working from a second barge follows up by setting the sheeting planks which are nailed to the walings above the waterline, and a dredger follows behind pumping fill inside and outside the cofferdam. Drainage holes are provided in the sheeting to draw down the water level in the fill as the cofferdam is pumped dry, so avoiding excessive hydrostatic pressure between the timber sheeted walls. The cofferdam is removed by a reverse process to its installation. A dredger pumps out the filling, starting at one end. A gang takes away the sheeting, then the framework is lifted by floating crane and dismantled section by section. The Ohio-type cofferdam is quick to install and requires no falsework but it is difficult to construct in a fast-flowing current. It is also sensitive to erosion, and heavy slope protection is required at critical points such as closure sections and corners.

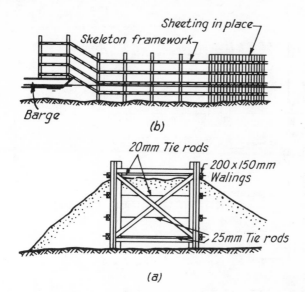

FIG. 10.7. CONSTRUCTING THE OHIO-TYPE COFFERDAM (WHITE AND PRENTIS[10.1])

## STEEL SHEET PILE COFFERDAMS

Steel sheet piling is widely used for cofferdams, including the deepest types, because of its structural strength, the watertightness given by its interlocking sections, and its ability to be driven to deep penetration in most types of ground. The deep penetration gives resistance to inward movement at the bottom of the excavation and sufficient cut-off to prevent piping in permeable ground. There are many types of rolled steel sections available for sheet piles. The dimensions and properties of some of these types are given in Table 10.1.

For low heads of water and shallow excavations, the cofferdam can consist of a single wall which is self-supporting by the cantilever

## Table 10.1

## SECTIONS AND PROPERTIES OF VARIOUS MAKES OF STEEL SHEET PILING

(a) Larssen Steel Sheet Piling (manufactured by British Steel Corporation)

| Section | b (mm) | h (mm) | d (mm) | t (mm nominal) | f (mm) flat of web | Sectional area (cm²/m of wall) | Weight kg/m | Weight kg/m² $W$ | Combined moment of inertia (cm⁴/m) | Modulus of section (cm³/m) $Z_p$ | Ratio $\dfrac{Z_p}{W}$ |
|---|---|---|---|---|---|---|---|---|---|---|---|
| 1A | 400 | 130 | 7.2 | 5.8 | 302 | 107 | 33.6 | 84 | 2 496 | 384 | 4.57 |
| 1B | 400 | 178 | 7.1 | 6.4 | 305 | 114 | 35.6 | 89 | 4 998 | 562 | 6.31 |
| 1GB | 400 | 130 | 8.1 | 5.8 | 302 | 115 | 36.2 | 90 | 2 729 | 419 | 4.66 |
| 1U | 400 | 130 | 9.4 | 9.4 | 302 | 135 | 42.4 | 106 | 3 184 | 489 | 4.61 |
| 2 | 400 | 200 | 10.2 | 7.8 | 270 | 156 | 48.8 | 122 | 8 494 | 850 | 6.97 |
| 2B | 400 | 270 | 8.6 | 7.1 | 248 | 149 | 46.7 | 117 | 13 663 | 1013 | 8.66 |
| 2N | 400 | 270 | 9.4 | 7.1 | 248 | 156 | 48.8 | 122 | 14 855 | 1101 | 9.02 |
| 3 | 400 | 247 | 14.0 | 8.9 | 248 | 198 | 62.0 | 155 | 16 839 | 1360 | 8.77 |
| 3B | 400 | 298 | 13.5 | 8.9 | 235 | 198 | 62.1 | 155 | 23 910 | 1602 | 10.34 |
| 3/20 | 508 | 343 | 11.7 | 8.4 | 330 | 175 | 69.6 | 137 | 28 554 | 1665 | 12.15 |
| 4A | 400 | 381 | 15.7 | 9.4 | 219 | 236 | 74.0 | 185 | 45 160 | 2371 | 12.82 |
| 4B | 420 | 343 | 15.5 | 10.9 | 257 | 256 | 84.5 | 201 | 39 165 | 2285 | 11.37 |
| 4/20 | 508 | 381 | 14.3 | 9.4 | 321 | 207 | 82.5 | 162 | 43 167 | 2266 | 13.99 |
| 4/20 | 508 | 381 | 15.7 | 9.4 | 321 | 218 | 86.8 | 171 | 45 924 | 2414 | 14.12 |
| 5 | 420 | 343 | 22.1 | 11.9 | 257 | 303 | 100.0 | 238 | 50 777 | 2962 | 12.45 |
| 6 | 420 | 440 | 22.0 | 14.0 | 248 | 370 | 122.0 | 290 | 92 298 | 4200 | 14.48 |
| 6 | 420 | 440 | 25.4 | 14.0 | 251 | 398 | 131.0 | 312 | 101 689 | 4618 | 14.80 |
| 6 | 420 | 440 | 28.6 | 14.0 | 251 | 421 | 138.7 | 330 | 109 968 | 5000 | 15.15 |
| 10A | 450 | 171 | 12.7 | 12.7 | 130 | 176 | 62.2 | 138 | 4 166 | 486 | 3.52 |
| 10B/20 | 508 | 171 | 12.7 | 12.7 | 273 | 167 | 66.4 | 131 | 6 054 | 706 | 5.39 |
| 10A-10B/20 | 450/508 | 108 | 12.7/12.7 | 12.7/12.7 | 130/273 | 171 | 62.2/66.4 | 134 | 2 250 | 356 | 2.66 |

(i)    (ii)    (iii)

*Note*

Fig. (i) refers to all Sections except 10A and 2(10A),

Fig. (ii) refers to Section 10A,

Fig. (iii) refers to Section 2(10A).

# Table 10.1 (cont.)

(b) Larssen-Stahlwände (manufactured by Thyssen Stahlunion-Export, Dusseldorf, West Germany)

| Section | $b$ (mm) | $h$ (mm) | $d$ (mm) | $t$ (mm) | Sectional area (mm² × 100/m of wall) | Weight kg/m | Weight kg/m² (W) | Combined moment of inertia cm⁴/m | Modulus of section (cm³/m) $Z_p$ | Ratio $\dfrac{Z_p}{W}$ |
|---|---|---|---|---|---|---|---|---|---|---|
| 20 | 500 | 220 | 7 | 6 | 101 | 39·5 | 79 | 6 600 | 600 | 7·59 |
| 21 | 500 | 220 | 8·2 | 8 | 121 | 47·5 | 95 | 7 700 | 700 | 7·37 |
| 22 | 500 | 340 | 10 | 9 | 155 | 61 | 122 | 21 250 | 1250 | 10·25 |
| 23 | 500 | 420 | 11·5 | 10 | 197 | 77·5 | 155 | 42 000 | 2000 | 12·90 |
| 24 | 500 | 420 | 15·6 | 10 | 223 | 87·5 | 175 | 52 500 | 2500 | 14·29 |
| 31 | 450 | 150 | 9·5 | 9·5 | 127 | 45 | 100 | 3 450 | 460 | 4·60 |
| 32 | 450 | 250 | 10·5 | 10·5 | 155 | 54·9 | 122 | 10 600 | 850 | 6·97 |
| III | 400 | 247 | 14·2 | 9·2 | 197 | 62 | 155 | 16 670 | 1350 | 8·71 |

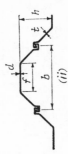

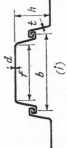

T. 10.1 (b)

*Note*
Fig. (i) refers to Section III.
Fig. (ii) refers to Sections 20–24, 31 and 32.

**Table 10.1 (*cont.*)**

(c) Frodingham Steel Sheeting Piling (manufactured by British Steel Corporation)

| Section | $b$ (mm) | $h$ (mm) | $d$ (mm) | $t$ (mm) | Weight | | Modulus of section (cm³/m) $Z_p$ | Ratio $\dfrac{Z_p}{W}$ |
|---|---|---|---|---|---|---|---|---|
| | | | | | kg/m | kg/m² (W) | | |
| 1A | 400 | 146 | 6·9 | 6·9 | 35·64 | 89·1 | 563 | 6·32 |
| 1B | 400 | 133 | 9·5 | 9·5 | 42·13 | 105·3 | 562 | 5·34 |
| 1BXN | 476 | 143 | 12·7 | 12·7 | 62·1 | 130·4 | 688 | 5·28 |
| 2N | 483 | 235 | 9·7 | 8·4 | 54·21 | 112·3 | 1150 | 10·24 |
| 3N | 483 | 283 | 11·7 | 8·9 | 66·15 | 137·1 | 1688 | 12·31 |
| 4N | 483 | 330 | 14·0 | 10·4 | 82·45 | 170·8 | 2414 | 14·13 |
| 5 | 425 | 311 | 17·0 | 11·9 | 100·76 | 236·9 | 3168 | 13·37 |

\* These sections have generally been superseded by Sections 2N, 3N and 4N and are therefore only available by special arrangement.

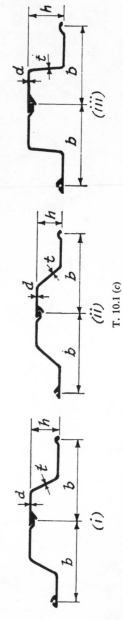

T. 10.1 (c)

*Note* Fig. (i) refers to Sections 1A, 2N, 3N and 4N; Fig. (ii) refers to Sections 1B and 1BXN; Fig. (iii) refers to Sections 2, 3, 4 and 5.

**Table 10.1** (*cont.*)

(*d*) Arbed-Belval Steel Sheet Piling (Selling agents—Columeta, Luxembourg)

| Section | $b$ (mm) | $h$ (mm) | $d$ (mm) | $t$ (mm) | Sectional area (cm² per m of wall) | Weight | | Combined moment of inertia cm⁴ per m | Modulus of section (cm³/m) $Z_p$ | Ratio $\dfrac{Z_p}{W}$ |
|---|---|---|---|---|---|---|---|---|---|---|
| | | | | | | kg/m | kg/m² (W) | | | |
| *BZ 0 | 500 | 135 | 9·5 | 9·5 | 132·5 | 52·00 | 104·0 | 3510 | 520 | 5·00 |
| *BZ 0R | 500 | 135 | 12·7 | 12·7 | 159·9 | 62·75 | 125·5 | 4120 | 610 | 4·86 |
| BZ IN | 420 | 165 | 8·0 | 8·0 | 127·4 | 42·00 | 100·0 | 5940 | 720 | 7·20 |
| BZ IRA | 420 | 167 | 9·5 | 9·5 | 150·3 | 49·56 | 118·0 | 7100 | 850 | 7·20 |
| BZ IR | 420 | 167 | 10·0 | 10·0 | 155·4 | 51·24 | 122·0 | 7180 | 860 | 7·05 |
| *BZ 250 | 500 | 240 | 8·5 | 8·5 | 142·9 | 56·10 | 112·2 | 14400 | 1200 | 10·70 |
| BZ IIN | 450 | 220 | 5·5 | 8·5 | 155·4 | 54·90 | 122·0 | 13200 | 1200 | 9·84 |
| BZ IIR | 450 | 222 | 11·0 | 10·0 | 178·3 | 63·00 | 140·0 | 15210 | 1370 | 9·79 |
| BZ 350 | 500 | 295 | 9·5 | 9·5 | 166·4 | 65·30 | 130·6 | 24630 | 1670 | 12·79 |
| BZ IIIN | 450 | 260 | 12·5 | 10·0 | 197·4 | 69·75 | 155·0 | 23270 | 1790 | 11·55 |
| BZ IVN-50 | 500 | 290 | 14·0 | 10·0 | 202·5 | 79·50 | 159·0 | 29720 | 2050 | 12·89 |
| BZ IIIR | 450 | 263 | 15·0 | 12·0 | 235·7 | 83·25 | 185·0 | 27750 | 2110 | 11·41 |
| BZ IVN | 450 | 300 | 14·0 | 10·0 | 224·2 | 79·20 | 176·0 | 35400 | 2360 | 13·41 |
| BZ IVNR | 450 | 302 | 15·2 | 10·2 | 236·3 | 83·47 | 185·5 | 37980 | 2515 | 13·56 |
| BZ VN | 500 | 350 | 20·0 | 12·0 | 301·9 | 118·50 | 237·0 | 65100 | 3720 | 15·70 |
| BZ VR | 500 | 354 | 24·0 | 14·0 | 346·5 | 136·00 | 272·0 | 74690 | 4220 | 15·51 |

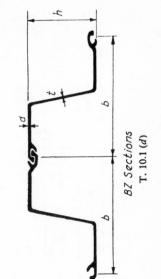

*BZ Sections*
T. 10.1 (*d*)

\* Sections similar to Frodingham 1B (Table 10.1*c*).

**Table 10.1 (cont.)**

(e) U.S.S. Steel Sheet Piling (Selling agents—United States Steel (New York) Inc.)

| Section index | $b$ (mm) | $h$ (mm) | $d$ (mm) | $t$ (mm) | Weight | | Modulus of section (cm³/m) $Z_p$ | Ratio $\frac{Z_p}{W}$ |
|---|---|---|---|---|---|---|---|---|
| | | | | | kg/m | kg/m² (W) | | |
| MZ-38 | 457 | 305 | 12·7 | 9·5 | 84·8 | 185·5 | 2516 | 13·6 |
| MZ-32 | 533 | 292 | 12·7 | 9·5 | 83·3 | 156·2 | 2060 | 13·2 |
| MZ-27 | 457 | 305 | 9·5 | 9·5 | 60·3 | 131·8 | 1624 | 12·3 |
| MZ-22 | 559 | 241 | 9·5 | 9·5 | 60·0 | 107·4 | 1022 | 9·5 |
| MP-117 | 381 | 84 | 9·5 | 9·5 | 57·7 | 151·3 | 382 | 2·5 |
| MP-113 | 406 | — | 12·7 | — | 55·5 | 136·7 | 134 | 0·98 |
| MP-112 | 406 | — | 9·5 | — | 45·7 | 112·3 | 129 | 1·1 |
| MP-110 | 406 | 152 | 12 | 9·5 | 63·5 | 156·2 | 823 | 5·3 |
| MP-116 | 406 | 127 | 9·5 | 9·5 | 53·6 | 131·8 | 575 | 4·4 |
| MP-115 | 498·5 | 82·5 | 12 | 9·5 | 53·6 | 107·4 | 290 | 2·7 |

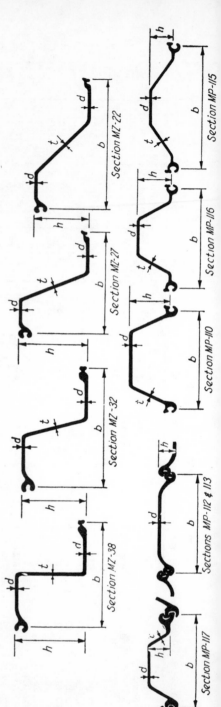

**Table 10.1 (cont.)**

(f) Krupp Steel Sheet Piling (Selling agents—Krupp Stahlexport, Dusseldorf, West Germany)

| Section index | b (mm) | h (mm) | t (mm) | d (mm) | Weight kg/m | Weight kg/m² (W) | Modulus of section (cm³/m) $Z_p$ | Ratio $\frac{Z_p}{W}$ |
|---|---|---|---|---|---|---|---|---|
| KSIa | 430 | 160 | 6·2 | 7·8 | 38·4 | 89 | 600 | 6·74 |
| KSI | 430 | 160 | 8 | 8·5 | 43·0 | 100 | 630 | 6·30 |
| KSIb | 430 | 160 | 9 | 9 | 45·6 | 106 | 660 | 6·23 |
| KSII | 430 | 180 | 10 | 11·7 | 52·5 | 122 | 850 | 6·97 |
| KII | 400 | 200 | 8 | 8·2 | 48·8 | 122 | 1100 | 9·02 |
| KIII | 400 | 240 | 9 | 10·5 | 62·0 | 155 | 1600 | 10·32 |
| KIIIb | 400 | 200 | 10 | 12 | 62·0 | 155 | 1350 | 8·71 |
| KIV | 400 | 280 | 10 | 13·3 | 74·0 | 185 | 2200 | 11·89 |
| KV | 360 | 320 | 12 | 14·5 | 85·7 | 238 | 3000 | 12·61 |

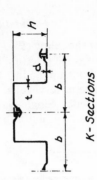

KS - Sections

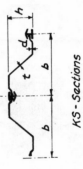

K - Sections

T. 10.1 (f)

action of the piling (Fig. 10.8 (*a*)). Higher heads can be withstood if a bank of earth is left on the inside face (Fig. 10.8 (*b*)). If an earthfill bank is built up against the inside face, instability may occur if the outside water level falls, when an unbalanced pressure will develop on the inside. Single-wall construction can also be used where it is possible to strut across the excavation. For low heads a single top

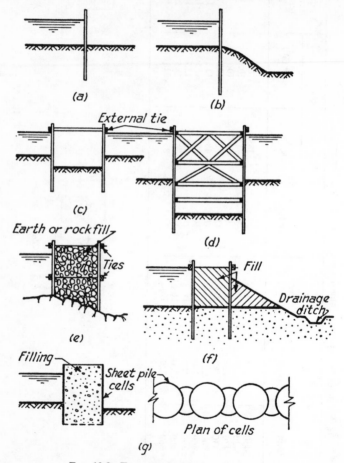

FIG. 10.8. TYPES OF SHEET PILE COFFERDAMS

    (*a*) Single wall.
    (*b*) Single wall with earth bank.
    (*c*) With single top frame.
    (*d*) With multiple frames.
    (*e*) Double wall.
    (*f*) Double wall on permeable soil.
    (*g*) Cellular.

frame can be used (Fig. 10.8 (c)) but for high heads or deep land cofferdams it is necessary to provide multiple frames (Fig. 10.8 (d)). Where the excavation is too wide for cross-bracing an earth- or rock-filled double-walled cofferdam is adopted (Fig. 10.8 (e)). Where such cofferdams are built on permeable ground it is usual to place earthfill on the inside, thus lengthening the seepage path and preventing piping (Fig. 10.8 (f)). The interior earth bank also gives added stability where there is a risk of tilting due to overturning moments on soils of moderate bearing capacity. Self-supporting cofferdams to withstand high heads of water are sometimes constructed in cellular form, the cells being filled with rock or earth (Fig. 10.8 (g)).

## Design of Single-wall Sheet Pile Cofferdams

Cofferdams must be designed to withstand the conditions—

1. Hydrostatic pressure of water outside cofferdam.
2. Hydrostatic pressure of water *inside* cofferdam if the water level outside falls at a faster rate than can be attained by pumping down or the discharge from valves or sluice gates.
3. Earth pressure outside cofferdam.

They must have overall stability against the following conditions—

1. Base failure from bottom heave.
2. Failure from inward yielding.
3. Failure from piping or blows.
4. Failure during removal.

The distribution of hydrostatic pressure on a cofferdam is triangular, whereas the distribution of earth pressure as measured by various observers is approximately trapezoidal (Fig. 9.23). However, hydrostatic pressure generally provides the major proportion of the external pressure on a cofferdam and is generally three or four times (or more in certain types of ground) the earth pressure at any given depth. It is therefore the normal practice to calculate earth pressure on cofferdams in the same way as retaining walls, i.e. a triangular pressure distribution calculated by the methods given in the *British Standard Code of Practice for Earth-retaining Structures*. It must be remembered that the density of a soil below the water table is taken as its submerged density which is approximately half its fully saturated density.

### SPACING OF FRAMES

For economy of materials and fabrication costs of bracing frames it is desirable to space the horizontal frames so that they each carry, as nearly as possible, an equal load from the hydrostatic pressure transmitted to them by the sheet piling. The exception is the top frame which is provided at or just above top water level as a guide frame and prevents inward movement when pumping down the cofferdam before the second frame is fixed. The required spacing of the frames for equal loading can be expressed in terms of multiples of the spacing between the first and second frames. Thus, if the top waling is set at water level and assuming the sheet piling to be simply-supported over the walings then—

Distance from top to 2nd waling $= h$

| | | | | | | | | |
|---|---|---|---|---|---|---|---|---|
| ,, | ,, | 3rd | ,, | $= 1{\cdot}60h$ ,, | ,, | 7th | ,, | $= 2{\cdot}97h$ |
| ,, | ,, | 4th | ,, | $= 2{\cdot}03h$ ,, | ,, | 8th | ,, | $= 3{\cdot}22h$ |
| ,, | ,, | 5th | ,, | $= 2{\cdot}38h$ , | ,, | 9th | ,, | $= 3{\cdot}45h$ |
| ,, | ,, | 6th | ,, | $= 2{\cdot}69h$ ,, | ,, | 10th | ,, | $= 3{\cdot}67h$ |

Where the strength of the sheet piling is the governing factor, the distance $h$ is determined by the moment of resistance of the piling. Allowable working stresses for sheet piling are usually selected within a range of values depending on the grade of steel. The lower figures in each range are adopted for deep cofferdams for which consequences of failure due, say, to separation of pile clutches in hard driving conditions would be serious. The higher figures in the range are used for cofferdams in which failure or yielding would not have serious consequences. The range of values corresponding to each grade of steel are shown below. Also shown is the formula for calculating $h_{,max}$ assuming the sheet piling to be simply supported at the walings, and values of $Z_p$, the combined modulus of section of the sheetpiling in cm³/m of wall.

| Grade of steel | Allowable tensile stress $(N/mm^2)$ | Distance from top 2nd waling $h_{max}^{(m)}$ |
|---|---|---|
| Mild steel (BS 4360 Grade 43) | 125 to 165 | $\sqrt[3]{0.1937 \times Z_p}$ <br> $\sqrt[3]{0{\cdot}2557 \times Z_p}$ |
| Medium tensile steel | 165 to 195 | $\sqrt[3]{0{\cdot}2557 \times Z_p}$ <br> $\sqrt[3]{0{\cdot}3022 \times Z_p}$ |
| High yield steel (BS 4360 Grade 50 B & C) | 175 to 230 | $\sqrt[3]{0{\cdot}2712 \times Z_p}$ <br> $\sqrt[3]{0{\cdot}3565 \times Z_p}$ |

Values of $h_{max}$ are plotted against $Z_p$ for the various allowable tensile stresses.

A severe condition of hydrostatic pressure may occur in deep cofferdams when the water level within the cofferdam is lowered to allow the second bracing frame to be fixed in the dry. At this stage there is an excess pressure between the inner water level and the point of fixity of the sheet piling in the ground equal to the difference in head between the inner and outer levels. Thus in a deep cofferdam the bending moments due to this excess pressure over the long span between the top waling and the point of fixity in the ground may be considerable, and may well be the most severe condition for the flexural stress in the piling and the loading on the top bracing frames. If the stresses in the sheet piling or the loading on the top frame are too severe for this pumped-down condition, then heavier section piling can be used or the distance between the top and second frame can be reduced. It is also possible to get over the difficulty by using divers to fix the second frame under water. In very deep cofferdams it is advisable to check the conditions for the top and second frames when the cofferdam is pumped down to fix the third frame.

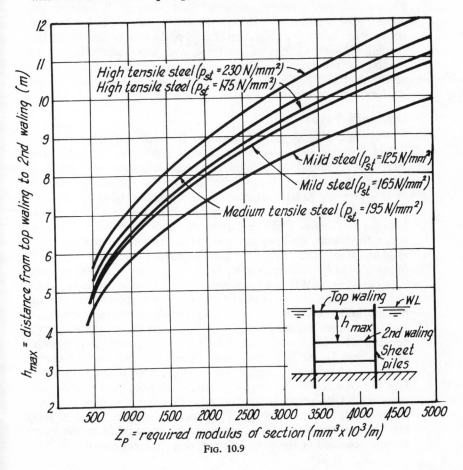

FIG. 10.9

This problem may not arise in tidal waters when the second frame can be fixed during neap tides or while the water level outside the cofferdam is at low water of spring tides. Sluices or valves of adequate size must be provided in the walls of the cofferdam to let the water flow out as the tide is falling, otherwise an internal pressure sufficient to burst the cofferdam may develop. It is always advisable to provide an external waling as a safeguard against outward movement of the piles due to unexpected head differences. The provision of sluices or valves to unwater a cofferdam on the falling tide also saves a considerable amount of unnecessary pumping and enables the cofferdam to be flooded rapidly if it shows signs of distress or bottom failure.

Driving in long lengths or to deep penetrations into difficult ground will require heavy sections of sheet piling or alternatively the adoption of medium or high tensile steel. Thus, if the full flexural strength of the heavy or high tensile steel piling is to be developed, the spacing between walings will be large, with a correspondingly high loading in the frames. The loading may be too great for the economical use of timber frames and it will be necessary to use steel or reinforced concrete.

### DESIGN OF FRAMES

Walings are designed as beams simply-supported between struts unless they are continuous over at least three spans or unless the joints are designed to develop the necessary shear and bending strength. In circular cofferdams on land the walings can be designed as ribs carrying radial thrust. This arrangement, with its freedom from cross-bracing, can give an economical design of cofferdam. Packshaw[10.2] states that the maximum diameter of cofferdams for which the frames are designed as circular ribs without cross-bracing is 45 to 60 m. The loads on the walings from trough-section sheet piling should be treated as a series of point loads in direct contact with the waling. Where walings act as struts to other walings (i.e. at corners) they should be designed to carry the combined stresses of bending and direct compression. Struts should be designed as round-ended members between walings or cross-members. If the length between cross-members is taken the connexions should be adequately braced both in the horizontal and vertical planes. The structural design requirements of timber, steel, or concrete bracing members is given in Chapter 9. Bracing frames designed as prefabricated units must be accurately constructed with tolerances to allow easy fitting inside the sheet piling. They should be made 25 to 50 mm smaller than the plan dimensions inside the sheet piling to allow for inward deflexion of the sheet piling during pumping down.

When considering the bending stresses on the sheet piling below the bottom frame, the point of fixity can be taken in good ground as one-tenth of the height of the piling, but in weak ground such as soft mud the point of fixity should be taken as 6 m below ground level or the depth to a firm stratum, whichever is the least. Below the bottom frame the pressure on the sheet piling is carried by the passive resistance of the soil below excavation level. The method of calculating this passive resistance is given in the *Code of Practice for Earth-retaining Structures.* Heavy and continuous pumping from a cofferdam founded on permeable ground will reduce the passive resistance of the soil below excavation level because the upward seepage towards the pumping sump will cause the soil to be in a partly "quick" or live condition. Piping or incipient "blows" will completely eliminate all passive resistance and the active earth pressure and hydrostatic pressure on the piling will be carried solely by cantilever action from the bottom frame.

### PIPING IN SINGLE-WALL COFFERDAMS

Stability against base failure by heaving and against inward yielding should be checked by the procedure described on pages 597 to 601. The stability against "piping" or "boiling" in the base resulting from heavy upward seepage of ground water into the cofferdam must be checked in cases where the sheet piles are not driven into an impermeable stratum. It is important either to prevent piping or to reduce it to an insignificant amount since severe piping can lead to loss of ground outside the cofferdam and even to undermining and collapse of the sheet pile wall. As already mentioned, it can cause loss of passive resistance of the ground to the inward thrust of the sheet piling. Piping occurs when the exit gradient, or the ratio of the head to the length of seepage path, at the point of outflow into the cofferdam reaches unity; at this stage the velocity of the upward flowing water within the cofferdam is sufficient to lift and displace the soil through which it is flowing. Since, by Darcy's law,

$$\text{Velocity} = \frac{\text{Constant} \times \text{Head}}{\text{Length of seepage path}}$$

it follows that the tendency to piping can be eliminated by lengthening the seepage path, for example by driving the sheet piling to a sufficient depth or if width is available by providing a bank of permeable soil within the cofferdam. The other method of preventing piping is to reduce the head of the water causing seepage; this can be done by pumping from wellpoints or deep wells placed at or below the level of the bottom of the sheet piles. This procedure is described in

Chapter 11. Minimum values for the depth of cut-off of sheet piling
are as follows—

| Width of cofferdam | Depth of cut-off $D$ |
|---|---|
| 2 $H$ or more | 0·4 $H$ |
| $H$ | 0·5 $H$ |
| 0·5 $H$ | 0·7 $H$ |

Piping is most likely to take place in loose fine sands which are
permeable enough to allow seepage through them but whose grain-
size is small enough to be disturbed by the seepage forces. Piping is
unlikely to occur in gravels since the draw-down in water level
outside the cofferdam as a result of their high permeability usually
lowers the head, so reducing the hydraulic gradient. Piping does not
take place in silty or sandy clays due to their low permeability.

Doubtful cases can be analysed by drawing flow nets similar to that
shown in Fig. 10.10. For a theoretical treatment of the subject of

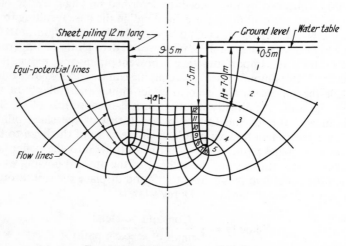

FIG. 10.10. FLOW NET FOR COFFERDAM

$$\text{Exit gradient} = \frac{H}{N_p \times a}$$

$$= \frac{7}{12 \times \frac{9 \cdot 5}{10}} = 0 \cdot 6$$

$$\text{Factor of safety against piping} = \frac{1}{0 \cdot 6} = 1 \cdot 7$$

seepage into sheeted excavations, the reader is referred to a paper by McNamee.[10.5]

If piping takes place unexpectedly, for example by an unforeseen increase in external water head due to abnormally high tides or flood levels, emergency action must be taken to prevent its spreading. A small localized inflow can soon erode a large channel into the cofferdam, causing undermining and collapse of the wall. If boiling is seen to occur in an isolated patch of more permeable soil it can sometimes be controlled by building a wall of clay bags around the seepage, thus reducing the effective head. However, this procedure often results in a boil breaking out in another place. The most effective procedure is to flood the cofferdam and then take measures to reduce the hydraulic gradient as already described.

### Construction of Single-wall Sheet Pile Cofferdams

To ensure verticality in pitching piles and to prevent them from moving off the vertical when driving past obstructions, it is most

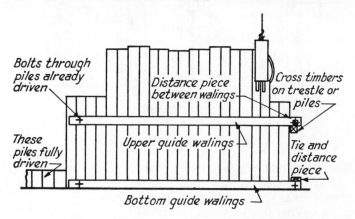

FIG. 10.11. GUIDE WALINGS FOR DRIVING SHEET PILES

important that sheet piles should be driven through guides. In the case of land cofferdams the guides are provided simply by a lower pair of guide walings at ground level and an upper pair at the highest level permitted by the position of the hammer on completion of the first stage of driving. These guide walings are supported at one end by bolts through the partly driven piling and at the other end by cross timbers (Fig. 10.11). Alternatively, a timber or steel trestle can be built and moved as a unit by crane (Fig. 10.12). Where sheet piles are driven by a frame it is only necessary to provide guide walings at the lower level. The upper part of the piles is kept in the vertical position by a toggle bolt passing through the leaders of the pile frame.

Where sheet piles are driven over water the guide walings are supported by timber or steel piled stagings constructed by floating plant. It is unsatisfactory to drive sheet piling by floating plant without fixed guides for the piles. The guide walings and staging can consist of pairs of guides at low water level and at top waling level (Fig. 10.13 (*a*)) or the cofferdam walings can be assembled in a

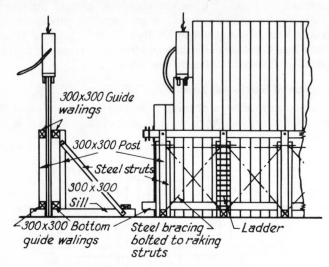

FIG. 10.12. GUIDE TRESTLE FOR SHEET PILES

prefabricated unit which is supported from the river bed (Fig. 10.13 (*b*)). Where the piles are driven by frame the guide walings need only be at top waling level (Fig. 10.13 (*c*)).

Guide walings should consist of substantial timbers, say 300 × 300 mm. Lighter timbers, say 300 × 150 mm, are only used for light section piling in short lengths. The walings are fixed at a distance 5 mm wider apart than the overall depth of the piles, and this dimension is maintained by timber distance pieces.

To ensure a good closure of sheet piling surrounding a cofferdam the piles should be pitched in panels of six to twelve piles interlocking with partly driven piles of adjacent panels (Fig. 10.11). Thus the last (and partly driven) pile serves as the guide pile for the next panel, and pitching and driving in panels continues around the cofferdam until it is closed by interlocking with the first pile driven. If the piles have crept out of verticality there will be difficulty in making the closure. A slope of more than 1 in 300 will give difficulty in closing, depending on the length of the piles, their flexibility, and the ground conditions. Corrections in verticality can be made by driving with an eccentric blow or by straining the piles by block and tackle. If these measures cannot give enough correction it will be necessary to use a tapered pile to make the closure. It is therefore convenient to

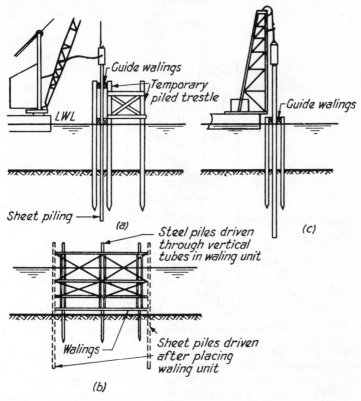

FIG. 10.13. DRIVING SHEET PILING OVER WATER

make the first pile to be pitched a corner pile, when a special section riveted or welded tapered corner pile can be provided as detailed in the handbooks of pile manufacturers. Accurate driving is facilitated by a spacer block (Fig. 10.14). The width of the block is equal to the overall depth of the piling less the web thickness. A cross-bar bolted to the block rests on the guide waling.

In small cofferdams it is advantageous to pitch and interlock all the piles before driving any of them. This is usually impossible in large cofferdams because of the length of guide walings required and the likely instability of a large area of unsecured piling exposed to flowing water in a river or tidal stream.

Piles are usually driven in pairs, except in hard driving conditions. However, they are usually pitched as single piles.

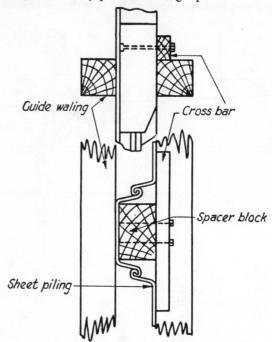

Guide waling

Cross bar

Spacer block

Sheet piling

FIG. 10.14. SPACER BLOCK FOR SHEET PILING

Sheet piles may be driven by drop-hammer or single-acting hammer operating in a pile frame or with false leaders, or by double-acting hammer with or without leaders. Double-acting hammers are generally preferred for speed and efficiency and this type functions well in most types of ground, especially in sandy and gravelly soils.

Double-acting hammers are preferred for use with floating plant, and Type "B" hammers have the advantage of being able to work under water to depths of up to 15 m. Single-acting hammers or drop hammers are preferable in some circumstances, especially when driving in heavy clays. Diesel operated single-acting hammers (*see* p. 465) are effective for hard driving conditions.

Vibratory hammers (p. 469) can be used for sheet pile driving. Their relatively low noise level is advantageous for pile driving in built-up areas. The Taylor-Woodrow "Pilemaster" pile-driving equipment operates on the principle of pushing sheet piles into the soil by hydraulic rams against a reaction provided by the skin friction developed on piles already in place. Initially this reaction is obtained by the penetration of the panel of piles under the 10 tonne mass of the equipment. As the piles in the panel are alternately pushed down the skin friction resistance is progressively increased. The maximum thrust of each of the eight rams is 2250 kN. The "Pilemaster" operates without ground vibrations and is virtually silent. The "Hush" piling system operated by Sheet Piling Contractors Ltd employs a drop hammer within a sound-absorbent box, which is also effective in achieving relatively quiet driving.

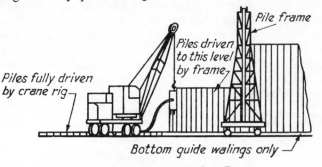

FIG. 10.15. TYPICAL TWO-STAGE PILE DRIVING

The noise from sheet pile driving is an important consideration in the selection of the type of hammer. At the present time increasing attention is being given to the enforcement of noise control regulations in rural areas as well as in towns. As yet there is no legislation in Britain for specific noise levels which must not be exceeded in areas accessible to the general public. Local authorities adopt their own standards and maximum day and night noise levels of 70 dBA and 60 dBA respectively are frequently stipulated for urban areas. Control of noise is also necessary to protect the health of site operatives. The Department of Employment recommends that no person should be exposed to a noise level of more than 90 dBA for 8 hours a day in a five-day week. It is recognized that pile driving noise exceeds 90 dBA but the operations are not continuous throughout the working day and the observed noise level can be converted to an equivalent sound level which takes account of the duration of noise emission.

Some observed noise levels from pile driving hammers are shown in Table 10.2. It will be seen that a distance of more than 1000 m is required from the noisiest group of hammers before the sound is attenuated to a permitted level of 70 dBA.

It is important to protect the heads of sheet piles during driving. Where double-acting hammers are used for driving piles singly or in pairs a double anvil block is supplied with the hammer. For driving with single-acting or drop hammers, a single or double cast steel driving cap should be used in conjunction with a hardwood or plastic dolly. Driving caps are sometimes used with the large double-acting hammers for driving heavy sections of Larssen piling.

Long lengths of sheet piling are conveniently driven in two stages. In the first stage the piles are pitched by long jib derrick or crawler crane and driven to part penetration by a light or medium weight hammer. In the second stage a heavy hammer suspended from a shorter jib crane (say a truck-mounted or locomotive crane) is used to complete the driving. Alternatively, the two-stage driving can be accomplished with two pile frames; the first a tall light frame and the second a short sturdy one. Using a pile frame for the first-stage driving facilitates placing the hammer on the pile, which is not an easy job for a man working high on a ladder lashed to a swaying pile when working without a frame. A typical method of two-stage driving is illustrated in Fig. 10.15.

Table 10.2
NOISE FROM PILE DRIVING OPERATIONS

| Type of hammer | Type of pile | Observed noise level | | Approx. distances (m) for noise levels of | |
|---|---|---|---|---|---|
| | | dBA | Distance from source (m) | 70 dBA | 90 dBA |
| Taylor Woodrow Pilemaster | Steel sheet | 70 | 1·5 | 1·5 | 0·15 |
| Vibratory (med. frequency) | H-section | 90 | 1 | 14 | 1 |
| Drop (in Hush Tower) | Steel sheet | 70 | 18 | 18 | 1·5 |
| Drop (internal) | Cased | 90 | 18 | 170 | 18 |
| Drop (5-ton) | Precast concrete | 98–107 | 7 | 200–400 | 20–50 |
| Diesel (light with shroud) | Steel sheet | 95 | 18 | 274 | 27 |
| Vibratory (high frequency) | Steel sheet | 113 | 2 | 287 | 29 |
| Diesel (light) | Steel sheet | 97 | 18 | 345 | 34 |
| Double-acting (air) | Steel sheet | 90 | 110 | 1050 | 110 |
| Single-acting (air) | Precast concrete | 90 | 140 | 1350 | 140 |
| Diesel (medium) | Steel sheet | 116 | 7 | 1400 | 150 |
| Diesel (medium) | Steel tubes | 121 | 7 | 2400 | 280 |

Where long runs of sheet piling have to be driven, the two-stage method, with simultaneous driving of the two stages, gives rapid progress. Another method is to use specially designed travelling rigs incorporating multiple hammers.

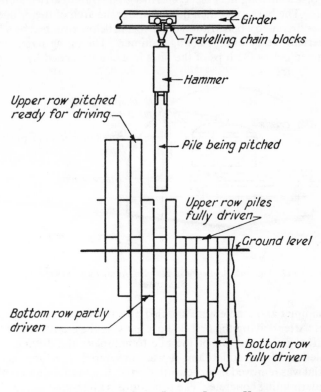

FIG. 10.16. DRIVING SHEET PILES IN LIMITED HEADROOM

### DRIVING WITH LIMITED HEADROOM

Difficult problems arise when piles have to be driven where there is limited headroom in which to pitch the piles and place the hammer. One method is to drive the piles in two lengths with dovetailed joints. Alternate piles are driven one or two metres deeper than the adjoining ones; the upper row of piles can then be interlocked with the upstanding portions (Fig. 10.16) and the two lengths driven down together. Where watertightness is required the butt joint must be welded up. If it is desired to utilize the full flexural strength of the piling it may be necessary to add fishplates.

A typical case of restricted headroom conditions occurs in the case of a cofferdam constructed around a pier to an arch bridge to enable the foundations to be underpinned. The procedure adopted for the underpinning of Cavendish Bridge, Leicestershire, was to pitch a panel of 4·25 m long steel sheet piles in a guide frame carried alongside a barge. The barge was then floated under the arch of the bridge and the piles driven to a penetration of 1·5 to 2 m below river bed by a No. 6 McKiernan–Terry double-acting hammer. The piling hammer was suspended below the tops of the piles in a cradle carried by the piles.

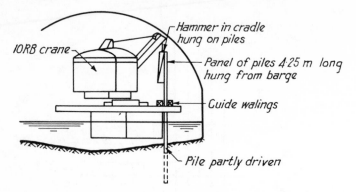

FIG. 10.17. DRIVING SHEET PILES BENEATH ARCH OF CAVENDISH BRIDGE, SHARDLOW

The hammer and cradle were handled by a 10RB crane carried on the barge. After driving the first 0·5 to 1 m using the cradle, the hammer was lifted on to the top of the pile to complete the driving. After completion of the cofferdam, it was unwatered, the loose scoured material was removed from beneath the pier foundations and replaced by underpinning concrete. The procedure is illustrated in Fig. 10.17.

### Examples of Single-wall Cofferdam Design

The cofferdam for the south main pier of the Forth Road Bridge[10.6] constructed in 1959–60 by John Howard & Co. provides an interesting example of the modern techniques of prefabrication. The purpose of this sheet pile cofferdam was to enable the caissons forming the base of the main pier to be sunk as an open-well structure, so avoiding the difficulties and expense of working under high air pressures. The cofferdam was the shape of a figure-8 in plan designed to accommo-date the two circular caissons (Fig. 10.18).

The first stage was to float out a prefabricated waling unit to the construction site. This unit consisted of a hollow box-section bottom waling made up from steel plates with internal stiffening forming a watertight ring, together with a top waling consisting of a pair of I-sections with angle lacings. The two walings were connected together by tubular diagonal bracing. The buoyant unit was sunk on the falling tide and held in position by piles dropped through prepared openings. Larssen No. 4 sheet piles 24·4 m long were then pitched around the unit and driven 3 to 6 m into the boulder clay.

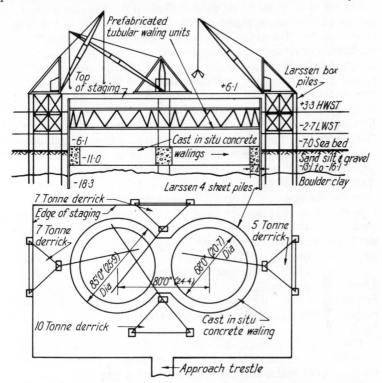

FIG. 10.18. COFFERDAM FOR SOUTH MAIN PIER, FIRTH OF FORTH ROAD BRIDGE

The silt was excavated from within the cofferdam by grabs operated by derricks on piled staging erected around the cofferdam and, on reaching the level of the boulder clay, formwork was assembled for the cast-in-situ concrete ring waling. The timber-faced formwork for the 2·4 m wide by 4·9 m deep ring beam was prefabricated in panels and lowered by derrick for assembly within the cofferdam above low-water level. It should be mentioned that the cofferdam at this stage was open to the tides since the sheet piling could not withstand the 15 m or so head of external water pressure until the concrete waling had been completed. After assembly of the form-work panels the whole unit was lowered and final connexions made under water by divers. The concrete was placed by "pre-packed" methods (*see* p. 662) and, after the concrete had hardened, the coffer-dam was pumped down, the formwork removed, and the surface of the boulder clay trimmed to level to receive the caisson shoes.

The 68 m long by 30 m wide cofferdam for the east anchorage pier of the Delaware Memorial Bridge ranks as one of the largest ever built.[10.7] The sheet piles were driven around a prefabricated steel framework incorporating the walings. The foundations were designed to be excavated under water and a tremie concrete seal was placed in the cofferdam before it was pumped dry. The bracing frameworks were built on shore and transported to the site by barge in four sections, each 15 m deep. They incorporated walings and horizontal bracing at four levels. Cross-bracing was in the form of fully welded vertical panels at 5·5 m centres in both directions, thus forming 5·5 m square bays for grab excavation and concreting. The site was prepared by dredging to 12·8 m below mean low-water and six spud piles were driven for each of the four bracing units as guides for lowering the units and supporting them clear of the mud on the river bottom. The first section was completely fabricated on shore, skidded on to a barge, and floated out to site where it was lifted off the barge and lowered into position by three revolving cranes, two of 50 tonne and one of 75 tonne capacity. The crane capacity was the governing factor in the size of the bracing units, which weighed about 130 tonne each. The remaining three units were only partly fabricated ashore, the remaining work being carried out on the barges. Underwater bolted connexions between the units were made by divers.

The 30·5 m long sheet piles were pitched by a floating crane with a 50 m jib, and the piles were driven by a floating rig with a 18·3 m long hanging spud leader and heavy double-acting hammer.

Excavation in sand and clay was carried out by underwater grabbing with floating cranes. The material around the bracing frames and in other inaccessible parts was cleared by washing down with high-pressure water jets and raised to the surface by airlift pumps.

After completion of the excavation the bottom was inspected by divers before placing the 8 m thick tremie concrete seal. The seal was placed in four equal lifts in seven and one-half days. The total quantity of 20 560 m³ of concrete was mixed in one 137 m³ per hour and one 46 m³ per hour floating batching and mixing plants working in two eleven-hour shifts. After a seven-day waiting period from completion of the seal, the cofferdam was pumped dry and the exposed parts of the bracing cut free and wholly removed. The general arrangement of the cofferdam and tremie concrete seal is shown in Fig. 10.19.

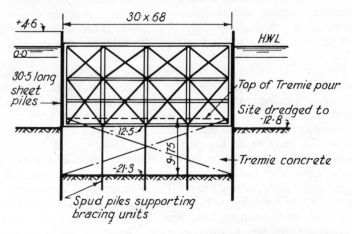

FIG. 10.19. COFFERDAM FOR EAST ANCHOR PIER, DELAWARE MEMORIAL BRIDGE

### Double-wall Sheet Pile Cofferdams

Double-wall sheet pile cofferdams are essentially free-standing walls used for wide excavations where cross-bracing would be uneconomically long. Cofferdams of this type are not used for land excavations since in these conditions support to a single wall can be given by raking shores, as described on pages 579 to 581. Double-wall cofferdams consist of two lines of steel sheet piling (or for low heights an outer line of steel and an inner line of timber sheet piling) driven into the ground and tied together at the top by walings and tie bolts. For high heads it may be necessary to install sets of walings and tie bolts at lower levels. Dams on impermeable soil need not have an inner banking but, on permeable soils and soils of moderate bearing capacity, an inner banking is a desirable addition (Fig. 10.8 (*f*)). The space between the piling is filled with sand, gravel, crushed rock, or broken bricks. The depth of penetration of the piles depends on the pressure exerted by the filling and on the need to prevent horizontal sliding. Each line of sheet piling is considered to be anchored at the top or intermediate levels and restrained at the bottom by the passive resistance of the soil. Where cofferdams are constructed on permeable soils, the depth of penetration of the piles is also governed by considerations of piping. White and Prentis[10.1] have made an extensive study of double-wall cofferdams on such ground and they take the view that lengthening the seepage path in a horizontal direction is more effective and is more economical than lengthening it by deeper penetration of the sheet piling. They regard the inner earth banking as an essential feature in the stability of double-wall cofferdams against collapse following on piping. Another important feature is the wide drainage ditch (Fig. 10.8 (*f*)) carefully laid to falls with check weirs as necessary to keep the ditch full of water and the velocity of flow low enough to avoid erosion.

White and Prentis state that the inner row of sheet piles contributes nothing to the watertightness of the dam and that its main function is to prevent collapse in the event of overtopping causing erosion on the inside face. Their double-wall cofferdams for the work on the Mississippi River were designed to be overtopped during the flood season and they make the point that it is important to provide adequate sluices through the walls to allow the interior to be flooded as the water level outside rises, so reducing the risk of erosion or piping under high external heads. The need for rapid lowering of the internal water level during the period of a falling river level is also important, as the reverse head may cause collapse of a cofferdam which is not designed for this condition. Generally, the detailed and practical observations of White and Prentis on these double-wall cofferdams are of absorbing interest and should be studied carefully by engineers concerned with major cofferdam construction.

FILLING MATERIALS

Where double-wall dams are constructed on unstable soils it is necessary to excavate between the sheet pile rows and remove the soft material before placing the filling. This procedure is facilitated by providing diaphragms between the rows at a spacing of four to eight times the width. Individual cells between diaphragms can then be pumped down and excavated. Clay and other materials which must consolidate before they offer much resistance to external pressure should not be used as filling. Watertightness is given by the outer row of sheet piles and not by the filling material. Weep holes should be provided at various levels in the inner wall to drain down the filling thus avoiding internal hydrostatic pressure. Rubber washers can be provided around the tie bolts between the external walings at the face of the sheet piling for added watertightness.

The sheet piling of double-wall cofferdams founded on rock must be restrained from outward movement by banks of earth or rockfill or by bagged concrete on both inner and outer faces (Fig. 10.20). The pressure exerted by the filling can be reduced by using concrete in the lower part (Fig. 10.21). The risk of sliding on a sloping rock

bottom can be prevented by a bank of rockfill on the inner face or by
dowelling a base slab of concrete to the rock by means of short steel
rods or old rails fixed into holes drilled in the rock.

The double-wall cofferdam shown in Fig. 10.22 was constructed by
the author's firm for the Pitlochry Dam and Power Station, Scotland,
in difficult conditions of bedrock covered by gravel and large

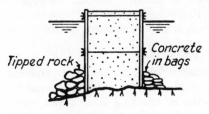

FIG. 10.20

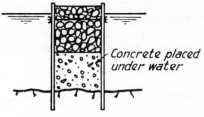

FIG. 10.21

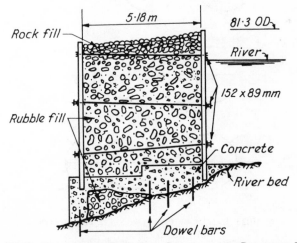

FIG. 10.22. DOUBLE-WALL SHEET PILE COFFERDAM FOR PITLOCHRY DAM
(BENNETT[10.8])

boulders.[10.8] Rock level in the bed of the River Tummel fell steeply towards the excavation. The cofferdam was constructed at a low stage in the river and diaphragms permitted individual cells to be pumped out and excavated to rock level. Sealing concrete was rammed under the piles and dowel bars were used to key the dam to the rock. Further concrete was placed beneath the inner row of piles. Records of the flow in the river showed the depth to vary between 0·3 and 3·8 m. Flows higher than 2·4 m were infrequent and the cofferdam was designed to be overtopped at this level.

### Cellular Sheet Pile Cofferdams

Cellular cofferdams for work in rivers and the sea consist of complete circles of interlocking piling connected by short arcs (Fig. 10.23 (*a*)) or a series of arcs in a double wall connected by straight diaphragms (Fig. 10.23 (*b*)) or modified circles (Fig. 10.23 (*c*)).

They have the advantage that little falsework is required in their construction; the only requirements are top and bottom templates for pitching the piles. They can be constructed working out from land, each successive cell, after filling, forming the working platform for driving the next (Fig. 10.24). Trough-shaped piling is unsuitable

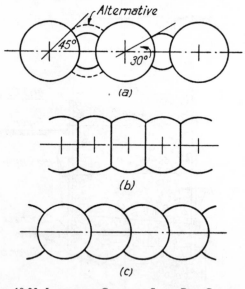

FIG. 10.23 LAYOUT OF CELLULAR SHEET PILE COFFERDAMS
    (*a*) Circular cells.
    (*b*) Diaphragm cells.
    (*c*) Modified circular cells.

and special straight web sections must be used. Sand, gravel, crushed stone, or broken bricks are suitable materials for filling. Clay is unsuitable for the reasons already stated for double-wall cofferdams. Cellular cofferdams can be used on an irregular rock bed when the sheet pile lengths can be tailored to suit the rock profile. They are also suitable for founding on stiff clays or sandy or gravelly soils. In the latter two cases it is usually necessary to provide an inner earth banking to give the necessary length of seepage path to avoid failure by piping.

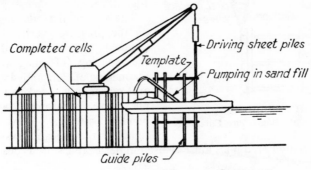

FIG. 10.24. CONSTRUCTING CELLULAR COFFERDAMS

Cellular cofferdams suffer from an important hazard in that a major failure at any interlock may result in complete failure of a cell with serious consequences. Thus it is inadvisable to use cellular construction on ground containing boulders or other obstructions which might cause splitting of the piles or parting of the interlocks. Great care must also be taken in the accurate pitching and driving of the piles. Packshaw[10.2] states that the ratio of the average width (i.e. the area of a cell divided by the distance between centres of cells) to the height should be 0·85 or 0·9 if the filling is sand, or 0·8 to 0·85 if the filling is rock. Cellular cofferdams should be stable against bodily sliding and against tilting and distortion. The detailed structural design of cellular cofferdams is rather complex and the reader is referred to papers by Cummings[10.9] and Swatek[10.9a] for an account of the structural problems involved.

## CONCRETE-WALLED COFFERDAMS

### Bored Cast-in-situ Piling

A cofferdam formed by a row of bored and cast-in-situ piles sunk in close contact with one another is a useful construction expedient for situations where headroom limitations prevent the driving of steel sheet piling or where it is necessary to avoid vibrations from pile driving. Bored pile cofferdams can also be used in ground containing boulders which would split steel sheet piles or cause

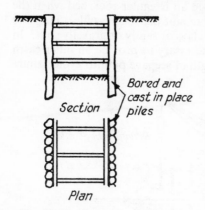

them to come out of interlock. However, bored piles sunk in bouldery ground are in themselves a costly form of construction. A typical bored pile cofferdam is shown in Fig. 10.25.

*Bored and cast in place piles*

*Section*

*Plan*

FIG. 10.25. BORED PILE COFFERDAM

The size of the piles depends on the pressure exerted by the retained water and soil and the spacing of the walings. Diameters of 300 and 450 mm are commonly used and the piles are reinforced against bending stresses. For water-tightness the "secant" system of interlocking bored piles must be used in permeable soils as described in Chapter 5.

### Continuous Diaphragm Walls

The use of grabbing and drilling methods to excavate trenches supported by bentonite mud for the construction of basement walls has been described on pages 286 to 287. Similar techniques can be used for the construction of con-

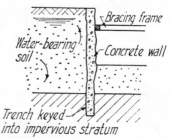

crete-walled cofferdams. The ground within the cofferdams is subsequently excavated and support given to the concrete walls by strutting (Fig. 10.26) or tied-back anchorages (p. 584).

*Bracing frame*

*Water-bearing soil*

*Concrete wall*

*Trench keyed into impervious stratum*

FIG. 10.26. CONCRETE WALL COFFER-DAM

As an alternative to placing concrete in the mud-filled trench, stiffened steel lining plates can be used in a narrow trench. In fairly small circular excavations, the lining plates can be designed to be self-supporting. Armco pressed steel culvert sections have been used in this way.

Another method of forming a watertight diaphragm is the E.T.F. process. This employs a heavy steel H-section which is driven with a guide device to the required penetration. Clay-cement grout is then injected at the bottom through a pipe fixed to the web of the H-section. The section is withdrawn while injection is continued; thus the grout fills the void left on withdrawal to form a section of the continuous diaphragm (Fig. 10.27).

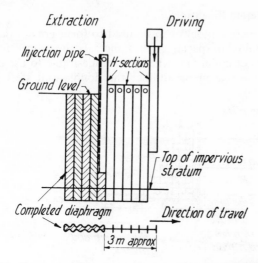

FIG. 10.27. CONTINUOUS DIAPHRAGM CONSTRUCTED BY THE E.T.F. PROCESS

In any form of diaphragm construction where a bentonite-filled trench is required to be left open before the concrete filling or other rigid membrane is placed, consideration must be given to the possibility of collapse of the walls of the trench while they are supported by the mud only. The problem of stability is very complex. The walls of the trench are supported by the fluid pressure of the bentonite, which normally has a lower density than the soil forming the trench walls. Additional support is given by the thixotropic or gel-forming properties of the bentonite and by the stabilizing action of the cake formed on the walls of the trench by the penetration of the mud into the interstices of the soil. In a permeable soil the penetration may be of the order of several metres. The possibility of inward collapse of the trench walls is most likely to occur in loose saturated sands, and the addition of heavy particles to the mud may be necessary. Conversely, in very soft organic clays the bentonite may push back the trench walls. For a mathematical treatment of the stability problem, the reader is referred to the *Proceedings of the Symposium on Grouts and Drilling Muds in Engineering Practice,* 1963.[10.9b]

If the soil is suitable, a diaphragm wall can be made by stabilizing the soil in situ with cement using a churn drill or a rotary drill fitted with a fish-tailed drilling bit. This method can be used in sands or gravels.

### Precast Concrete Blockwork

Precast concrete blocks can be used to form gravity dams. This method is limited to special circumstances, such as repetition work in short lengths of cofferdam where it is undesirable to use bracing or where for one reason or another the double-wall steel sheet pile

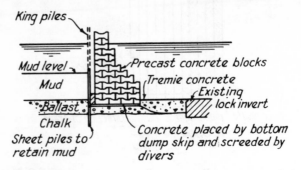

FIG. 10.28. PRECAST CONCRETE BLOCKWORK DAM AT GALIONS LOWER ENTRANCE (MALCOLM AND LEWIS[10.10])

cofferdam cannot be adopted. As blockwork dams are heavy and sensitive to fairly small differential settlements which might cause the blockwork to open at the joints, they cannot be used on ground of low bearing capacity.

It is normally necessary to construct the blocks to fine tolerances with joggled or dovetailed joints to give watertightness and stability against sliding. They must also be set on an accurately screeded tremie concrete bed, and successive tiers must be carefully placed to ensure close joints. This involves much work by divers and the slinging and setting of heavy units. Therefore blockwork dams are generally a costly expedient only used in special circumstances.

A blockwork cofferdam was used to close the entrance to the Galions entrance lock of the Lower Albert Dock, London,[10.10] where the foundation conditions, consisting of a thin layer of sandy gravel overlying chalk, were good and where the existing entrance walls and sill of the lock provided sound abutments. In all, thirteen courses of blockwork were placed for the 15·5 m high dam. Watertightness was ensured by lowering long canvas bags down recesses formed in the blocks and grouting the bags with cement. A cross-section of the dam is shown in Fig. 10.28.

## Concrete Wall Cofferdams

Where high heads and water velocities must be resisted, elaborate forms of cofferdams are necessary. Circular and semicircular concrete shells were used for the Kariba Dam.[10.11] The most spectacular of these was the 115 m diameter by 43 m high circular cofferdam for the construction on the right-hand bank. The downsteam section of the concrete wall was 3·6 m thick at the base, decreasing to 1·2 m at the top. These dams successfully withstood unprecedented floods in the Zambesi River.

### Prestressed Concrete Frames

An unusual form of cofferdam was used for the foundation of the Riveres Dam across the Tarn River in France.[10.12] A mass concrete base 3·2 m wide with minimum and maximum thicknesses of 0·65 and 2·65 m respectively was constructed on the cleaned-off surface of the rock. The upper surface of this base had pairs of pockets at 2·25 m centres to receive the feet of 4·10 m high by 2·55 m wide rectangular braced precast concrete frames. After the frames were erected a pair of cables was passed through holes in the upper interior corner of each frame and the cables were led through ducts in the base to anchorages in the rock. Additional pairs of anchor cables secured the base to the rock. In all there were six anchor cables each stressed to 199 kN per 2·25 m length of cofferdam. Finally, precast concrete slabs were inserted in the recesses cast in the vertical members of the frames and filling was placed between them. The assembly of frames on the base is shown in Fig. 10.29. The prestressing was by Freyssinet methods.

## MOVABLE COFFERDAMS

Where there is a considerable amount of repetition work in underwater foundations, such as in the piers of multi-span river bridges or in long jetties, it is economical to design the cofferdams to be moved as a single unit from one foundation to another. A simple type of movable cofferdam in the form of a steel cylinder was used by the author's firm to construct bases to precast concrete columns supporting a jetty at Bonahaven, Islay, Scotland. The cylinder which was 1·37 m in diameter was divided into two sections by a flanged circumferential joint. The lower section was first lifted by crane, lowered on to the sea bed and held in position by 300 × 300 mm timber guides. The upper section was then bolted on and the cylinder

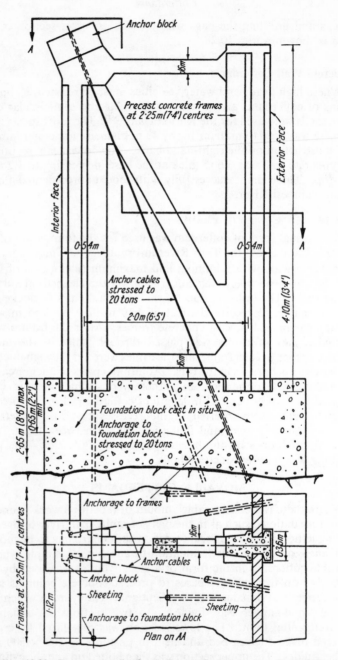

FIG. 10.29. PRESTRESSED CONCRETE FRAME COFFERDAM FOR RIVERES DAM

was sunk through silt, sand, gravel, and boulders on to bedrock. The sinking was achieved by breaking up boulders with a heavy rock chisel, and removing the fragments and small boulders with an orange-peel grab. The silt, sand, and gravel were cleaned out by a

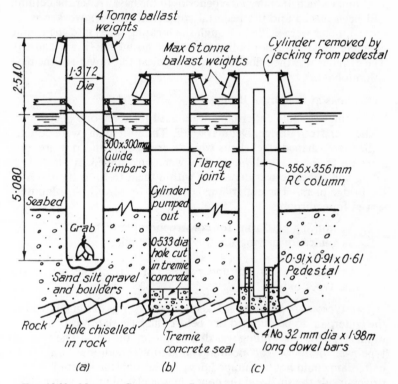

FIG. 10.30. MOVABLE CYLINDRICAL COFFERDAM FOR BONAHAVEN PIER, ISLAY

compressed-air/water ejector (*see* p. 351 for description). The downward movement of the cylinder was aided by hanging ballast weights totalling 4 tonne on to brackets on the top edge of the cylinder (Fig. 10.30 (*a*)).

After bedrock had been reached, a 0·51 m deep by 1·37 m diameter hole was excavated in the rock. Tremie concrete was then placed to a level 0·3 m above the cutting edge of the cylinder. Three days after the concrete had set, a further 2 tonne of ballast weights were added and the cylinder was pumped out. A 533 mm diameter by 300 mm deep socket to receive the 356 × 356 mm precast concrete column was then made in the concrete base by drilling close-spaced holes around a steel template and breaking out the core within the circle of drill holes (Fig. 10.30 (*b*)). Steel formwork was then placed on the base to form a 0·91 m square pedestal. The formwork unit had locating pipes for four 32 mm diameter by 1·98 m long steel bolts which anchored the pedestal to the base. After the column had been placed and the pedestal concreted, the formwork was removed, holes were drilled through the locating tubes into the tremie concrete, and the anchor bolts were set and grouted in (Fig. 10.30 (*c*)). The cylinder was then flooded and lifted clear for moving to the next column base.

### Cofferdams at Storstrøm Bridge

Floating movable cofferdams were used for forty-one of the piers of the Storstrøm Bridge, Denmark.[10.13] The cofferdams were double-walled oval-shaped steel shells which were floated into position and sunk on to the sea bed where they were surrounded by steel sheet piling and concrete was deposited within them to form the bases of the bridge piers. The cofferdams, designed by Mr. G. A. Maunsell, served four purposes—

1. As working platforms for construction plant.
2. As guides for driving the rings of sheet piles.
3. As cofferdams.
4. As formwork for the underwater portions of the pier shafts (external types only).

Two types were provided. The internal type was designed to allow the cofferdam to be pumped dry before the base slab was concreted; in this type the sheet piling was driven outside the unit. The external type was designed for poorer foundation conditions where the cofferdam could not be pumped dry; in this unit the sheet piling was driven inside the shell and the concrete was placed under water. Two internal units were provided for twenty-seven piers and two external units for the remaining fourteen.

The first step was to drive a ring of timber piles, using floating plant, around the pier site. The tops of the piles were carefully levelled at or close to the sea bed by divers. The cofferdam unit with a crane mounted on it was then floated out and sunk until it came to rest on top of the timber piles. Sinking was achieved by exhausting air from the compartments between the steel skins. In some cases sheet piles were assembled around the units before they left the harbour, and in other cases they were pitched after sinking the unit. In the case of the external units they were hung around the inside skin. The sheet piles were then driven by underwater double-acting hammer until their tops were level with the bottom strake of the

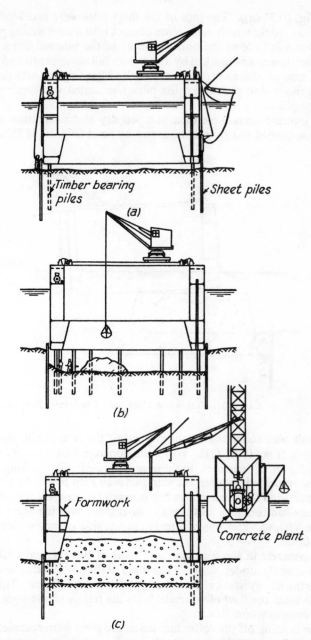

Timber bearing piles

Sheet piles

*(a)*

*(b)*

Formwork

Concrete plant

*(c)*

FIG. 10.31. CONSTRUCTING PIERS WITH MOVABLE COFFERDAMS, STORSTRØM BRIDGE, DENMARK (MAUNSELL AND PAIN[10.13])

unit (Fig. 10.31 (*a*)). The tops of the sheet piles were provided with hardwood blocks which made close contact with a steel waling placed around the outside of the bottom strake of the internal units. The remaining space was caulked by divers with tallow-impregnated rope. In the case of the external units the V-shaped space between the sloping inner skin plates and the piles was sealed with underwater concrete placed by divers.

The internal units were then pumped dry and excavation of the pier base carried out by grabbing and by hand (Fig. 10.31 (*b*)). The

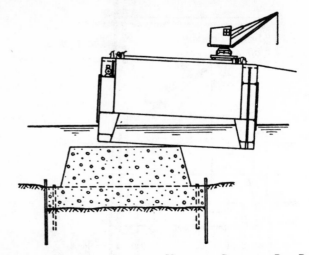

Fig. 10.32. Careening Cofferdam Unit over Completed Pier Base

base slab was concreted in the dry using the inner skin plates as formwork (Fig. 10.31 (*c*)). When the concrete had been placed to within 2·5 m of sea level, the unit was floated off. Jacking posts were incorporated between the skin plates to help break the bond of the concrete to the inner plates but generally these were not needed. The units had too deep a draught to float them over the pier tops on an even keel, so water was pumped in at one side to careen them over (Fig. 10.32).

The concrete in the base slab and shaft of the external units was placed entirely under water. The base slab was divided into ten compartments by vertical formwork panels set by divers. This was done to limit the flow of concrete from the tremie pipe to not more than 3 m in any direction.

After floating off the cofferdam units, the piers were completed by floating out and sinking on to the shaft, a precast concrete shell section forming the "middle body" of the pier (Fig. 10.33). This was filled with concrete and bonded to the pile shaft after which the upper portions of the piers were concreted between formwork in the usual way.

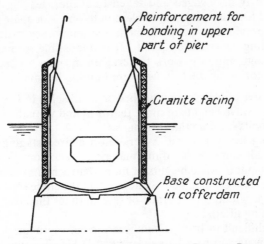

FIG. 10.33. CROSS-SECTION OF MIDDLE BODY OF PIER

## UNDERWATER FOUNDATION CONSTRUCTION

The following are some notes on methods of concreting under water and on underwater construction generally. Typical circumstances for the adoption of underwater construction are in relatively small-scale or non-repetitive foundation work in deep water where the cost of cofferdams or other temporary work might greatly exceed that of the permanent foundation structures; or on sites where stability conditions for cofferdams or caissons are such that security against "blows" or piping can only be obtained at a high cost. Other underwater work includes fixing bracing to piles driven from floating plant or stagings; cutting off sheet piling or bearing piles when removing temporary structures or in site clearance; and underwater drilling and shot firing for rock removal.

Underwater construction demands a special technique and the permanent work should be designed with this in view. Simplicity is the essential feature, for example mass concrete instead of reinforced concrete and simple outlines to avoid complex underwater formwork. Although underwater work can proceed with little hindrance in sheltered waters, such work in the open sea is entirely at the mercy of the weather. The scheme should allow for the occurrence of the worst predicted storms during the construction period. It is folly merely to trust to luck that such storms will not occur if their effect would be to wreck the construction plant and partly completed work. The safe method is to design the work so that construction vessels can be quickly disengaged and taken to shelter, leaving the partly constructed foundations in a stable condition. Adequate fendering should be provided to the permanent and temporary structures and to the floating construction plant. It is impossible to make a hard and fast programme for work undertaken in open waters. Even if storms do not occur the following are limiting factors—

(a) Transfer of men from launches or small ships to fixed stagings is difficult in wave heights of more than 1 m and virtually impossible in wave heights of more than 1·5 m.

(b) Lifting heavy material by crane on a fixed staging from the deck of small ships or handling materials by a pontoon-mounted crane is difficult in wave heights of more than 1 m and dangerous in waves more than 1·5 m high. "Snatching" of the crane rope can result in a temporary load on the crane of several times the dead weight of the load being lifted.

(c) It is difficult to bring divers wearing conventional diving suits out of the water on to a launch or fixed ladder in wave heights of more than 1 m although they can work in rather more severe conditions in self-contained equipment.

(d) Diving operations are difficult in currents of more than 2 knots.

(e) Divers cannot undertake long spells of work in water deeper than about 15 m without long decompression periods during their ascent or in decompression chambers on the site.

Much useful information on underwater construction is given in a paper by Malcolm and Lewis.[10.10]

**Excavation**

Excavation in limited areas on foundation work is normally carried out by grabbing, with the cranes operating from pontoons or stagings. Small quantities of excavation can, however, be dealt with by divers using air- or water-lift equipment of the types illustrated on page 351.

Where it is necessary to drill and blast rock under water, the work is carried out wholly by divers if the area to be excavated is small. Divers can drill with hand-held jackhammers in depths of water up to 15 m without modification to standard tools, but it may be desirable to carry a large diameter exhaust pipe up to the surface to prevent exhaust bubbles from obscuring the diver's vision and to overcome back pressure on the tool. In deep water it is advantageous to increase the pressure of the air supply to ensure efficient operation of the tools. Underwater drilling with hand-held jackhammers is not difficult in hard rocks but in soft rocks, such as weathered sandstone, marl, or soft limestone, the tools are liable to clog and jam and the diver has not the sensitivity of touch nor the ability to ease up a heavy drill to free the drill steel. Excavation by divers in soft rocks produces such turbidity in the water that visibility is nil and the divers rely entirely on feel. Soft and slurried material should be cleaned off by air/water jet and raised to the surface by an ejector. For drilling and blasting in large areas the most efficient method is to drill from pontoons or barges with multiple drills mounted on them or from transportable stagings lifted and moved from point to point by floating crane.

## Underwater Concreting

Concrete deposited under water is never as sound as that placed in the dry. There is always a tendency for cement to be washed away or for the fine aggregate to become segregated from the coarse. Therefore, underwater concrete should normally be regarded as a sealing layer to enable a cofferdam, caisson, or hollow box foundation to be pumped dry for subsequent placing of the main structural concrete. However, where the circumstances are such that the whole of the concrete work must be carried out under water, every care must be taken to ensure a sound job. Extra cement over and above that required for compressive strength alone should be added to the mix, but too much cement results in excessive laitance forming on the surface of the layers. It is also important to place underwater concrete on a clean firm surface. After dredging, the surface should be levelled by dragging a heavy steel beam across it. If the surface is on rock, any high spots shown by the drag should be dressed down by a diver. If the surface is on clay, mud, or loose sand, a blanket of crushed graded rock should be placed and levelled by drag. Where the surface has to be levelled accurately to receive a box caisson or block-work, it should be screeded by divers working with a strike-off template across a pair of carefully-levelled steel screed rails. A blinding layer of concrete or sand-cement grout over the crushed stone layer is advisable where blockwork or reinforced concrete has to be placed.

### Formwork

For small thicknesses of concrete where the outline need only be rough, such as sea-bed protection to piles or piers, the formwork can consist of concrete in bags (Fig. 10.34 (*a*)). Greater heights of lift, or successive lifts, can be achieved with formwork provided by precast concrete blockwork (Fig. 10.34 (*b*)). Steel formwork is required for high lifts and for all underwater structures where regularity of outline is required. The forms should be designed to be assembled in units above water, preferably with the reinforcement fixed within them before the whole assembly is lowered to the bottom.

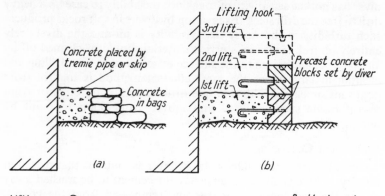

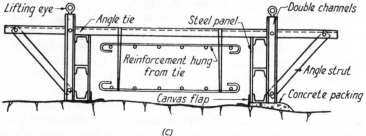

FIG. 10.34. TYPES OF UNDERWATER FORMWORK

(*a*) Concrete bagwork.
(*b*) Precast concrete blocks.
(*c*) Braced steel panels.

Gaps between the bottom of the forms and the crushed rock bed or blinding layer can be filled with bagged concrete or heavy canvas or rubber flaps. The forms should not be designed to be shored up externally but as self-supporting units with the thrust on the panels carried by cross ties above or below the finished surface (Fig. 10.34 (*c*)). Any underwater connexions made between formwork units should be as simple as possible with pins or toggle connexions rather than bolts.

PLACING

Underwater concreting is carried out by the following methods—

(*a*) Bags
(*b*) Bottom-dumping skips

(c) Tremie pipe

(d) Grouting pre-placed aggregate (prepacked concrete).

Concrete placed by divers emptying it from *bags* is limited to small quantities since the work is slow and laborious. The bags are made of canvas about 0·5 m in diameter and 1·2 m long. The bottom is closed by a length of chain, or rope, with a slip knot which is released by the diver. Where the concrete is built up in *bagwork* the bags should only be partly filled (two-thirds to three-quarters). The diver builds the bags up in bonded courses with the mouths of the sacks away from the face. The bags are rammed flat while laying them. Steel spikes may be driven through successive courses to hold them together.

*Bottom-dumping skips* are designed to discharge their contents after being lowered on to the bottom. The door release mechanism can be actuated by the skip coming to rest on the bottom, or the skip can be provided with an outside latch operated by diver or by a trip wire to the surface. The skips should be provided with canvas covers to stop cement being washed away as they are lowered through the water. The concrete must not be dropped through the water, and the mechanism should be checked to ensure that the door has opened before the skip is raised through the water.

A *tremie pipe* is made up from a number of lengths of 150 to 250 mm diameter steel pipes with quick release joints. A receiving hopper is fixed to the upper end. The tremie pipe is slung from a crane or gantry and lowered until the lower end is almost touching the bottom (Fig. 10.35). A stopper of old cement bags or straw or an expendable steel plug is placed in the top of the pipe and concrete is dumped into the hopper. This forces down the stopper until it is expelled from the bottom of the pipe and the concrete flows out. Another method of preventing segregation in the first charge of concrete is to introduce a bubble of compressed air into the tremie pipe just below the concrete.* As it is essential to keep the bottom of the pipe buried in concrete the hopper must be kept well charged and, if there is any sign of the pipe emptying, it must be lowered quickly to close the bottom. If there is any tendency for the concrete to jam in the pipe, the tremie must be "dollied" up and down to release it. For concreting in large areas a number of tremie pipes are set at 2·5 to 5 m centres, the object being to limit the flow of concrete in a horizontal direction so preventing the build-up of excessive laitance. Concrete is placed in the hoppers one by one in turn, moving to the next one as soon as the level of concrete has been raised by 0·5 to 1 m.

* A plug of vermiculite granules can also be used as a stopper. The granules become dispersed in the concrete.

The tremie pipe should be emptied after each turn and the paper or straw stopper used for the refilling. If the area is not large enough to warrant a number of pipes, it should be compartmented by steel or precast concrete slab panels to ensure that the concrete does not have to flow laterally by more than about 3 m.

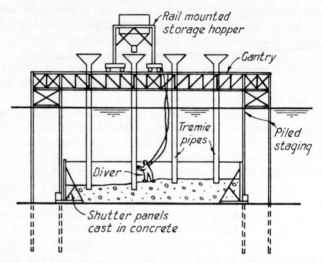

FIG. 10.35. TREMIE PLANT FOR LARGE AREA OF UNDERWATER CONCRETING

Concrete for placing by tremie should have adequate workability (125 to 200 mm slump) to allow it to flow readily. Malcolm and Lewis[10.10] state that underwater concrete made with rapid-hardening cement develops much more laitance than normal Portland cement concrete. They quote the case of a 1·8 m thick layer of concrete placed in 15 m of water to seal a 4·4 m diameter cylinder, when a 0·6 m thick layer of laitance was formed. Further use of this type of cement was abandoned and high alumina cement was substituted (presumably for its rapid-hardening properties). The laitance with the high alumina cement was much less and was in the form of a thin sludge which was pumped out. Bouvier[10.14] has made a detailed study of mix design and operational techniques for tremie concrete.

*Prepacked concrete* has its advantages in underwater construction, since the volume of materials to be passed through the mixer is only one-third of the total volume of concrete placed. This can give worthwhile savings in the size of the mixing and batching plant which, in turn, saves in the size of pontoons or barges or temporary stagings. These savings are important in work over water, where the cost of purchase or hire of floating plant represents a high proportion of the cost of the work.

Grout pipes in the form of perforated steel tubes or cylinders made up from expanded metal are placed at intervals over the area to be concreted. Then coarse aggregate of 12·5 mm or preferably 25 mm minimum size is dumped inside the formwork by skip or chute. The grout injection pipes are lowered down the perforated pipes until their ends are nearly touching the bottom. Alternatively, the injection pipes can be used without the perforated outer casings. Grout is then pumped in and displaces the water as the level rises. The injection pipes are slowly raised until the whole mass has been grouted. Soundings are taken in intermediate perforated pipes to check that an even flow is being maintained. The grout consists of a mixture of cement and sand and sometimes pulverized fuel ash (fly-ash). Workability aids are often added to improve flow characteristics. The grout is mixed in an ordinary grout pan and transported by cementation pump, or in a colloidal mixer with an attached displacement pump.

The method must be used with caution in flowing water, or in water containing silt or organic matter, since there is a risk of the grout being washed away from the aggregate or of the latter becoming coated with silt or other material which would prevent a proper bond with the grout. Silty coatings on aggregates are liable to occur when underwater excavation has been undertaken in soft rocks such as chalk or marl. Although the silt tends to settle slowly and eventually the water will clear, subsequent placing of the aggregate would stir up the silt layer on the bottom and cause it to be deposited on the lower layers of the aggregate. Drilling inspection holes into the prepacked concrete of a pier of the Arthur Kill bridge in New York[10.15] showed that the 2300 m³ pier base consisted of layers or pockets of loose aggregate surrounded by hard concrete. The mass of the material could not be relied upon to carry the loading from the bridge structure and it was necessary to drill large-diameter holes through it to enable the pier base to be underpinned by piles.

In tropical waters there is a risk of marine growth around the aggregate occurring in a relatively short period and therefore the grouting should be done within a few days of placing the aggregate.

Because of troubles with excess of laitance or of the possibility of patches of aggregate remaining ungrouted, the author would not recommend the prepacked method for structures constructed entirely underwater with relatively thin bases or walls where external water pressure must be resisted or for any structure where high strength concrete is required. The process is best suited to mass concrete work, such as the hearting of piers or piles, where the material is placed within a structural shell. In all cases careful selection of materials and close supervision of the work are required, ensuring a uniform rise in grout level over the whole area being concreted.

In some circumstances it is advantageous to place mass filling as a pumped sanded grout without any coarse aggregate.

### Wharf at Nanaimo, Vancouver

A good example of the possibilities of underwater construction is the erection of cylindrical piers for the foundations of a 115 m long by 18 m wide wharf near Nanaimo, Vancouver Island, British Columbia.[10,16] A total of sixteen 3·0 m diameter piers were provided at 15 m centres longitudinally and 12 m transversely. The first operation was to excavate a 5 m diameter hole in the sea-bed rock to a minimum depth of 1·2 m by underwater drilling and blasting, the debris being removed by clam shell grab. A barge was then centred over the excavation by theodolite and a 150 mm diameter hole was drilled at the centre of the cylinder site to a depth of 1·5 m into the rock. A piece of small-diameter pipe was placed in the drill hole to serve as a locator for a 127 mm diameter centering pipe pile. The next stage was to fabricate and place a reinforcing cage. This was made up on shore and consisted of fourteen 89 kg/m rails standing vertically around a circle and joined by rings of 25 mm by 75 mm bars at 6·1 m centres. The rings were held to a true circle by 25 mm radial rods. The lowermost (fourth) ring was 0·91 m from the bottom and it contained a steel cone at its centre designed to be lowered over the centering pile to locate the cage. A crane barge lowered the 8-tonne cage over the centering pile and it was held vertically by wire ropes to 10-tonne precast concrete anchor blocks. Adjustment to the true vertical was by divers operating screw jacks on the ends of five of the rails.

Formwork for the concrete cylinder was then set as shown in Fig. 10.36. The base unit was a 3·0 m diameter by 0·9 m high precast concrete ring. An angle ring was fixed around the top of the precast unit to hold the feet of 6·1 m long 100 × 150 mm timber staves which provided the outer sheeting of the formwork. The staves were held in position by a further four steel angle rings. The lifts of formwork comprising the precast concrete ring and two 6·1 m lifts of timber staves were assembled above water and lowered as a single unit on to brackets projecting from the reinforcing cage and centred by bars fixed to the cage. Some cylinders required a third lift of staves. Jacking off the cage was required to force down the wood formwork, which was buoyant. The spaces between the staves were not sealed, but in the cylinders exposed to the waves plywood was tacked around the outside at the waterline to prevent loss of fines from the concrete which was placed by 254 mm diameter tremie pipe.

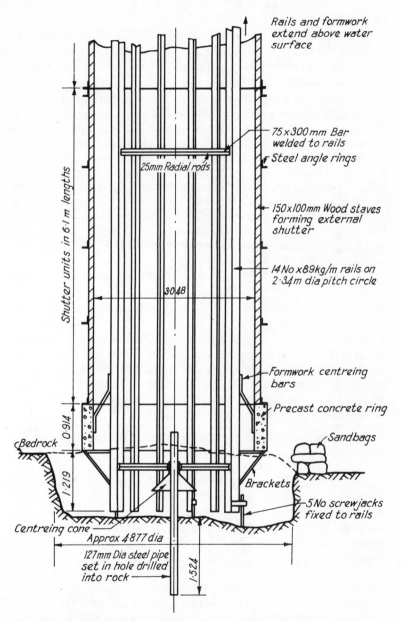

Rails and formwork
extend above water
surface

75 × 300 mm Bar
welded to rails

Steel angle rings

25mm Radial rods

150 × 100mm Wood staves
forming external
shutter

Shutter units in 6·1 m lengths

14 No × 89kg/m rails on
2·34m dia pitch circle

30·48

Formwork centreing
bars

Precast concrete ring

Sandbags

0·914

Bedrock

1·219

Brackets

5 No screwjacks
fixed to rails

Centreing cone

Approx 4·877 dia

127mm Dia steel pipe
set in hole drilled
into rock

1·524

FIG. 10.36. REINFORCEMENT AND FORMWORK FOR UNDERWATER CONCRETING
FOR CYLINDRICAL PIERS AT NANAIMO WHARF, BRITISH COLUMBIA[10.15]

## EXAMPLES ON CHAPTER 10

### EXAMPLE 10.1

The cofferdam shown in Fig. 10.37 (*a*) is to be constructed in sheltered tidal waters. The tidal range is 7·6 m at springs and 1·5 m at neaps. Excavation level is in stiff clay at 1·6 m below sea-bed level or 9·3 m below highest high water.

The cofferdam must be designed for the maximum head of water which occurs at times of highest high water (8·3 m above datum). At this stage the head is 9·3 m above excavation level when the cofferdam is completed and dewatered. Since the piles need not be driven deeply below sea-bed level and the overall length is not great, we can work to the higher range of stress for mild steel and use a fairly light section, say, Larssen No. 2 (section modulus $= Z_p = 850 \text{ cm}^3/\text{m}$), or Frodingham No. 2N ($Z_p = 1150 \text{ cm}^3/\text{m}$). From p. 628 depth from top to second waling $= h_{max} = \sqrt[3]{(0·2557 \times 850)} = 6·0$ m for Larssen No. 2 piles. The maximum depth to the third waling $= 1·6 \times 6·0 = 9·6$ m. A fourth waling is not required. See Fig. 10.37 (a) for actual positions of walings.

From the pressure diagram (Fig. 10.37 (*b*)) load on second waling

$$= \frac{4·15 \times (26·0 + 67·5)}{2} = 194 \text{ kN per m run}$$

This is carried as a series of point loads on the waling equal to the distance between centres of the troughs, i.e. at 400 mm centres. We can consider struts at 1·5 m centres for 300 × 300 mm walings (timber bracing will be preferable to steel for this small "one-off" structure). Thus, on a 1·5 m span we get three point loads each of $194 \times 0·4 = 77·6$ kN. For a simply supported waling—

Bending moment at midspan taking a symmetrical arrangement for the three point loads on the 1·5 m span

$$= 0·75 \left( 77·6 + \frac{77·6}{2} \right) - (0·4 \times 77·6) = \underline{\underline{56·3 \text{ kNm}}}$$

The walings will be continuous over more than three spans and therefore we can take approximately two-thirds of this bending moment for continuity. Therefore,

Bending moment for continuous spans $= \frac{2}{3} \times 56·3 = 37·5$ kNm

The moment of resistance of a 300 × 300 mm timber is 55·7 kNm for a maximum fibre stress in bending of 12·4 N/mm². The bending moments on the end spans of the walings will be rather higher than 37·5 kNm but these spans are only about 1·2 m. The arrangement of

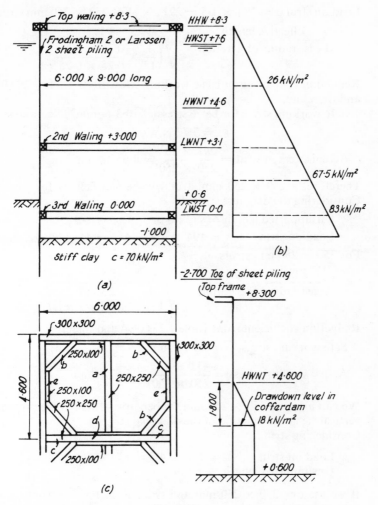

FIG. 10.37

(a) Cross-section. (Note: Vertical bracing members and other details not shown.)
(b) Pressure diagram.
(c) Half plan showing layout of struts and walings. Vertical bracing members not shown.
(d) Pressure conditions before fixing second frame.

667

walings and struts shown in Fig. 10.37 (*c*) will give economy in length of struts and maximum clear space for excavation and concreting.

Load on strut *a* = 194 × 1·5 = 291 kN. For 250 × 250 mm strut—

$$\frac{\text{Effective length}}{\text{Least radius of gyration}} = \frac{4 \cdot 1}{\sqrt{\left(\dfrac{1}{12} \times \dfrac{0 \cdot 25 \times 0 \cdot 25^3}{0 \cdot 25 \times 0 \cdot 25}\right)}} = 57$$

Reduction coefficient on basic working stress from Table 7.2 is 0·75 and therefore,

Safe working stress for basic stress of 10·3 N/mm² in compression

$$= 7 \cdot 72 \text{ N/mm}^2$$

$$\text{Actual stress in strut} = \frac{291 \times 10^3}{250 \times 250} = 4 \cdot 65 \text{ N/mm}^2$$

Therefore, a 250 × 250 mm strut will be satisfactory for struts *a*. Considering the diagonal struts *b*—

Unsupported length = say 1·8 m

Load on strut　　　= 194 × 1·5 × $\sqrt{2}$ = 411 kN

For 250 × 250 mm struts,

$$\frac{\text{Effective length}}{\text{Least radius of gyration}} = \frac{1 \cdot 8}{\sqrt{\left(\dfrac{1}{12} \times \dfrac{0 \cdot 25 \times 0 \cdot 25^3}{0 \cdot 25 \times 0 \cdot 25}\right)}} = 25$$

Reduction coefficient from Table 7.2 is 0·94 and therefore,

Safe working stress　　= 9·7 N/mm²

$$\text{Actual working stress} = \frac{411 \times 10^3}{250 \times 250} = 6 \cdot 57 \text{ N/mm}^2$$

We can also use 250 × 250 mm timbers for struts *c* if we provide a vertical tie at the junction of the diagonal struts.
Considering struts *d*—

Load on strut　　　= 194 × 4·5 = 873 kN
Unsupported length = 1·2 m

If we use one 250 × 250 mm and two 250 × 100 mm timbers and assuming the members are securely bolted to act together—

$$\frac{\text{Effective length}}{\text{Least radius of gyration}} = \frac{1 \cdot 2}{\sqrt{\left(\dfrac{1}{12} \times \dfrac{0 \cdot 25 \times 0 \cdot 45^3}{0 \cdot 25 \times 0 \cdot 45}\right)}} = 9$$

Reduction coefficient from Table 7.2 is 0·98 and therefore,
Safe working stress = 10·1 N/mm²

Actual working stress $= \dfrac{873 \times 10^3}{450 \times 250} = 7\cdot76 \text{ N/mm}^2$

A 250 × 100 mm stretcher can be placed at $e$ to carry the thrust from the diagonal struts.

Considering the bearing pressures on walings from struts—

Load on struts $a$ $\qquad\qquad = 291 \text{ kN}$

Bearing pressure on waling $= \dfrac{291 \times 10^3}{250 \times 250}$

$\qquad\qquad\qquad\qquad\qquad = 4\cdot65 \text{ N/mm}^2$

which is only slightly greater than the allowable pressure perpendicular to the grain of $4\cdot1$ N/mm². It will not therefore be necessary to insert a hardwood packer.

Consider the conditions below the bottom frame. If it is assumed that water seeps down a slight gap between the clay and the sheet piles there will be hydrostatic pressure on the outside of the piles in addition to active earth pressure. This will be resisted by the counter-balancing hydrostatic pressure on the inside and the passive earth resistance. From pressure diagram—

Hydrostatic pressure at 3rd frame $= 83\cdot0 \text{ kN/m}^2$
Hydrostatic pressure at bottom
 of sheet piling 11·0 m long $\quad = 110 \text{ kN/m}^2$
Total hydrostatic pressure $\quad = \underline{260 \text{ kN per m run}}$

Active earth pressure at level of 3rd frame is negligible. Active earth pressure at bottom of sheet piling by Bell's equation

$\qquad = \gamma z - 2c$
$\qquad = 8\cdot8 \times 3\cdot3 - 2 \times 70$, which is negative.

Therefore, only hydrostatic pressure has to be resisted. Counter-balancing hydrostatic pressure at bottom of excavation is zero.

Counter-balancing pressure at bottom of sheet piling, assuming seal into clay at this point,

$$= 10\cdot0 \times 1\cdot7 = 17\cdot0 \text{ kN/m}^2$$

Total counter-balancing hydrostatic pressure

$$= \tfrac{1}{2} \times 1\cdot7 \times 17\cdot0 = 14\cdot5 \text{ kN per m run}$$

Passive earth resistance at bottom of sheet piling

$$= \gamma z + 2c$$
$$= 8\cdot8 \times 1\cdot7 + 2 \times 70$$
$$= 155 \text{ kN/m}^2$$

Passive earth resistance at excavation level

$$= 2 \times 70 = 140 \text{ kN/m}^2$$

Total passive resistance

$$= \tfrac{1}{2} \times (140 + 155) \times 1\cdot7 = 251 \text{ kN per m run}$$

Total passive resistance plus counter-balancing hydrostatic pressure = $251 + 14\cdot5 = 265\cdot5$ kN per m run which exceeds the hydrostatic pressure on the outside.

Consider finally the conditions for dewatering the cofferdam to fix the second frame.

If this is done over the neap tide period, the head of water outside cofferdam at high water neap tides, when water level inside cofferdam is lowered to level of 2nd frame, is 1·8 m (Fig. 10.37 (*d*)). Therefore, Total excess pressure on outside of sheet piles

$$= \tfrac{1}{2} \times 1\cdot8^2 \times 10\cdot0 + 1\cdot8 \times 10\cdot0 \times 2\cdot2 = 55\cdot8 \text{ kN per m}$$
$$\text{run of wall}$$

Span of sheet piling from top frame to sea-bed level $= 7\cdot7$ m

Effective span $= 7\cdot7 + 0\cdot1 \times 7\cdot7 = 8\cdot47$ m

Approximate maximum bending moment on sheet piling from excess pressure assuming piling to be fully fixed in the ground and simply supported at the top waling = 65·4 kNm per m run of wall.

Required section modulus of piling for 165 N/mm² safe stress

$$= \frac{65\cdot4 \times 10^6}{165} = 397 \times 10^3 \text{ mm}^3 \text{ per m run of wall}$$

Therefore, the No. 2 Larssen piling ($Z_p = 850 \text{ cm}^3/\text{m}$) is amply strong for this stage of dewatering. However, it would be unwise to unwater the cofferdam to $+2\cdot8$ m level at the spring tide periods, unless the work of fixing the waling was done over the $+6$ to $0$ range only and the cofferdam allowed to partly refill as the rising tide approached the $+6$ level.

### EXAMPLE 10.2

The 21 m by 9 m cofferdam for the piers of a river bridge shown in Fig. 10.38 (*a*) is sited in 15 m of water at highest estimated flood level. The river bed consists of 5·5 m of soft mud overlying water-bearing dense sand. Borings show that the maximum head of water in the sand layer is 12·2 m above river bed level. It is necessary to found the

pier in the dense sand stratum, taking the foundation level 1·0 m into
the sand.

In the conditions shown in Fig. 10.38 (*a*) it will clearly be impossible to unwater the cofferdam to place the base concrete in the dry. In the first place, pumping down the level to fix the first bracing frame will give excessive bending moments in the piling unless an

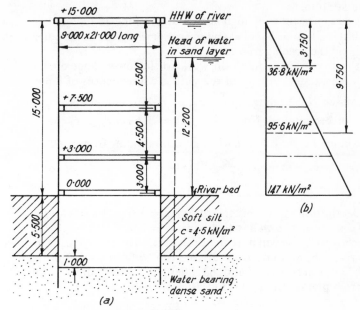

(*a*) Cross-section.

(*b*) Pressure diagram.

(*c*) Layout of walings and struts.

Fig. 10.38

(*a*) Cross-section. (Note: Vertical bracing members and other details
    not shown.)

(*b*) Pressure diagram.

(*c*) Layout of walings and struts.

uneconomical close spacing of frames is adopted, and in the second place, the sheet piles would have to be driven to at least 15 m below excavation level in order to avoid piping after pumping down. This would be impossible in the ground conditions. Therefore the coffer-dam must be designed for the base slab to be concreted under water. The sheet piling can be driven around a prefabricated bracing frame hung on to bearing piles driven through the soft mud into the dense sand stratum.

A heavy section of high tensile steel piling is required in view of the length to be handled and to economize in the underwater work in fixing the bracing frames.

It will also be desirable to work to the lower range of stress for high tensile steel in view of the serious consequences of failure.

If Larssen No. 5 piling is adopted, $Z_p = 2962$ cm³ per m run

or Frodingham No. 5      $Z_p = 3168$ cm³ per m run

Maximum height between top and second waling from p. 628

$$= h_{max} = \sqrt[3]{0.2712 \times 2962})$$
$$= 9.3 \text{ m}$$

**Depth** from top waling to 3rd frame $= 1.6 \times 9.3 = 14.9$ m
**Depth** from top waling to 4th frame $= 2.03 \times 9.3 = 18.9$ m
The fourth frame will have to be raised to 15 m level to bring it above the river bed and no further frames can be fixed until after the base slab has been concreted and the cofferdam pumped down.

From pressure diagram (Fig. 10.38 (*b*))—

$$\text{Average pressure on 2nd frame} = \frac{3.75 \times 9.81 + 9.75 \times 9.81}{2}$$

$$= 66.2 \text{ kN/m}^2$$

Therefore,    Total load on 2nd waling $= 66.2 \times 6.0$
$$= 397.2 \text{ kN per m}$$
$$\text{run of waling}$$

For struts at 3 m centres, it will be satisfactory to assume a uniformly distributed load.

Bending moment for simply supported spans

$$= \frac{397.2 \times 3^2}{8} = 447 \text{ kNm}$$

Taking two-thirds of this value for continuous spans,

$$\text{Bending moment} = \tfrac{2}{3} \times 447 = 298 \text{ kNm}$$

For 165 N/mm² safe working stress in mild steel bracing, required modulus of section, $= 1\cdot81 \times 10^3$ cm³.

Structural steel handbooks show that two $389 \times 154$ mm by 67 kg Universal Beams can be used (net $Z = 2 \times 1\cdot095 \times 10^3 = 2\cdot19 \times 10^3$ cm³).

Checking shear stress,

$$\text{Maximum shear on walings} \quad = \frac{397\cdot2 \times 3}{2} = 596 \text{ kN}$$

$$\text{Shear stress on webs of walings} = \frac{596 \times 10^3}{2 \times 9\cdot7 \times 389} = 78\cdot9 \text{ N/mm}^2$$

which is within safe limits.

If two rows of longitudinal struts are provided, effective length of cross struts will be about 2·7 m. Maximum load on struts is 595 × 2 = 1190 kN. It will be convenient for detailing the steelwork not to have the struts deeper than the walings. A Universal Column 254 × 254 mm by 73 kg in mild steel will support a safe concentric load of 1240 kN with an effective length of 2·7 m.

It will be necessary to provide web stiffness to the walings at the junctions with the struts and diagonal bracing in a vertical plane between the four frames to give the necessary stiffness against distortion. Diagonal bracing in a horizontal plane is undesirable in this case since it will obstruct the 3 m square bays through which underwater grabbing and concreting must take place. The frames should be designed to be assembled and lifted from a barge on to the river bed by floating crane. The number of units into which the whole assembly is divided will be governed by the capacity of the crane. The general arrangement of the completed bracing frames is given in Fig. 10.38 (c).

It will also be advisable to check the overall stability of the cofferdam against overturning from the forces of winds, waves, and currents.

We will now consider the problems concerning the tremie concrete slab. Its thickness is given by the weight required to hold down 18·7 m artesian head of water in the sand stratum after the cofferdam has been pumped down.

$$\begin{aligned}\text{Maximum uplift pressure on underside of slab} &= 9\cdot81 \times 18\cdot7 \\ &= 183 \text{ kN/m}^2\end{aligned}$$

Required thickness of concrete assuming density of $2.40$ Mg/m$^3$

$$= \frac{183}{2.40 \times 9.81} = 7.80 \text{ m}$$

This will come above the fourth frame which will have to be either left buried in the concrete or raised above tremie concrete level. Checking stresses in sheet piling between 4th frame raised to $1.8$ m above mud level and bottom of excavation before placing tremie concrete—

Hydrostatic pressures are balanced (assuming water levels inside and outside cofferdam are kept the same).

Earth pressure at 4th frame is zero.

Earth pressure at excavation level (by Bell's equation)

$$= \gamma z - 2c = 8.8 \times 6.5 - 2 \times 4.5 = 48.2 \text{ kN/m}^2$$

Total pressure on sheet piling $= \frac{1}{2} \times 48.2 \times 6.5$
$$= 157 \text{ kN per m run of piling}$$

Approx. maximum bending moment $= 0.128 \times 157 \times 8.3$
$$= 167 \text{ kNm}$$

Required modulus of section $= \dfrac{167 \times 10^6}{175} = 0.9 \times 10^3$ cm$^3$ per m run.

The modulus of section of Larssen No. 5 piling is 2962 cm$^3$ per m run, which is adequate for this condition.

## REFERENCES

10.1  WHITE, L. and PRENTIS, E. A., *Cofferdams* (New York, Columbia Univ. Press, 1950).

10.2  PACKSHAW, S., Cofferdams, *Proc. Inst. C.E.*, **21**, pp. 367–398 (Feb., 1962).

10.3  FOWLER, C. E., *Engineering and Building Foundations*, **1**, pp. 72–76 (New York, John Wiley, 1920).

10.4  BERTLIN, D. P. and OLIVIER, H., Owen Falls; constructional problems, *J. Inst. C.E.*, **3**, Pt. 1, pp. 670–701 (Nov., 1954).

10.5  McNAMEE, J., Seepage into a sheeted excavation, *Geotechnique*, **1**, No. 4, pp. 229–241 (Dec., 1949).

10.6  ANDERSON, J. K., *et al.*, Forth Road Bridge, *Proc. Inst. C.E.*, **32**, pp. 321–512 (Nov., 1965).

10.7  DAVIES, A. L., Construction of the Delaware Bridge anchorage cofferdam, *Eng. News Rec.*, **144**, No. 4, pp. 28–30 (26th Jan., 1950).

10.8  BENNETT, J. A., *Pitlochry Dam and Power House and Clunie Dam, Symposium of Four Notes on Contractors' Site Layouts*, Inst. C.E. Works Constr. Div. (1949).

10.9 CUMMINGS, E. M., Cellular cofferdams and docks, *Proc. A.S.C.E.*, *Paper No. 1366*, **83** (WW3) (1957).

10.9a SWATEK, E. P., Cellular cofferdams, design and practice, *Proc. A.S.C.E.*, Paper No. 5398, WW3, p. 109 (Aug., 1967).

10.9b *Proceedings of the Symposium on Grouts and Drilling Muds in Engineering Practice* (London, Butterworth, 1963).

10.10 MALCOLM, J. R. and LEWIS, J. A., Civil engineering construction under water, *Proc. Inst. C.E.*, **3**, Pt. 3, pp. 738–788 (Dec., 1954).

10.11 COYNE, A., Le Barrage de Kariba, *Travaux*, No. 297, 43 année, pp. 395–413 (July, 1959).

10.12 LE BAILLY, P. and MAZEAN, J., The Tarn Barrage, *Travaux*, Pt. 159, pp. 54–55 (Jan., 1948).

10.13 MAUNSELL, G. A. and PAIN, J. F., The Storstrøm Bridge, *J. Inst. C.E.*, **11**, No. 6, pp. 391–448 (1938–39: April, 1939).

10.14 BOUVIER, J., Étude et perfectionnement d'une technique de béton immergé, *Ann. de l'Inst. Technique du bâtiment et des travaux Publics*, 13e Ann., No. 146, pp. 151–180 (Feb., 1960).

10.15 THORNLEY, J. H., Building a foundation through a foundation, *Eng. News Rec.*, **161**, No. 9, pp. 40–46 (28th Aug., 1958).

10.16 WILSON, F. P., Bare rock bottom is tough pier site, *Eng. News Rec.*, **153**, No. 13, pp. 33–34 (23rd Sept., 1954).

# 11

# The Control of Ground Water
# in Excavations

GROUND water is usually regarded as one of the most difficult problems in excavation work. Heavy and continuous pumping from excavations is a costly item and the continual flow from the surrounding ground may cause settlement of adjacent structures. Heavy inflow is liable to cause erosion or collapse of the sides of open excavations. In certain circumstances there can be instability of the base due to upward seepage towards the pumping sump, or instability can occur if the bottom of an excavation in clay is underlain by a pervious layer containing water under artesian pressure. However, from a knowledge of the soil and ground water conditions and an understanding of the laws of hydraulic flow, it is possible to adopt methods of ground water control which will ensure a safe and economical construction scheme in any conditions. The important thing is to obtain all the necessary information before commencing work. All too often it happens that after an excavation is commenced ground water is met in larger quantities than anticipated, more pumps are brought to the site, and with a great struggle the excavation is taken deeper until the inflow is so heavy that the sides start collapsing with imminent danger to adjoining roads and buildings; or "boiling" of the bottom is so widespread that a satisfactory base for foundation concreting cannot be obtained. At this stage the contractor gives up the struggle and calls for outside help in installing a wellpointing or bored well system of ground water lowering or resorts to underwater construction. The ground water lowering systems may do the work efficiently but the overall cost of abortive pumping, extra excavation of collapsed material, making good the damage and standing time of plant and labour will have been much higher than if the ground water lowering system had been used in the first instance. There have also been cases where, due to lack of knowledge of the capabilities of modern ground water lowering systems, caissons have been used for foundations in water-bearing soils where conventional construction with the aid of such systems would have been perfectly feasible and much less costly.

### Seepage of Water into Excavations

The flow line of ground water under a fairly low head into an open excavation in a permeable soil is shown in Fig. 11.1 (*a*). The water

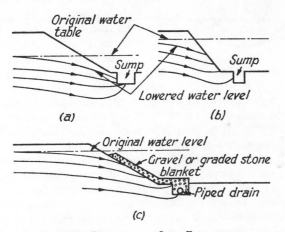

Fig. 11.1. Seepage into Open Excavations
(*a*) Stable conditions.
(*b*) Unstable conditions.
(*c*) Increasing stability of slope by blanketing.

surface is depressed towards the pumping sump and, because of the low head and flat slope, the seepage lines do not emerge on the slope and the conditions are perfectly stable. If, however, the head is increased or the slopes are steepened, the water flows from the face, and if the velocity is high enough it will cause movement of soil particles and erosion down the face leading to undermining and collapse of the upper slopes (Fig. 11.1 (*b*) and Plates XV and XVI). The remedy is to flatten the slopes and to blanket the face with a graded gravelly filter material which allows the water to pass through but traps the soil particles (Fig. 11.1 (c)). The design of graded filters is referred to on page 693. This form of instability by erosion is most liable to occur in fine or uniformly graded sands. There is much less risk of trouble with well-graded sandy gravels since these materials act as filters in themselves, and the draw-down given by their higher permeability prevents the emergence of the flow lines on the excavated face.

In the case of close-timbered or sheet piled excavations, the flow

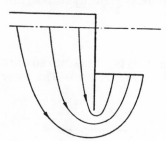

lines run vertically downwards behind the sheet piling and then upwards into the excavation (Fig. 11.2). This condition of upward seepage is particularly liable to cause instability, referred to as "piping" or "boiling," when the velocity of the upward flowing water is high enough to bring the soil particles into suspension (p. 631).

FIG. 11.2. SEEPAGE INTO SHEETED EXCAVATION

Methods of preventing instability by increasing the length of the seepage path have been described in Chapter 10.

The foregoing cases are mainly applicable to ground water flow in permeable soils such as sands and gravels, or similar materials containing fairly low proportions of silt and clay. Little or no trouble occurs with excavations in clays. Where ground water is present it will usually seep from fissures and it can be dealt with by pumping from sumps. The velocity of flow is usually so low that there is no risk of erosion. Silts, on the other hand, are highly troublesome. They are sufficiently permeable to allow water to flow through them, but their permeability is low enough to make any system of ground water lowering by wellpoints or bored wells a slow and costly procedure. Ground water in rocks usually seeps from the face in the form of springs or weeps from fissures or more permeable layers. There is no risk of instability except where heavy flows take place through a weak, shattered rock. Generally, water in rock excavations can be dealt with by pumping from open sumps, and the only trouble is given when foundation concrete is designed to be placed against the rock face. If the springs or weeps are strong the water will wash out the cement and fines from the unset concrete and flow out through the surface of the concrete layer. The usual procedure is to construct the pumping sump at the lowest point in the excavation and continue to pump from it until the concrete has hardened, while at the same time allowing seepage to take place from the face towards the sump through a layer of "no fines" concrete, or behind corrugated sheeting, or bituminous or plastic sheeting fixed to a wire mesh frame (Fig. 11.3). After completion of the concrete work the space behind the sheeting is grouted through pipes left for this purpose. Occasional weeps can often be dealt with by plastering with quick-setting cement mixtures, or by placing dry cement on the face before placing the concrete.

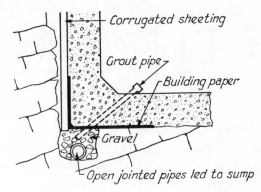

FIG. 11.3. CONCRETING ADJACENT TO WATER-BEARING ROCK FORMATION

## Calculation of Rates of Flow of Seepage into Excavations

In large excavations it is necessary to estimate the quantity of water which has to be pumped to draw down the water below formation level. This quantity must be known so that the required number and capacity of pumps can be provided. A commonly used method of calculation is by the formula of Du Puit–Forchheimer—

$$Q = \pi K \frac{h_e^2 - h_w^2}{\log_e \frac{r_e}{r_w}} \qquad . \qquad . \qquad . \quad (11.1)$$

where $Q$ = discharge from well per unit time

$K$ = permeability constant of water-bearing medium

$h_e$ = value of $h$ when $r = r_e$ (Fig. 11.4)

$h_w$ = height of water in well above impermeable stratum during pumping

$r_e$ = external radius of assumed flow system

$r_w$ = radius of well.

It is necessary to know the coefficient of permeability of the ground. In loose uniform soils it may be calculated approximately by Hazen's formula—

$$\text{Coefficient of permeability} = K = C_1 D_{10}^2 \text{ cm/sec} \qquad (11.2)$$

where   $C_1$ = a factor varying between 100 and 150

and   $D_{10}$ = effective grain size* in cm

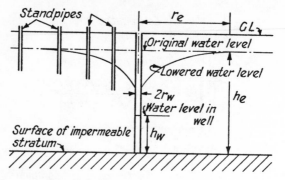

FIG. 11.4. FLOW INTO A PUMPED WELL

In variable or irregularly stratified soils it may be sufficient to make a rough estimate of $K$ from the average grading of the deposits. On more important work field tests for permeability may be justified. The ideal procedure is to conduct a full-scale pumping test from a bored well with standpipes at intervals to measure the draw-down curve (Fig. 11.4). Knowing the water levels in the observation stand-pipes and the yield of the test well, the average permeability of the soil within the draw-down zone can be calculated by the method described by Boulton.[11.1] It should be noted from Fig. 11.4 that the draw-down water table (the "phreatic line") cuts the well at a higher level than the pumping level in the well. In ground of moderate to low permeability the seepage line into the well may be a considerable distance above the pumping level. It is difficult to estimate the shape of the draw-down curve in non-homogeneous material by calculation, and for this reason the author would always like to have a full-scale pumping test on an important project.

Other methods of field permeability test consist in pumping from a single well over a known filter length without observation wells, or pumping into the ground through a known length of filter. These procedures are referred to on page 45.

---

* *Effective grain size* is the grain size corresponding to the 10 per cent retention on the grading curve of the soil.

In the case of wellpointing schemes, it will normally be found that firms hiring the various proprietary wellpoint systems will, from their knowledge and experience, be able to give a fairly close estimate of the required number of wellpoints and pumping capacity, provided that they are supplied with borehole records and particle-size distribution curves of the soil strata.

## METHODS OF GROUND WATER CONTROL

The following methods of ground water control and associated geotechnical processes can be used in excavation work—

1. Pumping from open sumps
2. Pumping from wellpoints
3. Pumping from bored wells
4. Pumping from horizontal wells
5. Electro-osmosis.

Elimination or reduction of ground water flow by—

6. Grouting with cement, clay suspensions, or bitumen
7. Chemical consolidation
8. Compressed air
9. Freezing.

The choice of method depends to a great extent on site conditions. For example, pumping from open sumps can be used in most ground conditions provided that the site area is large enough to permit the excavation to be cut back to stable slopes, and that there are no important structures close to the excavation which might be damaged by settlement resulting from erosion due to water flowing towards the sump. Wellpointing or bored wells can be used in more restricted site conditions, and the special processes such as grouting, chemical consolidation and freezing are used where it is necessary to safeguard existing structures, or in particular ground or rock conditions where pumping is impracticable.

The soil characteristics, and especially the particle-size distribution of the soil, also influence the choice of method. The range of soil types over which the various processes are applicable have been classified by Glossop and Skempton,[11.2] and are shown on the particle-size distribution curves in Figs. 11.5 and 11.6. To use these curves, the particle-size distribution of the soil is obtained by sieving tests and the grading curve is plotted on one or other or both of the charts. For example, the coarse gravel (Soil A in Fig. 11.5) may be unsuitable for wellpointing because of the heavy flow through the highly permeable ground. However, reference to the chart in Fig. 11.6 shows that the gravel is amenable to treatment by cement grouting to eliminate or greatly reduce the flow into the excavation. The coarse to fine sand (Soil B) is suitable for wellpointing, but if there should be a risk of damage to adjacent structures due to lowering of the ground water table, Fig. 11.6 shows that chemical consolidation can be used to solidify the soil and greatly reduce or prevent inflow. The sandy

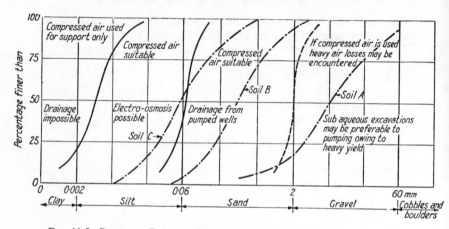

FIG. 11.5. RANGE OF PARTICLE SIZE FOR VARIOUS GROUND WATER LOWERING PROCESSES (GLOSSOP AND SKEMPTON[11.2])

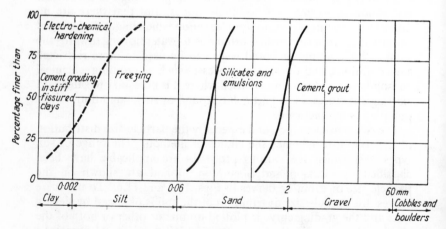

FIG. 11.6. RANGE OF PARTICLE SIZE FOR VARIOUS GEOTECHNICAL PROCESSES (GLOSSOP AND SKEMPTON[11.2])

silt (Soil C) is too fine for wellpointing, but we could use electro-osmosis, or the freezing process, or compressed air.

## Pumping from Open Sumps

This is the most widely used of all methods of ground water lowering. It can be applied to most soil and rock conditions, and the costs of installing and maintaining the plant are comparatively low. The method is essential where wellpointing or bored wells cannot be used because of boulders or other massive obstructions in the ground, and it is the only practical method for rock excavations. However, it has the disadvantage that the ground water flows *towards* the excavation; with a high head or steep slopes there is a risk of collapse of the sides. There is also the risk in open or timbered excavations of instability of the base due to upward seepage towards the pumping sump.

The essential feature of the method is a sump below the general level of the excavation at one or more corners or sides. To keep the floor of the excavation clear of standing water a small grip or ditch is cut around the bottom of the excavation, falling towards the sump. In large excavations which have to remain open over long periods, it is advantageous to pay special attention to the design of these drainage ditches. They should be sufficiently wide to keep the velocity low enough to prevent erosion. Further safeguards against erosion can be given by check weirs (boards placed across the ditch), by stone or concrete paving, or by laying open-jointed pipes surrounded by graded stone or gravel filter material. Where the ground water is present in a permeable stratum overlying a clay, with the excavation taken down into the latter material, it is preferable to have the pumping sump at the base of the permeable stratum. This procedure reduces the pumping head, and avoids softening of the clay in the base of the excavation. The drain at the base of the permeable stratum above excavation level is known as a *garland drain*. Typical details of a garland drain for (*a*) open excavation over a timbered excavation, (*b*) a wholly timbered excavation, and (*c*) in rock excavation are shown in Fig. 11.7. The greatest depth to which the water table may be lowered by the open sump method is not much more than 8 metres below the pump, depending on its type and mechanical efficiency. For greater depths of excavation it is necessary to reinstall the pump at a lower level, or to use a sinking pump or submersible deep well pump suspended by chains and progressively lowered down a timbered shaft or perforated steel tube. It is sometimes a useful procedure to sink the pumping sump for the full depth of the excavation by means of a timbered shaft with spaces between the runners or poling boards to allow the water to flow into the shaft.

Gravel filter material can be packed behind the timbers if excessive fine material is washed through. This method ensures dry working conditions for the subsequent bulk excavation, and it also provides an exploratory shaft for obtaining information on ground conditions to supplement that found from borings.

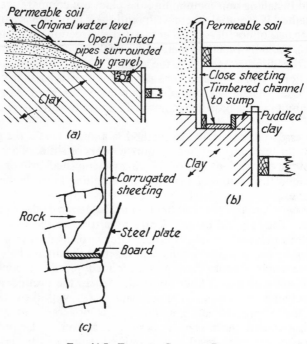

FIG. 11.7. TYPES OF GARLAND DRAIN

PUMPING PLANT

Whenever flooding of an excavation can cause damage to partly constructed works, or where pumps have been installed below ground water level, it is important to provide adequate standby pumping plant of a capacity at least 100 per cent of the steady pumping rate. It will often be found that the pumping capacity required to lower the ground water is twice the capacity required to hold it down at a steady rate of pumping. Therefore, if double the required steady rate capacity is installed, the full installation can be used in the initial draw-down period, and then half the pumps can be shut down and used as the emergency standby and for regular maintenance. If the main pumps are electrically driven, it is useful to have the standby pumps driven by diesel or steam engines in case of failure of the main electricity supply.

Types of pumps suitable for operating from open sumps are—

*Hand-lift diaphragm.* Output from 20 l/min for 30 mm suction, up to 250 l/min for 100 mm suction. Suitable for intermittent pumping in small quantities.

*Motor-driven diaphragm.* Output from 350 l/min for 75 mm suction up to 600 l/min for 100 mm suction. Can deal with sand and silt in limited quantities.

*Pneumatic sump pumps.* At 7 bar air pressure outputs range from 450 l/min against 15 m head to 900 l/min against 3 m head. Useful for intermittent pumping on sites where compressed air is available. Can deal with sand and silt in limited quantities.

*Self-priming centrifugal.* Widely used for steady pumping of fairly clean water. Smallest units can be carried by one man. Outputs range from 750 l/min for 50 mm suction to 7000 l/min for 200 mm suction. Sand and silt in water cause excessive wear on impeller for long periods of pumping, therefore desirable to have efficient filter around sump or pump suction.

*Rotary displacement (Monopump).* Can deal with considerable quantities of silt and sand. Output for 75 mm pump is 550 l/min against 6 m head.

*Sinking pumps.* Suitable for working in deep shafts or other confined spaces where pumps must be progressively lowered with falling water table. Can be vertical spindle centrifugal pump or steam-operated pulsometer type. Outputs range from 300 l/min for 50 mm suction to 4000 l/min for 150 mm suction. Can pump against 60 m head.

### Pumping from Wellpoints

The wellpoint system of ground water lowering comprises the installation of a number of filter wells, usually 1 m long, around the excavation. These are connected by vertical riser pipes to a header main at ground level which is under vacuum from a pumping unit. The water flows by gravity to the filter well and is drawn by the vacuum up to the header main and discharged through the pump. The wellpointing system has the advantage that water is drawn *away* from the excavation, thus stabilizing the sides and permitting steep slopes. Indeed, slopes of 1 in ½ (vertical to horizontal) are commonly used when wellpointing in fine sands, whereas with open-sump pumping where the water flows towards the excavation, the slopes must be cut back to 1 in 2 or 1 in 3 for stability. Thus, wellpointing gives a considerable saving in total excavation and permits working fairly confined spaces. The installation is very rapid and the equipment is reasonably simple and cheap. There is the added advantage that the water is filtered as it is removed from the ground and carries little or no soil particles with it. Thus the danger of subsidence of the surrounding ground is very much less than with open-sump pumping. One disadvantage of the system is its limited suction lift. A lowering of 5 to 5·5 m below pump level is generally regarded as a practical

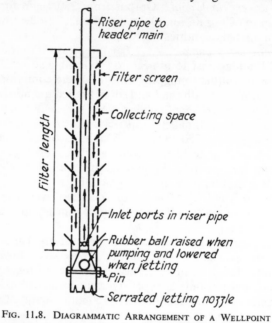

FIG. 11.8. DIAGRAMMATIC ARRANGEMENT OF A WELLPOINT

limit. Attempts at greater lowering result in excessive air being drawn into the system through joints in pipes, valves, etc., with consequent loss in pumping efficiency. For deeper excavations the wellpoints must be installed in two or more stages. Also, in ground consisting mainly of large gravel, stiff clay, or sand containing cobbles or boulders, it is impossible to jet down the wellpoints and they have to be placed in boreholes or holes formed by a "puncher" with consequent increase in installation costs.

The filter wells or wellpoints (Fig. 11.8) usually consist of a 1 m long and 60 to 75 mm diameter gauze screen surrounding a central riser pipe. Where wellpoints are required to remain in the ground for a long period, e.g. for dewatering a drydock excavation, it may be economical to use disposable plastic wellpoints. These consist of a nylon mesh screen surrounding a flexible plastic riser pipe. Water drawn through the screen falls in the space between the gauze and the outside of the riser pipe to holes drilled in the bottom of this pipe and thence to the surface. The wellpoints are installed by jetting them into the ground, when the jetting water flows freely from the serrated nozzle. Various proprietary systems concentrate the jetting water through the nozzle rather than allowing it to be dissipated through the filter.

The capacity of a single wellpoint with a 50 mm riser is about 10 l/min. Their spacing around the excavation depends on the permeability of the soil and on the time available to effect the draw-down. In fine to coarse sands or sandy gravels a spacing of 0·75 to 1 m is satisfactory. In silty sands of fairly low permeability a 1·5 m spacing will be satisfactory. In permeable coarse gravels they may need to be as close as 0·3 m centres. The normal set of wellpointing equipment comprises 50 to 60 points to a single 150 or 200 mm pump with a separate 100 mm jetting pump. The wellpoint pump has an air/water separator and a vacuum pump as well as the normal centrifugal pump.

INSTALLATION

Water at a pressure of up to 15 bar is required for jetting down wellpoints, and up to 1000 l of water are required for a single point. If a layer of clay overlies the water-bearing stratum it is often more convenient to bore through the clay by hand auger rather than to attempt jetting through it. When the wellpoint has been jetted down to the required level, the jetting water supply is cut down to a low velocity sufficient to keep the hole around the point open. Coarse sand is then fed around the annular space to form a supplementary filter around the point, and the water is then cut off. This process, known as "sanding-in" the points, is an important safeguard against drawing fine material from the ground which might clog the system or cause subsidence. A wellpoint with a gauze fine enough to screen out the finest particles would have insufficient capacity. Sanding-in also increases the effective diameter of the wellpoint and hence its output. Therefore, sanding-in should never be neglected. There may be difficulty in sanding-in a wellpoint in highly permeable gravels when the jetting water is dissipated into the surrounding ground and does not reach the surface around the riser pipe. Normally, a wellpoint does not need sanding-in in these conditions but it sometimes happens that coarse gravels are overlying sand with the wellpoints terminating in the latter. In such cases the wellpoint must be inserted in a lined borehole, the lining tubes being withdrawn after the filter sand is placed. Wellpoints act most effectively in sands and in sandy gravels of moderate but not high permeability. The draw-down is slow in silty sands but these soils can be effectively drained. There have been instances of silts and sandy silts being drained by the "vacuum process," where the upper part of the riser pipe is surrounded by clay to maintain a high vacuum surrounding the wellpoint by means of which the soil is slowly dewatered.

Wellpoints are installed in the "progressive" or "ring" systems. The progressive system is used for trench work (Fig. 11.9). The

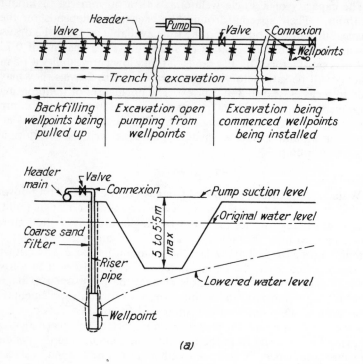

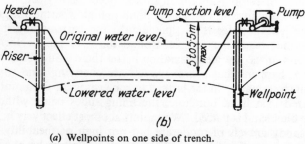

(a) Wellpoints on one side of trench.
(b) Wellpoints on both sides of wide excavation.

header is laid out along the sides of the excavation, and pumping is continuously in progress in one length as further points are jetted ahead of the pumped-down section and pulled up from the completed and backfilled lengths. For narrow excavations it is often sufficient to have the header on one side only (Fig. 11.9 (*a*)). For wide excavations or in soil containing bands of relatively impervious material, the header must be placed on both sides of the trench (Fig. 11.9 (*b*)).

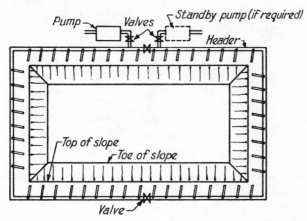

FIG. 11.10. SINGLE-STAGE WELLPOINT INSTALLATION BY THE RING SYSTEM

In the ring system (Fig. 11.10) the header main surrounds the excavation completely. This system is used for rectangular excavations such as for piers or basements.

### WELLPOINTING OF DEEP EXCAVATIONS

The limitation in the draw-down of water-level to 5 to 5·5 m below pump level has already been mentioned; if deeper excavation below standing water level is required, a second or successive stages of wellpoints must be provided. A section through a three-stage installation is shown in Fig. 11.11. There is no limit to the depth of draw-down in this way, but the overall width of excavation at ground level becomes very large. The upper stages can often be removed or reduced when the lower ones are working.

It is often possible to avoid two or more wellpoint stages by excavating down to water level before installing the pump and header. The procedure in its simplest form is shown in Fig. 11.12. A more complex case was provided in the excavation for the intake pumphouse for the Ferrybridge "B" Power Station. At this site there were two water tables, the upper one in a layer of ash and clinker fill being separated from deeper water-bearing sands and silts by a stratum of impervious soft clay. The head of water in the lower strata was 4·3 m above excavation level. The upper water table was cut off by light section sheet piling driven into the clay. Excavation

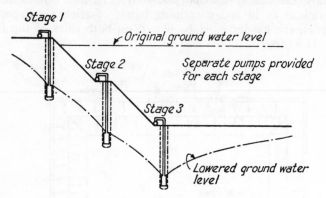

FIG. 11.11. THREE-STAGE WELLPOINT INSTALLATION

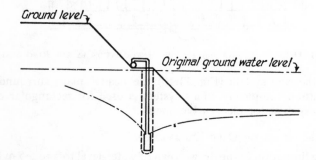

FIG. 11.12. REDUCTION IN GROUND LEVEL BEFORE INSTALLATION OF WELLPOINT

was then taken down into the clay until a level was reached at which the weight of clay just counterbalanced the head of water in the underlying silty sands and sandy gravels. Wellpoints were installed at this level and the head in the water-bearing strata was lowered before the excavation was completed. A cross-section through the site is shown in Fig. 11.13.

In the case of wellpointing used in sheet piled excavations (Fig. 11.14) it will be noted that the wellpoints are placed close to the toes of the sheet piles.

This is done to ensure lowering the water level between the sheet pile rows. It is not necessary to lower the water table down to the tops of the wellpoints. Wellpoints are provided in conjunction with the sheet piles either to prevent "boiling" of the bottom when the piles are of limited penetration, or to eliminate hydrostatic pressure on the back of a sheet pile cofferdam thus allowing lighter bracing to be used. If wellpoints are provided for the latter purpose it is essential that standby pumping plant is provided, otherwise collapse of the cofferdam would quickly follow if pumping were to cease. In very permeable soil the water can rise to its original level in a matter of

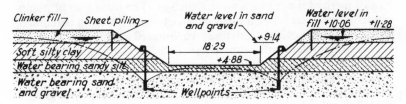

FIG. 11.13. WELLPOINT INSTALLATION FOR INTAKE PUMPHOUSE, FERRYBRIDGE "B" POWER STATION

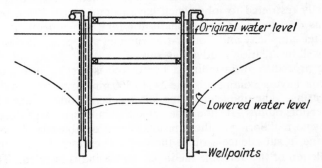

FIG. 11.14. WELLPOINTS IN SHEET PILED EXCAVATION

minutes. For this reason on completion of a dewatering scheme the wellpoints should always be shut off one by one to allow the water table to come gradually back to its normal level.

Very thin impervious layers of silt or clay are often met in water-bearing sandy soils. Layers as thin as 2 mm if continuous can be very troublesome in a dewatering scheme, causing breaks in the draw-down curve. These troubles can largely be overcome by jetting holes on the side of the wellpoints away from the excavation and filling them with coarse sand. These sand columns provide a path down which the water can seep to the wellpoints more readily than towards the sides of the excavation; thus weeping from the sides of the excavation is prevented. Difficulties can also be caused by layers of highly permeable material when the water will tend to by-pass the wellpoints. This situation can be dealt with by jetting at close intervals in a row around the excavation to cause intermingling of the various layers.

### Pumping from Wells

Pumping from wells can be undertaken by surface pumps with their suction pipes installed in bored wells. The depth of draw-down by this method is not much more than 8 m. The main uses of pumping from wells are when a great depth of water lowering is required or where an artesian head must be lowered in permeable strata at a considerable depth below excavation level. In such cases electrically powered submersible pumps are installed in deep boreholes with a rising main to the surface. Wells can be installed in a wider variation of ground conditions than is possible with wellpoints, since heavy boring plant is used to sink the wells enabling boulders, rock, or other difficult ground to be penetrated. The cost of installation of a deep well system is relatively high. Therefore, the process is generally restricted to jobs which have a long construction period such as dry docks or access shafts for long sub-aqueous tunnels, when the simplicity and trouble-free running of a properly designed deep well installation is advantageous.

The procedure in installing a bored well is first to sink a cased borehole having a diameter some 200 to 300 mm larger than the inner well casing. The diameter of the latter depends on the size of the submersible pumps. It should be noted that sinking a large-diameter well by normal boring methods results in considerable loss of ground, resulting in subsidence around the well. Therefore, large-diameter completion of the borehole the inner well casing is inserted. This is provided with a perforated screen over the length where dewatering of the soil is required and it terminates in a 3 to 5 m length of unperforated pipe to act as a sump to collect any fine material which may be drawn through the filter mesh. The perforated screen may consist of ordinary well casing with slots or holes burned through the wall and brass mesh spot-welded round the outside. A cheaper and quite effective well screen consists of slotted P.V.C. tube surrounded by a filter in the form of a nylon or terylene mesh sleeve. Slots are preferable to holes, since there is less risk of blockage from round stones. The effective screen area can be increased by welding rods longitudinally or spirally on to the casing to provide a clear space between the mesh and the casing. As an alternative to the mesh screen, purpose-made slotted casing with fine openings is marketed and is advantageous in many cases.

After the well casing is installed, graded gravel filter material is placed between it and the outer borehole casing over the length to be dewatered. The outer casing is withdrawn in stages as the filter material is placed. The remaining space above the screen is backfilled with any available material. The water in the well is then

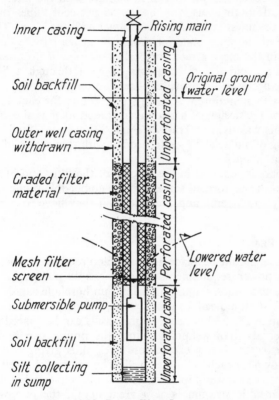

FIG. 11.15. BORED WELL INSTALLATION

"surged" by a boring tool to promote flow back and forth through the filter, and at the same time any unwanted fines which fall into the sump are cleaned out by bailer before the submersible pump is installed. This is the last operation before putting the well into commission. The completed installation is shown in Fig. 11.15.

DESIGN OF FILTER

The grading of the filter material is determined from the average grading of the soil to be dewatered. Sieve analyses are made on a number of samples, and an average grading curve is drawn, or in the case of a variably graded soil, the grading curves of the coarsest and finest layers are drawn. Then by Terzaghi's rules the filter material should be selected so that its grain-size at the 15 per cent "finer than" size (D.15) should be at least four times as large as the 15 per cent size of the coarsest layer of soil in contact with the filter, and not more than four times as large as the 85 per cent "finer than" size (D.85) of the finest layer of soil in contact with the filter. The maximum size of the filter material should be at least twice that of the openings in the mesh screen (or perforated pipe if no mesh is provided). To avoid too great a loss of head through a filter it is frequently necessary to provide more than one layer of graded filter material with a minimum thickness of 150 mm for each layer. An example of the design of a two-layer graded filter is shown in Fig. 11.16. This was used at Trafford Park, Manchester, for bored well dewatering of a glacial clay interbedded with thin seams of a water-bearing fine sand.

Great care is required in the placing of the filter and in avoiding damage to the perforated screen, since submersible pumps are very susceptible to clogging and breakdown if they have to pump dirty water.

PUMPING PLANT

Reference should be made to manufacturers' catalogues for the sizes and power requirements of submersible pumps for various duties. As examples, a pump in a 150 mm borehole can deliver 350 l/min against 30 m head, or a pump in a 350 mm borehole can raise 7 500 l/min against 30 m head. Bored wells can be spaced at much wider intervals than wellpoints, since the pumps can be installed at greater depths below excavation level, thus giving a wide area of draw-down for each individual well. The depth of the well depends on the depth to a lower impermeable stratum. Thus, in Fig. 11.17 (*a*), the impermeable stratum is at a great depth, the pumps can be placed well below excavation level, and a wide spacing can be adopted. In Fig. 11.17 (*b*), the impermeable stratum is at a shallow depth below excavation level and there is no point in placing the filter screen below the permeable stratum. This limits the depth of draw-down, hence a close spacing must be adopted. The shape of the draw-down curve depends on the permeability of the soil. For a coarse sandy gravel the draw-down curve is flat (Fig. 11.18 (*a*)), and the free water surface is drawn well down towards the pumping level in the borehole, so a wide spacing is possible (though the pumping rate is correspondingly high). In the case of a soil of fairly low permeability, say a silty sand, the free water surface is not drawn

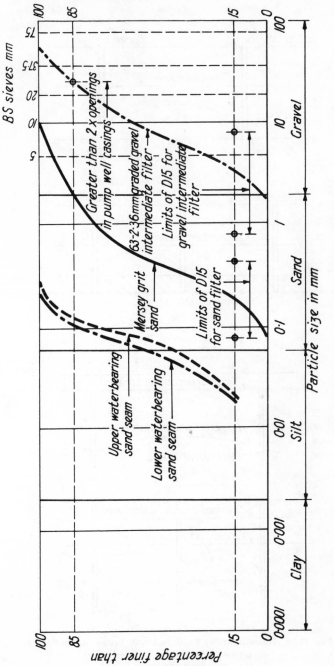

FIG. 11.16. EXAMPLE OF DESIGN OF 2-LAYER GRADED FILTER

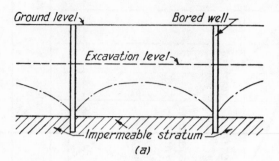

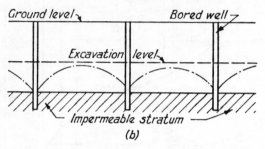

FIG. 11.17. SPACING OF BORED WELLS

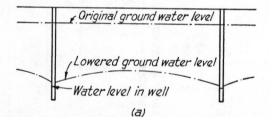

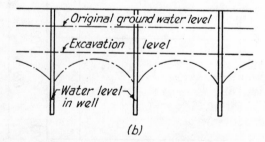

FIG. 11.18. DRAW-DOWN IN PERMEABLE AND SEMI-PERMEABLE SOILS
(a) Draw-down in sandy gravel.
(b) Draw-down in silty sand.

down to the pumping level in the well necessitating a closer spacing of wells, but with a lower output per well (Fig. 11.18 (*b*)).

The spacing of the wells should not be so wide that shutting an individual well down for repairs to the pump will cause the water level to rise above excavation level. In fact, the installation should be designed so that individual wells can be shut down as required for cleaning out and maintenance of the pumps. Where the electric power is supplied from the mains, standby diesel or steam-powered generators should be provided. If the installation has its own

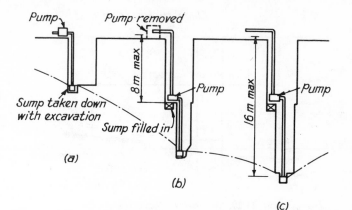

Fig. 11.19. Stages in Sinking Pumping Well with Suction Lift Lumps

(*a*) First-stage well partly sunk.
(*b*) Second-stage well partly sunk.
(*c*) Completed deep well.

generating plant there should be ample standby capacity for the generators and prime movers. This standby capacity need not be 100 per cent of the maximum power requirements. As already mentioned in the case of pumping from open sumps, maximum power is only required during the time of lowering the water from its standing level to the fully drawn-down state. Thereafter the power required is considerably less and might be as little as 50 per cent of the maximum.

Ordinary centrifugal pumps limited to about 8 m suction lift can be used for deep well pumping if the wells are sunk in stages and the pumps re-installed at each stage (Fig. 11.19). This method  has certain advantages in that ordinary pumps are cheaper in the first cost, they give less trouble in operation, and are readily accessible for maintenance. However, the cost of sinking the wells is greater since they must necessarily be of much larger plan area.

## Pumping from Horizontal Wells

This process is applicable only in the special circumstances where wellpointing or bored well water lowering cannot be used. Typical of these conditions is where a deep excavation is to be sunk through heavily water-bearing ground and founded on or just within an impermeable stratum (Fig. 11.20). Because of the great depth or possible obstructions sheet piling cannot be driven to give a cut-off in the impermeable layer. Bored wells cannot lower the ground water completely down to the rock stratum because of the shape of the

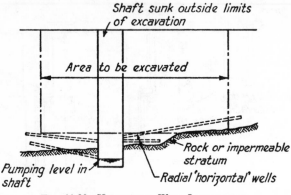

FIG. 11.20. HORIZONTAL WELL INSTALLATION

draw-down curve. The procedure is then to sink a lined shaft by boring methods into the clay layer. The shaft is large enough to allow men to go down and install horizontal wells which are jacked or jetted out into the ground. These wells consist of an outer and inner casing, the space between them being filled with a gravel filter. They are provided with valves where they pass through the wall of the shaft, to allow them to be shut off until all are installed. The valves are then opened and pumping takes place from the shaft using a sinking pump or submersible pump.

## Ground Dewatering by Electro-Osmosis

The various methods of ground dewatering described in the previous pages are used mainly in gravels and sands. Soils of finer particle-size, i.e. silts and clays, are more troublesome to drain because capillary forces acting on the pore water prevent its flowing freely under gravity to a filter well or sump. The vacuum process of wellpointing in silts has already been mentioned, but if this process is ineffective and if, for some reason or another, sheet piling cannot be used then electro-osmosis is a possible expedient and may well prove to be less expensive than the last resort of freezing the ground. In the electro-osmosis system direct current is made to flow from anodes which are steel rods driven down into the soil, to filter wells forming cathodes. The positively charged particles of water flow through the pores in the soil and collect at the cathodes where they are pumped to the surface. Casagrande[11.3] has shown that the equation of flow is similar to Darcy's law, the rate of flow being dependent on the porosity of the soil and the electrical potential. In the few recorded instances of the process a current of 100 amps has been used, the power requirements being some 0·5 to 1·3 kw per cubic metre of soil dewatered for large excavations and as much as 13 kw per cubic metre for small excavations.

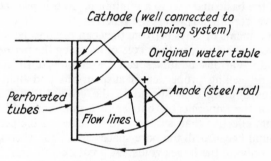

FIG. 11.21. ELECTRO-OSMOSIS INSTALLATION

A typical layout of an installation is shown in Fig. 11.21. The anodes are placed nearest to the excavation causing the ground water to flow away from the slopes, which effectively stabilizes them and permits steep slopes even in soft water-bearing silts. The anodes corrode and require constant replacing but the cathodes remain serviceable for long periods. The process was developed in Germany during the 1939–45 war, and was used to stabilize a railway cutting at Salzgitter and in the construction of U-boat pens and other works at Trondhjem.[11.3] So far it has been employed to remedy a difficult situation where other methods have failed rather than as a construction process in its own right. The main drawback is its high installation and initial running costs, but the power consumption, and hence running costs, decrease considerably after the ground is stabilized.

### Reduction or Elimination of Ground Water Flow by Grouting

In ground where the permeability is so high that wellpointing or bored wells need a very high pumping capacity, or in water-bearing rock formations where wellpointing cannot be used and bored wells are very costly, other expedients must be sought to control the ground water. One method is to inject fine suspensions or fluids into the pore spaces, fissures or cavities in the soil or rock, so reducing their permeability. The type of injection material is governed by the particle size distribution of the soil or the fineness of fissuring in rock strata. Reference to Fig. 11.6 (p. 682) will give a guide to the suitability of various injection processes for soils. Another guide for the suitability of *suspension* grouts is given by the "groutability ratio." Thus for a soil to accept a suspension grout the ratio of the $D_{15}$ size of the soil to the $D_{85}$ size of the grout must be greater than 11 to 25 for cement grouts and greater than 5 to 15 for clay grouts.

Grouting is a fairly costly process. The aim should be to keep the volume of the basic material to a minimum. In this respect chemical grouts have certain advantages. Whereas they cost considerably more than cements or clays per ton, they can be considerably diluted and still work effectively in their role of reducing the permeability of the ground. Various additives can be employed to control the viscosity and gelling properties of suspensions and fluid chemical grouts, thus limiting their spread in the ground and keeping the thickness of the impermeable barrier to a minimum. Fluid grouts can be more effective than suspensions in reducing the permeability of the ground because all the pore spaces are filled, whereas suspensions may only fill the larger voids. A great deal of useful information on the principles and practices of grouting are included in the *Proceedings of the Symposium on Grouts and Drilling Muds in Engineering Practice*[10.9b] and in Code of Practice *CP 2004*.

Care is needed in the adoption of injection processes, especially when working close to existing underground structures, since large quantities of materials injected into the ground under pressure must inevitably cause some displacement. The injected material tends to travel along the more permeable layers or along planes of weakness, often emerging at a considerable distance from the point of injection. Thus, a watch must be kept on sewers or cellars if any are existing in the vicinity of the work, and continuous records must be kept of surface levels.

CEMENT GROUTING

Cement is suitable for injection where strengthening is required in addition to a reduction in the permeability of soil or rock strata. It is necessary for soil to have a very coarse grading (*see* Fig. 11.6) to permit effective grouting with cement. The process is largely ineffective in sands, except for its consolidating or compacting effect when injected at close intervals. In coarse materials or rocks the excavation is surrounded by a "grout-curtain" consisting of two rows of primary injection holes at 2·5 to 5 m centres in both directions, with secondary holes (and possibly tertiary holes) between them (Fig. 11.22).

Cement grouting was used for the foundation excavations for extensions to the North Point Generating Station, Hong Kong. This site was on ground which had been reclaimed by tipping granite-rubble sea walls and filling up the ground behind them with sand and clay. A series of such reclamations had been made on the generating station site, which was crossed by three buried rubble

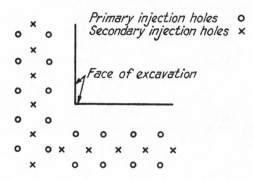

FIG. 11.22. LAYOUT PLAN OF GROUT INJECTION HOLES TO FORM "GROUT CURTAIN" AROUND EXCAVATION

walls. These walls intersected at right angles a wharf wall of granite masonry built on a rubble mound (Fig. 11.23). It was necessary to sink a number of shafts through two of the buried walls to enable piles to be driven for the foundations of the generating station buildings and plant. It was clearly impossible to drive piles through the rubble, which included 5-tonne boulders. It was equally impossible to drive sheet piles around the shaft excavations to exclude the ground water. Accordingly, it was decided to excavate in timbered shafts. The site investigation showed that ground water in the rubble mounds had a connexion to the sea in the harbour through the wharf wall. Therefore, in order to avoid pumping large quantities of water from the shafts, a grout curtain was formed across the two buried rubble walls close to their intersection with the wharf wall. A single row of 9 m deep holes was drilled at 3·7 m centres to form each curtain. The first holes drilled took about 30 tonne of cement but the quantities for succeeding holes became less, and in all, over 150 tonne of cement were used for the two grout curtains. To economize in cement a sanded grout was used in the proportions of three parts of cement to one part of sand. The effectiveness of the grout curtain can be judged from the fact that only two 150 mm pumps were needed to dewater the shafts nearest the harbour, with a single 150 mm pump for the shafts further away. A total of twenty-two shafts was excavated to a maximum depth of 8·5 m.

## CLAY GROUTING

Injections of bitumen emulsion or slurries of clay or bentonite, sometimes with added chemicals to aid dispersion and suspension of these materials, have been used in ground where the grading is too

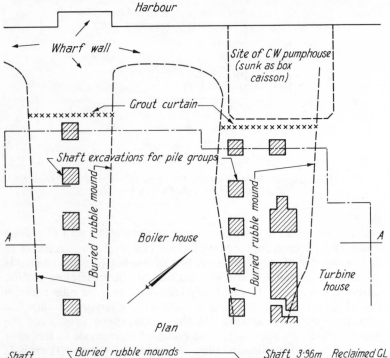

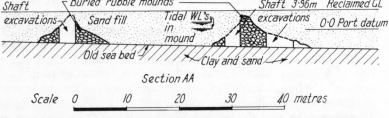

FIG. 11.23. GROUTING OPERATIONS FOR SHAFT EXCAVATIONS, NORTH POINT GENERATING STATION, HONG KONG

fine for cement grouting, and in gravels where reduction in permeability is required without the need for any strengthening of the ground. Grouting with a slurry of chemically-treated bentonite clay has been used extensively for creating impermeable cut-offs in alluvial strata beneath dam foundations, and to create impermeable barriers around excavations in water-bearing alluvial strata. The principle of the method is to use bentonite clay in combination with Portland cement, soluble silicates, and other agents in differing proportions to produce a grout, the characteristics of which can be varied to suit the permeability of the ground into which it is injected. The larger voids are first filled with clay/cement grout followed by clay/ chemical grouting to fill the spaces in the finer materials.

Its use in the construction of the Dartford–Purfleet vehicular tunnel has been described by Kell.[11.4] The 8·58 m internal diameter cast-iron lined tunnel was driven through silt and peat, Thames gravel, and then into chalk. Where the tunnel was driven through chalk the ground was treated by grouting with cement from a 3·66 m diameter pilot tunnel. The cement injection holes were drilled 1·5 m beyond the lining to seal fissures and broken rock in the zone of weathered chalk immediately below the Thames gravel.

Where the upper part of the tunnel face was in gravel, the Soletanche process was used to form a 6 m wide wall of treated ground along both sides of the tunnel. This wall formed a seal between the silt above and the chalk below and thus reduced the quantity of compressed air needed for driving the tunnel through the gravel stratum, with a consequent reduced risk of "blows." Where the gravel ran out above the face of the tunnel the treated zones were merged to form a continuous block of grouted ground extending to a point where the bottom of the gravel stratum was 1·5 m above the tunnel. The procedure adopted is shown in Fig. 11.24. The injection points were at 3 m centres in both directions, in two double rows. On the Essex shore the treated ground extended under the river, and the injection holes were sunk from timber piled stagings one of which was built 120 m out from high water mark.

The injection holes were made by first sinking a 75 mm diameter cased borehole by normal methods to the full depth of the gravel. A 38 mm diameter sleeved injection tube was inserted in the borehole and the annular space was filled with a plastic grout designed to be fluid but thick enough to prevent its permeating the gravel when the 75 mm borehole casing was withdrawn. The injection tube* (Fig. 11.25) was provided with groups of radial perforations at 300 mm intervals, each perforated section being covered by a flexible rubber sleeve fitting closely around the tube. Then a 25 mm diameter inner

* Commonly known as the tube-à-manchette.

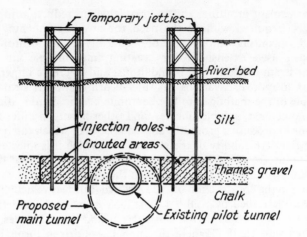

FIG. 11.24. CLAY INJECTIONS FOR DARTFORD–PURFLEET TUNNEL (KELL[11.4])

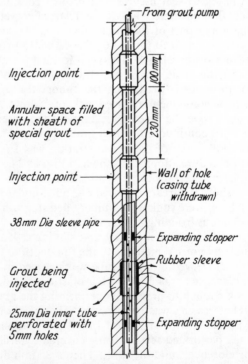

FIG. 11.25. THE SOLETANCHE GROUTING TUBE (TUBE-À-MANCHETTE)

tube was lowered down the injection tube. This inner tube had a closed end but the lower part was perforated, with expanding rubber packer rings above and below the perforated section. To grout the ground at a particular level the perforated section of the inner tube was raised or lowered to bring it opposite a sleeved perforated section of the injection tube. Grout was then pumped down the inner tube lifting the rubber sleeve and rupturing the plastic grout to penetrate into the surrounding ground. Normally, with this method grouting starts at the bottom and proceeds upwards, but the principle of the sleeved tube enables grouting to be made at selected locations, the grout mixtures being varied to suit the grading of the soil at the particular level.

CHEMICAL CONSOLIDATION

The chemical injection process or chemical consolidation is applicable to sandy gravels, and sands of all but the finest gradings (*see* Fig. 11.6). The chemical most commonly used is sodium silicate which in conjunction with other chemicals forms a fairly hard and insoluble "silica-gel." In the "two-shot" process, pipes are driven into the ground about 0·5 m apart and calcium chloride is injected down one and sodium silicate down the other as the pipes are slowly withdrawn in stages. Alternatively, one chemical can be injected as the pipe is driven down followed by the other chemical as it is withdrawn.

The "two-shot" method has been largely superseded by the "one-shot" technique in which all chemicals are mixed together immediately before injecting them. The grout is formulated so that the gel formation is delayed for a sufficient time to allow for complete penetration of the ground. Many other chemical processes based on the "one-shot" principle have been developed with the aim of obtaining a very low viscosity at the time of injection with only a slow increase in viscosity until gelation occurs, thus ensuring maximum penetration. The chemicals include acrylic polymers, resins and lignins.

A typical example of the use of chemical consolidation has been given by Harding.[11.5] On a site in London it was necessary to sink a shaft through 8·5 m of sand and gravel into London Clay. Because of the site conditions, pumping from an open excavation was prohibited, and for the same reason the vibrations from driving sheet piling would have been detrimental. It was also important to avoid a "blow" into the excavation through possible gaps between sheet piles resulting from "declutching" under hard driving. An outer ring of injection pipes was first driven around the 3·0 m diameter shaft, followed by an inner ring (Fig. 11.26). The inner injection pipes were inclined as necessary to clear the spread of chemicals from the first stage injection, caused by an intermediate clay layer. Shaft sinking in rings of cast-iron segments was then undertaken without difficulty. When the London Clay was reached the quantity of water seeping from the treated gravel was only 180 l/min under

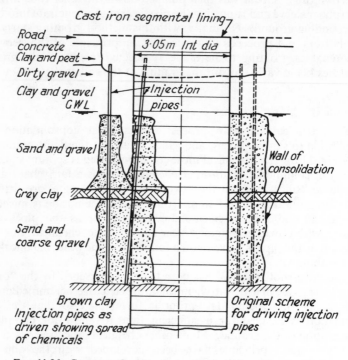

FIG. 11.26. CHEMICAL CONSOLIDATION AROUND 10-FT DIAMETER SHAFT (HARDING[11.5])

5·5 m head, compared with the 45 40 l/min which would have had to be pumped without chemical consolidation.

Complete cut-off of water by chemical consolidation or clay injection can only be obtained by repeated injections at close-spacing over a considerable width of treated ground. The cost of such work is rarely justifiable and in most practical cases a partial cut-off, say 80 to 95 per cent, is all that is required. It must be remembered that permeable water-bearing soils contain some 30 to 40 per cent void spaces, which must be filled with expensive chemicals. Thus, considering the volume of ground to be treated in a grout curtain some 2 to 2·5 m thick, the process is necessarily an expensive one, costing some two to five times more than grouting with cement. Clay grouting is cheaper than cement injections, particularly if locally-excavated clay can be used. At the other end of the scale, resin and acrylic polymer grouting may cost 10 to 20 times as much as cement grouting per cubic metre of ground treated.

## Excavation under Compressed Air

The use of compressed air for excluding water from foundation excavations in caissons and shafts has been described in Chapter 6.

## The Freezing Process

Because of its high cost, freezing of the ground to prevent inflow of water into excavations is usually regarded as a last resort when all other expedients have failed or are impracticable for one reason or another. The high cost of the freezing method is due to the necessity of sinking a large number of boreholes at close spacing around the excavation. The boreholes must be drilled to a high order of accuracy in verticality to avoid the risk of a gap in the enclosure of frozen ground, and the refrigeration plant is costly to install and maintain. The system also has the drawback that it takes some six months to drill the holes, install the plant, and freeze the ground; also, freezing certain types of ground causes severe heaving. There are difficulties in operating compressed-air tools in the low temperatures prevailing in the excavation, and there are also difficulties in concreting the permanent work. Nevertheless, in some situations freezing is the only practicable method of dealing with ground water, such as in very deep shaft excavations where the pressure of water is too high to allow men to work in compressed air and where fissures in rock are too fine for injection.

Basically, the system involves sinking a ring or rectangle of boreholes at 1 to 1·5 m centres around the excavation. The boreholes are lined with 100 to 150 mm steel tubing with closed bottoms, and inner tubing of 38 to 75 mm diameter open at the bottom is then inserted. The tops of the inner tubes are connected to a ring main carrying chilled brine from the refrigeration plant. The brine used to freeze the ground, is pumped down the inner tubes and rises up the annular space between them and the outer casing; it then returns to the refrigeration plant via the return ring main. Usually it takes some two to four months to freeze the ground. A borehole lined with perforated pipes is drilled near the centre of the treated area to act as a tell-tale. As the ice wall forms and closes up it compresses the ground water within the wall. When the water rises up the tell-tale pipe and overflows at ground level, the ice wall has closed and excavation can commence.

It is most important when using the freezing process to ensure that the ice wall is continuous before commencing excavation. Difficulties which were encountered when excavating in an incomplete ice wall have been described by Ellis and McConnell.[11.6] A number of examples of its use in civil engineering works have been given by Mussche and Waddington.[11.7]

The freezing process was employed in an unusual way in the construction of the Stockholm Underground Railway in 1954–55. Part of the railway constructed in cut and cover ran close to existing buildings, and it was rightly feared that the yielding (which normally occurs in excavating sheet piled trenches no matter how carefullly they are timbered) might cause settlement of the adjacent ground surface and buildings. It was therefore decided to form a solid plug of frozen ground between the double sheet pile walls on both sides of the excavation to prevent inward yielding as the ground was excavated between the sheet pile rows.

The soil conditions consisted of a 3·5 to 7·5 m thick surface layer of filling followed by 5 to 10 m of soft clay (shear strength 10 to 30 $kN/m^2$), then 1 to 3 m of fine sand overlying granite bedrock. It was desired to avoid dangerous frost expansion of the upper soft clay stratum, so the freezing units were only 1·8 m long and were lowered down the outer casing with the object of maintaining an insulating air gap between the upper part of the casing and the flow and return pipes of the chilled brine.

The freezing wells (Fig. 11.27) were installed at 0·75 m centres down the bosoms of the sheet piles on both sides of the double wall. The wells were first installed in the inside of the trench but later they were put down outside.

The freezing period was four to five weeks, after which excavation was taken down between the sheet piles in lengths of 10 m between sheet pile bulkheads, and bracing frames were set at the positions shown in Fig. 11.28 (*a*). The next step was to cast a 1 to 1·5 m thick concrete beam between the sheet piles at the position previously occupied by the plug of frozen ground. This beam was anchored to bedrock by steel bars grouted into holes drilled in the rock (Fig. 11.28 (*b*)). Then the inner rows of sheet piles were withdrawn and the dumpling removed, after placement of a top bracing frame (Fig. 11.28 (*c*)). A lower frame suspended from the top frame was installed after the dumpling had been taken out to a depth of 9 m, and the excavation was completed (Fig. 11.28 (*d*)).

Considerable savings in time of freezing can be achieved by using liquid nitrogen fed directly into pipes driven into the ground. Liquid nitrogen is expensive but the installation costs may be considerably lower than those of the brine method, and its use may therefore be more economical than brine installation where a short-term expedient is required to overcome a localized patch of bad ground. It was used for this purpose in the construction of working shafts for a watertunnel.[11.8]

### The Settlement of Ground Adjacent to Excavations Caused by Ground Water Lowering

The problems of settlement of the ground surface adjacent to excavations due to piping of soil beneath sheet piling, erosion from

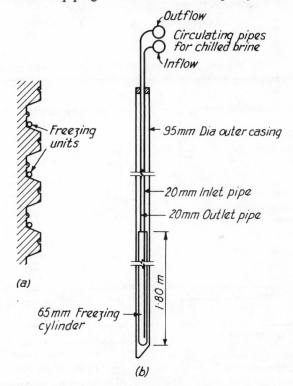

Fig. 11.27. Arrangement of Freezing Units for Stockholm Underground Railway

sloping sides of excavations, and infiltration of fines into unscreened pumping wells has been mentioned in the preceding pages. However, there is one cause of ground settlement which is liable to occur in some types of soil no matter how carefully the ground water lowering is executed. This type of settlement is due to an increase in density of the soil as a result of a general lowering of the water table. Thus, at a point $A$ near an excavation where the ground water is being lowered by pumping from a sump (Fig. 11.29 (*a*)) or at $B$ adjacent to a wellpoint system (Fig. 11.29 (*b*)), the effective overburden pressure before lowering the ground water table is given by

$$p_e = \gamma_{sub}H + \gamma_{sat}h$$

and after ground water lowering $p_e$ becomes

$$p'_e = \gamma_{sat}(H + h)$$

which is an increase in pressure of $\gamma_{sat}H - \gamma_{sub}H$

$$= (\gamma_{sub} + \gamma_w)H - \gamma_{sub}H$$
$$= \gamma_w H$$

In other words, the effective pressure at $A$ or $B$ is increased by an amount equivalent to the head of water which existed above these

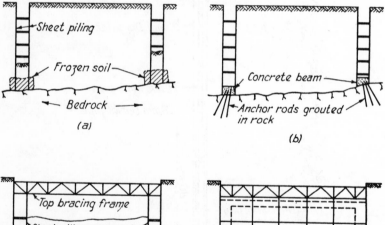

(a)

(b)

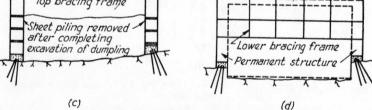

(c)

(d)

Fig. 11.28.  Excavating for Stockholm Underground Railway
(*a*) Excavation in sheet piled trenches.
(*b*) Anchoring bottom of sheet piles.
(*c*) Removal of dumpling.
(*d*) Completion of excavation.

levels before dewatering. If compressible clay or peat layers exist above the water-bearing layer the increase in their effective weight causes them to consolidate, with accompanying settlement of the ground surface. Similarly, the increase in effective pressure on compressible strata below the lowered water table will also cause consolidation of these strata with corresponding settlement at ground level.

Although the effects are severe in soft clays and peats, appreciable settlement can occur in sands, especially if they are loose and if the lowered water table is allowed to fluctuate. Little or no trouble need be feared with dense sands and gravels, provided that the ground water lowering system has efficient filters to prevent loss of fines from the soil. Consideration must be given to the possibility of the

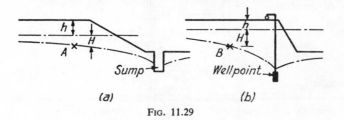

(a)                    (b)

Fig. 11.29

settlement of piled foundations if they are bearing on compressible materials, when the lowering of the water table will cause negative skin friction or drag-down on the piles. If the increase in load on the piles is small, and if they are toed into stiff or hard clay, the resulting settlement may well be negligible. However, if the increase in load is sufficient to exceed their carrying capacity, heavy settlement is inevitable.

### RECHARGING WELLS

Precautions against such effects can be taken by a system of "recharging wells," i.e. by pumping water into the ground near the excavation to keep up the water table. This procedure was adopted for the basement excavation for the Tower Latino Americana in Mexico City.[11.9] Lowering of the deep water table in the city has caused heavy settlements of the lacustrine volcanic clays, and it was feared that a steep draw-down in the shallow water-bearing strata for the foundation excavations would cause serious settlement of neighbouring streets and buildings. The excavation, which was taken down almost to the top of the first water-bearing sand layer (about 2·5 m below ground level), was surrounded with tongued and grooved timber sheet piling (Wakefield piling) and four 35 m deep pump

wells were installed. The water level was then lowered to just below
the final excavation level of 12 m and the water was discharged into
an "absorption" ditch at ground level to maintain the existing ground
water conditions in the shallow deposits. It was also discharged into

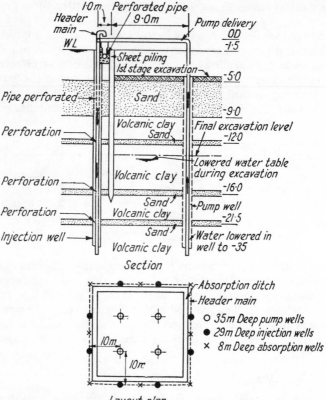

FIG. 11.30. PUMPING AND RECHARGE SYSTEM FOR BASEMENT EXCAVATION,
MEXICO CITY (ZEEVAERT[11.9])

injection or recharging wells to maintain the existing head in the
lower pervious layers (Fig. 11.30). These wells consisted of 75 mm
pipes perforated at 12, 16, 21, and 28 m where they passed through
the previous layers and were surrounded by a 90 mm thick sand filter.

The recharging process prevented settlement of adjacent structures,
and, at the same time, the increase in effective pressure on the clay
layer below basement level due to the reduction in the water table
compensated for the decrease in overburden pressure. Thus, no

swelling of the basement excavation occurred. The recharging process is standard practice in Mexico City.

Recharging wells were also used for the basement excavations for five blocks of flats at Coney Island, New York.[11.10] It was necessary to construct these fourteen-storey buildings on 4·9 m deep buoyancy raft foundations because of the risk of excessive settlement in underlying layers of compressible organic clay. Excavation for the basements involved lowering the ground water table by more than 3 m and it was decided that wellpointing methods were suitable. However, a general lowering of the water table over the whole area of the flats was accompanied by the risk of settlement of adjacent buildings

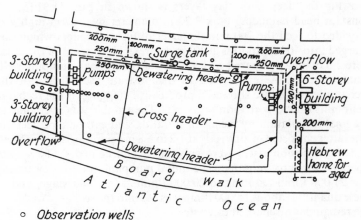

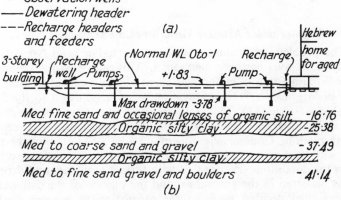

FIG. 11.31. DEWATERING ARRANGEMENTS FOR BASEMENT EXCAVATIONS AT CONEY ISLAND, NEW YORK (PARSONS, HEYMAN, AND WERBLIN[11.10])

(a) Layout of pumping and recharge headers.
(b) Section through site.

including six-storey flats. A lowering of 2·5 or 2·75 m below these buildings was anticipated. Accordingly, a system of recharging wells was adopted by which it was possible, by careful balancing of the flow between the pumping wellpoints and the recharge wells, to maintain the water level below the existing buildings close to its natural level which fluctuated under the tidal influence of the nearby Atlantic Ocean. This careful balancing was very necessary, since an excess of pumping over recharging would have resulted in a draw-down beneath the buildings, and the reverse would have given "quick" conditions beneath the building foundations with risk of disastrous settlement. The layout of the pumping and recharging wellpoints is shown in Fig. 11.31, and a section through the site showing the deep silty clay layers is shown in Fig. 11.31 (*b*). A constant head balancing tank 3·20 m diameter by 7·62 m high was provided to feed the 200 mm diameter diffusion headers which discharged into 400 wellpoints at 1·2 m centres. The screens of the latter were 2·5 m long compared with the normal 0·9 m long pumping wellpoint screens. A test section to demonstrate the efficacy of the recharging procedure showed a progressive clogging of the recharge wellpoints due to corrosion products. The trouble was overcome in the final installation by means of filtration and cathodic protection. The latter consisted of zinc rods at 1·2 to 1·8 m centres in the pipe lines, and the diffusion risers were galvanized and coated. The system operated for three months. The initial pumping rate for dewatering was 27 000 l/min reducing to 20 000 l/min at the later stage, and of these quantities about 15 000 l/min was fed into the recharge wells and the remainder discharged to waste.

### Ground Water under Artesian Head beneath Excavations

The problem of ground water under artesian head beneath an impervious layer has been mentioned. This caused partial failure of a cofferdam for a pumping station at Cowes Generating Station, Isle of Wight.[11.11] When excavation was almost down to the final level of −6·63 m O.D. (Fig. 11.32), the floor rose 100 to 150 mm in one corner and a crack opened up across this corner with water seeping up through it. Counterweighting of a 3·5 by 3·5 m area was carried out with steel plates and 6 tonne of kentledge, but over the next two days the conditions deteriorated with further cracking, and depressions occurred in the ground around the outside of the cofferdam. It was then decided to flood the excavation to prevent further deterioration. Subsequent borings showed a 1·2 to 1·8 m thick layer of fine sand beneath the clay at excavation level. This sand layer was charged with fresh water under a 10 m head. The artesian water had lifted the clay, opening up fissures through which water flowed, thus softening the clay and allowing inward yielding of the sheet piling.

The foundations were completed by casting the foundation slab under water and anchoring it to a lower stratum of bedrock by prestressing wires located inside steel box piles.

Similar problems, occurred in the intake pumphouse of Ferry-bridge "B" Power Station, but these were foreseen and the artesian head in the underlying permeable layer was lowered by wellpointing

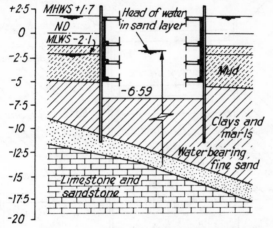

FIG. 11.32. GROUND CONDITIONS AT COWES GENERATING STATION (COATES AND SLADE[11.11])

as described on page 689. However, unforeseen trouble did occur in sheet piled excavations for the circulating water discharge culverts on the same site. They were excavated to a lesser depth than the intake pumphouse and it was thought that the weight of the 1·5 to 1·8 m layer of soft clay overlying the permeable layer, together with the adhesion of the clay to the sheet piles, was more than sufficient to counter-balance the 4·6 m head of water in the underlying water-bearing strata (Fig. 11.33). This proved to be the case but trouble was experienced at one location where sheet piles forming a bulkhead across the trench were withdrawn to allow the base slab of the culvert to be placed. Water boiled strongly up the holes left by the sheet piles in the clay. The difficulty was overcome by excavating ditches on each side of the trench bottom and these led the water to a pumping sump.

RELIEF WELLS

Ward[11.12] has described the use of simple relief wells to overcome the problem of artesian water below impervious layers. These were used for sewer construction at Millbrook, Southampton, where extensive heaving of the trench bottom and partly constructed sewer took place due to water under artesian head in laminated sands and silty clays. The relief wells took the form of hand auger boreholes filled with gravel and terminating in a layer of coarse gravel at trench bottom level. Artesian water flowing up these wells escaped through

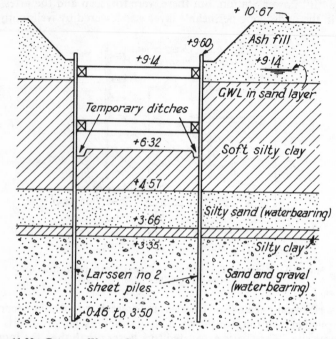

FIG. 11.33. GROUND WATER CONDITIONS AT FERRYBRIDGE "B" POWER STATION

the coarse gravel layer to a pumping sump. The flow was maintained through this layer by casting the concrete base slab for the sewer on building paper laid over a blinding of ashes on the coarse gravel.

It should be noted that relief wells cannot be used where the artesian head of water in the underlying permeable layers is such that flow up the wells causes erosion of the soil immediately beneath and surrounding the wells.

### The Use of Geotechnical Processes for Increasing Allowable Bearing Pressures

As well as their use in aiding excavation in water-bearing ground, the various injection processes can be used to increase the bearing capacity of the ground, thus permitting a reduction in the area of foundations or preventing excessive settlement. Because of the cost of these types of ground treatment they are not normally used, since it is usually much cheaper to increase the size of foundations or to use bearing piles. However, there are circumstances where it may be expedient to adopt such methods, for example where the area available for foundations is limited by the presence of existing structures, or where piling cannot be adopted because of risks of settlement due to vibrations or loss of ground.

Cement injections are likely to be the cheapest process if the ground is sufficiently permeable. Otherwise, chemicals can be injected. Such processes are, of course, inapplicable in fine-grained soils such as silts or clays.

Cement or chemical injections are a valuable construction expedient in underpinning, and their uses in this connexion will be described in the following chapter.

## Deep Vibration

Deep vibration can be used to improve the bearing capacity and reduce the compressibility of loose granular materials.

In Britain the method has been used to obtain a degree of uniformity in the density of existing materials, thus enabling strip foundations to be used for buildings instead of the more costly raft or piled foundations. For example, fill material resulting from site clearance of old houses consists of brick rubble, broken concrete, timber, tiles, paving materials, soil and other miscellaneous materials. Usually, little attention is paid to uniform compaction of such materials when clearing and levelling a site scheduled for urban re-development. However, by means of close-spaced insertions of a heavy high-frequency vibrating unit along the line of the proposed foundations, the materials are induced to attain a closer state of packing and voids formed by arching of the fill are broken down. Additional granular material is fed into the depression formed around the vibrator. By means of repeated insertions and withdrawals of the unit the granular material is compacted into any remaining voids, thus forming a strip of dense granular fill upon which the new foundations can be constructed without risk of appreciable differential settlement.

Two principal methods are used for deep compaction. In the vibroflotation process a heavy vibratory unit (Fig. 11.34) is jetted down into the soil (Fig. 11.35 (a)). On reaching the desired depth, the 22 kW rotating vibrating machine within the unit is set in motion and the direction of jetting is reversed to carry the soil particles downwards. The vibrator which has an amplitude of 20 mm compacts the soil to a radius of about 1·2 to 1·5 m around the unit and sand is shovelled in to fill the cone-shaped depression which appears at the surface (Fig. 11.35 (*b*)). The unit is withdrawn in 0·25 m stages, vibration being applied at each stage and ground surface made up as required. The unit is put down again about 2 or 2·5 m away and the

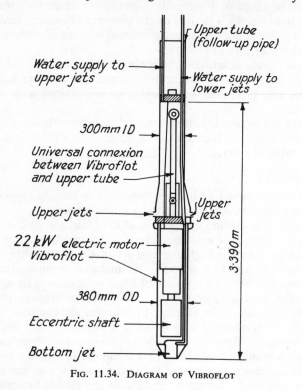

*Water supply to upper jets*

*Upper tube (follow-up pipe)*

*Water supply to lower jets*

*300mm ID*

*Universal connexion between Vibroflot and upper tube*

*Upper jets*

*Upper jets*

*22 kW electric motor*
*Vibroflot*

*3·390 m*

*380mm OD*

*Eccentric shaft*

*Bottom jet*

FIG. 11.34. DIAGRAM OF VIBROFLOT

process repeated until the whole area to be treated is covered by overlapping cylinders of compacted soil. The units can be jetted to a depth of about 10 m.

The vibroflot is most effective in clean sands or gravels or granular fills, but it can operate in silty or clayey sands containing up to 25 per cent of silt or 5 per cent of clay.

In the vibro-replacement process the vibratory unit consists of a large vibrating tube which relies on dead weight combined with high-frequency vibration to obtain the desired penetration. No water is used, otherwise the procedure is generally similar to vibroflotation.

Either process can be used to introduce strengthening materials into soft silts or clays to enable them to carry increased foundation loads. The vibratory units are used to form columns of clean graded stone or blastfurnace slag at a close spacing over the foundation area. The stone columns act in several ways. To some extent they act as bearing piles and also form zones of granular material having a higher shear strength than the surrounding soil, thus increasing the

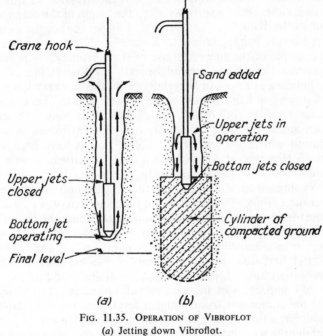

Crane hook —

Sand added

Upper jets in operation

Bottom jets closed

Upper jets closed

Bottom jet operating

Cylinder of compacted ground

Final level

(a)                    (b)

FIG. 11.35. OPERATION OF VIBROFLOT
(a) Jetting down Vibroflot.
(b) Withdrawal of Vibroflot.

capacity of the soil to resist general shear failure. The columns are unlikely to act effectively as vertical drains, numerous investigations have shown that vertical sand drains do not increase the rate of dissipation of pore-pressure when compared with the dissipation through natural drainage channels in soils, i.e. through fissures and laminations (Rowe[1.4]).

A disadvantage of this particular use of soil strengthening is the uncertainty of the extent to which the stone columns can be relied on to carry concentrated loading without excessive settlement. For this reason the author considers that the method is best applied to wide foundation areas where some differential settlement is not detrimental, e.g. to the foundations of embankment or steel storage tanks.

Large quantities of stone are required to form columns in very soft soils. In such conditions the process is only marginally cheaper than conventional piling, bearing in mind the higher working load which can be safely carried on a pile compared with a stone column. It should also be noted that a critical condition arises when stone columns are loaded to a stress at which there is simultaneous failure by bulging and yielding of the base. Hughes and Withers[11.13] showed that this critical state occurred at a vertical stress of 25 times the undrained cohesion of a soft clay when the length of the column was four times the diameter. A settlement of 58 per cent of the diameter occurred before bulging failure took place.

An example of the successful use of the vibroflotation process is the consolidation of the ground beneath the foundation of a 20-storey building at Lagos in Nigeria.[11.14] At this site very loose sand extended to a depth of 6 m, followed by denser sand to 12 m underlain by a considerable depth of soft to stiff clays alternating with mainly compact sands. It was calculated that the settlement of a raft foundation with a loading of 183 kN/m² would have been about 200 mm. However, it was estimated that the settlement would be reduced to about 100 mm by compacting the loose sand by vibroflotation. A comparison of costs showed that this method was very much cheaper than piling. The vibratory unit was inserted on a 1·90 m grid over the foundation area. Dynamic and static cone penetration tests made before and after vibration showed a threefold to fivefold increase in cone resistance between the depths of 2·1 and 6·1 m. It was found that little increase in density was achieved at depths shallower than 2 m. This suggests that it is desirable to provide other means of compaction of the shallow soil layers, or alternatively to operate the equipment from a higher level, then excavate down to the final formation level. Measurements of settlement of the 20-storey building were made up to a period of a year after completing the main structure. The maximum settlement was about 25 mm, although settlement was still continuing at a slow rate.

Another method of achieving deep compaction of loose or soft ground consists of dropping a very heavy weight from a considerable height on to the ground surface. Menard[11.15] has described the use of this process for compacting hydraulic fill some 9 to 10 m deep, by dropping 10 to 12 tonne weights from heights between 6 and 12 m. It is claimed that the process is effective in silty and clayey soils if time is allowed for dissipation of the pore pressures set up by the impact of the falling mass.

## REFERENCES

11.1  BOULTON, N. S., The flow pattern near a gravity well in a uniform water-bearing medium, *J. Inst. C.E.*, **36**, No. 10, pp. 534–550 (1950–51: Dec., 1951).

11.2 GLOSSOP, R. and SKEMPTON, A. W., Particle size in silts and sands, *J. Inst. C.E.*, **25**, No. 2, pp. 81–105 (1945–46: Dec., 1945).

11.3 CASAGRANDE, L., The application of electro-osmosis to practical problems in foundations and earthworks, *Building Research Tech. Paper No. 30* (London, H.M.S.O., 1947).

11.4 KELL, J., Pretreatment of gravel for compressed-air tunnelling under the River Thames at Dartford, *Chartered C.E.*, pp. 20–24 (March, 1957).

11.5 HARDING, H. J. B., The choice of expedients in civil engineering construction, *Inst. C.E. Works Constr. Div. Paper No. 6* (1946–47).

11.6 ELLIS, D. R. and McCONNELL, J., The use of the freezing process in the construction of a pumping station and storm-water overflow at Fleetwood, Lancashire, *Proc. Inst. C.E.*, **12**, pp. 175–186 (Feb., 1959).

11.7 MUSSCHE, H. E. and WADDINGTON, J. G., Applications of the freezing process to civil engineering works, *Inst. C.E. Works Constr. Div. Paper No. 5* (1945–46).

11.8 COLLINS, S. P. and DEACON, W. G., Shaft sinking by ground freezing, *Proc. Inst. C.E.*, Supp. Paper 7506S (May, 1972).

11.9 ZEEVAERT, L., Foundation design and behaviour of Tower Latino Americana in Mexico City, *Geotechnique*, **7**, No. 3, pp. 115–133 (Sept., 1957).

11.10 PARSONS, J. D., HEYMAN, S., and WERBLIN, D. A., Solution to wet foundation problem, *Eng. News Rec.*, p. 39 (12th April, 1956).

11.11 COATES, R. H. and SLADE, L. R., Construction of circulating water pumphouse at Cowes Generating Station, Isle of Wight, *Proc. Inst. C.E.*, **9**, pp. 217–232 (March, 1958).

11.12 WARD, W. H., The use of simple relief wells in reducing water pressure beneath a trench excavation, *Geotechnique*, **7**, No. 3, pp. 134–139 (Sept., 1957).

11.13 HUGHES, J. M. O. and WITHERS, N. J., Reinforcing of soft cohesive soils with stone columns, *Ground Engineering*, **7**, 3, pp. 42–49) (May, 1974).

11.14 GRIMES, A. S. and CANTLAY, W. G., A twenty-storey office block in Nigeria founded on loose sand, *Struct. Engr.*, **43**, 2, pp. 45–57 (Feb., 1965).

11.15 MENARD, L., The dynamic consolidation of recently placed fills and compressible soils, *Travaux*, 452 (1972).

# 12

# Shoring and Underpinning

SHORING of a structure is required—

(*a*) to support a structure which is sinking or tilting due to ground subsidence or instability of the superstructure;

(*b*) as a safeguard against possible settlement of a structure when excavating close to and below its foundation level;

(*c*) to support a structure while making alterations to its foundations or main supporting members.

Underpinning of a structure is required for the reasons given in (*a*) and (*b*) above and in addition—

(*d*) to enable the foundations to be deepened for structural reasons, for example to construct a basement beneath a building;

(*e*) to increase the width of a foundation to permit heavier loads to be carried, for example when increasing the storey height of a building;

(*f*) to enable a building to be moved bodily to a new site.

Shoring and underpinning are highly skilled operations and should be undertaken only by experienced firms. No one underpinning job is like another and each one must be given individual consideration for the most economical and safest scheme to be worked out. For this reason the author does not intend to describe the methods in detail but merely to state the general principles which are followed. Much interesting and detailed information is given in Prentis and White's book *Underpinning*[12.1] which is a classic work on the subject.

## METHODS OF SHORING

Shoring by external props is only required in connexion with underpinning work for structures which are out of plumb, or for structures which are sensitive to the effects of small settlements. It is generally unnecessary to provide extensive shoring to steel or reinforced concrete-framed buildings while excavating close to their foundations since the structural framework effectively ties the building together. It is, of course, necessary to support individual columns while underpinning their foundations. Buildings with load-bearing walls, if in sound condition, can generally be secured against

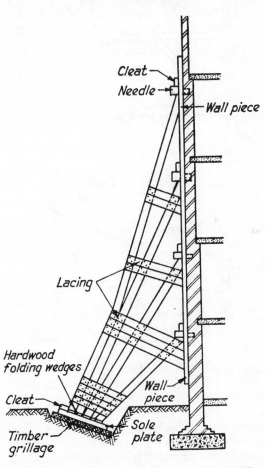

FIG. 12.1. ARRANGEMENT OF RAKING SHORES TO 5-STOREY BUILDING

harmful movement while underpinning by means of horizontal ties at the various floor and roof levels supplemented as necessary by internal bracings. These methods avoid obstructing the ground around the building where the underpinning operations or excavations are taking place.

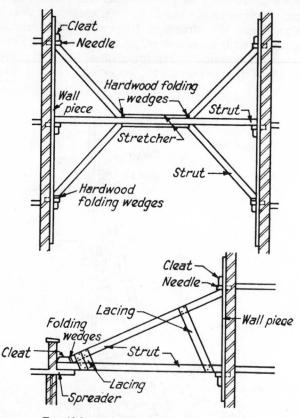

FIG. 12.2. ARRANGEMENTS OF FLYING SHORES

Shoring in connexion with underpinning work may also be avoided to a great extent if the underpinning system incorporates a jacking arrangement which ensures that the foundations remain at the same relative levels.

*Raking shores* (Fig. 12.1) are generally used where external support is necessary. The angle of the shores is generally 60° to 75°. If the feet of raking shores obstruct construction operations then *flying shores* (Fig. 12.2) can be used provided that there is a conveniently placed wall or other structure to strut against. For practical reasons the length of flying shores is generally limited to about 10 m. The levels of raking shores and flying shores are so arranged that they bear on the walls at the floor levels of the buildings. This ensures that the thrust is transmitted as far as possible to the whole structure and avoids putting a bending load on to a wall. If there is no floor at a suitable level at the end of a flying shore a stiff vertical member should be provided to distribute the load. Because flying shores do

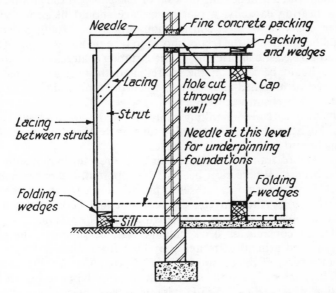

FIG. 12.3. ARRANGEMENT OF DEAD SHORES

not bear on the ground they cannot carry the weight of a wall; they merely provide a restraint against bulging or tilting. Support to the vertical load of a wall, where it is required in conjunction with flying shores or horizontal ties, can be given by means of *dead shores* (Fig. 12.3). Dead shores are vertical struts bearing on the ground at the required distance away from the wall to be clear of underpinning operations and surmounted by a horizontal beam or *needle* spanning between a pair of shores.

Raking or dead shores should be designed to carry the whole weight of the walls and any loads transmitted to them from the floors and roof of the building. The loading should be lightened as far as possible by removing machinery installations or stored materials. The needles are inserted through holes cut in the wall. A gap is left between the needles and the underside of the wall into which fine dry concrete or fairly dry mortar is rammed to ensure a good bearing over the full width of wall. Pad stones may be necessary to avoid concentrations of loading on the brickwork when supporting heavy walls. Where raking shores are used, wall pieces are placed over the needles and the upper ends of the shores are restrained from kicking up by means of *cleats* nailed to the wall pieces.

Raking and dead shores must be securely braced together and provided with a firm bearing on a *sill* or *sole plate*. If the ground has a low bearing capacity, a mat or grillage should be provided in timber, concrete, or steel construction. Hardwood folding wedges should be inserted at the feet of shores to take up any yielding of the ground and elastic shortening of the strutting materials. A careful watch should be kept on the shores, and the wedges should be tightened or loosened as necessary when the timber shrinks in dry weather or swells in wet weather.

Timber is suitable for raking shores for walls up to about 10 m high. Higher walls can be shored in tubular steel scaffolding or steel beams braced with channels or angles.

Columns of framed structures can be shored up individually by needle beams. Where steel beams are supported, cleats are bolted or welded to the opposite flanges to provide a bearing to the needles (Fig. 12.4 (*a*)). Alternatively, the beams at first floor level can be shored up and the column left hanging from them (Fig. 12.4 (*b*)). Reinforced concrete or brick columns can be supported by girts tightly bolted around them and prevented from slipping by chases cut in the faces of the columns (Fig. 12.5 (*a*)). Alternatively, chases or sockets can be cut in the sides of the column bases to permit the insertion of jacks (Fig. 12.5 (*b*)). It is preferable to place jacks between the needle beams and the cleats or girts. The pressure from the jacks is increased until upward movement of the column is just detected. This prestresses the supports to the needles and their bearing on the ground before the foundation of the column is cut away or undermined. After the needle system has been given time to settle down, the spaces between the needles and cleats can be packed and tightly wedged and the jacks removed.

Before any shoring work is commenced the building should be carefully surveyed. Records should be made of the levels of floors and the inclination of walls and sills, noting, marking, and photographing any cracks. Tell-tales and datum points should be placed where necessary for observing the movement of cracks and settlements. The records of levels, photographs, and notes should be agreed between the building owners, engineers, and contractors. The observations and measurements should be continued throughout the

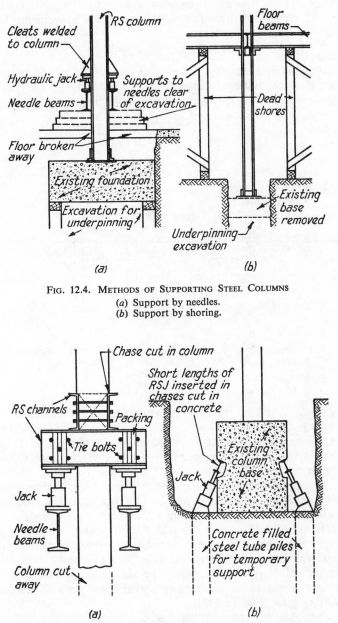

FIG. 12.4. METHODS OF SUPPORTING STEEL COLUMNS

(a) Support by needles.
(b) Support by shoring.

FIG. 12.5. METHODS OF SUPPORTING REINFORCED CONCRETE OR BRICK
COLUMNS

period of shoring and any subsequent excavation or underpinning, and until such time thereafter as all detectable movements have ceased.

## METHODS OF UNDERPINNING

Before undertaking any scheme of underpinning whether in connexion with adjacent construction operations, or to prevent further settlement as a result of ground subsidence or overloading of

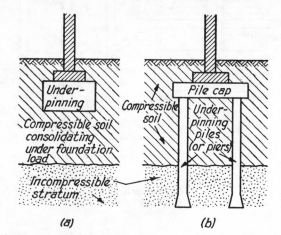

FIG. 12.6. UNDERPINNING TO ARREST SETTLEMENT DUE TO CONSOLIDATION OF SOIL UNDER FOUNDATION LOADING
(a) Incorrect method.
(b) Correct method.

foundations, it is important to carry out a careful soil investigation by means of borings or trial pits with laboratory tests on soil samples to determine allowable bearing pressures for the new foundations.

If underpinning is necessary to arrest settlement it is essential that the underpinned foundations should be taken down to relatively unyielding ground below the zone of subsidence. For example, if the bearing pressures of existing foundations are such that excessive settlement is occurring due to consolidation of a compressible clay soil it is quite useless simply to widen the foundations by shallow underpinning. This will merely transmit the pressures to the same compressible soil at a lower level (Fig. 12.6 (a)) and the cycle of settlement will start all over again. The underpinning must be taken down to a deeper and relatively incompressible stratum, if necessary by piers or piles (Fig. 12.6 (b)).

It is essential to recognize the true cause of settlement. Shallow underpinning may be quite satisfactory if the settlement is due to shrinkage of a clay soil due to dry weather; for example if settlement has occurred due to soil shrinkage in London Clay it is sufficient to underpin the foundations to a depth of 1·2 m. If, however, the soil shrinkage is due to the drying action of the roots of trees or hedges the underpinning will have to be taken well below the root system (*see* p. 159).

Underpinning is ineffective if the settlement is due to some deep seated cause such as coal mining. In such cases all that can be done is to wait for the movement to cease, then restore the structure to level (if practicable) before repairing it. Alternatively, a jacking system can be installed to maintain the foundations at a constant level (*see* p. 180).

**Underpinning to Safeguard Against the Effects of Adjacent Excavations**

It has been noted in Chapter 9 that cracking of the ground surface adjacent to deep excavations is generally found at a point given by the

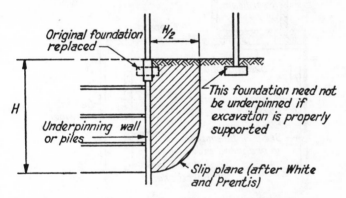

FIG. 12.7. UNDERPINNING CLOSE TO DEEP EXCAVATION

intersection of a line drawn at a slope of 1 vertically in ½ horizontally from the base of the excavation with the ground surface (Fig. 9.31, p. 601). This gives a guide to the width of the ground outside the excavation which is likely to be subjected to appreciable settlement. Prentis and White[12.1] suggest that movements within this zone take place along the path shown in Fig. 12.7. The theoretical studies of Bjerrum and Kirkedam (p. 594) indicate a similarly shaped slip plane. The author recommends that as a general guide in *stable* ground conditions foundations closer to an excavation than half its depth should be underpinned to the full depth of the excavation, but many authorities prefer to see underpinning of foundations closer to the excavation than the full depth (e.g. a 1 in 1 slip plane). Certainly if there is doubt about the stability of the ground and the condition of the existing structure, the author would recommend underpinning within the 1 in 1 line. Beyond a distance equal to the depth or half the depth of the excavation whichever rule is followed, no underpinning should be necessary provided that—

(*a*) the excavation is properly sheeted and strutted to prevent collapse of the sides and progressive slipping back from the face; or

(*b*) the sides of the excavation are cut back to a stable slope.

Underpinning to a greater distance from the face may be necessary if a ground water lowering system is in operation unless other safeguards are taken (*see* p. 709), or for very deep excavations where there may be appreciable settlement at a distance back from the face equal to 2 or 3 times the excavation depth (Fig. 9.30).

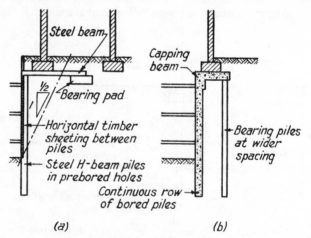

FIG. 12.8. METHODS OF UNDERPINNING BY PILING ADJACENT TO DEEP EXCAVATIONS

If the structure to be underpinned is close to the excavation it is often convenient to combine the underpinning with the supports to the excavation. For example, the supports can consist of steel Universal beam soldiers inserted in pre-bored holes with horizontal sheeting members. The load of the building can then be transferred to the tops of the piles (Fig. 12.8 (*a*)). Alternatively a system of close-spaced bored piles can be used (Fig. 12.8 (*b*)).

In all cases where underpinning is provided close to excavations it is important to design the underpinning members to carry any lateral loads transmitted to them from the retained earth or ground water. An example of the complexities of underpinning before undertaking basement excavations within an existing building is given in a paper by Slatter and Brown.[12.2]

### Underpinning by Continuous Strip Foundations

In its simplest form, underpinning consists in excavating rectangular pits or "legs" at intervals beneath the existing strip foundation. The pits are then filled with concrete or brickwork up to the underside of the existing foundation, after which the intervening legs are excavated and the concrete or brickwork constructed within them to bond on to the work already in place, so forming a continuous strip

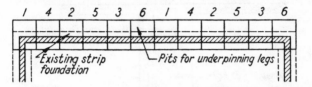

FIG. 12.9. SEQUENCE OF EXCAVATING UNDERPINNING LEGS FOR CONTINUOUS STRIP FOUNDATION

of underpinning at the required depth. The maximum length of wall which can be left unsupported above each leg is usually taken as 1·2 to 1·5 m for brick walls of normal construction. The unsupported lengths should be equally distributed over the length of the wall and in no circumstances should the sum of the unsupported lengths exceed one-quarter of the total length of the structure. Jordan[12.3] recommends that the legs should be dealt with in groups of six in the sequence 1, 2, 3, 4, 5, 6 (Fig. 12.9), the legs of the same number being excavated simultaneously.

If the wall is heavily loaded or shows signs of structural weakness, the unsupported length at any given point should not exceed one-fifth to one-sixth of its total length.

The concrete should be placed as quickly as possible after completion of excavation in each leg. If there is likely to be any delay in commencing concreting, the last 100 to 150 mm of soil should be left and removed only when the concreting is ready to start. Alternatively, a layer of sealing concrete can be placed at the bottom.

Concrete underpinning should be carried up to within 50 to 100 mm of the underside of the existing foundation, then left to set and shrink before fine dry concrete or mortar is rammed in to make full contact with the old and new work. Chases or pockets should be left in the vertical stop ends of the legs to bond in with the concrete of the adjacent legs. Horizontal chases can conveniently be formed by the walings supporting the poling boards lining the excavation.

Brickwork can be used to fill the spacing between the top of the underpinning concrete and the underside of the existing foundation. The bricks should be bedded in cement mortar and well rammed into position. Underpinning in wide foundations should be undertaken in steps working from back to front.

Excavation for intermediate legs will throw additional load on to legs already in place. Therefore, to avoid lateral flow of soil from

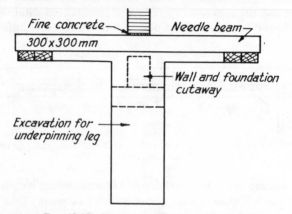

Fig. 12.10. Supporting Wall by Needling

beneath the first series legs, the excavation for the second series legs should not be taken as deep as that for the first series.

Sometimes as a final stage in underpinning, pressure grouting of any remaining voids between the old and new work is carried out. This gives some measure of prestressing the ground beneath the new foundation. Pressure grouting is not normally used for ordinary walls but it may be advantageous for wide foundations or irregular shapes where it is difficult to ensure thorough packing of the underpinning concrete or brickwork beneath the structure. Generally, dry packing gives a sounder job than grouting.

If it is desired to excavate beneath brick walls to lengths greater than 1·2 to 1·5 m or if the load distribution is not uniform, it may be necessary to give direct support to the walls by needle beams (Fig. 12.10).

### Underpinning with Piers or Bases

If a building has a framed structure with the wall loading transferred to the columns, it is convenient to underpin the columns in individual pits beneath each column foundation. The columns or column bases are shored up or supported by needles as described on page 726 while the pit is dug to the required level and backfilled with the underpinning material. It may be convenient to break out the bases of steel columns and construct entirely new ones.

Pier foundations may be a desirable method of underpinning walls where deep excavations are required in difficult ground, for example

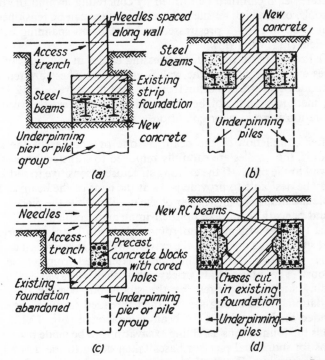

Fig. 12.11. Methods of Underpinning Wall Foundations using Beams Spanning between Piers or Piles

water-bearing or bouldery soils. This method should only be considered where there is a stratum of good bearing capacity at a reasonable depth, because heavy loads will have to be carried by the piers. It is necessary to provide a beam beneath the wall to transfer the load to the piers. The beam can be constructed in a number of ways; these include—

(a) Supporting the wall by needles for the full length between piers and inserting steel or precast concrete beams (Fig. 12.11 (a)).

(b) Inserting steel beams into chases cut into both sides of the wall foundation (Fig. 12.11 (b)).

(c) Inserting precast concrete blocks or stools into pits excavated beneath the walls in the manner described for underpinning wall foundations by continuous strips. The blocks are provided with longitudinal holes which are lined up to form continuous ducts along the length of the beam. Mild or high tensile steel rods or wires are threaded through the ducts. Either a normal reinforced concrete beam can then be formed by concreting around the blocks or stools, or the high tensile steel rods or wires can be tensioned and grouted up to form a prestressed concrete beam spanning between the piers (Fig. 12.11 (*c*)).

(*d*) Providing tie rods or prestressing cables at the sides of or in chases cut in the sides of the wall foundation. These are tensioned to produce a prestressed beam from the wall structure (Fig. 12.11 (*d*)). This method would not be contemplated if the existing wall and foundation were in poor condition.

After completion of the beam by one or another of the above methods, the needles are carefully removed to transfer the weight of the wall to the piers. If the existing structure is sensitive to settlement it may be desirable to provide jacks at the ends of the beams. These enable the wall to be lifted clear of the needles while the piers and the ground beneath them take up their immediate settlement.

The Pynford system of underpinning[12.4] with beams comprises as a first step cutting pockets in the existing wall to take precast concrete stools. The stools are 762 mm deep assembled from five separate sections. The intermediate brickwork is then cut away leaving the building supported entirely by the stools but bearing on its old foundation. Reinforcing steel is then threaded through the spaces provided in the stool and the beam is concreted (Fig. 12.12). This stiffens the foundations, enabling excavations to be made beneath the beams for individual piers or bases taken down to the desired level for underpinning. Finally the load is transferred to the piers or bases to complete the underpinning.

Piers or bases are constructed in concrete or brickwork in timbered shafts. Alternatively, cylindrical shafts can be sunk with cast iron or precast concrete segmental lining (*see* p. 318) backfilled with concrete. In difficult ground compressed-air caissons have been used for underpinning but such methods would only be considered if underpinning by piles were impractical due to the site conditions.

### Underpinning by Piles

Underpinning by piles is similar in principle to the method of piers described above. It is a convenient method to use if the bearing stratum is too deep for economical excavation in shafts or if the ground conditions are difficult for hand excavation.

Where walls are underpinned by piles, the piles can be placed at close centres when they are relatively short. If, however, the piles must be taken down to a considerable depth to reach a satisfactory bearing stratum it will be more economical to space them widely with a corresponding increase in working load. Where the piles are closely spaced, the wall and its foundation, if in good condition, can

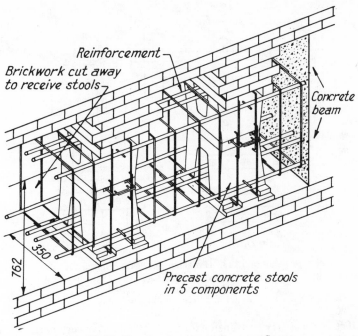

FIG. 12.12. UNDERPINNING WITH PYNFORD STOOLS

be relied upon to span between the piles. For widely spaced piles a beam will have to be provided by one of the methods described on page 544.

Underpinning piles to walls are normally provided in pairs, one on each side of the wall (Fig. 12.13 (*a*)). Piles underpinning columns are placed in groups around or at the sides of the column (Fig. 12.13 (*b*)). If, due to access conditions, it is impractical to install piles within a building it is necessary to provide them in pairs on the outside with a cantilevered capping beam (Fig. 12.13 (*c*)).

Bored piles (pp. 527 to 530) are generally used since they cause little or no noise and vibration and the piling rig can be operated in conditions of low headroom. In water-bearing sandy soils a careful boring technique is required to prevent sand being drawn into the borehole from the surrounding ground. It is not desirable to pump from the pile shaft before concreting as this may cause settlement for the reasons described on page 709. Uncased augered holes are suitable for underpinning in stiff clays, for example where settlement has occurred due to deep-seated soil shrinkage resulting from the drying action of tree roots.

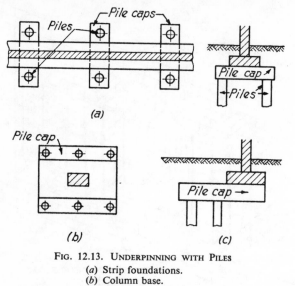

FIG. 12.13. UNDERPINNING WITH PILES
(a) Strip foundations.
(b) Column base.
(c) Cantilevered pile cap.

If it is necessary to transfer load to the pile at a very early age it may be desirable to leave the casing in the borehole or to use Universal beams or precast concrete columns inserted in prebored holes. Steel tube or Universal beam piles are useful where bending moments or lateral loads are carried, for example where underpinning piles are used as retaining walls for basements or where they are required to carry cantilevered loads at an early age.

JACKED PILES

Piles can be installed directly beneath foundations if jacked types are used, when the weight of the building provides the reaction for the jacks. The Franki Miga system employs a proprietary form of jacked pile which consists of a number of 305 × 305 × 762 mm long precast concrete units with a 50 mm diameter hole running down the centre (Fig. 12.14). The piles are installed by first excavating a pit beneath the foundation. The bottom pile section, which has a pointed end, is placed in the pit and a hydraulic jack, with steel packing plates and short steel beam sections to spread the load, is used to force the pile into the ground until it is nearly flush with the ground at the bottom of the pit. The jack is removed, the next section is added, and the process repeated until the desired pile-carrying capacity is reached. Adjacent units are bonded together by

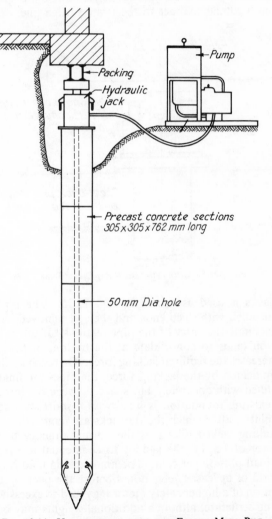

Pump

Packing

Hydraulic jack

Precast concrete sections
305 x 305 x 762 mm long

50 mm Dia hole

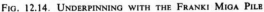

FIG. 12.14. UNDERPINNING WITH THE FRANKI MIGA PILE

grouting short lengths of steel tube into the central hole at each stage. When the pressure gauge on the jack indicates that the required pile-carrying capacity has been reached (i.e. working load plus a safety factor) short lengths of steel beam or rail are driven hard between the head of the pile and the existing foundation. The jack is then removed and the head of the pile and packings are solidly concreted.

In America it is the usual practice to jack down pipe piles in short sections in a similar manner to the Franki Miga pile, except that a

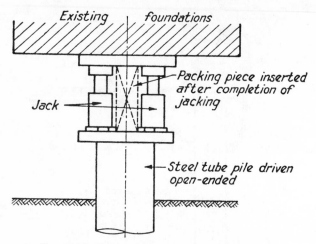

FIG. 12.15. UNDERPINNING WITH STEEL TUBE PILES

pair of jacks is used as shown in Fig. 12.15. The pipe piles are usually installed with open ends and the soil removed from time to time to facilitate the entry of the pipe sections. If this is not done a plug of soil tends to consolidate at the bottom of the pile, which greatly increases the required jacking force. On reaching the required level as indicated by the jacking force, the pipes are finally cleaned out and filled with concrete. The space between the top of the pipe and the existing foundation is filled with a short steel column and packing plates, after which the the jacks are removed.

In installing jacked piles it is the normal practice to work to a safety factor of 1·5, i.e. the jacking force is equal to the calculated working load plus 50 per cent. The final jacking load is maintained for a period of at least twelve hours before the packing is inserted. The adoption of a higher safety factor may lead to excessive loads on the existing structure, although additional weights may be added to increase the jacking reaction.

It is important to insert the packing between the pile and the structure *before* releasing the load on the jacks. In this way elastic rebound of the pile is prevented and the settlement minimized. A method of forcing up the head of a pile into contact with a structure above it is shown in Fig. 12.16. This shows the device as used for piles supporting tunnel sections beneath the River Maas at Rotterdam. The head of the pile is connected to the lower part only by a peripheral nylon sleeve. Cement grout is injected under pressure into the space between the two components, thus lifting the pile head and forcing it into contact with the superstructure.

### "Pretest" Methods of Underpinning

Mention has been made in the preceding pages of the use of jacks in underpinning work. By jacking between the existing structure and the new underpinning, the underlying ground is preloaded before the load of the structure is finally transferred to the underpinning. This method has been given the name "pretest" by its originators, Messrs. Spencer White and Prentis of New York, although several proprietary underpinning systems involve the use of jacks. The application of the pretest method to piled underpinning has already been described. The "legs" are brought up to the required level and, after hardening, jacks are installed and a series of beams are placed on top of the jacks. A layer of concrete is then deposited on top of the beams. Before this sets the beams are jacked up, thus bringing the concrete into close contact with the underside of the existing foundations. The concrete is then allowed to harden after which the loads on the jacks are increased to the desired pretest value. Brickwork or steel pinning is then built up on both sides of the jacks to enable them to be released and removed. The spaces occupied by the jacks are filled with further pinning or, if continuing movements of the underlying strata are expected, they can be left open to serve as jacking pockets. The jacks are reinstalled in the pockets from time to time, as required to correct further settlement.

The time required to install jacks and underpinning beams can be shortened, if required, by the use of proprietary brands of rapid-hardening cement for the concrete work.

The required jacking loads should be carefully calculated, due allowance being made for the number of legs which are open at any given time. It may be necessary to adjust the jacking loads as the work proceeds and extensometers or strain gauges have been used as an accurate means of controlling the jacking operations.

There are various patented systems of jacking which involve interconnexions of the jacks in conjunction with a centralized pumping plant and a hydraulic accumulator. The Pynford Pedatifid system,[12.5] referred to on page 180 in connexion with mining subsidence, is controlled by water-level gauges at various jacking points around the building. These gauges actuate electrical relays which control the motor-operated jacks.

Hydraulic jacks used in ordinary underpinning work should preferably have screwed rams fitted with collars. The collars are kept screwed down against the cylinders so that in the event of failure in the hydraulic pressure the ram will not fall. The Freyssinet "Flat Jack," a hollow light-gauge metal canister, has useful applications to underpinning work. Its shallow depth enables it to be inserted into small spaces. The jack is designed to be expendable. Air introduced under pressure expands the thin metal box, which jacks up the structure to the desired amount. Cement grout is then introduced and the injector-pressure pipe is sealed off.

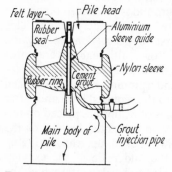

FIG. 12.16. UNDERPINNING PILE WITH ADJUSTABLE HEAD

Complications resulting from the installation of underpinning piles outside the existing foundation structure, or from pits beneath the structure, can be avoided by using "Pali Radice" (root-piles). This proprietary system of Fondedile Foundations Ltd. involves the rotary drilling of relatively small-diameter holes *through* the foundation structure and underlying soil to the bearing stratum. Reinforced concrete is cast-in-place in the drilled holes, which are arranged at various angles to provide support across the full width of the foundation. This system has the advantages of not requiring any excavations or shoring, and the piles are bonded to the whole mass of the existing structure through which they are installed. However, care must be taken to obtain sound concrete especially when forming piles in loose or water-bearing ground.

### Underpinning by Injections

Injections of the ground with cement or chemicals to fill voids or to permeate and strengthen the ground are sometimes used as a means of underpinning. The work may be done wholly by injections or the ground treatment may be used as a means of temporary strengthening while excavating for normal underpinning legs or shafts.

Cases have occurred where pressure grouting has been wrongly applied. For example it has been used in cases where slow consolidation of a compressible soil has caused settlement of structures. Soils showing long-term consolidation effects, however, are always fine-grained and cement or chemicals cannot be injected into the void spaces (*see* p. 681). (see p. 681) Cement grout introduced under pressure beneath the foundations merely forms a thin layer which may lift the foundations to restore the level to some extent, and it may cause a short-term acceleration in the normal consolidation process. However, after a time the slow consolidation takes effect once more, and settlement of the structure recommences.

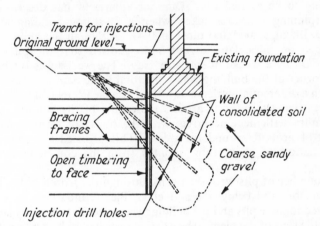

FIG. 12.17. UNDERPINNING BY CHEMICAL INJECTIONS

Cement-grouting is a useful expedient to fill voids in the ground beneath foundations which have been caused by erosion or by vibration effects in loose granular soils. It is also a useful means of strengthening old rubble masonry foundation walls before excavating beneath them for normal underpinning operations. Cement grouting can be used to consolidate open-textured gravel soils beneath machinery foundations in cases where settlement is occurring due to vibration effects.

Chemicals can be used for injection into coarse sands or sandy gravels to produce a wall or block of consolidated ground beneath the foundations to the desired level for underpinning. In favourable ground conditions this is a useful method of underpinning in connexion with deep excavations close to existing structures. The injections are made from ground level, thus avoiding the necessity of shoring or needling, and the wall of consolidated ground acts as a retaining wall when excavating close to the existing foundations (Fig. 12.17). The consolidated ground is supported where necessary by bracing frames but the need for sheet piling or close timbering is often eliminated. The range of soil types in which chemical consolidation can be used is given in Fig. 11.6 (p. 682).

### The Use of the Freezing Process in Underpinning Work

The applications of the freezing process to excavation work has been described on pages 707 to 709. Freezing has been used to solidify ground which was consolidating beneath the foundation loading, thus arresting further settlement and enabling permanent underpinning to be carried out. Dumont-Villares[12.6] has described the underpinning measures taken when a 26-storey building at São Paulo, Brazil, settled and tilted in 1941. Although the building was founded on piles, later investigation showed that the piles were underlain by a wedge of soft silty clay. The wedge was thickest at one corner of the building where the total settlement was nearly 0·3 m with a differential settlement (tilting) almost as great. The freezing was restricted to an area around the corner of the building where maximum settlement occurred, with the object of forming a solid block of ground around the piles. This arrested the settlement in a period of about three months from the commencement of freezing.

A number of pits were then sunk through the frozen ground to a stratum of sand below the soft clay. Pier foundations were constructed in these pits and the building was restored to level by jacking from the tops of the piers. The existing piles had to be cut free where necessary as the building was raised. Selected piles were restored to use by inserting precast concrete sections (Franki–Miga–Hume piles) between the old piles and the underside of the building. The precast sections were jacked down to the required pretest load. No further settlement was recorded over a ten-year period following the completion of the underpinning work.

### MOVING BUILDINGS

Underpinning methods are normally used in connexion with moving buildings (without demolition) from one site to another. The weight of the buildings is transferred to a system of beams placed on both sides of the walls and wheeled carriages or rollers are installed beneath the beams running on rail tracks laid in the desired direction. Changes in direction of movement along the rails can be achieved by jacking up the carriages in turn and rotating them in another direction to run on a new set of tracks.

These operations are usually undertaken by specialist firms who adopt a careful technique based on a thorough survey of the building, accurate calculation of loads, a detailed soil investigation along the line of the tracks and at the new site of the building, and controlled jacking in conjunction with strain measuring and equalizing devices.

When buildings with load-bearing walls are moved, holes are cut in the walls and needles are inserted at the appropriate spacings over which the brickwork can safely span. Longitudinal beams are then laid on each side of the wall and jacked up against the needles, shims and wedges being added as necessary to ensure even distribution of the load. Where necessary individual pairs of jacks can be provided between each needle and the beams. The carriages and rollers are then installed beneath the longitudinal beams, or a second set of girders can be provided beneath the wall beams in order to reduce the number of carriages and hence the number of tracks.

The system of support used by Messrs. Christiani and Nielsen for moving houses near Paris has been described by Olsen[12.7] and is illustrated in Fig. 12.18. Three pairs of steel beams were placed alongside the longitudinal walls and short needles were fixed to their lower flanges at two intermediate points on these walls. Two pairs of main cross girders were then laid over the longitudinal beams, one pair to each end wall. Wheeled carriages were placed at four points, i.e. at the ends of the outer cross girders as shown in Fig. 12.18. The pairs of longitudinal girders were "preflexed" by small hydraulic jacks placed at six points above the short needle beams on the longitudinal walls and at four points on the end walls. When the total load on these small jacks equalled the total load of the building, the jacks were locked and the load was transferred through the cross girders to the four main jacks and through them to the carriages. Two of the main jacks were coupled together to enable them to act as one unit. Thus the system was on a statically-determinate three-point support. If one of the two jacks sank due to unevenness or settlement of the track the pressure in the cylinder fell, causing oil to flow from the cylinder of the other jack. Thus the first jack was raised again while the other fell by a corresponding amount to equalize the movement of the pair of supports.

Olsen also mentioned the alternative method of supporting a load-bearing wall by prestressing it. Two rolled steel beams were placed to act as ties, one on each side of the wall. Short cross beams were fixed at the ends of the beams and jacks were placed between the cross beams and the wall to induce a compressive stress in the wall.

The thrust required to move structures along the tracks is usually provided by long-stroke hydraulic jacks. The cylinders are fixed to the rails and the rams operate against the carriages. Jacking is

preferable to winching, since the stretch and snatch of the cables of
the latter method are liable to set up a dangerous jerky motion.

Prentis and White[12.1] state that the propulsive force to start the
movement need only be 1 to 2 per cent of the weight of the structure,
using steel rollers on a well-laid track bearing on a good foundation.
The force to keep the building moving may only be about two-thirds
of the force required to start the movement.

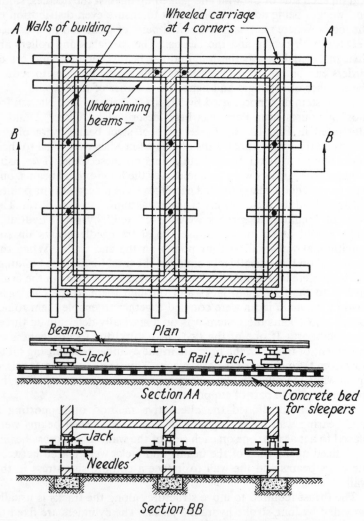

FIG. 12.18. MOVING A HOUSE ON FOUR CARRIAGES (OLSEN[12.7])

Framed buildings are moved by needling and propping individual columns, and installing roller carriages either under each column or under a combined support to a row of columns. Olsen[12.7] has described the installation of temporary struts and ties in the lower storey of a four-storey warehouse to enable the loading of fifty-five columns to be transferred to twenty-two main jacking points in two rows as shown in Fig. 12.19. The twenty-two jacks were provided

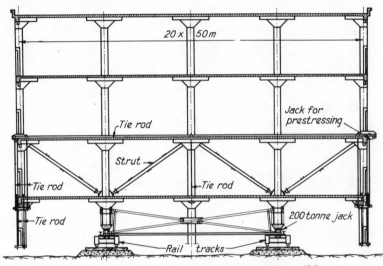

FIG. 12.19. MOVING A 5-STOREY WAREHOUSE (OLSEN[12.7])

with equalizing connexions forming three independent groups, so giving the desirable three-point support previously mentioned. The warehouse, which measured 100 × 20 m, was split into two sections. Each section of 2500 tonne mass was moved half a mile including the crossing of a road and a railway. The propulsion was by six 50-tonne jacks.

### REFERENCES

12.1   PRENTIS, E. A. and WHITE, L., *Underpinning*, 2nd ed. (New York, Columbia Univ. Press, 1950).

12.2   SLATTER, F. W. and BROWN, A., Foundations, underpinning and structural problems at the Daily News Building in the City of London, *Structr. Engr.*, **32**, No. 10, pp. 264–273 (Oct., 1954).

12.3   JORDAN, S. K., Foundations for basement buildings adjoining existing property, *J. Inst. C.E.*, **15**, No. 2, pp. 119–140 (Dec., 1940).

12.4   ARCHITECT'S JOURNAL, *Library of Information Sheets* 26.E.2, Pynford method of underpinning (1949).

12.5 PRYKE, J. F. S., Eliminating the effects of subsidence, *Colliery Engineering*, **31**, No. 37, pp. 501–507 (Dec., 1954).

12.6 DUMONT-VILLARES, A., The underpinning of the 26-storey "Companhia Paulista de Seguros" Building, São Paulo, Brazil, *Geotechnique*, **6**, No. 1, pp. 1–14 (March, 1956).

12.7 OLSEN, K. A., The re-siting of structures, *Inst. Struct. Eng. 50th Anniversary Conference*, pp. 364–371 (Oct., 1958).

# 13

# Protection of Foundation Structures Against Attack by Soils and Ground Water

FOUNDATIONS are subject to attack by destructive compounds in the soil or ground water, by living organisms, and by mechanical abrasion or erosion. Thus, timber piles in jetties are attacked by organisms in the soil and water causing decay of the timber; they suffer from the depredations of termites and the insect-like marine "borers"; they are abraded by ships, ice or other floating objects and they may suffer severe damage by the movement of shingle if they are sited on beaches exposed to wave action. Concrete in foundations may have to withstand attack by sulphates in the ground or in chemical wastes. Steel piles are subject to corrosion. The severity of attack on foundations depends on the concentration of the aggressive compounds, the level of and fluctuations in the ground water table and the climatic conditions. Immunity against deterioration can be given to a varying degree by protective measures. Some of these may be very costly and the engineer may have to seek a compromise between complete protection over the working life of the structure and partial protection at a lower cost but with the added expense of periodical repairs and renewals.

**Soil and Ground Water Investigations**

In considering protective measures the first step is to undertake a detailed investigation of the soil and ground water conditions. The latter are of particular importance in evaluating the risk of attack on timber, concrete, or steel structures. Generally the required data can be obtained in conjunction with the general investigations for foundation design using the methods described in Chapter 1. Samples of the ground water can be taken for chemical analysis, and portions of the disturbed and undisturbed soil samples can be set aside for this purpose.

If necessary stand-pipes should be left in boreholes for long-term measurements of the ground water table. It is important to establish the highest level to which the ground water can rise, either from the stand-pipe recordings or the results of local inquiry. The possibility should be borne in mind of marked changes in the ground water level occurring at some time in the future, say as a result of drainage or irrigation schemes.

In considering sulphate attack on concrete foundations it is usually sufficient to determine the sulphate content and pH value of the soil and ground water. If the sulphate content is found to be high it will be advisable to determine the concentrations of the relevant cations. A full chemical analysis is required where the soil or ground water is contaminated with chemical wastes in order to identify compounds potentially aggressive to concrete.

SULPHATES IN SOILS

In Great Britain sulphates occurring naturally in soils are generally confined to the Keuper Marl, the Lias, Oxford, Kimmeridge, Weald, Gault and London Clays. The superficial deposits or drift are generally free of sulphates except where they are in close proximity to sulphate-bearing soils. Some peats have a high sulphate content. Sulphates occur in Europe, U.S.A., and in the semi-arid gypsiferous soils of the Middle East.

Because of wide variations in the sulphate content of soils, the best indication of possible aggressive conditions is given by analysis of the ground water. The highest concentrations of sulphates in the ground water will occur towards the end of a long dry spell. If the sampling is done during heavy winter rains the concentration may be unrepresentative of the most severe conditions. In hilly ground where there is a flow of ground water down the slope across sulphate-bearing soils, the highest concentration of sulphates will be on the downhill side. Flow of ground water from sulphate-bearing soils will result in concentration of sulphates in soils which are not naturally sulphate-bearing. An account of the distribution of sulphates in various ground conditions in Britain is given in a paper by Bessey and Lea.[13.1]

INVESTIGATIONS FOR CORROSION

For investigating the possibility of corrosion of buried steel structures the most rapid and economical method is to carry out an electrical resistivity survey of the site by the method described in Chapter 1 (p. 47). The readings of the Megger Earth Tester or other apparatus used give the conductivity of the soil which is a measure of the concentration of soluble salts in the soil and which in turn is a measure of its corrosive action. The presence in the soil of sulphate-reducing bacteria causes serious corrosion which commonly occurs in tidal mud flats contaminated by sewage or in ground containing organic refuse. In these conditions a bacteriological analysis is required, for which purpose the soil must be sampled using the techniques described on pages 18 to 25 but with the added precaution of using sterilized unoiled tubes. The ends of the tubes must be waxed immediately on withdrawal from the ground.

Sea water should be sampled in tidal rivers, estuaries or the open sea at various stages of the tide both at neap and spring tide conditions to determine the worst conditions of salinity and bacteria content. Again sterilized bottles should be used if bacteriological examination is thought necessary. A full chemical analysis together with determinations of pH value is required on the water samples.

## PROTECTION OF TIMBER PILES

Nowadays the only timber in foundations is in piles or in bracing to piled structures. Biological decay of buried timber does not occur if the timber is kept wholly wet but the decay may be severe if the timber is kept in a partly wet and partly dry (or moist) state, for example in the zone of a fluctuating water table for buried timber piles, or in the half-tide zone for piles in the sea or rivers. Timber which is properly air-seasoned will, if kept dry, be immune to biological decay.

To ensure freedom from decay and infestation of timber, precautions must be taken from the time that the timber is felled. Dry rot fungus is present in forests due to the accumulation of dead wood, and it may also occur in heaps of sawdust and scrap wood in timber yards. Therefore, felled timber should be cleared from the forests as quickly as possible and stacked in the timber yards on firm well-drained elevated ground from which all vegetable soil has been removed. The ground beneath and around the stacks should be kept clear of weeds.

Timber should be stacked clear of the ground and placed so that air can circulate freely around all baulks or planks. It should season in the stacks until the moisture content of the outer layers is less than 30 per cent, when it is ready for treatment by creosote or other preservative.

Alternatively, if the timber is to be used in permanently water-logged ground it can be stored wholly immersed in water.

**Preservation Methods**

Impregnation with creosote under pressure is the most effective method of preserving timber in foundations against decay and it gives a degree of protection against termites and some marine borers. Creosote is preferable for foundation work to other preservatives such as water-soluble and solvent types. Softwoods can be completely penetrated by pressure treatment, but hardwoods such as Douglas fir can only be properly impregnated by incising them and subjecting them to long sustained pressure. Even with this treatment the heartwood cannot be fully penetrated. In piling work the absorption and penetration of the creosote is greatly improved by the use of round piles in which the outer sapwood is retained. Richardson[13.2] states that the sapwood is absorptive to creosote and with Scots pine or Baltic redwood an outer band of creosoted wood of up to 75 mm depth is readily obtained which will protect the piles for a very long time. He points out the disadvantage of using squared timber for piles (a common British practice) which results in most of the sapwood being cut away, thus exposing the heartwood which in practice rarely receives adequate creosote treatment. Because complete impregnation of hardwoods cannot be obtained, all bolt holes and incisions made by cant hooks, dogs or slings should subsequently be re-creosoted. Creosote should be poured by funnel down bolt holes, or better still they should be given pressure treatment by specially designed equipment. Particular attention should be given to the end-grain.

**Protection by Concrete**

Because of the likelihood of severe decay of timber piles in the zone of a fluctuating water table, the creosote treatment is not likely to be effective in this zone over the life of the structure. If the water table is fairly shallow the piles can be cut off at the lowest water level and the pile cap taken down to this level. If the lowest water level is too deep for this to be economical it will be advisable to use composite piles, the portion permanently submerged being in timber and the upper portion in concrete similar to those illustrated in Figs. 8.38 and 8.39 (p. 539).

### Action of Marine Borers

The burrowing of molluscan and crustacean organisms which inhabit saline or brackish waters is responsible for the most severe damage of piles and fendering in marine and river work. An illustrated account of the species of these organisms with photographs of their depredations and an account of protective methods is given in an article by Chellis.[13.3] He lists the principal species as follows—

*Molluscan borers*

Teredo ("shipworm")
Bankia
Xylophaga dorsalis
Lyrodus
Pholadidae
Martesia
Hiata

*Crustacean borers*

Limnoria ("gribble" or "sea-louse")
Chelura
Sphaeroma

The molluscan borers enter through minute holes when young and grow to a size of up to one inch in diameter and three to four feet long, destroying the wood as they grow. The crustaceans are mainly surface workers and form a network of branching and interlacing holes. The borers are found throughout the oceans of the world. Some of the known locations are named by Chellis. Salinity, temperature, current action, depth of water, pollution, pH value, dissolved oxygen and sulphuretted hydrogen, all affect the presence or absence of borers. Usually saline or brackish water with salinities of more than 15 parts per 1,000 (sea water normally has a salinity of 30 to 35 parts per 1,000) is essential to their survival, but *Sphaeroma* are found in almost fresh tropical waters in South America, South Africa, India, Ceylon, New Zealand, and Australia.

The destructive action of marine borers can be extremely rapid. Timber jetties have been destroyed after only a few months of exposure, therefore some protection is necessary in all cases where timber piles are driven in salt or brackish water. Such protection should only be omitted if there is strong evidence that borers do not exist in a particular locality. The investigation should cover an examination of all timber structures and driftwood and advice should be sought from a marine biologist.

### PROTECTION AGAINST MARINE BORERS

The best protection is to use a timber which is known to be resistant to borers. Chellis gives a list of immune woods including greenheart in Europe and America, billian in the China Seas, turpentine in New South Wales, black cypress and ti-tree in Queensland, spotted gum in Tasmania, and teak in India. Jarrah, blue gum, and greenheart show greater immunity in the cold British waters than in warmer seas. The *Code of Practice on Foundations* mentions greenheart, pyinkado, turpentine, totara, and jarrah.

Creosote is poisonous to *Teredo* and *Martesia* borers but not to *Limnoria*. Roe and Hochman[13.4] suggest that inorganic copper and mercury compounds and copper chelates are effective against Limnoria. However, the efficacy of preservative treatments depends on their complete continuity over the outer layer of the timber. If the treated shell is perforated by lifting hooks or by saw cuts or bolt holes, the borers can make an entry. Even though such cuts or abrasions are treated before the piles are finally driven, there is still the possibility of damage by floating objects or by the erosive action of shingle.

Some hardwoods cannot be impregnated with creosote and in these cases protection can be given by jacketing the piles with concrete. Chellis describes several methods of jacketing including placing concrete inside movable steel forms or precast concrete shells. The use of gunite (sand-cement mortar sprayed on to the timber) is also mentioned. The essential practice is any form of concrete jacketing is to provide a dense fairly rich mix which will not craze or crack.

Chellis states that metal sleeving is not used to any great extent because of the impossibility of finding a corrosion-resistant metal at an economical price and difficulties at joints and bracing connexions.

## PROTECTION OF STEEL PILING AGAINST CORROSION

Corrosion of iron or steel in an electrolyte (for example, soil or water) is an electrochemical phenomenon with different areas of the metal surface or structure acting as an anode and a cathode in cells. Pitting will occur at the anodic areas, and rust will be the final product in the cathodic areas. Both air and water are essential to the occurrence of corrosion. The general wastage of bare structural steel in dry unpolluted climates is practically nil, but it can be nearly 1 mm per year in humid and saline conditions on tropical surf beaches. Pollution is an important factor in atmospheric corrosion, the rate of which is greatly accelerated by the presence of dust, acids (derived from smoke), and sodium chloride (from sea spray). The rate of corrosion in soils in a function of the electrical conductivity of the soil but other factors, including the presence in the soil of sulphate-reducing bacteria can greatly accelerate corrosion.

The relative aggression of water depends on the salinity, pollution if any, temperature and oxygen content.

Fancutt and Hudson[13.5] quote the following rates of corrosion of bare steel—

In disturbed soil—0·008 to 0·08 mm per year (tests by National Bureau of Standards in America; in British soils it is in the lower half of this range).

Normal sea water—0·013 to 0·13 mm per year.

Industrial atmosphere in Britain—0·08 to 0·13 mm per year.

It is the normal practice to apply a protective coating to piles driven into the soil, but it must be realized that this gives only partial protection since the coating is liable to be stripped off by stones or other obstructions in the soil. However, if the higher range of 0·08 mm wastage per year is taken a steel pile with a web thickness of 20·6 mm will have a life of more than sixty years before 50 per cent of its thickness is lost (although there is likely to be some deeper local pitting). Since the stresses on the cross-sectional area of the steel are generally low there is unlikely to be failure of the pile due to over-stressing. Romanoff[13.6] examined many steel piles which had been in the ground for periods up to 40 years. The examination showed that where the piles had been driven into *undisturbed* soil, i.e. where no oxygen was present, the corrosion of the steel was so light that it had no significant effect on the life of the piling. This indicates that where piles are driven wholly in undisturbed soil no form of protection need be given in the portion below the ground surface. However, as already mentioned, there are certain factors, such as the presence of sulphate reducing bacteria, which thrive in the absence of oxygen and can greatly accelerate corrosion. In these cases additional protection, for example jacketing H-beam piles, filling hollow piles with concrete or applying cathodic protection, must be considered.

For piles projecting above the soil line, a good paint treatment will give adequate protection of the exposed portion, provided that the paintwork can be renewed from time to time. However, maintenance of paintwork is impossible below the water line in jetty structures, and the paintwork in this part of a pile is especially liable to damage by the action of waves, barnacles and floating objects. Therefore additional protection, usually in the form of cathodic protection, is necessary where a long life is required from the piles.

## Protection by Paint Treatment

The first step in the paint treatment is to clean the piles thoroughly, removing all rust, dirt, and mill-scale. The most effective cleaning method is by abrasive blasting, for example shot blasting. After cleaning to the "white metal" condition, all dust and grit should be removed by vacuum or air blast. While the pile is still dry it should be given a priming coat with the primer appropriate to the finishing coat, and then the finish coat or coats of hot coal tar and bituminous enamel paint should be heavily applied by brush or swab to build up a finished coating thickness of 1·5 to 2·5 mm. Elaborate precautions should be taken to avoid damage to the coating.

In very severe corrosive conditions, for example in ground containing acids, special treatments such as epoxide resin paints or neoprene coatings should be considered and advice on their application sought from the manufacturers.

## Cathodic Protection

The principle of cathodic protection is the utilization of the characteristic electrochemical potential possessed by all metals. The behaviour of any two metals in the presence of an electrolyte (that is, in a cell) is governed by their relative electropotentials. For example, where zinc and iron are the electrodes in a cell, zinc, being higher in the electromotive series, will act as the anode. In this way a complete structure can be protected by connecting it electrically to anodes at suitable intervals. The current escapes to the soil or solution by way of the anode, making the whole structure cathodic and so preventing the escape of metallic ions from the structure to the soil or solution. In time this action causes polarization of the surface of the structure which prevents rusting and thus provides an additional benefit.

Cathodic protection can be applied either by using sacrificial anodes or by a power-supplied system. Sacrificial anodes consist of large masses of metal which corrode away in the course of their protective action and have to be replaced from time to time. They must be higher in the electromotive series than the structure being protected. Magnesium anodes are generally used for the protection of steel structures.

In the power-supplied (or current-impressed) systems the anodes take the form of large pieces of scrap-iron or lumps of carbon. The d.c. current required for flow from the anode to the cathode is supplied from the mains through a transformer/rectifier or directly from a d.c. generator.

The rate of wastage of anodes or the power requirements for power-supplied systems can be minimized by keeping the area of exposed steel as small as possible. The cathodic protection does not supplant proper paint or other surface treatment of the metal. The more this surface coating can be kept intact the less will be the wastage of anodes and, in the case of power-supplied systems, the requirements for power. Thus thorough treatment by paint or bituminous enamel should be given to the piles as described above. It is particularly important to ensure thorough surface protection between high and low water mark in marine structures and in the "splash zone" above, since cathodic protection is ineffective above water level and the unprotected parts, if uncoated, may act anodically to the parts below water with accelerated corrosion.

## PROTECTION OF CONCRETE STRUCTURES

The principal cause of deterioration of concrete in foundations is attack by sulphates present in the soil, in the ground water, or in sea water. Other agencies causing deterioration include chemical wastes, organic acids, frost, sea action, certain deleterious aggregates, and corrosion of reinforcement.

### Sulphate Attack

Sulphates in solution react with Portland cement to form insoluble calcium sulphate and calcium sulpho-aluminate. Crystallization of the new compounds is accompanied by an increase in molecular volume which causes expansion and disintegration of the concrete at the surface. This disintegration exposes fresh areas to attack and if there is a flow of ground water bringing fresh sulphates to the affected area, the rate of disintegration can be very rapid. Easily-soluble sulphates such as those of magnesium, sodium, and ammonium are more aggressive than calcium sulphate (gypsum). Insoluble sulphates do not attack concrete.

The sulphate content of sea water expressed as $SO_3$ is about 230 parts per 100,000, which is greatly in excess of the figure regarded as marginal between aggressive and non-aggressive in ground water (*see* Table 13.1). However, sea water is not regarded as being markedly aggressive to concrete because sodium chloride has an inhibiting or retarding action on the expansive reaction of the sulphates. It is usually satisfactory to adopt a good quality rich mix using normal Portland cement, although, in the case of reinforced concrete structures in sea water it is advisable to adopt the added precaution of using sulphate-resisting cement. This will prevent cracking of the concrete followed by corrosion of the reinforcement.

In the soil or in ground water, the higher the concentration of sulphates the more severe is the attack. The disintegration is particularly severe if the foundation structure is subjected to one-sided water pressure, for example a basement or culvert with a head of ground water on the outside. Other factors increasing the severity of attack are porosity of the concrete, the presence of cracks, and disruption of the surface by barnacles and similar growths.

Attack does not take place if there is no ground water and for the disintegration to continue there must be replenishment of the sulphates. If the ground water is absolutely static the attack does not penetrate beyond the outer skin of concrete. Thus there is little risk of serious attack on structures buried in clay soils provided that there is no flow of ground water such as might occur along a loosely back-filled foundation trench. There is a risk of attack in clayey soils in certain climatic conditions, for example when hot, dry conditions cause an upward flow of water by capillarity from sulphate-bearing waters below foundation level. Similar conditions can occur when water is drawn up to the ground floor of a building due to the drying action of domestic heating or furnaces.

## PROTECTION AGAINST SULPHATE ATTACK

Recommendations on precautions to be taken against sulphate attack on concrete structures have been published by the Building Research Station.[13.7] However, it is important to note that the recommended minimum cement contents, if adopted, will result in concrete which has a very low workability. It will be quite impossible to place such concrete in thin reinforced members, bored piles and other confined spaces, without the risk of honeycombing. The essential feature of resisting sulphate attack is to produce a dense, impermeable concrete. Accordingly the author has prepared Table 13.1 which recommends minimum cement contents for a range of concrete situations in four classifications of sulphate concentrations. These recommendations should be more helpful than those given in the Building Research Station Digest, which take little account of the situation in which the concrete is placed.

## SULPHATE-RESISTING AND OTHER CEMENTS

It will be noted from Table 13.1 that normal Portland and sulphate-resisting cements are satisfactory for moderate concentrations of sulphates. High-alumina and supersulphate cements give practically complete immunity against attack from the severest conditions normally encountered in the ground or in sea water. Supersulphate cement is however, attacked by ammonium sulphate. It is not manufactured in Britain at the present time and the imported brands are expensive.

High alumina cement also suffers from the disadvantage that the compressive strength of concrete made with it can fall drastically, due to a phenomenon known as "conversion"[13.8]. The fall can occur at any time in the life of the structure and is accompanied by a marked decrease in the resistance of the concrete to sulphate attack. This disadvantage can be overcome to some extent if over-rich mixes are avoided and precautions are taken to prevent the exposure of concrete to heat. Steam curing must not be used and stocks of piles made with high alumina cement should be shaded from the sun in the casting yard and on site. Piles should be driven when they are between the ages of three and seven days. It should be noted that high alumina cement concrete even when it has undergone "conversion" possesses a residual strength which may be adequate for the working stresses in the structural member. However, collapses of a few high alumina concrete structures in Britain in 1973–4 led to withdrawal of Code of Practice approval of this cement for structural concrete which includes the foundations. Accordingly, the use of high alumina cement for protection against sulphate attack has not been shown in Table 13.1. The best form of protection for high sulphate concentrations in ordinary foundation work is to use well-compacted dense impermeable concrete made with sulphate resisting cement.

OTHER FORMS OF PROTECTION

Asphalt tanking gives complete protection against sulphate attack and if basements are tanked, in the manner described in Chapter 5, no other form of protection is needed in sulphate-bearing ground water. Concrete in strip or pad foundations can be protected by wrapping them with bituminous felt or plastic sheeting. The self-adhesive types of plastic sheeting are very suitable for this purpose. Bituminous emulsion does not provide a satisfactory coating.

In conditions where ground water can be drawn up to ground floor slabs by heat in buildings, adequate protection can be given by bitumen dampcourse material or polyethylene sheeting laid below the ground slab.

Ordinary concrete foundations above the ground water table in Kuwait (where the soils are heavily gypsiferous) have been given satisfactory protection by a heavy coat of hot bitumen on the exposed surfaces.

# CLASSIFICATION OF SULPHATES IN SOILS AFFECTING

| Classifications of soil conditions | | | | Recommended |
| --- | --- | --- | --- | --- |
| $SO_3$ in g.w. (Parts $SO_3$ per $10^5$) | $SO_3$ in soil | | Precast concrete products[1] (piles, cylinders, blockwork) | Massive concrete in foundations[3] (including pile caps) |
| | Total (%) | In 1:1 aqueous extract (g/l) | | |
| Less than 30 | Less than 0·2 | — | No special precautions. | (a) If foundations wholly above the water-table[2], no special precautions necessary.<br>(b) If foundations are in contact with a fluctuating water-table use normal Portland cement (cement content not less than 310 kg/m³ Max. $W/C$ 0·55). |
| 30 to 120 | 0·2 to 0·5 | — | (a) If structures wholly above the water-table[2] use normal Portland cement (cement content not less than 310 kg/m³ Max. $W/C$ 0·50).<br><br>(b) If structures are in contact with a fluctuating water table use normal Portland cement (cement content not less than 350 kg/m³ Max. $W/C$ 0·50), or sulphate-resisting cement (cement content not less than 310 kg/m³ Max. $W/C$ 0·50). | (a) If foundations wholly above the water-table[2] use normal Portland cement (cement content not less than 330 kg/m³ Max. $W/C$ 0·50).<br><br>(b) If foundations are in contact with a fluctuating water-table use normal Portland cement (cement content not less than 350 kg/m³ Max. $W/C$ 0·50), or sulphate-resisting cement (cement content not less than 310 kg/m³ Max. $W/C$ 0·50). |
| 120 to 250 | 0·5 to 1·0 | 2·5 to 5·0 | (a) If structures wholly above the water-table[2] use normal Portland cement (cement content not less than 380 kg/m³ Max. $W/C$ 0·50) or sulphate-resisting cement (cement content not less than 340 kg/m³ Max $W/C$ 0·50).<br><br>(b) If structures are in contact with a fluctuating water-table use sulphate-resisting cement (cement content not less than 350 kg/m³ Max. $W/C$ 0·50). | (a) If foundations wholly above the water-table[2] use normal Portland cement (cement content not less than 400 kg/m³ Max. $W/C$ 0·50), or sulphate-resisting cement (cement content not less than 390 kg/m³ Max. $W/C$ 0·50).<br><br>(b) If foundations are in contact with a fluctuating water-table use sulphate-resisting cement (cement content not less than 390 kg/m³ Max. $W/C$ 0·50). |

| Precautions | |
|---|---|
| thin concrete sections in basements,[1] culverts, pipes, manholes | Concrete in cast-in-place piles[1] |
| (a) If structures wholly above the water-table[2] use normal Portland cement (cement content not less than 310 kg/m$^3$, Max. $W/C$ 0·55). <br><br> (b) If structures are subjected to external water pressure use normal Portland cement (cement content not less than 370 kg/m$^3$, Max. $W/C$ 0·55). Alternatively, apply asphalt or other membrane as tanking. | (a) If piles wholly above the water-table use normal Portland cement (cement content not less than 330 kg/m$^3$, Max. $W/C$ 0·55). <br><br> (b) If piles are in contact with a fluctuating water-table use normal Portland cement (cement content not less than 370 kg/m$^3$, Max. $W/C$ 0·55). |
| (a) If structures wholly above the water-table[2] use normal Portland cement (cement content not less than 370 kg/m$^3$, Max. $W/C$ 0·50). <br><br> (b) If structures are subject to external water pressure, use normal Portland cement (cement content not less than 380 kg/m$^3$, Max. $W/C$ 0·50), or sulphate-resisting cement (cement content not less than 340 kg/m$^3$, Max. $W/C$ 0·50). Alternatively, apply asphalt or other membrane as tanking. | (a) If piles wholly above the water-table use normal Portland cement (cement content not less than 370 kg/m,$^3$ Max. $W/C$ 0·50). <br><br> (b) If piles are in contact with a fluctuating water-table use normal Portland cement (cement content not less than 380 kg/m$^3$, Max. $W/C$ 0·50) or sulphate-resisting cement (cement content not less than 340 kg/m$^3$, Max. $W/C$ 0·50). |
| (a) If structures wholly above the water-table[2] use normal Portland cement (cement content not less than 400 kg/m$^3$, Max. $W/C$ 0·50), or sulphate-resisting cement (cement content not less than 350 kg/m$^3$, Max. $W/C$ 0·50). <br><br> (b) If structures are subjected to external water pressure use sulphate-resisting cement (cement content not less than 380 kg/m$^3$, Max. $W/C$ 0·50). Alternately apply asphalt or other impervious membrane as tanking. | (a) If piles wholly above the water-table use normal Portland cement (cement content not less than 400 kg/m$^3$, Max. $W/C$ 0·50), or sulphate-resisting cement (cement content not less than 350 kg/m$^3$, Max. $W/C$ 0·50). <br><br> (b) If piles are in contact with a fluctuating water-table use sulphate-resisting cement (cement content not less than 390 kg/m$^3$, Max. $W/C$ 0·50) for end bearing piles only[3]. |

## CLASSIFICATION OF SULPHATES IN SOILS AFFECTIN(

| Classifications of soil conditions | | | Precast concrete products[1] (piles, cylinders, blockwork) | Recommende(  Massive concrete in foundations( (including pile caps) |
|---|---|---|---|---|
| $SO_3$ in g.w. (Parts $SO_3$ per $10^5$) | $SO_3$ in soil | | | |
| | Total (%) | In 1:1 aqueous extract (g/l) | | |
| 250 to 500 | 1·0 to 2·0 | 5·0 to 10·0 | (a) If structures are wholly above the water-table[2] use sulphate-resisting cement (cement content not less than 380 kg/m$^3$ Max. $W/C$ 0·45). <br><br> (b) In contact with a fluctuating water-table use metal or plastics sheathing over sulphate-resisting cement concrete (cement content, Min. 390 kg/m$^3$, Max. $W/C$ 0·40) | (a) If foundations are wholly abov( the water-table[2] use normal Por( land cement (cement content no( less than 400 kg/m$^3$ Max. $W/C$ 0·45) or sulphate-resisting cement (ce( ment content not less than 35( kg/m$^3$ Max. $W/C$ 0·45). <br><br> (b) If foundations are in contact wit( a fluctuating water-table it will b( necessary to determine the cations( thence to decide whether sulphate resisting cement[4] or supersulphat( cement[5] or sheathing is necessary |
| Above 500 | Above 2·0 | Above 10 | (a) Above the water-table[2] use sulphate-resisting cement (cement content not less than 390 kg/m$^3$, Max. $W/C$ 0·40). <br><br> (b) In contact with a fluctuating water-table use metal or plastics sheathing over sulphate-resisting cement concrete (cement content, Min. 390 kg/m$^3$, Max. $W/C$ 0·40) | (a) If foundations are wholly abov( the water-table use normal Portland cement (cement content not less than 400 kg/m$^3$, Max. $W/C$ 0·40), o( sulphate-resisting cement (cemen( content not less than 350 kg/m$^3($ Max. $W/C$ 0·40). <br><br> (b) If foundations are in contact with a fluctuating water-table use sulphate–resisting cement (cemen( content not less than 390 kg/m$^3$ Max. $W/C$ 0·40) and protect by( asphalt or plastics sheathing). |

*Notes*

(1) The cement contents recommended in the above table are suitable for concrete mixes having workabilities as follows:

Precast concrete products }  
Massive concrete in foundations } low workability (10 to 24 mm slump)

Thin concrete sections—medium workability (50 to 75 mm slump)  
Concrete in cast-in-place piles—fairly high workability (100 mm slump)

Cement contents lower than those stated in the table are possible if the placing conditions permit concrete of lower workability to be used in each class, but in all cases the concrete must be capable of being fully compacted to produce a dense impermeable mass. The maximum water/cement ratio is shown above as Max. $W/C$.

**13.1** (*cont'd*)

## CONCRETE AND RECOMMENDED PRECAUTIONS

| precautions | |
|---|---|
| Thin concrete sections in basements,[1] culverts, pipes, manholes | Concrete in cast-in-place piles[1] |
| (a) If foundations are wholly above the water-table[2] and the soil will always remain dry, use normal Portland cement (cement content not less than 400 kg/m³, Max. $W/C$ 0·45), or sulphate-resisting cement (cement content not less than 350 kg/m³, Max. $W/C$ 0·45).<br><br>(b) If foundations are in contact with fluctuating water-table it will be necessary to determine the cations; thence to decide whether sulphate-resisting cement[4] or supersulphate cement[5] is necessary, or whether asphalt or other impervious membrane should be applied as a tanking. | (a) If piles are wholly above the water-table and the soil will always remain free of seepage water use normal Portland cement (cement content not less than 400 kg/m³, Max. $W/C$ 0·45), or sulphate-resisting cement (cement content not less than 350 kg/m³, Max. $W/C$ 0·45).<br><br>(b) Sulphate contents of ground water much in excess of 300 parts per 100,000 are severely aggressive. Special precautions are required, e.g. use of supersulphate cement, or membrane protection to shaft of end-bearing piles. The type of cement will depend on the cations. |
| (a) If foundations are wholly above the water-table[2] and the soil will always remain dry, use normal Portland cement (cement content not less than 400 kg/m³, Max. $W/C$ 0·45), or sulphate-resisting cement (cement content not less than 350 kg/m³, Max. $W/C$ 0·45).<br><br>(b) If foundations are in contact with a fluctuating water-table use sulphate-resisting cement (cement content not less than 390 kg/m³, Max. $W/C$ 0·40) and protect by asphalt tanking or adhesive plastics sheathing. | (a) If piles are wholly above the water-table and the soil will always remain free of seepage water use normal Portland cement (cement content not less than 400 kg/m³, Max. $W/C$ 0·45), or sulphate-resisting cement (cement content not less than 350 kg/m³, Max. $W/C$ 0·45).<br><br>(b) Sulphate contents of ground water much in excess of 300 parts per 100,000 are severely aggressive. Special precautions are required, e.g. use of supersulphate cement, or membrane protection to shaft of end-bearing piles. The type of cement will depend on the cations. |

(2) If surface water is likely to collect and remain in backfilled zone around structure then precautions as for structures in contact with fluctuating water-table or subject to external water pressure should be adopted.

(3) It is possible that sulphate attack on the surface of the pile shaft may form a soft skin which reduces the skin friction on the shaft. Therefore the precautionary measures stated here apply only to end-bearing piles.

(4) Sulphate-resisting cement can be used in acidic soil conditions where pH value is not less than 6.

(5) Supersulphate cement can be used in acidic soil conditions where pH value is not less than 3·5. No admixtures of any kind should be used with sulphate-resisting, or supersulphate, cements.

### Sea Action on Concrete

The main cause of deterioration of concrete structures exposed to sea water is spalling of the surface due to corrosion of the reinforcement. Other causes are attack by sulphates in the sea water, disruption by marine growths, and erosion by wave action. Deterioration from almost all these causes can be prevented by providing 50 mm or more cover to the reinforcement and by using a rich mix (not leaner than $1 : 1\frac{1}{2} : 3$) well compacted to give a dense impermeable concrete. Sea water is not recommended for mixing in reinforced concrete structures because of the risk of corrosion of the reinforcement. It is, however, satisfactory for mass concrete.

Erosion at beach level due to shingle moving under wave action may be severe. Protection can be given by dumping mass concrete or rubble around vulnerable points.

### Organic Acids

The naturally occurring organic acids are mainly lignic or humic acids found in peaty soils and waters. These acids form insoluble calcium salts by reaction with free lime of normal Portland cements, so that the risk of attack is slight with dense concrete which is relatively impermeable. Therefore no special precautions are necessary in foundation concrete above the water table or in soils of low to moderate permeability, provided that attention is paid to quality in mixing, placing, and compacting.

In certain marsh peats, oxidation of pyrites or marcasite can produce free sulphuric acid which is highly aggressive to concrete. The presence of free sulphuric acid is indicated by pH values lower than 4·3 and a high sulphate content. Where the foundation concrete is exposed to freely flowing ground water with a pH value of less than 5, there could be leaching of the concrete. Therefore either supersulphated cement should be used, or the concrete should be protected by a membrane.

### Chemical and Industrial Wastes

Aggressive chemicals present in the ground in chemical works or in waste dumps give the most difficult problems in protecting foundation structures. These problems usually require the help of specialist advice. The chief difficulty is in identifying the full range of deleterious compounds from a limited number of samples and the concentration of the chemicals can vary widely from point to point. Another complication is given by some of the chemical processes, for example the foundations may incorporate underground tanks containing hot acids or alkalis. High alumina and supersulphate cements can withstand attack by acids having pH values as low as

3·5 but high-alumina cement cannot be used where alkalis are in strong concentrations.

Industrial wastes such as slag, burnt colliery shale, and fly ash used as filling below floors can cause dangerous concentrations of sulphates in ground floor slabs as a result of the drying action previously described. Cases have occurred where colliery shale fill containing sulphates has caused the expansion of ground floor concrete resulting in outward tilting of foundation walls. This trouble can be overcome by providing bituminous or plastic sheeting below the floors and carried through to the damp-proof course in the walls.

### Frost Action

Concrete placed 300 mm or more below ground level in Great Britain is unlikely to suffer any deterioration from frost. However, for severe conditions of exposure careful attention must be paid to the design of the mix and the placing of the concrete. The disruptive effect of frost is due to expansion of the water while it is freezing in the pores in the concrete. The effect is most severe if the freezing is rapid when there is no time for water to be extruded from the surface or into the interior of the mass.

For severe exposure conditions Murdock[13.9] recommends using the lowest possible water–cement ratio compatible with having sufficient workability for compaction. He states that a water–cement ratio of less than 0·5 can be regarded as safe against frost damage, between 0·5 and 0·6 there is a risk in isolated cases and above 0·6 the risk becomes progressively greater. Air entraining agents are reputed to increase the frost resistance of concrete.

### Corrosion of Reinforcement

This occurs as a result of insufficient cover, through the presence of chlorides in the aggregates and in certain proprietary chemical admixtures, and through the penetration of water into cracks and honeycombed concrete. Stray electric currents can also cause electrolytic corrosion. It can be avoided by using the correct cover (*see* Chapters 4 and 8), by careful selection of aggregates and by the use of dense well-compacted concrete.

### REFERENCES

13.1 BESSEY, G. E. and LEA, F. M., The distribution of sulphates in clay soils and ground water, *Proc. Inst. C.E.*, **2**, Pt. 1, No. 2, pp. 159–181 (March, 1953).

13.2 RICHARDSON, N. A., Wood preservation, *Proc. Inst. C.E.*, **2**, Pt. 1, No. 6, pp. 649–678 (Nov., 1953).

13.3 CHELLIS, R. D., Finding and fighting marine borers, *Eng. News Rec.* (4th March, 18th March, 1st April, and 15th April, 1948, pp. 344–347, 422–424, 493–496 and 555–558, respectively).

13.4 ROE, T. and HOCHMAN, H., Harbour screening tests of marine borer inhibitors—VII, *U.S. Naval Civil Engineering Laboratory, Technical Report* R. 380 (May, 1965).

13.5 FANCUTT, F. and HUDSON, J. C., The choice of protective schemes for structural steelwork, *Proc. Inst. C.E.*, **17**, pp. 405–430 (Dec., 1960).

13.6 ROMANOFF, M., Corrosion of steel pilings in soils, *National Bureau of Standards*, NBS Monograph 58, U.S. Dept. of Commerce, Washington D.C. (1962).
and, Performance of steel pilings in soils, Proc. 25th Conf. Nat. Assoc. Corrosion Eng., Houston, pp. 14–22 (1969).

13.7 H.M. STATIONERY OFFICE, *Building Research Station Digest*, No. 90, second series (Feb., 1968).

13.8 NEVILLE, A. M., *Properties of Concrete*, pp. 82–91, 2nd ed. (London Pitman, 1973).

13.9 MURDOCK, L. J. and BLACKLEDGE, G. F., *Concrete Materials and Practice*, 4th ed. (London, Arnold, 1968).

# Appendix A

# Properties of Materials

| Material | Density when drained above ground water level ($\gamma$) (Mg/m³) | Density when submerged below ground water level ($\gamma_{sub}$) (Mg/m³) |
|---|---|---|
| Gravel | 1·60–2·00 | 0·90–1·25 |
| Hoggin (Gravel-sand-clay) | 2·00–2·25 | 1·00–1·35 |
| Coarse to medium sands | 1·70–2·10 | 0·90–1·25 |
| Fine and silty sands | 1·75–2·15 | 0·90–1·25 |
| Loose fine sands | down to 1·50 | down to 0·90 |
| Stiff boulder clay | 2·00–2·30 | 1·00–1·35 |
| Stiff clay | 1·80–2·15 | 0·90–1·20 |
| Firm clay | 1·75–2·10 | 0·80–1·10 |
| Soft clay | 1·60–1·90 | 0·65–0·95 |
| Peat | 1·05–1·40 | 0·05–0·40 |
| Granite | 2·50* | — |
| Sandstone | 2·20* | — |
| Basalts and dolerites | 1·75–2·25 | 1·10–1·60 |
| Shale | 2·15–2·30 | 1·20–1·35 |
| Stiff to hard marl | 1·90–2·30 | 1·00–1·35 |
| Limestone | 2·70* | — |
| Chalk | 0·95–2·00 | 0·30–1·00 |
| Broken brick | 1·10–1·75 | 0·65–0·95 |
| Ashes | 0·65–1·00 | 0·30–0·50 |
| Pulverized fuel ash | 1·20–1·50 | 0·65–0·80 |

* Measured in the solid (i.e. not crushed or broken).

**VALUES OF $K_a$ FOR COHESIONLESS SOILS (FOR CALCULATING ACTIVE PRESSURE ON VERTICAL WALLS WITH HORIZONTAL GROUND SURFACE)**

| Values of $\delta$ | Values of $K_a$ for values of $\phi$ of: | | | | |
|---|---|---|---|---|---|
| | 25° | 30° | 35° | 40° | 45° |
| 0 | 0·41 | 0·33 | 0·27 | 0·22 | 0·17 |
| 10° | 0·37 | 0·31 | 0·25 | 0·20 | 0·16 |
| 20° | 0·34 | 0·28 | 0·23 | 0·19 | 0·15 |
| 30° | — | 0·26 | 0·21 | 0·17 | 0·14 |

# Appendix B

# Conversion Tables

*Imperial–Metric*

| Imperial | Metric (or metric force) | S.I. |
|---|---|---|
| 1 in | 25·4 mm | |
| 1 ft | 304·8 mm | |
| 1 yd | 914·4 mm | |
| 1 in² | 645·16 mm² | |
| 1 ft² | 92903 mm² | |
| 1 yd² | 0·8361 m² | |
| 1 in³ | 16387 mm³ | |
| 1 ft³ | 0·028317 m³ | |
| 1 yd³ | 0·7645 m³ | |
| 1 ft³ of fresh water | 28·32 l | |
| 1 Imperial gallon | 4·546 l | |
| 1 lb | 0·4536 kg | 4·44822 N (= 1 lbf) |
| 1 ton (2240 lb) | 1016·05 kg | 9·96402 kN (= 1 tonf) |
| 1 lbf/in² | 0·0703 kgf/cm² | 6·89476 kN/m² |
| 1 lbf/ft² | 4·882 kgf/m² | 47·8803 N/m² |
| 1 lb/ft³ | 16·02 kg/m³ | |
| 1 ft³/S | 0·0283 m³/S | |
| 1 Imperial gall/min | 4·546 l/min | |
| 1 in unit of Moment of Inertia | 41·6198 × 104 mm units | |
| 1 in unit of Moment of Inertia | 16·3860 × 10² mm units | |

| *Metric–Imperial* | | |
|---|---|---|
| 1 mm | 0·03937 in | |
| 1 m | 39·37 in = 3.281 ft = 1·0936 yd | |
| 1 mm² | 0·00155 in² | |

| S.I. | Metric (or metric force) | Imperial |
|---|---|---|
| | 1 m² | 10·764 ft² = 1·196 yd² |
| | 1 mm³ | 0·061 0 × 10⁻³ in³ |
| | 1 m³ | 35·315 ft³ = 1·308 yd³ |
| | 1 m³ of fresh water | 220·4 Imp gall = 2204 lb |
| | 1 l | 0·220 Imp gal = 61·026 in³ |
| 1 kgf = 9·806 65 N | 1 kg | 2·204 6 lb |
| | 1 tonne | 1000 kg = 0·984 3 ton (long) |
| | 1 kgf/cm² | 14·22 lbf/in² |
| | 1 kg/m³ | 0·062 45 lb/ft³ |
| | 1 m³/s | 35·315 ft³/s = 132 27 Imp gal/min |
| | 1 l/s | 0·22 Imp gal/s |
| | 1 mm unit of Moment of Inertia | 0·024 03 × 10⁻³ in units |
| | 1 mm unit of Modulus of section | = 0·061 03 × 10⁻² in unit |
| 1 N | 0·101 97 kgf | 0·224 81 lbf |
| 1 bar | 10197 kgf/m² | 14·503 8 lbf/in² |
| 1 kN/m² | 101·97 kgf/m² | 20·885 4 lbf/ft² |
| 1 kN | 101·64 kgf | 0·100 36 tonf |

*Metric–U.S.A.*

1 tonne = 1·102 USA ton
1 litre = 0·264 2 USA liquid gallon

*U.S.A.–Metric*

1 USA ton = 907·18 kg
1 USA liquid gallon = 3·785 litres

## U.S.A. EQUIVALENTS OF THE MOST FREQUENTLY USED BRITISH STANDARD SIEVES

| British Standard sieves | | American Standard sieves | |
|---|---|---|---|
| Sieve number or size | Sieve opening (microns)* | Sieve opening (microns)* | Sieve number |
| 6·3 mm | 6300 | 6350 | No. 3 (¼ in.) |
| 5 mm | 5000 | 4760 | No. 4 |
| 3·35 mm | 3350 | 3360 | No. 6 |
| 2·36 mm | 2360 | 2380 | No. 8 |
| 1·18 mm | 1180 | 1190 | No. 16 |
| 600 $\mu$m | 600 | 590 | No. 30 |
| 425 $\mu$m | 425 | 420 | No. 40 |
| 300 $\mu$m | 300 | 297 | No. 50 |
| 212 $\mu$m | 212 | 210 | No. 70 |
| 150 $\mu$m | 150 | 149 | No. 100 |
| 75 $\mu$m | 75 | 74 | No. 200 |

* 1 micron = 0·001 mm.

British Standard sieve openings are as given in B.S. 410.

# Index

ꞁ

PLATE I

LIGHT SHELL AND AUGER BORING RIG

PLATE II

PILCON "WAYFARER" SOIL EXPLORATION RIG
WITH DIAMOND CORE DRILLING ATTACHMENT

PLATE III
HEAVY ROTARY DIAMOND CORE DRILLING RIG

PLATE IV

TUBULAR STEEL PLATFORM FOR EXPLORATORY BORING OVER WATER

PLATE V

SWALLOW HOLES IN CHALK FORMATION FILLED WITH CLAY

PLATE VI
REINFORCED CONCRETE CELLULAR BUOYANCY RAFTS FORMING FOUNDATIONS TO POWER
STATION AT GRANGEMOUTH, SCOTLAND
Two rafts have been sunk to final level, the other two are partially sunk.

PLATE VII

(*a*)  LOWERING PNEUMATIC CAISSON SHOE INTO THE RIVER CLYDE PREPARATORY TO TOWING
TO SINKING SITE AT PLANTATION QUAY, GLASGOW

(*b*) INTERIOR OF PNEUMATIC CAISSON AT PLANTATION QUAY, GLASGOW
Note precast concrete blocks to arrest sinking of caisson on reaching required
founding level.

PLATE VIII
BRITISH STEEL PILING CO. 32 M PILE FRAME

PLATE IX
HIGHWAY MECHANICAL AUGER

PLATE X

CALWELD ROTARY DRILLING RIG FOR LARGE-DIAMETER BORED PILES

The casing tube is being handled by the rig. Note the bucket auger on the right of the rig.

PLATE XI

BENOTO GRAB-TYPE DRILLING RIGS FOR LARGE-DIAMETER BORED PILES

PLATE XII

MINOR SLIPPING FROM 1 : ½ SLOPE IN STIFF FISSURED LONDON CLAY, MIDDLESEX
Note smooth appearance of fissure planes.

PLATE XIII

VERTICAL FACE OF STIFF BOULDER CLAY IN EXCAVATIONS FOR DRY DOCK AT SOUTH
SHIELDS

PLATE XIV
STABLE SLOPES IN SANDY GRAVEL FOR BASEMENT EXCAVATION, HAMMERSMITH, LONDON.
PUMPING IN PROGRESS FROM TIMBERED SUMP